The Psychology of Language
From Data to Theory

Trevor A. Harley

*Department of Psychology, University of
Warwick, Coventry, UK*

Erlbaum (UK) Taylor & Francis

Erlbaum (UK) Taylor & Francis, Publishers
27 Church Road
Hove
East Sussex, BN3 2FA
UK

British Library Cataloguing in Publication Data

A catalogue record for this book is available from the British Library

   ISBN 0-86377-381-1 (hbk)
   ISBN 0-86377-382-6 (pbk)

Cover design by Joyce Chester
Printed and bound in the United Kingdom by BPC Wheatons Ltd., Exeter

Contents

To Siobhan

Preface

"It is nothing other than words which has made us human."
(Pavlov, 1927 / 1960)

Although language might not be all that makes us human, it is hard to imagine being human without it. Given its importance in our behaviour, it is perhaps surprising that until recently relatively scant attention has been paid to it in undergraduate courses. Often at best it has been studied as part of a general course on cognitive psychology. That situation is changing. Furthermore, the research field of psycholinguistics is blossoming, as evinced by the growth in the number of papers on the subject, and indeed, in the number of journals dedicated to it. With this growth and this level of interest, it is perhaps surprising that there are still relatively few textbooks devoted to psycholinguistics. I hope this book fills this gap. It is aimed at second and third year undergraduates, although new postgraduates might also find it useful, and I would be delighted if it found other readers.

I have tried to make as many of the references as possible towards easily obtainable material. I have therefore avoided citing unpublished papers, doctoral theses, and conference papers. New papers are coming out all the time, and if I were going to make this book completely up-to-date, I would probably never stop! Therefore I have decided to call a halt, with a few exceptions, at material published in 1994. Of course, given current publication lags, much of this material would actually be done some years before, and the current state of people's thinking and work, as discussed at conferences and seminars, might be very different from the positions attributed to them in this book. Furthermore, some very important ideas cannot be included. This is most unfortunate, but unavoidable. I have however tried to provide a flavour of where the subject is going in the final chapter.

I think the organisation of the book is obvious. I start with "low level" processes such as recognising individual spoken and written words, and then deal with words in combination. I then look at how the meaning of words and text is represented, and move back out from the central systems to look at speech production. The final chapters deal with developmental issues, and the relationship between language and thought. Neuropsychological issues are dealt with as they arise. There is only one chapter whose contents and location might not be intuitive, and that is Chapter 9, on the architecture of the language system. This contains material that is first, integrative, and second, relevant to more than one other chapter. For example, ambiguity is a topic that, for me at least, stands alone. Also, most of what can be said about ambiguity in spoken word recognition also applies to ambiguity in visual word recognition. This arrangement is not ideal: it does mean that material on spoken or visual word recognition, and on parsing, is spread across more than one chapter, but I obviously think it is the best. Many thanks to Gerry Altmann for making me think about this more. The formal details of connectionist models are in the Appendix; I hope this does not mean that it will not be read. I toyed with a structure where the technical details were given when the class of model was first introduced, but a more general treatment seemed more appropriate. Alan Kennedy swayed me. Although I think the book is best read more or less in the given order, I have tried to make each chapter as independent as possible. However, for someone with *no* background in the area, it would probably be best to read Chapter 1 first as this introduces a number of technical terms. Throughout, technical terms are italicised when they are introduced.

I would welcome feedback, corrections (although hopefully few or none of these will be necessary!), and suggestions for any future editions. In particular, however hard one tries, the content is I suspect bound to be biased towards one's own teaching preferences. Therefore suggestions on topics I have omitted or under-represented would be particularly welcome. The hardest bit of writing this book has been deciding what to leave out. I am sure that some courses will cover some material in much more detail than has been possible to provide here. I would be interested to hear however of any major differences of emphasis. I am best reached in cyberspace, on the Internet via my e-mail address: psrds@csv.warwick.ac.uk.

A number of people have read portions or all of this book. I would like to thank: Gerry Altmann, Helen Bown, Gordon Brown, Alan Kennedy, Don Mitchell, Siobhan MacAndrew, Nadine Martin, and Julian Pine. George Dunbar created the sound spectrogram for Fig. 2.1 using MacSpeechLab. I have not always taken their advice, but I thought about all the points they have raised. This book would be much worse without their help. I am of course responsible for any errors or omissions that remain.

Finally, many thanks to the people at Erlbaum (UK) who made this book possible—and also who made it happen so quickly. In particular, I would like to mention Jane Charman, Paul Dukes, and Rohays Perry.

Trevor A. Harley
May 1995

CHAPTER ONE

What is language?
What is psycholinguistics?

INTRODUCTION

Although we often take language for granted, a moment's reflection will show how important it is in our lives. In some form or another it dominates our social and cognitive processes. It is difficult to imagine what life would be like without it. Indeed, most of us consider it to be an essential part of what it means to be human, and in part it is what sets us apart from other animals. Not surprisingly then, it is a major component of understanding human behaviour. *Psycholinguistics* is the name given to the study of the psychological processes involved in language. Psycholinguists study understanding, producing, and remembering language. We are concerned with listening, reading, speaking, writing, and memory for language. We are further interested in how we acquire language, and the way in which it interacts with other psychological systems.

One reason why we take language for granted is that it usually happens so effortlessly, and, most of the time, so accurately. Indeed, when you listen to someone speaking, or look at this page, you cannot help but understand it. It is only in exceptional circumstances that we might become aware of the complexity involved: if we are searching for a word but cannot remember it; if a relative or colleague has had a stroke which has affected their language; if we observe a child acquiring language; if we try to learn a second language ourselves as an adult; or if we are visually or hearing-impaired or if we meet someone else who is. As we shall see, all of these examples of what might be called *language in exceptional circumstance* reveal a great deal about the processes involved in speaking, listening, writing, and reading. But given that language processes are normally so automatic, we also need to carry out careful experiments to get at what is happening in them.

Because of this, psycholinguistics is closely related to other areas of cognitive psychology, and as such relies to a large extent upon the experimental method. From experimental results we construct models of what we think is going on. Hence the subtitle of this book; we use observational and experimental data to construct theories. This book will examine some of the experimental findings psycholinguistics has given us, and the theories that have been proposed to account for those findings. The emphasis of this book is cognitive; it is concerned with understanding the *processes* involved in using and acquiring language. This is not just my personal bias; I believe that all our past experience has shown that the problems of studying human behaviour have yielded and will continue to yield to a cognitive analysis.

It might seem natural at this point to state exactly what is meant by the term *language*. Clearly we all have some intuitive notion of what it is: a simple definition might be "a system of symbols and rules that enable us to communicate". Symbols are things that stand for other things: words, either written or spoken, are symbols. The rules specify how words are ordered to form sentences. However, providing a formal definition of language is not as straightforward as it might first appear. Consider other systems that at first sight are related to human spoken language. Are the communication systems of monkeys a language? What about the "language" of dolphins, or the "dance" of honey bees that communicates the location of sources of nectar? Is the signing of the deaf a language? It should be apparent that the issue is a complex one, and we will address it again shortly.

We can describe language at a number of levels. We can talk about the sounds of the language, or the meaning of words, or the grammar that determines the order of words. These types of distinctions are fundamental in linguistics, and these different aspects of language have been given special names. We can distinguish between *semantics* (the study of meaning), *syntax* (the study of word order), *morphology* (the study of words and word formation), *pragmatics* (the study of language use), *phonetics* (the study of raw sounds), and *phonology* (the study of sounds within a language). The usage of syntax and semantics should be apparent, and if not should certainly be clarified by example in the next few chapters. Morphology is concerned with the way that complex words are made up of simpler units, called *morphemes*. There are two types of morphology: *inflectional morphology*, which is concerned with changes to a word that do not alter its underlying meaning or syntactic category; and *derivational morphology*, which is concerned with changes that do. Pluralisation (e.g. "house" becoming "houses", and "mouse" becoming "mice") and verb tense changes (e.g. "kiss" becoming "kissed", and "run" becoming "ran") are examples of inflectional changes. "Develop" becoming "development", "developmental", or "redevelop" are all examples of derivational changes. The distinction between phonetics and phonology, which are both ways of studying sounds, will be examined in more detail in the next chapter.

In this book, we will start with what appear to be the simplest or lowest level processes and work towards more complex ones. Hence we will first look at how we recognise and understand single words. Although these first chapters are largely about recognising words in isolation in the sense that only one word is present at a time, the influence of context is an important consideration, and we will look at this also. The next chapter looks at the speech system and how we identify spoken words. The third chapter looks at how we recognise printed words, and the fourth how we pronounce them, together with disorders of reading (the dyslexias). It also looks at how we learn to read. We then move on to how we understand words strung together to form sentences. This brings us to the issue of how language is stored, and how we represent the meaning of words and text, and how sentences are strung together to form larger units of discourse or text. Then we will consider the process in reverse, and examine language production and its disorders (types of aphasia). By this stage we will have an understanding of the processes involved in understanding language, and these processes must be looked at in a wider context. First, we will look at the structure of the language system as a whole, and the relationship between the parts. Next, we will look in detail at the more general role of language, by examining the relationship between language and thought. We will examine the biological, cognitive, and social precursors of language: what other faculties must be in place (if any) before a child can start acquiring language? Then we will then look at how children acquire language. We will also look at what can be learned from language acquisition in exceptional circumstances, including the effects of linguistic deprivation, and looking at how bilingual children can learn two languages. The final chapter looks again at the themes raised in this chapter, and discusses some exciting new developments.

There are five issues that will recur throughout this book. The first is that we will emphasise uncovering the actual *processes* involved in language. The second issue is that of how apparently different language processes are related to one another. At a gross level of analysis, this means things like: to what extent are the same processes involved in reading also involved in speaking? The third issue is whether or not processes in language operate independently of one another, or whether they interact. This is the issue of *modularity*, which we will look at in more detail later in this chapter. One important aspect of this issue is, for a particular process, at what stage does context have an effect? For example, does the meaning of a sentence help in recognising the sounds of a word or in making decisions about how the words are ordered? Fourth, how sensitive are the results of our experiments to the particular techniques employed? That is, do we get different answers to the same question if we do our experiments in a different way? To anticipate, the answer is often "yes": at first sight, the answers we get depend upon the way we find the answers out. This obviously can make the interpretation of findings quite complex, and we find that the experimental techniques themselves come under close scrutiny. In this respect, the distinction between data and theory is blurred.

Finally, it should be obvious that psycholinguistics should have *applications*. Although language comes naturally to most humans most of the time, there are many occasions when it does become a problem: in learning to read, in overcoming language disabilities, in rehabilitating patients with brain damage, and in developing computer systems that can understand and produce language. Advances in the theory of any subject such as psycholinguistics should have practical applications. For example, in Chapters 3 and 4 we will look in detail at the research on visual word recognition and reading. There are obvious benefits to be had from any sophisticated model of these processes. Learning to read is a remarkably difficult task, and anything which facilitates it is obviously desirable. A good theory of reading should cast light on how it should best be taught. It should indicate the best strategies that can be used to overcome difficulties in learning to read, and thereby help children with a specific learning disability in reading. It should specify the most advantageous method of dealing with adult illiteracy. Furthermore, it should help in the rehabilitation of adults who have difficulty in reading as a consequence of brain damage, showing what remedial treatment would be most useful and which strategies would maximise any preserved reading skills. This is not to say that any of the current theories can already do all of these things, but it is a goal for which we should aim, and which our experimental studies should help us reach.

In the next part of this chapter we will search for a formal definition of language. It is particularly useful in this context to look at the controversial topic of whether non-human primates, particularly chimpanzees, can be taught a human-like language. We can then discuss the various methods available to us in studying language. First, we consider the origin and history of language.

The origin of language

Where did language come from? Much about its origin and evolution is unclear. Unlike with the evolution of the hands and the use of tools, there is no fossil record available for study. The capacity for language and symbol manipulation must have arisen as the brain increased in size and complexity between 2 million and 300,000 years ago as *Homo sapiens* became differentiated from other species. There are indications that Broca's area, a region of the brain associated with language, was present in the brains of early hominids as long as two million years ago. The vocal apparatus has become particularly well adapted for making speech sounds in a way that is not true of animals: our teeth are upright, our tongues relatively small and flexible, the larynx (or voice-box) lower in the throat, and the musculature of the lips is more finely developed. The fundamental structures of language appear unchanged over the last 60,000 years.

Language need not and indeed could not have arisen in a vacuum. The social set-up of early man might have helped, but many other animals, particularly primates, have complex social organisations yet did not develop language. Other primates have a rich repertoire of alarm calls, gestures, and other sounds (see below). Some words might have been *onomatopoeic*—that is, they sound like the things to which they refer. For example, "cuckoo" sounds like the call of a bird, "hiss" sounds like the noise a snake makes, and "ouch" sounds like the exclamation we make when there is a sudden pain. The idea that language evolved from mimicry or imitation has been called, tongue in cheek, the "ding-dong", "heave-ho", or "bow-wow" theory. However, such similarities can only be attributed to a very few words, and many words are very different in different languages. Furthermore, there is much more to language than using words in isolation. What gives human language its power is the ability to combine words together by use of a *grammar*, and it is the evolution of this that is the most contentious issue.

So murky is the origin of language that it is even an issue whether its grammar arose by Darwinian natural selection. At first sight some strong arguments have been proposed against this: there has not been enough time for something so complex to evolve since the evolution of man diverged from that of other primates; it cannot exist in any intermediate form; and possessing a complex grammar confers no obvious selective advantage, so it could not have been selected for. The alternative explanation to evolution by selection is that language arose as a side-effect of the evolution of something else, such as the ability to use more complex manual gestures, or to use tools, or even just as a by-product of other evolutionary forces such as an increase in overall brain size (e.g. Chomsky, 1988; Piattelli-Palmarini, 1989). Paget (1930) proposed that language evolved in intimate connection with the use of hand gestures, so that vocal gestures developed to expand the available repertoire. Corballis (1992) argued that the evolution of language freed the hands from having to make gestures to being able to make tools at the same time. On the other hand, Pinker and Bloom (1990) argued that grammar could have arisen by Darwinian natural selection. They argued that there was indeed sufficient time for grammar to evolve, that it evolved to communicate existing cognitive representations, and that the ability to communicate thus confers a big evolutionary advantage to those that can. To give their example, it obviously makes a big difference to your survival if an area has animals that you can eat, or animals that can eat you. The arguments that a specific language faculty could have arisen through natural selection and evolution are also covered by Pinker (1994). It has been further argued that the evolution of language was related to the evolution of consciousness (Jaynes, 1977). As can be seen, this whole topic is very speculative; indeed, as Corballis (1992) notes, the Société de Linguistique de Paris banned all debate on the origins of language! And we shall not mention it again, apart from to point out that if it can be shown to have evolved, then some portion of it must be genetically transmitted. This is an important topic to which we shall return.

Although the way in which language evolved may be unclear, it is clear that it has changed. Many languages are related to each other. This relationship is apparent in the similarity of many of the words of some languages (e.g. "mother" in English is "Mutter" in German, "moeder" in Dutch, "mère" in French, "maht" in Russian, and "mata" in Sanskrit). It has been shown by more detailed analyses along these lines that most of the languages of Europe, and parts of west Asia, derive from a common source called proto-European. All the languages that are derived from this common source are therefore called Indo-European. Indo-European has a number of main branches: the Romance (such as French, Italian, and Spanish), the Germanic (such as German, English, and Dutch), and the Indian languages. (There are some exception languages, which are European languages that are not part of the Indo-European family. Finnish and Hungarian are part of the Finno-Ugric family, which is related to Japanese. Basque meanwhile is unrelated to any other language.) Languages change over relatively short time spans: clearly Chaucerian and Elizabethan English are substantially different from today, and even Victorian speakers would sound decidedly odd to us today. At the very least we have to coin new words or new uses of old words when necessary (e.g. "television", "telephone", "rap").

Differences between languages should not be glossed over. Although they have arisen over a relatively short time compared with the evolution of man, we cannot assume that there are no processing differences between speakers of different languages. Whereas it is likely that the great bulk of the mechanisms involved are the same, there might be some differences, and this is most apparent in the processing of written or printed words. Writing is a recent development compared with speech, and while visual word processing might be derived from object recognition, there might also be important differences. As we shall see in Chapter 3, there are important differences in the way that different written languages map written symbols into sounds, and different strategies for dealing with this have arisen between people from different linguistic communities. Nevertheless it appears to be the case that there is an important core of psychological mechanisms common to the processing of all languages.

ANIMAL LANGUAGE?

Is language an ability that is uniquely human? We will examine both naturally occurring animal communications systems, and a number of attempts to teach animals (particularly chimpanzees) a human-like language. There are a number of reasons why this topic is important. First, it provides a focus for the issue of what we mean by the term *language*. Second, it informs debate on the extent to which language might have a genetic basis. Third, it might tell us about what other social and cognitive processes are necessary for a language to develop. Finally, of course, the question is of great intellectual interest. The idea of being able to "talk to the animals" like the fictional Dr. Dolittle fascinates both adults and children alike. It can become an emotive subject, as it touches upon the issue of animal rights, and whether man is clearly distinct from other animals.

Animal communication systems

It is without question that some animals possess surprisingly rich communication systems. *Communication* is much easier to define than *language*: it is the transmission of a signal that conveys information, usually such that the sender benefits from the recipient's response (see Pearce, 1987). A wide range of methods is used to convey information, even in insects. For example, ants rely a great deal upon chemical messengers or pheromones. Honey bees produce a complex "dance" in a figure-of-eight shape to other members of the hive (von Frisch, 1950, 1974): the direction of the straight part of the dance (or the axis of the figure-of-eight) represents the direction of the nectar relative to the sun, and the rate at which the bee wiggles during the dance represents its distance. As we move up the evolutionary ladder, primates use a wide variety of calls to symbolise a range of threats. For example, a vervet monkey produces a snake chutter to warn others that a snake is nearby, and a distinct eagle call when an eagle is overhead. Each type of call elicits different responses from other nearby vervets (Demers, 1988).

It is a widespread belief that whales and dolphins possess a language. However, the research on this does not support this belief, and the topic is controversial. There are many methodological problems with this type of research. In the wild, it is often difficult to locate the individual responsible for a sound within a group. It is not clear whether dolphins employ sequences of subunits which convey particular messages, in rather the same way as we combine words to form sentences to convey messages; there is currently no evidence to suggest that they do. Hump-backed whale song does consist of ordered subparts, but their function is unknown (see Demers, 1988).

But even if a communication system such as that of a hump-backed whale were well understood, how would we decide if it had crossed the boundary to be counted as a language?

Defining language

Is the difference between a communication system and a language just a matter of degree? The dictionary defines language as "human speech . . . an artificial system of signs and symbols, with rules for forming intelligible communications for use e.g. in a computer" (*Chambers Twentieth Century Dictionary*, 1977). Many introductions to the study of language, linguistics, avoid giving a definition, or consider it to be so obvious that it does not need to be defined. To some extent the aim of modern theoretical linguistics is to offer an answer to this question (Lyons, 1977a).

Design features.   One attempt to side-step the thorny issue of providing a definition of language was that of Hockett (1960). Rather than provide a definition, he listed 16 general properties or *design features* of spoken human language (see Table 1.1). The emphasis of this system is very much upon the physical characteristics of spoken languages. Furthermore, I would not wish to say that they are essential defining characteristics—human written language does not display "rapid fading" yet clearly we would not want to say that this should not count as a language! Nevertheless, design features provide a useful

TABLE 1.1
Hockett's (1960) Design features of human spoken language

1. Vocal-auditory channel
   (communication occurs by the producer speaking and the receiver hearing)

2. Broadcast transmission and directional reception
   (a signal travels out in all directions from the speaker but can be localised in space by the hearer)

3. Rapid fading
   (once spoken, the signal rapidly disappears and is no longer available for inspection)

4. Interchangeability
   (adults can be both receivers and transmitters)

5. Complete feedback
   (speakers can access everything about their productions)

6. Specialisation
   (the amount of energy in the signal is unimportant; a word means the same whether it is whispered or shouted)

7. Semanticity
   (signals mean something: they relate to the features of the world)

8. Arbitrariness
   (these symbols are abstract; except with a few onomatopoeic exceptions, they do not resemble what they stand for)

9. Discreteness
   (the vocabulary is made out of discrete units)

10. Displacement
    (the communication system can be used to refer to things remote in time and space)

11. Openness
    (the ability to invent new messages)

12. Tradition
    (the language can be taught and learned)

13. Duality of patterning
    (only combinations of otherwise meaningless units are meaningful—this can be seen as applying both at the level of sounds and words, and words and sentences)

14. Prevarication
    (language provides us with the ability to lie and deceive)

15. Reflectiveness
    (we can communicate about the communication system itself, just as this book is doing)

16. Learnability
    (the speaker of one language can learn another)

framework for thinking about how animal communication systems differ from human language.

To do this, we can take each feature and ask whether animal communication systems possess them. All communication systems possess some of the features. For example, the red belly of a breeding stickleback is an arbitrary sign. Some of the characteristics are more important than others; we might single out semanticity, arbitrariness, displacement, openness, tradition, duality of patterning, prevarication, and reflectiveness. These features have in common that they relate to the fact that language is about meaning, and provide us with the ability to communicate about anything. To this list we might add others that emphasise the creativity and meaning-related aspects of language. Marshall (1970) points out the important fact that language is under our voluntary control; it is *intentional* in that we intend to convey a particular message. Anderson (1985) added iteration and recursion, syntactic rules that enable us to construct potentially infinitely long sentences by devices such as combining portions of sentences with the conjunction "and", or embedding sentence fragments in other sentences (such as "The cat the dog chased escaped"). This is important because, as we shall see, the linguist Chomsky argues that these features are essential in making language the powerful tool that it is.

It should be emphasised that we can use language to communicate about anything, however remote in time and space. Hence whereas a parrot uses the vocal-auditory channel and satisfies most of the design characteristics up to number thirteen, it cannot lie or reflect about its communication system, or talk about the past. Whereas monkeys are limited to chattering and squeaking about immediate threats such as snakes in the grass and eagles overhead, we can express novel thoughts; we can make up sentences that convey ideas that have never been expressed before. This cannot be said of other animal communication systems. Bees will never dance a book on the psychology of the bee dance. Human language achieves its power by combining a limited number of words according to a finite number of syntactic rules to produce an infinite number of sentences.

In summary, although many animals possess a rich symbolic communication system which enables them to convey messages to other members of the species, which affects their behaviour, and which possesses many of Hockett's design features, the communication systems all fall short of the richness of human language. This richness is manifested by our limitless ability to talk about anything, starting from a finite number of words and rules to combine those words.

Teaching language to apes (and other animals)

Is it just an historical accident that animals have not evolved a language, or are they in principle incapable of learning one? This question is just one reason for the recent interest in attempts to teach language to animals. Most research has focused upon apes, particularly chimpan- zees, as they are highly intelligent animals and convenient to teach.

The cognitive abilities of apes, while obviously inferior to those of humans are not very different from those of very young children.

What are the cognitive abilities of other animals? The perceptual abilities of a chimpanzee named Viki at 3½ years were generally comparable to those of a child of a similar age on a range of perceptual tasks such as matching and discrimination, but broke down on tasks involving counting (Hayes & Nissen, 1971). Experiments on another chimp named Sarah also suggested that she was performing at levels close to that of a young child on tasks such as conservation of quantity (if she could see the transformation occurring), and, more controversially, that she was able to make inferences about people's mental states (e.g. see Premack & Woodruff, 1978; Woodruff & Premack, 1981). More generally, the short-term memory span of apes is very limited, and they have particular problems with tasks involving self-reference, identification, causality (what causes what), and temporal sequencing (what comes before what). They learn slowly, need careful training, and are inflexible in the test conditions and their responses (see Cohen, 1983, for a more detailed discussion). The point is, however, that it is not immediately obvious that the cognitive abilities of apes are wildly discrepant from those of young children, apart from their native language abilities. This decoupling of linguistic and other cognitive abilities has important implications. First, it suggests that on many basic cognitive tasks language is not essential. Second, that there are prerequisites to linguistic development (particularly of syntax) other than cognitive ones. Third, it suggests that cognitive limitations in themselves might not be able to account for failure of apes to learn language.

There have been a number of examples where humans have tried to teach apes a human-like language. It is useful to bear in mind the distinction between teaching word meaning and syntax. As we have seen, it is an essential feature of human language that it involves both associating a finite number of words with particular meanings or concepts, and using a finite number of rules to combine those words into a potentially infinite number of sentences. We would have to show that apes can do both of these things before we could conclude that they have learned a language. I will simply describe some of the attempts to teach primates language first, and then look at some methodological problems with this research.

Talking chimps: Gua and Viki. The earliest attempt was that of Kellogg and Kellogg (1933), who raised a female chimpanzee named Gua along with their own son. (This type of rearing is called cross-fostering.) Gua never produced recognisable words, and appeared to understand only a few. Hayes (1951) similarly brought up a chimp named Viki as a human child and attempted to teach her to speak. This also was unsuccessful, as after six years the chimpanzee could produce just four poorly articulated words ("mama", "papa", "up", and "cup") using her lips. Even then, Viki could only produce these in a guttural croak, and only the Hayes' could understand them easily. With a great deal of training she understood more words, and some combinations of words. These early studies have a fundamental limitation. The vocal tracts of chimps are physiologically unsuited to producing speech, and it is likely that this was the main block to progress. Hence nothing can be concluded about the language abilities in general of primates from these early failures. On the other hand, chimps have high manual dexterity. Hence later attempts were based on systems using either a type of sign language, or that involved manipulating man-made symbols.

Washoe.   Perhaps the most famous example of trying to teach an ape language is that of Washoe. Washoe was a female chimpanzee who was caught in the wild when she was approximately one year old. She was then brought up as a human child (cross-nurtured), doing things such as eating, toilet training, playing, and other social activities (see, for example, Gardner & Gardner, 1969, 1975). In this context she was taught American Sign Language (AMESLAN). AMESLAN is the standard sign language for the deaf in use in North America. Just like spoken language, it has words and a syntax.

At the age of four, Washoe could produce 132 signs, and comprehend more; a few years later this had increased to 200 (Fouts, Shapiro & O'Neil, 1978). These words came from many syntactic categories, including nouns, verbs, adjectives, negatives and pronouns. It was claimed that she made over-generalisation errors similar to those of young children (for example, in using the sign for "flower" to stand for flower-like smells, or "hurt" to refer to a tattoo). It was further claimed that when she did not know a word, she could coin a new one. When she first saw a duck and had not learnt a sign word for it, she coined a phrase combining two signs she did have, producing "water bird". Furthermore, she combined signs and used them correctly in strings up to five items long. Examples of Washoe's speech include: "Washoe sorry", "Baby down", "Go in", "Hug hurry", and "Out open please hurry". She could answer some questions that use what are called WH-words (so called because in English most of the words that are used to start questions begin with WH). She was particularly good at understanding questions starting with "what", "where", or "who", but she had problems with questions involving "how", "where", or "why". These latter WH-words concern causality and temporal-spatial sequencing, and as we have just seen, the limited short-term memory capacity of apes seems to lead to particular difficulties with these tasks. She displayed some sensitivity to word order in that she could distinguish between "You tickle me" and "I tickle you". Hence at first sight Washoe appears to have acquired the use of words and their meanings, and at least some rudimentary syntax—that is, a sensitivity to word order in both production and comprehension.

Sarah. A rather different approach was taken by Premack (1971, 1976; see also 1985, 1986a). Sarah was a chimpanzee trained in a laboratory setting to manipulate small plastic symbols that varied in shape, size, shape, and texture. The symbols could be ordered in certain ways according to rules; together the symbols and the rules form a language called Premackese. One advantage of this set-up is that as the array is always in front of the animal the memory load required is less, as the language signal here does not display rapid fading. She produced mainly simple *lexical concepts* (strings describing simple objects or actions), and could produce novel strings of symbols. On the whole, however, these were only at the level of substituting one word for another. For example, "Randy give apple Sarah" was used as the basis of producing "Randy give banana Sarah". She produced sentences that were syntactically quite complex (for example, producing logical connectives such as "if . . . then"), and showed metalinguistic awareness (reflectiveness) in that she could talk about the language system itself using symbols that meant " . . . is the name of".

Nim. Terrace, Petitto, Sanders, and Bever (1979) described the linguistic progress of a chimpanzee named Nim Chimpsky (a pun on the name of the linguist Noam Chomsky). They taught Nim Chimpsky a language also based upon AMESLAN. They found that there was regularity of order in two word utterances—for example, place was usually the second thing mentioned—but that this broke down with longer utterances. Longer utterances were largely characterised by more repetition ("banana me eat banana eat") rather than displaying real syntactic structure. Terrace et al. were far more pessimistic about the linguistic abilities of apes than either the Gardners or Premack. However, O'Sullivan and Yeager (1989) pointed out that Nim's linguistic skills might have been limited by the type of training she received. They found that she performed better in a conversational setting than in a formal training session.

Some other attempts. Savage-Rumbaugh, Rumbaugh, and Boysen (1978) reported attempts to teach the chimpanzees Lana, Sherman, and

Austin language, using a computer-controlled display of symbols structured according to an invented syntax called Yerkish. The symbols that serve as words are called *lexigrams*. Other primates such as gorillas have also been studied (e.g. Koko, reported by Patterson, 1981). One interesting line of research has been the investigation of whether chimps who have been taught language will then go on in turn to teach their own offspring, or whether the offspring can learn it by observing their parents. This is an important question, because as we shall see in later chapters, there is little evidence that human children are explicitly taught language by their parents. It has been noted that Washoe's adopted son Loulis both spontaneously acquired signs from Washoe and was also seen to be taught by Washoe. Although this is a clear indication of cultural transmission, it is still not clear whether it is a language that has been transmitted, or just a sophisticated transmission system. (Fouts, Fouts, & van Cantford, 1989).

Finally, there has been some research on non-primates. For example Herman, Richards, and Wolz (1984) taught two bottle-nosed dolphins, Phoenix and Akeakami, an artificial language. However, this research tested only the animals' comprehension of the artificial language, not their ability to produce it. From the point of view of answering our original questions on language and animals it is clearly important to examine both comprehension and production.

Interim summary.   At first sight then these attempts to teach apes a human-like language look interesting and quite convincing. If we look at them in terms of Hockett's design features, at first sight all the important ones appear to be present. Specific signs are used to represent particular words (discreteness), and apes can refer to objects that are not in view (displacement). The issue of semanticity, whether or not the signs have meaning for the apes, is a controversial one to which we shall return. At the very least we can say that they have learnt associations between objects and events and responses. Sarah could discuss the symbol system itself (reflectiveness). Signs could be combined in novel ways (openness). The reports of apes passing signs on to their young satisfies the feature of tradition. Most importantly, it is claimed that the signs are combined according to specified syntactic rules of ordering: that is, they have apparently acquired a grammar. Maybe then these animals can learn language, and the difference between apes and humans is only a matter of degree.

Problems with the earlier work.   There are many problems with some of this research, particularly the early, pioneering work. The literature is full of argument and counter-argument, and this makes it difficult to come to a definite conclusion. Criticisms arise in two ways: first, methodological criticisms of the training and particularly the testing procedures involved; second, argument over how the results should be interpreted. We will start with the methodological criticisms.

First, it has been claimed that AMESLAN is not truly symbolic (see Savage-Rumbaugh et al., 1978; Seidenberg & Petitto, 1979), in that many of the signs are icons standing for what is represented in a non-arbitrary way. For example, the symbol for "give" looks like a motion of the hand towards the body reminiscent of receiving a gift, and "drive" is a motion rather like turning a steering wheel. If this were true then this research could be dismissed as irrelevant because the chimps are not learning a symbolic language. Clearly it is not true; not all the attempts mentioned above used AMESLAN—Premack's plastic symbols, for example, are very different. In addition, the force of this objection can be largely dismissed on the grounds that not all AMESLAN symbols are like this, and that deaf people clearly use it in a symbolic way. No-one would say that deaf people using AMESLAN are not using a language. Nevertheless, AMESLAN is different from spoken language in that it is more condensed—articles such as "the" and "a" are omitted—and this clearly might affect the way in which animals use the language. And in Washoe's particular signing at least, a great proportion of her signing seemed to be based upon these "onomatopoeic" signs that do resemble natural gestures. This brings us to another problem, that of over-interpretation by the trainers. This might be interpretation of gestures as signs, or even wishful thinking that a particular movement was indeed an appropriate sign. Again, these criticisms are hard to justify against the lexigram-based studies, although Brown (1973) noted that Sarah's performance deteriorated when her trainer changed. More worryingly, in these early studies reporting of signing behaviour was anecdotal, or limited to cumulative vocabulary counts and lists. No-one ever produced a complete corpus of all the signs of a signing ape in a pre-determined period of time with details of the context in which the signs occurred (Seidenberg & Petitto 1979). This has a number of consequences which make interpretation difficult. For example, the "water bird" example would be less interesting if Washoe had spent all day making signs such as "water shoe", "water banana", "water fridge", and so on. In addition, the data presented are "reduced" so as to eliminate the repetition of signs thus producing summary data. Repetition in signing is quite common, leading to long sequences such as "me banana you banana me give", which is a less impressive syntactic accomplishment, and not at all like the early sequences produced by human children. Imitations of humans' immediately preceding signs abound, while genuinely creative signing is rare. (For details of these methodological problems, see Bronowski & Bellugi, 1970; Seidenberg & Petitto 1979; and Thompson & Church, 1980.)

There are also a number of differences between the behaviour of apes using language and of children of about the same age, or with the same vocabulary size. The utterances made by chimps are tied to the spatio-temporal context, with utterances involving temporal displacement (talking about things remote in time) particularly rare. There is a lack of syntactic structure and the word order used is inconsistent, particularly with longer utterances. Fodor, Bever and Garrett (1974) pointed out that there appeared to be little comprehension of the syntactic relationships between units, and that it was difficult to produce a linguistic syntactic analysis of their sentences. Hence, if they had "acquired" a sentence structure as in the string of words "Insert apple dish", there was little evidence that this would help or transfer to the producing the new sentence "Insert apple red dish". Unlike humans, chimpanzees cannot reject ill-formed sentences. They rarely ask questions, which of course is an obvious characteristic of the speech of young children. Chimps do not spontaneously use symbols referentially—that is, they need explicit training to go beyond merely associating a particular symbol or word in a particular context. Young children behave quite differently. Finally, it is not clear that chimps use language to help them to reason.

Quite naturally, these criticisms have not gone unchallenged. Premack (1976) addressed some of the earlier criticisms, and Savage-Rumbaugh (1987) pointed out that it is important not to generalise from the failure of one ape to the behaviour of others. Furthermore, many of these early studies were pioneering and later studies learned from their failures and difficulties. Perhaps the major challenge to the critical point of view, however, has come from more recent studies involving pygmy chimpanzees.

Kanzi. Much of this early work then is of limited value because it is not clear that it tells us anything about the linguistic abilities of apes; if anything, it suggests that they are rather limited. More recently strong claims have been made about the performance of Kanzi (Savage-Rumbaugh, McDonald, Sevcik, Hopkins, & Rupert, 1986). While earlier studies used the common chimpanzee (*Pan troglodytes*), comparative studies of animals suggest that the bonobo or pygmy chimpanzee (*Pan paniscus*) is more intelligent, has a richer social life, and a more extensive natural communicative repertoire. Kanzi is a pygmy chimpanzee, and it is claimed he has made a vital step in spontaneously acquiring the understanding that symbols refer to things in the world, behaving far more like a child. Unlike other apes, Kanzi did not receive formal training by reinforcement with food upon production of the correct symbol. He first acquired symbols by observing the training of his mother (called Matata), and then interacted with people in normal daily activities.

However, even this work is not without its critics (Seidenberg & Petitto, 1987). The argument depends upon whether Kanzi's behaviour is too context-independent—for example, using "strawberry" as a name, as a request to travel to where the strawberries grow, as a request to eat strawberries, and so forth. In reply Savage-Rumbaugh (1987) and Nelson (1987) argued that the critics under-estimated the abilities of the chimpanzees, and over-estimated the appropriate linguistic abilities of very young children.

Evaluation of work on teaching apes language. Most people would agree that in these studies we have taught some apes something, but what exactly? Clearly apes can learn to associate names with actions and objects, but there is more to language than this. Problems concerning the definition of language still arise. It is useful to think about the distinction between word meaning and syntax again.

Let us take word meaning first. This raises the issue of how we use names—in what way is it different from simple association? Pigeons can be taught to respond differentially to pictures of trees and water (Herrnstein, Loveland, & Cable, 1977). So it is an easy step to imagine that we could condition pigeons to respond in one way (e.g. pecking once) to one printed word, and in another way (e.g. pecking twice) to a different word, and so on. We could go so far as to say these pigeons would be "naming" the words! So in what way is this naming behaviour different from ours? One obvious difference is that we can do more than name words: we also know their meaning. For example, we know that a tree has leaves and roots, that an oak is a tree, that a tree is a plant, and so on. That is, we know how the word tree is conceptually related to other words (see Chapter 5 on meaning). Another important point is that we know what a "tree" looks like. By examining its pecking behaviour, we could infer that the best a trained pigeon might manage is to indicate that the word "tree" looks more like "tee" than "horse". Is the use of signs by chimpanzees on a par with pigeons or with us? There are two key questions which would clearly have to be answered "yes" before most psycholinguists would agree that these primates are using words like us rather than like our pigeons. First, can apes spontaneously learn that names refer to objects in a way that is constant across contexts? For example, we know that a strawberry is a strawberry whether it's in front of us in a bowl covered in cream and sugar, or whether it's in a field attached to a strawberry plant half covered in soil. Furthermore, do the categories which they use correspond to the way in which we use them? Despite the recent promising work with Kanzi, there are no unequivocal answers to these questions. For example, Nim could sign "apple" or "banana" correctly if these fruits were presented to him one at a time, but was unable to respond correctly if they were presented together. This suggests that he did not understand the meaning of the signs in the way that humans do. More recent work by Savage-Rumbaugh on chimpanzees called Sherman, Austin, and especially Kanzi suggests that apes do understand the meaning of at least some of the signs they use. For example, Sherman and Austin could group lexigrams into the proper superordinate categories even when the objects to which they referred were absent. For example, they could group "apple", "banana", and "strawberry" together as "fruit". However, this finding is controversial. (See Savage-Rumbaugh, 1987, and Seidenberg & Petitto, 1987, for details of this debate.)

Now let us look at chimps' syntactic abilities. Has it been demonstrated that apes can combine symbols in a rule-governed way to form sentences? In as much as they might appear to do so, it has been proposed that the "sentences" are simply generated by "frames". That is, it is nothing more than a sophisticated version of conditioning, and does not show the creative use of rules. It is as though we have now trained our pigeons to respond to whole sentences rather than just individual words. Such pigeons would not be able to recognise that the sentence "The ghost chased the dog" is related in meaning to "The dog is chased by the cat", or has the same structure as "A vampire loved a ghost".

A great deal comes down to a comparison of the performance of apes with that of children, and there is considerable disagreement on how well apes come out of this comparison. Obviously children are not as good at language as adults; to some extent they are somewhere between us (adult humans) and our pigeon example, depending on their age. Therefore one obvious problem is that it is unclear with which age group of children the chimpanzees should be compared. When there is more work on linguistic apes bringing up their own offspring, the picture should be clearer. However, this research is difficult to carry out, is expensive, and difficult to obtain funding for, so we might have to wait some time for these answers. Until then we can merely say that the case is "not proven".

Why is the issue so important?   As we saw earlier, there is more to the issue of a possible animal language than simple intellectual interest. First, it provides a deeper insight into the nature of language and what is important about it. This discussion should have clarified what makes human language different from vervets "chuttering" when they see a snake. Second, the influential American linguist Noam Chomsky has claimed that human language is a special faculty that has a specific biological basis and that has evolved only in humans. Language arose because the brain passed a threshold in size, and only human children can learn language because only they have special innate equipment necessary to do so. This hypothesis can be summed up by the phrase "language is species-specific and has an innate basis", and we will return to it later (Chapter 10). Even Premack (1985, 1986a, 1990) has since become far less committed to the claim that apes can learn language just like human children. Indeed, he also has come to the conclusion that there is a major discontinuity between the linguistic and cognitive abilities of children and chimpanzees, with children possessing innate, "hard-wired" abilities which other animals lack.

THE HISTORY AND METHODS OF PSYCHOLINGUISTICS

Now we know something about what language is, let us look at how modern psycholinguistics studies it. We can get a better understanding of the modern methods if we look briefly at the history of the subject.

A brief history of psycholinguistics

Given the subjective importance of language, it is surprising that the history of psycholinguistics is a relatively recent one. Although it is often traced to a conference on psycholinguistics held in Cornell, USA, in the summer of 1951, as reflected in its use in Osgood and Sebeok's (1954) book describing that conference, the approach was certainly used before. For example, in Germany at the end of the last century, Meringer and Mayer (1895) analysed slips of the tongue in a remarkably modern way (see Chapter 8).

As its name implies, psycholinguistics has its roots in two disciplines, linguistics and psychology. *Linguistics* is the study of language itself, the rules which describe it, and our knowledge about the rules of language. In modern linguistics the primary data which linguists use are *intuitions* about what is and is not an acceptable sentence. For example, we know that (1) is acceptable, but most of us would reject (2) as ungrammatical. On what grounds? Can we formulate general rules to account for our intuitions?

1.   What did the pig give to the donkey?
2.   *What did the pig chase to the donkey?

(Ungrammatical constructions are conventionally marked by an asterisk.) The primary concerns of early linguistics were rather different from what they are now. Comparative linguistics was concerned with comparing and tracing the origins of different languages. In particular, the American *Bloomfieldian* tradition emphasised comparative studies of indigenous North American Indian languages. This led to an emphasis upon what is called *structuralism*, in that a primary concern was to provide an analysis of the appropriate categories of description of the units of language (see, for example, Harris, 1951).

Early psychological approaches to language saw it as a simple device which could generate sentences by moving from one state to another. There are two strands in this early work, to be found in information theory (Shannon & Weaver, 1949) and behaviourism. Information theory, which emphasised the role of probability and redundancy in language, developed out of the demands of the early telecommunications industry. In the middle part of this century, the dominant tradition in psychology was behaviourism. This emphasised the relationship between an input (or stimulus) and output (response), and how these associations were formed (conditioning, reinforcement). Intermediate constructs (the mind) were rejected. For behaviourists, the only valid subject matter for psychology was behaviour, and language was a behaviour just like any other. Its acquisition and use could therefore be explained by standard techniques of reinforcement and conditioning. This approach perhaps reached its acme in 1957 with the publication of B. F. Skinner's famous (or to linguists, notorious) book *Verbal behaviour*.

Attitudes changed very quickly: in part this was due to a devastating review of Skinner's book by the young American linguist Noam Chomsky (1959). This was one of the rare occasions when the review of a book is probably more influential than the book itself. Chomsky showed that behaviourism was incapable of dealing with natural language. He went on to propose a new type of linguistic theory called transformational grammar that provided both an account of the underlying structure of language and also of people's knowledge of their language (see Chapter 5 for more details). Psycholinguistics blossomed in attempting to test the psychological implications of this linguistic theory. The enterprise was not wholly successful, and experimental results indicated that although linguistics might tell us a great deal about our knowledge of our language and about the constraints on children's language acquisition, it is limited in what it can tell us about the processes involved in speaking and understanding. To a large degree psycholinguistics was absorbed into mainstream cognitive psychology in the 1970s. In this, the information processing or computational metaphor was supreme, and much work during this time primarily attempted to show how one level of representation of language is transformed into another. Information processing approaches to cognition view the mind rather like a computer. The mind uses rules to translate an input (albeit speech or vision) into a symbolic representation. This gives rise to the view that cognition is symbol processing. This can perhaps be seen at its clearest in a computational account of vision, such as that of Marr (1982), where the representation of the visual scene becomes increasingly abstract from the retinal level up through increasingly sophisticated representations. The computational metaphor is clearly influential in modern psycholinguistics, as most models are phrased in terms of the description of levels of processing and the rules or processes that determine what happens in between.

As a consequence of the influence of the computational metaphor, and with the development of suitable experimental techniques, psycholinguistics gained an identity independent of linguistics. However, modern psycholinguistics is primarily an experimental science, and as in much of cognitive psychology, experiments measuring reaction times have been particularly important. There is a particular danger in language research however. When we run experiments, not only do we have to sample randomly from among subjects, we also usually have to sample randomly from the set of possible words. This leads to particular dangers in interpretation and analysis. Clark (1973) advocated the use of a particular statistic called *min F'* (pronounced "min F prime"), which takes account of both of these considerations together. A less stringent constraint is to report analyses by ANOVA by subjects (F_1) and by materials (F_2). The analysis by subjects corresponds to the conventional statistical analysis used in most other areas of psychology, where scores for each subject are averaged across items in each condition. An analysis "by materials" is the inverse of this, averaging scores for each item across subjects in each condition. *Min F'* is a compound of these.

The "cognitive science" approach

Recently the term cognitive science has come to cover the multi-disciplinary approach to the study of the mind, including adult and developmental psychology, philosophy, linguistics, anthropology, neuropsychology and particularly artificial intelligence (AI). We have already mentioned the influence of linguistics upon psycholinguistics; its influence has been particularly strong upon syntax. Philosophy has played an important role in our understanding of meaning. AI involves getting computers to do things that appear to need intelligence, such as understanding a story, or understanding speech. Apart from the obvious technological uses of AI, the hope has been that it will increase our understanding of how humans do such tasks. Traditional AI involves computer modelling of human behaviour emphasising rules, plans and goals. It has the great advantage of implementation; when you write a computer program, you have to be explicit about everything. There are no hidden assumptions in models that are implemented as programs.

If you have seen Kubrick's film *2001: A space odyssey*, you will probably remember HAL, the talking, listening, thinking computer. HAL's linguistic abilities are what researchers in AI hope to emulate. Early successes in this approach to language led to great optimism that this was a readily realisable goal. Among the earliest of these was Weizenbaum's (1966) program called ELIZA. This simulated a non-directive, Rogerian therapist. In the following example, the output of the computer—the ELIZA program—are in capitals.

Men are all alike.
IN WHAT WAY
They're always bugging us about something or other.
CAN YOU THINK OF A SPECIFIC EXAMPLE
Well, my boyfriend made me come here.
YOUR BOYFRIEND MADE YOU COME HERE
He says I'm depressed much of the time.
I AM SORRY TO HEAR THAT YOU ARE DEPRESSED
It's true that I am unhappy.
DO YOU THINK COMING HERE WILL HELP YOU NOT TO BE UNHAPPY
I need some help, that much seems certain.
WHAT WOULD IT MEAN IF YOU GOT SOME HELP
Perhaps I could learn to get along with my mother.
TELL ME MORE ABOUT YOUR FAMILY

The program worked in a very simple way using a few tricks such as matching sentences to pre-stored structures of templates, producing pre-determined responses to a few keywords (such as mother), and repeating what was input to it back with a few appropriate changes in word order. Nevertheless people became very attached to it, even if they knew it was only a machine. Some even wanted to consult regularly with it in private. This however says more about human concerns than it does about how language is produced. In the 1960s there were a number of variants of ELIZA, such as PARRY (Colby, 1975), which "simulated" the output of a paranoid schizophrenic. The next influential program was SHRDLU (Winograd, 1972). This program could represent and answer questions about an imaginary world called "blocksworld". Blocksworlds are occupied by small red pyramids sitting on top of big blue cubes. SHRDLU's success in being able to "understand" sentences such as "move" was much hailed at the time. It soon became clear that understanding language was much more difficult than this. These early demonstrations worked only for very simple, limited domains, and the programs had no real understanding of what was happening. SHRDLU could not answer questions about elephants, or even what "block" means. Its knowledge is limited to the role of blocks within blocksworld.

These early attempts did have the virtue of demonstrating the enormity of the task in understanding language. They also revealed the main problems which have to be solved before we can talk of computers understanding language. In principle, there is an infinite number, and in practice, a very large number of sentences, of varying degrees of complexity. We can talk about and understand potentially anything. The roles which context and world knowledge play in understanding are very important; potentially anything might be necessary to understand a particular sentence. The conventional AI approach still has some influence on psycholinguistic theorisation, particularly on how we understand syntax (see the section on augmented transition networks in Chapter 5) and how we make inferences in story comprehension (see Chapter 6).

More recently an approach called variously *connectionism*, *parallel distributed processing*, or *neural networks* has assumed great importance. We will look at particular models in some detail, but they all have in common that they involve many very simple, richly interconnected neuron-like units working together without an explicit governing plan. Instead, rules and behaviour emerge from the interactions between these many simple units.

One concept is central in connectionism, and has applications throughout this book. This is the idea of *activation*. In fact it did not originate with connectionism; the idea has been around for a long time. Activation is a continuously varying quantity, and can be thought of as a property rather like heat. We also talk of how activation can spread from one unit or word or point in a network to another.

Although the goal of this book is to explain how humans understand and produce language, we will be eclectic about the evidence we will consider. The bulk of our data comes from traditional psychology experiments, particularly involving reaction times. This is not the only source of data, however; among other things, we also use observational studies and linguistic intuitions. Much has been learnt from computer modelling, and this will be discussed when relevant.

Cognitive neuropsychology

Cognitive neuropsychology is another recent development that has led to advances in our understanding of psycholinguistics. Traditional neurology and neuropsychology have been concerned primarily with questions to do with which parts of the brain control different sorts of behaviour (that is, with the *localisation of function*), and with working out how complex behaviours map onto the flow of information through brain structures. In one of the best known traditional neuropsychological models of language, the Wernicke-Geschwind model, language processes basically flow from the back of the left hemisphere to the front, with high-level planning and semantic processes towards the rear, low-level sound retrieval and articulation towards the front. The emphasis of cognitive neuropsychology is rather different: the goal is to relate brain-damaged behaviour to models of normal processing. For example, research on impaired reading (or dyslexia) has contributed to our understanding of the processes of normal reading, and research on impaired speech (or aphasia) has contributed to our understanding of the processes of speech production. Shallice (1988) argued that cognitive neuropsychology can be distinguished from traditional neuropsychology in three crucial respects. First, it has made a theoretical advance in relating neuropsychological disorders to cognitive models. Second, it has made a methodological advance in stressing the importance of single case studies, rather than group studies of neuropsychological impairment. That is, the emphasis is upon providing a detailed description and explanation of individual patients, rather than comparing groups of patients who might not have the same underlying deficit. Third, it has contributed a research programme in that it emphasises how models of normal processing can be informed by studying brain-damaged behaviour. Cognitive neuropsychology has contributed a great deal to our understanding of language, and we will discuss it on a number of occasions. However, Shallice (1988) argues that in some respects this approach has been taken too far, and identifies this position as that of *ultra-cognitive neuropsychology*. First, it has gone too far in arguing that group studies cannot provide any information appropriate for constructing cognitive models. This proposal has led to a heated controversy (see, for example, Bates, McDonald, MacWhinney, & Appelbaum, 1991; Caramazza, 1986, 1991; McCloskey & Caramazza, 1988). Second, it has gone too far in claiming that information about the localisation of function is irrelevant to our understanding of behaviour (e.g. Morton, 1984). Third, it has under-valued clinical information about patients. Seidenberg (1988) points to another problem, which is that cognitive neuropsychology places too much emphasis on uncovering the *functional architecture* of the systems involved. That is, the organisation of the components involved is emphasised at the cost of exploring the processes actually involved. This leads to the construction of "box-and-arrow" diagrams with little advance in our understanding of what goes on inside the boxes.

At times it will appear that I have adopted the ultra-cognitivist stance: I will primarily discuss single case studies, I will rarely refer to brain topology, and I will not discuss additional clinical information. This arises more as a combination of reflecting the dominant paradigm in the literature and concentrating upon the results of cognitive neuropsychology as it informs our models of normal processing than because of my particular theoretical stance. Certainly more emphasis is now being placed on understanding not just how components are related to one another, but also on what happens inside the components. This has particularly been the case since connectionist modelling has been applied to cognitive neuropsychology.

An additional concept important in both traditional and cognitive neuropsychology is that of the *double dissociation*. Consider two patients A and B given two tasks I and II. Patient A performs normally on task I but cannot perform task II. Patient B displays the reverse pattern of behaviour, in performing normally on task I but not on task II (see Fig. 1.1). If this is the case, the two tasks are said to be doubly dissociated. We can then conclude that different processes underlie each task. If we further find that patients A and B have lesions to different parts of the brain we will be further tempted to draw a conclusion about where these processes are localised.

Some care is necessary with inferences from neuropsychological data. Some researchers have questioned the whole enterprise of trying to find out about normal processing by studying brain-damaged behaviour. Deutsch (1960) made the analogy of attempting to find out how a radio set works by removing its components. He pointed out that if we did this, we would conclude that the function of a capacitor was to inhibit loud wailing sounds! Furthermore the categories we will discuss are not always clearly recognisable in the clinical setting. There is often much overlap between patients, with the more pure cases usually associated with smaller amounts of brain damage. Finally, the position subsequent to damage is not static; intact processes reorganise, and some recovery of function often occurs, even in adults. Fortunately we find that neuropsychological and other data usually converge to suggest the same model.

Modularity and interaction. At the beginning of this chapter I said that modularity and interactions between systems would be a recurring theme in this book. The existence of a double dissociation is often taken

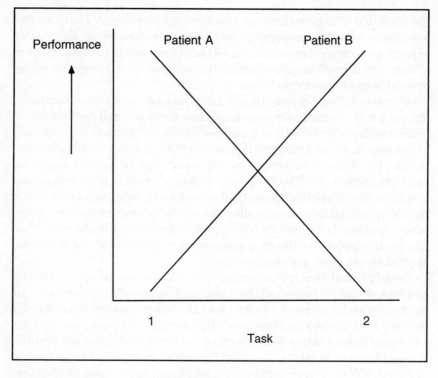

FIG. 1.1. Illustration of a hypothetical double dissociation.

as evidence of the *modularity* of the processes involved. This concept of modularity is important in psycholinguistics. A module is a self-contained set of processes: it converts an input to an output without any outside help on what goes on in-between. Another way of putting this is that the processes inside a module are "independent" of processes outside the module. Yet another way is to say that processing is purely *bottom-up*. The opposing view is that processing is interactive. We can see interactive processes as involving *feedback* or *reverse information flow*. For example, does knowledge about what a word might be influence the recognition of its component sounds or letters? Fodor (1983) clarified modularity as a major research theme for cognitive psychology, and the same questions arise in psycholinguistics. Are the processes of language self-contained, or do they interact with one another? For example, we shall see that a major issue in how we process information about word order is the extent to which we use information about meaning. Tanenhaus and Lucas (1987) identified two main predictions of the modularity hypothesis: First, the information accessed during each processing stage should be invariant across all contexts; second, the speed with which information becomes available should not be influenced by context from outside that processing stage. As we shall see, the role of context and feedback are fundamental issues in the study of language.

When we consider the neuropsychology of modularity, however, we must remember that we can talk both about physical modularity (are psychological processes localised in one part of the brain?) and processing modularity (in principle a set of processes might be distributed across the brain yet have a modular role in the processing model). It makes sense however from the point of view of the design of the cognitive system if the two are related; that is, cognitive modules correspond to neuropsychological modules. However, Farah (1994) criticises this "locality" assumption, and considers neuropsychological dissociations from the viewpoint of interactive, connectionist systems.

At the moment, the issue of modularity makes psycholinguists perhaps more agitated than anything else, and to the outsider it is sometimes difficult to see why. According to many researchers, we should start with the assumption that processes are modular or non-interactive unless there are very good reasons to think otherwise. There are a number of reasons for this assumption. The first is simplicity: modular models generally involve fewer processes and connections between systems. The second is a belief that evolution favours modules. However, the controversy really gets going when it comes to agreeing what a "very good reason" to think otherwise might be. It is always possible to come up with an *auxiliary hypothesis* (Lakatos, 1970) that can be used to modify and hence save the original modularity hypothesis. We will see this time and time again: in word recognition, the saving hypothesis is to postulate post-access processes; in syntax and parsing, it is to propose parallel processing with deferred decision making; and in word production, it is to propose an editor, or to stress the role of working memory, or to claim that some kinds of data (e.g. picture naming times) are more fundamental than others (e.g. speech errors). Researchers can get very hot under the collar about this.

There are broader implications of modularity, too. Generally those most committed to the claim that language processes are highly modular also argue that a great deal of our language capacity is innate. The argument is essentially that nice, clean-cut modules must be hard-wired, and complex, messy systems must reflect learning. Finally, both Fodor (1983, 1985) and Pinker (1994), arch-exponents of modularity and innate processes in language, give a broader philosophical view: modularity is inconsistent with *relativism*, the idea that anything goes (particularly in the social sciences). Modules provide a fixed framework in which to study the mind.

In the end, of course, you should listen to the data, and ask in each case: is this auxiliary hypothesis more plausible than the non-modular alternative?

CONCLUDING SUMMARY

In this chapter we have tried to answer the two questions "what is language?" and "what is psycholinguistics?" Psycholinguistics is the scientific study of the psychological processes involved in producing, understanding, and remembering language. Although it uses data from a number of sources, the emphasis in this book at least is upon a cognitive approach. The main types of evidence with which we will be concerned will be experiments (particularly involving reaction times), computer simulations, and neuropsychological case studies. Another bias of this book is that it emphasises how modern psycholinguistics is actually done: what are the experimental techniques in use, what are their advantages and limitations, and what things affect subjects' performance in experiments.

A ready formal definition of *language* is surprisingly elusive. Language is a system of communication based upon words. Words have meaning, and are combined together according to the syntactic rules of our grammar to create an infinite number of sentences. This enables us to communicate about anything. Naturally occurring animal communication systems are limited in a number of ways. Although there have been several attempts to teach non-human primates a human-like language, there is as yet no unequivocal evidence that these have been successful. At present the most promising work is with pygmy chimpanzees. Hence we cannot yet reject the idea that language is a special faculty unique to humans. We shall return to these themes in later chapters when we examine the relationship between language and thought, and the way in which children acquire language.

Finally, we traced the history of psycholinguistics. We looked at the role of other disciplines, such as neuropsychology. We also saw why modularity is given such prominence in current research.

FURTHER READING

For a summary of the early history of psycholinguistics, see Fodor, Bever and Garrett (1974), and of linguistics, Lyons (1977a). If you wish to find out more about linguistics, you might try Fromkin and Rodman (1978) or Yule (1985). Aitchison (1994) covers many of the issues concerning the representation and processing of single words with a strong linguistic emphasis. A general survey of cognitive science is provided by Stillings et al. (1987). There are many introductory textbooks on traditional AI, including Boden (1977) and Winston (1984). Two recent introductions to connectionism are Quinlan (1991) and Bechtel and Abrahamsen (1991). Traditional neuropsychology and the Wernicke-Geschwind model are described in detail by Kolb and Whishaw (1990). If you want to find out more about cognitive neuropsychology in general, try Ellis and Young (1988) or Shallice (1988).

Dennett (1991) discusses the evolution of language, and its possible relationship to consciousness. For a more detailed review of animal communication systems and their cognitive abilities, see Pearce (1987). A detailed summary of early attempts to teach apes language is provided by Premack (1986a). More recent analyses of Washoe's signs are reported by Gardner, van Cantford, and Gardner (1992). Premack's later stance is critically discussed in a review by Carston (1987) and Walker (1987); see also the debate between Premack (1986b) and Bickerton (1986) in the journal *Cognition*. A popular and contemporary account of Kanzi is given by Savage-Rumbaugh and Lewin (1994). See Klima and Bellugi (1979) for more on sign language in humans.

An up-to-date review of most of psycholinguistics is provided by Gernsbacher (1994). This is a collection of review articles, each written by a leading researcher in the field, that covers every major topic in psycholinguistics.

A number of journals cover the field of psycholinguistics. Many relevant experimental articles can be found in journals such as the *Journal of Experimental Psychology* (particularly the sections entitled *General* and *Language, Memory and Cognition*, and, for lower level processes such as speech perception and aspects of visual word recognition, *Human Perception and Performance*), the *Quarterly Journal of Experimental Psychology, Cognition, Cognitive Psychology, Cognitive Science*, and *Memory and Cognition*. Two journals with a particularly strong language bias are the *Journal of Memory and Language* (formerly called the *Journal of Verbal Learning and Verbal Behavior*) and *Language and Cognitive Processes*. Theoretical and review papers can often be found in *Psychological Review, Psychological Bulletin*, and the *Behavioral and Brain Sciences*. The latter includes critical commentaries on the target article, plus a reply to those commentaries, that can be most revealing. Articles on AI approaches to language can be found in *Cognitive Science* again, and sometimes in *Artificial Intelligence*. Many relevant neuropsychological papers can be found in *Brain and Language* and *Cognitive Neuropsychology* and sometimes in *Brain* and *Cortex*. Papers with a biological or connectionist angle on language can sometimes also be found in the *Journal of Cognitive Neuroscience*. Journals rich in good papers on language acquisition are *Journal of Child Language* and *First Language*; see also *Child Development*.

CHAPTER TWO

The speech system and spoken word recognition

INTRODUCTION

Speech is at the very heart of our language faculties. This chapter is about the raw sounds of language, how we say them, and how we understand them. How do we produce sounds? How do we recognise them? How do we recognise spoken words?

At the outset we should make a distinction between speech perception, and spoken word recognition. The former is about how we identify or perceive the sounds of language, while the latter is about a higher-level process, how we recognise the words which they make up. Although this is a convenient distinction to make, it should become clear that it is perhaps a rather artificial one. We cannot just assume that we identify all the sounds of a word, and then put them together to recognise the word. Knowing the word may help us to identify their constituent sounds; as we shall see, this is an important and controversial topic. We may not even need to hear all the sounds of a word before we can identify it.

At this point it is useful to introduce the concept of the *lexicon*. This can be thought of as a mental dictionary. It is hypothesised to contain all the information we know about a word, including its sounds (phonology), meaning (semantics), written appearance (orthography), and the syntactic roles in which it can partake. Word recognition can be thought of as rather like looking a word up in a dictionary; when we know what the word is, we then have access to all the information about it, such as what it means. So when we see or hear a word, how do we access its representation within the lexicon? How do we know whether an item is stored there or not? What are the differences between understanding speech and understanding visually presented words? The processes of lexical access and how items are represented there are of fundamental interest to psycholinguists.

Words and their structure.   The idea of a *word* also merits some consideration. Like the word "language", the word "word" turns out on closer examination to be a somewhat slippery notion. The dictionary definition is that a word is "a unit of language". For now we can think of a word as the smallest self-contained unit of language that has some meaning. A word can be analysed at a number of levels. At the lowest, it is made up out of sounds and their components. Sounds combine together to form syllables. Hence the word "cat" has three sounds and one syllable; "houses" has two syllables; "syllable" has three syllables. It is also useful to introduce another concept, that of a unit of structure that reflects meaning. This unit is called a *morpheme*. Consider a word like "ghosts". This is made up out of two units of meaning: the idea of "ghost", and then the plural ending ("-s"), or inflection, which conveys the idea of number, that there is more than one ghost. Therefore we say that "ghosts" is made up out of two morphemes, the "ghost" morpheme and plural morpheme "s". The same can be said of past tense endings or inflections: "kissed" is also made up out of two morphemes, "kiss" plus the "-ed" ending that signifies the event happened in the past. Notice that irregular forms that do not obey the general rule of forming plurals by adding an "-s" to the end of a noun or forming the past tense by adding a "-d" or "-ed" to the end of a verb also contain at least two morphemes: "gave" contains two morphemes, the idea of "give" plus the idea of the past tense. Hence "house", "mouse", and "do" are made up out of one morpheme, whereas "houses", "mice" and "does" are made up out of two. "Rehoused" is made up out of three morphemes: "house" plus "re-" added through mechanisms of derivational morphology, and "-ed" added by inflection. The children's favourite "antidisestablishmentarianism" is made up of six, and so on.

In this chapter we will look first at the speech system. We will consider its anatomy, and the way in which different sounds are made. Then we look at a notation for representing sounds. After this we will examine the processes of speech perception and spoken word recognition. As we have already noted, this is a convenient if rather arbitrary division. We will start with the lower-level, apparently simpler processes.

THE ANATOMY OF SPEECH AND
REPRESENTING SOUNDS

In the previous chapter, we mentioned that there are two approaches to the study of sounds, phonology and phonetics. A gross characterisation is that phonology is the higher level study of sounds, whereas phonetics studies them at a lower level. In particular, phonology studies sound in the context of a particular language, whereas phonetics looks at them more absolutely. This should be made clear with an example. Consider the sound "p" in the English words "pin" vs. "spin". The actual sounds are different; you can tell this by putting your hand up to your mouth as you say them. You should be able to feel a breath of air going out as you say "pin", but not as you say "spin". The "p" sound in "pin" is said to be aspirated, and that in "spin" unaspirated. In English it does not make any difference to the meaning of the word which you use, even though the sounds are different—if you could manage to say "pin" with an unaspirated "p" it might sound a little odd, but to your listeners it would still have the same meaning as "pin" as when said normally. In some languages however aspiration does make a difference to the meaning of words. In Thai, for example "paa" (unaspirated) means "forest", "paa" (aspirated) means "to split". The two "p"s are acoustically different—they are said to be different *phones*. These different phones or sounds are said to be the same *phoneme* of a particular language if the difference between them never makes a difference to the meaning of words. So a phoneme is a basic unit of sound in a particular language. In English then the two sorts of "p" are the same phoneme, whereas in Thai they are different phonemes. To take another example, the sounds "l" and "r" are clearly different phones, and in English they are also different phonemes. In Japanese however they represent the same phoneme. Different phones that are understood as the same phoneme in a language are called *allophones*. Hence in English aspirated [pʰ] and unaspirated [p] are allophones of /p/. A special notation is used for distinguishing between phones and phonemes. Conventionally, square brackets are used to designate [phones], whereas slanting lines are used for /phonemes/. Broadly speaking phonetics is the study of phones, and phonology is the study of phonemes. There are in fact three different types of phonetics depending upon which emphasis is taken: articulatory (which emphasises how sounds are made), auditory/perceptual (which emphasises how sounds are perceived), and acoustic (which emphasises the sound waveform and physical properties). In this book we mainly use the articulatory approach, and will largely be concerned with the phonemes and phonology of English. The concept of a phoneme is an extremely important one in both the psychology of speech recognition and production. There is an even lower level of analysis of sounds, acoustics, which is concerned with the physics of the sounds. Generally we shall not be much concerned with acoustics in this book.

Acoustic information about sounds can be depicted in a number of ways. One of the most commonly used is a sound *spectrogram* (see Fig. 2.1). This shows the amount of energy present in a sound when frequency is plotted against time. The bursts of energy are called *formants*.

Sounds do not always correspond in languages such as English to individual letters. The letter "o" represents a number of different sounds (such as in the words "mock", "moon", and "mow"). It would be convenient to have a system of representing individual sounds with specific symbols. Because of these sorts of ambiguities, letters are not suitable. Such a system is the *International Phonetic Alphabet* (or IPA for short). The symbols of the IPA and examples of the sounds they represent are shown in Table 2.1. The sounds which these symbols

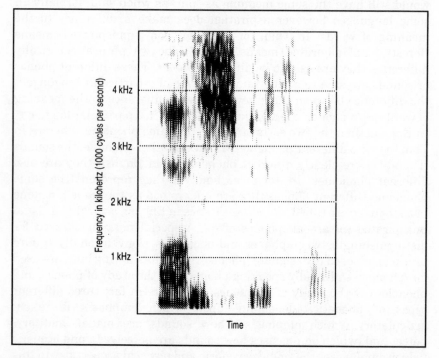

FIG. 2.1. Sound spectrogram for the word *hospital*. The burst of noise across a wide range of frequencies corresponds to /s/; the noticeable gaps are the stop consonants /p/ and /t/. In normal speech the final vowel is barely represented.

TABLE 2.1
The International Phonetic Alphabet (IPA) with alternative symbols shown in parentheses. Main examples are for most speakers of British English; the far right symbols for vowels and diphthongs are for most speakers of American English

Consonants		
p	*p*at	*p*ie
b	*b*at	*b*a*b*ble
t	*t*ie	to*t*
k	*k*id	*k*ic*k*
d	*d*id	*d*ee*d*
g	*g*et	ke*g*
s	*s*un	*p*sychology
z	ra*z*or	pea*s*
f	*f*ield	lau*gh*
v	*v*ole	dro*v*e
m	*m*ole	*m*u*m*
n	*n*ot	*n*u*n*
ŋ	si*ng*	thi*n*k
θ	*th*igh	mo*th*
ð	*th*e	*th*en
ʃ (š)	*sh*e	*sh*ield
ʒ (ž)	vi*s*ion	mea*s*ure
l	*l*ie	*l*ead
w	*w*e	*w*itch
ʌ	*wh*en	*wh*ale
r	*r*at	*r*an
j (y)	*y*ou	*y*oung
h	*h*it	*h*im
tʃ (č, t̠š)	*ch*eese	*ch*ur*ch*
dʒ (ǰ, dž)	ju*dg*e,	reli*g*ion
x	lo*ch*	(Scottish pronunciation)
ʔ	bo*tt*le	(glottal pronunciation)

TABLE 2.1 (continued)

Vowels

British English			American English
i	r*ee*d	b*ea*t	i
ɛ	b*e*d	s*ai*d	ɛ
ɪ (I)	d*i*d	b*i*t	ɪ
eɪ (e)	m*a*y	b*ai*t	eɪ
æ	r*a*t	*a*nger	æ
ɔ	s*aw*	*au*thor	ɔ (in s*aw*)
ɑ (a)	h*ar*d	c*ar*	ɑr
ɒ	p*o*t	g*o*t	ɑ
oɷ (o)	g*o*	b*oa*t	oɷ
u	wh*o*	b*oo*t	u
ɷ (U)	c*ou*ld	f*oo*t	ɷ
ə	b*i*rd	sof*a**	ər
ʌ	h*u*t	t*ou*gh	ʌ

Diphthongs

aɪ (ay)	r*i*se	b*i*te	aɪ
aɷ (æw)	c*ow*	ab*ou*t	aɷ
ɔɪ (ɔy)	b*oy*	c*oy*	ɔɪ
ɪə	h*ere*	m*ere*	ɪr
ɛə	m*are*	r*are*	er
aɪɔ	h*ire*	f*ire*	aɪr
ju	n*ew*,	French t*u*	

**Note:* This is the *schwa*, a weak, central, neutral vowel often used to replace unstressed vowels.

represent are illustrated by the examples of common words. However, it should be apparent that the ways in which these words are pronounced can vary greatly. These examples are based upon received pronunciation in English; American English is noticeably different in its pronunciation of vowels. In addition to the regular differences in the pronunciation of phonemes, there might also be different irregular pronunciations; for example, American English tends to drop the initial /h/ in "herbs". Of course, words might be pronounced differently within the same country—this is known as a *dialect* difference. (It is important to note that these examples do not mean that these are the correct ways of pronouncing words.) The advantage of the IPA is that it is possible to represent these different ways of pronouncing the same thing.

Speech is produced by the vocal tract, including the lips, teeth, tongue, mouth, and voice box or larynx (see Fig. 2.2). Sounds are produced by changing the shape of the vocal tract in some way. There are two different major types of sounds. *Consonants* (such as p, b, t, d, k) are made by closing or restricting some part of the vocal tract. *Vowels* are made by modifying the shape of the vocal tract which remains more or less open while the sound is being produced. This suggests one way of examining the relationship between sounds; we can look at their *place of articulation*—that is, the place where the vocal tract is closed or restricted.

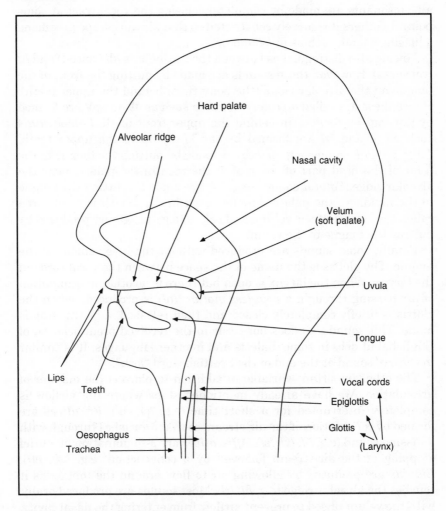

FIG. 2.2. The structure of the vocal tract.

Consonants

We can classify consonants depending upon the place of articulation. For example, /p/ and /b/ are called *bilabial* sounds and are made by closing the mouth at the lips; /t/ and /d/ by putting the tongue to the back of the teeth. How do /b/ and /p/ differ? In one case (/b/), the vocal chords are closed and vibrating from the moment the lips are released; they are said to be *pronounced with voice* or just *voiced*. In the other case, (/p/) there is a short delay, as the vocal chords are spread apart as air is first passed between them. Hence they take some time to start vibrating. These are said to be produced without voice, voiceless, or unvoiced. Not all consonants are made by completely closing the vocal tract at some point. In others it is merely constricted so that air can escape producing a hissing sound, such as in /s/ and /z/.

Voicing also distinguishes between the consonants /d/ (voiced) and /t/ (voiceless). However, these sounds are made by putting the front of the tongue on the alveolar ridge (the bony ridge behind the upper teeth). Hence these are called *alveolars*. *Dentals* such as /θ/ and /ð/ are formed by putting the tongue tip behind the upper front teeth. *Labiodentals* such as /f/ and /v/ are formed by the lower lip to the upper teeth. *Alveo-palatal* sounds (e.g. /ʃ/, /ʒ/) are made by putting the tongue to the front of the hard part of the roof of the mouth, the palate, near the alveolar ridge. *Palatal* sounds (e.g. /y/) are made by putting the tongue to the middle of the palate. Further back in the mouth is a soft area called the soft palate or velum, and *velars* (e.g. /k/, /g/) are produced by putting the tongue to the velum.

Finally, some sounds are produced without the involvement of the tongue. The glottis is the name of the space between the vocal cords in the larynx. When the larynx is open but there is no other manipulation of air passing through, a *voiceless glottal* (/h/) is produced. When the glottis is briefly completely closed and then released, a glottal stop is made. This sound (/x/) does not occur in the received pronunciation of English, but does in some dialects and in other languages. It is similar to the /ch/ sound at the end of the Scottish word "loch".

The other important variable in addition to place is the manner of articulation. We have already mentioned stops where the airflow is completely interrupted for a short time (e.g. /p/, /b/). *Fricatives* are formed by constriction of the air-stream so that air rushes through with a hissing sound (e.g. /f/, /v/, /s/). *Affricatives* are a combination of a brief stopping of the air-stream followed by a constriction (e.g. /dʒ/, /tʃ/). *Liquids* are produced by allowing air to flow around the tongue as it touches the alveolar ridge (e.g. /l/, /r/). Most sounds are produced orally, with the velum raised to prevent airflow from entering the nasal cavity. If it does and air is allowed to flow out through the nose we get nasal sounds (e.g. /m/, /n/). *Glides* or semi-vowels are transition sounds produced as the tongue moves from one vowel position to another (e.g. /w/, /y/).

In summary, it is possible to build up a table that distinguishes between consonants according to different combinations of such distinguishing phonological features (see Table 2.2).

Vowels

Different features are necessary to describe vowels. Vowels are made with a relatively free flow of air, and are determined by the way in which the shape of the tongue modifies the airflow. Table 2.3 provides a classification of verbs depending on the position (which can be raised, medium, or lower) of the front, central, or rear portions of the tongue. For example, the /i/ sound in "meat" is a high front vowel because the air flows with the front part of the tongue in a raised position.

Finally, there are combined vowel sounds that contain two sounds. These special types of vowels are called *diphthongs*. They begin with a vowel sound and end with a glide. Examples are the sounds in "my", "cow", and "boy".

It should be reiterated that whereas the pronunciation of consonants is relatively constant across speakers, that of vowels can differ greatly across dialects. Also whereas the choice of consonants within a word is constant across dialects, the vowels are not. For example, for any particular word the consonants are identical in British English and American English; it is the vowels that differ.

TABLE 2.2
English consonants as combinations of distinguishing phonological features

PLACE	stop		fricative		affricative		nasal		liquid glide		glide	
	+V	–V	+V	–V	+V	–V	+V	–V	+V	–V	+V	–V
bilabial	b	p					m				w	
labiodental			v	f								
dental			ð	θ								
alveolar	d	t	z	s			n					
alveopalatal			ʒ	ʃ	dʒ	tʃ			l, r		y	
velar	g	k					ŋ					
glottal		ʔ									h	

TABLE 2.3
Vowels as combinations of distinguishing phonological features

	Front	Central	Back
High	i		u
	ɪ		ω
Mid	eɪ	ə	oω
	ɛ		ɔ
Low	æ	ʌ	ɑ

Further phonetic considerations

When two words in a language differ apart from one sound, they are called *minimal pairs*. Examples are "dog" and "cog", "bat", and "pat", "fog" and "fop". We can extend this to talk about minimal sets of words (e.g. "pat", "bat", "cat", "hat"), all of which differ by only one phoneme, in the same position. We have already seen that making a difference to meaning is part of the definition of a phoneme. Substituting one phoneme for another by definition leads to a change in the meaning, whereas just changing one phone for another (e.g. aspirated for unaspirated [p]) need not necessarily do so.

Higher level structure

You will remember that words can be divided into syllables. For example, the word syl—la—ble has three. Many words are monosyllabic—they only have one syllable, and indeed a great deal of psycholinguistic research has been carried out on monosyllabic words. Syllables can be analysed in terms of a hierarchical structure intermediate between words and phonemes (see Fig. 2.3).

The *onset* is an initial consonant or cluster (e.g. /cl/); the *rime* consists of a nucleus which is a vowel or syllabic consonant, and a *coda*, which is a final consonant. Hence in the word "rime" "r-" is the onset, and "-ime" the rime, which in turn can be analysed into a nucleus ("i"), and coda ("m"). All of these components are optional, apart from the nucleus, which is present in all English words. Rules concerning how syllables combine differ across languages—for example, Japanese words cannot have codas.

Finally, features of words and syllables that may span more than phoneme, such as pitch and stress, are called *suprasegmental* features.

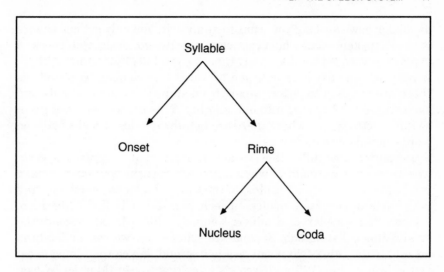

FIG. 2.3. The tree structure of syllables.

SPEECH PERCEPTION

It is useful to distinguish two sorts of code in speech perception. At the lower level we have the *pre-lexical* (or *phonetic*) code which is sound representation prior to lexical access when the word is identified. At a higher level we have the *post-lexical* (or *phonological*) code, a representation that is available only after lexical access. Foss and his colleagues (Foss & Blank, 1980; Foss & Gernsbacher, 1983) have argued for a dual-code theory where speech processing employs both codes. It is possible to manipulate the difficulty of *phoneme monitoring task*, where subjects have to press a button as soon as they hear a particular sound, by manipulating how plausible the target word is in the context of the sentence, or the clarity of the speech signal. As this task requires subjects to access the prelexical code directly, they can only do this in relatively easy conditions. Hence subjects respond to the prelexical code when the phoneme monitoring task is easy, but to the postlexical code when the task is difficult. An important task for understanding speech recognition is to specify the nature of the prelexical code. As we shall see, one aspect of this is the issue of whether or not phonemes are represented explicitly in this representation.

Preliminary findings and problems in speech perception

Speech perception is a more difficult task than visual word perception. The most obvious difference between the tasks is that spoken words are present only very briefly, while a written or printed word is there in front of you for however long you want to analyse it. You only get one chance with a spoken word, but you can usually go back and check a visually-presented word as many times as you like. Furthermore, there is not such an easy segmentation of words into component sounds as there are words into letters; apart from stop consonants, sounds and even words tend to slur into one another. This can be seen clearly in sound spectrograms, where there are not always clear breaks between words, yet alone sounds.

In spite of these difficulties, we are rather good at recognising speech. The process is automatic; when you hear speech, you cannot make yourself not understand it. Most of the time it happens effortlessly and with little apparent difficulty. Speech perception is fast (Liberman, Cooper, Shankweiler, & Studdert-Kennedy, 1967). In one second, the brain cannot distinguish 10 separate sounds; yet we can understand speech at the rate of 20 phonemes per second. We can recognise most words in less than 125 milliseconds after their onset (Marslen-Wilson & Welsh, 1978). (The millisecond, a thousandth of a second, is the standard unit of measurement in psycholinguistics.) Furthermore, speech sounds seem to be at an advantage over non-speech sounds when heard against background noise. Miller, Heise, and Lichten (1951) found that the more words there are to choose from a predetermined set (as they put it, the greater the information transmitted per word), the louder the signal had to be relative to the noise for the subjects to identify them equally well. Bruce (1958) showed that words in a meaningful context are recognised better against background noise than words out of context. Therefore, despite all the problems we will look at, there is clearly some advantage to speech that makes it easier to recognise than non-speech. What might this advantage be? It is obtained in spite of the fact that the mapping from the physical acoustic level to the sounds we hear is far from straightforward.

Acoustic signals and phonetic segments.   The acoustic properties of phonemes are not fixed. They vary with the context they are in, and they even vary acoustically depending upon the speaking rate (Miller, 1981). This makes identifying phonemes a complex task, as it means that they cannot be identified by comparison with a "perfect exemplar" of that phoneme, or a *template*. There is an analogy with recognising letters; there are lots of perfectly acceptable ways of writing the same letter. This variation is most clear in the context of different phones that are the same phoneme, such as the two forms of /p/. Yet we successfully map these different phones onto one phoneme.

If we look at the physical acoustic signal and the sounds conveyed by the signal, it is apparent the relationship between the two is a complex one. In their review of speech perception, Miller and Jusczyk (1989) point out that this complexity arises because of two main features which must act as major constraints on theories of speech perception. These features are both facets of the lack of identity or isomorphism between the acoustic and phonetic levels of language. They are the *segmentation* and *invariance* problems. The segmentation problem is that sounds slur together and cannot easily be separated. The invariance problem is that the same phoneme can sound different depending upon the context in which occurs. Let us look at these problems in more detail.

The segmentation problem is that is not easy to separate sounds in speech as they run together (except for stop consonants and pauses). This problem does not just apply to sounds within words; in normal conditions, words also run into each other. To take a famous example, in normal speech the strings "I scream" and "ice cream" sound indistinguishable. The acoustic segments visible in spectrographic displays do not map in any easy way into phonetic segments. There are a number of possible strategies available for coping with this, such as initiating lexical access anew for every phoneme we hear, or only after possible words have been found. Current evidence suggests that syllable boundaries are important in solving this problem (see Altmann, 1990). However, the strategies speakers develop depend upon exposure to a particular language. In English, the main strategy employed is that what are called *strong syllables*—those that bear stress and are not shortened to schwas (see Table 2.1)—are likely to be the initial syllables of main content-bearing words, while weak syllables are either not word initial, or start a grammatical word (Cutler & Butterfield, 1992; Cutler & Norris, 1988). It is possible to construct experimental materials that violate these expectations, and these reliably induce mishearings in listeners. This type of procedure, whereby listeners segment speech by identifying stressed syllables, is called *stress-based segmentation*. An alternative mechanism, used in languages such as French which have very clear and unambiguous syllables, is called *syllable-based segmentation*, based, as its name implies, on detecting syllables. In stress-based languages such as English syllable boundaries are often unclear, and identifying the syllables is hence not reliable. Hence the segmentation strategy is determined by the form of the language (Cutler, Mehler, Norris, & Segui, 1986). English-French bilingual speakers segment depending on their primary or dominant language: only English-dominant speakers show stress-based segmentation with English language materials, and never show syllable-based segmentation, whereas only French-dominant speakers show syllabic segmentation, and only with French materials (Cutler, Mehler, Norris, & Segui, 1992).

Acoustic invariance arises because the details of the realisation of a phoneme varies in the context of others. This means that phonemes take on some of the acoustic properties of their neighbours, a process known as *assimilation*. Hence the /ɪ/ phoneme is usually produced without nasal quality, but in words such as "pin" and "sing" the way in which the vocal tract anticipates the shape it needs to adopt for the next phoneme means that /ɪ/ takes on a nasal quality. That is, there are *coarticulation* effects in that as we produce one sound our vocal apparatus has just moved into position from making another sound, and is preparing to change position again to make the subsequent sound. This means that information about the identity of phonetic segments may be spread over several acoustic segments. This has the consequence that phonemes vary slightly depending upon the context. This property has the advantage however that we do not gather information about only one phoneme at any one time; they provide us with some information about the surrounding sounds (a feature known as *parallel transmission*). For example, the [b] in "bill", "ball", "bull" and "bell" are all slightly different, and tell us about what is coming next. The disadvantage is that there is no single invariant property of the acoustic signal that serves as a necessary and sufficient cue to the identity of the phonetic segment.

Categorical perception.   Even though there is all this variation in the way in which phonemes can sound, we do not appear to notice these differences. We classify speech sounds as one phoneme or another; there is no half-way house. This phenomenon is known as categorical perception of phonemes. It was first demonstrated by Liberman, Harris, Hoffman, and Griffith (1957). They used a speech synthesiser to create a continuum of artificial syllables which differed in the place of articulation. In spite of the continuum, subjects placed these syllables into three quite distinct categories beginning with /b/, /d/, and /g/. Another further example of categorical perception is voice onset time (abbreviated to VOT). You will remember from our discussion of how consonants are made that for some consonants, the voiced consonants (e.g. /b/ and /d/), the vocal cords start vibrating as soon as the vocal tract is closed, whereas for others (the unvoiced consonants, such as /p/ and /t/) there is a delay of about 60 milliseconds. The pairs /p/ and /b/, and /t/ and /d/ differ only in this minimal feature of voicing. Voicing actually lies on a continuum; it is possible to create sounds with a VOT of, for example, 30 milliseconds. Although this is midway between the two extremes, we actually categorise such sounds as being either simply voiced or unvoiced. (Exactly which may differ from time to time and person to person, and we shall see that people can actually be biased towards one end of the continuum or the other. Categorical perception is also influenced by contextual factors such as speaking rate; see Miller & Jusczyk, 1989.) Hence even though speech stimuli may be physically continuous, perception is categorical.

At first, researchers thought that listeners were actually unable to distinguish between slightly different members of a phoneme category. However, this does not appear to be the case. Pisoni and Tash (1974) found that subjects were faster to say that two /ba/ syllables were the same if the /b/s in each were acoustically identical, than if the /b/s differed slightly in VOT. Hence subjects are in fact sensitive to differences within a category.

Finally, it should be noted that the importance of categorical perception has recently come into question. It is possible that many phenomena in speech perception are better described in terms of continuous rather than categorical perception, and although our phenomenal experience of speech identification is that sounds fall into distinct categories, the evidence that early sensory processing is really categorical is much weaker (Massaro, 1994). Nevertheless, the idea of categorical perception remains popular in psycholinguistics.

The pre-lexical representation.   Most researchers believe that there is a stage of phonetic representation intermediate between the acoustic input and words. That is, that we identify phonetic features or phonemes before we identify words. This view is not however unanimous. Klatt (1979, 1980) proposed a one-stage perceptual model that made no use of phonetic representations. He pointed out that models that posit intervening stages must discard information present in the perceptual input to construct the abstract representation, and that such information might be useful for relatively high-level tasks. Savin and Bever (1970) argued for the non-perceptual reality of the phoneme. They asked subjects to respond as soon as they heard a particular unit, which was either a single phoneme or a syllable. They found that subjects responded more slowly to phoneme targets than to syllable targets. They concluded that phoneme identification is subsequent to the perception of target phonological units. This conclusion was queried by Foss and Swinney (1973). They argued that the phoneme and syllable monitoring task used by Savin and Bever did not directly tap into the perception process. That is, just because we can become consciously aware of a higher unit first does not mean that it is processed perceptually earlier. Young children also find words are easier to segment into syllables than phonemes (I. Liberman, Shankweiler, Fischer, & Carter, 1974). Illiterate speakers have particular difficulty with phonemes, yet they can manipulate other phonological characteristics of speech such as syllables (Morais, Bertelson, Cary, & Alegria, 1986). Speakers of

Chinese, who use a non-alphabetic writing system where there is no correspondence between written symbols and individual sounds (see next chapter), are also less aware of individual phonemes (Read, Zhang, Nie, & Ding, 1986).

In summary, it seems likely that we do indeed first identify something, such as phonemes, on the way to identifying words, although this view is not without its dissenters. That is, phonemes are explicitly represented in the pre-lexical code. Furthermore, syllables do not seem to be part of the pre-lexical code for English speakers, although they may be for French speakers (Cutler et al., 1986; Mehler, Dommergues, Frauenfelder, & Segui, 1981).

Recently, however, Marslen-Wilson and Warren (1994) have provided extensive experimental evidence on a range of tasks that there is no intervening level of phoneme classification, and argue that lexical representations are directly accessed from featural information in the sound signal. At the very least, we seem to be less aware of phonemes than other phonological constituents of speech. A possible solution to these apparently contradictory data might be provided by suggestion by Morais and Kolinsky (1994) that there are two quite distinct representations of phonemes: an unconscious system operating in speech recognition and production, and a conscious system developed in the context of the development of literacy (reading and writing). On this scheme, the evidence for the conscious representation is much stronger than for the unconscious representation.

The pre-lexical code: Evidence from infant perception.   Even though they have not yet learned to talk, babies have surprisingly sophisticated speech recognition abilities. Pre-linguistic infants have sophisticated perceptual systems that can make subtle phonetic distinctions. It is obviously difficult to carry out research on the perceptual abilities of such very young children. A commonly used technique is known as the sucking habituation paradigm. In this procedure, experimenters measure the sucking rate of infants on an artificial teat. Babies prefer novel stimuli, and as they become habituated to the stimulus presented, their rate of sucking declines. If they then detect a change in the stimulus, their sucking rate will then increase again. In this way it is possible to measure whether the infants can detect differences between pairs of stimuli. Using techniques such as this, it has been shown that they are sensitive to speech sounds, as distinct from non-speech sounds, from birth. Indeed, it has been argued that infants between one and four months of age, and perhaps even younger, are sensitive to all the acoustic differences used later to signal phonetic distinctions (Eimas, Miller, & Jusczyk, 1987). For example, they are capable of the categorical perception of voicing, place, and manner of articulation. Cross-linguistic studies, which compare the abilities of infants growing up with different linguistic backgrounds, show common categorisation by infants, even when there are differences in the phonologies of the adult language. This suggests that these perceptual mechanisms might be innate.

Early on, infants discriminate sounds regardless of whether or not these sounds are to be found in the surrounding adult language. The innate perceptual abilities are then modified by exposure to the adult language. For example, Werker and Tees (1984) showed that infants born into English-speaking families in Canada could make phonetic distinctions present in Hindi at the age of six months, but this ability declined rapidly over the next two months. A second example is that two month old Kikuyu infants in Africa can distinguish between [p] and [b]. If not used in the language into which they are growing up, this ability is lost by about the age of one year or even less (Werker & Tees, 1984). (Adults can learn to make these distinctions again, so these findings are more likely to reflect a reorganisation of processes rather than complete loss of ability.)

Infants are sensitive to features other than phonetic discriminations. Mehler et al. (1988) showed that neonates (new-born infants) prefer to listen to parental rather than non-parental speech. Neonates aged three days prefer the mother's voice to that of others (DeCasper & Fifer, 1980). This raises the possibility that the neonate has been exposed to some features of language in the womb, and this exposure affects its preferences after birth. The sensitivity of babies to language extends between simple sound perception; infants aged eight months are sensitive to cues to such as the location of important syntactic boundaries in speech (Hirsh-Pasek et al., 1987).

Just because some mechanisms of speech perception are innate does not mean in this case that they are necessarily species-specific. Kuhl (1981) showed that chinchillas (a type of South American rodent) display categorical perception of VOT in syllables such as /da/ and /ta/ in the same way as humans do. It is less clear whether monkeys also show categorical perception of place of articulation as do humans (Miller & Jusczyk, 1989). However, even if animals can perform these perceptual distinctions, it does not necessarily follow that the perceptual mechanisms they employ are identical to those of humans.

Finally, there is some evidence that for a while children subsequently regress in their speech perception abilities (Gerken, 1994). It is not clear whether this is an artefact of using more stringent tasks to test older children, or perhaps more likely because the child's language perception is shifting in emphasis from making contrasts between phonemes to recognising whole words, and that whole words comprise phonological segments.

The role of context in speech recognition

In Chapter 1, we saw that the effect of context on language processing and the modularity of the language system would be important recurring themes in this book. The role of context on speech recognition is of central importance, and has been hotly debated. Put simply, the issue is "is speech recognition a purely bottom-up process, or can top-down information influence its outcome?" If we can show that the word which a sound is in, or indeed the meaning of the whole sentence, can influence the recognition of a particular sound, we have shown a top-down influence on sound perception. We have shown that it is in part at least an interactive (as opposed to independent) process; knowledge about whole words is influencing our perception of their component sounds.

The first piece of relevant evidence is based upon the observation that sounds varying along a continuum are perceived categorically. For example, although [p] and [b] differ in VOT between 0 and 60 milliseconds, sounds in between will be assigned to one or the other category. It was mentioned above that to precisely which category they would be assigned varied, and could be prejudiced by various factors. One such factor is word context. Ganong (1980) varied an ambiguous phoneme along the appropriate continuum (e.g. /k/ to /g/), and inserted this in front of a context provided by a word-ending (e.g. "—iss"), and found that context affected the perceptual changeover point. That is, subjects are willing to put a sound into a category they would not otherwise do if the result makes a word: "kiss" is a word, "giss" is not, and this influences our categorical perception of the ambiguous phoneme. In this respect, word context is influencing our categorisation of sounds. This technique was developed by Connine and Clifton (1987) to strengthen further the argument that lexical knowledge— information about words—is available to early perceptual processing. They showed that other processing advantages accrue to the ambiguous stimuli when this lexical knowledge is invoked, but not at the ends of the continuum, where perceptual information alone is sufficient to make a decision. Connine (1990) also found that the context provided by the meaning of the whole sentence, sentential context, behaves differently to lexical context, the context provided by the word the ambiguous phoneme is in. The sentential effect seems sensitive to post-perceptual factors. Even so, there are problems with even this interpretation. Some phonemes—such as fricatives—suffer more interference from noise than others. (For further details and a recent review see Tyler, 1990.)

A classic psycholinguistic finding known as the *phoneme restoration* effect appears to extend this finding (Obusek & Warren, 1973; Warren, 1970; Warren & Warren, 1970). Subjects were presented with sentences such as "The state governors met with their respective legi*latures convening in the capital city". At the point marked with an asterisk *, a 0.12 second portion of speech corresponding to the /s/ phoneme had been cut out and replaced with a cough. Nevertheless, subjects could not detect that a sound was missing from the sample. That is, they appear to restore the /s/ phoneme to the word "legislatures". The effect is quite dramatic. Subjects continue to report that the deleted phoneme is perceptually restored even if they know it is missing. Moreover, subjects cannot correctly locate the cough in the speech. The effect can still be found if an even larger portion of the word is deleted (as in le***latures). Warren and his colleagues argued that subjects are using semantic and syntactic information far beyond the individual phonemes in their processing of speech. In an even more dramatic example, subjects were presented with the four sentences (1) to (4) below.

1.   It was found that the *eel was on the orange.
2.   It was found that the *eel was on the axle.
3.   It was found that the *eel was on the fishing-rod.
4.   It was found that the *eel was on the table.

The tapes to which subjects listened were constructed so that the only thing that differed between the four sentences was the last word; in each case a different final word was spliced onto a physically identical beginning. This is important because it means that there can be no subtle phonological or intonational differences between the sentences that might cue subjects. Again, the phoneme at the beginning of *eel was replaced with a cough. It was found that the phoneme which subjects restored depended upon the semantic context provided four words later with the final word of the sentence. Subjects restored a phoneme that would make an appropriate word. These are "peel" in (1), "wheel" in (2), "reel" in (3), and "meal" in (4).

The actual sound used is not critical; a buzz or a tone elicits the effect as successfully as a cough. There are limits on what can be restored, however; replacing a deleted phoneme with a short period of silence is easily detectable and does not elicit the effect.

At first sight it seems then that the perception of speech can be constrained by higher level information such as semantic and syntactic considerations. This interpretation of these results has been questioned by Fodor (1983). In the case of the phoneme restoration effect, is the restoration at the phonological processing level, or is at a higher-level?

Perhaps it is just the case, for example, that subjects guess the deleted phoneme. The guessing does not even need to be conscious. Another way of putting this issue is does the context affect the actual perception or some later process? The pendulum has recently swung away from the perceptual interpretation. Recent work by Samuel (1981, 1987, reviewed by Samuel, 1990) examined effects of adding noise to the segment instead of just replacing the segment with noise. If phoneme restoration is truly perceptual, subjects should not be able to detect any difference between these conditions; in each case they will think they hear a phoneme plus sound. On the other hand, if the effect is post-perceptual, there should be good discrimination between the two conditions. Samuel further used signal detection analysis to try to prise apart the separate effects of lexical and sentential context. He concluded that lexical context affects true phoneme recognition (pre-lexical processing) but sentence context does not, and affects only post-lexical processing.

How does the effect of lexical context operate here? As we have noted, this central issue of the autonomy of processing, and the locus at which different types of context have an effect, is a recurring theme in modern psycholinguistics. Does context affect which *candidates* for the word being processed are *generated* in the process of accessing the lexicon, or merely which are *selected* and what happens to them after selection? Either it contributes to the lower level directly (the interactionist position) or it simply aids in evaluating the output (the autonomy position). For example, it might suggest a re-evaluation of the sensory input. That is, does context operate pre-lexically or post-lexically? We would need precise temporal data to distinguish between these possibilities, which we do not yet have. Many of the questions concerning the effect of context on phoneme perception therefore remain unresolved.

Models of speech perception

Not surprisingly, there is much overlap between models of speech perception and of spoken word recognition. Here we will concentrate upon models of the lower level processes. Before we can start the processes of accessing the lexicon, we have to translate the output of the auditory nerves from the ear into a suitable form. Speech perception is concerned with this early stage of processing. It is obviously an important topic for machine recognition, as there would be many obvious advantages if computers and other machines could understand speech. There is considerable effort underway to create a computer operating system that takes its commands as speech rather than input from the keyboard or mouse.

Early models of recognition examined the possibility of *template matching*. Targets are stored as templates, and identification made when a match is found. However, there is far too much variation in speech for this to be plausible in all apart from the most restricted domains. Speakers differ in their dialect, pitch, basic speed of talking, and in many other ways. One person can produce the same phoneme in many different ways—you might be speaking loudly, or more quickly than normal, or have a cold, for example. The number of templates that would have to be stored would be prohibitively large. Generally, template models are not realistic in psycholinguistics. Nevertheless, variants of the basic idea exist and are more successful. Klatt (1989) has proposed a very sophisticated version for speech perception called the LAFS model (which stands for "Lexical Access From Spectra").

One of the most influential models of speech perception has been the idea of *analysis-by-synthesis* (Halle & Stevens, 1962; Liberman et al., 1967; Stevens, 1960). The basis of this is that we recognise speech by reference to the actions necessary to produce a sound. This model proposes that when we hear speech, we produce or synthesise a succession of speech sounds until we match what we hear. The synthesiser does not randomly generate candidates for matching against the input; it creates an initial "best guess" constrained by acoustic cues in the input, and then attempts to minimise the difference between this and the input. Your initial reaction to this model might be one of surprise that such a model has been taken far more seriously than the template one. The approach however has a number of advantages. First, it copes easily with intra-speaker differences, because the listeners are generating their own candidates. Second, it is easy to show how constraints of all levels might have an effect; the synthesiser only generates candidates that are plausible. It will not, for example, generate sequences that are illegitimate within that language. One variant of the model, the *motor theory*, proposes that the speech synthesiser models the articulatory apparatus and motor movements of the speaker. It effectively computes which motor movements would have been necessary to create those sounds. Some evidence for this is that our classification of sounds is based more upon how they are made rather than how they sound. For example, all /d/'s are made by closing the sound against the alveolar ridge. Note that the specification of the motor movements must be quite abstract; mute people can understand speech perfectly well (Lenneberg, 1962). We can understand speech we cannot ourselves produce (e.g. that of people with stutters, foreign accents). Hence only a weak version of the analysis-by-synthesis model, that the motor specifications are abstract, is acceptable. However, it has been argued that a weak version is under-specified and has little predictive power (see Clark & Clark, 1977). Some of these criticisms have been addressed in a recent resurgence of interest in this approach (A. Liberman & Mattingly, 1986). Another approach has been to search for acoustic properties of speech that are invariant and can be uniquely identified from the speech signal (Blumstein & Stevens, 1979). This would greatly simplify the recognition task. There is little doubt that analysis-by-synthesis has proved one of the most influential models of speech perception.

With recent advances in computer modelling techniques, there are now a number of competing models of speech perception, including updated versions of analysis-by-synthesis. Most of these are too technical and mathematical to describe here. Descriptions can be found in the recent good if technical review by Klatt (1989).

SPOKEN WORD RECOGNITION

There are two main issues in spoken word recognition. The first is deciding upon the phases involved in recognition, and the second is determining whether and how context affects each of these phases. The models that have been proposed to account for spoken word recognition differ in the way they address these issues. The main models we will look at in detail here are the cohort model of Marslen-Wilson and his colleagues, and the connectionist model called TRACE. Frauenfelder and Tyler (1987) provide an excellent summary of these models and the issues which they address.

The stages of spoken word recognition

The terms *word recognition* and *lexical access* are often used in the spoken word recognition literature to refer to different processes (Tanenhaus & Lucas, 1987), and so it is best to be clear in advance about what our terms mean. We can outline three stages of identification: initial contact, lexical selection, and word recognition (Frauenfelder & Tyler, 1987). These stages might overlap; whether they do or not is an empirical question, and is an aspect of our core concern with modularity. Recognising a spoken word begins when some representation of the sensory input makes initial contact with the lexicon. This is the *initial contact phase*. What is the form of the representation that makes contact with the lexicon? The precise form depends on our preferred model of speech perception, and as we have seen a number of alternatives have been described. These include a motor representation (as in analysis-by-synthesis models), temporally defined spectral templates (e.g. see Klatt, 1989); abstract units such as phonemes (e.g. Pisoni & Luce, 1987); or syllables (e.g. Mehler, 1981). Once lexical entries match the contact representation, they change in some way; they become "activated". The activation might be all-or-none (as is the case in the original cohort model described later); or their relative status might depend upon properties of the words (such as word frequency, as in Forster's serial search model to be discussed in the next chapter); or words may be activated in proportion to the current goodness of fit with the sensory data (as in the more recent cohort model, or in the connectionist TRACE model). In the *selection phase*, sensory input continues to accumulate until one lexical entry is selected. *Word recognition* is the end point of the selection phase. The point at which this happens, the word recognition point, generally happens before listeners have heard the word completely. In the simplest case the word recognition point corresponds to its uniqueness point, where the word's initial sequence is common to that word and no other. For these two points to be equal assumptions must be made about the order in which the signal is processed: it is possible that recognition may be delayed until after the uniqueness point, and in principle we might recognise a word before its uniqueness point—in strongly biasing contexts for example. Lexical access refers to the point at which all the information—phonological, semantic, syntactic, pragmatic—about a word become available following its recognition. In the cohort model all stored information becomes simultaneously available upon initial contact: that is, lexical access precedes recognition. The process of *integration* that then follows is the start of the comprehension process proper, where the semantic and syntactic properties of the word are integrated into the higher-level sentence representation. Models of speech recognition have little to say about integration and there are no differences between them concerning this phase.

Context effects in speech recognition

Does context affect spoken word recognition? *Context* refers to all of the information not in the immediate sensory signal. It includes information available from the previous sensory input (the prior context) to higher knowledge sources (e.g. lexical, syntactic, semantic, and pragmatic information). To show that context affects recognition, we need to show top-down influences upon the bottom-up processing of the acoustic signal. We have already examined whether context affects low-level perceptual processing; this section is concerned with the possible effects of context upon word identification. The issues involved are more complex than the question as posed at the start of this paragraph: even if there are some contextual effects, we would still need to determine which types of context have an effect, at what stage or stages they have an effect, and how they have this effect.

We have already noted that there are two opposed positions upon the role of context which can be called the autonomous and interactionist positions. Let us try to characterise them more fully. The *autonomous* position says that context cannot have an effect prior to word recognition. It can only contribute to the evaluation and integration of the output of lexical processing, not its generation. The lateral flow of information is however permitted in these models. For example, information flow is allowed within the lexicon, but not from the lexicon to lower level processes such as word identification. On the other hand, *interactive* models allow different types of information to interact with one another. In particular, there may be feedback from later levels of processing to earlier ones. For example, information about the meaning of the sentence or the pragmatic context might affect perception.

This way of putting the distinction is the most clear-cut. However, perhaps the autonomous and interactive models should be looked at as the extreme ends of a continuum of possible models rather than the two poles of a dichotomy. There might be some restrictions on permitted interaction in interactive models. For example, context can propose candidates for what word the stimulus might be before sensory processing has begun (Morton, 1969), or it might be restricted to disposing of candidates and not proposing them (Marslen-Wilson, 1987). Because there are such huge differences between models it can be difficult to test between them. However, it is strong evidence for the interactionist view if context has an effect before or during the access and selection phases. In an autonomous model, context can only have an influence after a word has emerged as the best fit to the sensory input.

Frauenfelder and Tyler (1987) distinguish between two types of context which they call structural and non-structural. *Non-structural context* is that which does not result in a higher level representation. *Structural context* is that which concerns how words can be combined into higher level units.

Non-structural context is not used to bear on the construction of a higher-level representation. Speech comprehension can be thought of as a hierarchical process: phonemes are used to construct words, and words are used to construct sentences. Non-structural context can be thought of as information from the same level of processing as what is currently being processed. An example is facilitation in processing arising from intra-lexical context, such as associative relationship between two words such as "doctor" and "nurse". It can be explained in terms of relations within a single level of processing and hence need not violate the principle of autonomy: As we shall see in the next chapter, it can be explained in terms of spreading activation within the lexicon. Alternatively, associative facilitation can be thought of as occurring because of hard-wired connections between similar things at the same level. According to autonomy theorists such as Fodor (1983) and Forster (1981b) this is the only type of context that can affect processes prior to recognition.

Structural context involves higher-level information. If we find evidence for this, such processing is clearly top-down and involves multiple levels of processing. There are a number of possible types. Word-knowledge, or lexical context, might be used to identify phonemes, or sentence-level knowledge, or sentence context, might be used to identify individual words. We have discussed the possible effects of lexical context on speech perception above. Another type of structural context is syntactic context. Imagine you have heard the start of a sentence which goes "The dog chased". You might predict a determiner ("the", or "a") next, and this might facilitate the perception of a "th" sound if that does indeed come next. Current indications are however that syntactic context has very little effect. This makes sense, because most of the time syntactic context is not actually very useful. The rules of our grammar are so complex that many different syntactic categories can follow a particular word. Even our apparently straightforward fragment might have continued "The dog chased everything that moved." Just think how many legitimate continuations there are in a sentence starting with the word "the"!

The most interesting types of structural context are those based on meaning. Two sub-types have been distinguished, semantic and interpretative (Frauenfelder & Tyler, 1987). Semantic context is based upon word meanings. There is much evidence that this affects word processing. Words which are appropriate for the context are responded to faster than those which are not across a range of tasks which we will discuss in more detail later, such as phoneme monitoring, shadowing, naming, and gating (e.g. Marslen-Wilson, 1984; Marslen-Wilson & Tyler, 1980; Tyler & Wessels, 1983). But it is not clear whether structural and non-structural semantic context effects can be distinguished, or at which stages they operate. Furthermore, these effects must be studied using tasks that minimise the chance of post-perceptual factors operating. This might happen for example if there is too long a delay between the stimulus and the response. Subjects have a chance to reflect upon and maybe alter their decisions, which would obviously reflect late-stage, post-access mechanisms.

Interpretative context involves more high-level information, such as pragmatic, discourse, and world knowledge. For example, suppose you hear a sentence which begins "Every morning, the businessmen on the train all ...". Now you might use your world knowledge to work out that "read newspapers" is a likely continuation. If you can show that this information influences the early stages of word recognition, before a single candidate is selected, then you would have demonstrated an early effect of world-knowledge context. Such a successful demonstration would be very bad news for autonomy theorists. As yet there has been no unambiguous demonstration of such an effect. In part the problem is that it is difficult to find world-knowledge context that might not also involve intra-lexical or associative cues. Perhaps there is a simple low-level association between "businessmen" and "read". We shall return to this issue in Chapter 9.

Evaluation of context effects.   It is difficult to draw any definite conclusions about the role of context in spoken word recognition, but this is still very much a live issue. As with phoneme perception, to resolve these questions we need more detail on the time course of the different stages of word recognition. Hence we do not yet have the relevant data, and there are many methodological pitfalls in doing these experiments. In particular, it is difficult to be sure that these experiments are tapping processes before the selection of a unique candidate rather than reflecting post-access effects. Tanenhaus and Lucas (1987) argued that most of the currently used experimental tasks that are on-line—that is, that attempt to investigate speech recognition as it happens rather than afterwards by say, examining memory—do not distinguish between perceptual processes (which can be equated with the access and selection phases) and post-perceptual processes (which can be equated with the integration phase). There is some argument that only the tasks described above used by Samuel (1990) and Connine (1990) escape this criticism (although we saw that even this is debatable). If these tasks are giving the correct answer, then the data suggest that the role of sentential context is very limited. After some years when the interactionists held the roost, there seems to be a shift in opinion happening at the moment to a more autonomous position whereby structural context can only have post-access effects.

TRACE
This is a highly interactive model of spoken word recognition (McClelland & Elman, 1986), derived from the McClelland and Rumelhart (1981) interactive activation model of letter and visual word identification (see Chapter 3). Here we will outline only the principal features of the model, but the mathematical details are given in the Appendix. The most important characteristic of TRACE is that it emphasises the role of top-down processing (context) on word recognition. Hence lexical context can assist directly acoustic-perceptual processing, and information above the word level can directly influence word processing.

TRACE is a connectionist model, and as such is made up of lots of simple processing units connected together. These units are arranged in three levels of processing. It assumes some early, fairly sophisticated perceptual processing of the acoustic signal. The level of input units represent phonological features; these are connected to phoneme units which in turn are connected to the output units which represent words. Input units are provided with energy or "activated", and this energy or *activation* spreads along the connections in a manner determined by the equations shown in the Appendix, with the result that eventually one output unit is left activated. All connections between levels are bi-directional, in the sense that information can flow along them in both directions. This means that both bottom-up and top-down processing can occur. There are inhibitory connections between units in each level which has the effect that once a unit is activated, it tends to inhibit its competitors. This mechanism therefore emphasises the concept of competition between units at the same level. However, there are no inhibitory connections between levels (unlike the visual word recognition model of McClelland & Rumelhart, 1981). The model is implemented in the form of computer simulations, and trials under different conditions are compared with what happens in normal human speech processing. It shows how lexical knowledge can aid perception—for example, if an input ambiguous between /p/ and /b/ is given followed by the ending corresponding to –LUG, then /p/ is "recognised" by the model. Categorical perception arises in the model as a consequence of within-level inhibition.

Evaluation of TRACE.   As with all computer models, TRACE has the advantage of being explicit. However, there are many parameters which can be manipulated in the model, and it is possible to level the criticism that TRACE is too powerful in that it can accommodate any result. By adjusting some of the parameters, can the model be made to simulate any data from speech recognition experiments, whatever they show? Moreover, the way in which the model deals with time, simulating it as discrete slices, is very implausible.

Massaro (1989) provided a detailed experimental critique of the TRACE model. He made predictions from TRACE about the behaviour of ambiguous phonemes between /l/ and /r/ based upon signal detection theory. He showed that subtle interactions with context were not then verified in experiments with human subjects. McClelland's (1991) reply accepted many of his points, and tried making the model's output probabilistic (or *stochastic*). But Massaro and Cohen (1991) showed that even after this modification problems remained. Massaro's work is important in that it shows that it is possible to make falsifiable predictions about connectionist models such as TRACE. Massaro argues for a model where phonetic recognition uses features which serve as an input to a decision strategy involving variable conjunctions of perceptual features called *fuzzy prototypes* (see Klatt, 1989, for more detail). Choosing between these models is difficult, and it is not clear that they are addressing precisely the same issues: TRACE is concerned with the time course of lexical access, whereas the fuzzy logic model is more concerned with decision-making and output processes (McClelland, 1991).

However, the main problem with TRACE is that it is based upon the idea that top-down context permeates the recognition process. This is not consistent with the experimental findings that suggest that the role of context is much more limited. In direct support of TRACE, Elman and McClelland (1988) reported some evidence for interactive effects on speech recognition. They show that between-level processes can affect within-level processes at a lower level. In particular, they showed that illusory phonemes created by top-down, lexical knowledge (in a manner analogous to phoneme restoration) can affect co-articulation (the influence of one sound on a neighbouring sound) operating at the basic sound perception level. Such findings are at present the exception. Indeed, Marslen-Wilson and Warren (1994) report auditory lexical decision and gating data inconsistent with TRACE. (These tasks are described in more detail later.) As we saw above, they conclude that there is no role for a phoneme level in speech recognition.

The cohort model of word recognition

The *cohort model* of spoken word recognition was proposed by Marslen-Wilson (1973, 1975; for a review of these earlier versions, see Marslen-Wilson, 1984, 1987, 1989). The central idea of the model is that as we hear speech, we set up a cohort of possible items the word could be. Items are then eliminated from this set until only one is left. This is then taken as the word currently trying to be recognised. We should distinguish an early version of the model, which permitted more interaction, and a late version, which was more autonomous. Let us look at the model in more detail.

We can distinguish three stages. First, there is an *access* stage when the perceptual representation is used to activate lexical items, and therefore generate a candidate set (or cohort) of items. The beginning of the word is particularly important in generating this cohort. Second, there is a *selection* stage when one item only is chosen from this set. Third, there is an *integration* stage; this is the way in which the semantic and syntactic properties of the chosen word are utilised—for example, in integrating the word into a complete representation of the whole sentence. The access and selection stages are pre-lexical, and the integration stage post-lexical. Like Morton's logogen model (see Chapter 3), the original cohort model is based upon parallel, interactive, direct access. It is said to be "active" as against Morton's "passive" logogen model. Logogens passively accumulate positive evidence, but cohorts actively seek to eliminate themselves. On the presentation of the beginning of a word, a "word-initial cohort" of candidate words is set up. These are then actively eliminated by all possible means, including further phonological evidence, and semantic and syntactic context. In particular, as we hear increasing stretches of the word, candidates are eliminated.

An important concept in this model is the *uniqueness* point. This is the point at which a word can be distinguished uniquely from all similar words. It is after this has been identified that we "recognise" the word, and it is around this point that the most intense processing activity occurs. Consider the following increasing segments of a word (5–9). Obviously when we hear /d/ alone (5) there are many possible words—the cohort will be very large. The next segment (in 6) reduces the cohort somewhat, but it will still be very large. With more information (7) the cohort of possible items is reduced still further, but there are still many items the word might be ("dry", "dries", "drive", "driving", "driver"). (8) reduces the size of the cohort yet more, but is only at (9) that the cohort is reduced to one—"driving". This point then is this word's uniqueness point.

5. /d/
6. /dr/
7. /dry/
8. /drive/
9. /drivi-/

The dependence of the on-line recognition point upon when the target diverges unambiguously from similar neighbours is an important characteristic which distinguishes this model from others. It is important to note that the recognition point does not have to coincide with the uniqueness point. Suppose we heard the start of a sentence "The lorry driver was dr–". In the early version of this model, at this point the context might be sufficiently strong to eliminate all other words apart from "driving" from the cohort. Hence it could be recognised before its uniqueness point. The early version of the model was very interactionist in this respect; context is clearly affecting the pre-lexical stages in that it is affecting the selection stage.

In the revised version of the model, context only affects the integration stage. Context cannot be used to restrict which items form the initial cohort, or context cannot be used to get rid of members of the cohort before the uniqueness point. This change is motivated by experimental data detailed below that suggest the role of context is more limited than was originally thought. Another important modification is that the elimination of candidates from the cohort no longer becomes all or none. This counters one objection to the original model: What happens if the start of a word is distorted or misperceived? This would have prevented the correct item from being in the word-initial cohort, yet we can sometimes overcome distortions even at the start of a word. In the absence of further positive information, candidates gradually decay back down to their normal resting state. They can be revived again by subsequent positive information. Furthermore, the frequency of a word affects the activation level of candidates in the early stages of lexical access (Zwitserlood, 1989). That is, there are relative frequency effects within the initial cohort, so that entry in the cohort cannot be all-or-none, but varies along a continuum. We say that some candidates are more activated than others. The most recent version of the model (Marslen-Wilson & Warren, 1994) stresses the direct access of lexical entries on the basis of an acoustic analysis of the incoming speech signal, without any intervening phonological representation.

Experimental tests of the cohort model.   Four main experimental tasks have been used by Marslen-Wilson and his colleagues to provide evidence for the cohort model and for an interactive view of language processing. We shall look at three here, and one, the sentence continuation task, in our discussion of syntactic ambiguity in Chapter 9.

Marslen-Wilson and Welsh (1978) used a technique known as *shadowing*. In this task, subjects have to listen to continuous speech and repeat it back as quickly as possible (e.g. 250 milliseconds). The speech has deliberate mistakes in it—distorted sounds so that certain words are mispronounced. Subjects are not told that there are mispronunciations, but are told they have to repeat back the passage of speech as they hear it But Marslen-Wilson and Welsh found that subjects often (about 50% of the time) repeat these back as they should be rather than as they are. That is, we find what are called fluent restorations, such as producing "travedy" as "tragedy". The more distorted a sound is (the more "distinctive features" are changed), the more likely you are to get an exact repetition. In their experiment there were three variables of interest. These were the number of phonological features changed in the deliberate error (one or three), the *lexical constraint*, which reflects the number of candidates available at different positions in the word by manipulating the syllable position upon which the error was located (first or third), and the context (the word involved was a probable or improbable continuation of the start of the sentence). They found that most of the fluent restorations were made when the distortion was slight, when the distortion is in the final syllable, and the word is highly predictable from its context. On the other hand, most of the exact reproductions occur with greater distortion when the word is relatively unconstrained by context. That is, these factors interact. Later shadowing experiments showed that both syntactic and semantic analyses of speech start to happen almost instantaneously, and are not delayed until a whole clause (syntactic unit) has been heard (Marslen-Wilson, 1973, 1975, 1976).

We do not pay attention equally to all parts of a word. The beginning of the word, particularly the first syllable, is especially salient. This was demonstrated by the "listening for mispronunciations" task of Cole (1973; see also Cole & Jakimik, 1980). In this task subjects listen to speech where a sound is distorted (e.g. "boot" is changed to "poot"), and detect these changes. Consistent with the shadowing task, subjects are more sensitive to changes on the beginning of the words. Cole and Jakimik also argue that context is important in word recognition.

The *gating* task of Grosjean (1980) and Tyler and Wessels (1983) involves presenting gradually increasing amounts of a word, as in examples (5) to (9) above. This task enables the recognition point of words to be found. It again shows the importance of context: subjects need an average of 333 milliseconds to identify a word out of context, but only 199 milliseconds in an appropriate context. On the other hand, these studies also show that candidates are generated that are compatible with the perceptual representation up to that point, but which could be ruled out as incompatible with the context. Hence context is not affecting the generation phase.

Finally, a technique known as *cross-modal priming* enables the measurement of contextual effects at different times in recognising a word (Zwitserlood, 1989). This technique will be described in detail in the next chapter, but it involves subjects listening to speech over headphones while simultaneously looking at a computer screen to monitor the screen for particular words. The relationship between the word on the screen and the speech, and the precise time relationship between the two, can be systematically varied. The results of these experiments suggest that the role of context was over-estimated in the early version of the cohort model. Context does not have an effect on word recognition until after a word's uniqueness point.

Evaluation of the cohort model.   The cohort model has changed over the years in the light of more recent data to place less stress upon the role of context. In the early recent version of the model, context cannot affect the access stage, but it can affect the selection and integration stages. In the later version of the model, context cannot affect selection but only affects integration. In the revised version (Marslen-Wilson, 1987), elements are not either "on" or "off", but have an activation level proportional to the goodness-of-fit between the element and the acoustic input, so that a number of candidates may then be analysed further in parallel. This permits a gradual decay of candidates rather than immediate elimination. The model does not distinguish between provisional and definite identification; there are some probabilistic aspects to word recognition (Grosjean, 1980). The later version, by replacing all-or-none elimination from the cohort with gradual elimination, also better accounts for the effects of frequency on word recognition and the ability of the system to recover from errors.

Lexical neighbourhoods.   In the cohort model, evaluation of competitors to the target word takes place in parallel. For example, if "speed" is the target, after /sp-/, then the competitors include "specious", "speech", and "spray", among many others. That is, the number of competitors at any time should not, according to Marslen-Wilson (1987), have any effect on the recognition of the target. Data from Marslen-Wilson (1987) suggest that cohort size does not affect the time course of word recognition, but data from Luce, Pisoni and Goldinger (1990) suggests that it does; also that the characteristics of the competitors (such as their frequency) is very important. In a similar way, Goldinger, Luce and Pisoni (1989) used auditory priming to test predictions of the *neighbourhood activation model*. Luce and his colleagues argue that the number of competitors, what they call the *neighbourhood density*, influences the decision.

Marslen-Wilson (1990) examined the effect of the frequency of competitors upon recognising words. He found that the time it takes you to recognise a word such as "speech" does not just depend on the relative uniqueness points of competitors (such as "speed" and "specious") in the cohort, but also on the frequency of those words. Hence you are faster to identify a high frequency word which only has low frequency neighbours than vice versa. The rise in activation of a high frequency word is much greater than for a low frequency one. Obviously more work is necessary here, but neighbourhood effects are emerging as an increasingly important concept in word recognition.

Comparison of models of speech recognition

Let us first return to the three phases of speech recognition we identified and see what different models have to say about them. The precise format of the contact representation has implications for what happens next, as the richer the representation, the more discriminating it is, and the smaller the number of lexical entries that are likely to be contacted. Furthermore, the amount of speech needed to compute the contact representation determines when initial contact can occur. In Klatt's (1989) LAFS model, contact can be made after the first 10 milliseconds. Models such as the syllable-based models, which need larger units of speech, will obviously take longer to get started. Different models also emphasise how representations make contact with the lexicon. Hence in the cohort model temporally early information (the first 150 milliseconds) is used first to access the word. In other models (e.g. Grosjean & Gee, 1987), the more salient or reliable parts of the word, such as the most stressed syllable, are used to make first contact. All of these models where initial contact is used to generate a subset of lexical entries have the disadvantage that it is difficult to recover from a mistake (e.g. a mishearing). Models such as TRACE, where there is not a unique contact for each word, do not suffer from these problems. Each identified phoneme—the whole word—contributes to the set of active lexical entries. The cost of this is that these sets may be very large and this might be computationally costly.

However, because it provides a better fit with the data on the role of contexts, we must conclude that at present the revised cohort model is currently our best account of what happens in spoken word recognition.

THE NEUROPSYCHOLOGY OF SPOKEN WORD RECOGNITION

Some difficulty in speech recognition is quite common in adults with a disturbance of language functions caused by brain damage. Varney (1984) reported that 18% of such patients had some problem in discriminating speech sounds. We shall see in our discussions of the neuropsychology of language that there are many varieties of disorder. In line with this, brain damage can affect most levels of the word recognition process, including certainly the pre-lexical and perhaps the post-lexical codes.

There are many cases of patients who have difficulty in constructing in the pre-lexical code. These are reviewed by Caplan (1992). For example, disturbances can affect the earliest stages of acoustic-phonetic processing of features such as VOT, or the later stages involving the identification of sounds based on these features (Blumstein, Cooper, Zurif, & Caramazza, 1977).

Patients with *pure word deafness* can speak, read, and write quite normally, but cannot understand speech, even though their hearing is otherwise normal (see Saffran, Marin, & Yeni-Komshian, 1976, for a case history). These patients however cannot repeat speech back, and which suggests disruption to a pre-lexical, acoustic processing mechanism. A variant of this which is very rare (and controversial) is called word meaning deafness. Such patients show the symptoms of pure word deafness but have intact repetition. The most famous case of this was a patient living in Edinburgh in the 1890s (Bramwell, 1897/1984), although more recent cases have been reported by Franklin, Howard, and Patterson (1994), and Kohn and Friedman (1986). We shall see in Chapter 9 that such disturbances tell us about the organisation of the lexicon. Pure word deafness shows that we can produce words without necessarily being able to understand them.

Only one patient (referred to as EDE; neuropsychology case studies are conventionally referred to by initials) shows intact acoustic-phonetic processing and therefore the ability to construct a pre-lexical code, but who then still has apparent difficulties in lexical access (Berndt & Mitchum, 1990). This patient performed well on all test of phoneme discrimination and acoustic processing, yet made many errors in deciding whether a string of sounds made up a word or not (e.g. "horse" is a word, but "hort" is not). Nevertheless EDE generally performed well in routine language comprehension, and Berndt and Mitchum interpreted her difficulties with this particular task in terms of a short-term memory deficit rather than in terms of lexical access. As yet there have been no reports of patients who have completely intact phonetic processing but who cannot access the post-lexical code. If our models are correct, then this is because so far we have not looked hard enough, or perhaps have just been unlucky.

CONCLUDING SUMMARY

This chapter examined the properties of speech, and some low level processes of speech perception. A major difference between the processing of speech and that of visual language is that in the former case the speech stimulus fades rapidly. We introduced the notion of the lexicon, our mental dictionary where all information about words is stored. Word recognition therefore involves lexical access. Lexical access is made on the basis of a pre-lexical code. We looked at evidence from experiments on infants and cross-linguistic comparisons that reveal something of the nature of this code. We saw that constructing this code is a difficult task because of difficulties in segmenting speech, and in the way in which sounds vary depending on the acoustic context in which they occur. Nevertheless, most of the time speech recognition is very fast and accurate and appears to be effortless.

We looked at a number of models of speech recognition. A recurring question is whether processes in spoken word recognition interact, or whether they are autonomous (or independent, or modular, all of which mean much the same thing).

A tentative conclusion is that both lexical (or word-level knowledge) and sentence context can affect processing, but in different ways. Spoken word recognition is essentially modular. Prior to lexical access, the pre-lexical code can only make direct use of nonlexical information. Higher level information, such as lexical knowledge, can only affect post-access processes such as checking. Sentence information can only affect the late stage of integration. There is now an increasing realisation that the number and nature of words similar to the target, the lexical neighbourhood, is also very important. The notions of competition and neighbourhood effects are emerging as important concepts.

We looked at the TRACE and cohort models of spoken word recognition. TRACE is a connectionist model, and allows interaction between all levels of processing. The cohort model (although it has changed over the last few years) is far more restrained in when context can have an effect. It provides a better fit for the data we currently have.

Finally, there are a variety of disturbances that can affect different aspects of speech recognition in adults caused by brain damage.

There is, not surprisingly, some overlap between models of spoken and visual word recognition. Certainly the same themes recur through both sets of literature. We shall now turn in detail to visual word recognition and reading.

FURTHER READING

An introduction to acoustics, the low level processes of hearing, and how the ear works, can be found in Luce (1993). The classic textbook by Clark and Clark (1977) has a good description of the earlier models of speech perception, particularly analysis by synthesis. The paper by Frauenfelder and Tyler (1987) in a special issue on spoken word recognition in the journal *Cognition* is an introduction to the issues involved in spoken word recognition. All of the articles in that special

issue are relevant to this topic. Two recent collections of papers on
speech processing are to be found in Altmann (1990) and Altmann and
Shillcock (1993). The first chapter in each book provides an overview.
The collection edited by Marslen-Wilson (1989) contains material on
both spoken and visual word recognition. Massaro (1989) provides a
critique of connnectionist models in general and TRACE in particular.
Frauenfelder and Peeters (1990) explore the TRACE model further.
There are alternative connectionist models which cannot be discussed
here. For example, Norris (1990) presents what he calls a dynamic net
model of speech recognition.

Advanced reviews of the field can be found in Remez (1994), Kluender
(1994), Massaro (1994), and Lively, Pisoni, and Goldinger (1994). Caplan
(1992, Chapter 2) includes a detailed review of the neuropsychology of
spoken word recognition.

CHAPTER THREE

Visual word recognition

INTRODUCTION

How do we recognise visually presented words—that is, words that are written or printed? When we see or hear a word, how do we access its representation within the lexicon? How do we know whether an item is stored there or not? Although strictly *recognition* means identifying an item as familiar, we will use the term slightly more widely. We are interested not only in discovering how we decide if a printed string of letters is familiar or not, but how all the information that relates to a word becomes available. For example, when you see the string of letters "g h o s t", you know more than that they make up a word. You know what the word means, that it is a noun and can therefore occupy certain roles in sentences but not others, what it means, and how the word is pronounced. You further know that its plural is formed regularly as "ghosts". This knowledge results from lexical access. I will use the terms *recognition* and *identification* interchangeably. In this and the next chapter we look at the answers to some of the foregoing questions. In this chapter we focus upon how we recognise a word, how we assess its familiarity, and how lexical access takes place. In particular, how is the meaning of a word made available? In the next, we concentrate on one important aspect, that of how we pronounce the word.

Visual word recognition has been a very popular topic in psycholinguistics. Although reading might not be the most fundamental or natural of language processes — that accolade applies to speech — to say that it is exceptionally useful is surely an understatement. Civilisation is built upon reading. Imagine what it would be like if you could neither read nor write. Now although we very rarely find adults who have not learned to speak or understand speech, we find many people who have never learned to read or write. As we saw in Chapter 1, the study of word recognition should have many implications for teaching children to read, for the remediation of illiteracy, and for the rehabilitation of people with reading difficulties.

Many of the experiments that are described in these two chapters involved recognising single words, presented in isolation, out of context. You might think this is an artificial task; however, there are two reasons for its popularity. First, these are relatively easy experiments to perform; all you need is a computer and timer. Second, reducing the task to isolated words simplifies the interpretation of the results. We assume that the same basic processes operate when we see single words as when we see a whole page of words. The effect of context on visual word recognition is as important a topic as it is in spoken word recognition. In the experiments discussed here, *context* is often reduced to one word. We therefore further assume that the context of many words operates in the much the same way as the context of one word. Of course there are important differences, and there are other processes involved. We will look at these in following chapters, when we consider how words combine to form sentences, and how we extract the meaning from these.

It is instructive to take the three stages we identified as occurring in speech recognition: initial contact, lexical selection, and word recognition. Although the processing of spoken language has a great deal in common with the processing of visual language, we saw in the last chapter that one important difference is that the speech signal is only available for a short time, while under normal conditions a written word is available for as long as the reader needs it. This makes a big difference to the initial contact and selection phases, because all the information necessary is more or less immediately available. Hence the distinction between the uniqueness and recognition points is no longer relevant; all written or printed words are almost immediately perceptually unique, and all that matters therefore is the recognition point.

METHODS AND FINDINGS

There are six main methods that have been used to explore visual word recognition. These are brain scanning or imaging techniques, eye movements, tachistoscopic identification, and measuring naming, lexical decision, and categorisation times.

In tachistoscopic identification, subjects are shown words for very short presentation times. Researchers in the past used a piece of equipment designed for presenting pictures of words for very short durations called a tachistoscope; now computers are often used instead, but the name is still used to refer to the general methodology. The experimenter records the threshold at which subjects can no longer confidently identify items. The extreme version of this task is commonly known as *subliminal perception*. In this case the items are presented for such a short duration that subjects are not aware that anything has been presented at all.

The other techniques involve reaction times. In the *naming* task, subjects are given visual presentation of a word which they then have to name, and then the *naming latency* is measured. That is, how long does it take a subject to pronounce the word aloud from when it is first presented? This is typically in the order of 500 milliseconds.

In the *lexical decision* task the subject must decide whether a string of letters is a word or nonword. In the more common visual presentation method the words are displayed visually, on a computer screen or tachistoscope (auditory versions also exist). For example, you would press one key in response to the word "nurse" and another key in response to the nonword "murse". The experimenter measures reaction times and error rates. One problem with this task is that experimenters must be sensitive to the problem of finding speed–error trade-offs (such that the faster subjects respond the more errors they make; see Pachella, 1974), and therefore you must be careful about the precise instructions the subjects are given. Response times vary, as we shall see, according to a host of factors, and of course there are marked individual differences, but are typically in the order of 500 milliseconds to about one second.

Higher-level tasks might involve getting a subject to perform a semantic categorisation task. For example, is the word "apple" a "fruit" or a "tree"? Is the object referred to by the word smaller or bigger than a chair?

In the reaction time methods the absolute time taken to respond is not particularly useful. We are concerned with differences between conditions. We assume that our experimental manipulations change only particular aspects of processing, and everything else remains constant and therefore cancels out. For example, we assume that the time subjects take to locate the word on the screen and turn their attention to it—the fixation time—is constant (unless of course we are deliberately trying to manipulate it).

Two fairly new techniques are those of brain scanning or imaging, and examining the eye movements that accompany reading. We will look at brain scans, which give us a way of looking directly at the brain's activity, in the final chapter. We will also come across eye movements again, when we look at understanding sentences (Chapters 5 and 9). Both techniques need special, relatively expensive apparatus. Eye movement studies need a specially adapted pair of spectacles attached to a computer screen and display. Eye movements are recorded by an infra-red beam bounced off the eye ball. The technique is founded upon the observation that when we read, we do not read smoothly. We go in jumps called *saccades* of about 25 milliseconds, with intervals ranging from 200 to 250 milliseconds in between when the eye is still. These still periods are called *fixations*. The information that can be taken in within a fixation is limited — 15 characters to the right and only 3–4 to the left in English speakers (Rayner, Well, & Pollatsek, 1980). This asymmetry is reversed for Hebrew readers, who read from right to left (Pollatsek, Bolozky, Well, & Rayner, 1981). Ehrlich and Rayner (1981) showed we spend more time looking at less predictable words; indeed, we might skip highly predictable ones altogether. Of course, sometimes we make mistakes, and have to look backwards. The study of regressive eye movements—which indicate rereading of material so briefly that we might not be aware of it—provides important information about how we disambiguate ambiguous material.

By far the most studies have used the naming and lexical decision tasks. Different techniques do not however always give the same results, and this is particularly true of these two tasks. They seem to tap different aspects of processing. We shall defer discussion of this until we have considered what these tasks have revealed.

Preliminary findings
In this section we will look at some of the main findings on visual word recognition. You should bear in mind that many of these phenomena also apply to spoken word recognition. In particular, frequency effects and semantic priming are found in both spoken and visual word recognition.

Semantic priming.   Meyer and Schvaneveldt (1971) provided one of the first demonstrations of what is one of the most robust and important findings in word recognition. The identification of a word is made easier if a word related in meaning is presented just before it. They used a lexical decision task, but the effect can be found, with differing magnitudes of effect, across many tasks, and is not limited to visual word recognition. We are faster to say yes to "doctor" as a word if it is preceded by the word "nurse" than if it is preceded by a word unrelated in meaning, such as "butter", or than if it is presented in isolation. "Butter" does however speed up the recognition of words related to it in meaning, such as "bread". This phenomenon is commonly known as *semantic priming*.

At this point it is useful to make a few important distinctions. The word *priming* is best reserved for the methodology of investigating what happens when one word precedes another. If there is an effect, there are of course two ways in which it might turn out. The first word, or *prime*, might speed up recognition of the second word, or *target*, in which case we talk of *facilitation*. In some cases however we find that a prime can slow down the identification of the target, in which case we talk of *inhibition*. Most of the time *semantic priming* is used to refer to semantic facilitation, but not always. As we shall see, there are types of priming other than just semantic, although this is the most important and most researched.

Semantic priming can be thought of as the consequence of a particular type of context. One can also see that the effect makes some processing sense. Words are rarely read (or heard) in isolation, and neither are words randomly juxtaposed. Words related in meaning tend to co-occur in sentences. Hence processing can perhaps be speeded up if words related to the word you are currently reading are somehow made more easily available, as they are more likely to come next than random words. How does this happen? We shall return to this question throughout this chapter.

Frequency and related effects. The frequency of a word is a very important factor in word recognition. Commonly used words are easier to recognise and are responded to more quickly than less commonly used words. It was first demonstrated in tachistoscopic recognition (Howes & Solomon, 1951), but has since been demonstrated for a wide range of tasks. Whaley (1978) showed that frequency is the single most important factor in determining the speed of responding in the lexical decision task. Forster and Chambers (1973) found the effect in the naming task. These effects are not just due to differences between frequent and very infrequent words (e.g. "year" versus "hermeneutic") where you would obviously expect a difference, but also between common and slightly less common words (e.g. "rain" versus "puddle"). It is therefore essential to control for frequency in psycholinguistic experiments, ensuring that different conditions are matched. There are a number of frequency counts available; Kuçera and Francis (1967; see also Francis & Kuçera, 1982) is one of the most popular of these, listing the occurrence per million of a large number of words.

The effect of frequency is all pervasive, and as you might expect a number of other variables correlate with it. For example, common words tend to be shorter. If you wish to demonstrate an unambiguous effect of frequency, you must be careful to control for these other factors. Indeed, it may be the case that word frequency is not the main reason for why high frequency words are apparently accessed more easily; it could be that one of the factors which is highly correlated with it is actually responsible. This has been argued most convincingly for two variables: the familiarity of a word, and the age at which you first learn it. The importance of familiarity is based on the observation that there is a great deal of variation in the experiential familiarity of the low frequency words. Some words with recorded low frequency (such as "mumble", "giggle", and "drowsy") are rated as more familiar than other of similar frequency (such as "cohere", "rend", and "char"). Gernsbacher (1984) argued that *familiarity* is a more fundamental processing variable than frequency. Familiarity can be thought of as a measure of personal frequency. Hence psychologists might be very familiar with a word such as "behaviourism", even though it has quite a low frequency in the general language. Certainly not all low-frequency words are alike, and this might need to be considered in designing experiments. The age-of-acquisition of a word is when you first learn a word (Gilhooly, 1984). On the whole, children learn more common words first, but there are exceptions: for example, "giant" is generally learned early although it is a relatively low frequency word. Brown and Watson (1987), and Morrison, Ellis, and Quinlan (1992), argued that age-of-acquisition is more fundamental than familiarity frequency, at least in naming words and pictures of objects.

Although either or both of these proposals may turn out to be correct, the dominant position is to accept that frequency is a fundamental variable on word recognition whose effect must be explained by any model. The question then arises at what stage does frequency act? Is it inherent in the way words are stored, or does it merely affect the way in which subjects respond in experimental tasks? An early indication that it might be the latter could be found in an experiment by Goldiamond and Hawkins (1958). The first part of this experiment was a training phase. Subjects were exposed to nonwords (such as "lemp" and "stunch"). Frequency was simulated by giving a lot of exposure to some words (mimicking high frequency), and less to others (mimicking low frequency). For example, if you see "lemp" a lot of times relative to "stunch", then it becomes a higher-frequency item for you, even though it is a nonword. In the second part of the experiment, subjects were tested for tachistoscopic recognition at very short intervals. Although the subjects were told to expect the words that they were trained on, only a blurred stimulus that they had not seen before was in fact presented. Nevertheless, subjects generated the trained nonwords even though they were not present, but also with the same frequency distribution as they were trained on. That is, they responded with the more frequent words more often even though nothing was actually present. It can be argued from this that frequency does not have an effect on the perception or recognition of a word, only on the later output processes. That is, frequency affects our *response bias*. This is sometimes called a *guessing model*. In fact, this type of experiment only shows that frequency can affect the later, response stages. It does not show that it does not involve the earlier recognition processes as well. Indeed, Morton (1979a) showed how mathematical modelling suggests that sophisticated guessing cannot explain the normal word frequency effect. Bradley and Forster (1987) also argued that frequency is a real access effect which has a major influence on lexical access. This is an important issue to which we will return.

A frequency effect could arise in two ways. A word could become more accessible because we see (or hear) frequent words more than we see (or hear) less frequent ones, or because we speak (or write) frequent words more often. Of course, most of the time these two possibilities are entangled; we use much the same words in speaking as we are exposed to as listeners. Another way of putting this is to ask if frequency effects arise through recognition or generation. Morton (1979a) disentangled these two factors. He concluded that the data are best explained by models whereby the advantage of high frequency words is that they need less evidence to reach some threshold for identification. The effect of repeated exposure to a word is therefore to lower this threshold. These mechanisms form a central part of his logogen model to be discussed below. The later recognition of a word is facilitated every time we are exposed to it, whether through speaking, writing, listening, or reading. Hence frequency of experience and frequency of generation are both important.

Word–nonword effects.   Words are generally responded to faster than nonwords. Less plausible nonwords are rejected faster than more plausible nonwords (Coltheart, Davelaar, Jonasson, & Besner, 1977). Hence in a lexical decision task we are relatively slow to reject a nonword like "siant" (which might have been a word, and indeed which looks like one, "saint"), but very quick to reject one such as "tnszv". Nonwords that are plausible—that is, that follow the rules of word formation of the language in that they do not contain illegal strings of letters—are sometimes called pseudowords.

Interfering with identification.   We can slow down the process of word identification by making it harder to recognise the stimulus by degrading its physical appearance. This is called *stimulus degradation*.

We can do this by means such as breaking up the letters that form the word, by reducing the contrast between the word and the background, or by rotating the word to an unusual angle.

Along similar lines, presenting another stimulus immediately after the target interferes with the recognition process. This is called *backwards masking*. There are two different ways of doing this. If the masking stimulus is unstructured—for example if it is just a patch of randomly positioned black dots, or just a burst of light—then we call it *energy* (or brightness, or random noise) masking. If the masking stimulus is structured (for example, if it comprises letters or random parts of letters) then we call it *pattern masking* (or feature masking). These two types of mask have very different effects (Turvey, 1973). Energy masks operate on the visual feature detection level by causing a visual feature shortage and making feature identification difficult. Feature masks cause interference at the letter level and limit the time available for processing.

Masking is implicated in one of the greatest of all psycholinguistic controversies, that of *perception without awareness*. Perception without awareness is a form of subliminal perception. Studies such as Allport (1977) and Marcel (1983a, b) have found an effect whereby words that have been masked so that subjects report that they are not aware of their presence, nevertheless produce activation through the word identification system, even to the level of semantic processing. That is, items can access semantic information without there being any awareness of that item. The techniques involved are notoriously difficult; the results questioned by, among others, Ellis and Marshall (1978) and Williams and Parkin (1980). Holender (1986) provides a critical review of the field. Problems with the methodology include titrating the level of conscious awareness for each individual subject such that it is the same, and ensuring that subjects are equally dark-adapted during the preliminary establishing of individual thresholds and the main testing phase of the experiment. Otherwise we cannot be sure that information is not reaching conscious awareness in the testing phase, even though we think we might have set the time for which the target is presented to a sufficiently short interval. The window between presenting a word quickly enough for it not to become available to consciousness, and not so quickly that subjects really do see nothing at all, is very small. As yet it is unclear whether we can identify and access meaning-related information about words without conscious awareness, although the balance of evidence is probably that we can. Such a finding does not pose any real problem for our models of lexical access.

Repetition priming.   Once you have seen a word, it is easier to identify the next time. The effects of this are surprisingly long-lasting. You might expect that having just seen a word will make it easier to recognise straightaway, but periods of facilitation caused by repetition have been reported over several hours or even longer. The technique of facilitating recognition by repeating a word is known as repetition priming. Repetition interacts with frequency. In a lexical decision task, repetition priming effects are stronger for low frequency words than for high frequency ones (Forster & Davis, 1984). Forster and Davis also pattern-masked the prime in an attempt to wipe out any possible episodic memory of the prime. They concluded that repetition effects have two components: a very brief lexical access effect, and a long-term episodic effect, with only the latter sensitive to frequency.

Length effects.   Gough (1972) argued that letters are taken out of the visual buffer one-by-one at 15 milliseconds per letter. This transfer rate is slower for poor readers. Therefore it would not be at all surprising if long words are harder to identify than short words. However, a length effect independent of frequency has proved surprisingly elusive. One complication is that there are three different ways of measuring word length: how many letters there are in a word, how many syllables, and how long it takes you to say it. Henderson (1982) concluded that generally word length affects naming but not lexical decision, an instance of the claim to which we shall return that not all experimental tasks give the same results. This conclusion should be treated with caution, as Whaley (1978) did find word length effects upon lexical decision.

Generally, the naming time increases as a function of the number of syllables in a word (Eriksen, Pollack, & Montague, 1970). There is at least some contribution from preparing to articulate these syllables in addition to any perceptual effect. We find a similar effect in picture naming, whereby we take longer to name pictures of the object depicted by long words compared with pictures of the objects depicted by short words, and longer to read numbers that have more syllables in their pronunciation, such as the number 77 compared with the number 16 (Klapp, 1974; Klapp, Anderson, & Berrian, 1973).

Summary.   The ease of word recognition is affected by a number of variables. There are others that should be mentioned, including syntactic class (see West & Stanovich, 1986), and the frequency of individual letters and letter clusters within a word. The imageability, meaningfulness and concreteness of a word may have an effect on its identification (see Paivio, Yuille, & Madigan, 1968). In a review of 51 properties of words, Rubin (1980) concluded that frequency, emotionality, and pronunciability were the best predictors of commonly used experimental tasks. Whaley (1978) concluded that frequency, meaningfulness, and the number of syllables had most effect upon lexical decision times. Masking can dramatically affect the speed and accuracy of word recognition. Any model of word recognition must be able to account for how these variables have their effect. Furthermore, the models must be able to account for how variables combine together to have an effect; that is, how they interact.

Attentional processes in visual word recognition

The first thing to note is that reading is essentially a mandatory process; when you see a word, you cannot help but identify it. In addition to introspection, further evidence comes from the Stroop phenomenon: naming the colour that a word is written in is impaired if the colour name and word conflict (e.g. "red" written in green ink).

We have seen that priming can alter the ease with which we can identify a word. The prime will facilitate the recognition of the target if it is related to it in meaning (semantic priming), is the same word as the target (repetition priming), or looks similar to it (form-related priming). Is a single mechanism involved in priming? Here we will focus upon how the most studied of these, semantic priming, operates. In a classic experiment, Neely (1977) argued that there were two different attentional modes of priming. His findings relate to a distinction made by Posner and Snyder (1975) and Schneider and Shiffrin (1977) between automatic and attentional (or controlled) processing. *Automatic processing* is fast, parallel, not prone to interference from other tasks, does not demand working memory space, cannot be prevented, and is not directly available to consciousness. *Attentional processing* is slow, serial, sensitive to interference from competing tasks, does use working memory space, can be prevented or inhibited, and its results are often (but not necessarily) directly available to consciousness.

Neely used the lexical decision task to investigate how priming occurs. He manipulated four variables. The first was whether or not there was a semantic relationship between the prime and target, so that in the related condition a category name acting as prime preceded the target. Second, he manipulated the subjects' conscious expectancies. Third, he varied whether or not subjects' attention had to be shifted from one category to another between the presentation of the prime and the presentation of the target. Finally, he varied the *stimulus onset asynchrony* (SOA). This is the time between the beginning of the presentation of the prime to the beginning of the presentation of the target. In his experiment it varied between 250 milliseconds (a very short SOA) and 2000 milliseconds (a very long SOA).

Discrepancies between what subjects were led to expect from the instructions given to them before the experiment started, and what actually happened in the experiment, were an important factor. Subjects were told, for example, that whenever the prime was "BIRD", to expect that a type of bird would follow; but that whenever the prime was "BODY", a part of a building would follow. Hence their conscious expectancies determined whether they had to expect to shift or not shift their attention from one category name to members of another category. Examples of stimuli in the key conditions are given in Table 3.1.

He found that the pattern of results depended upon the SOAs. The crucial condition is what happens after "BODY". At short SOAs, "HEART" is facilitated relative to the baseline condition, whereas "SPARROW" is about the same as the baseline. At long SOAs, "HEART" is inhibited — that is, subjects are actually slower to respond to it than they are to the baseline condition. On the other hand, at short SOAs, "DOOR" is not facilitated, but at long SOAs, it is.

These results were interpreted that two different processes are operating at short and long SOAs. At short SOAs, there is fast-acting, short-lived facilitation of semantically related items, irrespective of the

TABLE 3.1
Examples of materials in Neely's (1977) experiment

1.	BIRD	ROBIN	R	E	NS
2.	BODY	DOOR	UR	E	S
3.	BIRD	ARM	UR	UE	NS
4.	BODY	SPARROW	UR	UE	S
5.	BODY	HEART	R	UE	S
6.	CONTROL:	to measure the base-line, use XXXX–ROBIN			

Key

R	semantically related
UR	semantically unrelated
E	as expected from instructions
UE	unexpected from instructions
S	shift of attention from one category to another
NS	no shift of attention from one category to another

subjects' expectations. This facilitation is based upon semantic relationships between words. There is no inhibition of any sort at short SOAs. This is called *automatic priming*. "HEART" cannot help but be primed by "BODY" even though the participant is trying not to. But at long SOAs, there is a slow build-up of facilitation which is dependent upon your expectancies. This leads to the inhibition of responses to unexpected items, with the cost that if you do have to respond to them then responding will be retarded. This is *attentional priming*. To summarise, two different processes are involved in priming: short-lived automatic facilitatory semantic priming, and slow build-up expectancy-based attentional priming. Normally, these two types of priming are confounded, and work together. In a semantic priming task at intermediate SOAs (around 400 milliseconds) both automatic and attentional priming will be co-operating to speed up responding. One can also conclude from this experiment, on the basis of the unexpected-related condition, that the meanings of words are accessed automatically.

Further evidence for a two-process priming model.   The idea that two processes are involved in priming has been developed since Neely's original experiment, although the underlying principle remains sound. Whereas Neely used category-instance associations (e.g. "BODY–ARM") which are not particularly informative (any part of the body could follow "BODY"), Antos (1979) used instance–category associations (e.g. "ARM–BODY"), which are highly predictive. He then found evidence of inhibition (relative to the baseline) in the "trick condition" at shorter SOAs (at 200 milliseconds), suggesting that inhibition may not just arise from attentional processes, but may also have an automatic component. Antos also showed the importance of the baseline condition, a conclusion supported by de Groot (1984). A row of X's, as used by Neely is a very conservative baseline, and tends to delay responding; it as though subjects are waiting for the second word before they respond. It may be more appropriate to use a neutral word (such as "BLANK", or "READY") as the neutral condition. If this is done, we find inhibition at much shorter SOAs. Antos also argued that even Neely found evidence of cost at short SOAs, but that this was manifested in increase in the error rate rather than a slowing of reaction time. This is evidence of a speed–error trade-off in the data. Generally, in psycholinguistic reaction time experiments, it is always important to check for differences in the error rate as well as reaction times across conditions.

Den Heyer (1985), and Den Heyer, Briand, and Dannenbring (1983) looked at what is called the *proportion effect*. This is when the amount of priming found increases as the proportion of associated words in the experiment increases. If priming were wholly automatic, then the amount found should remain constant across all proportions of associated word pairs. Similarly, Tweedy, Lapinski and Schvaneveldt (1977) varied *cue validity*. Both the proportion effect and cue validity basically reflect manipulation of the subjects' expectancies by varying the proportion of valid primes. If there are a lot of primes that are actually unrelated to the targets, subjects quickly learn that they are not of much benefit. This will then wipe out the contribution of attentional priming. Nevertheless, in those cases where primes are related to the target, automatic priming still functions. The distinction between automatic and attentional processing in priming has also been supported by further experiments by Fischler and Bloom (1979), and Hoffman and MacMillan (1985). Hence we can conclude that priming has both an automatic and attentional component. The work by Antos and de Groot suggests that inhibition might be automatically generated when the prime is inappropriate for the target: that is, that both components may lead to inhibition of inappropriate words.

Summary. There are two attentional processes operating in semantic priming. A short-lived, automatic, facilitatory process that we cannot prevent happening, and an attentional process that depends upon our expectancies and which is much slower to get going. The benefits of priming are not however without their costs; attentional priming certainly involves inhibition of unexpected alternatives, and if one of these is indeed the target than recognition will be delayed. There is probably also an inhibitory cost associated with automatic priming. Automatic priming probably operates through spreading activation.

We can extend our distinction between automatic and attentional processes to word recognition itself. As we have seen, there is clearly an automatic component to recognition, because this processing is mandatory. Intuitively there is also an attentional component. If we misread a sentence, we might consciously choose to go back and reread a particular word. To take this further, if we provisionally identify a word which seems incompatible with the context, we might check that we have indeed correctly identified it. These attentional processes operate after we have first contacted the lexicon, and hence we also talk about automatic lexical access and non-automatic post-access effects. Attentional processes are important in word recognition, and may play different roles in the tasks used to study it.

In summary, both word recognition and priming have automatic and attentional components.

Differences between methodologies

Unfortunately the interpretation of results in the word recognition field is particularly muddied by the contribution of the specific tasks used to investigate the processes. We are not just studying word recognition pure and simple; we are studying word recognition plus measurement tasks that are not themselves that well understood. Worse, the tasks interact with what is being studied. It is rather like using a telescope to judge the colour of stars when the glass of the telescope lens changes colour depending on the distance of the star—and we don't realise it. For example, Bowles and Poon (1985) showed that unlike in lexical decision (where it has a facilitatory effect), semantic priming has an inhibitory effect upon retrieving a word given its definition. However, by far the most controversy surrounds the naming and lexical decision tasks. Which of these gives the most straightforward results in the sense that it taps automatic processes?

Lexical decision has been particularly criticised as being too sensitive to post-access mechanisms. It reflects too much of subject strategies rather the automatic processes of lexical access (e.g. see Balota & Lorch, 1986; Neely, Keefe, & Ross, 1989; Seidenberg, Waters, Sanders, & Langer, 1984), and measures subject decision-making times in addition to the pure lexical access times (Balota & Chumbley, 1984; Chumbley & Balota, 1984). Subjects do not always respond as soon as lexical access occurs; instead, attentional or strategic factors may come into operation which delay responding. (You do not need to be aware of these post-access mechanisms; remember, not all attentional processes are directly available to consciousness). Two types of strategy used by subjects have been proposed, and of course it is possible that both might be operating in a particular experiment. First, as we have seen, subjects have *expectancies* which affect processing. In a lexical decision experiment, subjects usually notice that some of the prime–target word pairs are related. So when they see the prime, they can generate a set of possible targets themselves. Hence they can make the "word" response faster if the actual target matches one of their generated words than if not. The second is a *post-lexical* or *post-access checking* strategy. Subjects might use information subsequent to lexical access to aid their decision. The presence of a semantic relationship between the prime and target suggests that the prime must be a word, and hence they respond "word" faster in a lexical decision task. There can be no semantic relationship between a word and nonword. That is, using post-lexical checking, subjects are responding on the basis of an estimate of the semantic relationship between prime and target, and not directly on the outcome of the attempt to access the lexicon for the target.

What is the evidence that word naming is less likely to engage subject strategies than lexical decision? First, inhibitory effects are small or non-existent in naming (Lorch, Balota, & Stamm, 1986; Neely et al., 1989). Second, it has been argued that mediated priming between pairs of words that are connected only through an intermediary (e.g. "winter" primes "summer" which primes "swim") has to be automatic. Mediated priming is found in the naming task but not in lexical decision (Seidenberg et al., 1984). Third, backwards semantic priming of words which are only associated in one direction but not another (see below) is found in lexical decision but is not normally found in the naming task (Seidenberg et al., 1984). This type of priming is thought to arise through post-access checking.

There has been considerable debate recently on whether these tasks are differentially sensitive to word frequency (Balota & Chumbley, 1984, 1985, 1990; Monsell, Doyle, & Haggard, 1989). Balota and Chumbley argued that as frequency had no effect on semantic categorisation, a task that very clearly must involve lexical access, it must arise because of post-access processes, such as checking and articulation. They also showed that the magnitude of the frequency effect depended upon subtle differences in the stimulus materials in the experiment (such as length differences between words and nonwords). This can be explained if the effect is mediated by subjects' strategies. Furthermore, at first sight the magnitude of the frequency effect is much greater in lexical decision than naming. The argument is that this is because it is has two components: a small (or even non-existent) automatic effect, and a large attentional, strategic component. Lexical decision is more sensitive to strategic factors; therefore lexical decision is more sensitive to frequency.

Contrary to this, Monsell et al. (1989) showed that frequency effects in naming can be inflated to a similar level to that found in lexical decision by manipulating the regularity of the pronunciation of words (see next chapter). It may be that frequency effects are absorbed by other components of the naming task (Bradley & Forster, 1987). Furthermore, delaying subjects' responses virtually eliminates the frequency effect (Savage, Bradley, & Forster, 1990). Delaying responding does not of course eliminate any articulatory effect, as although responses can be prepared, they must still be spoken. This casts doubt on the claim that there is a major articulatory component to the effect of frequency on naming, and suggests that the effect must be earlier.

A further complication was introduced by Grainger (1990; see also Grainger, O'Regan, Jacobs, & Segui, 1989), who reported experiments that addressed both the locus of the frequency effect and also task differences between lexical decision and naming. He showed that response times to words are also sensitive to the frequency of the neighbours of the target words. Remember that the neighbours of a word are those that similar to it in some way—in the case of visually presented words, it is visual or *orthographic* similarity that is important. For example, there is much overlap in the letters and visual appearance of "blue" and "blur". Grainger showed that when the frequency of the lexical neighbourhood of a word is controlled, the magnitude of the effect of frequency in lexical decision is reduced to that of the naming task. Responses to words with a high frequency neighbour were slowed in the lexical decision task and facilitated in the naming task. He argued that as low frequency targets necessarily tend to have more high frequency neighbours, previous studies had confounded target frequency with neighbourhood frequency. Furthermore, he argued that the usual finding that frequency effects are stronger in lexical decision than naming cannot necessarily be attributed to task-specific post-access processes, as they arise instead because of this confound with neighbourhood frequency.

Summary.   Lexical decision and naming do not always give the same results. Although there is still some debate, the differences probably arise because while naming times are a relatively pure measure of the time it takes for automatic access to the lexicon, lexical decision times may include a substantial amount of attentional processing. Hence the differences in reaction times between the tasks may reflect differing accounts of post-access rather than access processes. This is perhaps not surprising if you reflect upon the nature of the tasks. In lexical decision, not only do you need to access the word in your lexicon, you then have to make a binary response (such as deciding between word–nonword). However, we have just seen that there are some recent data that suggest that frequency effects can be inflated in naming, and other data which suggest that they can be reduced in lexical decision. This clearly challenges the view that lexical decision alone is particularly sensitive to post-access processing.

Even if we accept the view that in most cases naming times may preferable, we must remember that naming also is more than just accessing the lexicon. Naming times also include the time it takes to access the sound of a word, its *phonological code*, after the word has been identified. This means it is sensitive to a different set of factors. For example, Henderson (1982) concludes that word length affects naming but not lexical decision. Indeed, as we shall see in the next chapter, it has been argued that it is possible to access this phonological code before the word is recognised. However, most experimentalists believe that the naming task does routinely involve lexical access (e.g. Forster & Chambers, 1973).

MEANING-BASED FACILITATION OF VISUAL WORD RECOGNITION

We have seen that semantic priming is one of the most robust effects upon word recognition. It is time to look at different types of semantic priming; they do not have equal effects.

Types of semantic priming

The distinction between automatic and attentional priming is also useful for thinking about semantic priming. One obvious issue concerning semantic priming is whether all types of semantic relationship are equally successful in inducing priming. Obviously the closer the meanings of the two words are, the bigger the size of the priming effect found. We can also distinguish between *associative* and *non-associative* semantic priming. Two words are said to be associated if subjects produce one in response to the other in a word association task. This can be measured by word association norms such as that of Postman and Keppel (1970). Norms such as these list the frequency of responses to a number of words in response to the instruction "Say the first word that comes to mind when I say . . . doctor". If you try this, you will probably find words such as "nurse" and "hospital" come to mind. Non-associative semantically-related words are those which still have a relationship in terms of meaning to the target, but are not produced as associates. Consider the words "dance" and "skate". They are clearly related in meaning, but "skate" is rarely produced as an associative of the prime. "Bread" and "cake" are an example of another pair of semantically related but unassociated words. Superordinate category names (e.g. "animal") and category instances (e.g. "fox") are clearly semantically related, but not always strongly associated. Members of the same category (e.g. "fox" and "camel" are both animals) are clearly related, but are not associated. Finally, some words are produced as associates of words that are not related in meaning: an example might be "waiting" generated in response to hospital.

Non-associative semantic priming could occur by words contacting a higher level representation outside of the lexicon. For example, "camel" might contact "animal", which then contacts all other animals, including "fox". We shall return to this question of the organisation of meaning in Chapter 6.

Most studies of semantic priming have looked at word pairs that are both associatively and semantically related. However, we can examine the differential contributions of association and pure semantic relatedness to priming. Lupker (1984) found virtually no semantic priming of non-associated words in a naming task. The word pairs were related in his experiment by virtue of being members of the same semantic category but were not commonly associated (e.g. "ship" and "car" are related by virtue of both being types of vehicles). Shelton and Martin (1992) showed that automatic priming is obtained only for associatively related word pairs in a lexical decision task, and not for words that are semantically related but not associated. Hence automatic priming occurs only within the lexicon by virtue of associations between words. Moss and Marslen-Wilson (1993) also report how semantic associations and semantic properties have differential priming effects in a cross-modal priming task (see also Chapter 9). They also concluded that associative priming does not reflect the operation of semantic representations, but is a low level, intra-lexical automatic process. Kiger and Glass (1983) placed the primes immediately after the target; they then found *backwards priming*, of the target, but only for word-pairs that were associated. In this task the time interval probably did not give time for attentional priming to develop before subjects had responded.

On the other hand, Hodgson (1991) found no priming for semantically related pairs in a naming task, but significant priming for the same pairs in a lexical decision task. However it is likely that the instructions in his lexical decision task encouraged non-automatic processing (Shelton & Martin, 1992). As an aside, this reiterates the importance of the details of the instructions given to subjects in psycholinguistic experiments. Both Fischler (1977) and Lupker (1984) found some priming effect of semantic relationship without association, also in a lexical decision task. As we have just seen, the lexical decision task seems to be a less pure measure of automatic processing than naming, and hence this priming might have arisen through non-automatic means. Although Shelton and Martin (1992) also used lexical decision, they designed their experiment to minimise attentional processing. Rather than passively reading a prime and then responding to the target, subjects made rapid successive lexical decisions to individual words. On a small proportion of trials two successive words would be related, and the amount of priming to the second word could be recorded. This technique of minimising non-automatic processing produced priming only for the associated words and not for the non-associated related words.

Given that facilitation largely appears to be based on association, it is important to note that not all associations are equal in both directions.

"Bell" leads to "hop" but not vice versa: hence "bell" facilitates "hop", but "hop" does not facilitate "bell". However, Koriat (1981) and Seidenberg et al. (1984) showed that "backward" priming can arise from non-automatic, attentional priming as a result of a post-lexical checking strategy.

In summary, the data are not wholly clear, but the results on the whole indicate that automatic priming occurs within the lexicon rather than at a semantic level, at least in low-level tasks that tap the processes of lexical access. This means that this type of priming can be explained by associations between words rather than mediation based upon word meaning. "Doctor" primes "nurse" because these words frequently co-occur together, leading to the strengthening of connections in the lexicon, rather than because of an overlap in their meaning, or the activation of an item at a higher level of representation. You do not need to step outside the lexicon to explain automatic priming; it can remain a closed module. On the other hand, non-associative semantic priming only occurs via attentional processes such as expectancies or checking. Maybe the term "semantic priming" is something of a misnomer. To tap true automatic semantic processing, you should use true semantic tasks such as semantic categorisation. These results show how modularity can be preserved in the face of apparently contrary priming evidence.

Sentence context effects in visual word recognition

Priming from sentence context is that contributed over and above that of the associative effects of individual words in the sentence. The beginning of the sentence "It is important to brush your teeth every single__" facilitates the recognition of a word such as "day", which is a highly predictable continuation of the sentence, compared with a word such as "dog", which is not. The sentence context facilitates recognition even though there is no semantic relationship between "day" and other words in sentence. This is *contextual facilitation* or priming. How does sentence context have its effect? Does it operate before or after lexical access? Given our conclusion that there is no automatic non-associative semantic priming, it would be surprising if we find an automatic effect of sentence context. Instead, we should expect this effect to be attentional. Also in comparison with non-associative semantic priming, we might expect different tasks to give different results.

Sentence context effects were first demonstrated by Schuberth and Eimas (1977) They presented incomplete context sentences followed by a word or nonword. Subjects had to make a lexical decision response to this final word. Response times speeded up if the target word was congruent with the preceding context. West and Stanovich (1978) demonstrated similar facilitation by congruent contexts on word naming. Later studies have revealed limitations to when and how much contextual facilitation can occur.

Fischler and Bloom (1979) used a paradigm similar to that of Schuberth and Eimas. They showed that response times are only speeded up if the target word was a highly probable continuation of the sentence. For example, consider the sentence "She cleaned the dirt from her__ ". The word "shoes" is a highly predictable continuation here; the word "hands" is an unlikely but not anomalous continuation; while "terms" would clearly be an anomalous ending. (We do not need to rely on our intuitions here; we can ask a group of other subjects to give a word to end the sentence and count up the numbers of different responses.) Compared to a baseline condition, we find that an appropriate context has no effect on the recognition of the congruent but unlikely words (e.g. "hands"), but a facilitatory effect on the highly predictable congruent words ("shoes") and an inhibitory effect (that is, responses are slower than in the neutral condition) to the anomalous words (e.g. "terms"). As there is no direct associative relationship between "shoes" and other words in the sentence, this seems to be attributable to priming from sentential context.

Stanovich and West (1979, 1981; see also West & Stanovich, 1982) found contextual effects are also larger for words that are harder to recognise in isolation. Contextual facilitation was much larger when the targets were degraded by reduced contrast. In clear conditions, we find mainly contextual facilitation; in conditions of target degradation, we find contextual inhibition. Children, who of course are less skilled at reading words in isolation than adults, also display more contextual inhibition.

As hinted at above, the main two tasks used also yield different results. Naming tasks tend to find more facilitation of congruent words, whereas lexical decision tasks tend to find more inhibition of incongruent words. The inhibition is most likely to arise because lexical decision is again tapping post-access, attentional processes. It is likely that these processes involve integrating the meanings of the words accessed with a higher-level representation of the sentence. West and Stanovich (1982) argue that the facilitation effects found in the naming task arise through simple associative priming from preceding words in the sentence. It is very difficult to construct testing materials that eliminate all associative priming from the other words in the sentence to the target.

In summary, it seems that contextual priming probably occurs through post-lexical rather than lexical mechanisms. Any facilitation found is probably simply a result of associative priming from the other words in the sentence. Sentence context operates by the post-access inhibition of words incongruent with the preceding context, and this is most likely to be detected with tasks such as lexical decision that are more sensitive to post-access mechanisms. Forster (1981b) also noted that using context is not straightforward, and often likely to use cognitive resources. This in itself is enough to suggest that contextual effects should at least sometimes be non-automatic. This means that it is perhaps not worth the language processor using context routinely, limiting it to difficult circumstances, such as when the stimulus is degraded.

Summary of meaning-based priming studies

We have distinguished between automatic and attentional priming and lexical access mechanisms. The only type of priming for which there is fairly unambiguous evidence that it is automatic is associative priming arising from associative connections between words that frequently co-occur. Other types of priming such as semantic priming without association, and contextual priming, probably only occur through attentional processes. These speed up post-access processing; those mechanisms that operate after the lexicon has been accessed. These processes include checking that the item accessed is the correct one, and integrating the word with higher-level, syntactic and semantic representations of the sentence being analysed. In this way we can also maintain the position that processing within the lexicon is modular; that the processes of lexical access cannot be directly influenced by higher-level information. We shall return to this topic in Chapter 9 when we consider the modularity of the language system in more detail.

MODELS OF WORD RECOGNITION

In this section we will look at some models that have been proposed to account for how lexical access occurs and to explain the phenomena we have described. Many models of visual word recognition have been proposed, and we cannot describe all of them, so we will concentrate instead upon the most influential. All of them have in common that they take as input a perceptual representation of the word, and output desired information such as meaning, sound, and familiarity. An important issue is how we derive a word's phonological form. We will defer discussion of this until the next chapter. Here we concentrate on what Carr and Pollatsek (1985) call *lexical instance* models. These models all have in common that there is simply perceptual access to a memory system, the lexicon, where individual words are stored, and do not have any additional rule-based component which converts individual letters into sounds.

We can distinguish two main types of lexical instance model. These differ in whether they employ the concept of the direct, multiple activation of units, or the concept of serial search. Direct access, activation-based models include the logogen model, connectionist models, and the cohort model. The best known instance of a search model is the bin-based serial search model. On the fringes and more difficult to fit into this simple scheme are hybrid or verification models (which combine direct access and serial search) and distributed connectionist models (which although very similar to the logogen model do not have simple lexical units at all).

In this chapter we will focus upon the bin-based serial search and the logogen models. In many ways these are at opposite ends of the spectrum, and make the difference involved very clear. We will also look at an interactive activation model and the verification model.

Forster's autonomous serial search model

Forster (1976, 1979) proposed a model of serial search through the lexicon. This is very like trying to identify a word by searching through a dictionary; you search through the entries, which are arranged to facilitate search on the basis of visual characteristics (that is, they are in alphabetical order), until you find the right entry. The entry in the dictionary gives you all the information you need about the word: its meaning, pronunciation, and syntactic class. This model also argues that perceptual processing of words occurs independently of any other process. Another commonly used analogy here is that of searching though card catalogues to find the location of a book in the library. The model is a two-stage one; you can use the card catalogue to find out where the book is, but you still have to go to the shelf, find the book's actual location, and extract information from it. In this model the card catalogue system corresponds to what are called *access files*, and the shelves full of books to the *master file*.

The model is based upon this dictionary-search idea but incorporates many extensions to account for the data we have been examining in this chapter. Perceptual processing is followed by the sequential search of access files which point to an entry in the lexicon. Access files are modality-specific: there are different ones for orthographic, phonological, and syntactic-semantic (used in speech production) sources. These access files give pointers to a master file in the lexicon which stores all information to do with the word, including its meaning. To speed up processing, these access files are sub-divided into separate bins on the basis of the initial sound or letter of a word. Items within these bins are then ordered in terms of frequency, such that the more frequent items are examined first. Automatic priming occurs by intra-lexical spreading activation and is analogous to cross-references in the master file. The model is summarised in Fig. 3.1.

The model is said to be autonomous because there can be no leakage of information between levels. The only type of context that can operate

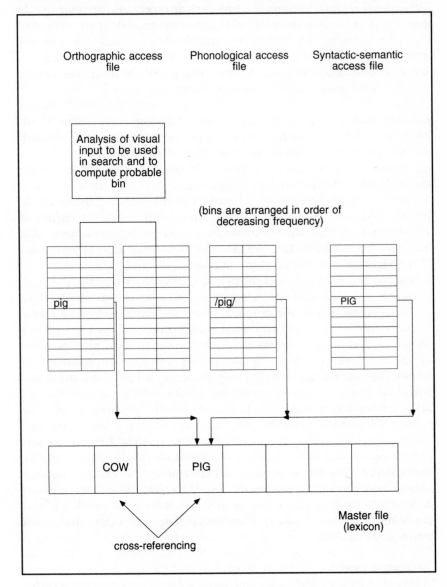

FIG. 3.1.   Forster's serial search model of lexical access. (Based on Forster, 1976, p. 268.)

on lexical access in that of associative priming within the master file. Hence there is no early role for sentence context effects. These can only have an effect through post-access mechanisms such as checking the output of lexical access against the context and integration with higher-level representations. Factors such as repetition can temporarily change the order of items within bins, thereby providing an account of repetition priming. Entries in the master file can only be accessed through one access file at a time. Nonwords are only rejected after a fairly exhaustive search of the lexicon. The model has been extended by Bradley and Forster (1987) to speech recognition as well.

Evaluation of the serial search model.   Glanzer   and   Ehrenreich (1979) proposed that we have two mental dictionaries at our disposal: one contains information on only common, high-frequency words; the other contains information on all words (duplicating the high frequency ones). Using a lexical decision task, they concluded that within a dictionary, search time does not vary with frequency. This result is known as *frequency blocking.* In reply, Forster (1981a) used a variety of naming tasks to show that there is only evidence for one lexicon, and that frequency is important within this. He argued that Glanzer and Ehrenreich's results were a result of post-access processes.

Another criticism concerns the plausibility of serial search. Although introspection suggests that word recognition is direct rather than involving serial search, we cannot rely on this sort of data. The model accounts for the main data in word recognition, and makes a strong prediction that priming effects should be limited to associative priming within the lexicon. There should be no top-down involvement of extra-lexical knowledge in word recognition. As we have seen, so far this prediction has been largely borne out. However, other models that do not depend on lexical search could account for the data equally well. The account of within-lexical priming seems rather ad hoc. Carr and Pollatsek (1985) show that serial search models have problems accounting for the recognition of long and morphologically complex words. And finally, the model does not convincingly account for how we process and pronounce nonwords. Forster (1994) addresses some of these problems. This model has proved very influential and is a useful standard: Are lexical access mechanisms more complex than those used here really justified?

The logogen model

In this model every word we know has its own simple feature counter or *logogen* corresponding to it. A logogen accumulates evidence until its individual threshold level is reached. When this happens, the word is recognised. Lexical access is therefore direct, occurs simultaneously and in parallel for all words, and is said to be passive, as unlike words in the cohort model, logogens just accumulate evidence, rather than seeking to disallow themselves on the basis of a mismatch. Proposed by Morton (1969, 1970), it was related to the information processing idea of features and demons (described in Lindsay & Norman's classic, 1977, textbook). It was originally formulated to explain context effects in tachistoscopic recognition, but has been extended to account for many word recognition phenomena. It has undergone considerable revision since its original formulation, and we will look at the motivation for the most important change. The full mathematical model is presented in Morton (1969), but a simplified account can be found in Morton (1979a).

Each logogen unit has a resting level of energy called activation. As it receives corroborating evidence that it corresponds to the stimulus presented, its activation level increases. Hence if a "t" letter is identified in the input, the activation levels of all logogens which correspond to words containing a "t" will increase. If the activation level manages to pass a threshold, the logogen "fires" and the word is "recognised". Evidence which will increase the activation level can be either perceptual or contextual. That is, there is no distinction between evidence for a word from external and internal sources. Context increases a logogen's activation level just as relevant sensory data does. Any use of the logogen will give rise to subsequent facilitation by lowering the threshold of that logogen. More frequent items have lower thresholds. Nonwords will be rejected if no logogen has fired by the time a deadline has passed. Logogens compute phonological codes from auditory and visual word analysis, and also pass input after detection to the cognitive system. The cognitive system does all the other work, such as semantic information. Of course, these connections are bi-directional, as semantic and contextual information from the cognitive system can affect logogens. (See Fig. 3.2 for a depiction of the early version of the logogen model.)

Note that in many ways the logogen model is similar to the cohort model. However, logogens passively accumulate activation until a threshold is passed, while rivals are actively deleted from the cohort. Bradley and Forster (1987) argue that the context-sensitivity of units in the cohort model is an important distinguishing feature: the original cohort model could not recover if it misidentifies the first segment of a spoken word. However, logogens can recover from any setback if they accumulate enough activation from other sources.

Problems with the original logogen model. The original logogen model conceptualised a single logogen carrying out all language tasks

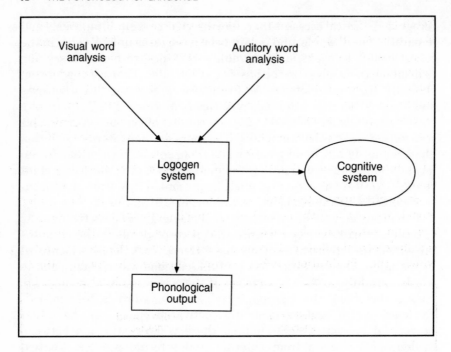

FIG. 3.2. The original logogen model of lexical access. (Based on Morton, 1979b, p. 260.)

for a particular word. That is, the same logogen would be used for recognising speech and visually presented words, and for speaking and for writing. This arrangement is said to be *amodal*. This is clearly the most economical arrangement, and it has the clear prediction that the source of activation—the modality—of a logogen should not matter. For example, visual recognition of a word should be as equally facilitated by a spoken prime as by a visual prime. Subsequent experiments however contradicted this prediction.

Winnick and Daniel (1970) showed that tachistoscopic recognition of a printed word was facilitated by the prior reading aloud of that word. However, naming a picture or producing a word in response to a definition produced no subsequent facilitation of tachistoscopic recognition of those words. That is, different modalities produce different amounts of facilitation. Indeed, Morton (1979b) reported replications of these results, clearly necessitating the need for a revision of the logogen model. (For further details of the experiments, see also Clarke and Morton, 1983; Warren and Morton, 1982). Hence Morton divided the word recognition system into different sets of logogens for different modalities (e.g. input and output). Morton (1979b) also showed that although the modality of response appears to be immaterial (reading or speaking a word in the training phase), the modality of training did matter. The model was revised so that instead of one logogen for each word, there were two, modality-specific ones (see Fig. 3.3). The consequence of this change ensured that only visual inputs could facilitate subsequent visual identification of words, and that only auditorily presented primes would not facilitate visually presented targets in tachistoscopic recognition. Subsequent evidence suggests that four logogen systems are necessary: an input (for listening and reading) and output (for speaking and writing) verbal and *orthographic* (for all written and printed material) lexicon. This issue is discussed in more detail in Chapter 9.

Some have argued that Morton was too hasty in giving up the simpler model, arguing that the possible ways in which the primes and targets are represented in the tachistoscopic results means that no firm conclusion can be drawn (P. Brown, 1991), or about the precise way in which the facilitation effect occurs (Besner & Swan, 1982).

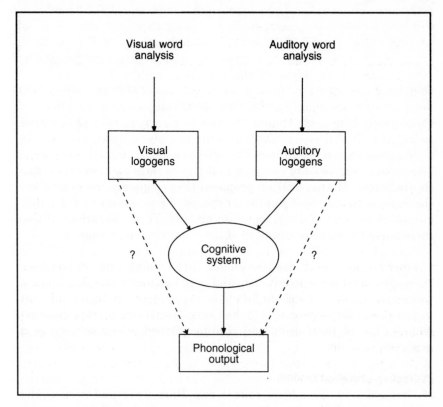

FIG. 3.3.   The revised logogen model of lexical access. (Based on Morton, 1979b, p. 265.)

Neuropsychological evidence seems consistent with the splitting or *fractionation* of the logogen system however, and this is currently the dominant view.

Interaction of variables in the logogen model. As we have seen, frequency and context are handled in the same way in the logogen model. Hence they should show similar patterns of interaction with any other variable. For example, stimulus quality (whether or not the stimulus is degraded) should behave in the same way with context as with frequency. If Morton's model is correct they should all combine together and act similarly; we should get an interaction. If lexical access is a two-stage process with frequency and context affecting different stages, they will behave differently in combination with stimulus quality. If there is more than one stage and frequency and stimulus quality interact, we should only find that context and stimulus quality are additive. The findings here are complicated and contradictory. Some researchers find an interaction; Meyer, Schvaneveldt and Ruddy (1974) found that the less legible were the stimuli, the more beneficial the effects of context. Others have found them to be additive (Becker & Killion, 1977; Stanners, Jastrzembski, & Westwood, 1975). Later experiments by Norris (1984) to some extent clarified these results. He showed that frequency and stimulus quality can interact, but that the interaction between stimulus quality and context is still larger and more robust. Of course, if stimulus degradation affects a very early encoding stage prior to lexical access, these results tell us nothing about lexical access.

In summary, it is very difficult to draw conclusions from this research. The issues involved are complex and the experimental results often contradictory. Morton (1979a) proposed that frequency does not affect the logogen system itself, but rather the cognitive systems to which they output at the end of the recognition process. The implications of this revision make the interpretation of these data yet more complex.

Later revisions to the logogen model. The logogen model has been developed in response to criticism and contradictory findings. Although this means that it can account for all the experimental data, it is difficult to pin down. To some extent it has been overtaken by connectionist models of word recognition and reading. Indeed, it can be seen as a precursor of them.

Interactive activation models
McClelland and Rumelhart (1981) and Rumelhart and McClelland (1982) developed a model called *interactive activation* with competition (IAC). It is one of the earliest connectionist models. The original purpose

of this model was to account for word context effects on letter identification. Reicher (1969) and Wheeler (1970) showed that in tachistoscopic recognition, letters are easier to recognise in words than when seen as isolated letters; this is known as the *word superiority effect*. However, the model can be seen as a component of a general model of word recognition. We will look at the general principles of the model here, but the technical details, including the equations, are given in the Appendix.

The model consists of many simple processing units arranged in three levels. There is an input level of visual feature units, a level where units correspond to individual letters, and an output level where each unit corresponds to a word. Each unit is connected to each unit in the level immediately before and after it. Each of these connections is either *excitatory* (that is positive, or *facilitatory*), if it is an appropriate one (e.g. the letter "T" would excite the word units "TAKE" and "TASK" in the level above it), or *inhibitory* (negative), if it is inappropriate (e.g. "T" would inhibit "CAKE" and "CASK" above it). Excitatory connections make the destination units more active, inhibitory connections make them less active. Furthermore, each unit is connected to each other unit within the same level by an inhibitory connection. This introduces the element of competition. The basic arrangement of the network, its *architecture*, should be made clear by Fig. 3.4.

When a unit becomes activated, it sends off energy, or activation, in parallel, along the connections to all the other units to which it is connected. If it is connected by a facilitatory connection, it will have the effect of increasing activation at the unit at the other end of the connection, whereas if it is connected by an inhibitory connection, it will have the effect of decreasing the activation at the other end. Hence if the unit corresponding to the letter "T" in the initial letter position becomes activated, it will increase the activation level of the word units corresponding to "TAKE" and "TASK", but decrease the activation level of "CAKE"—just as you would expect. But because units are connected to all other units at the same level by inhibitory connections, as soon as a unit (e.g. a word) becomes activated, it starts inhibiting all the other units at that level. Hence if the system "sees" a "T", then "TAKE", "TASK" and "TIME" will become activated, and immediately start inhibiting words without a "T" in them, like "CAKE", "COKE" and "CASK". As activation is also sent back down to lower levels, all letters in words beginning with "T" will become a little bit activated and hence "easier" to "see". Furthermore, as letters in the context of a word receive activation from the word units above them, they are easier to see in the context of a word than when presented in isolation, when they receive no supporting top-down activation—hence the word superiority effect.

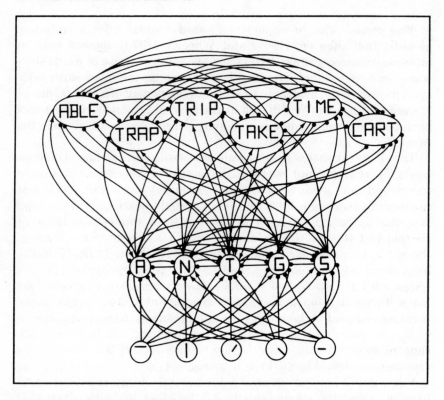

FIG. 3.4. Fragment of an interactive activation network of letter recognition. (Reprinted from McClelland, J. L., & Rumelhart, D. E., 1981. An interactive activation model of context effects in letter perception: Part 1. An account of the basic findings. *Psychological Review, 88*, 375–407, p.380. © 1981 by the American Psychological Association. Reprinted by permission.) Arrows show excitatory connections; filled circles inhibitory connections.

Equations described in the Appendix determine the way in which activation flows between units, is summed by units, and is used to change the activation level of each unit at each time step.

Then suppose the next letter to be presented is an "A". This will activate "TAKE" and "TASK" but inhibit "TIME", which will then also in turn be inhibited by within-level inhibition from "TASK" and "TIME". The "A" will of course also activate "CASK" and "CAKE", but these will already be some way behind the two words starting with a "T". If the next letter is a "K", then "TAKE" will be the clear leader. Time is divided into a number of slices called processing cycles. Over time, the pattern of activation settles down or relaxes into a stable configuration so that only "TAKE" remains activated, and hence is the word "seen" or recognised.

Evaluation. The interactive activation model of letter and word recognition has been highly influential. There are two ways in which it has been developed. First, as we saw in the previous chapter, the TRACE model of speech recognition is an obvious extension into the domain of speech. Second, we can view the word units as analogous to logogens. There is no reason why in principle the model could not be extended so that the word units output to other units which represent the meaning of words, or why they should not receive inputs from other types of context. As in the logogen model, there is no distinction between input to a word or letter unit based upon perceptual information and input based upon top-down or contextual information. As the very name implies, this type of model is heavily interactive. Hence any evidence that appears to place a restriction on the role of context is problematic for this model.

The other problem is that the connection strengths have to be determined arbitrarily, or such that the simulations produce the desired phenomena. For this reason models where the connection strengths are learned have become more popular. We shall consider a connectionist learning model of word recognition and naming in the next chapter.

Other models

Logogen and connectionist models are one extreme type of model, and search-based another. There are a number of models, most of which lie in between these two extremes. We will look briefly at some of these.

Becker's verification model. Becker's (1976, 1980) verification model is a hybrid model, involving elements of direct access of units and serial search. In this model, bottom-up stimulus-driven perceptual processes cannot recognise a word on their own. A process of top-down checking or *verification* has the final say. Rough perceptual processing generates a candidate or *sensory set* of possible lexical items. This sensory set is ordered by frequency. Context generates a contextual or *semantic set* of candidate items. Both the sensory and semantic set are compared and *verified* by detailed analysis against the visual characteristics of the word. The semantic set is verified first; verification is serial. If a match is not found, then the matching process proceeds to the sensory set. This process will generate a clear advantage for words presented in an appropriate context. The less specific the context is, the larger is the semantic set, and the slower the verification. As the context precedes the target word, the semantic set is ready before the sensory set is ready. Versions of the verification model have also been presented by Paap, Newsome, McDonald, and Schvaneveldt (1982). The process of verification can be extended to include any model where verification or checking that the output of the bottom-up lexical access processes is correct.

Norris's (1986) model.   Norris (1986) also envisaged a central role for *post-access checking.* The main idea is that a post-access checking mechanism checks the output of lexical access against context and resolves any ambiguity. A primary source of data accounted for by this model is context and frequency effects, and the interaction between them. Frequency does not affect the processes of candidate selection, but the processes of post-selection checking: a candidate is more likely to be accepted as the correct analysis of the sensory input the higher it is in frequency. This model maintains autonomy of lexical processing in the same general way as serial search; contextual priming effects arise from processes operating after lexical access.

Comparison of models
There are two dichotomies that could be used to classify these models. The first is between interactive and autonomous models. Interactive models permit context to affect lexical access directly; autonomous models do not. In these models non-associative context can only affect post-access processes. The second dichotomy is between whether words are accessed directly or through a process of search. The logogen and interactive activation models are both interactive direct access models; the serial search model is autonomous and obviously search-based. The crucial data are the evidence for non-associative priming. At present the balance is that this has no automatic, pre-access effect. On the other hand, simple serial search models have their own problems. Some type of hybrid, verification-based model is probably currently the most promising. However, we have not yet examined how these models deal with pronouncing words.

CONCLUDING SUMMARY

In this chapter we have examined the main processes involved in visual word recognition, and considered the factors that can make recognition easier or harder. Context undoubtedly has an effect, but how and when? The central issue is whether it affects the perceptual processing of the stimulus and lexical access, or whether it affects post-lexical processing such as checking, subject's expectancies, or integration into higher-level representations.

There are two types of theory. According to interactive models such as the logogen model, the early cohort model, and connectionist models, all types of context and expectancies can affect all levels of processing, including those of perceptual processing and generating candidates. That is, context can have pre-lexical effects. On the other hand, according to the autonomy position, such as advocated by Forster, only associations can influence pre-lexical processing. Other types of context (sentence context, subjects' expectancies) are restricted to post-lexical processes.

We have also distinguished between automatic and attentional priming and lexical processing. There is only clear evidence that associative priming is automatic, and affects automatic, pre-lexical processes. Contextual priming (including non-associative semantic and contextual priming) is attentional and only unambiguously affects post-access processes. These results favour the autonomy position.

Different experimental tasks sometimes give different results. This is because they tap differentially pre- and post-access processes. Lexical decision appears to be particularly sensitive to post-access processes. The naming task gives a more pure measure of lexical access.

Some of the issues raised here are almost certainly applicable to spoken word recognition. Hence it is almost certain that both priming effects and identification processes have an automatic and attentional component. Spoken word recognition tasks might be differentially sensitive to them, in the way that naming and lexical decision are in visual word recognition.

It is possible that the depth of lexical access can vary. Intuitively this seems an appealing idea. This was first proposed by Johnson-Laird (1975), who noted that sometimes we retrieve hardly any information for a word. This idea has been extended by Gerrig (1986), who argued there are different "modes of lexical access" in different contexts. This idea merits further investigation.

The processing of more than one word at a time in sequence in text poses problems for all these models (Carr & Pollatsek, 1985). Eye movement research has shown that many words, particularly long words, may need more than one eye fixation, and there may be overlap between fixations. Hence it is not clear that the word rather than some sub-word unit is a basic unit of processing. We have noted that there is a bias—for good reasons—in the literature to single word processing.

Finally, it is worth considering how our reading ability might have come about. While there has been plenty of time for speech to evolve (see Chapter 1), reading is a much more recent development. It therefore seems unlikely that a specific system has evolved to deal with visual word recognition. It seems more likely that the word recognition system must be tacked onto other cognitive and perceptual processes. In particular, word recognition must be like any other form of object recognition where the objects in question have similar characteristics to words, a point often overlooked. However, words are unusual: we are exposed to them a great deal, they have meaning over all, and most importantly, in alphabetic writing systems at least they are composed of units which have another correspondence—to sounds. It is time to examine the translation of words into sounds in detail.

FURTHER READING

Henderson (1987) provides an historical overview of visual word recognition. A recent advanced review of the whole field can be found in Balota (1994). The book by Rayner and Pollatsek (1989) reviews the whole field of visual word recognition and reading, including its impairments and development. It will therefore also be useful reading for Chapters 4, 5, and 12. Coltheart (1987a) edited a collection of more advanced papers based upon the XIIth meeting of *Attention and Performance* that will similarly be useful.

See Harris and Coltheart (1986) for explanations of the word-superiority effect in these terms, and other types of masks. See Humphreys and Bruce (1989) for further details of Turvey's (1973) experiments. Monsell (1991) provides an up-to-date review of the locus of the frequency effect in word recognition, and Monsell (1985) reviews work on repetition priming. Monsell argues that connectionist learning models provide new insights into how frequency effects arise and operate. Neely (1991) gives a detailed and comprehensive review of semantic priming in visual word recognition. References to more recent work on perception without awareness can be found in the papers by Doyle and Leach (1988) and Dagenbach, Carr, and Wilhelmsen (1989). The literature on attentional processes in priming is reviewed by Humphreys (1985). Neely (1991) provides a wide-ranging review of semantic priming. For discussion of whether associative priming occurs through a mechanism of spreading activation or some more complex process, see McNamara (1992, 1994). An excellent review of models of word recognition was carried out by Carr and Pollatsek (1985); they provide a useful diagram showing the relationship of all types of recognition model. Other reviews and comparisons of models can be found in Forster (1989) and Norris (1986). See McClelland (1987) for a review of evidence favouring the interactive position. See Garnham (1985) for more detail on the interactions between frequency, context, and stimulus quality.

CHAPTER FOUR

Word pronunciation and dyslexia

INTRODUCTION

In the previous chapter we looked at how we recognise words. In this chapter we will be concerned with one very important thing we do with words: how we read or pronounce them. How do we turn words into sounds? We will also look at how children learn to read. A complete theory of reading should indicate how the teaching of reading can be improved, and how difficulties in learning to read be best overcome.

The basic unit of written language is called the *grapheme*. This can be defined as a letter or combination of letters that represent phonemes. For example, the word "ghost" contains five letters and four graphemes ("gh", "o", "s", and "t"), representing four phonemes. There is much more variability in the structure of written languages than there is in spoken languages. Whereas all spoken languages utilise a basic distinction between consonants and vowels, there is no such common thread to the world's written languages. The most familiar sorts of written language are *alphabetic scripts*, such as English uses. In alphabetic scripts, the basic unit represented by a grapheme is essentially a phoneme. However, the nature of this correspondence can vary. In *transparent* languages such as Serbo-Croat and Italian there is a one-to-one grapheme-phoneme correspondence, so that every grapheme is realised by only one phoneme, and every phoneme is realised by only one grapheme. In languages such as English this relationship can be many-to-many: a phoneme can be realised by many different graphemes (e.g. the long /ai/ phoneme in the written words "mine", "pie", "my"), and a grapheme can be realised by many different phonemes (e.g. the letter "a" in the words "fate", "pat", and "father"). Some languages lie between these extremes. In French a grapheme has only one pronunciation, but a phoneme may have different graphemic realisations (e.g. the graphemes "o", "au", "eau", "aux", and "eaux" all represent the same sounds). In *consonantal scripts*, such as Hebrew and Arabic, not all sounds are represented, as vowels are not written down at all. In *syllabic scripts* (such as the Indian language Kanaada), the written units represent syllables. Finally, some languages do not represent any sounds. In *ideographic languages* (sometimes also called logographic languages), such as Chinese and the Japanese script Kanji, each symbol equals basically a whole word.

Unlike speech, writing and hence reading is a relatively recent development. The emergence of the alphabetic script can be traced to ancient Greece about 1000BC. The development of one-to-one correspondence in English orthography primarily arose between the fifteenth and eighteenth century, as a consequence of the development of the printing press and the activities of spelling "reformers" who tried to make the Latin and Greek origins of words more apparent in their spellings (see Ellis, 1993, for more detail). Therefore it is perhaps not surprising that reading is actually quite a complex cognitive task. There is a wide variation in reading abilities, and many types of reading disorder arise as a consequence of brain damage.

A preliminary model of reading

Introspection can provide us with a preliminary model of reading. Consider how we might name or pronounce the word "beef". Words like this are said to have a regular spelling-to-sound correspondence. That is, the graphemes map onto phonemes in a totally regular way; you need no special knowledge about the word to know how to pronounce it. If you had never seen the word "beef" before, you could still pronounce it correctly. Some other examples of regular word pronunciations include "hint" and "rave". In these words, there are alternative pronunciations (as in "pint" and "have"), but "hint" and "rave" are pronounced in accordance with the most common pronunciations. These are all *regular words*.

Not all words are regular, however. Some are *irregular or exception words*. Consider the word "steak". This has an irregular spelling-to-sound (or grapheme-to-phoneme) correspondence: the grapheme "ea" is not pronounced in the usual way, as in "streak", "sneak", "speak", "leak", and "beak". Other exceptions to a rule include "have" (an exception to the rule that leads to the regular pronunciations "gave", "rave", "save" and so forth) and "vase" (in British English, an exception to the rule that leads to the regular pronunciations "base", "case", and so forth). English has many irregular words as a consequence of the many-to-many grapheme correspondence rules. Some words are even more irregular, containing unusual patterns of letters that have no close neighbours, such as "island", "aisle", "ghost", and "yacht". These words are sometimes called *lexical hermits*.

Some words such as "bow", "row", and "tear", have different pronunciations but are written in the same way. These are called *homographs*. How do we select the appropriate pronunciation? Consider sentences (1) and (2).

1. When his shoelace came loose, Vlad had to tie a bow.
2. At the end of the play, Dirk went to the front of the stage to take a bow.

In this case we appear to use the meaning to select the pronunciation, but at what stage? This is an example of lexical ambiguity, an issue to which we will return in detail in Chapter 9.

Finally, we can pronounce strings of letters such as "nate", "smeak", "fot", and "datch" even though we have never seen them before. These are all pronounceable *nonwords* or *pseudowords*, yet we can still pronounce them, and we all agree on how they should be pronounced. (Of course, not all nonwords—e.g. "xzhgh"—are pronounceable.) If you hear nonwords like these, you can spell them correctly; you assemble their pronunciations from their constituent letters (graphemes).

Our ability to read nonwords on the one hand, and irregular words on the other suggests the possibility of a *dual-route model* of naming. We can assemble pronunciations for words or nonwords we have never seen before, yet also pronounce correctly irregular words which must need information specific to those words (that is, *lexical information*).

The classical dual-route model (see Fig. 4.1) has two routes to turning words into sounds. Route (1) is a direct access or lexical route, which is needed for irregular words. This must at least in some way involve reading via meaning. That is, with this route we need to go through the lexicon to retrieve the sound of a word. Route (2) is the *grapheme-to-phoneme* conversion (GPC) route (also called the non-lexical or sublexical route), and is used for reading nonwords. This route does what is called *phonological recoding*. It does not involve lexical access at all. The non-lexical route was first proposed in the early 1970s (e.g. Gough, 1972; Rubenstein, Lewis, & Rubenstein, 1971). It cannot in itself be sufficient for reading, as it cannot account for irregular words or words of differing meaning with the same pronunciation (these are called *homophones*, such as "there" and

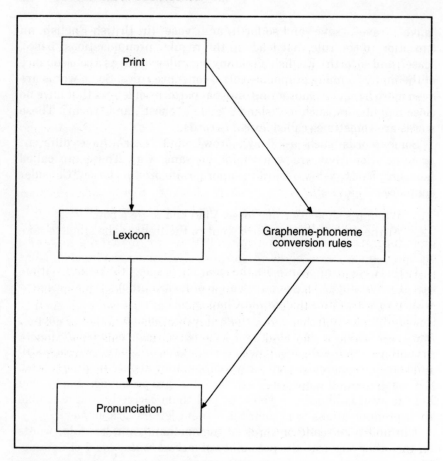

FIG. 4.1. A simplified version of the dual-route model of reading.

"their"). Another important justification for a grapheme-to-phoneme conversion route is that it is useful for children learning to read by spelling out words letter by letter.

Given that neither route can in itself adequately explain reading performance, it seems that we must use both. Modern dual-route theorists see reading as a race between these routes. When we see a word, both routes start processing it. Most of the time the direct route is much faster, so this will usually "win" the race. Irregular words only produce conflict in exceptional circumstances, such as for very unfamiliar words, or with an unusual task (e.g. lexical decision). Then the direct and GPC routes will produce different pronunciations, and these words would therefore be harder (Coltheart, Besner, Jonasson, & Davelaar, 1979). Notice that we do not have to posit there is a race; we could say that words are read by the direct route and nonwords by the GPC route. This is only plausible if we assume in the first instance that everything we come across is a word until we try to read it lexically, and if we fail to find a matching lexical item then we use the non-lexical route. No current model of reading has proposed this approach.

Relationship of the dual-route model to other models.   In the previous chapter we examined a number of models of word recognition. These can all be seen as theories of how the direct, lexical access reading route operates. The dual-route is the simplest version of a range of possible *multi-route* or *parallel coding* models, some of which posit more than two reading routes. Do we really need a non-lexical route at all? Although we appear to need it for reading nonwords, this seems a costly procedure. We have a mechanism ready to use for something we rarely do—pronouncing new words or nonwords. Perhaps it is a left-over from the development of reading, or perhaps it is not as costly as it first appears. We will see later that the non-lexical route is also apparently needed to account for the neuropsychological data. As we shall see, this issue is complex and there are other interpretations. Whether or not two routes are necessary for reading is a central issue of this topic. Models that propose that we can get away with only one (such as connectionist and some direct access models) must produce a satisfactory account of how we pronounce nonwords.

THE PROCESSES OF NORMAL READING

The strong dual-route model says there are two independent routes when naming a word and accessing the lexicon: a lexical or direct access route and a non-lexical or grapheme–phoneme conversion route. What is the experimental evidence for this model from the normal processing of words and nonwords? Is it a plausible model of normal word naming?

Nonword processing

According to the dual-route model, the pronunciation of all nonwords should be assembled using the GPC route. This means that all nonwords should be alike and their similarity to words should not matter. There are some problems with this hypothesis.

The pseudohomophone effect.   Pseudohomophones are nonwords which sound like words when pronounced (such as "brane", which sounds like the word "brain" when spoken). The behaviour of the pseudohomophone "brane" can be compared with the very similar nonword "brame", which does not sound like a word when it is spoken. Rubenstein, Lewis and Rubenstein (1971) showed that pseudo-homophones are more confusable with words than other types of nonwords. Subjects are faster to name them but slower to reject them as nonwords than control nonwords. Although E.V. Clark (1973) argued that this effect was due to a subset of items in the original experiment, the effect is very robust.

Is the effect due to phonological or visual similarity between the nonword and word? Martin (1982) and Taft (1982) argued that it is visual similarity which is important. Pseudohomophones are more confusable with words than other nonwords because they look more similar to words than non-pseudohomophones, rather than because they sound the same. Pring (1981) alternated case of letters within versus across graphemes, such as the "AI" in "grait", to produce "GraIT" or "GRaiT". These then look different but still sound the same. Alternating letter cases within a grapheme or spelling unit (aI) eliminates the pseudohomophone effect; alternating letters elsewhere in the word (aiT) does not. Hence we are sensitive to the visual appearance of spelling units of words.

In summary, recent research shows that the pseudohomophone effect does appear to be real, but that it is found only in restricted conditions (Laxon, Masterson, Pool, & Keating, 1992). It does however suggest that not all nonwords are equal. The importance of the visual appearance of the nonwords further suggests that something else apart from phonological recoding is involved here. It remains to be seen whether the phonological recoding route is still necessary, but if it is then it must be more complex than we first thought.

Glushko's (1979) experiment: Results from nonwords.   Glushko (1979) performed a very important experiment on the effect of the regularity of the word neighbours of a nonword on its pronunciation. Consider the nonword "taze". Its word neighbours include "gaze", "laze", and "maze"; these are all themselves regularly pronounced words. Now consider the word neighbours of "tave". These also include plenty of regular words ("rave", "save", and "gave") but there is an exception word neighbour, "have". As another example, compare the nonwords "feal" and "fead": both have regular neighbours ("real", "seal", "deal", "bead", "read") but the pronunciation of "fead" is influenced by its irregular neighbour "dead". Glushko (1979) showed that naming latencies to nonwords such as "tave" were significantly slower than to ones such as "taze". That is, reaction times to nonwords which have orthographically irregular spelling-to-sound correspondence word neighbours are slower than to other nonword controls. Also, people make pronunciation "errors" with such nonwords:

"pove" might be pronounced to rhyme with "love" rather than "cove"; and "heaf" might be pronounced to rhyme with "deaf" rather than "leaf". In summary, Glushko found that the pronunciation of nonwords is affected by the pronunciation of similar words, and that nonwords are not the same as each other. Indeed, subsequent research has shown that the number of regular pronunciations of nonwords increases as the number of orthographic neighbours increases (McCann & Besner, 1987). Another way of putting this is that there are lexical effects upon nonword processing.

Other data.   Consider the nonword "yead". This can be pronounced to rhyme with "bead" or "head". Kay and Marcel (1981) showed that its pronunciation can be affected by the pronunciation of a preceding prime word: "bead" biases a subject to pronounce "yead" to rhyme with it, whereas the prime "head" biases subjects to the alternative pronunciation. Rosson (1983) primed the nonword by a semantic relative of a phonologically related word. So the task was to pronounce "louch" when preceded either by "feel" (which is associated with "touch") or by "sofa" (which is associated by "couch"). In both cases "louch" tended to be pronounced to rhyme with the appropriate relative.

Finally, nonword effects in complex experiments are sensitive to many factors such as the pronunciation of the surrounding words in the list. This also suggests that nonword pronunciation involves more than simple grapheme–phoneme conversion.

Evaluation of research on nonwords.   These data do not fit the simple version of the dual-route model. The pronunciation of nonwords is affected by the pronunciation of visually-similar words. That is, there are lexical effects in nonword processing; the lexical route seems to be affecting the non-lexical route.

Word processing

According to the original dual-route hypothesis, all words are accessed directly by the direct route, perhaps using a mechanism such as we discussed in the previous chapter. This means that all words should be treated the same in respect of the regularity of their spelling-to-sound correspondences. An examination of the data reveals that this prediction does not stand up.

One problem for this model is that pronunciation regularity affects response times. An early demonstration of this was provided by Baron and Strawson (1976), who showed that a list of regular words was named faster than a list of frequency-matched exception words (e.g. "have"). This task is a simplified version of the naming task, with response time averaged across many items rather than taken from each one individually. There have been many other demonstrations of regularity upon naming time (e.g. Forster & Chambers, 1973; Frederiksen & Kroll, 1976; Stanovich & Bauer, 1978). On the other hand, it is not clear whether there are regularity effects upon lexical decision. They have been obtained by, for example, Stanovich and Bauer (1978), but not by Coltheart et al. (1977), or Seidenberg, Waters, Barnes and Tanenhaus (1984). In particular, a word such as "yacht" looks unusual, as well as having an irregular pronunciation. The letter pairs "ya" and "ht" are not frequent in English; we say they have a low *bigram frequency*. Obviously the visual appearance of words is going to affect the time it takes for direct access, so we need to control for this when searching for regularity effects. Once we control for the generally unusual appearance of irregular words, regularity and consistency only seem to affect naming times, not lexical decision times.

In general, regularity effects seem to be more likely to be found when subjects have to be more conservative, such as when accuracy rather than speed is stressed. However, we have seen in the previous chapter that the naming task is a better measure of automatic lexical access than lexical decision, and the finding that regularity affects naming times at all is problematic for the dual-route model. Seidenberg et al. (1984) found that pronunciation regularity interacts with frequency, such that irregularity is more of a handicap for low-frequency words. That is, common words are named equally quickly regardless of their regularity. This finding makes sense if there is a race between the direct and indirect routes. The pronunciation of common words is retrieved quickly and directly, before the indirect route can construct any conflicting pronunciation. Conflict arises when the lexical route is slow, as when retrieving low frequency words, and when its pronunciation conflicts with that of the nonlexical route (see Norris & Brown, 1985).

Glushko's (1979) experiment: Results from words.   In the same experiment as we looked at above in the context of nonwords, Glushko (1979) also found a corresponding effect on words. That is, the naming times of words are affected by the phonological consistency of neighbours. The naming of a regular word is slowed down relative to that of a control word of similar frequency if the test word has irregular neighbours. For example, the word "gang" is regular, and all its neighbours (such as "bang", "sang", "hang", and "rang") are also all regular. Consider on the other hand "base"; this itself has a regular pronunciation (compare it with "case"), but it is *inconsistent*, in that it has one irregular neighbour, "vase" (in British English pronunciation). We could say that "vase" is an *enemy* of "base". This leads to a slowing of naming times. In addition, Glushko found true naming errors of over-regularisation: for example "pint" was sometimes given its regular pronunciation, to rhyme with "dint".

Pronunciation neighbourhoods. Continuing this line of research, Brown (1987) argued that the number of consistently pronounced neighbours (*friends*) determines naming times, rather than whether a word has *enemies* (that is, whether or not it is regular). This result has however been disputed by Kay and Bishop (1987), and by Jared, McRae, and Seidenberg (1990). Current evidence suggests that both whether a word has enemies and whether it has friends are important (see Brown & Watson, 1994).

Andrews (1989) reported that there were effects of neighbourhood size on both naming and lexical decision tasks. Words with large neighbourhoods were responded to more rapidly than words with small neighbourhoods (although this may be moderated by frequency, as suggested by Grainger, 1990). Not all readers produce the same results. Barron (1981) found that good and poor elementary school readers both read regular words more quickly than irregular words. However, once he controlled for neighbourhood effects, he found that there was no longer any regularity effect in the good readers, although it persisted in the poor readers.

Parkin (1982) found more of a continuum of ease-of-pronunciation, rather than a simple division between regular and irregular words. All this work suggests that a binary division into words with regular and irregular pronunciations is no longer adequate. Patterson and Morton (1985) provided a more satisfactory but complex categorisation rather than a straightforward dichotomy between *regular* and *irregular* words (see Table 4.1). This classification reflects two factors: first, the regularity of the pronunciation with reference to spelling-to-sound correspondence rules; second, the agreement with other words that share the same *body* . (This is the end of a monosyllabic word, comprising the central vowel plus final consonant or consonant cluster). We need to consider not only whether a word is regular or irregular, but also whether its neighbours are regular or irregular. The same classification scheme can be applied to nonwords.

The role of sound in accessing meaning. So far then the data indicate that the regularity of a word affects naming. While at first sight this is may not seem to you to be surprising, it is problematic for any model that suggests we only use the direct, lexical route for words. It is a defining characteristic of the direct route that you do not need to access the sound of a word in order to access its meaning. Some recent

TABLE 4.1
Classification of word pronunciations depending upon regularity and consistency
(based on Patterson & Morton, 1985)

Word type	Example	Characteristics
consistent	gaze	all words receive the same regular pronunciation of the body
consensus	lint	all words with one exception receive the same regular pronunciation
heretic	pint	the irregular exception to the consensus
gang	look	all words with one exception receive the same irregular pronunciation
hero	spook	the regular exception to the consensus
gang without a hero	cold	all words receive the same irregular pronunciation
ambiguous: conformist	cove	regular pronunciation with many irregular exemplars
ambiguous: independent	love	irregular pronunciation with many regular exemplars
hermit	yacht	no other word has this body

experiments suggest however that a word's sound may have some influence on accessing the meaning (van Orden, 1987; van Orden, Johnstone, & Hale, 1988; van Orden, Pennington, & Stone, 1990). In a category decision task subjects have to decide if a target word is a member of a preceding category. (For example, given "A type of fruit" you would respond "yes" to "pear", and "no" to "pour"). If the "no" word is a homophone of a "yes" word (e.g. "pair"), subjects make a lot of false positive errors—that is, they respond "yes" instead of "no". Subjects seem confused by the sound of the word, and category decision clearly involves access to meaning. The effect is most noticeable when subjects have to respond quickly, and Jared and Seidenberg (1991) showed that it only happens with low-frequency homophones.

These experiments however do not necessarily suggest that we have to access meaning via sound under certain conditions. These results could be explained by feedback from the speech production system to the semantic system. Alternatively it may be that the (non-semantic) direct access route causes inner speech that interferes with processing.

Evaluation of research on words. Just as not all nonwords behave in the same way, neither do all words. The regularity of pronunciation of a word affects the ease with which we can name it. In addition to the pronunciations of the words themselves that we are trying to read, the pronunciations of their neighbours are important. For this reason, and the reasons we have seen in previous chapters, the study of *lexical neighbourhoods* and *consistency* effects is now an important research topic in contemporary psycholinguistics.

The notion of lexical neighbourhoods in naming was formalised by Coltheart et al. (1977). They described a statistic called the *N-value* of a word, which is the number of other words that can be produced by considering each letter position in a word in turn, and substituting all other letters in the alphabet. It is hence an approximate measure of the visual distinctiveness of a word. The word "bank" has an N-value of 20, but "abhorrence" only has an N-value of 1. (The related word is "abhorrency".)

Evaluation of experiments on normal reading

There are two major problems with our simple dual-route model. First, we have seen that there are lexical effects on reading nonwords, which should be read by a non-lexical route insensitive to lexical information, and there are effects of regularity of pronunciation on reading words, which should be read by a direct, lexical route insensitive to phonological recoding.

Note that this second point is also a problem for all single route, lexical access models. At this juncture neighbourhood effects come to the rescue. We can attempt to explain all regularity effects in terms of neighbourhood density. Regular words share their spelling and visual appearance with many other words with the same spelling-to-sound correspondence; they have a dense, consistent neighbourhood. Irregular words on the other hand must have a sparsely populated neighbourhood. Hence regularity effects may arise not because of interference from sound, but from inconsistent neighbours. However, Barron's (1981) experiment is problematic for this interpretation, because he showed that regularity effects remained in poor readers after neighbourhood density was controlled.

THE NEUROPSYCHOLOGY OF READING DISORDERS: DYSLEXIA

What can studies of brain-damaged reading tell us about the reading process? This section is concerned with disorders of processing written language. We must distinguish between acquired disorders (which as a result of head trauma such as stroke, operation, or head injury, lead to disruption of processes that were functioning normally beforehand) and developmental disorders (which do not result from obvious trauma and which disrupt the development of a particular function). Disorders of reading are called the *dyslexias*; disorders of writing are called the *dysgraphias*. Broadly, damage to the left hemisphere will result in dyslexia, but as the same sites are involved in speaking, dyslexia is often accompanied by disorders of speech as well as disorders of writing. However, as mentioned in the introduction, we are not concerned with localisation of function in this book. Our emphasis is upon what examining brain-damaged reading can tell us about the processes involved in reading.

It is convenient to distinguish between central dyslexias, which involve central, high-level reading processes, and *peripheral dyslexias*, which involve lower-level processes. These include visual dyslexia, attentional dyslexia, letter-by-letter reading, and neglect dyslexia. As our focus is upon understanding the central reading process, we will limit discussion here to the central dyslexias. In addition, we will only look at adult disorders in this section, and defer discussion of developmental dyslexia until our examination of learning to read.

If the dual-route model of reading is along the right lines, then we should expect to find a double dissociation of the two routes. That is, we should find some patients have damage to the lexical route but can still read by the non-lexical route only; whereas we should be able to find other patients who have damage to the non-lexical route but can read by the lexical route only. As such the existence of a double dissociation is a strong prediction of the dual-route model, and a real challenge to any single-route model.

Surface dyslexia

Surface dyslexics have a selective impairment in the ability to read irregular (exception) words. Hence they would have difficult with "steak" compared with a regular relative such as "speak". Early case histories; were reported by Marshall and Newcombe (1973), and Shallice and Warrington (1980). When they can make attempts at irregular words, surface dyslexics make "over-regularisation" errors on them: for example, they pronounce "broad" as "brode", "steak" as "steek", and "island" as "eyesland". On the other hand, their ability to read regular words and nonwords is intact. In terms of the dual-route model, the most obvious explanation of surface dyslexia is that they can only read via the indirect, non-lexical route: that is, it is an impairment of the lexical (direct access) processing route.

The effects of brain damage are rarely localised to highly specific systems, and in practice patients are not as clear-cut as the ideal of totally preserved regular word and nonword reading, and total loss of irregular words. The clearest case yet reported is that of a patient referred to as MP (Bub, Cancelliere, & Kertesz, 1985). She showed completely normal accuracy in reading nonwords, and hence her non-lexical route was totally preserved. She was not the best possible case of surface dyslexia, however, since she could read some irregular words (with an accuracy of 85% on high frequency items, and 40% on low frequency exception words). This means that her lexical route must have been partially intact. Other patients are considerably less clear than this, with even better performance on irregular words, and some deficit in reading regular words. The more pure cases are rarely found.

The comprehension of word meaning is intact in these patients. They still know what an "island" is, even if they cannot read the word; they can still understand it if you say the word to them. If patients are reading through a non-lexical route, we would not expect lexical variables to affect the likelihood of reading success. Kremin (1985) found no effect on reading success of word frequency, part of speech (noun versus adjective versus verb), or whether or not it is easy to form a mental image of what is referred to (called imageability). Although patients such as MP, from Bub et al. (1985) show a clear frequency effect in that they make few regularisations of high frequency words, other patients, such as HTR, from Shallice, Warrington, and McCarthy (1983) do not. Patients also make homophone confusions (such as reading "pane" as "to cause distress").

More recently, there has been some debate as to whether surface dyslexia is a unitary category. Shallice and McCarthy (1985) distinguished between Type I and Type II surface dyslexia. Both types are, of course, poor at reading exception words. The more pure case, known as Type I patients, are highly accurate at naming regular words and pseudowords. Other patients, known as Type II, also show some impairment at reading regular words and pseudowords. The reading performance of Type II patients may be affected by lexical variables such that they are better at reading high frequency, high imageability words, better at reading nouns than adjectives and better at reading adjectives than verbs, and better at reading short words than long. This is interpreted as meaning that Type II patients must have an additional, moderate impairment to the non-lexical route. This pattern can still be explained by the dual-route model.

Phonological dyslexia

Phonological dyslexics have a selective impairment in the ability to read pronounceable nonwords or pseudowords (such as "sleeb"), while their ability to read matched words (e.g. "sleep") is preserved. Phonological dyslexia was first described by Shallice and Warrington (1979, 1980), Patterson (1980) and by Beauvois and Derouesné (1979). Irregular words are no harder than regular words for phonological dyslexics. These symptoms suggest that these patients can only read using the lexical route, and that phonological dyslexia is impairment of the non-lexical (GPC) processing route. As with surface dyslexia, the "perfect patient", who in this case would be able to read all words but no nonwords, has yet to be discovered. The clearest case yet reported is that of patient WB (Funnell, 1983), who could not read nonwords at all; hence the non-lexical GPC route must have been completely abolished. He was not the most extreme case possible of phonological dyslexia, however, because there was also an impairment to his lexical route; his performance was about 85% correct on words. Most patients are less extreme than this.

For those patients who can pronounce some nonwords, nonword reading is improved if the nonwords are pseudohomophones (such as "nite" for "night", or "brane" for "brain"). For those patients who also have difficulty in reading words, they have particular difficulty in reading the words that do the grammatical work of the language. (These are called function words, and tend to be short words that do not have much meaning in themselves, like "the", "and", "in", "so", and "why". We shall meet these words again.) Low frequency, low imageability words are also poorly read, although neither frequency nor imageability seems to have any overwhelming role in itself. They also have difficulty in reading morphologically complex words—words have syntactic modifications called inflections. On these words, they sometimes make what are called *derivational errors*, where they read a word as a grammatical relative of the target, such as reading "performing" as "performance". Finally, they also make visual errors, in which a word is read as another with a similar visual appearance, such as reading "perform" as "perfume".

Deep dyslexia

Surface and phonological dyslexia would appear to exhaust the possibilities in terms of the consequences of damage to the dual-route model. There is however another, even more surprising type called deep dyslexia. Early accounts of this were first provided by Marshall and Newcombe's (1966, 1973) description of two patients, GR and KU, although it is now recognised in retrospect that the syndrome had been observed in patients before this (Marshall & Newcombe, 1980). In many respects deep dyslexia resembles phonological dyslexia. Patients have great difficulty in reading nonwords, and considerable difficulty in reading the grammatical, function words. Like phonological dyslexics, they make visual and derivational errors. However, the defining characteristic of deep dyslexia is the presence of semantic reading errors or *semantic paralexias.* This is when a word related in meaning to the target is produced instead of the target, as in examples (1) to (4).

1. DAUGHTER   → "sister"
2. PRAY   → "chapel"
3. ROSE   → "flower"
4. KILL   → "hate"

The imageability of a word is a very important determinant of the probability of reading success. The easier it is to form a mental image of a word, the easier it is to read. Like phonological dyslexics, deep dyslexics obviously have some difficulty in obtaining non-lexical access to phonology via grapheme–phoneme recoding, but they also have some disorder of the semantic system. An important question that naturally arises is whether a single underlying cause leads to both of these impairments.

The right hemisphere hypothesis. Does deep dyslexia reflect attempts by a greatly damaged system to read normally, as has been argued by Morton and Patterson (1980), among others? Or does it instead reflect the operation of an otherwise normally suppressed system coming through? It has been suggested that deep dyslexics do not always use the left hemisphere for reading. The more of the left hemisphere that is damaged, the greater the degree of deep dyslexia (Jones & Martin, 1985; but see Marshall & Patterson, 1985). Instead then, it is argued, they use a reading system based in the right hemisphere that is normally suppressed (Coltheart, 1980; Saffran, Bogyo, Schwartz, & Marin, 1980; Zaidel & Peters, 1981). The reading performance of deep dyslexics resembles that of split-brain patients when words are presented to the left visual field, and therefore the right hemisphere. Under such conditions they also make semantic paralexias, and have an advantage for concrete words. Patterson, Vargha-Khadem, and Polkey (1989) describe the case of a patient called NI, a 17-year-old girl who had had her left hemisphere removed for the treatment of severe epilepsy. After some recovery, she retained some reading ability, but this resembled that of deep dyslexics. Nevertheless, this hypothesis has never won wide acceptance. In part this is because the hypothesis is considered a negative one in that if it is correct, deep dyslexia would tell us nothing about normal reading. In addition, deep dyslexics read much better than the right hemisphere of split-brain patients. Also the right hemisphere advantage for concrete words is rarely found, and the imageability of the target words used in these experiments might have been confounded with length (Patterson & Besner, 1984; Ellis & Young, 1988).

Summary of research on deep dyslexia.   There has been debate as to whether the term *deep dyslexia* is a meaningful label. This is because it refers to a syndrome; that is, to a cluster of symptoms. The central issue is whether they must necessarily co-occur because they have the same underlying cause. Are semantic paralexias always found associated with impaired nonword reading? So far they seem to be; semantic paralexias have been associated with all the other symptoms in all reported cases. How then can deep dyslexia be explained by one underlying disorder? In terms of our dual-route model, we would appear to posit difficulties at two loci: with the non-lexical route (to explain the difficulties with nonwords) and the semantic system (to explain the semantic paralexias and the imageability effects). As we shall see, connectionist models have cast valuable light on this question. A second issue is whether we can make inferences from deep dyslexia as we can the other types. We have seen that the dual-route model readily explains surface and phonological dyslexia, and that their occurrence is as expected if we were to *lesion* that model by removing one of the routes. Hence it is reasonable to make inferences about normal reading on the basis of data from such patients. There is some doubt however as to whether we are entitled to do this in the case of deep dyslexia; if the right hemisphere hypothesis proves correct, it is likely that deep dyslexia will tell us little about normal reading. Perhaps fortunately, the balance of evidence is at present that deep dyslexia does not reflect right hemisphere reading, but does indeed reflect reading by a greatly damaged left hemisphere. In this case, deep dyslexia suggests that normally we can in some way read through meaning; that is, we use the semantic representation of a word to obtain its phonology.

Non-semantic reading

If we can read via meaning, what happens if this route is disrupted? Schwartz, Marin, and Saffran (1979), and Schwartz, Saffran, and Marin (1980) describe WLP, an elderly patient suffering from progressive dementia. WLP had a greatly impaired ability to retrieve the meaning of written words; for example, she was unable to match written animal names to pictures. But she could read the words out aloud almost perfectly, getting 18 out of 20 correct and making only minor errors, even on low frequency words. She could read irregular words and nonwords. In summary, WLP could read words without any comprehension of their meaning. This means that we must have a direct access route from orthography to phonology that does not go via semantics. Coslett (1991) describes a patient, WT, who is virtually unable to read nonwords, suggesting an impairment of the indirect route, but despite having an additional semantic impairment, is able to read words quite proficiently.

This also suggests words can be read through a non-semantic route which has been preserved in WT's case. Taken together with deep dyslexia, this is evidence for a fractionation of the direct access route into semantic and non-semantic routes.

Summary of the interpretation of the dyslexias

We have looked at four main types of adult central dyslexia: surface, phonological, deep, and non-semantic reading. Our primary interest is on how these can be related to a model of the processes involved in reading. We have seen how a dual-route model explains surface dyslexia as an impairment of the lexical, direct access route, and explains phonological dyslexia as an impairment of the non-lexical, phonological recoding route. Deep dyslexia and non-semantic reading suggest that the simple dual-route model needs refinement. In particular, the direct route must be split into two: a direct access route that retrieves phonology given orthography, and a second lexical route, reading through semantics.

Dyslexia in other languages.   Languages such as Italian, Spanish, or Serbo-Croat which have totally transparent or *shallow* alphabetic orthographies—that is, where every grapheme is in a one-to-one relationship with a phoneme can show phonological and deep dyslexia, but not surface dyslexia, if we define this strictly as an inability to read exception words (Patterson, Marshall, & Coltheart, 1985). We can however find the symptoms that can co-occur with an impairment of exception word reading, such as homophone confusions, in the languages that permit them (Masterson, Coltheart, & Meara, 1985).

Whereas languages such as English has a single, alphabetic script, Japanese has two different scripts, *Kana* and *Kanji* (see Coltheart, 1980; Sasanuma, 1980). Kana is a syllabic script, and Kanji a logographic or ideographic script. Therefore words in Kanji convey no information on how a word should be pronounced. While Kana is designed to allow non-lexical processing, Kanji must be directly accessed. The right hemisphere is better at dealing with Kanji, and the left hemisphere is better at Kana. Generally Kana appears to be more prone to disruption by left hemisphere damage. A dual-route model is clearly advocated by these data. The analogue of deep dyslexia is a selective impairment of Kana, while Kanji is preserved. The analogue of surface dyslexia is the reverse; these patients must rely on Kana. Chinese is also an ideographic language, and Butterworth and Wengang (1991) report evidence of two routes in reading in Chinese.

The study of other languages which have different means of mapping orthography onto phonology is still at a relatively early stage, but it is likely to greatly enhance our understanding of reading mechanisms. So far it provides support for at least two reading routes.

MODELS OF NAMING

Both the classic dual-route and single route, *lexical instance* models face a number of problems. First, there are lexical effects for nonwords and regularity effects for words, and therefore reading cannot be a simple case of automatic grapheme-to-phoneme conversion for nonwords, and automatic direct access for all words. Single route models on the other hand provide no account of nonword pronunciation, and it remains to be demonstrated how neighbourhood effects operate to affect a word's pronunciation. Second, any model must also be able to account for the pattern of dissociations found in dyslexia. While surface and phonological dyslexia indicate that two reading mechanisms are necessary, other disorders suggests that these will not suffice. At first sight it is not obvious how a single route model could explain these dissociations at all.

Theorists have taken two different approaches depending upon their starting point. One possibility is to refine the dual-route model. Another is to show how word neighbourhoods can affect pronunciation and how pseudowords can be pronounced in a single route model. This led to the development of analogy models. More recently, a connectionist model of reading has been developed that takes the single route, analogy-based approach to the limit.

The revised dual-route model

We can save the dual-route model by making it more complex. Morton and Patterson (1980) and Patterson and Morton (1985) describe a three route model (see Fig. 4.2). First, there is the usual non-lexical route for assembling pronunciations from sublexical grapheme–phoneme conversion. The non-lexical route now consists of two subsystems. A standard grapheme–phoneme conversion mechanism is supplemented with a *body* subsystem that makes use of information about correspondences between orthographic and phonological rimes. Second, there is a direct route between orthography and phonology that does not access word meanings. In some ways, this route resembles the original logogen model. Third, there is a second direct route which involves reading through meaning, called the lexical-semantic route. This route accesses the meaning of imageable words.

The three route model can account for the data as follows. The lexical effects on nonwords and regularity effects on words are explained in this

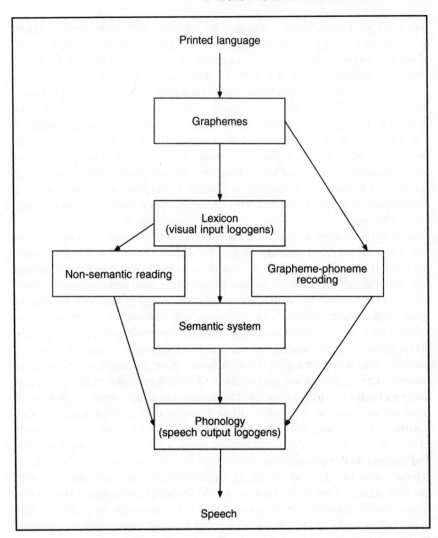

FIG. 4.2. The *three route* model of reading.

model by cross-talk between the lexical and non-lexical routes. Two types of interaction are possible: interference during retrieval, and conflict in resolving multiple phonological forms after retrieval. The two subsystems of the non-lexical route also give the model greater power. Surface dyslexia is the loss of the ability to make direct contact with the orthographic lexicon, and phonological dyslexia is the loss of the indirect route. Non-semantic reading is a loss of the lexical-semantic route. Deep dyslexia remains rather mysterious. First, we have to argue that these patients can only read through the lexical-semantic route. While accounting for the symptoms that resemble phonological dyslexia, it still does not explain the semantic paralexias. One possibility is that this route is normally, but not always, successful, and needs additional information (such as from the non-lexical and non-semantic direct route) to succeed. So when this information is no longer available it functions imperfectly. It gets us to the right semantic area, but not necessarily to the exact item, hence giving paralexias. This additional assumption seems somewhat ad hoc. An alternative idea is that paralexias are due to additional damage to the semantic system itself. Hence a complex pattern of impairments is still necessary to explain deep dyslexia, and there is no reason to suggest why these are not dissociable, as appears to be the case.

Multi-route models are becoming increasingly complicated as we find out more about the reading process (for example, see Carr & Pollatsek, 1985). It now seems that multiple levels of spelling-to-sound correspondences combine in determining the pronunciation of a word. In Norris's (1994) *multiple levels* model, different levels of spelling-to-sound information, including phoneme, rime, and word level correspondences, combine in an interactive activation network to determine the final pronunciation of a word. Such an approach develops earlier models which make use of knowledge at multiple-levels such as Brown (1987), Patterson and Morton (1985), and Shallice, Warrington, and McCarthy (1983). Furthermore, it is still possible to provide a spirited defence of a sophisticated version of the dual-route model. Coltheart, Curtis, Atkins, and Haller (1993), and Coltheart and Rastle (1994) describe a *dual-route cascaded model*. This model maintains the basic architecture of the dual-route model, but makes use of cascaded processing; as soon as there is any activation at the letter level, activation is passed on to the word level. The model also splits the lexical route into one route which goes through the semantic system and one which does not. As we shall see, connectionist modelling suggests a further alternative to the dual-route model.

The analogy model

This model was first proposed by Glushko (1979), Henderson (1982), Kay and Marcel (1981), and Marcel (1980). This is a form of single route model that provides an explicit mechanism for how we pronounce nonwords. It proposes that we pronounce nonwords and new words by analogy with other words. When a word (or nonword) is presented, it activates its neighbours, and these all influence its pronunciation. For example, "gang" activates "hang", "rang", "sang", and "bang"; these are all consistent with the regular pronunciation of "gang", and hence assembling a pronunciation is straightforward. When presented with "base", however, "case" and "vase" are activated; these conflict and hence the assembly of a pronunciation is slowed down until the conflict is resolved. A nonword such as "taze" is pronounced by analogy with the consistent set of similar words ("maze", "gaze", "daze"). A nonword such as "mave" activates "gave", "rave", and "save", but it also activates the conflicting enemy "have", which hence slows down pronunciation of "mave". In order to name by analogy, you have to find candidate words containing appropriate orthographic segments (like "-ave"); obtain the phonological representation of the segments; and assemble the complete phonology ("m + ave").

While attractive in the way that it deals with regularity and neighbourhood effects, early versions of analogy models suffered from a number of problems. First, the models did not make clear how the input is segmented in an appropriate way. Second, the models make incorrect predictions about how some nonwords should be pronounced. Particularly troublesome are those based upon *gangs*; "pook" should be pronounced by analogy with the great preponderance of the gang comprising "book", "hook", "look", and "rook", yet it is given the "hero" pronunciation—which is in accordance with grapheme–phoneme correspondence rules—nearly 75% of the time (Kay, 1985). Analogy theory also appears to make incorrect predictions about how long it takes us to make regularisation errors (Patterson & Morton, 1985). Finally, it is not clear how analogy models account for the dissociations found in acquired dyslexia.

Connectionist models: Seidenberg and McClelland (1989)

The analogy model can be seen as a precursor of Seidenberg and McClelland's (1989) connectionist model of reading. This model shares many features with the interactive activation model of letter recognition discussed in the previous chapter, and the technical details are given in the Appendix. It has three levels, each containing many simple units. These are the input, hidden, and output layers (see Fig. 4.3). Each of the units in these layers has an activation level, and each unit is connected to all the units in the next level by a weighted connection, which can be either excitatory or inhibitory. An important characteristic of this type of model is that the weights on these connections are not set by the modellers, but are learned. This network learns to associate phonology with orthography by being given repeated exposure to word–pronunciation pairs. It learns using an algorithm called back-propagation.

Seidenberg and McClelland's (1989) model of naming and word recognition is a back-propagation net which learns to associate spellings

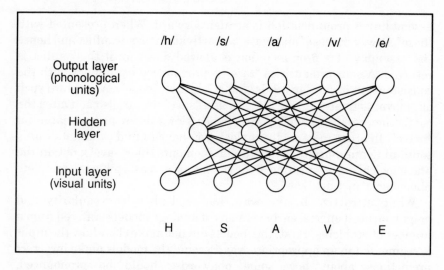

FIG. 4.3. Simplified architecture of the Seidenberg and McClelland model of single word reading. (Based on Seidenberg & McClelland, 1989, pp. 526–527.)

(input) with pronunciations (output). The model provides an account of how readers recognise letter strings as words and pronounce them. They used 400 units to code orthographic information for input and 460 units to code phonological information for output, mediated by 200 hidden units. Phonemes and graphemes were encoded as a set of triples, so that each grapheme or phoneme is specified with its flanking grapheme or phoneme. This is a standard device to represent position-specificity; the representation for phonemes is traditionally known as *Wickelphones* (see Wickelgren, 1969). For example, the word "have" is represented by the triples "#ha", "hav", "ave", "ve#", with "#" representing a blank space. Each Wickelphone was encoded as a pattern of activation distributed over a set of units representing phonetic features. A non-local representation was used: the graphemic representations were encoded as a pattern of activation across the orthographic units rather than corresponding directly to particular graphemes. The underlying architecture was not a simple feed-forward one in that the hidden units fed back to the orthographic units, mimicking top-down word-to-letter connections in the IAC model of word recognition. However, there was no feedback from the phonological to the hidden units, so phonological representations could not directly influence the processing of orthographic level representations.

The training corpus comprised all 2897 uninflected monosyllabic words of at least three or more letters in the English language present in the Kuçera and Francis (1967) word corpus. Each trial consisted of the presentation of a letter string that was converted into the appropriate pattern of activation over the orthographic units, which then feeds forward to the phonological units by way of the hidden units. In the training phase, words were presented a number of times with a probability proportional to the logarithm of their frequency. This means that the ease with which a word is learnt by the network, and the effect it has on similar words, depends to some extent upon its frequency. About 150,000 learning trials were needed to minimise the error score.

After training, the network was tested by the presentation of letter strings and computing the orthographic and phonological error scores. The error score is a measure of the average difference between the actual and desired output of each of the output units, across all patterns. The orthographic error scores were interpreted as a measure reflecting the performance of the model in a lexical decision task, while the phonological error scores were interpreted as reflecting performance on a naming task. Seidenberg and McClelland showed that the model fitted human data on a wide range of inputs. For example, regular words (such as "gave") were pronounced faster than exception words (such as "have").

Note that the Seidenberg and McClelland model uses a single reading mechanism. There is only one set of hidden units, and only one process is used to name regular, exception, and novel items. (In the complete architecture proposed—but not implemented—by Seidenberg & McClelland, there is an additional reading route through semantics.) Furthermore, as the model uses a distributed representation, there is no one-to-one correspondence between hidden units and lexical items; each word is represented by a pattern of activation over the hidden units. According to Seidenberg and McClelland, lexical memory does not consist of entries for individual words. Orthographic neighbours do not influence the pronunciation of a word directly at the time of processing; instead, regularity effects in pronunciation derive from statistical regularities in the words of the training corpus—all the words we have learned—as implemented in the weights of connections in the simulation. Lexical processing on this account involves the activation of information, and is not an all-or-none event.

Evaluation of the Seidenberg and McClelland model.   Coltheart et al. (1993) criticise important aspects of the Seidenberg and McClelland model. They formulate six questions about reading which any account of reading must answer. First, how do skilled readers read exception words aloud? Second, how do skilled readers read nonwords aloud? Third, how do we do visual lexical decision? Fourth, how does surface dyslexia arise? Fifth, how does phonological dyslexia arise? Sixth, how does developmental dyslexia arise? Coltheart et al. then argue that Seidenberg and McClelland's model only answers the first of these questions, whereas a version of the dual-route model answers all of them. They instead proposed a new version of the dual-route model they called the *dual-route cascaded model.*

Besner, Twilley, McCann, and Seergobin (1990) provided a detailed critique of the Seidenberg and McClelland model, although a reply by Seidenberg and McClelland (1990) answered some of these points. First, Besner et al. argued that in a sense the model still possesses a lexicon, where instead of a word corresponding to a unit, it corresponds to a pattern of activation. Second, they pointed out that the model "reads" nonwords rather poorly. In particular, it only produced the "correct", regular pronunciation of a nonword under 70% of the time. This contrasts with the model's excellent performance on its original training set. Hence the model's performance on nonwords is impaired from the beginning (Seidenberg & McClelland, 1990, pointed out in reply that their model was trained upon only 2987 words, as opposed to the 30,000 words which people know, and that this may be responsible for the difference). Hence the model simulates the direct lexical route rather better than it simulates the indirect grapheme–phoneme route. If this is the case, then any disruption of the model will give a better account of disruption to the direct route—that is, of surface dyslexia. They also point out that, unlike humans, the model performs badly with *pseudohomophones.* This again suggests that the non-lexical route has been more weakly instantiated in learning than the direct route, and this may account for the particular susceptibility of the latter. Finally, the assumption that lexical decision performance is determined by the degree of overlap in the orthographic error scores between nonwords and words is questionable (Fera & Besner, 1992).

Forster (1994) critically evaluates the assumptions behind connectionist modelling of visual word recognition. He makes the point that showing that a network model can successfully learn to perform a complex task such as reading does not mean that that is the way that humans actually do it. Finally, Norris (1994) argues that a major stumbling block for the Seidenberg and McClelland model is its inability to account for the ability of readers to shift strategically between relying on lexical and sublexical information.

A revised connectionist model performs much better (Plaut & McClelland, 1993). This uses different input and output representations, and gives a much better account of nonword processing (Seidenberg et al., 1994). Connectionist models of reading are at an early stage, but they have contributed enormously to our understanding of normal reading. But can they also provide any account of the dissociations found in dyslexia?

Connectionist models of dyslexia

Over the last few years connectionist modelling has contributed to our understanding of deep and surface dyslexia. We will look at two influential models.

Surface dyslexia. Patterson, Seidenberg, and McClelland (1989) artificially damaged or "lesioned" the Seidenberg and McClelland (1989) network after the learning phase by destroying hidden units or connection weights, and then observing the behaviour of the model. Its performance, it was claimed, then resembles that of a surface dyslexic. Patterson et al. (1989) explored three main types of lesion: damage to connections between the orthographic input and hidden units (called by them *early weights*); damage to the hidden to output (phonological) units (*late weights*), or damage to the hidden units themselves. Damage was inflicted by probabilistically resetting a proportion of the weights or units to zero. The greater the amount of damage being simulated, the higher the proportion of weights that were changed. The consequences were measured in two ways. First, the damage was measured by the phonological error score, which as we have seen reflects the difference between the actual and target activation values of the phonological output units. Obviously, high error scores reflect impaired performance. Second, the damage was measured by the *reversal rate*. This corresponds to a switch in pronunciation by the model, so that a regular pronunciation is given to an exception item (for example, "have" is pronounced to rhyme with "gave"). It is defined as the simulation producing a lower phonological error score for a non-target pronunciation.

Increasing damage at each location produces near-linear increases in the phonological error scores of all types of word. On the whole, though, the lesioned model generally performed better with regular than exception words. The greater the degree of damage the higher was the reversal rate, but nevertheless there were still more reversals occurring on exception words than on regular words. Damage to the hidden units in particular produced a large number of instances where exception words were produced with a regular pronunciation; this is similar to the result whereby surface dyslexics over-regularise their pronunciations. However, the number of regularised pronunciations that were produced by the lesioned model was significantly lower than that produced by surface dyslexic patients. No lesion made the model perform selectively worse on nonwords. Hence the behaviour of the lesioned model resembles that of a surface dyslexic.

Patterson et al. also found that word frequency was not a major determinant of whether a pronunciation reversed or not. (It did have some effect, so that high-frequency words were generally more robust.) As we have seen, some surface dyslexics show frequency effects on reading, while others do not. They found that the main determinant of reversals was the number of vowel features by which the regular pronunciation differs from the correct pronunciation. This finding leads to clear predictions that were verified against the neuropsychological data. Hence here the connectionist model has contributed to an important new line of research.

An additional point of interest is that the lesioned model produced errors that have traditionally been interpreted as "visual" errors. These are mispronunciations that are not over-regularisations and which were traditionally thought to result from an impairment of early graphemic analysis. If this analysis is correct, then Patterson et al. should only have found such errors when there was damage to the orthographic units involved. In contrast, they found them even when the orthographic units were not damaged. This is an example of one strength of the connectionist approach; the same mechanism explains what were considered previously to be disparate findings. Here visual errors result from the same lesion that causes other characteristics of surface dyslexia, and it is unnecessary to resort to more complex explanations involving additional damage to the graphemic analysis system.

There are three main problems with this particular account. First, the original Seidenberg and McClelland model is relatively bad at producing nonwords before it is lesioned. We might say that the original model is already operating as a phonological dyslexic. Second, the model does not really over-regularise, it just changes the vowel sound of words. Third, Behrmann and Bub (1992) report data that are inconsistent with this model. In particular, they showed that the performance of the surface dyslexic MP on irregular words does vary as a function of word frequency. They interpret this frequency effect as problematic for connectionist models.

Phonological dyslexia.   Patterson et al. (1989) are quite explicit in simulating only surface dyslexia; their model does not address phonological dyslexia. However, given that the account of surface dyslexia is based upon Seidenberg and McClelland's original model, which claims to be a complete single-mechanism account of the reading process, we might wonder why a simulation of phonological dyslexia cannot be obtained from this architecture. If the argument is that an account of phonological dyslexia presupposes explicit modelling of non-lexical mechanisms, then the completeness of the original

Seidenberg and McClelland model merits re-examination. Indeed, Seidenberg and McClelland (1990) say that to give a complete account of the reading process it might be necessary to simulate reading via a second route, one involving going from orthography to phonology through a semantic system, instead of merely through hidden units. As yet then there is no widely reported model of phonological dyslexia.

Deep dyslexia.   Hinton and Shallice (1991) have lesioned another connectionist model to simulate deep dyslexia. Their model is trained by back-propagation to associate word pronunciations with a representation of the meaning of words. This model is particularly important, because it shows that one type of lesion can give rise to all the symptoms of deep dyslexia, particularly both paralexias and visual errors.

The underlying semantic representation of a word is specified as a pattern of activation across semantic units or *sememes*. These correspond to *semantic features* or primitives such as "main-shape-2D", "has-legs", "brown", and "mammal". These can be thought of as atomic units of meaning, and we will discuss them in more detail in Chapter 6. The architecture of the Hinton and Shallice (1991) model comprised 28 graphemic input units and 68 semantic output units with an intervening hidden layer containing 40 intermediate units. The model was trained to produce an appropriate output representation given a particular orthographic input using back-propagation. The model was trained on 40 uninflected monosyllabic words.

The structure of the output layer is quite complex. First, there were inter-connections between some of the semantic units. The 68 sememe units were divided into 19 groups depending on their interpretation, with inhibitory connections between appropriate members of the group. For example, in the group of semantic features that define the size of the object denoted by the word, there are three sememes: "max-size-less-foot", "max-size-foot-to-two yards", and "max-size-greater-two-yards". Each of these features inhibits each other in the group, because obviously an object can only have one size. Second, an additional set of hidden units called *cleanup units* were connected to the semantic units. These permitted more complex inter-dependencies between the semantic units to be learned, and have the effect of producing structure in the output layer. This results in a richer semantic space where there are strong *attractors*. An attractor can be seen as a point in semantic space to which different states of the network are attracted; it resembles the bottom of a valley or basin, so that objects positioned on the sides of the basin tend to migrate towards the lowest point. This corresponds to the semantic representation ultimately assigned to a word.

As in Patterson et al.'s (1989) simulation of surface dyslexia, a number of different types of lesion were possible. There are two dimensions to remember: one is *what* is lesioned, the other is *how* it is lesioned. The connections involved were the grapheme–intermediate, intermediate–sememe, and sememe–cleanup. Three methods of lesioning the network were used. First, each set of connections were taken in turn, and a proportion of their weights were set to zero, or *disconnected*. Second, random noise was added to each connection. Third, the hidden units (the intermediate and cleanup units) were *ablated* by destroying a proportion of them.

The results showed that the closer the lesion was to the semantic system, the more effect it had. The lesion type and site interacted in their effects; for example, the cleanup circuit was more sensitive to added noise than disconnections. Lesions resulted in four types of error: semantic (where an input gave an output word that was semantically but not visually close to the target; these resemble the classic semantic paralexias of deep dyslexics), visual (words visually similar but not semantically), mixed (where the output is both semantically and visually close to the target), and others. All types of lesion site and type (except disconnecting the semantic and cleanup units) produced the same broad pattern of errors. Finally, on some occasions the lesions were so severe that the network could not generate an explicit response. In these cases Hinton and Shallice tested the below-threshold information left in the system by simulating a forced choice procedure. They achieved this by comparing the residual semantic output to a set of possible outputs corresponding to a set of words, one of which was the target semantic output. The model behaved above chance on this forced-choice test in that its output semantic representation tended to be closer to that of the target than the alternatives.

Hence the lesioned network behaves rather like a deep dyslexic. In particular, it makes semantic paralexias. These occur because semantic attractors cause the accessing of feature clusters close to the meanings of words that are related to the target. A "landscape" metaphor may be useful. Lesions can be thought of as having the results of destroying the ridges that separate the different basins of attraction. The occurrence of such errors does not seem to be crucially dependent upon the particular lesion type or site under consideration. Furthermore, this account provides an explanation of why different error types, particularly semantic and visual errors, nearly always co-occur in such patients. Two visually similar words can point in the first instance to nearby parts of semantic space, even though their ultimate meanings in the basins may be far apart; if you start off on top of a hill, going downhill in different directions will take you to very different ultimate locations. Lesions modify semantic space so that visually similar words are then attracted to different semantic attractors.

Hinton and Shallice's account is important for cognitive neuropsychologists for a number of reasons. First, it provides an explicit mechanism whereby the characteristics of deep dyslexia can be derived from a model of normal reading. Second, it shows that the actual site of the lesion is not of primary importance. This is mainly because of the "cascade" characteristics of these networks. Each stage of processing is continually activating the next, and is not dependent upon the completion of processing by its prior stage (McClelland, 1979). Therefore, effects of lesions at one network site are very quickly passed on to surrounding sites. Third, it shows why symptoms that were previously considered to be conceptually distinct necessarily co-occur. Semantic and visual errors can result from the same lesion. Fourth, it thus revives the importance of syndromes as a neuropsychological concept. If symptoms necessarily co-occur as a result of any lesion to a particular system, then it makes sense to look for and study such co-occurrences.

Plaut and Shallice (1993a) extended this work to examine the effect of word abstractness upon lesioned reading performance. As we have seen, the reading performance of deep dyslexics is significantly better on more imageable than less imageable words. Plaut and Shallice show that the richness of the underlying semantic representation of a word is an analogue of imageability. They hypothesised that the semantic representations of abstract words contain fewer semantic features than those of concrete words; that is, the more concrete a word is, the richer its semantic representation. Jones (1985) showed that it was possible to account for imageability effects in deep dyslexia by recasting them as *ease-of-predication* effects. Ease-of-predication is a measure of how easy it is to generate things to say about a word, or *predicates*, and is obviously closely related to the richness of the underlying semantic representation. It is easier to find more things to say about more imageable words than less imageable words. Plaut and Shallice (1993a) showed that when an attractor network similar to that of Hinton and Shallice (1991) is lesioned, concrete words are read better than abstract words. One exception was that severe lesions of the cleanup system resulted in better performance on abstract words. Plaut and Shallice argue that this is consistent with patient CAV (Warrington, 1981), who showed such an advantage. Hence this network can account for both the usual better performance of deep dyslexics on concrete words, and the rare exception where the reverse is the case.

Connectionist modelling has advanced our understanding of deep dyslexia in particular, and neuropsychological deficits in general. The finding that apparently unrelated symptoms can necessarily co-occur as a result of a single lesion is of particular importance. It suggests that deep dyslexia may after all be a unitary condition.

Comparison of models

A simple dual-route model provides an inadequate account of reading, and needs an additional lexical route through imageable semantics. The more complex a model becomes, the greater the worry that routes are being introduced on an ad hoc basis to account for particular findings. Analogy models have some attractive features, but their detailed workings are vague and they do not seem able to account for all the data. Connectionist modelling has provided an explicit, single-route model which covers most of the main findings, but has its problems. Yet at the very least it has clarified the issues involved in reading. Its contribution goes beyond this, however. It has set the challenge that only one route is necessary in reading words and nonwords, and that regularity effects in pronunciation arise out of statistical regularities in the words of the language. It may not be a complete or correct account, but it is certainly a challenging account. At present these models are in a relatively early stage of development, and it would be premature to dismiss them because they cannot yet account for all the data.

Finally, all of these models—particularly the connectionist ones—are limited in that they have focused upon the recognition of morphologically simple, often monosyllabic words. The recognition of morphologically complex words provides useful data for deciding between models of word recognition (see Carr & Pollatsek, for a review, particularly on experiments on what is called *prefix stripping*). The study of these more complex words has not been ignored altogether; Taft (e.g. 1985, 1987; see also Marslen-Wilson, Tyler, Waksler, & Older, 1994; Taft, 1985, 1987) has developed a model that tackles these issues head on.

LEARNING TO READ AND SPELL

How do we learn to read? Unlike speaking and listening, reading and writing are clearly not easy tasks to learn, as manifested by large numbers of people who find them difficult, and the amount of explicit tuition apparently necessary. Here we will concentrate on the most fundamental aspect of reading development, how we learn to recognise words. Reading development is closely associated with skills such as spelling, and we will also examine this. Finally, difficulty in learning to read and spell—developmental dyslexia and dysgraphia—are relatively common, and we will examine these in the context of a model of normal reading development. Developmental dyslexias can be categorised in a similar way to acquired dyslexia, which has been used as further justification for a dual-route model of reading.

"Normal" reading development

Reading is a complex skill which many find difficult, and the complexities of a language such as English make it even harder. It seems likely that children learn to read in a series of stages, although as Rayner and Pollatsek (1989) point out, it is likely that these stages reflect the use of increasingly sophisticated skills and strategies, rather than the type of biologically and environmentally driven sequence of stages that might underlie cognitive development. Marsh and his colleagues (Marsh, Desberg, & Cooper, 1977; Marsh, Friedman, Welch, & Desberg, 1981) proposed that reading emerges in four stages. Stage one is called *linguistic guessing*; this involves looking at words and guessing what they might be on the basis of the linguistic context. Rote learning of how some words are pronounced plays a role here. Stage two is *discrimination net guessing*, where more sophisticated guessing is used, based upon the visual appearance of the letters. Stage three is *sequential decoding*, where the reader learns grapheme–phoneme conversion rules; at this stage, the interpretation of each grapheme depends on its context. Finally, stage four is *hierarchical decoding*, where the reader is capable of skilled reading, using an analogy strategy. Frith (1985) developed this scheme, distinguishing in sequence a *logographic* stage based on direct access of some familiar words using their salient visual features, an *alphabetic* stage where the learner makes use of information about letters and how they are pronounced; and finally an *orthographic* stage where words access their pronunciations in a systematic and adult-like way. Within the alphabetic stage there is probably an order of how spelling-to-sound correspondences are acquired: the correspondences between sounds and the rimes of syllables are probably the first to be acquired (Goswami, 1993). However, whether reading by analogy precedes alphabetic reading is currently unclear (see Coltheart & Leahy, 1992; Goswami, 1988, 1993; Laxon, Masterson, & Coltheart, 1991; Marsh et al., 1981).

At some point all children appear to go through a stage of alphabetic reading where they make use of grapheme–phoneme correspondences, yet skilled readers eventually end up making use of the direct route. Hence learning skilled reading at first sight involves a developmental shift away from reading through grapheme–phoneme conversion to reading by direct access. However, more detailed examination of the evidence suggests that, if anything, the shift is the other way round; the use of grapheme–phoneme correspondences follows direct access (Barron, 1986; Rayner & Pollatsek, 1989). For example, Barron and Baron (1977) showed that concurrent articulation had no effect on extracting the meaning of a printed word, even in early readers who should have been relying on grapheme–phoneme correspondences. Instead, it seems that the development of the awareness of the role of phonological correspondence in reading is quite a late and sophisticated skill. Although later research questions whether concurrent articulation has any effect on grapheme–phoneme conversion, the conclusion stands (Bryant & Bradley, 1983; Goswami & Bryant, 1990).

Phonological awareness.   An important concept in learning to read is *phonological awareness*, which is awareness of the sounds of a word. It can be measured by a number of tasks, including segmenting words (asking children to divide a spoken word into its phonemes and then do something with them, such as count them or rearrange them), rhyming, and blending sounds to form a more complex one. These tasks probably all measure the same thing (Stanovich, Cunningham, & Cramer, 1984). Beginner readers have difficulty with these tasks, but their performance improves with age. It seems that developing phonological awareness improves reading skills, and that as children learn to read, their phonological awareness increases. The evidence is reviewed by Rayner and Pollatsek (1989); although there are some contradictions in the data, phonological awareness does appear to play a central and primary role. Training on phonological awareness can lead to an improvement in segmenting and reading skills in general (Bradley & Bryant, 1983). Perhaps the most detailed account of phonological awareness and its importance in learning to read is that of Goswami and Bryant (1990). In summary, phonological awareness is a central concept in reading and is absent or impoverished in non-skilled readers.

Teaching reading.   Traditionally there are two main approaches to teaching reading and word recognition. These correspond to the two routes of the routes in the dual-route model. In the *look-and-say* or *whole word* method, children learn to associate the sound of a word with a particular visual pattern. This corresponds to emphasising the lexical or direct access route. In the alternative *phonic method*, children are taught to associate sounds with letters and letter sequences, and use this to build up the pronunciations of words. This corresponds to emphasising the non-lexical or grapheme–phoneme conversion route.

It is generally agreed that the phonic method gives better results. Indeed, many studies show that discovering the alphabetic principle (that letters correspond systematically to sounds) is the key to learning to read (see Backman, 1983; Bradley & Bryant, 1978, 1983; Rayner & Pollatsek, 1989). Furthermore, as we have seen, training on phonological awareness improves reading skills.

The age at which children start to learn to read seems to be relatively unimportant—indeed, even when it is delayed until age seven, there are no serious or permanent side-effects (Rayner & Pollatsek, 1989). In fact, older children learn to read more quickly by comparison (Feitelson, Tehori, & Levinberg-Green, 1982). As a corollary of this, very early tuition does not provide any obvious long-term benefits, as late starters catch up so easily.

Spelling.   Spelling is an important skill associated with learning to read and with the emergence of phonological awareness and the skills that reflects. Spelling can be thought of as the reverse of reading: instead of having to turn letters into sounds, you have to turn sounds into letter. Indeed the classic model of spelling is a dual-route model which is the inverse of the dual-route model of reading (see Brown & Ellis, 1994). In this model there is a spelling-to-sound or assembled or non-lexical route, which can only work for regular words, and a direct or addressed or lexical route, which will work for all words. The order in which these routes are acquired is controversial. According to Frith (1985), children spell logographically before they spell alphabetically, but this is disputed by Goswami and Bryant (1990), who found little evidence for a logographic stage in spelling development at all. Given the similarities between reading and spelling, it is no surprise that same sorts of issues are found in spelling research as in reading research, and that the two areas are closely connected.

Developmental dyslexia

Developmental dyslexia refers to an impairment in acquiring reading abilities. Whereas acquired dyslexia involves damage to reading systems that were known to be functionally normal before the brain trauma, developmental dyslexics grow up such that the normal acquisition of reading is impaired. The reasons for this impairment are currently poorly understood. In the popular press, the term is often used to refer to difficulties with writing and poor spelling. Strictly, this is developmental dysgraphia, although naturally developmental dyslexia and dysgraphia usually occur together. Here we will consider only difficulties in reading. It would bolster our model of reading if it could account for the varieties of developmental dyslexia that are found.

It is clear that developmental dyslexia comes in a number of varieties. Frith (1985) related different types to her model of reading development outlined above. In particular, she stressed the importance of progressing from logographic stage to the alphabetic stage. She argued that classic developmental dyslexics fail to make this progression. Less severe are readers who are arrested at the alphabetic stage and cannot progress onto the orthographic stage. Less severe still is what is called *type-B spelling* disorder, where there is a failure of orthographic access for spelling but not for reading.

There is another way of looking at the types of developmental dyslexia other than relating them immediately to a particular model of reading development. A number of researchers have pointed out that there are similarities between acquired and developmental dyslexia. Jorm (1979) compared developmental dyslexia with deep dyslexia. In both cases grapheme–phoneme conversion is impaired, which leads to a particular difficulty with nonwords. He concluded that the same part of the parietal lobe of the brain was involved in each case; it was damaged in deep dyslexia, and failed to develop normally in developmental dyslexia. However, Baddeley, Ellis, Miles and Lewis (1982) found that although the phonological encoding of developmental dyslexics was greatly impaired, they could do some tasks that necessitate it. For example, they could read nonwords at a much higher level than deep dyslexics, although of course nowhere near as well as age-matched controls. Developmental dyslexics also rarely make semantic paralexias, so perhaps they resemble phonological dyslexics rather more? Campbell and Butterworth (1985), and Butterworth, Campbell, and Howard (1986) describe the case of RE, who resembled a phonological dyslexic (although this did not prevent her becoming a successful university student!) RE could only read a new word once she had heard someone else say it. She could not inspect the phonological form of words, and could not "hear words in the head". Such a skill may be necessary for the development of the phonological recoding route. In addition, she had an abnormally low digit span. Temple and Marshall (1983) describe another case of developmental dyslexia that resembles phonological dyslexia, whereas Coltheart, Masterson, Byng, Prior and Riddoch (1983) report a case resembling surface dyslexia. Castles and Coltheart (1993) examined the reading of 56 developmental dyslexics, and argued that they did not form a homogeneous population, showing instead a clear dissociation between surface and phonological dyslexic reading patterns. They concluded that such a dissociation is the norm in developmental dyslexia. In this interpretation, the types of develop-mental dyslexia correspond to a failure to "acquire" normally one of the two routes of the dual-route model.

Hence the process of learning to read seems prone to the same types of disruption as are found when the mature reading system is lesioned.

However, Snowling (1983, 1987) has urged caution in comparing types of acquired and developmental dyslexia. In particular, she argued that the best comparison in understanding what has gone wrong is not between developmental and acquired dyslexics, but between developmental dyslexics and reading age-matched controls. That is, if someone has a reading age of 10, they should be compared with normal readers of 10. Bryant and Impey (1986) reported such a comparison, and found that the "normal" children made exactly the same types of reading error as the dyslexic children. If dyslexic and normal children make the same types of error then this weakens the argument that developmental dyslexia arises from the same type of brain damage as acquired dyslexia. In addition, we find large differences in normal young readers. Bryant and Impey suggest that there are many different reading styles, and some children adopt styles that lead them into difficulty. Indeed, Baron and Strawson (1976) showed reading differences in adults, with some relying more on phonological rules, others relying more upon the direct route. Nevertheless, the precise way in which these difficulties become manifest remains to be explained (see Coltheart, 1987b, and Temple, 1987, for detailed replies) Both Seymour (1987, 1990) and Wilding (1990) conclude that most impairments in developmental dyslexia lie upon a continuum, rather than falling into two neat categories. Others cases lie well outside this continuum; Johnston (1983) described a developmental deep dyslexic.

Another problem that arises when trying to infer the properties of the reading system from cases of developmental dyslexia is that the developing reading system may be very different from the final, adult version. For example, grapheme–phoneme conversion might play a larger role in children. Furthermore, this is likely to interact with the way in which the children are taught to read. The *look and say* method emphasises the role of the direct access route, and the *phonic* method grapheme–phoneme conversion.

The relationship between these disorders and other cognitive abilities is complex (Ellis, 1993). Some developmental dyslexics have other language problems, such as in speaking or object naming. Identifying developmental dyslexics is complex: by definition, they read worse than age-matched controls, but how much worse do you have to read to be a developmental dyslexic, rather than just a poor reader? At present it looks as though dyslexics are indeed worse at both tasks involving phonological awareness (Goswami & Bryant, 1990) and nonword reading (Rack, Snowling, & Olson, 1992). A complete model of reading should be aim to account for any differences between good and poor readers.

CONCLUDING SUMMARY

If we look at the relationship between a word's orthography (spelling and the visual appearance of a word) and phonology, there are two types of word in English. Some have a regular spelling-to-sound correspondence, and some have an irregular correspondence. In addition, we can pronounce pseudowords and words we have never seen before. The simplest account is that we can read through two routes, a lexical, direct access one (which corresponds to the direct access or lexical instance models, such as the logogen model, we examined in the previous chapter), and a non-lexical route which assembles pronunciations from grapheme–phoneme correspondences. This dual-route model can account for the basic dissociation displayed between surface and phonological dyslexia. However, there are lexical effects upon reading nonwords, and regularity effects on reading words. The characterisation of words into regular and irregular is too simple. In addition, the pattern of dissociations found in dyslexia suggest that a third reading route is necessary, involving reading through imageable semantics. Alternatively, direct access models explain these effects in terms of lexical neighbourhood effects, and argue that nonwords are pronounced by analogy with words. Analogy models provide a mechanism for pronouncing nonwords by analogy with words. They are now largely replaced in popularity by connectionist models of reading, which make the mechanisms which operate quite explicit. According to connectionist models, only one reading route is necessary between orthography and phonology. Furthermore, regularity effects arise because of statistical regularities in the language that we learn. It is possible to lesion connectionist models to simulate surface and deep dyslexia; the connectionist account of deep dyslexia is particularly compelling. On the other hand, dual-route and race models have become more complicated in response to these data. As yet it is too early to say whether connectionist models or multi-route parallel coding models will win the day; the race is on. Models of reading can also be applied to children learning to read and the difficulties they encounter.

FURTHER READING

There are a number of works that describe the orthography of English, and discuss the rules whereby certain spelling-to-sound correspondences are described as regular and others irregular. One of the best known of these is Venezky (1970).

Patterson and Coltheart (1987) give a tutorial review on the role of phonological processes in reading. A vigorous debate between proponents and opponents of the dual-route model was carried out in the pages of the journal *The Behavioral and Brain Sciences* in 1985 (see Humphreys & Evett, 1985).

For a general introduction to reading, writing, spelling, and their disorders, see Ellis (1993). This includes an excellent description of developmental dyslexia. For more discussion of dyslexia, including peripheral dyslexias, see Ellis and Young (1988). Two volumes (entitled *Deep dyslexia*, 2nd ed., by Coltheart, Patterson, & Marshall, 1987, and *Surface dyslexia* by Patterson, Marshall, & Coltheart, 1985) cover much of the relevant material. Barry and Richardson (1988) review the literature on imageability effects on reading in deep dyslexia. Among the works on developmental dyslexia, Snowling (1987) is very approachable, and Olson (1994) provides an up to date review. For general overviews of learning to read, with emphasis on individual differences in reading ability, see Goswami and Bryant (1990), McShane (1991), Oakhill (1994), and Perfetti (1994). For a popular account of connectionist models of reading, see Hinton (1992), and Hinton, Plaut, and Shallice (1993). Caplan (1992, chapter 5) reviews literature relevant to both this chapter and the previous one, with emphasis on the neuropsychology of reading. He also (chapter 6) reviews the recognition (and production) of morphologically complex words.

The processes involved in the unimpaired reading of Japanese Kanji characters are discussed by Flores d'Arcais, Saito, and Kawakami (1995).

In addition, many of the references at the end of Chapter 3 will also be relevant here. In particular, the review by Carr and Pollatsek (1985) also covers pronunciation and parallel coding models.

A recent special issue of the *Journal of Experimental Psychology: Human Perception and Performance* (1994, volume 20, whole section 6) is devoted to models of visual word recognition and reading, and brings many of the issues discussed in this and the previous chapter up to date. In addition to papers previously mentioned, these include papers by Jacobs and Grainger (1994), which reviews models of word recognition; Massaro and Cohen (1994), which extends Massaro's fuzzy logic model of speech perception discussed in Chapter 2 to reading; Seidenberg, Plaut, Petersen, McClelland, and McRae (1994), exploring how connectionist models should best deal with the pronunciation of nonwords; and van Orden and Goldinger (1994), who discuss a complex systems, ecological approach to perception and reading.

Eysenck and Keane (1995) and Rayner and Pollatsek (1989) provide introductory coverage of learning to read. Brown and Ellis (1994) review research on spelling.

CHAPTER FIVE

Syntax and parsing

INTRODUCTION

So far we have looked at how we recognise individual words. When we access the lexical entry for a word, two major types of information become available: information about a word's meaning, and information about the syntactic roles which a word can take. The first step in understanding a sentence is to work out what is the subject (what is doing the principal action), what is the object (what is having something done to it), and what is the main action. At the very least this means identifying whether each word is a noun, verb, adjective, adverb, and so on. From such information about individual words we start to construct a representation of the meaning of the sentence we are reading or hearing. The next two chapters are about the process of assembling this representation.

When we hear and understand a sentence, information about the word order is often crucial. This of course is information about the *syntax* of the sentence. Sentences (1) and (2) have the same word order structure but different meanings; (1) and (3) have different word order structures but the same underlying meaning.

1. The ghost chased the vampire.
2. The vampire chased the ghost.
3. The vampire was chased by the ghost.

The process of computing the syntactic structure of a sentence is called *parsing*. Hence when we parse a sentence, we must assign each word to a syntactic category such as noun, verb, or adjective. As these examples show, parsing is often an essential step in obtaining the intended meaning of a sentence.

A number of important questions arise about parsing and the human sentence parsing mechanism, or HSPM for short. How does parsing operate? Why are some sentences more difficult to parse than others? What happens to the syntactic representation after parsing? Why are sentences assigned the structures or *phrase markers* they are? In particular, how do we cope with ambiguity? Does syntactic processing use semantic information to construct parses, or is it restricted to using syntactic information? This last question is reminiscent of the issue of independence in lexical access, and is indeed another manifestation of the issue of whether language processes are modular or not. Is there an enclosed syntactic module which uses only syntactic information to parse a sentence, or can other types of information guide the parsing process? The final two questions together address a fundamental issue in the psychology of parsing: How do we cope with ambiguous syntax? This issue will be a focal topic of Chapter 9.

It must be remembered that the goal of understanding is to extract the meaning from what we hear or read. Syntactic processing is only one stage in doing this, but it is nevertheless an important one. Whether it is always an essential one is an important issue in itself. There is, however, another reason why we should study syntax. Fodor (1975) argued that there is a "language of thought" which bears a close resemblance to our surface language. In particular, the syntax that governs the language of thought may be very similar to or identical with that of external language. Studying syntax may therefore provide a window onto fundamental cognitive processes.

Finally, it should be pointed out that syntax is a relatively technical area, with what at first sight appears to be a lot of jargon and a rather daunting number of symbols. This is necessary, however, to make sense of the subject, and in order to specify exactly what it is that is that has to be explained. It is worth persevering.

LINGUISTIC APPROACHES TO SYNTAX

We first need a language for talking about syntax, and linguistics provides such a language. The contribution of linguistics to our understanding of parsing and the limitations of different types of parsing systems has been enormous. In particular, the work of the

American linguist Noam Chomsky has dominated the field. We must look at this work in some detail.

The linguistic theory of Chomsky

It is convenient to consider two aspects to Chomsky's work, although of course these are closely related. We will examine the relationship between language and thought and his views on language acquisition in later chapters. Chomsky argues that language is a special feature which is innate, species-specific, and biologically pre-programmed, and which is a faculty independent of other cognitive structures. Here we will be primarily concerned with the more technical aspect of his theory.

For Chomsky, the goal of linguistics is to describe the grammar that enables us to produce and understand language. Chomsky (1968) pointed out that it is important to distinguish between our idealised *linguistic competence*, and our actual *linguistic performance*. Our linguistic competence is what is tapped by our intuitions as to which are acceptable sentences in the language, and which are ungrammatical strings of words. Hence we know that the sentence "The vampire the ghost loved ran away" is grammatical, even if we never produce it in practice, while we also know that "The vampire the ghost the cat loved ran away" is ungrammatical. *Competence* concerns our abstract knowledge of our language. It is about the judgements we would make about language if we had sufficient time and memory capacity. In practice, of course, our actual linguistic *performance*—the sentences which we actually produce—is limited by these factors. Furthermore, the sentences we actually produce often use the more simple grammatical constructions. Our speech is full of false starts, hesitations, speech errors, and corrections. The actual ways in which we produce and understand sentences are also in the domain of performance. Although these factors are of prime interest to the psycholinguist, they muddy the waters of linguistic competence a great deal. As a generalisation we can say that psycholinguists are more interested in our linguistic performance, and linguists in our competence. Nevertheless many of the issues of competence are relevant to psychologists. In particular, linguistics provides a framework for thinking about syntax, and its theories place constraints upon language acquisition.

The main goals of linguistics then are to develop a theory of *grammar*, which involves producing an appropriate description and analysis of the syntactic rules of a language. A grammar is a formal device that uses a finite number of rules that in combination can generate all the sentences of a language. Obviously we could produce a device that could emit words randomly, and this would not be acceptable. For example, "dog vampire cat chase" is a non-sentence in English. Hence our grammar must also produce no non-sentences. For Chomsky, a theory of language must do several things. It must describe the complete set of rules which will generate all of the sentences of the language, but no non-sentences. It must give an account of the underlying syntactic structure of sentences. As we shall see, this is done by what are called *tree diagrams* or *phrase markers*. The sentence structures that we create should capture our intuitions about how sentences and fragments of sentences are related. Finally, the theory should also explain how children can acquire these rules.

It should be pointed out that Chomsky's linguistic theory has evolved greatly over the years. The first version was widely available in a book called *Syntactic structures* (1957). The (1965) version became known as the "standard theory"; this was followed in turn by the "extended standard theory", "revised extended standard theory", and currently "government and binding" (or GB) theory (Chomsky, 1981). The essence has nevertheless remained the same. The central theme is that language is rule-based, and that our knowledge of syntax can be captured in a finite number of syntactic rules. A moment's reflection should show that language involves rules, even if we are not always aware of them. How else would we know that "Vlad bought himself a new toothbrush" is acceptable English but "Vlad bought himself toothbrush new a" is not?

Phrase structure grammar

How then should these rules be described? Chomsky proposed that *phrase structure rules* are an essential component of our grammar. The central idea is that sentences are built up hierarchically from smaller units. A phrase structure grammar comprises what are known as *rewrite rules*. These are simply rules which translate a symbol on the left-hand side of the rule into those on the right-hand. There are two main types of symbol: terminal elements (consisting of the sentence symbol S at the top end, and vocabulary items or words at the lowest) and non-terminal elements (everything else). The units should be familiar to anyone with a smattering of knowledge of grammar. At the lowest are the individual words, which fall into classes such as nouns (words used to name objects and ideas, both concrete and abstract), adjectives (words used to describe), verbs (words describing actions or states, or an assertion), adverbs (words qualifying verbs), determiners (words limiting the nouns they modify), prepositions (words such as "in", "to", and "at"), conjunctions (words such as "and", "because", and "so") and so on. This should be clear from the examples in Table 5.1, which is an example of a grammar that accounts for a fragment of English. Words combine to make phrases which express a single idea. For example, "Vlad", "the vampire", "the old vampire", and "the grouchy old vampire" are all examples of noun phrases—they can all take the part of nouns in sentences. For example, they all make acceptable beginnings to the sentence fragment "__ bought a new toothbrush". *Phrases* in turn combine to make clauses. *Clauses* contain a *subject* (something doing the action), and a *predicate* (a verb relating to the subject). Sentences contain at least one clause but may contain many more. The essential idea of a phrase structure grammar is the analysis of the sentence into its lower-level constituents, such as noun phrases, verb phrases, nouns, and verbs; because of this, this approach is sometimes called *constituent analysis*. Formally, constituents are units that can be replaced by a single word—not necessarily with the same meaning. Hence in the sentence "The nasty vampire laughed at the poor ghost", "The nasty vampire" is a constituent (as it can be replaced by, for example, "Vlad"), whereas "The nasty" is not; "laughed at the poor ghost" is a constituent (for example, it can be replaced by just "laughed"), but "at the" is not.

Even the simple grammar in Table 5.1 can be used to generate a number of simple sentences. Let us start by applying some of these rewrite rules to show how we can generate a sentence (see example 4). The goal is to show how a particular sentence can be made up from the lowest level constituents (the terminal elements).

TABLE 5.1
A grammar for a fragment of English

S	$\rightarrow$ NP + VP	(A)
NP	$\rightarrow$ DET + N	(B)
NP	$\rightarrow$ N	(C)
VP	$\rightarrow$ V + NP	(D)
VP	$\rightarrow$ V	(E)
N	$\rightarrow$ Vlad, Boris, poltergeist, vampire, werewolf, ghost ...	
V	$\rightarrow$ loves, hates, likes, bites, is ...	
DET	$\rightarrow$ the, a, an ...	

Abbreviations	
S	sentence
NP	noun phrase
VP	verb phrase
N	noun
V	verb
DET	determiner

4. Starting with S, rule (A) from Table 5.1 gives us NP + VP.
    Rule (B) gives us DET + N + VP.
    Rule (D) gives us DET + N + V + NP.
    Rule (C) gives us DET + N + V + N.
    Then the substitution of words gives us the example sentence:
    "The vampire loves Boris."

This is obviously an extremely limited grammar. The most obvious omission is perhaps that we cannot construct more complex sentences with more than one clause in them. We could, however, do this by introducing conjunctions. A slightly more complex example would be using a relative clause with a relative pronoun (such as "which", "who", and "that") to produce sentences such as (5).

5. The vampire who loves Boris is laughing.

Chomsky showed that if we had a sufficiently complex phrase structure grammar, with many more rules, and more detailed restrictions on when particular rules could and could not be applied, we would satisfy our basic criterion in that we would have a description of a grammar that could generate all of the sentences of a language and none of the non-sentences. (Obviously another language, such as French or German, would have a different set of phrase structure rules.) We noted in Chapter 1 that there are potentially an infinite number of sentences in real languages, and you might wonder how we can get an infinite number of sentences from a finite number of rules and words. We can do this because of special rules based upon what are known as *iteration* and *recursion*. Iteration enables us to carry on repeating the same rule, potentially for ever. For example, we can use iteration to conjoin sentences such as (6):

6. The vampire loves the ghost and the ghost loves the werewolf and the werewolf loves the ghoul and ...

Recursion is even more important. Recursion is when a rule calls itself. The most important use of this is that we can embed a sentence within another sentence. We can use recursion to produce *centre-embedded sentences*. Examples (8) and (9) are based on (7).

7. The vampire loved the ghoul.
8. The vampire the werewolf hated loved the ghoul.
9. The vampire the werewolf the ghost scared hated loved the ghoul.

This process of centre-embedding could continue potentially for ever, and the sentence would still be perfectly well-formed; that is, it would still be grammatical. Of course, we would soon have difficulty in understanding such sentences, for we would soon lose track of who scared whom and who loved what (many people have difficulty with sentence 9!), and we might never produce even simple sentences of this type, but our grammar must be capable of producing them. Given a piece of paper and sufficient time, you could still parse sentences of this type. This reflects the distinction between competence and performance mentioned above: we have the competence to understand these sentences, even if we never produce them in actual performance.

However, remember that we desire more of a grammar than it merely being able to generate sentences. We need a way to describe the underlying syntactic structure of sentences. This is particularly important for syntactically ambiguous sentences. These are sentences which have more than one interpretation, such as example (10). This could be paraphrased as either "When I was flying to America, I saw the witches" or "There I was standing on the ground when I looked up and there were the witches flying off to America". A phrase structure grammar also enables us to describe the syntactic structure of a sentence by means of a tree diagram, as shown for our ambiguous sentence in Fig. 5.1. The points on the tree corresponding to constituents are called *nodes*. Nodes which are either at the top of the tree (the sentence or S node) or the bottom (corresponding to words) are called *terminal nodes*; all the others, corresponding to constituents such as NP and VP, are *non-terminal nodes*.

10.   I saw the witches flying to America.

Such tree diagrams are very important in the analysis of syntax and it is important to be clear as to what they mean. The underlying structure of a sentence or phrase is sometimes called its phrase structure or *phrase marker*. It should be reiterated that the important idea is capturing the underlying syntactic structure of sentences; it is not our goal to explain how we actually produce or understand them. Furthermore, at this stage directionality is not important; the directions of the arrows in Table 5.1 do not mean that we are limited to talking about sentence production. Our discussion at present applies equally to production and comprehension. Phrase structure rules provide us with the underlying syntactic structure of sentences we both produce and comprehend.

There are actually different types of phrase structure grammar. Context-free grammars contain only rules that are not specified for

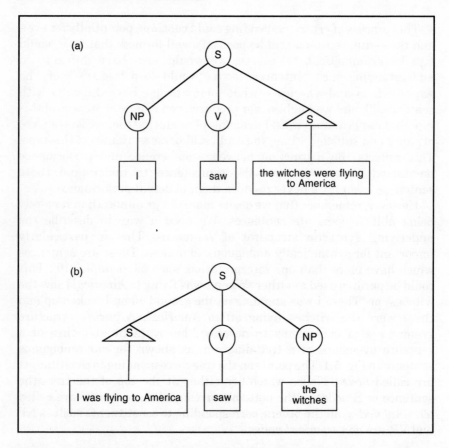

FIG. 5.1. Tree diagram of the alternative structures of sentence (10), "I saw the witches flying to America". The tree diagram captures the important distinction of exactly who was "flying to America".

particular contexts, while context-sensitive grammars contain at least some rules that can only be applied in certain circumstances. In a context-free rule, the left-hand symbol can always be rewritten by the right hand one regardless of the context in which it occurs. This is an important general problem but it even arises in our simple little grammar. The writing of a verb in its singular or plural form depends on the context of the preceding noun phrase (e.g. "Boris loves Vlad", but "The werewolves love Vlad").

Transformations. Chomsky argued that powerful as phrase structure grammar is, it is not up to the job of capturing our linguistic competence. Although it can produce any sentence of the language and none of the non-sentences, and also provide an account of the structure of sentences, it cannot explain the relationship between related sentences. Consider sentences (11) and (12).

11. The vampire chases the ghost.
12. The ghost is chased by the vampire.

Clearly our linguistic intuitions tell us that sentence (11) is related to sentence (12), but how can we capture this relationship in our grammar? There is no way of doing this in phrase structure grammar. Chomsky (1957) showed that this could be achieved by the introduction of special rewrite rules known as *transformations*. Transformations are so central to the theory that the whole approach became known as *transformational grammar*. A normal rewrite rule takes a single symbol on the left-hand side (e.g. S, NP, VP), and rewrites it as something else more complex. A transformation is a special type of rewrite rule that takes a string of symbols (i.e. more than one symbol) on the left-hand side, and rewrites this string as another string on the right-hand side. Sentences (11) and (12) above are related to each other by what is called the *passivisation* transformation; (12) is the passive form of the active form (11). The transformation that achieves this change looks like (13):

13. $NP_1 + V + NP_2 \rightarrow NP_2 + \text{auxiliary} + V^* + by + NP_1$

(where an *auxiliary* is a special verb, here "is", and the asterisk indicates that it is necessary to change the form of the main verb, here by changing the "–s" ending to an "–ed" ending).

There are many other types of transformations. For example, we can turn a declarative form of a sentence (11) into an interrogative or question form (14), or its affirmative form into a negative form (15). We can also combine transformations—for example, to form a negative question, as in (16).

14. Does the vampire chase the ghost?
15. The vampire is not chased by the ghost.
16. Does the vampire not chase the ghost?

Not only do transformations capture our intuitions about how sentences are related but they also enable the grammar to be greatly simplified, primarily because rules which enable us to rewrite strings as other strings capture many of the aspects of the dependencies between words (the context-sensitive aspect described above). Of course, in a fully fledged grammar the rules would be much more numerous and much more complex. For example, we have not addressed the issue of the details of the changes to the form of the verb, or specified the types of sentences to which passivisation can be applied.

Kernel sentences.   Chomsky (1957) distinguished between optional and obligatory transformations. In a way the passive transformation is optional; the active form of the sentence is perfectly grammatical, and we do not need to apply the transformation (although there might be good pragmatic reasons for doing so, such as to emphasise the object of the sentence). Some of the transformations Chomsky discussed are obligatory in that the sentence would be ungrammatical without them: examples include transformations introduced to cope with number agreement between nouns and verbs, and the introduction of "do" into negatives and questions. Generalised transformations (such as conjunctions) enable us to combine strings so as to produce sentences such as (17):

17.   The vampire chased the ghost and the werewolf chased the ghoul.

Chomsky defined a subset of sentences that he called kernel sentences, as they form the *kernel* of the language. Kernel sentences are those to which only obligatory transformations have been applied, and no optional or generalised transformations. They are therefore the active, affirmative, declarative form of English sentences. The concept of a kernel sentence proved important for early psycholinguistic experiments motivated by transformational grammar.

Surface and deep structure.   Chomsky (1965) presented a major revision of the theory. The changes were primarily concerned with, first, the structure of the linguistic system, and second, the nature of the syntactic rules.

In the later model there are three main components. First, a semantic system (which had no real counterpart in the earlier model) that assigns meaning to the syntactic strings; second, a phonological component that turns syntactic strings into phonological strings; and third, a syntactic component concerned with word ordering. This in turn has two components, a set of base rules (roughly equivalent to the earlier phrase structure rules), and transformational rules.

Perhaps the most important extension of the later theory was the introduction of the distinction between *deep structure* and *surface structure* (now called *d-structure* and *s-structure*). To some extent this was implicit in the earlier model with the concept of kernel sentences, but the revised model goes beyond that, in that every sentence has a deep structure and a surface structure. Furthermore there is no longer a distinction between optional and obligatory transformations. In a sense all transformations became obligatory, in that markers for them are represented in the deep structure.

In the standard theory, the syntactic component generates a deep structure and a surface structure for every sentence. The deep structure is the output of the base rules and the input to the semantic component; the surface structure is the output of the transformational rules and the input to the phonological rules. (It is important to note that this implies no processing order.) The syntactic and semantic primacy of the deep structure gives rise to two main advantages. First, some surface structures are ambiguous in that they have two different deep structures. Second, what is the subject and what is the object of the sentence is often unclear in the surface structure. Sentence (18) is ambiguous in its surface structure. However, there is no ambiguity in the corresponding deep structures, which can be paraphrased as (19) and (20).

18. The hunting of the vampires was terrible.
19. The way in which the vampires hunted was terrible.
20. It was terrible that the vampires were hunted.

Sentences (21) and (22) have the same surface structure, yet completely different deep structures.

21. Vlad is easy to please.
22. Vlad is eager to please.

In (21), Vlad is the object of please; in (22), Vlad is the subject of please. This can be made apparent in that it is possible to build a deep structure corresponding to (21) of the form of (22), but not for (22), as (24) is clearly ungrammatical in isolation. (This is indicated by the convention of the asterisk.)

23. It is easy to please Vlad.
24. * It is eager to please Vlad.

Later revisions. Chomsky's theory has continued to evolve. Although the basic goals of linguistics are the same, many of the features of the grammars have changed. In more modern versions of the grammar the rules are phrased in terms of what is called $\overline{X}$ (pronounced "X bar") syntax (Jackendoff, 1977; Kornai & Pullum, 1990). The most recent version of the theory is known as *government and binding* theory.

There have been five central moves in the more recent versions of the theory. First, with time, the number of transformations has steadily dwindled. Second, related to this, the importance of deep structure has also dwindled (Chomsky, 1991). Third, when constituents are moved from one place to another, they are hypothesised as leaving a *trace* (sometimes called a *gap*) in their original position. (This has nothing in common with the TRACE model of spoken word recognition.) Fourth, special emphasis is given to the most important word in each phrase. For example, in the noun phrase "the vampire with the garlic", the most important noun is clearly "vampire", not "garlic". (This should be made clear by the observation that the whole noun phrase is about the vampire, not the garlic.) The noun "vampire" is said to be the *head* of the noun phrase. Fifth, the revised theory permits units intermediate in size between nouns and noun phrases, and verbs and verb phrases. This makes the structure of phrase structure trees more complex. These intermediate units are called $\overline{N}$ (pronounced noun bar) and $\overline{V}$ (verb bar). They are made up of the head of a phrase plus any essential *arguments* or role players. Hence "king" is an N and the head of the phrase, "king of Transylvania" an $\overline{N}$ (because Transylvania is the argument of "king", the place which the king is king of), and "king of Transylvania with a lisp" an NP. This approach distinguishes between essential arguments (such as "of Transylvania") and optional *adjuncts* or modifiers (such as "with a lisp"). The same applies to verbs, which also have obligatory arguments (even if they are not always stated) and optional modifiers. The advantage of this description is that it captures new generalisations such as that if a noun phrase contains both arguments and adjuncts, the argument must always be closer to the head than the adjunct: "The king with a lisp of Transylvania" is distinctly odd. It is an important task of linguistics to capture and explain such generalisations. It also enables the specification of a very general rule such as (25).

25. $\overline{X} \rightarrow X + ZP*$

That is, any phrase (X-bar) contains a head followed by any number of modifiers. Such an abstract rule is a blueprint for the treatment of both noun phrases and verb phrases, and captures the underlying similarity between them. It shows that English is a *head-first* language. Japanese, on the other hand, is a head-last language. Nevertheless, both languages distinguish between heads and modifiers; this is an example of a very general rule that Chomsky argues must be innate. The *parameter* that specifies head-first or head-last is acquired through exposure to a particular language (Pinker, 1994).

Other linguistic approaches to syntax

All linguistic approaches to syntax show a debt to Chomsky's approach. In all of them idea of phrase structure rules is paramount. Other approaches differ in the extent to which they emphasise the role of semantics in syntactic processing, or the extent to which they emphasise transformations. One of the most influential early alternatives was that of *generative semantics* (Fillmore, 1968). This emphasised the role of the semantic component in grammar, and the way in which words in a sentence are assigned to semantic roles, or *cases*, as well as to syntactic roles. We will consider this in more detail in the next two chapters. The *lexical functional grammar* approach of Kaplan and Bresnan (1982; see also Bresnan, 1978) has enjoyed recent popularity. This takes the gradual down-grading of transformations that has been apparent in the evolution of Chomsky's ideas to the limit: surface structures are generated by phrase structure rules without any transformational component. The work is done instead by the specification of lexical roles and the appropriate expression of the agent and arguments. In addition, the lexicon has a much larger syntactic role to play. It contains information about the grammatical roles in which each word can partake and how a word is modified for tense and number, if this is applicable. Each sentence is given two types of syntactic description: first, a conventional phrase or constituent structure analysis of the surface structure; and second, a functional structure description which represents the grammatical relations in a sentence such as subject, object, predicate, and tense. The functional structure is partly determined by the lexical form of the main predicate. In constructing the constituent structure, the phrase rules are annotated by the appropriate functional relationships.

The formal power of grammars: Automata theory

This section is relatively technical and can be skipped, but the ideas discussed are useful for understanding the motivation of how powerful a grammar that can account for natural language has to be. It also reveals something of the difficulty of the task confronting the child who is trying to learn language. The study of different types of grammar and the devices that are necessary to produce them is part of the branch of mathematical linguistics or computational theory (a subject which combines logic, linguistics, and computer science) called *automata theory*. An automaton is a device, that can, among other things, produce grammars. It can be thought of as a type of machine, in the sense that a computer is a machine. It takes an input and performs some elementary operations according to some previously specified instructions to produce an output. It is not necessary to go into detail here, but the topic is of some importance because if we know how complex natural language is, we might expect this to place some constraints on the power of the grammar necessary to cope with it.

We have already defined a grammar as a device that can generate all the sentences of a language, but no non-sentences. In fact, there are many possible grammars which fall into a small number of distinct categories, each with different power. Each corresponds to a particular type of automaton, and each produces an increasingly complex language.

We cannot produce all the sentences of natural language simply by listing them, because there are an infinite number of grammatically acceptable sentences. We have seen that this is because the grammatical rules for human language include iteration and recursion. Hence our grammar must be capable of producing these rules. We have also seen that some rules appear to need to be sensitive with respect to the context in which the symbols they manipulate occur. Context-free and context-sensitive grammars simply differ in whether they need rules that can be specified independently of the context in which the elements occur. How powerful is natural language, and how powerful is the grammar that produces it?

The simplest type of automaton is known as a finite-state device. This is a simple device that moves from one state to another depending on only its present state and current input, and produces what is known as a Type 3 grammar. The present state is determined by some finite number of previous symbols (words). Type 3 grammars are also known as right-linear grammars, because every rewrite rule can only be of the form $A \rightarrow B$ or $A \rightarrow xB$, where x is a terminal element. This produces right-branching tree structure trees. Next up in power is a push-down automaton. This is an improvement on a finite-state device because it has a memory; the memory is limited, however, in that it is only a push-down stack. A push-down stack is a special type of memory where only the last item stored on the stack can be retrieved; if you want to get at something stored before the last thing, everything stored since will be lost. It produces Type 2 grammars which can parse context-free languages. Next in power is a linear-bounded automaton, which has a limited memory, but can retrieve anything from this memory. It produces Type 1 grammars, parsing context-sensitive languages. Finally, the most powerful automaton, a Turing machine, has no limitations, and produces a type 0 grammar.

Chomsky (1957) showed that natural language cannot be characterised by a finite-state device. In particular, it cannot produce arbitrarily long sequences of multiple centre-embedded structures. In addition to centre-embedding, there are other more complex relationships between words in a sentence. For this, recursion is necessary, and recursion is beyond the scope of finite state devices. Although this might seem obvious to you now, at the time, it was surprising: theories of language were dominated by behaviourism and information theory, and it was thought that knowledge of the previous states was all that was necessary to account for human language. In effect Chomsky showed that no matter how many previous words were taken into account, a finite state device cannot produce or understand natural language. An important extension of this argument is that children cannot learn language simply by conditioning. But Chomsky went further and argued that neither context-free nor context-sensitive grammars provided an account of human language. He showed that it is necessary to add transformations to a phrase structure grammar; the resulting grammar is then a Type 0 grammar, and can only be produced by a Turing machine. We have seen that one reason why Chomsky thought that transformations were necessary is that they are needed to show how sentences are related to each other. Also, they simplify the phrase structure rules necessary and provide a more elegant treatment of the language. Finally, there is some linguistic evidence that seems to show that no context-free or context-sensitive grammar can account for certain constructions found in natural language. For example, Postal (1964) argued that the Mohawk language contains *intercalated dependencies*, in which words are cross-related (such as a1 a2 ... an b1 b2 bn, where a1 relates to b1, and so on). Hence it seems that natural human language can only be produced by the most powerful of all types of grammar.

Although this conclusion was accepted for a long time, it has recently become an issue of debate. First, it is not clear that all the complex dependencies between words described by Chomsky and Postal are necessarily grammatical. Second, there is a surprising formal demonstration by Peters and Ritchie (1973) that context can be taken into account without exceeding the power of a context-free grammar. The trend in modern linguistics then is once again towards examining less powerful grammars.

Psycholinguistic evaluation
So far we have seen how linguistics has captured the syntactic structure of language. Although this is necessary for a complete theory of language, does this approach contribute anything to our understanding of the processes involved in producing and understanding syntactic structures? Early on, when Chomsky's work first appeared, there was great optimism that it would also be an account of the processes involved in producing and understanding syntax. Two ideas attracted particular interest and were considered easily testable: these were the *derivational*

theory of complexity (DTC), and the *autonomy of syntax*. The idea of the derivational theory of complexity is that the more complex is the syntactic derivation of a sentence—that is, the more transformations are necessary to form it—the more complex the psychological processing necessary to understand or produce it. This means that transformationally complex sentences should be harder to process than less complex sentences, which could be detected by an appropriate measure such as reaction times. The psychological principle of the autonomy of syntax takes Chomsky's assertion that syntactic rules should be specified independently of other constraints further, to mean that syntactic processes operate independently of other ones. This is another manifestation of the principle of autonomy that has recurred throughout earlier chapters.

Miller and McKean (1964) tested the idea that the more transformations there are in a sentence, the more difficult it is to process. They looked at "detransformation" reaction times to the sentences such as in (26) to (30). Subjects were told that they would have to make a particular transformation, and then press a button when they had done so. Miller and McKean measured these times.

26.   The robot shoots the ghost.
       0 transformations (active affirmative)
27.   The ghost is shot by the robot.
       1 transformation (passive affirmative)
28.   The robot does not shoot the ghost.
       1 transformation (active negative)
29.   The ghost is not shot by the robot.
       2 transformations (passive negative)
30.   Is the ghost not shot by the robot?
       3 transformations
       (passive negative question)

Sentence (26) is the starting point—it is the kernel sentence in the terminology described above, and of course has no (optional) transformations in its syntactic representation. We can derive increasingly complex sentences from this kernel: for example, (29) is derived from (26) by the application of three transformations: passivisation, negativisation, and question formation. Miller and McKean found that the time it took to detransform sentences with transformations back to the kernel was linearly related to the number of transformations in them. That is, the more transformations a subject has to make, the longer it takes them to do it. This was interpreted as supporting the psychological reality of transformational grammar.

Other experiments around this time appeared to corroborate this result. Savin and Perchonock (1965) found that sentences with more transformations in them took up more memory space. The more transformationally complex a sentence was, the fewer items could subjects simultaneously remember from a list of unrelated words. Mehler (1963) found that when subjects made errors in remembering sentences, they tended to do it in the direction of forgetting transformational tags, rather than adding them. It was as though subjects remembered sentences in the form of "kernel plus transformation".

Problems with transformational grammar.   The tasks that appear to support transformational grammar all involved somewhat odd or indirect tasks. If we ask subjects explicitly to detransform sentences, it is perhaps not surprising that the time it takes to do this reflects the number of transformations involved. This is not a task we routinely do in language comprehension, however. Would we still find for the derivational theory of complexity if we do not explicitly demand this of our subjects? Furthermore, memory measures are not an *on-line measure* of what is happening in sentence processing; at best they are reflecting a side-effect. What we remember of a sentence need have no relationship with how we actually processed that sentence. Other findings that were difficult to fit into this framework soon emerged.

Slobin (1966a) performed an experiment similar to the original detransformation experiment of Miller and McKean, in which he examined the processing of what are called *reversible* and *irreversible passive* sentences. A reversible passive is one where the subject and object of the sentence can be reversed and the sentence still makes sense. An irreversible passive is one which does not make sense after this reversal. If you swap the subject and object in (31) you get (33), which makes perfect sense, whereas if you do this to (32) you get (34), which although not ungrammatical, is rather odd—it is said to be *semantically anomalous*.

31.   The ghost was chased by the robot.
32.   The flowers were watered by the robot.
33.   The robot was chased by the ghost.
34.   ? The robot was watered by the flowers.

In the case of an irreversible passive, you can work out what is the subject of the sentence and what is the object by semantic clues alone. With a reversible passive, you have to do some syntactic work. Slobin found that Miller and McKean's results could only be obtained for reversible passives. Hence detransformational parsing only appears to be necessary when there are not sufficient cues to the meaning of the sentence from elsewhere. This result means that the derivational theory of complexity is not always true: complexity only involves parsing in the absence of semantic cues.

Slobin's result that the depth of syntactic processing is affected by semantic considerations is also counter to the idea of the autonomy of syntax. This conclusion was supported by an experiment by Wason (1965) on the relationship between the structure of a sentence and its function. He measured how long it took subjects to complete sentences describing an array of eight coloured circles, seven of which were red and one of which was blue. It is more natural to use a negative in a context of "plausible denial"—that is, it is more appropriate to say "this circle is not red" of the exception than of each of the others "this circle is not blue". That is, the time it takes to process a syntactic construction such as negative-formation depends upon the semantic context.

In summary, early claims supporting the ideas of derivational complexity and autonomy of syntax in linguistic performance that were derived from Chomskyan grammar were at best premature, and perhaps just wrong.

Evaluation of linguistic approaches

Linguistic approaches have given us a useful terminology for talking about syntax. It also illuminates how powerful the grammar that underlies human language must be. Chomsky's theory of transformational grammar also had a major influence upon the way in which psychological syntactic processing was thought to take place. In particular, the ideas of the autonomy of syntax and the derivational theory of complexity were put to the empirical sword. However, despite initial promise, later experiments provided negative evidence for their psychological reality as processing features. Chomsky and other linguists had a simple retreat available: linguistic theories describe our linguistic competence rather than our linguistic performance. That is, transformational grammar is a description of our knowledge of our language, and the constraints upon language acquisition, rather than an account of the processes involved in parsing on a moment to moment basis. This has effectively led to a separation of linguistics and psycholinguistics, with each pursuing these different goals. Miller, who first provided apparent empirical support for the psychological reality of transformation grammar, later came to believe that all the time taken up in sentence processing was used in semantic operations.

ARTIFICIAL INTELLIGENCE (AI) APPROACHES TO PARSING

Many of the psycholinguistic ideas about parsing and syntax have been borrowed from other areas. We have seen that linguistics had a strong influence in the 1960s, and we shall now see that artificial intelligence was influential during the 1970s.

The earliest AI parsers, such as ELIZA and SHRDLU discussed in Chapter 1, had very primitive syntactic processing abilities. ELIZA used templates for sentence recognition, and cannot really in any sense be said to have parsed sentences. SHRDLU was a little more sophisticated, containing a syntactic processor, but this was dedicated to the extraction of the limited semantic information necessary to move around "blocksworld". It cannot be said to illuminate any aspect of real syntactic parsing. Indeed, early AI parsers lacked the computational power of transformational grammar. This was first obtained with augmented transition networks.

Augmented Transition Networks (ATNs)

Augmented transition networks (abbreviated to ATNs) are parsing devices with a computational power equivalent to transformational grammar. Hence they are powerful enough in principle to parse any sentence; the question is do they do so in a way similar to humans? The first ATN was constructed by Woods (1970), but they were introduced into the mainstream psycholinguistic literature by Kaplan (1972). An ATN can be thought of as a network of networks, each of which can do a simple parsing task, such as recognising a noun phrase. An example is given in Fig. 5.2.

Each of these small networks that carry out specific tasks is called a transition network, and each of these is equivalent in power to a finite state device. ATNs comprise a recursive hierarchy of these networks. At the lowest level, they are made up out of states corresponding to syntactic constituents such as NP, VP, N, or V, joined by what are called *arcs*. They parse *top-down*, in that they start with the sentence S constituent and work down through smaller and smaller constituents until they find a match. So for example, they might begin looking for a NP; to do this they might look for a determiner; if the first word of the sentence is a determiner then all well and good: the determiner forms the first item of the parse tree and the ATN moves on to try and parse the second word. If it is not a determiner, the ATN has to back-up and try something else—for example, trying to parse the first word as a proper noun. If this does not work then an initial parse other than an NP will have to be tried. This type of repetitive process is very well suited

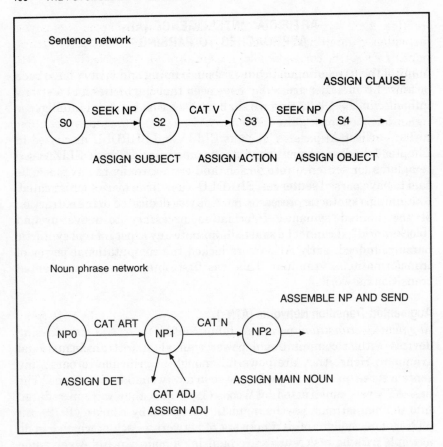

FIG. 5.2. A simplified augmented transition network (ATN). (Based on Wanner & Maratsos, 1978, p. 124.)

to computer simulation. Transitions to other sub-networks can occur when a phrase or word is analysed. ATNs are one-stage parsing devices, in that the parser attempts to build the parse tree in one go; it does not first build a number of sub-trees which it tries to assemble later.

As such, a recursive network of networks is equal in power to a context-free phrase structure. What gives ATNs their particular power is that there can be conditions on the arcs between states and actions to be performed when arcs are transversed. These conditions are what augment the power of the network and gives them their names. These conditions perform the work of transformations. Examples include SEEK NP, ASSIGN SUBJECT, and IF ENCOUNTER PASSIVE VERB THEN RELABEL SUBJECT AS OBJECT. The last example, for example, mimics the action of the passivisation transformation. There are five main types of arc: CAT (which is transversed whenever particular grammatical lexical categories such as N, V, or ADJ are found), SEEK (the corresponding arc for phrasal categories such as NP and VP); WORD (an action to be performed when a special word is found, such as "by"); JUMP (enabling the parser to move between two states without finding a constituent); and SEND (which returns control to higher level network). Of course an ATN for a real language would be much more complex than Fig. 5.2.

As with many theories, ATNs have become considerably more complex since their initial formulation. For example, the PARSIFAL parser of Marcus (1980) combines the top-down parsing of the original design with bottom-up processing which uses the syntactic category of particular words to generate hypotheses about what constituent is involved. For example, if you identify the first word of a constituent as a determiner (e.g. "the"), it is likely that you have encountered a noun phrase.

Psycholinguistic evaluation of ATNs. There is no doubt that from an AI perspective, ATNs are a useful technology for parsing sentences. But are the mechanisms they employ anything like what humans do in parsing? Wanner and Maratsos (1978) tested predictions from ATNs about parsing performance. They measured the processing load while subjects were parsing sentences by interrupting these sentences at different points and presenting a set of unrelated words which the subjects later had to recall. These measures of transient processing load accorded with how ATNs behave: in an ATN, constituents which were held in buffers while sub-networks were being transversed would obviously decrease spare memory capacity for other, unrelated words.

The problem with this type of experiment is that it is likely that any other model of parsing will give the same result. We would expect our processing resources to be used most at syntactically difficult parts of the sentence. Another problem is that any type of parser which is top-down is implausible as a model of how we parse. Just think of how many different possible syntactic ways there are of starting a sentence; an ATN can only really get to work when it has hit upon assigning the initial constituent to the correct syntactic category. Generally, this type of parser is likely to involve far too much back-tracking—going back and trying a different parse until it gets it right. It is likely that human parsing involves a much greater bottom-up component. Mixed parsers, such as PARSIFAL, fare better. So although AI has been very useful in making us think explicitly about the exact mechanisms involved in parsing, we must look at some of the techniques we actually use.

PSYCHOLINGUISTIC APPROACHES TO PARSING

We have looked at both the linguistic and AI approaches to parsing, and found them wanting as full accounts of the human sentence parsing mechanism. We shall now look at some specifically psycholinguistic approaches.

What size are the units of parsing?

What are the constituents in parsing, and how big are they? Jarvella (1971) showed that listeners only begin to purge memory of the details of syntactic constituents after a sentence boundary has been passed. Once a sentence has been processed, verbatim memory fades very quickly after. Hence, perhaps not surprisingly, the sentence is a major processing unit. Beneath this, the clause also turns out to be an important unit. A clause is a part of a sentence which has both a subject and predicate—that is, a noun phrase plus verb phrase. Both Caplan (1972) and Jarvella (1971) showed that there was a clause boundary effect in recalling words: it is easiest to recall words from within the current clause, independent of the number of words in the clause. Also, the processing load is highest at the end of the clause, and eye fixations are longer on the last word (Just & Carpenter, 1980). We probably do not sit idly by while we wait for the clause to finish: Ford, Besnan, and Kaplan (1982) emphasise the importance of building up the parse tree incrementally—that is, on a word-by-word basis, rather than waiting until a whole clause is available. This makes a lot of sense from a processing point of view.

For early psycholinguists still influenced by ideas from transformational grammar such as the autonomy of syntax, the process of language understanding went something like this. First, we identify the words using only perceptual data. Recognition and lexical access give us access to the syntactic category of the words. We can use these to build a parse tree for each clause. It is only when each clause is completely analysed that we finally start to build a semantic representation of the sentence. This, of course, is the extreme autonomy viewpoint.

Click displacement studies.   One of the most controversial techniques used to explore the size of the syntactic unit in parsing, and that purported to show that syntactic units were extremely important from the earliest stages of processing, was the *click displacement technique* (Fodor & Bever, 1965; Garrett, Bever, & Fodor, 1966). The basic idea of this is that major processing units resist interruption: we finish what we are doing, and then process other material at the first suitable opportunity. Subjects heard speech over headphones in one ear, and at certain points in the sentence, extraneous clicks were presented in the other ear. Even if the click falls in the middle of a real constituent, it should be perceived as falling at a constituent boundary. That is, the clicks should appear to migrate according to listeners' reports. This is what was observed.

35.   That he was* happy was evident from the way he smiled.

For example, a click presented at * in (35) migrated to after the end of the word "happy". This is at the end of a major constituent, at the end of the clause. The original study was claimed to show that the clause is a major perceptual unit. The same results were found when all non-syntactic perceptual cues, such as intonation and pauses, were removed. This suggests that the clause is a major unit of perceptual and syntactic processing.

This interpretation may however be premature. The subjects' task is a complex one: they have to perceive the sentence, parse it, understand it, remember it, and give their response. Click migration could occur at any of these points, not just perception or parsing. Reber and Anderson (1970) carried out a variant of the technique in which subjects listened to sentences which actually had no clicks at all. They were told that it was an experiment on subliminal perception, and asked to say where they thought the clicks occurred. Subjects still placed the non-existent clicks at constituent boundaries. This suggests that click migration occurs in the response stage: subjects are intuitively aware of the existence of constituent boundaries and have a response bias to put clicks there. Wingfield and Klein (1971) showed that the size of the migration effect is greatly reduced if subjects can point to places in the sentence on a visual display at the same time as they hear them, rather than having to remember them. It was also unclear whether intonation and pausing are as unimportant in determining structural boundaries as was originally claimed.

In summary, the clause is doubtless an important unit in sentence processing. It is less clear that this is because of the importance of syntactic processing from the earliest stages, independent of perceptual and semantic characteristics. Major syntactic units usually correspond to major semantic units, and it can be quite difficult to disentangle these components.

Surface structure strategies

Both autonomists and interactionists would accept that we use both syntactic and semantic information to construct a representation of the underlying meaning of the sentence which we are reading or hearing. An autonomist would argue that we start work on the semantic representation after we have constructed a syntactic representation of the current clause, while an interactionist permits semantic information to guide parsing within the clause. A more extreme version is that we construct the semantic representation directly, using syntactic information only when necessary. Nevertheless, although the relative importance of syntactic and semantic information may differ between the two positions, both would agree that at least some of the time we have to identify the syntactic constituents of the sentence. Now, the surface structure of the sentence often provides a number of obvious cues to the underlying syntactic representation. One obvious approach is to use these cues, and use a number of simple strategies that enable us to compute the syntactic structure.

The earliest detailed expositions of this idea were by Bever (1970) and Fodor and Garrett (1967). These researchers detailed a number of parsing strategies that used only surface structure cues. Perhaps the simplest example is that when we see or hear a determiner such as "the" or "a", we know a noun phrase has just started. A second example is based upon the observation that although word order is variable in English, and transformations such as passivisation can change it, the common structure noun–verb–noun often maps on to what is called the *canonical sentence structure* SVO (subject–verb–object). That is, in most sentences we hear or read, the first noun is the subject, and the second one the object. In fact, if we made use of this strategy we could get a long way in comprehension. This is called the canonical sentence strategy. Comprehenders try the simpler strategies first, and if these do not work, they try other ones. If the battery of surface structure strategies become exhausted by a sentence, they must try something else, and these are the sentences that we find harder to understand.

This type of approach was developed by Fodor, Bever, and Garrett (1974), which is one of the most influential works in the history of psycholinguistics. They argued that the goal of parsing was recovering the underlying, deep structure of a sentence. As it had been shown that this was not done by explicitly undoing transformations, it must be done by perceptual heuristics; that is, our surface structure cues. However, there is little evidence that deep structure is represented mentally independently of meaning (Johnson-Laird, 1983). Nevertheless, the general principle that when we parse we use surface structure cues, has remained influential, and has been increasingly formalised.

Kimball's seven principles of surface structure parsing

Kimball (1973) extended the surface structure cue approach, and proposed seven principles of parsing to explain the behaviour of the human sentence parsing mechanism. He argued that we initially compute the surface structure of a sentence guided by rules that are based upon psychological constraints such as minimising the load on working memory. He argued that these principles answered the three main questions about parsing we raised above: Why are sentences assigned the structure or phrase markers that they are? Why are we biased to parse many structurally ambiguous sentences in a certain way? And why are some sentences harder to parse than others? The seven principles are as follows; naturally there is overlap with the perceptual strategies described by Bever.

1. Parsing is top-down.   This principle says that parsing is top-down, except when a conjunction (such as "and") is encountered. It means that we start from the sentence node and predict constituents, as do ATNs, rather than combining lower level constituents until we reach the sentence node. However, to avoid an excessive amount of back-tracking, the parser employs limited *lookahead* of one or two words. In effect this means that you might examine the first word of the next constituent, see it is "the", and then you know that a noun phrase is coming next, which means that the next word will be either a noun or an adjective.

2. Right association.   Right association says that new words are preferentially attached to the lowest possible non-terminal node in the partially constructed phrase marker. This is one of the most important and influential of the seven principles. Consider the ambiguous sentence (36).

36.   Vlad figured that Boris wanted to take the pet rat out.

Here we attach "out" to the right-most available constituent, "take" rather than "figure". That is, although this structure is ambiguous, we prefer the interpretation "take out" to "figured out" (see Fig. 5.3). This places less of a load on memory. Right association gives English its typically right branching structure, and it also explains why sentence (37) is difficult. The most plausible semantic interpretation necessitates attaching "out" to high in the parse tree, contrary to the preferred right attachment.

37.   Boris figured that Vlad wanted to take the plane to Quito out.

3. New nodes.   Function words (small words that do the grammatical work of the language, such as determiners like "the", "a", prepositions, and conjunctions) signal a new phrasal node—either a NP (noun phrase), PP (prepositional phrase), or embedded S (embedded

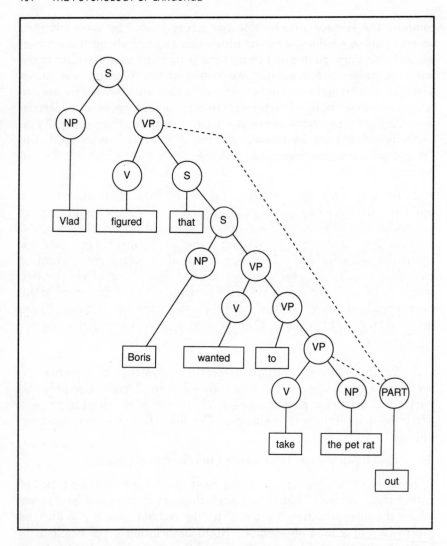

FIG. 5.3. Alternative structures for the sentence "Vlad figured that Boris wanted to take the pet rat out", showing how right association leads us to attach "out" to the right-most verb phrase node, "take", rather than to the higher verb node, "figured". (S = sentence, NP = noun phrase, VP = verb phrase, V = verb, PART = participle.)

sentence). Complementisers ("which", "that") are particularly important in that they signal that a sentence is embedded within another. For example, in constituent analysis the sentence "The vampire that the ghost laughed at felt sad" really contains two sentences: "The vampire felt sad" and "The ghost laughed at the vampire"; although the vampire in question is of course the same in both sentences.

4. Principle of two sentences.   At any one time, the parser can only cope with nodes associated with two sentence nodes. For example, centre-embedding splits up noun phrases and verb phrases associated with the sentences so that they have to be held in memory; when there are two embedded clauses, *daughters* of three sentence nodes will have to be kept active at once. Daughters are nodes immediately dominated by sentence nodes. Hence sentences of this sort (e.g. 38) will be difficult. Corresponding right-branching paraphrases such as (39) cause no difficulty, because the sentence nodes do not need to be kept open in working memory.

38.   The vampire the ghost the witch liked loved died.
39.   The witch liked the ghost that loved the vampire that died.

It is important to bear in mind here the distinction between daughters and lower level constituents. This principle explains why multiple centre-embedded constructions cause us particular difficulty.

5. Principle of closure.   The parser prefers to close a phrase as soon as is possible. Bever's canonical sentence strategy is a special case of this.

6. Fixed structure.   Having closed a phrase, it is computationally costly to reopen it and reorganise the previously closed constituents, and so this is avoided if possible. This principle explains our difficulty with *garden path* sentences where a preferred structure is assigned to a temporarily ambiguous sentence fragment (such as 40). Garden path sentences are discussed in detail in Chapter 9.

40.   The old man the boats.

7. Processing.   When a phrase is closed it exits from short-term memory and is passed onto a second stage of deeper, semantic processing. This principle underlies the earlier principles of new nodes, two sentences, closure, and fixed structure. Short-term memory of course has limited capacity. As we shall see in Chapter 7, details of the syntactic structure of a sentence are very quickly forgotten.

Evaluation of Kimball's principles.   These principles do a good job of explaining a number of properties of the HSPM. However, given that the principle of processing underlies so many of the others, perhaps the model can be simplified even further to reflect this? In addition, there are some problems with particular strategies. For example, eye fixation research shows that we may not always gaze at some function words. Hence their role in parsing might not be as important as Kimball thought.

This type of model is still autonomous: the syntactic structure is computed according to surface structure syntactic cues, and only after the closure of major syntactic units are the results shunted off to the stage of semantic analysis.

Fodor and Frazier and the sausage machine

Frazier and Fodor (1978) simplified Kimball's account by proposing a model they nicknamed the "sausage machine", because it divides the language input into something that looks like a link of sausages. The sausage machine is a two-stage model. The first stage is the called the *preliminary phrase packager*, or PPP, which is followed by the *sentence structure supervisor*, or SSS. The PPP has a limited viewing window of about six words, and cannot attach words to structures that reflect dependencies longer than this. The SSS assembles the packets produced by the PPP, but cannot itself undo the work of the PPP. The idea of the limited length of the PPP, and a second stage of processing which cannot undo the work of the first, makes concrete how Kimball's "processing" principle operates.

There is an additional constraint, originally called *minimal attachment* (Frazier & Fodor, 1978), which says that if there is a choice of ways of attaching a new node to the partial phrase marker, the simpler structure is preferred. *Simpler* is then defined as the structure which results in there being fewer nodes intervening between the new node and the existing phrase marker. But because the PPP which does this has a view limited to six words, it can only be simpler in a local context.

This two-stage, limited window architecture leads to the development of parsing strategies. Right association arises because the PPP can only see six words of a sentence; therefore it cannot attach a new word to any node that has fallen off to the left of the window. Minimal attachment arises because of a race. The first combination of syntactic rules to incorporate the current word into the phrase structure wins, and the fewer the nodes to be processed, the sooner the new item is likely to be incorporated into the parse tree. Principles such as right association then emerge without the principle having to be stated explicitly. Therefore Frazier and Fodor argue that the sausage machine provides a more parsimonious account than Kimball's seven principles. Furthermore, they argue that it provides a better reading of some sentences, such as (41).

41.   Vlad bought the stake for Boris.

As this fits in the six-word window, we prefer the simpler structure, even though it is not the right associated structure, "bought for Boris". That is, we prefer to attach "for Boris" to "bought", as minimal attachment predicts, rather than "the stake", as right association predicts (see Fig. 5.4).

In longer sentences such as (42), however, there is no option but to go for the lower, right attachment, as the alternative node is out of the limited window of the PPP and has been passed onto the SSS.

42.   Vlad bought the stake that I had been trying to obtain for Boris.

In this case the PPP cannot see the higher available node. Thus the sausage machine appears to conform implicitly to right association in longer sentences.

The limited parsing window of the PPP also explains why multiple centre-embedded sentences are hard, as they exceed its capacity. It also explains why if phrases are lengthened so that each one can be closed in a window, they can be passed on to be assembled correctly by the SSS. In (43) the phrases (with boundaries marked by |) can each be closed within a single window.

43.   The very beautiful young witch | the vampire the girl loved | met on a flight to Quito | died of sunstroke in 1872.

These types of sentence are much harder if the function words are deleted. This makes the task of the PPP much more difficult. The sausage machine also provides an account of the parsing of temporary ambiguity.

Evaluation of the sausage machine.   Wanner (1980) provided a detailed critique of the sausage machine, arguing that ATNs can do the same thing as the sausage machine, only better. He listed a number of problematical sentences for the sausage machine. For example, there are some six word sentences which are triply embedded, but because they are so short, should fit easily into the PPP window (e.g. 44). Nevertheless, we still find them difficult to understand.

44.   Vampires werewolves rats kiss love sleep.

Furthermore, there are some six word sentences where right association operates when minimal attachment is unable to choose between the alternatives, as they both involve the same number of intervening nodes (45).

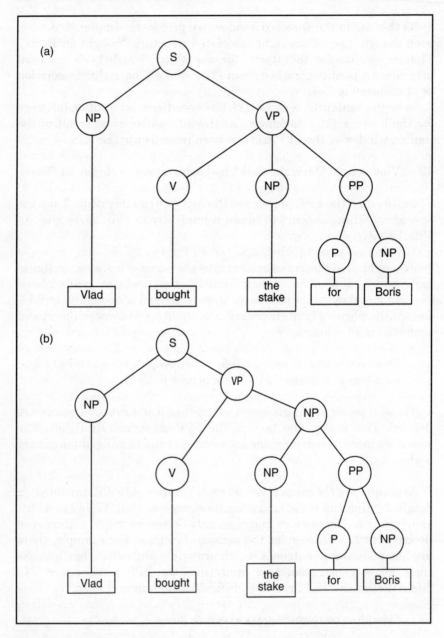

FIG. 5.4. Minimal attachment (a) versus right association (b) interpretations of the sentence "Vlad bought the stake for Boris". (a) is simpler than (b) because there are fewer nodes under the VP node. (S = sentence, NP = noun phrase, VP = verb phrase, V = verb, PP = prepositional phrase, P = preposition.)

45.   Vlad said that Boris cried yesterday.

Here we prefer the interpretation "cried yesterday" to "said yesterday". The sausage machine cannot account for the preference for right association in some six word sentences.

In reply, Fodor and Frazier (1980) conceded that right association does not arise directly from the sausage machine's architecture. Instead, they added a new principle that governs the performance of the sausage machine, which says that right association operates when minimal attachment cannot determine where a constituent should go. Right association refers to the original principle proposed by Kimball (1973), whereas *local association* is the specific principle attributed to the limited capacity of the PPP. Another refinement was proposed by Milsark (1983), who argued that the window of the PPP was limited to a single clause, not to six words.

These changes make the sausage machine less attractive, as one of its primary motivations was to provide a parsimonious account of parsing: the principles that appear to govern parsing should be derived from the architecture of the parsing system. Nevertheless the model remains one of the most comprehensive and clearly motivated that we have of the syntactic approach to comprehension. The principles of *minimal attachment* ("do not postulate any unnecessary nodes") and *late closure* ("if grammatically possible, attach new items into the phrase or clause currently being processed") still play an influential if controversial role in parsing preferences (Frazier, 1987a).

The main challenge facing all of these syntactic accounts of parsing is to show first of all that syntactic cues or principles, or the architecture of the parser, can account for our preferences and difficulties in parsing. Perhaps it is also the case, however that semantic considerations determine or contribute to these. Perhaps semantic considerations even determine how the parse tree is constructed.

Recent advances in understanding parsing

Even if the sausage machine is an incomplete account of parsing, it is clear that working memory constraints play an important role (MacDonald, Just, & Carpenter, 1992). Listeners do not hold all possible parses of a sentence in memory in parallel; instead, we parse *depth first*, choosing the most plausible parse until there is reason to change it. What determines what is most plausible is discussed in our analysis of garden path sentences in Chapter 9. This means that the way in which readers parse sentences depends upon their reading working memory capacity, so that readers with a larger capacity can hold alternative representations of an ambiguous sentence for longer than readers with smaller capacities. Hence analysis of parsing strategies can tell us something about what distinguishes good from poor readers.

In recent years there has been something of an explosion in experimental work on parsing. Two main experimental techniques have been popular, and each tells us how much time readers are spending analysing different parts of the sentence. The first is *self-paced reading*. In this technique subjects read a computer display and press a key every time they are ready for a new word. The second is the study of *eye movements*. In addition to telling us how long subjects are spending looking at each part of the sentence, this technique has the advantage that it tells us if subjects look back to earlier parts of the sentence (that is, whether or not and where they make regressive movements).

Recent work supports the idea that parsing is a two-stage process (Crain & Steedman, 1985; Mitchell, 1987), although the nature of the stages is different from that in the sausage machine. In the first stage or pass, words are assigned an immediate syntactic categorisation, and this is used to construct a single preliminary phrase structure. In the second stage, this initial structure is checked for consistency against other information, such as the structure assigned to other parts of the sentence, and semantic or contextual information. At this stage the initial working hypothesis is either retained, or a decision made to construct an alternative. The first stage is called the *director* or *assembler*, and the second stage the *monitor*. As we shall see in Chapter 9, the first stage of parsing may make use of detailed lexical information about words—such as the detailed types of structures that different verbs can take part in, called the *subcategorisation* information of the verb, or *verb control* information (see Clifton, Frazier, & Connine, 1984; Ford, Bresnan, & Kaplan, 1982; Mitchell & Holmes, 1985; Mitchell, 1987; and Tanenhaus & Carlson, 1989, for a review). The issue here is whether the initial stage operates in serial, constructing a single syntactic representation solely on the basis of syntactic information, or whether it generates the alternatives in parallel and then uses thematic information to choose among them, or whether it uses some hybrid strategy (Mitchell, 1994). The second stage of parsing may also make use of verb control information to evaluate alternative structures, such as how best gaps should be filled (Frazier, Clifton, & Randall, 1983; Mitchell, 1987). In any case, many consider that detailed information about words, or *lexical guidance*, is more important in determining parsing preferences than general parsing strategies such as minimal attachment (Holmes, 1987; Holmes, Kennedy, & Murray, 1987; but see Frazier, 1987a, for a dissenting view).

There is also an accumulation of evidence for the importance of gaps or traces and the dislocated constituents that fill them. First, traces place a strain on memory: the dislocated constituent has to be held in memory until the trace is reached. Second, processing of the trace can be detected in measurements of the brain's electrical activity (Garnsey, Tanenhaus, & Chapman, 1989; Kluender & Kutas, 1993). Third, the parser ranks tying to assign fillers to gaps as extremely important, an idea called the *active filler hypothesis* (Frazier & Clifton, 1989). Fourth, all languages seem to employ a *recent filler* strategy whereby in cases of ambiguity a gap is filled with the most recent grammatically plausible filler (Frazier, 1987a). Fifth, traces can prime or facilitate the recognition of the dislocated constituents or antecedents with which they are associated (Bever & McElree, 1988). Hence in a sentence (46) the (astute lawyer) is the antecedent of the trace [t]; in the corresponding control sentence (47) there is no trace, as no constituent has been moved.

46.   (The astute lawyer), who faced the female judge, was certain [$_t$] to argue during the trial.

47.   The astute lawyer, who faced the female judge, hated the long speeches during the trial.

We find that the gap in (46) does indeed facilitate the recognition of a probe word from the antecedent (e.g. "astute"), compared with the control sentence (47). This is strong evidence for the psycholinguistic reality of traces: when we find a trace, we retrieve its associated antecedent—a process known as binding the dislocated constituent to the trace, thereby making it more accessible. Priming effects are still found when possible confounding differences between the test and control sentences are eliminated (MacDonald, 1989).

It should also be noted that sometimes the gap is ambiguous: that is, there is choice in how it should be filled. Most current work on parsing revolves around how we cope with syntactic ambiguity: how we choose among alternatives, what determines our parsing preferences, and how we deal with temporary ambiguity (garden path sentences). This topic will be discussed in detail in Chapter 9, when we examine the autonomy of the syntactic processor. Is parsing a self-contained module, or does it also recruit other types of information?

CONCLUDING SUMMARY

Syntax concerns the rules that govern word order. Both linguistics and artificial intelligence have had a strong influence upon the approaches taken to investigating syntax, but a pure psycholinguistic approach has emerged, perhaps not surprisingly, as the approach most suited to investigating syntactic processing. Linguistic theories such as *transformational grammar* were not supported by experimental data. This is because such theories provide an account of our linguistic competence rather than our actual performance.

Any account of parsing must answer three questions: Why are sentences assigned the structure that they are? Why are we biased to parse structurally ambiguous sentences in a certain way? Why are some sentences harder to parse than others? Psycholinguistic approaches emphasise the role of particular cues and strategies in parsing, and show how these answer these questions. Kimball detailed seven principles that give a good account of parsing. Frazier and Fodor's sausage machine showed how these principles could be simplified in that they are a consequence of the architecture of a two-stage parser where the first stage has a limited window. Even so, the sausage machine cannot account for all of our parsing behaviour; an additional rule, local attachment, emphasising the simplicity of syntactic structures within a local context, must be introduced. At present, the data favour a model where parsing occurs in two stages. In the first stage, the parser constructs an initial phrase structure, perhaps using only syntactic information. In a second stage, other information is used to evaluate this initial structure, and if necessary the input is reanalysed. The extent to which parsing makes use of principles such as minimal attachment and late closure, or detailed syntactic information accessed from the lexicon, remains controversial.

One of the most important current topics in the psychology of syntax is how we resolve syntactic or structural ambiguity. We will look at this in detail in Chapter 9. In the first stage of parsing, does the parser construct one initial representation or does it consider the alternatives in parallel? Garden path sentences suggest that initially only a single syntactic structure is generated in the first pass. Whether we resolve ambiguity by purely syntactic factors, or allow semantic cues to guide parsing, is of fundamental importance. Processes such as holding dislocated constituents in working memory until the appropriate trace is reached place additional strain on the parser.

What happens in the comprehension process after we have parsed the constituents? We have examined the computation of the syntactic structure, and the processes that affect this. Syntax is only an intermediary in extracting the meaning of a sentence; as we will see in Chapter 7, our memory for syntax is very short. We use it in combination with the meanings of words to construct a mental representation of the meaning of the sentence.

Finally, as Mitchell (1994) points out, most of the work in parsing has examined a single language. There are exceptions, including work on Dutch (Frazier, 1987b; Frazier, Flores d'Arcais, & Coolen, 1993), French

(Holmes & O'Reagan, 1981), German (Bach, Brown, & Marslen-Wilson, 1986), Hungarian (MacWhinney & Pleh, 1988), Japanese (Mazuka, 1991), and Spanish (Cuetos & Mitchell, 1988), but the great preponderance of the work has been on English alone. It is possible that this restriction is giving us at best a restricted view of parsing, and at worst a misleading view.

FURTHER READING

Fabb (1994) is a workbook of basic linguistic and syntactic concepts, and makes the meaning of grammatical terms very clear (although most of the book avoids using the notion of a verb phrase on the controversial but defensible grounds that verb phrases are not as fundamental as other types of phrases). Details of syntactic terminology and an analysis of English grammar can be found in Huddleston (1984). Borsley (1991) provides excellent coverage of contemporary linguistic approaches to syntax, and Radford (1981) provides detailed coverage of the linguistic aspects of Chomsky's extended theory. See Jackendoff (1977) for a technical treatment of $\overline{X}$-syntax; however, Pinker (1994) gives a brief and accessible description. The *generalised phrase structure grammar* (GPSG) of Gazdar, Klein, Pullum and Sag (1985) is an attempt to go back to a less powerful grammar which does not need a transformational component.

Greene (1972) covers the early versions of Chomsky's theory, and detailed coverage of early psycholinguistic experiments relating to it. Johnson-Laird (1983) provides technical analysis of the psychological relevance of linguistic theory. If you want to find out more about the relationship between linguistics and psycholinguistics, read the debate between Berwick and Weinberg (1983a,b) and Garnham (1983a), and the article by Stabler (1983) with the following peer commentary. An introduction to automata theory is also provided in Johnson-Laird (1983); a more detailed and mathematical treatment can be found in Wall (1972). Garnham (1985) discusses AI approaches to parsing in more detail.

See Clark and Clark (1977) for a detailed description of surface structure parsing cues. A review of the experimental methods used in looking at syntactic processing is provided by Haberlandt (1994); this also describes the methodologies used in word recognition, so is relevant to the previous two chapters as well. Frazier (1987a) and Mitchell (1987, 1994) review the literature on the psycholinguistic approach to syntax, the latter with particular reference to syntactic ambiguity. See also the references in Chapter 9 on syntactic ambiguity.

Finally, the extreme view of *cognitive linguistics* (Langacker, 1987) dispenses with formal linguistic rules altogether, focusing instead upon the communicative conventions of particular languages.

CHAPTER SIX

Semantics

INTRODUCTION

How do we represent the meaning of words? How is our knowledge of the world organised? These are issues concerned with the study of meaning, or *semantics*. In the previous chapter we saw how the sentence processing mechanism parses sentences to construct a representation of the syntactic relationships between words. Important as this stage might be, it is only an intermediate step towards the real goal of comprehension, constructing a representation of the meaning of the sentence. In this chapter we shall look at how the meaning of individual words are represented, and in the next how we combine these meanings to form a representation of the *meaning* of the whole sentence and beyond.

Our discussion of non-semantic reading in Chapter 4 showed that words and their meanings can be dissociated. There is further intuitive evidence to support this dissociation (Hirsh-Pasek, Reeves, & Golinkoff, 1993). First, we can translate words from one language to another. Furthermore, not every word meaning is represented by a simple, single word in every language (see Chapter 10 for further discussion of this). Second, there is an imperfect mapping between words and their meanings such that some words have more than one meaning (ambiguity) while some words have the same meaning (synonymy). Third, the meaning of words to some extent depends upon the context.

The word "big" means different things in the phrases "the big ant" and "the big rocket".

Tulving (1972) drew what is now regarded as a fundamental distinction between *episodic* and *semantic* memory. Episodic memory is our memory for events and particular episodes; semantic memory is, in simple terms, our general knowledge. Hence my knowledge that the capital of France is Paris is stored in semantic memory; my memory of learning as a child in a geography lesson at school when the Eiffel Tower was built is an instance of an episodic memory. Semantic memory develops from or is abstracted from episodes which may be repeated many times. I cannot now recall when I learnt the name of the capital of France, but clearly I must have been exposed to it at least once. We have already seen that our mental dictionary has been given the name *lexicon*, and similarly our store of semantic knowledge can be called our mental *encyclopaedia*. Clearly there is a close relationship between the two, both in development and in the developed system, but they must also be separable for the reasons given above. Neuropsychology reveals important dissociations in this respect. We have seen that words and their meanings can be dissociated; but we must be wary of confusing a loss of semantic information with the inability to access or use that information. This problem is particularly important when we consider semantic neuropsychological deficits.

The notion of meaning is closely bound to that of *categorisation*. Concepts are very closely related to meaning. A concept refers to a mental representation that determines how things are related or categorised. It enables us to group things together, so that instances of a category all have something in common. Thus concepts somehow specify category membership. All words have an underlying concept, but not all concepts are labelled by a word. We have a word "dog" which we can use about certain things in the world, but not others. There are two fundamental questions about this. We can say that the philosophical question is: how does the concept of "dog" relate to the members of the category dog? The psychological question is: how is the meaning of "dog" represented, and how do we pick out instances of dogs in the environment? As just hinted, we could in principle have a word, say "brog", to refer to brown dogs. That we do not have such a term is probably because this is not a particularly useful concept in this domain. Rosch (1978) pointed out that categorisation is not arbitrary, but determined by two important features of our cognitive system. First, the categories we form are determined in part by the way in which we perceive the structure of the world. Perceptual features are tied together because they form objects and have a shared function. How the categories we form are determined by the biological factors is an important topic, about which little is known. We shall return to this with the example of colour in our discussion of the relationship between language and thought in Chapter 10. Second, the structure of categories might be determined by a principle known as *cognitive economy*. This states that semantic memory is organised so as to avoid excessive duplication. Of course we cannot be too economical, as we often need to make distinctions between members of some categories more than others. Rosch proposed that this compromise resulted in a *basic level* of categorisation which tends to be the default level at which we categorise and think unless there is particular reason to do otherwise. Unless given reason to do otherwise, we use the basic level of "chairs", rather than the lower level of "armchairs" or the higher level of "furniture".

It should be obvious that the study of meaning therefore necessitates capturing the way in which words refer to things that are all members of the same category and have something in common, yet are different from non-members. (Of course something can belong to two categories at once: we can have a category labelled by the word "ghost", and another by the word "invisible", and indeed we can join the two to form the category of invisible ghosts labelled by the words "invisible ghosts".) There are two issues here. First, what distinguishes items of one category from items of another? Second, how are hierarchical relationships between categories to be captured? There are category relationships between words. For example, the basic level category "dog" has a large number of category *superordinate* levels above it (such as "mammal", "animal", "animate thing", and "object") and *subordinates* (such as "terrier", "rottweiler", and "alsatian"—these are said to be category co-ordinates of each other).

Hierarchical relationships between categories are one clear way in which words can be related in meaning, but there are other ways that are equally important. Some words refer to properties of things referred to by other words (e.g. "dog" and "paw"). Some words (*antonyms*) are opposites in meaning (e.g. "hot" and "cold"). We can attempt to define many words: for example, we might offer the definition "unmarried man" for "bachelor". Another fundamental issue for semantics concerns how we should capture all these relationships.

It should by now be clear that semantics is in many ways the interface between language and the rest of perception and cognition. This relationship is made explicit in the work of Jackendoff (1983), who proposed a theory of the connection between semantics and other cognitive, perceptual, and motor processes. From these considerations, he proposed two constraints on a general theory of semantics. The grammatical constraint says that we should prefer a semantic theory that explains otherwise arbitrary generalisations about syntax and the lexicon. Both some AI theories and theories based on logic (in particular, a form of logic known as predicate calculus) fail this constraint as to work at all they both have to make up entities that do not correspond to anything real. The cognitive constraint says that there is a level of representation where semantics must interface with other psychological representations such as those derived from perception.

In this chapter we will focus upon two main topics. First, how do we represent the meaning of words? In particular, how does a model of meaning deal with the issues we have just raised? Second, what does the neuropsychology of meaning tell us about its representation and its relationship with the encyclopaedia? We will consider the development of meaning, and how it is related to exposure to specific episodes, in Chapter 12.

CLASSICAL APPROACHES

It is useful to distinguish immediately between a word's *denotation* and its *connotation*. The denotation of a word is its core, essential meaning. The connotations of a word are all of its secondary implications, or emotional or evaluative associations. For example, the denotation of the word "dog" is its core meaning: it is the relation between a word and a class of objects to which it can refer. The connotations of "dog" might be "nice", "frightening", or "smelly". Put another way, everyone agrees on the denotation, but the connotations differ from person to person. Here we are primarily concerned with denotation, although the distinction can become quite hazy.

Ask a person on the street what the meaning of "dog" is, and they might well point to one. This theory of meaning that words mean what they refer to is one of the oldest, and is called the *referential theory*. There are two major problems with this lay theory, however. First, it is not at all clear how such a theory treats abstract concepts. How can you point to "truth", yet alone point to the meaning of a word such as "whomsoever"? Second, there is a dissociation between a word and the things to which it can refer. Consider the words "Hesperus" (Greek for "The Evening Star") and "Phosphorus" (Greek for "The Morning Star"). They have the same reference or extension in our universe, namely the planet Venus, but they have different senses or *intensions*. Indeed, the ancients did not know that they were the same thing, so even though the words "Hesperus" and "Phosphorus" actually refer to the same thing (the planet Venus), the words have different senses. "Hesperus" could only be used to refer to a planet in the evening sky, and "Phosphorus" could only be used to refer to a planet in the morning sky. This distinction was made explicit in the work of Frege (1892/1952), who distinguished between the *sense* (often called the *intension*) of a word and its *reference* (often called its *extension*). The intension is its abstract specification or meaning, determining how a word is related in meaning to other words, and which specifies the properties an object must have to be a member of the class, while the extension is what it stands for in the world, that is the objects picked out by that intension. These notions can be extended from words or descriptive phrases to expressions or sentences. Frege took the extension of a sentence to be its truth value (which is simply whether it is true or not), and its intension to be its underlying sense that was derived by combining the intensions of the component words. This formal semantics approach of building logical models of meaning has been developed by logicians into complex systems of meaning known as *model-theoretic semantics*. (Because of the importance of truth in these theories, it is sometimes known as truth-theoretic semantics.) Although the original idea was to provide an account of logic, mathematics, and computing languages, its application has been extended to natural language.

The importance of formal approaches to meaning for psycholinguistics is not clear. Although they help refine what meaning might be, they appear to say little about how we represent or compute it.

SEMANTIC NETWORKS

One of the most influential of all processing approaches to meaning is based on the idea that the meaning of a word is embedded within a network of other meanings. In a semantic network, knowledge is given meaning only by the way in which it relates to other knowledge. Some of the earliest theories of meaning, from Aristotle to the Behaviourists, viewed meaning as deriving from a word's *association*. From infancy, we are exposed to many episodes involving the word "dog". For the behaviourists, the meaning of the word "dog" was simply the sum of all our associations to the word: it obtains its meaning by its place in a network of associations. The meaning of "dog" might involve an association with "barks", "four legs", "furry", and so on. It soon became apparent that association in itself was insufficiently powerful to be able to capture all aspects of meaning. There is no structure in an associative network, with no relationship between words, no hierarchy of information, and no cognitive economy. In a semantic network, this additional power is obtained by making the connections between items do something—they are not merely associations representing contiguity of frequent co-occurrence, but themselves have a semantic value. That is, in a semantic network the links have meaning.

The Collins and Quillian semantic network model

Perhaps the best known example of a semantic network is that of Collins and Quillian (1969). The idea arose from an attempt to develop a *teachable language comprehender* to assist machine translation between languages.

A semantic network is particularly useful for representing information about natural kind terms. These are words that refer to naturally occurring categories and their members—such as types of animal or metal or precious stone. The scheme attributes fundamental importance to their inherently hierarchical nature: for example, a bald eagle is a type of eagle, an eagle is a type of bird of prey, a bird of prey is a bird, and a bird is a type of animal. This hierarchical format suggests a straightforward way to implement cognitive economy. If you store the information that birds have wings at the level of bird, you do not need to repeat it at the level of particular instances (e.g. eagles, bald eagles, and robins). An example of a fragment of such a network is shown in Fig. 6.1. In the network, *nodes* are connected by links which specify the relationship between the linked nodes; the most common link is an ISA link which means that the lower level node "is a" type of the higher level node. Attributes are stored at the lowest possible node at which they are true of all lower nodes in the network.

The sentence verification task. One of the most commonly used tasks in semantic memory research is that of *sentence verification*. Subjects are presented with simple "facts" and have to press one button if the sentence is true, another if it is false. The reaction time is an index of how difficult the decision was. Collins and Quillian (1969) presented subjects with sentences such as (1) to (4).

1. A robin is a robin.
2. A robin is a bird.
3. A robin is an animal
4. A robin is a fish.

Sentence (4) is of course false. Sentence (1) is trivially true, but it obviously still takes subjects some time to respond "yes"; clearly they have to read the sentence and initiate a response, but it does provide a baseline measure. The response time to (1) is less than to (2), which in turn is less than that to (3). Furthermore, the difference between the reaction times is about the same—that is, there is a linear relationship.

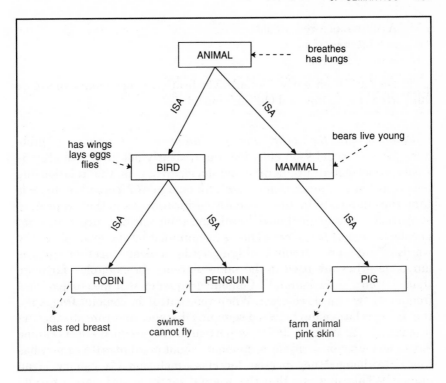

FIG. 6.1. Example of a hierarchical semantic network. (Based on Collins & Quillian, 1969, p. 241.)

Why do we get these results? According to this model, subjects produce responses by starting off from the node in the network that is the subject in the sentence (here "robin"), and travelling through the network until they find the information necessary. As this travelling takes a fixed amount of time for each link, the further away the information is, the slower the response time. To get from "robin" to "bird" involves travelling along only one link, but to get from "robin" to "animal" necessitates travelling along two links. That is, the semantic distance between "robin" and "animal" is greater than that between "robin" and "bird". If the information is not found the "no" response is made. The characteristic of property inheritance also shows the same pattern of response times, as we have to travel along links to retrieve the property from the appropriate level. Hence reaction times are fastest to (5), as the "red-breasted" attribute is stored at the "robin" node, slower to (6), as "has wings" is stored at the "bird" level above "robin", and slowest to (7), as this information is stored two levels above "robin" at the "animal" level.

5.   A robin has a red breast.
6.   A robin has wings.
7.   A robin has lungs.

These data from early sentence verification experiments therefore supported the Collins and Quillian model.

Problems with the Collins and Quillian model.   A number of problems for this model soon emerged. First, clearly not all information is easily represented in hierarchical form. What is the relationship between "truth", "justice" and "law", for example? A second problem is that the materials in the sentence verification task that appear to support the hierarchical model confound semantic distance with what is called *conjoint frequency*. This is exemplified by the example of the words "bird" and "robin"; these words appear together in the language—they are used in the same sentence for example—far more than do "bird" and "animal". Conjoint frequency is a measure of how frequently two words co-occur. When you control for conjoint frequency, the linear relationship between semantic distance and time disappears (Conrad, 1972; Wilkins, 1971); in particular hierarchical effects can no longer be found for verifying statements about attributes ("a canary has lungs") although they persist for class inclusion ("a canary is an animal"). This suggests that the original sentence verification results were found simply because the sentences that give the faster verification times contain words which are more closely associated. Another possible confound in the original sentence verification experiments is with category size; the class of "animals" is by definition bigger than the class of "birds", so perhaps this is why it takes longer to search (Landauer & Freedman, 1968). However, they did not properly control for typicality and semantic distance (see Rips, Shoben, & Smith, 1973; Smith, Shoben, & Rips, 1974).

Third, the hierarchical model makes some incorrect predictions. We find that a sentence such as (8) is verified much faster than (9), even though animal is higher in the hierarchy than mammal (Rips et al., 1973).

8.   a cow is an animal
9.   a cow is a mammal

We do not reject all untrue statements equally slowly. Sentence (10) is rejected faster than (11), even though both are equally untrue (Schaeffer & Wallace, 1969, 1970; Wilkins, 1971). This is called the *relatedness effect*: the more related two things are, the harder it is to disentangle them, even if they are not ultimately from the same class.

10. a pine is a chair
11. a pine is a flower

Neither are all true statements involving the same semantic distance responded to equally quickly. Sentence (12) is verified faster than (13), even though both involve only one semantic link (Rips et al., 1973), and a "robin" is judged to be a more typical bird than a "penguin" or an "ostrich" (Rosch, 1973). This is called the *prototypicality effect*.

12. a robin is a bird
13. a penguin is a bird

In summary there are too many problematical findings from sentence verification experiments to accept the hierarchical network model in its original form. We shall see that of these troublesome findings, the prototypicality effect is particularly important.

Revisions to the semantic network model. Collins and Loftus (1975) proposed a revision of the model based upon the idea of spreading activation. The structure of the network became more complex, with the links between nodes varying in strength or distance (see Fig. 6.2). Hence "penguin" is more distant from "bird" than is "robin". The structure is no longer primarily hierarchical, although hierarchical relationships still form parts of the network. Access and priming in the network occur through a mechanism of spreading activation. The concepts of activation travelling along links of different strengths and many simple units connected together in complex ways are of course important concepts in connectionist models.

SEMANTIC FEATURES

A different approach to semantic memory views the meaning of a word as encoded not by the position of a word in a network of meaning, but by its decomposition into smaller units of meaning called *semantic features*. This works very well for some simple domains where there is a clear relationship between the terms: one such domain much studied by anthropologists is that of kinship terms. A simplified example is shown in Table 6.1. Here the meanings of the four words "mother", "father", "son" and "daughter" can be captured by combinations of the three features "human", "male" or "female", and "older" or "younger". We *could* provide hierarchical arrangement of these features (e.g. human → young and old; young → male or female, and old → male or female) but this would either be totally unprincipled (there is no reason

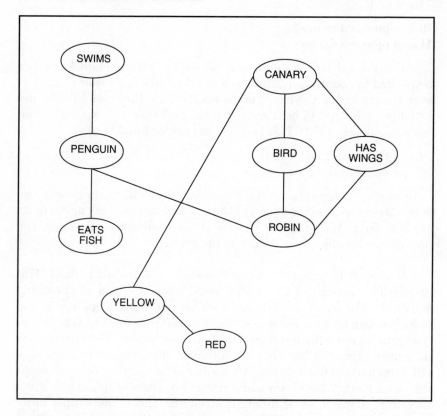

FIG. 6.2. Example of a spreading activation semantic network. (Based on Collins & Loftus, 1975, p. 412.) It should be noted that two dimensions cannot do justice to the necessary complexity of the network.

why adult/young should come before male/female, or vice versa) or involve duplication (if we store both hierarchical forms). Instead, we can list the meaning in terms of a list of features, so that father is (+ human, + male, + older).

TABLE 6.1
Decomposition of kinship terms into semantic features

FEATURE	Father	Mother	Daughter	Son
Human	+	+	+	+
Older	+	+	–	–
Female	–	+	+	–

We can take the idea of semantic features to the limit by trying to represent the meanings of all words in terms of combinations of as few semantic features as possible. When we use features in this way it is as though they become atoms of meaning, and are called *semantic primitives*. This approach has been particularly influential in AI. For example, Schank (1972, 1975) argued that the meaning of sentences could be represented by the *conceptual dependencies* between the semantic primitives underlying the words in the sentence. All common verbs can be analysed in terms of 12 primitive actions which concern the movement of objects, ideas, and abstract relations. For example, there are five physical actions (called "expel", "grasp", "ingest", "move", and "propel"), and two abstract ("attend", and "speak"). Their names are fairly self-explanatory, but it is not necessary to go into detail of their meanings here. Wilks (1976) described a semantic system where the meaning of 600 words in the simulation can be reduced to combinations of only 80 primitives. In this system the action sense of "beat" is denoted by ("strike" [subject—human] [object—animate] [instrument—thing]). The semantic representation and syntactic roles in which the word can partake are intimately linked.

Early decompositional theories: Katz and Fodor

Because this approach is based on decomposing the meaning of a word into simpler constituents, such theories are sometimes said to be *decompositional* theories of meaning. One of the earliest of these was that of Katz and Fodor (1963). The emphasis of this theory was to show the meanings of sentences could be derived by combining the semantic features for each individual word in the sentence, with particular emphasis on showing how we understand ambiguous words in different contexts. Consider examples (14) and (15). A different sense of "ball" is used in each sentence. Consider further (16), which is semantically anomalous.

14. The witches put on their football strips and kicked the ball.
15. The witches put on their party frocks and went to the ball.
16. ? The rock kicked the ball.

There are no syntactic cues to be made use of here, so how do the meanings of the words in the sentence combine to resolve the ambiguity in (14) and (15) and identify the anomaly in (16)? First, Katz and Fodor postulated a decompositional theory of meaning so that the meanings of individual words in the sentence are broken down into their component semantic features (called *semantic markers* by Katz and Fodor). Second, the combination of features across words is governed by particular constraints called *selection restrictions*. There is a selection restriction on the meaning of "kick" such that it must take an animate subject and an optional object, but if there is an object then it must be a physical object. An ambiguous word such as "ball" has two sets of semantic feature, one of which will be specified as something like (sphere, small, used in games, physical object ...), the other more like (dance, event ...). Only one of these contains the "physical object" feature, so kick picks out that sense. Similarly there is a selection restriction on the verb "went" such that it picks out locations and events, which is contradictory with the "physical object" sense of "ball". Finally, we have already mentioned that "kick" has a selection restriction specifying an animate subject, and the underlying semantic features of "rock" are incompatible with this. As there are no other possible subjects in this sentence we consider it anomalous.

Feature list theories and semantic verification: Feature comparison

We have seen that decompositional theories of meaning enable us to list the meanings of words as lists of semantic features. What account does such a model give of performance on the sentence verification task, and in particular what account does it give of the problem to which hierarchical network models fall prey? Rips et al. (1973) proposed that there are two types of semantic feature. *Defining features* are essential to the underlying meaning of a word and relate to properties that things must have to be a member of that category (for example, a bird is living, it is feathered, lays eggs, and so forth), whereas *characteristic features* are usually true of instances of a category but are not necessarily true (for example, most birds can fly but penguins and ostriches cannot).

Sentence verification in feature list theories. According to the characteristic-defining feature list theory, sentence verification involves making comparisons of the feature lists representing the meaning of the words involved in two stages. For this reason this is called the *feature comparison* theory. In the first stage, the overall featural similarity of the two words is compared, including both the defining and characteristic features. If there is very high overlap, we respond "true"; if there is very low overlap, we respond "false". If we compare "robin" and "bird", there is much overlap and no conflict in the complete list of features, so we can respond "true" very easily; with "robin" and "pig" there is very little overlap and a great deal of conflict, so we can respond "false" very quickly. However, if the amount of overlap is neither very high or low, we then have to go on to a second stage of comparison (which obviously takes additional time) where we consider only the defining features. An exact match on these is then necessary to respond "true".

For example, when we compare "penguin" and "bird", there is a moderate amount of overlap and some conflict (on flying, for example). An examination of the defining features of "penguin" then reveals that it is, after all, a type of bird.

Evaluation of decompositional theories

The appeal of decompositional theories is mixed. This is a difficult area in which to carry out experiments, and we must consider other lines of evidence. Indeed, Hollan (1975) argued that it is impossible to devise an experiment to distinguish between feature list and semantic network theories because they are formally equivalent in that it is impossible to find a prediction that will distinguish between them (but see Rips, Smith, & Shoben, 1975, for a reply).

On the one hand, such theories have an intuitive appeal, and they make explicit how we make inferences based upon the meaning of words in sentence verification task. In reducing meaning to a small number of primitives, it is very economical. On the other hand, it is difficult to construct decompositional representations for even some of the most common words. Some categories do not have any obvious defining features that are common to all their members. The most famous example of this was provided by Wittgenstein (1953), who asked what all games have in common, and therefore how "game" should be defined—that is, how it should be decomposed into its semantic primitives. There is no clear complete definition; instead, it is as though there are many different "games" which have in common a *family resemblance*. So if we cannot define an apparently simple concept such as this, how are we going to cope with more complex examples? A glance at the examples we mentioned above should reveal another problem: even when we can apparently define words, the features which we come up with are not particularly appealing or intuitively obvious; one suspects that an alternative set could be generated with equal facility. It is not even clear that our definitions are complete: often it is as though we have to anticipate all possible important aspects of meaning in advance. Bolinger (1965) criticised Katz and Fodor's theory with the example of (17).

17.   He became a bachelor.

The word "bachelor" is ambiguous between the senses of "unmarried man who has never been married" and "a person with a degree". Why do we select the second interpretation in the case of (17)? You might say that it is because we know that you cannot become an unmarried man who has never been married. So does that mean that "impossible to become" is part of the underlying meaning of this sense of bachelor—that is, that this is one of its semantic features? This seems very implausible. Generally, interpretation of word meaning is very sensitive to world knowledge. Is it part of the meaning of "pig" that it does not have a trunk? This also seems most unlikely. If we consider that such problems are solved by making an inference rather than simple access to semantic memory, then the problem becomes more much more complex.

The feature-comparison theory has additional problems. First, it is very specific to the sentence verification task. Second, there are some methodological problems with the Smith et al. (1974) experiments. Semantic relatedness and stimulus familiarity were confounded in the original experimental materials (McCloskey, 1980). Moreover, Loftus (1973) showed that if you reverse the order of the nouns in the sentences used in sentence verification, you find effects not predicted by the theory. If we only compare lists of features for the instance and class nouns, their order should not matter. Hence (18) "Is a robin a bird?" should be verified in the same time as (19) "Is a bird a robin?".

18.   Is a robin a bird?
19.   Is a bird a robin?

She found that order is important and the verification times were a function of how often the category was given for a particular instance for sentences such as (18), but were a function of how often the instance was given for the category in sentences such as (19). However, the task involved in verifying sentences such as (19) seems unnatural compared with that of (18). Fourth, Holyoak and Glass (1975) showed that people may have specific strategies for disconfirming sentences, such as thinking of a specific counter-example, rather than carrying out extensive computation. Finally, and most tellingly, it is not easy to distinguish empirically between defining and characteristic features. Hampton (1979) showed that in practice defining features do not always define category membership. The model still cannot easily account for the finding that some categories have unclear or *fuzzy* boundaries. McCloskey and Glucksberg (1978) showed that although subjects agree on many items as members of categories, they also disagree on many. For example, although all subjects agree that "cancer" is a disease and "happiness" is not, half think that "stroke" is disease and about half think that it is not. Similarly, about half the subjects think that "pumpkin" is a type of fruit and half do not. Labov (1973) showed that there is no clear boundary between membership and non-membership of a category for a simple physical object like a "cup": "cup" and "bowl" vary along a continuum, and different subjects put the cut-off point in different places. Furthermore, this point can be altered by asking subjects to focus on different aspects of the object; if they are asked to imagine an object which is otherwise half way between a cup and a bowl as containing mashed potato, subjects are more likely to think of it as a bowl.

Is semantic decomposition obligatory?   Another important issue for feature theories is whether the decomposition of a word into its component semantic features is obligatory. That is, when we see a word like "bachelor", is the retrieval of its features an automatic process? In featural terms, the meaning of the unmarried man sense of "bachelor" must clearly contain features that correspond to (+ unmarried, + man), although these in turn might summarise decomposition into more primitive features, or there might be others (see above). In any case, on the decompositional account, when you see or hear or think the word "bachelor", you automatically have to decompose it. Therefore you will draw automatically all the valid inferences that are implied by its featural representation—for example, the feature (+unmarried) automatically becomes available in all circumstances.

Automatic decomposition is a very difficult theory to test experimentally. However, Fodor, Fodor and Garrett (1975) observed that some words have a negative implicit in their definition. They called these *partial definitional negatives* (PDNs for short). For example, the word "bachelor" has such an implicit negative in (+unmarried), which is equivalent to (not married). It is well-known that double negatives, two negatives together, are harder to process than one alone. Fodor et al. compared sentences (20), (21), and (22).

20.   The bachelor married Sybil.
21.   The bachelor did not marry Sybil.
22.   The widow did not marry Sybil.

According to decompositional theories, (20) contains an implicit negative in the form of the PDN in "bachelor". If this is correct, and such features are accessed automatically, then (21) is implicitly a double negative and should be harder to understand than a control sentence such as (22), which contains only an explicit negative and no PDN. Fodor, Fodor, and Garrett could find no processing difference between sentences of the types of (21) and (22). They concluded that features are not accessed automatically, and instead proposed a non-decompositional account in which the meaning of words is represented as a whole. To draw an inference such as "a bachelor is unmarried", you have to make a special type of inference called a *meaning postulate*. We do this only when required. However, it is difficult to make up good controls (for example, sentences matched for length and syntactic complexity) for this type of experiment (see Katz, 1977).

Fodor, Garrett, Walker, and Parkes (1980) examined the representation of *lexical causatives*. These are verbs that bring about or cause new states of affairs. In a decompositional analysis such verbs would contain this in their semantic representation. For example, "kill" would be represented as something like (cause to die). In Fig. 6.3, (a) shows the surface structure for the two sentences with the apparently similar verbs "kiss" and "kill". For the control verb "kiss", the deep structure analysis is the same, but if "kill" is indeed decomposed into (cause to die), its deep structure should be like that of (b). Fodor et al. asked subjects to rate the perceived relatedness between words in these sentences. In (b), "Vlad" and "Agnes" are further apart than they are in the deep structure of "kissed", as there are more intervening nodes. Therefore "Vlad" and "Agnes" should be rated as less related in the sentence with the causative verb "Vlad killed Agnes" than with a non-causative verb as in "Vlad kissed Agnes". However, they found no difference in the perceived relatedness ratings in these sentences, and therefore no evidence that subjects decompose lexical causatives.

There are a number of assumptions in this analysis. The finding was questioned by Gergely and Bever (1986). In particular, they questioned whether perceived relatedness between words truly is a function of their structural distance. They provided experimental evidence to support their contention, concluding that the technique of intuitions about the relatedness of words cannot be used to test the relative underlying complexity of semantic representations. The conclusion also depends on a failure to show a difference rather than on obtaining a difference, which is always less satisfactory.

Whereas some studies have concluded that complex sentences which are hypothesised to contain more semantic primitives are no less memorable or harder to process than simpler sentences which presumably contain fewer primitives (Carpenter & Just, 1977; Kintsch, 1974), there are counter-arguments that these experiments confounded the number of primitives with other factors (Gentner, 1981). Sentences that contain primitives that facilitate interconnections between elements of the other sentence are recalled better than those which do not. For example, "give" decomposes into the notion of transferring the ownership of objects between participants in the sentence, while "sold" decomposes into the notion of transferring the ownership of objects plus an exchange of money between participants. Hence sentences of the type "Vlad sold the wand to Agnes" are remembered more accurately than

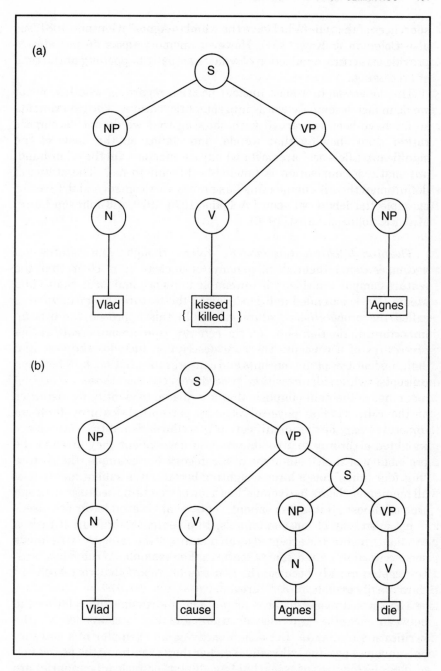

FIG. 6.3. Examples of analysis of semantics of causative verbs showing different deep structure distances. (Based on Fodor, Garrett, Walker, & Parkes, 1980, pp. 289–292.)

sentences of the type "Vlad gave the wand to Agnes" (Gentner, 1981; see also Coleman & Kay, 1981). However, memory tasks do not always provide an accurate reflection of what is actually happening at the time of processing.

This leaves us in a most unclear position regarding whether or not we do in fact decompose words into semantic features. The experiments so far have been concerned with showing that we do not decompose rather than showing that we do, and claims on the basis of "no significant difference" are never wholly satisfactory. On the other hand, automatic decomposition is fiendishly difficult to test. The status of definitional theories of meaning has proved very controversial. (See, for example, the debate between J.A. Fodor, 1978, 1979, and Johnson-Laird; Miller & Johnson-Laird, 1976).

The probabilistic feature model.   Even   though   the   status   of decompositional theories in general is unclear, it is clear that the feature-comparison theory is untenable in its original form. Smith and Medin (1981) extended and modernised the feature theory in what is called the *probabilistic feature model*. In this approach there is an important distinction between the *core descriptions* and *identification procedures* of a concept. The core description includes the essential defining features of the concepts and captures the relationships between concepts, while identification procedures concern those aspects of meaning, as the name implies, that are related to identifying instances of the concept. For physical objects, perceptual features form an important part of the identification procedure. Semantic features are weighted according to a combination of how salient they are and the probability of their being true of a category. For example, the feature "has four limbs" has a large weighting because it is salient and true of all mammals; "bears live young" has a lower weighting because although true of almost all it is less salient; "eats meat" is even lower because it is not even true of most mammals. In a sentence verification task, a candidate instance is accepted as an instance of the category if it exceeds some critical weighted sum of features. For example, "a robin is a bird" is accepted quickly because the features of "robin" that correspond to "bird" easily exceed "bird's" threshold.

The revised model has the advantage of stressing the relationship between meaning and identification, and can account for all the verification time data. Because identifying an exemplar of a category only involves passing a threshold rather than examining the possession of defining features, classes that have "fuzzy" or unclear boundaries are no longer problematic. At this point it becomes difficult to distinguish empirically between this model and the prototype model to be discussed next. The probabilistic feature model is still developing and it is at present premature to evaluate its success.

FAMILY RESEMBLANCE AND PROTOTYPES

We have seen that one of the problems of the decompositional theory of semantics is that for many words it is surprisingly difficult to come up with an intuitively appealing list of semantic features. Furthermore, many categories seem to be defined by a *family resemblance* between their members rather than the specification of defining features which all members must possess. On this view, a *prototype* is an average family member (Rosch, 1978). Potential members of the category are identified by how closely they resemble the prototype or category average. Some instances of a category are judged better exemplars than others. The prototype is the "best example" of a concept, and is often a non-existent, composite example. For example, a robin is very close to being a prototypical bird; it is of average size, has wings, feathers, can fly, and has average features in every respect. A penguin is a long way from being a prototypical bird, and hence we take longer to verify that it is indeed a member of the bird category. The idea of a prototype has arisen from many different areas of psychology. Posner and Keel (1968) showed subjects abstract patterns of dots. Unknown to the subjects, the patterns were distortions of just one underlying pattern of dots which the subjects did not see in the first instance. The underlying pattern of dots corresponds to the category prototype. Even though subjects never saw this pattern, they later treated it as the best example, responding to it better than the patterns they did see. We shall discuss the related work of Rosch on prototypes and colour naming in Chapter 10.

More formally, we can say that a prototype is a special type of *schema*. A schema is a frame for organising knowledge which can be structured as a series of slots plus fillers (see next chapter for more detail). A prototype is a schema with all the slots filled in with average values. For example, the schema for "bird" comprises a series of slots such as "can fly?" ("yes" for robin and wren, "no" for penguin and emu), "bill length" ("short" for robin, "long" for curlew), and "length" ("short" for robin, "long" for stork). The bird prototype will have the most common or average values for all these slots (can fly, short bill, short legs). Hence a robin will be closer to the prototype than an emu. Category boundaries are unclear or "fuzzy". For some items, it is not clear which category they should belong in; and in some extreme cases, some instances may be in two categories (for example, a tomato may be categorised as both a vegetable and a fruit).

There is a wealth of evidence supporting prototype theory. Rosch and Mervis (1975) measured family resemblance among instances of concepts such as fruit, furniture, and vehicles by asking subjects to list their features. Although some features were given by all subjects for particular concepts, these were not technically defining features, as they did not distinguish the concept from other concepts. For example, all subjects might say of "birds" that "they're alive", but then so are all other animals. The more specific features that were listed were not shared by all instances of a concept—for example, not all birds fly.

A number of results demonstrate the processing advantage of a prototype over particular instances (see for example Mervis, Catlin, & Rosch, 1975). Sentence verification time is faster for prototypical members of a category. Prototypical members can swap for category names in sentences whereas non-prototypical members cannot. Words for typical objects are learnt before words for atypical ones. In a free recall task, adults retrieve typical members before atypical ones (Kail & Nippold, 1984). Prototypes share more features with other instances of the category but minimise the featural overlap with related categories (Rosch & Mervis, 1975). Hence "apple" is a prototypical "fruit" (Battig & Montague, 1969), and is similar to other fruit and dissimilar to "vegetables", but "tomato" is a peripheral member and indeed overlaps with "vegetable". There are prototypes which possess an advantage over other members of the category even when they are all formally identical. Subjects consider the number "13" to be a better "odd number" than "23" or "501" (Armstrong, Gleitman, & Gleitman, 1983), and "mother" is a better example of "female" than "waitress". These typicality effects can also be found in sentence verification times.

Basic levels.   In the introduction to this chapter we saw that there is a basic level of categorisation which is particularly psychologically salient. The basic level is the level that has the most distinctive attributes and provides the most economical arrangement of semantic memory. There is a large gain in distinctiveness from the basic level to levels above, but only a small one to levels below. For example, there seems to be a large jump from "chairs" to "furniture" and other types of furniture such as "tables", but a less obvious difference between different types of chair. Objects at the basic level are readily distinguished from each other, but objects in levels beneath the basic level are not so easily distinguished from each other. It is the level at which we think in the sense that those are the labels we choose in the absence of any particular need to do otherwise. The basic level is the most general category for which a concrete image of the whole category can be formed (Rosch, Mervis, Gray, Johnson, & Boyes-Braem, 1976).

Rosch et al. (1976) showed that basic levels have a number of advantages over other categories: subjects can easily list most of the attributes of the basic level; it is the level of description most likely to be spontaneously used by adults; sentence verification time is faster for basic level terms; and it is typically acquired first by children. We can also name objects at the basic level faster than at the superordinate or subordinate levels (Jolicoeur, Gluck, & Kosslyn, 1984).

Problems with the prototype model. Although the prototype is now generally considered to be the best approach to the representation of meaning that we have, it is not without its criticisms. Hampton (1981) pointed out that not all concepts have prototype characteristics: abstract concepts in particular are difficult to fit into this scheme. What does it mean, for example, to talk about the prototype for "truth"? The prototype model does not explain why categories cohere: Lakoff (1987) points to some examples of very complex concepts for which it is far from obvious how there could be a prototype—the Australian Aboriginal language Dyirbal has a coherent category of "women, fire, and dangerous things" marked by the word "balan". It cannot explain why typicality judgements vary systematically depending on the context (Barsalou, 1985). Finally, the characterisation of the basic level as that of the most psychologically fundamental is not quite as clear cut as at first sight. The amount of information we can retrieve about subordinate levels varies with our expertise (Tanaka & Taylor, 1991). Birdwatchers, for example, know nearly as much about subordinate members such as blackbirds, jays, and dartford warblers, as they do about the basic level. Komatsu (1992) describes these problems in detail.

NEW APPROACHES TO SEMANTICS

Recent work questions the necessity of whether *abstraction* is an essential component of conceptual representation. An alternative view is that of representing exemplars without abstraction: each concept is representing a particular, previously encountered instance. This has been called the *instance approach* (Komatsu, 1992). There are different varieties of the instance approach depending on how many instances are stored, and on the quality of these instances. (See, for example, Hintzman, 1986; Murphy & Medin, 1985; Nosofsky, 1991; Smith & Medin, 1981; and Whittlesea, 1987). The instance approach provides greater informational richness at the expense of cognitive economy.

Connectionism has not yet had as much impact on high level processes such as semantic memory as it has had on lower level processes such as word recognition. Nevertheless there has already been some interesting work in this area. We saw in Chapter 4 how Hinton and Shallice (1991) and Plaut and Shallice (1993) incorporated the semantic representation of words into a model of the semantic route of meaning. In this model meaning is represented as a pattern of activation across a number of semantic feature units, or *sememes*, such as "hard", "soft", "maximum-size-less-foot", "made-of-metal", and "used-for-recreation". No-one is claiming that the semantic features that they use in their simulations are necessarily those which humans use, but there is some evidence for this sort of approach from recent data on word naming by Masson (1995). Indeed, the semantic features that underlie word meaning may not have any simple linguistic encoding. (If there are many features corresponding to quite low-level information they are sometimes called *micro-features*.) The semantic level is more complex than this, however, because the semantic units do not stand in isolation. First, they are grouped together so that features that are mutually excluded inhibit each other so that only one can be active at any one time. For example, an object cannot be both "hard" and "soft", or "maximum-size-less-foot" and "maximum-size-greater-two-yards" at the same time. Second, they are operated upon by another set of units called "clean-up" units that modify their activation. These allow combinations of sememes to influence each other. Although their description is couched mathematically in terms of multidimensional vector spaces, as we saw in Chapter 4, it can be thought of as a landscape with many hills and valleys. The bottom of each valley corresponds to a particular word meaning. Words that are similar in meaning will be in valleys that are close together. The initial pattern of activation produced by a word when it first activates the network might be very different from its ultimate semantic representation, but as long as you start somewhere along the sides of the right valley, you will eventually find its bottom. The valley bottoms which correspond to particular word meanings are called *attractors*, and for this reason this type of network is called an *attractor network*.

Note that this approach is not necessarily a competitor to the prototype theory; one instance of a category might cause one pattern of activation across the semantic units, another instance will cause another, similar pattern, and so on. We can talk of the prototype that defines that category as the average pattern of activation of all the instances.

At this stage it is too early to say exactly how such an approach would deal with particular semantic processing tasks, such as sentence verification and categorisation, although it is fairly straightforward to see how it might be done in terms of comparing patterns of activation.

Such comparisons are a move away from viewing all processing as occurring through the interaction of many simple units. Systems that combine connectionist networks with complex, rule-based operations are called *hybrid* models. It is possible that the future of semantic memory lies with these.

THE NEUROPSYCHOLOGY OF SEMANTICS

Can we learn anything about the representation of word meaning by looking at how it breaks down as a result of brain damage? It is a recurring theme of this book that brain damage can selectively impair a range of language functions. Of course, just because a subject cannot name a word or object does not mean that the semantic representation of that word has been lost or damaged. We have seen in our discussions of both dyslexia and anomia that subjects can fail to access the phonology of a word while they still have access to its semantic representation. We know this for a number of reasons: they may have access to part of the phonological form, they might be able to comprehend the word in speech if they cannot read it, they might be able to produce it spontaneously, they know what to do with the objects in real life, and they can group appropriate pictures together. Nevertheless there are some instances where the semantic representation is disrupted. In Chapter 8 we shall look in detail at Howard and Orchard-Lisle's (1984) patient JCU who has a general semantic disorder such that she was unable to distinguish object names from close semantic relatives. But can neuropsychology tell us anything about the organisation of semantic memory?

Category-specific semantic disorders

Perhaps the most intriguing and hotly debated phenomenon in this area is *category-specific disorders*. In these cases some semantic categories are disrupted, whereas other related ones are preserved. For example, Warrington and Shallice's (1984) patient JBR had a semantic category-specific impairment, such that he performed much better at naming inanimate objects than animate objects. He also had a relative comprehension deficit with living things. At first sight this suggests that semantic memory is organised in terms of categories, and that it is divided into animate and inanimate object categories. JBR's brain damage has caused the loss of the animate category. There are even more precise disorders. Hart, Berndt, and Caramazza (1985) reported a patient MD who also had specific difficulties in naming fruit and vegetables. Difficulties with a particular semantic category are not restricted to naming pictures of its members: they arise across a range of tasks, also including picture–name matching and carrying out gestures appropriate to the object (Warrington & Shallice, 1984).

There are three possible explanations for category-specific disorders. The first is the obvious one I have just mentioned, that different types of semantic information are located at different sites in the brain, so that brain damage destroys some types and not others. On this view, information about fruit and vegetables is stored specifically in one part of the brain. If this explanation is correct then category-specific disorders are important because they reveal the structure of the categories as represented by the brain. Hence the distinction between living and non-living things would be a fundamental organising principle in semantic memory. Problems with this localisation theory are discussed in detail by Farah (1994), but in summary it is argued that it goes against everything we know about the organisation of the brain. The second possible explanation is that the categories that are disrupted share some incidental property that makes them susceptible to loss. Riddoch, Humphreys, Coltheart, and Funnell (1988) proposed that categories that tend to be lost tend to include many similar and confusable items. However, it is not clear that these patients have any perceptual disorder (Caplan, 1992). The third, which we shall examine shortly, is that members of the lost category share other characteristics other than being simply animate or inanimate.

The third possible explanation, then, is that the differences between the categories are mediated by some other variable. One particular proposal is that the underlying distinction between animate and inanimate objects might be one based on the observation that artefacts are distinguished from one another in terms of their functional properties, while items within biological categories tend to be differentiated primarily in terms of their physical properties (Warrington & McCarthy, 1987; Warrington & Shallice, 1984; and see below). Hence JBR, who generally showed a deficit for living things, also performed poorly on naming musical instruments, precious stones, and names of fabrics. What these things all have in common is that, like living things, they are recognised primarily in terms of their perceptual characteristics, rather than being distinguished from each other on largely functional terms.

There are a number of methodological problems in studying category-specific disorders. Funnell and Sheridan (1992) reported an apparent category-specific effect whereby their patient, SL, appeared to show a selective deficit in naming pictures and defining words for living versus non-living things. However, when they controlled for the familiarity of the stimulus, this effect disappeared. They went on to make a more general observation about the materials used for these types of experiment. Most experiments use as stimulus materials a set of black-and-white line drawings from Snodgrass and Vanderwart (1980). Some examples are given in Fig. 6.4. Funnell and Sheridan (1992) showed that within this set there were more pictures of low frequency animate objects than there were low frequency inanimate objects. There were few low-familiarity non-living things and few high-familiarity living things. That is, a random sample of animate things is likely to be of overall lower frequency than a random sample of inanimate objects. Hence if frequency is important in brain-damaged naming, an artefactual effect will show up unless care is taken to control for frequency across the categories. Furthermore, there were two anomalous sub-categories: human body parts (high familiarity but a sub-category of living things) and musical instruments (low frequency but inanimate). These were the two anomalous categories mentioned by Warrington and Shallice (1984) in their description of JBR.

Stewart, Parkin, and Hunkin (1992) also argued that there had been a lack of control of name frequency, but pointed out in addition that the complexity and familiarity of the pictures used in these experiments varied between categories. In reply, Sartori, Miozzo, and Job (1993), analysing data from their patient "Michelangelo" concluded that Michelangelo had a real category-specific deficit for living things even when you control for these factors. The debate continued in Parkin and Stewart (1993), and Job, Miozzo, and Sartori (1993), particularly illustrating the need for better measures of visual featural complexity and similarity.

Many of the counter-arguments are weakened by the presence of double dissociations between the observed categories. Warrington and McCarthy (1983, 1987) describe patients who are the reverse of JBR in that they perform better on living objects than inanimate objects. It is

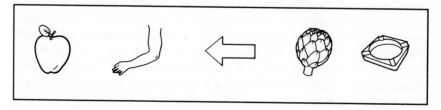

FIG. 6.4. Examples of line drawings from the Snodgrass and Vanderwart set. (Reprinted from Snodgrass, J. G., & Vanderwart, M., 1980. A standardised set of 260 pictures: Norms for name agreement, image agreement, familiarity, and visual complexity. *Journal of Experimental Psychology: Human Learning and Memory, 6,* 174–215, p. 197. © 1980 by the American Psychological Association. Reprinted by permission.)

necessary however to examine the detailed pattern of performance in these cases. Their patient YOT, for example, who generally had an impairment in naming inanimate objects relative to animate ones, on closer examination could identify large outdoor objects such as buildings and vehicles. There also appears to be a distinction between small and large man-made artefacts.

Finally, Farah, Hammond, Mehta, and Ratcliff (1989) showed that control subjects were poor at answering questions on the perceptual features of both living and non-living objects (e.g. "Are the hind legs of kangaroos larger than their front legs?"). This suggests we do not know much about the visual details of low frequency objects because, perhaps, they are never examined closely.

Modality-specific disorders

How many semantic systems are there? So far there has been little discussion of how meanings are accessed across different modalities. We have discussed semantic information as though there is only one semantic store, regardless of how it is accessed. Paivio (1971) has instead proposed a *dual-code theory* of semantic representation, with a perceptual code for the perceptual characteristics of a concept, and a verbal code for the abstract, non-sensory aspects of a concept. Experimental tests of this hypothesis have produced mixed results (Snodgrass, 1984). For example, subjects are often faster to access abstract information from pictures than from words (see for example Banks & Flora, 1977).

The idea of modality-specific semantic stores, whereby verbal (words) and non-verbal (pictures) material are separated, has enjoyed something of a resurgence owing to data from brain-damaged subjects. There are three main reasons for this (Caplan, 1992). First, priming effects have been discovered which have been found to be limited to verbal material. Second, cases of anomia have been discovered where it is limited to one sensory modality rather than the more common case when it is found across all modalities. Third, there is a finding that patients with semantic deficits are not always equally impaired for verbal and visual material (e.g. Warrington, 1975). Warrington and Shallice's (1979) patient JBR showed a much larger benefit from cueing in reading a written word than in naming the corresponding picture. They interpreted this finding as evidence for separate verbal and visual conceptual systems. However, as Caplan (1992) points out, there is no demonstration that automatic retrieval as manifested by short onset priming is impaired.

Alternative explanations have been offered for these early studies. Riddoch et al. (1988) argued that patients who perform better on verbal material may have a subtle impairment of complex visual processing. This idea is supported by the finding that this disturbance in processing pictures is worse for categories where there are many visually similar objects (for example, fruit and vegetables). The reverse dissociation of better performance on visual material may arise because of the abundance of indirect visual cues in pictures. For example, Caplan (1992) points out that the presence of a large gaping mouth and heavy paws in the picture of a lion is an excellent indirect cue to how to answer a comprehension question such as "Is it dangerous or not?" even if you do not know it is a picture of a lion.

Nevertheless, some more recent work is more difficult to explain away. Bub, Black, Hampson, and Kertesz (1988) describe the case of MP, who showed very poor comprehension of verbal material, and did not show automatic semantic priming, but much better comprehension of pictures. The nature of the detailed information MP was able to provide about the objects in the pictures, such as the colour of a banana from a black-and-white line drawing, could not easily be inferred from perceptual cues without access to semantic information about the object. Warrington and Shallice (1984) found high item consistency as long as modality was held constant, again suggesting different semantic systems were involved. Finally, supportive evidence comes from modality-specific anomia, in which the naming disorder is confined to one modality. For example, in *optic aphasia* (Beauvois, 1982) patients are unable to name objects when presented visually, but can if they are exposed to them through other modalities. The interpretation of these data is controversial. Riddoch and Humphreys (1987) argue that optic aphasia is a disorder of accessing a unitary semantic system through the visual system, rather than disruption to a visual modality-specific semantic system. Much hangs upon the interpretation of gestures made by the patient. Do they indeed reflect preserved visual semantics—so that patients understand the objects they see—with disruption of verbal semantics, or are they merely inferences from perceptual attributes of objects? Certainly Riddoch and Humphreys' patient JV produced only the most general of gestures to objects, and other experiments indicated a profound disturbance of comprehension of visual objects. Of course, we must remember the caveat that different patients display different behaviours, and one must be wary of drawing too general a conclusion from a single patient.

Caplan (1992) proposes a compromise position whereby only a subset of semantic information is dedicated to specific modalities. The perceptual information necessary to identify an object is certainly only a subset of the meaning of a concept, and this might well differ from the verbal semantic information elicited by that concept.

Modality-specific and category-specific effects   Is there any relationship between these findings of modality-specific and category-specific effects? Farah and McClelland (1991) argued that there is, in that damage to a modality-specific semantic memory system can lead to category-specific deficits. The architecture of their connectionist model comprises three "pools" of units: verbal input and output units (corresponding to name units), visual input and output units (picture units), and semantic memory units (divided into visual and functional units). The network was then taught to associate the correct semantic and name pattern when presented with each picture pattern, and to produce the correct semantic and picture pattern when presented with each name pattern. They then lesioned this network. They found that damage to visual semantic units primarily impairs knowledge of living things, while damage to functional semantic units primarily impairs knowledge about non-living things. Hence it is possible that semantic category-specific anomia arises not directly because knowledge about animate and inanimate objects is stored in different parts of the brain and can therefore be selectively erased, but because knowledge of animate objects is derived primarily from visual information, whereas knowledge of inanimate objects is derived primarily from functional information.

Access versus degradation

How can we tell when a concept is truly lost (or at least is degraded) from when there is difficulty in gaining access to it? Shallice (1988) and Warrington and Shallice (1979), among others, discuss five criteria to distinguish problems associated with the loss of a representation from problems of accessing it. First, performance should be consistent across trials. If an item is permanently lost, it should obviously never be possible to access it. If an item is available on some trials rather than others the difficulty is one of access. Second, superordinate information should be relatively well-preserved. Warrington (1975) found that superordinate information (e.g. that a lion is an animal, when "lion" is lost) may be preserved when more specific information is lost. She proposed that the destruction of semantic memory occurs hierarchically, from the bottom (more specific levels) up. Impaired access should affect all levels equally. Third, low frequency items should be lost first. Low frequency items should be more susceptible to loss, whereas problems of access should affect all levels equally. Fourth, priming should no longer be effective. If an item is lost it cannot be primed. Fifth, if the knowledge is lost then performance should be independent of the presentation rate, while disturbances of access should be sensitive to the rate of presentation of the material.

There has been considerable debate about how reliably these criteria do in fact distinguish access disorders from loss. It has been claimed that there are ways of presenting difficulties in access such that the same pattern of results could be found as if items were lost. See Shallice (1988) and Caplan (1992) for more detail, but in general to infer loss of items one needs to see at least consistent failure to access items across tasks. More recent work on this dichotomy is becoming mathematically sophisticated (see Faglioni & Botti, 1993).

Dementia

Dementia is a generalised decay of cognitive functioning generally found in old age. Although its exact cause is as yet unknown, memory and semantic information are particularly prone to disruption. As such many of the characteristics we have just discussed are exemplified.

Chertkow and Bub (1990) showed that patients with a type of dementia known as Alzheimer's disease demonstrated no improvement in picture naming when cued. That is, saying of a picture of a lion "It's like a tiger" did not help performance. On the other hand, Chertkow, Bub, and Seidenberg (1989) found that the same group of patients showed a clear effect of semantic priming in a lexical decision task with an SOA (stimulus onset asynchrony; see Chapter 3) of 500 milliseconds. There are two conclusions to be drawn from this study. First, for short-term priming to be found suggests that the items could not have been lost, and therefore caution must be employed if one task (such as cueing) suggests that they are. Second, Caplan (1992) points out therefore that cueing, involving attentional processing, must be distinguished from what he refers to as true priming, which involves short-term automatic processing.

Research on the breakdown of semantic memory in dementia is a fairly recent development (see Nebes, 1989, for a review). It is likely that over the next few years this will contribute greatly to our understanding of the representation of meaning.

Evaluation of the neuropsychology of semantic memory

At first sight this research seems promising. The types of dissociations found in category-specific disorders might reveal the fundamental organising principles of semantic memory. Unfortunately caution is needed on two counts. First, the area is plagued by methodological difficulties. Second, the organising principles might not be what they first seem to be. For example, the loss of the animate category might be really attributable to difficulty in accessing perceptual features, and the loss of the inanimate category might be attributable to difficulty in accessing features to do with function. At this stage it would be premature to draw any firm conclusion: this has become a very complex area.

CONCLUDING SUMMARY

Semantics is the study of meaning, and is inextricably bound up with the study of concepts and categorisation. We must distinguish between the intensional and extensional aspects of a word's meaning. We have looked at three main psycholinguistic approaches to word meaning. First, the idea that the meaning of a word is to be found in the way in which that item is embedded within a network representing the meaning of everything we know. Second, the meaning of a word is decomposed into a set of semantic features. There are a number of problems with both of these approaches. Probably the best approach to meaning that is currently available is that of prototypes. Connectionist modelling has yet to make much impact in this area.

We have also considered the neuropsychology of meaning. We have seen how a word and its meaning can be dissociated. Category-specific disorders are potentially a useful source of information about the organisation of semantic memory. Their study is however fraught with methodological problems. Neither is it clear whether at present they signify problems specifically concerning a particular semantic category, or whether instead they represent problems with some more fundamental organising principle. There is also considerable current debate as to whether there is a unitary semantic system, or whether there are different semantic stores for the visual and verbal systems. The study of dementia is also important, but here we must be careful to distinguish between the loss of semantic information from loss of the ability to access that information.

In the next chapter we shall see how we combine the meanings of individual words with the syntactic representation to form a representation of the meaning of the whole sentence.

FURTHER READING

An good overview of cognitive psychology approaches to meaning and the representation of knowledge is provided by Eysenck and Keane (1995). The classic linguistics work on semantics is Lyons (1977b,c). Johnson-Laird (1983) provides an excellent review of a number of approaches to semantics, including the relevance of the more philosophical approaches. Perhaps its most detailed and formalised philosophical system of meaning is that of *Montague grammar* (Montague, 1974). Montague grammar shows how the meaning of sentences can be formally derived by combining model-theoretic representations of the meanings or intensions of their component words. Although the theory is too advanced to be considered here, an introduction can be found in Johnson-Laird (1983, Chapter 8).

General problems with network models are discussed by Johnson-Laird, Herrman, and Chaffin (1984). Chang (1986) reviews the experimental support for psychological models of semantic memory. Komatsu (1992) and Medin (1989) review the literature on concepts. For further discussion of connectionist approaches to semantic memory, see Quinlan (1991).

Caplan (1992) provides and extensive review of the neuropsychology of semantic memory. Other cases have been reported by Sartori and Job (1988), who describe patient "Michelangelo", and de Renzi and Lucchelli (1994), who describe patient "Felicia", both of whom have a relative deficit on naming animals, fruit, and vegetables. A special issue of the journal *Cognitive Neuropsychology* (1988, volume 5, issue 1) was devoted to the neuropsychology of this subject, particularly upon modality-specific effects. Davidoff and de Bleser (1993) review the literature on optic aphasia, and Plaut and Shallice (1993b) describe a connectionist model of it. See Shallice (1988) and Caplan (1992) for further discussion of criteria for distinguishing between the loss of information and difficulty in accessing that information.

CHAPTER SEVEN

Comprehension: Understanding and remembering the message

INTRODUCTION

In this chapter we will be concerned with the processes of comprehension. What do we do with what we hear and read after we have identified the words involved, accessed their meanings, and parsed as much of the syntactic structure of the sentence as is necessary? How do we build up a representation of the meaning of the whole sentence, given the meanings of the individual words? And then how do we combine sentences to construct a representation of the whole conversation or text?

One of the central themes in the study of comprehension is whether it is a *constructive* process or a *minimal* process. Do we, the readers and listeners, go far beyond the words actually present, and construct a model of what is being communicated? Or do we do as little work as possible in comprehension, just enough so as to be able to make out the sense? In either case, the main way in which we go beyond the communicated material is that we make *inferences*. When and how do we make these inferences that go beyond what we simply hear or read to the meaning that is not explicitly presented? In making inferences, we construct a model of the complete structure that is communicated by the words and sentences that are presented. We are faced with the additional problem of working out what the words in the incoming sentences refer to in this model. In this case, we actually use the model that we are constructing to help us make sense of the material. We shall see that it is possible to take this idea of comprehension as construction too far: we do not do more work than is necessary during comprehension. If comprehension for meaning is like building a house to live in, we do not build a mansion.

A number of terms have closely related meanings. As we will use it, the term *text* is used to present written material, usually longer than a sentence. A story is a particular, self-contained type of text. It should be noted that a story as used in a psycholinguistic experiment may only be two sentences long! *Discourse* is the spoken equivalent of text. Of course there may be many things in common in representing and understanding the two. Most of what will be discussed in this chapter (apart from the very last section on conversation) applies to both written and spoken language, and the terms text and discourse can be used almost interchangeably. *Conversations* are spoken interchanges where the topic may change as the conversation unfolds. Conversations have their own particular mechanisms for controlling coherence and who is talking.

It is convenient at this stage to distinguish between semantic and referential processing (Garnham & Oakhill, 1992). Semantic processing concerns working out what things mean in general; we examined how meaning is represented in the previous chapter. Referential processing concerns the particular meaning of words with reference to their role in the model. In general, semantic processing precedes referential processing. In incremental parsing models (such as Altmann & Steedman, 1988), semantic and referential processing occur on a word-by-word basis.

The organisation of this chapter is as follows. First, we will look at what determines what we remember of text. Then we will examine the process of inference making in comprehension in detail, with particular emphasis on the problems of deciding what words refer to in our model. Then we will review some influential theories of text comprehension. We will conclude by considering some problems that are specific to spoken conversations.

What makes comprehension more difficult?

Throughout this chapter we will come across a number of findings that point to ways of making comprehension easier or more difficult. Some of them are perhaps not surprising: for example, it is difficult to remember material if the sense of a story is jumbled. Thorndyke and Hayes-Roth (1979) showed that the structure of individual sentences can affect the recall of the whole story. In particular, they showed that repetition of the same sentence structure improves recall when the content of the sentences changes, as long as not too much information is presented using the same sentence structure—that is, if it is not repeated too many times with different content. Throughout this chapter, measures of how much we remember of a story are often used to tell us how difficult the material is. That is, it is reasoned that good memory equals good comprehension. However, this is rather different from the other measures we have considered in previous chapters, which have tended to be on-line in the sense that they measure processing at the time of presentation. Memory may reflect processing subsequent to initial comprehension.

The given-new contract. One of the most important factors that determines the comprehensibility of something is the order in which new information is presented relative to what we know already. Clearly this affects the ease with which we can integrate the new information into the old. It has been argued that there is a "contract" between the writer and the reader, or participants in a conversation, to present new information so that it can easily be assimilated with what people already know. This has been called the *given-new contract* (Clark & Haviland, 1977; Haviland & Clark, 1974). It takes less time to understand a new sentence when it explicitly contains some of the same ideas as an earlier sentence than when the relationship between the contents of the sentences has to be inferred.

MEMORY FOR TEXT AND INFERENCES

Verbatim memory is notoriously unreliable. If we needed to be prompted of this, Neisser (1981) provided a case study of the memory of John Dean. John Dean was an aide of President Richard Nixon at the time of the Watergate cover-up and scandal in the early 1970s. Unknown to Dean, the conversations in Nixon's office were tape-recorded, so his recall for them when testifying to the Watergate Committee in June 1973 could be checked against the tape recordings, nine months after the original events. His recall was highly inaccurate. Nixon did not say many of the things Dean attributed to him, and much was omitted. Dean's recall was only really accurate at a very general thematic level: the people involved did discuss the cover-up, but not in the precise way Dean said they had. It seems that Dean's attitudes influenced what he remembered. For example, Dean said that he wanted to warn the President the cover-up might fall apart, but in fact he did not; at the hearings, he said that he thought he had. In summary, assuming that Dean was being truthful about his recall of the events, we see that in spite of their belief to the contrary, speakers only remember the gist of previous conversations. We see a tendency to *abstract*, and to "remember" things that never actually happen. These are findings have been replicated many times, so they are clearly an important feature of memory. Another well-known example is that of eye-witness testimony; this is easily influenced by many factors (Loftus, 1979). So what determines what we remember and what we forget, and can we ever remember material verbatim?

As we mentioned in Chapter 5, people generally forget the details of word order very quickly: we remember only the semantics of what we read or hear, not the syntax. Sachs (1967) presented subjects a sentence such as (1) embedded in a story. She later tested their ability to distinguish it from possible confusion sentences (2 to 4):

1. He sent a letter about it to Galileo, the great Italian scientist. (Original)
2. He sent Galileo, the great Italian scientist, a letter about it. (Formal word order change)
3. A letter about it was sent to Galileo, the great Italian scientist. (Passive form: a syntactic change)
4. Galileo, the great Italian scientist, sent him a letter about it. (Semantic change)

She tested recognition after 0, 80, or 160 intervening syllables (which are equal to approximately 0, 25, or 50 second delays respectively), and found that the subjects' ability to detect changes to word order and syntax decreased very quickly. That is, subjects could not tell the difference between the original and the changed sentences (2) and (3). They were however sensitive to changes in meaning (such as in 4). Generally, we remember the gist of text, and very quickly dump the details of word order.

The details of the surface syntactic form are not always lost. Yekovich and Thorndike (1981) showed that we can sometimes recognise exact wording, up to at least one hour after presentation. Bates, Masling, and Kintsch (1978) tested subjects' recognition memory for conversations in television soap operas. As expected, memory for meaning straight after the programme was nearly perfect, but subjects could also remember the detailed surface form when it had some significance. This shows that there are differences between coherent naturalistic conversation and isolated artificial sentences. In real conversation (counting soap operas as examples of real conversation) quite often what might be considered surface detail serves a particular function. For example, the way in which we use pronouns or names depends in part on factors like how much attention we want to draw to what is being referred to. This result accords with our intuitions: although we often remember only the gist of what is said to us, on occasion we can remember the exact wording, particularly if it is important or emotionally salient.

How we can sometimes remember the exact surface form is not currently known. When is the decision taken to store it permanently? Neither is the relationship between our memory for surface form and the structure of the parser well understood. Clearly we can routinely remember more than the six word or one clause window of the PPP, even if there has been subsequent interfering material, so it cannot be simply that we forget surface form as it drops out of the PPP. The finding that we can sometimes remember surface form for some time suggests that the SSS can parse one sentence while storing details of another.

Importance

Not surprisingly people are more likely to remember what they consider to be the more important aspects of text. Johnson (1970) showed that subjects were more likely to recall ideas from a story that had been rated as important by another group of subjects. Keenan, MacWhinney, and Mayhew (1977) examined memory for a linguistics seminar, and compared sentences that were considered to be HIC (High Interactional Content—which is material having personal significance) sentences with LIC (Low Interactional Content—which is material having little personal significance) sentences.

5.   I think you've made a fundamental error in this study.
6.   I think there are two fundamental tasks in this study.

Sentences with high interactional content (such as 5) were more likely to be recalled by the appropriate participants in the seminar than sentences with low interactional content (such as 6).

Although it may not be surprising that more important information is recalled better, there are a number of reasons why it might be so. We might spend longer reading more important parts of the text; indeed, eye movement research suggests this is in part the case. In this case the better memory would simply reflect more processing time. However, Britton, Muth, and Glynn (1986) restricted the time subjects could spend reading parts of the text so that subjects spent equal amounts of time reading the more and less important parts of a story, and found that they still remembered the important parts better. Hence there is a real effect of the role the material plays in the meaning of the story. Important material must be flagged in comprehension and memory in some way.

The effects of prior knowledge

The effect of prior knowledge upon what we remember and upon the processes of comprehension was explored in an important series of experiments by Bransford and his colleagues. For example, Bransford and Johnson (1973) read subjects the following story (7):

7. "If the balloons popped, the sound wouldn't be able to carry far, since everything would be too far away from the correct floor. A closed window would also prevent the sound from carrying, since most buildings tend to be well insulated. Since the whole operation depends upon a steady flow of electricity, a break in the middle of the wire would also cause problems. Of course, the fellow could shout, but the human voice is not loud enough to carry that far. An additional problem is that a string could break on the instrument. Then there could be no accompaniment to the message. It is clear that the best situation would involve less distance. Then there would be fewer potential problems. With face-to-face contact, the least number of things could go wrong." (Bransford & Johnson, 1973, p.392.)

This story was specially designed to be abstract and unfamiliar. Bransford and Johnson measured subjects' ratings of the comprehensibility of the story and also the number of ideas recalled. Subjects were divided into three groups, called "no context", "context before", and "context after". The context here was provided in the form of a picture which makes sense of the story (see Fig. 7.1). Bransford and Johnson found that this context was only useful if it was presented before the story: the "no context" group recalled an average of 3.6 ideas out of a maximum of 14, the "context after" also 3.6 ideas, but the "context before" recalled an average of 8.0 ideas. Hence context must provide more than just retrieval cues; it must also improve our comprehension, and this must then improve our recall. Context provides a *frame* for understanding text. The role of context and background information is a recurring theme in understanding how we understand and remember text, and its importance cannot be underestimated.

In this experiment, the story and the context were novel. Bransford and Johnson (1973) also showed that knowing a well-known context can facilitate comprehension. They presented subjects with the following story (8).

8. "The procedure is actually quite simple. First you arrange things into two different groups. Of course, one pile may be sufficient depending on how much there is to do. If you have to go somewhere

FIG. 7.1. Picture context for the "balloon story" (7). (Reprinted from Bransford, J. D., & Johnson, M. K., 1973. Consideration of some problems of comprehension. In W. G. Chase (Ed.), *Visual information processing*, p. 396. New York: Academic Press. © 1973 by Academic Press. Reprinted by permission.)

else due to lack of facilities, that is the next step; otherwise you are pretty well set. It is important not to overdo things. That is, it is better to do fewer things at once than too many. In the short run this might not seem important, but complications can easily arise. A mistake can be expensive as well. At first the whole procedure will seem complicated. Soon, however, it will become just another facet of life. It is difficult to foresee any end to the necessity for this task in the immediate future, but then one can never tell. After the procedure is completed, one arranges the material into different groups again. Then they can be put into their appropriate places. Eventually they will be used once more, and the whole cycle will then have to be repeated. However, that is part of life." (Bransford & Johnson, 1973, p. 400.)

When you know that this is called the "clothes washing" story, it probably all makes sense. Those who read the passage without this context later recalled an average of only 2.8 out of a maximum of 18 ideas; those who had the context after reading it also recalled only on average 2.7 ideas. However, those given the context before the story recalled an average of 5.8 ideas. These experiments suggest that background knowledge by itself is not sufficient: you must recognise when it is applicable.

Appropriate context may be as little as the title of a story. Dooling and Lachman (1971) showed the effect of providing subjects with a title that helped them make sense of what was read, but once again it had to be given before reading the story (9).

9.   "With hocked gems financing him, our hero bravely defied all scornful laughter that tried to prevent his scheme. 'Your eyes deceive', he had said. 'An egg, not a table, correctly typifies this unexplored planet.' Now three sturdy sisters sought proof. Forging along, sometimes through vast calmness, yet more often over turbulent peaks and valleys, days became weeks as doubters spread fearful rumours about the edge. At last, from nowhere, welcome winged creatures appeared signifying monumental success."

Without the title of *Christopher Columbus's discovery of America*, the story makes little sense. In fact, "three sturdy sisters" refers to the three ships, the "turbulent peaks and valleys" to the waves, "the edge" to the supposed edge of a flat earth, and so on.

It might reasonably be objected that all these stories so far have been designed to be obtuse without a title or context, and are not representative of normal texts. What happens with less obtuse stories?

This can be seen in an experiment by Anderson and Pichert (1978), who showed how a shift in perspective provides different retrieval cues. Subjects read a story which is summarised in (10).

10.   Two boys played hooky from school. They go to the home of one of the boys because his mother is never there on a Thursday. The family is well off. They have a fine old home which is set back from the road and which has attractive grounds. But since it is an old house it has some defects: for example, it has a leaky roof, and a

damp and musty cellar. Because the family is wealthy, they have a lot of valuable possessions, such as ten-speed bike, a colour television, and a rare coin collection.

(A more colloquial British term for "playing hooky" is "skiving".) The story was 373 words long and contained 72 main ideas. These had been previously rated by other subjects according to their relevance to a potential house buyer or a potential burglar. For example, a leaky roof and damp basement are important features of a house to house buyers but not to burglars, while valuable possessions and the fact that no-one is in on Thursday are more relevant to burglars. The participants in the experiment read the story from either a "house buying" or "burglar" perspective in advance. Not surprisingly, the perspective influenced the ideas the subjects recalled. Half the subjects were then told the other perspective, while a control group of the other half of the subjects just had the first repeated. The shift in perspective improved recall: subjects could recall things they had previously forgotten. This is because the new perspective provides a plan for searching memory.

At first sight the findings of this experiment appear to contradict those of Bransford and Johnson. Bransford and Johnson showed that context has little effect when it is presented after a story, but Anderson and Pichert showed that changing the perspective after the story—which of course is a form of context—can improve recall. The difference is that, unlike the Bransford and Johnson experiments, the Anderson and Pichert story was easy to understand. It is hard to encode difficult material in the first place, yet alone recall it later. With easier material the problem is in recalling it, not encoding it. In an extension of this study, Baillet and Keenan (1986) looked at what happens if perspective is shifted after reading but before recall. Subjects who recalled the material immediately depended upon the retrieval perspective; however subjects who retrieved after a much longer interval (one week) were not affected by the retrieval perspective—only the perspective given at encoding mattered.

Finally, the importance of an idea relative to the rest of the story also affects its memorability (Bower, Black, & Turner, 1979; Kintsch & van Dijk, 1978; Thorndyke, 1977). As you might predict, the more important a proposition is, the more likely it is to be remembered. It is the task of various text processing theories to predict why one idea should be more "important" than another.

Prior knowledge as a source of errors.   Prior knowledge and context are not unalloyed blessings. Although they can help us to remember material that we would otherwise have forgotten, they can also make us think we have "remembered" material that was never presented in the first place! For example, Sulin and Dooling (1974) showed that background knowledge can also be a source of errors if it is applied inappropriately. Consider the following story (11).

11.   "Gerald Martin strove to undermine the existing government to satisfy his political ambitions. Many of the people of his country supported his efforts. Current political problems made it relatively easy for Martin to take over. Certain groups remained loyal to the old government and caused Martin trouble. He confronted these groups directly and so silenced them. He became a ruthless, uncontrollable dictator. The ultimate effect of his rule was the downfall of his country." (Sulin & Dooling, 1974, p. 256.)

Half of the subjects in their experiment read this story as above, with the name of the main actor in the story given as "Gerald Martin". The other half read it with the name "Adolf Hitler" instead. Subjects in the "Hitler" condition afterwards tended to believe incorrectly that they had read a sentence "He hated the Jews particularly and so persecuted them", more than a neutral control sentence such as "He was an intelligent man but had no sense of human kindness". That is, they made inferences from their background world knowledge that influenced their memory of the story. Subjects in the fictitious character condition were of course unable to use this background information.

Inferences

We make an inference when we go beyond the literal meaning of the text. A very simple example is in the story: "Vlad burned his mouth on his coffee. It was too hot." Here you probably made the inference that "it" refers to "the coffee", rather than "his mouth". A more complex example was shown in the Gerald Martin story in the "Adolf Hitler" condition. Hence inferences are not always correct. There are three types of inference. First, *logical inferences* follow from the meanings of words. For example, hearing "Vlad is a bachelor" enables us to infer that Vlad is male. Second, *bridging inferences* serve the function of relating new to previous information (Clark, 1977a,b). Another way of putting this is that texts have *coherence* in a way that randomly jumbled sentences do not have. We strive to maintain this coherence, and make inferences to this end. In this respect, one of the major tasks in comprehension is sorting out to what pronouns refer, as in the example of Vlad's coffee. Sometimes even more cognitive work is necessary to make sense of what we read or hear. How can we make sense of (12)? We can if we assume that the moat refers to a moat around the castle mentioned in the first sentence. This is an example of how we maintain coherence: we comprehend on the basis that there is continuity in the material that we are processing, and that it is not just a jumble of disconnected ideas. Bridging inferences provide links among ideas so that they maintain coherence.

12.   Vlad looked around the castle. The moat was dry.

Third, we make *elaborative inferences* when we extend the text with world knowledge. The Gerald Martin example is an (unwarranted) elaborative inference. This proves to be very difficult for AI simulations of text comprehension, and is known as the *frame problem*. Our store of world general knowledge is enormous, and potentially any of it can be brought to bear on a piece of text. Bridging and elaborative inferences have sometimes been called *backward* and *forward* inferences respectively, as backward inferences require us to go back from the current text to previous information, while forward inferences allow us to elaborate to the future. As we shall see, there are reasons to think that different mechanisms are responsible for these two types of inference. Taken together, all inferences that are not logical are sometimes called *pragmatic inferences*. (See Garnham, 1985, 1987, for further discussion of these issues.)

We have seen in the previous section, people cannot help but make inferences on the basis of their world knowledge. We have also seen that we only remember the gist of what we read or hear, not the detailed form. Taken together, these suggest that we should find it very difficult to distinguish the inferences we make from what we actually hear. This was demonstrated in an experiment by Bransford, Barclay, and Franks (1972), who showed that after a short delay the target sentence (13) cannot be distinguished from the valid inference (14):

13.   Three turtles rested on a floating log and a fish swam beneath them.
14.   Three turtles rested on a floating log and a fish swam beneath it.

If you swim beneath a log with a turtle on it, then you must swim beneath the turtle. If you change "on" to "beside", then subjects are very good at detecting this change, because the inference is no longer true and therefore not one likely to be made.

When are inferences made?   What determines whether we make an inference? Comprehenders are more likely to make inferences related to the important components of a story and not on incidental details

(Seifert, Robertson, & Black, 1985). The important components are the main characters and their goals, and actions relating to the main plan of the story.

We have seen that the most commonly held position is that inferences play a role in constructing a representation of the text. It should be pointed out that there is an alternative position. This is known as the *minimalist hypothesis*, and is held most forcefully by McKoon and Ratcliff (1992). According to this viewpoint, as few inferences are made as possible, and those that are made are kept as simple as possible and use only information that is readily available. In part the issue comes down to when the inferences are made. Is a particular inference made automatically at the time of comprehension, or is it made with prompting during recall? This debate might remind you of some of the issues involved in word recognition. On the one hand, we might equate the "all inferences are made during comprehension and used to construct a model of the text" position with interaction, and "only a few inferences are made automatically during actual comprehension" positions with autonomy.

You might have observed that all the experiments described so far have tested subjects' memory for what was presented. Hence any inference detected in this way might have been made during the act of recall rather than during the act of comprehension. There is some experimental evidence for this. Corbett and Dosher (1978) found that the word "scissors" was an equally good cue for recalling each of the sentences (15–17).

15.   The athlete cut out an article with scissors for his friend.
16.   The athlete cut out an article for his friend.
17.   The athlete cut out an article with a razor blade for his friend.

The mention of a "razor blade" in sentence (17) will have prevented any inference being drawn then about the use of scissors. The finding that "scissors" is just as effective a cue suggests that subjects are working backwards at recall from the cue to an action and then retrieving the sentence.

Memory measures then are indirect measures of comprehension and may give a distorting picture of the comprehension process. In particular, this may have led us to over-estimate the role of construction in comprehension. It now seems likely that only bridging or reference-related inferences necessary to maintain the coherence of the text are made automatically during comprehension, and elaborative inferences are generally only made later, during recall. For an inference to be made automatically, appropriate supporting associative semantic information must be present in the text. For example, McKoon and Ratcliff (1986, 1989) showed that in a lexical decision task, the recognition of a word likely to be inferred in a "strong association predicting context" (e.g. the word "sew" in [18]) is facilitated much more than the word which might be inferred in a "weak association context" (the word "dead" in [19]).

18.   The housewife was learning to be a seamstress and needed practice so she got out the skirt she was making and threaded her needle.

19.   The director and cameraman were ready to shoot close-ups when suddenly the actress fell from the 14th storey.

In both cases the target word is part of a valid inference from the original sentence, but whereas "sew" is a semantic associate of the words "seamstress", "threaded", and "needle" in (18), the word "dead" involves a bridging inference in (19)—the actress does not have to die as a result of this accident—and is not supported by a strong associative context. Such inferences do not therefore have to be drawn automatically. The recent development of on-line techniques of examining comprehension has generally supported this more limited conclusion, although there is still considerable debate as to how often elaborative inferences are made automatically (see Graesser, Singer, & Trabasso, 1994; McKoon & Ratcliff, 1992; Singer, 1994; Singer & Ferreira, 1983; Potts, Keenan, & Golding, 1988). The most commonly used on-line measure is reading time, under the assumption that automatic inferences take time, necessitating us to look at the guilty word for longer.

Practical implications of inferences.   Of course, there are some obvious implications for everyday life if we are continually making inferences on the basis of what we read and hear. A great deal of social interaction is based upon drawing inferences from other people's conversation—and we have seen, these inferences are not always drawn correctly. There are two main applied areas where elaborative inferences are particularly important, and those are methods of advertising and eyewitness testimony.

The work of Loftus (e.g. 1975, 1979) on eyewitness testimony is very well-known. She showed how unreliable eyewitness testimony actually was, and how inferences based upon the wording of questions could prejudice people's answers. For example, in one experiment subjects saw a film depicting a car crash and then answered questions about it immediately afterwards. One question had two variants: "Did you see a broken headlight?" and "Did you see the broken headlight?" The definite article "the" implies the existence of what is being referred to, and she duly found that subjects who were asked the "the" form of the question were more likely to answer "yes" than those who had been asked the "a" version of the question. (In fact no broken headlight was visible in the film.) Harris (1978) simulated a jury listening to courtroom witnesses, and found that although subjects were more likely to accept directly asserted statements as true than only implied statements for which they had to make an inference, there was still a strong tendency to accept the implied statements. Instructions to subjects telling them to be careful to distinguish asserted and implied information did not help, either. Furthermore, this test was only five minutes after hearing the statements, whereas in a real courtroom the delays can be weeks, and the potential problem much worse.

Similar results about people's difficulty in distinguishing assertions and implications in advertising claims have been found by Harris (1977). Subjects are best at distinguishing assertions from implications if they have been warned to do so before hearing the claim, and are asked about it immediately afterwards. Deviation from this pattern leads to a rapid impairment of our ability to distinguish fact from implication.

Anaphoric reference and ambiguity

Anaphoric reference describes the way in which material can refer to earlier material, or the *antecedent*, without any explicit repetition of it. The most common example is by the use of a pronoun such as "he" and "it" in (20). Here "Vlad" and "knife" are the antecedents of "he" and "it" respectively. Strictly speaking, anaphor is reserved for the pronoun following the antecedent; *cataphor* is the term for the less common case when the pronoun precedes its antecedent, as in (21). Furthermore, anaphoric reference does not have to involve pronouns; it can also involve other nouns referring to the same thing (22), or verbs (23).

20.   Vlad put the knife on the table. Then *he* forgot where *it* was.
21.   After *he* had finished with the knife, Vlad put *it* on the table.
22.   Vlad went to the cinema. The *vampire* really enjoyed the film.
23.   Vlad loves Boris and so *does* Dirk.

It is useful to distinguish between deep and surface anaphors (Hankamer & Sag, 1976; Sag & Hankamer, 1984). Surface anaphors relate in an obvious way to an omission from the surface structure of previous material; deep anaphors do not depend on the syntactic form, but depend upon special explicitly referring constructions and their role in a discourse model for their interpretation. There are several types of each: examples (24) to (26) illustrate deep anaphora, (27) to (29) surface anaphora. There is some evidence that deep and surface anaphors are processed differently, with deep anaphors insensitive to the syntactic form of the antecedent and necessitating access to a representation of the text (Mauner, Tanenhaus, & Carlson, 1995; Murphy, 1985; Tanenhaus & Carlson, 1990; but see Garnham, Oakhill, Ehrlich, & Carreiras, 1995). However, most of the literature concerns research on deep anaphors.

24. Vlad left. He was angry. (Definite pronoun)
25. Vlad bought a big castle. Boris bought a small one. (one pronominal)
26. Vlad knew who was hungry. But he wouldn't tell. (null complement)
27. Vlad caught a rat, and Boris __, a bat. (gapping)
28. Vlad built a new castle. Boris did __, too. (verb phrase ellipsis)
29. Someone just called Vlad, but I don't know who __. (sluicing)

The processing problem of anaphoric reference is to work out to what they refer—what their antecedents are. This process is called *resolution*. Anaphoric resolution is nothing other than a particular type of backward inference that we must do to maintain a coherent representation of the text. Anaphoric resolution is necessary on both the constructionist and minimalist accounts of comprehension.

Resolving anaphoric ambiguity. In many cases anaphoric resolution is straightforward. In a story such as (30) there is only one possible antecedent.

30. Vlad was happy. He laughed.

However, what makes anaphoric resolution difficult is that often it is not obvious what the antecent of the anaphor is. The anaphor is ambiguous when there are more than one possible antecedent, such as (31) .

31. Vlad stuck a dagger in the corpse. *It* was made out of silver. *It* oozed blood.

In this case we have no apparent difficulty in understanding to what each "it" refers. How do we do this? In more complex cases there might be a number of alternatives, or background or world knowledge is necessary to disambiguate.

We cope with anaphoric ambiguity by using a number of coping strategies. Whether or not these strategies are used to guide an explicit search process, or to exclude items from a search set, or both, or even to avoid an explicit search altogether, is at present unclear. We can distinguish two groups of strategies: those dependent on the meaning of the actual words used, or their role in the sentence; and those dependent on the emergent discourse model. Of the first of these, one of the most obvious is the use of gender (Corbett & Chang, 1983). In (32) it is clear that "he" must refer to Vlad, and "she" to Agnes. Although it might seem self-evident that gender should be used automatically, Garnham, Oakhill, and Cruttenden (1992) suggested that the use of gender cues might be under the comprehender's strategic control. Subjects can switch interpretation of the gender cues on or off depending on the precise experimental task. Subjects use gender cues when the task forces them to pay particular attention to the pronouns. Garnham et al. (1995) extend these results examining the role of the arbitrary gender of Spanish and French nouns.

32.   Agnes won and Vlad lost. He was sad and she was glad.

Different verbs however carry different implications about the how the actors involved should be assigned to roles. If subjects are asked to complete the sentences (33) and (34), they produce continuations in which "he" refers to the subject (Timmy) in (33), and the object (Boris) in (34). Verbs such as "sale" are called NP1 verbs, because causality is usually attributed to the first, subject, noun phrase; while verbs such as "blame" are called NP2 verbs, because causality is usually attributed to the second, object, noun phrase (Grober, Beardsley, & Caramazza, 1978).

33.   Timmy sold his broomstick to Boris because he ...
34.   Timmy blamed Boris because he ...

This gives a cue to anaphoric resolution called *parallel function*. We prefer to match anaphors to antecedents in the same relevant position. When this is violated anaphoric resolution is more difficult. In (35) and (36) the appropriate order of antecedents and pronouns differ. In (35) "he" refers to "Vlad", which comes first in "Vlad sold Dirk", but in (36) "he" refers to "Dirk", which comes second. Therefore (36) is harder to understand than (35). The role of the congruity of the pronoun with the bias of the verb does seem to be automatic (Garnham et al., 1992).

35. Vlad sold Dirk his broomstick because he hated it.
36. Vlad sold Dirk his broomstick because he needed it.

The second group of anaphoric resolution strategies concern those dependent upon the perceived prominence of possible referents in the emergent text model. We might be biased for example to select the referent in the model that is most frequently mentioned. Antecedents are generally easier to locate when they are close to their referents than when they are further away, in terms of the number of intervening words (Murphy, 1985). In more complicated examples alternatives can sometimes be eliminated using background knowledge and elaborative inferences, as in (37). Exactly how this background knowledge is used is unclear. In this case we infer becoming a vegetarian would not make someone want to buy piglets, but more likely to sell them, as they would be less likely to have any future use for them. Here constructionist models come into their own.

37. Vlad sold his piglets to Dirk because he had become a vegetarian.

Pronouns are read more quickly when the referent of the antecedent is still in the foreground or focus of the situation being discussed than when the situation has changed so that it is no longer in focus (Garrod & Sanford, 1977; Sanford & Garrod, 1981). Items in explicit focus are said to be *foregrounded* and have been explicitly mentioned in the preceding text. Such items can be referred to pronominally. Items in implicit focus are only implied by what is in explicit focus. Experiments on reading time suggest that implicit focus items are harder to process. Items are likely to stay in the foreground if it is an important theme in the discourse, and these items are likely to be maintained in working memory. Pronouns with antecedents in the foreground, or *topic antecedents*, are read quickly, regardless of the distance between the pronoun and referent (Clifton & Ferreira, 1987). These strategies are what we might expect: in conversation we do not normally start using pronouns for referents that we have not mentioned for some time.

Finally, in conversation there is an additional possible source of help in resolving anaphora: the speaker who made the original statement. Conversation is a collaborative enterprise, and speakers collaborate with listeners to ensure that their utterances are understood (Clark & Wilkes-Gibbs, 1986; Schober & Clark, 1989).

Accessibility.   The notions of topics and discourse foregrounds imply that some items are more accessible than others. We are faster at retrieving the referent of more accessible antecedents. At this stage some caution is necessary to avoid a circular definition of accessibility. Accessibility is a concept related both to anaphor and to the work on sentence memory. It can be measured by recording how long it takes subjects to detect whether a name presented while subjects are reading sentences is present in the sentence.

Generally we are biased to referring back to the subject of a sentence; there is also an advantage to *first mention*. This means that participants that are mentioned first in a sentence are more accessible than those mentioned second. Gernsbacher and Hargreaves (1988) showed that there was a real advantage for first mention, independent of other factors such as whether the words involved were subject or object. Gernsbacher, Hargreaves, and Beeman (1989) explored the apparent contradiction between first mention and recency, in that items that are more recent should also be more accessible. Gernsbacher and Hargreaves explained this with a constructionist, structure-building account: the goal of comprehension is to build a coherent representation (or model, or structure) of what is being comprehended. Comprehenders represent each clause of a multi-clause sentence with a separate sub-structure, and have easiest access to the sub-structure they are currently working upon. However at some point the earlier information becomes more accessible because it serves as a foundation for the whole sentence-level representation. So it is only as the representation is being developed that recency is important. Recency is detectable only when accessibility is measured immediately after the second clause; elsewhere first mention is important, and has the more long-lasting effect. This explanation is reminiscent of Kintsch's propositional model discussed below, and shows how it is possible to account for anaphoric resolution in terms of the details of the emergent comprehension model.

Summary of work on memory, inferences, and anaphora
Any model of comprehension must be able to explain the following characteristics. We read for gist, and very quickly forget details of surface form. Comprehension is to some extent a constructive process: we build a model of what we are processing, although the level detail involved is controversial. At the very least, we make inferences to maintain coherence. One of the most important mechanisms involved in this is anaphoric resolution. Inferences soon become integrated into our model as we go along, and we are very soon unable to distinguish our inferences from what we originally heard. There is a foreground area of the model such that important and recent items are more accessible.

MODELS OF TEXT REPRESENTATION
AND PROCESSING

In this section we will look at some models of how we represent and process text. An adequate model must explain those features summarised in the previous section. As with syntax, models of comprehension have been heavily influenced by AI. The ideas thus generated are interesting and explicit, but this has the disadvantage that as the specific mechanisms we use are unlikely to be exactly the same as the explicit mechanisms used to implement the AI concepts, these ideas can prove remarkably difficult to test.

Propositional network models of representing text

The meaning of sentences and text can be represented by a network where the intersections, or nodes represent the meaning of words, and the connections represent the relationships between words. The basis of this approach is Fillmore's (1968) theory of *case grammar*, which in turn was derived from a grammatical theory which emphasised the importance of semantics, known as *generative grammar* (see Chapter 5). Case grammar emphasises the roles or *cases* played by what the words refer to in the sentence. It stresses the relationship between verbs and the words associated with them—their arguments. Table 7.1 gives some examples of cases. One disadvantage of case grammar is that there is little agreement over exactly what the cases which describe the language should be, or even how many there should be. As you will observe, this lack of agreement about the basic units involved is endemic in models of comprehension.

In network models, sentences are first analysed into *propositions*. A proposition is the smallest unit of meaning with an internal structure: that is, they can be put in predicate-argument form, such as verbs operating on nouns. Another way of putting this is that a proposition

TABLE 7.1
Examples of grammatical cases

Agent	Instigator (usually animate) of the action of the verb
Object	Entity affected by action
Instrument	Object used in causing event
Locative	Place of event
Time	Time of event
Source	Place from which something originates or moves
Goal	Place to which something moves

has a truth value— that is, we can say whether it is true or false. For example, the words "witch" and "cackle" are not propositions: they are unitary and have no internal structure, and it is meaningless to talk of individual words being true or false. On the other hand, "the witch cackles" contains a proposition. This can be put in the predicate-argument form "cackle(witch)", which does have a truth value: the witch is either cackling or she isn't.

Propositions are connected together in propositional networks, as in Fig. 7.2. The model of Anderson and Bower (1973) has been particularly influential. Originally known as HAM (short for Human Associative Memory), the model evolved first into ACT (Anderson, 1976) and later ACT* (pronounced "ACT-star"; Anderson, 1983). These models combine a spreading activation model of semantic memory, combined later with a production system for executing higher level operations. A production system is a series of if-then rules: *if* x happens, *then* do y. ACT* gives a good account of explaining fact retrieval from short stories. Experiments showed that the reaction time for retrieving facts increased as a function of the number of times the items sought for were mentioned in the stories: the more unique something is, the easier it is to retrieve.

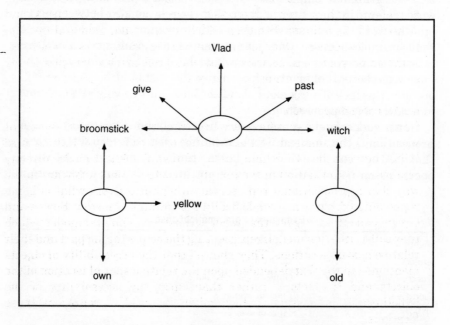

FIG. 7.2. An example of a simplified propositional network underlying the sentence "Vlad gave his yellow broomstick to the old witch". The ellipses denote objects and events, hence enabling a distinction between words and the concepts they denote.

Another influential network model has been the *conceptual dependency* theory of Schank (1975). As we saw in Chapter 6, this starts off with the idea that meaning can be decomposed into small, atomic units. Text is therefore represented by decomposing the incoming material into these atomic units and building a network that relates them. An important intermediate step is that the atomic units of meaning are combined into *conceptualisations* that specify the *actors* involved in the discourse and the actions that relate them. Once again, this approach has the advantage that as it has been implemented (in part) as a computer simulation: its assumptions and limitations are therefore very clear.

Evaluation of propositional network models.   Just as there is little agreement on the cases to use, there is little agreement on the precise types of roles and connections to use. If we measure propositional networks against the requirements at the end of the previous section, we can see that they satisfy some of the requirements, but leave a lot to be desired as models of discourse processing. They show how knowledge might be represented, but they have little to say about when or how we make inferences, or how some items are maintained in the foreground, or how we extract the gist from text. Johnson-Laird et al. (1984) and Woods (1975; but see Hendrix, 1979) provide detailed critiques of technical aspects of propositional network models. As we shall see, however, propositional networks may play a role in discourse processing as a means of representing knowledge.

Mental models approach

Comprehenders construct a *mental model* as they go along to represent what they hear and read. This approach is exemplified by Johnson-Laird (1983; but see also Garnham, 1985, 1987a). A mental model directly represents the situation in the text. Its structure is not arbitrary in the way that a propositional representation is, but mirrors what is being represented directly and analogically. For example, Morrow, Bower, and Greenspan (1989) argued that readers construct a mental model (which they call a situation model) representing the actors taking part and their relative spatial locations. They showed that the accessibility of objects mentioned in the text depended upon the relative spatial location of the objects and the actors, rather than upon the accessibility of the hypothesised propositions which might be used to represent those locations.

The mental models approach is thus an extreme version of a constructionist approach. Indeed, Brewer (1987) distinguishes mental models from other approaches by saying that rather than accessing pre-existing structures, mental models are specific knowledge structures constructed to represent each new situation using general information such as knowledge of spatial relationships, and human knowledge. Exactly how this construction takes place, and the precise nature of the representation, is sometimes unclear. Nevertheless, the idea is a useful one, and has motivated much important research, particularly the work by Garnham and his colleagues on anaphoric resolution.

Schema-based theories

The idea of a *schema* (plural: either schemata or schemas) was originally introduced by Bartlett (1932). A schema is an organised packet of knowledge that enables us to make sense of new knowledge. It is related to ideas in both AI on visual object recognition (Minsky, 1975) and experimental psychology (Posner & Keele, 1968; see also Chapter 6). The schema gives knowledge organising activation which means that the whole is greater than the sum of its parts. It can be conceptualised as a series of slots that can be filled with particular values. Ross and Bower (1981) provided support for this notion by demonstrating that, at least for words related in meaning, the whole representation is indeed greater than the sum of its components.

There are four central processes involved in schema formation. First, the appropriate aspects of the incoming stimuli must be selected. Second, the meaning must be abstracted, and syntactic and lexical details dispensed with. Third, appropriate prior knowledge must be activated to interpret this meaning. Finally, the information must be integrated to form a single holistic representation.

The idea of a schema cannot in itself account for text processing, but it is a central concept in many theories. Although it provides a means of organisation of knowledge, and explains why we remember the gist of text, it does not explain how we make inferences, how material is foregrounded, or why we sometimes remember the literal meaning. To solve these problems the notion must be supplemented in some way.

Scripts.   Scripts are a special type of schema, first proposed by Schank and Abelson (1977). They represent our knowledge of routine actions and familiar repeated sequences. Scripts include information about the usual roles, objects, and the sequence of events to be found in an action; they enable plans to be made and enable us to draw inferences about what is not explicitly mentioned. Two famous examples are the "restaurant script" and the "attending a lecture script" (see Table 7.2).

Psychological evidence for the existence of scripts comes from an experiment by Bower et al. (1979). Bower et al. asked participants to

TABLE 7.2
Examples of scripts (from Bower, Black, & Turner, 1979)
Items labelled (1) are considered most important in the script; (3) least important

Visiting a restaurant script		Attending a lecture script	
Open door	3	Enter room	1
Enter	2	Look for friends	2
Give reservation name	2	Find seat	1
Wait to be seated	3	Sit down	1
Go to table	3	Settle belongings	3
Be seated	1	Take out notebook	1
Order drinks	2	Look at other students	2
Put napkins on lap	3	Talk	2
Look at menu	1	Look at lecturer	3
Discuss menu	2	Listen to lecturer	1
Order meal	1	Take notes	1
Talk	2	Check time	1
Drink water	3	Ask questions	3
Eat salad or soup	2	Change position in seat	3
Meal arrives	3	Daydream	3
Eat food	1	Look at other students	3
Finish meal	3	Take more notes	3
Order dessert	2	Close notebook	2
Eat dessert	2	Gather belongings	2
Ask for bill	3	Stand up	3
Bill arrives	3	Talk	3
Pay bill	1	Leave	1
Leave tip	2		
Get coats	3		
Leave	1		

list about 20 events in activities such as visiting a restaurant, attending a lecture, getting up in the morning, visiting the doctor, or going shopping. Some examples are shown in Table 7.2: items labelled (1) were mentioned by the most subjects and are considered the most important actions in a script, items labelled (2) were mentioned by fewer subjects, and items labelled (3) were mentioned by the fewest number of subjects and are considered the least important parts of the script. The events are shown in the order in which they were usually mentioned. All of these events were mentioned by at least 25% of the subjects. Hence subjects agree about the central features that constitute a script and their relative importance.

Scripts are useful in explaining some results of experiments on anaphoric reference. Walker and Yekovich (1987) showed that a central concept of a script (such as a "table" in the restaurant script) was comprehended faster (regardless of whether it was explicitly mentioned in the story) than a peripheral concept. Peripheral concepts of scripts were dealt with particularly slowly when its antecedents were only implied. That is, we find it easier to assign referents to the important elements of scripts.

Furthermore, occasionally events turn up that are not in the script: for example, the waiter might spill the soup on you. Schank and Abelson (1977) refer to such interruptions as obstacles or distractions, because they get in the way of the main purpose of the script (here eating). Bower et al. made predictions about two types of event in stories relating to scripts. First, distractions that interrupt the purpose of the script should be more salient than the routine events and should therefore be more likely to be remembered. Second, events that are irrelevant to the purpose of the script (such as the colour of the waiter's shoes) should be poorly remembered. Both of these predictions were verified.

Schank (1982) refined the idea of scripts. Most of life is not governed by pre-determined, over-learned sequences such as is encapsulated in a script. Knowledge structures need to be flexible. Dissatisfied with this limitation of a script, Schank focused upon the role of reminding in memory. He argued that memory is a dynamic structure driven by its failures. Memory is organised into different levels, starting at the lower end with scenes. Examples of these in what would earlier have been a "going to the doctor script" include "reception room scene", "waiting scene", and "surgery scene". Scenes are organised into *memory organisation packets* or MOPs, which are all linked by being related to a particular goal. In any enterprise more than one MOP might be active at once. MOPs are themselves organised into meta-MOPs if a number of MOPs have something in common (for example, all MOPs involving going on a trip). At a higher level than MOPs and meta-MOPs are *thematic organisation points* or TOPs, which deal with abstract information independent of particular physical or social contexts.

There is some support for MOPs from a series of experiments by McKoon, Ratcliff, and Seifert (1989) and Seifert, McKoon, Abelson, and Ratcliff (1986). They showed that elements of MOPs could prime the retrieval of other elements from the same MOP. Subjects read a number of stories, some of which shared the same MOPs. They then had to make "old" or "new" recognition judgements about a number of test sentences, some of which had been and some of which had not been in the original stories. The test sentences were primed by other phrases. A priming phrase from the same story as the test sentence always produced facilitation. However, a priming phrase which had originally been in a different story to the test sentence also produced facilitation if it was in the same MOP as the test sentence. The amount of facilitation found was the same whether the original phrase was from a different story as from the same story. There was no facilitation if the priming phrase was from a different story and a different MOP to the test sentence.

Evaluation of script-based approaches. The primary accusation against schema and script based approaches is that they are nothing more than redescriptions of the data. This is quite difficult to rebuff. The experiment by Ross and Bower (1981) suggests that schemas have an organising ability beyond their constituents, but this has yet to be demonstrated of scripts, although the data from McKoon et al. could be interpreted in this way.

Although there are some experimental findings that support the idea that knowledge is organised around schema-like structures, they cannot as yet provide a complete account of text processing. They show how knowledge might be organised and what kinds of inference we can make, but at present they have little to say about how these inferences are made, how anaphoric resolution is done, or which items are foregrounded. To do this we must consider not only how knowledge is represented in memory, but also the processes that operate on that knowledge and relate it to incoming information.

Story grammars

Stories possess a structure: they have a beginning, a middle, and an end. This idea is taken to the extreme and made explicit in the idea of *story grammars*. The idea is based on an analogy with sentence grammar. Stories have an underlying structure, and the purpose of comprehension is to construct this underlying structure. This structure includes settings, themes, plots, and how the story turns out, its resolution. Story grammars make use of a generative grammar for stories based on schemas. The exact version of the story grammar varies from theorist to theorist, but important examples have been formulated by Mandler (1978), Mandler and Johnson (1977), Rumelhart (1975, 1977), and Thorndyke (1977).

Like sentence grammars, story grammars are made out of phrase structure rules (see the example in Table 7.3). The nature of the syntactic rules in Table 7.3 is expanded by a corresponding semantic rule: for example, once you have a setting then an episode is possible. You can draw tree structures just as with sentences, hence emphasising

TABLE 7.3
Example of a fragment of a story grammar (based on Rumelhart, 1975)
(Asterisks indicate that element can be repeated)

Story	→	Setting + theme + plot + resolution
Setting	→	Characters + location + time
Theme	→	(Event)* + goal
Plot	→	Episode*
Episode	→	Subgoals + attempt* + outcome

their hierarchical structure. The basic units, corresponding to individual words in sentence grammars, are propositions, which are eventually assigned the lowest level slots.

Findings accounted for by story grammars.   In the recall, paraphrasing, and summarising of stories, the less important details are omitted. Story grammar theoreticians claim that humans compute the importance of a sentence or fact by its height in the hierarchy; low nodes are omitted. However, all other hierarchical accounts (such as the Kintsch & van Dijk, 1978, model to be discussed next) predict the same. Cirilo and Foss (1980) showed that subjects spend more time reading sentences high in the structure than low down in the structure. A similar point could be made about this: any sensible theory of text processing should predict that we pay more attention to the important elements of a story.

Thorndyke (1977) presented subjects with one of two simple stories. The story "Circle Island" was about building a canal on an island, and a second story about an old farmer trying to put his donkey into a shed. One group of subjects heard these stories in their normal straightforward form. A second group heard a modified version of the stories where the story structure had been tampered with. The modifications included putting the theme at the end of the story (rather than before its plot, where it is most effective), deleting the goal of the story, or, in its most extreme version, presenting the component sentences in random order. Thorndyke found that the more the story structure was tampered with, the less subjects could subsequently recall of them. Hence jumbled stories are harder to understand and remember than originals. According to story grammar theory, this is because jumbling a story destroys its structure. Jumbling also however destroys referential continuity. Garnham, Oakhill, and Johnson-Laird (1982) restored referential continuity in jumbled stories; this greatly reduced the difficulty subjects have with them.

Evaluation of story grammars. The main problem is in getting agreement on what the elements, rules, and terminal elements of story grammars should be. There is little agreement on the intermediate categories. In a sentence grammar, the meaning of non-terminal elements such as "noun" and "verb" is independent of their content and well-defined. Neither of these is true for story grammars—hence the lack of agreement. Unlike with sentences, there are no formally agreed criteria for specifying a finite, well-specified set of terminal elements—there are a finite number of words, but an infinite number of propositions. There is no agreement on story structure: virtually every story grammatician has proposed a different grammar. Current story grammars only provide a limited account of a subset of all possible stories. Furthermore, the analogy of story categories with sentence grammars such as NP, VP, and their rules of combination, is very weak. There is much variation with stories, and unlike sentences, the analysis of stories is content-dependent.

Black and Wilensky (1979) argued that, as sentence grammars do not provide an account of how sentences are parsed, so story grammars also fail to provide an account of how stories are actually produced or understood.

These criticisms are discussed in more detail by Garnham (1983b), Johnson-Laird (1983), and Wilensky (1983); some of them were addressed in replies by Mandler and Johnson (1980) and Rumelhart (1980). However, given the fundamental nature of some of these difficulties, story grammars are no longer influential in comprehension research.

Kintsch's construction–integration model

Kintsch (1988; see also Kintsch & van Dijk, 1978, and Kintsch, 1979, for an earlier version of this model) provides a detailed and plausible model of spoken and written text comprehension known as the construction–integration model. This model emphasises how texts are represented in memory and understanding and how they are integrated into the comprehender's general knowledge base. The input is dealt with in processing cycles, and short-term memory acts as a buffer to store incoming material. We build up a representation of a story given two inputs: the story itself, and the goals of the reader. The goals and knowledge of the reader are represented by the *goal schema*, which does things such as stating what is relevant, sets expectations, and demands that certain inferences be drawn if needed facts are not explicitly stated.

Text is represented in the form of a network of connected propositions or facts called a coherence graph. Coherence is built up hierarchically. According to the model, text has both a microstructure and a macrostructure. The *microstructure* is this network of connected propositions. In processing text, we work through text in input cycles which usually correspond to a sentence, with an average size of seven propositions. In each cycle the overlap of the proposition arguments is noted; propositions are semantically related when they share arguments. If there is no overlap between incoming propositions and propositions currently in working memory, then the time consuming microprocesses of inference, recomputation, and reinstatement search (search of long-term memory) are used. If there is overlap, then the new propositions are connected to the active part of the coherence graph by *coherence rules*. The *macrostructure* concerns the higher level of description and the processes operating upon that. Relevant schemata are retrieved in parallel from long-term memory. These *macrorules* provide operations that delete propositions from microstructure; summarise propositions; and construct inferences (for reasons such as to fill gaps in the text). Script-like information would be retrieved at this stage.

As the text is being processed, certain propositions will be stored in working memory. As this has a limited capacity, what determines what goes into this buffer? First, recency is important. Second, the level of a proposition is important, with propositions higher in the coherence graph more likely to receive more processing cycles in working memory.

Evaluation of the construction–integration model. This model has explained many experimental findings, not all of which can be discussed in detail here. First, the more propositions there are in a passage, the longer it takes to read per word (Kintsch & Keenan, 1973). Second, we have just seen that there is a *levels effect* in the importance of a proposition owing to the multiple processing of high-level propositions. They are held in working memory longer, and elaborated more. Whenever a proposition is selected from working memory, its probability of being reproduced increases. Kintsch and van Dijk (1978) showed that the higher the level of a proposition, the more likely it is to be recalled in a free recall task.

Inferences are confused with original material because the propositions created as a result of inferences are stored along with explicitly presented propositions, and the two sorts of proposition are indistinguishable in the representation. That this depends upon the operation of goal and other schemata also explains why material can be hard to understand and remember if we do not know what it is about. We remember different things if we change perspective because different goal schemata become active.

Readability effects and the difficulty of the text are also explained by the model. Kintsch and van Dijk (1979) defined the readability of a story as the number of propositions in the story divided by the time it takes to read it. The best predictors of readability turn out to be the frequency of words in the text and the number of reinstatement searches that have to be made, as predicted from the model. Kintsch and Vipond (1979) confirmed that readability is not determined solely by the text, but is an interaction between the text and the readers. The most obvious example is that reinstatement searches are only necessary when a proposition is not in working memory, and obviously the greater the capacity of an individual's working memory, the less likely such a reader is to need to make reinstatement searches. Daneman and Carpenter (1980) also showed how individual differences in working memory size can affect reading performance. So if you want to write easily readable text, you should use short words, and try and write so as to avoid the reader having to retrieve a lot of material from long-term memory.

The model further explains differences between good and poor readers. Vipond (1980) showed that involvement of microprocesses predict the reading performance of less skilled readers, while macroprocesses predict the reading performance of better readers. He further showed that micro- and macroprocesses are completely independent, and use different cognitive resources.

Fletcher (1986) examined eight strategies that subjects might use to keep propositions in the short-term buffer. Four were local strategies ("most recent proposition"; "most recent topical"—the first agent or object mentioned in a story; "most recent containing the most frequent argument"; and "leading edge"—a combination of the most recent and important proposition) and four global strategies ("follow a script"; "correspond to the major categories of a story grammar"; "indicate a character's goal or plan"; "are part of the most recent discourse topic"). These were tested against twenty texts in a recall task and a "think-aloud protocol" task where subjects have to read the story and elaborate out loud. There was no clear preference for local versus global strategies, though the "plan/goal" strategy was top in both tasks, and story structure was also important. There are large task differences: for example, frequency was bottom in recall but third most used in the protocol task.

Comparison of models

We have looked at a range of models. Propositional networks and schema models, while providing useful constructs, are not in themselves sufficient to account for all the phenomena of text processing. Story grammars suffer from a number of problems: in particular, it is difficult to agree on what the terminal and non-terminal categories and rules of the grammar should be. Mental models stress the role of elaborative inferences too much. Of these models, Kintsch's model is the most promising, and as a consequence has recently received the most attention.

PRAGMATICS

Although this book focuses upon the processes of understanding and producing language, there is clearly more to being a skilled language user than these. The study of pragmatics looks at how we deal with those aspects of language that go beyond the simple meaning of what we hear and say. In a way we have already touched upon this in the discussion of inferences. In this section we will examine this topic in a little more depth. The issues are all related to the idea of how we get things done with language, and how we work out what the purpose is behind the speaker's utterance.

The study of pragmatics can be divided into two interrelated topics. The first is how hearers and speakers go beyond the literal meaning of what we hear to make and draw inferences. (Of course, not all inferences are always intended!). For example, if I say "Can you pass the salt?" I am usually not really asking you whether you have the ability to pass the salt; it is an indirect, polite way of saying, "Please pass the salt". Except perhaps in psycholinguistics experiments, we do not produce random utterances; we are trying to achieve particular goals when speaking. So how do we get things done with language? The second topic is how do we maintain conversations. To get things done, we have to collaborate; clearly we do not want to talk all at the same time. How do we avoid this? Do conversations have a structure that helps us to prevent this? And can we draw any inferences from apparent transgressions of conversational structure?

Pragmatics is a huge topic with many textbooks devoted to it alone, and we only have space here to look at the most important ideas. If there is a central theme to this research, it is that people are always making inferences at all levels on the basis of what they hear. Our utterances interact with the context in which they are uttered to give them their full meaning. This interaction, and the size of the context, makes the problem a difficult one for AI.

Making inference in conversations

We have seen that inferences have an important part to play in understanding text. They are equally important—perhaps more so—in conversation. We make inferences not just from what people say, but also from how they say it, and even from what they do not say.

Speech acts: Austin and Searle.   When we speak, we have goals and it is the listener's task to discover those goals. According to Austin (1962/1976) and Searle (1969), every time we speak we perform a *speech act*.

Austin (1976) began with the goal of exploring sentences containing *performative* verbs. These verbs perform an act in their very utterance, such as "I hereby pronounce you man and wife" (as long as the circumstances are appropriate—such as that I have the authority to do so; such circumstances are called the *felicity conditions*). He concluded that all sentences are performative, though mostly in an indirect way. That is, all sentences are doing something—if only stating a fact. For example, the statement "My house is terraced", can be analysed as "I hereby assert that my house is terraced." Austin distinguished three effects or forces each sentence possesses. The *locutionary force* of an utterance is its literal meaning, the *illocutionary force* is what the speaker is trying to get done with the utterance, and the *perlocutionary force* is the effect the utterance actually has on the actions and beliefs of the listener. For example, if I say (37) the literal meaning is that I am asking you whether you have the ability to pass the gin, the illocutionary force is that I hereby request you to pass the gin, and it might have the perlocutionary force of making you think that I am a drunken lush.

37.   Can you pass the gin?

Searle (1969, 1975) took this analysis further. When we speak, we make a series of speech acts. According to Searle, every speech act falls into one of five categories:

- *Representatives.* The speaker is asserting a fact and conveying his belief that a statement is true. ("Boris rides a bicycle.")
- *Directive.* The speaker is trying to get the listener to do something. (In asking the question "Does Boris ride a bicycle?", the speaker is trying to get the hearer to give information.)
- *Commissives.* The speakers commit themselves to some future course of action. ("If Boris doesn't ride a bicycle, I will give you a present.")
- *Expressives.* The speakers wish to reveal their psychological state. ("I'm sorry to hear that Boris only rides a bicycle.")
- *Declarative.* The speaker brings about a new state of affairs. ("Boris—you're fired for riding a bicycle!")

The categories of speech act used differ between theorists. For example, D'Andrade and Wish (1985) give seven types. They distinguished between assertions and reactions (such as "I agree") as representatives, and distinguish requests for information from other request directives. The lack of agreement and the lack of detailed criteria of what constitutes any type are obvious problems. Furthermore, some utterances might be ambiguous, and if so, how do we select the appropriate speech act analysis? A further challenge is that it needs to be made explicit how the listener uses the context to assign the utterance to the appropriate speech act type.

Direct speech acts are straightforward utterances where the intention of the speaker is revealed in the words, and *indirect speech acts* require some work on the part of the listener. The most famous example is "Can you pass the salt?", as analysed above. Speech acts can become increasingly indirect ("Is the salt at your end of the table?" to "This food is a bit bland"), often with increasing politeness. The less conventional they are, the more computational work is required by the listener. Over 90% of requests are indirect in English (Gibbs, 1986).

Of course, the meanings of very indirect speech acts are not always immediately apparent. Searle (1979) proposed a two-stage mechanism for computing the intended meaning. First, the listener tries the literal meaning to see if it makes sense in context. Only if it does not do they do the additional work of finding a non-literal meaning. There is an opposing one-stage model where people derive the non-literal meaning either instead of or as well as the literal one (Keysar, 1989). The evidence is conflicting but certainly the non-literal meaning is understood as fast as or faster than the literal meaning, suggesting a one-stage model. (See Taylor & Taylor, 1990, for a review.)

How to run a conversation: Grice's maxims.   Grice (1975) proposed that in conversations speakers and listeners are co-operating to make the conversation meaningful and purposeful. That is, we adhere to a *co-operative principle*. To comply with this, you must according to Grice "make your conversational contribution such as is required, at the stage at which it occurs, by the accepted purpose or direction of the talk exchange in which you are engaged." This is achieved by use of four conversational maxims. These are:

- *Maxim of quantity*. Make your contributions as informative as is required, but no more.
- *Maxim of quality*. Make your contribution true. Do not say anything that you believe to be false or for which you lack sufficient evidence.
- *Maxim of relevance*. Make your contribution relevant to the aims of the conversation.

- *Maxim of manner.* Be clear: avoid obscurity, ambiguity, wordiness, and disorder in your language.

Subsequently there has been some debate on whether there is any redundancy in these maxims. Sperber and Wilson (1986) argued that among them relevance is primary and the others can be deduced from it.

A few thought experiments should make it obvious that conversations quickly break down when we deviate from these maxims. However, we usually try to make sense of conversations which appear to deviate from them. We assume that overall the speaker is following the co-operative principle. To do this, we make a particular type of inference known as a *conversational implicature.* Consider the following conversational interchange:

38.   Vlad: Do you think my nice new expensive gold fillings suit me?
       Boris: Gee, it's hot in here.

This clearly violates the maxim of relevance. How can we explain this? Most of us would make the conversational implicature that in refusing to answer the question Boris is implying that he dislikes Vlad's new fillings and doesn't think they suit him at all, but for some reason doesn't want to say so to his face.

The structure of conversation
There are two different approaches to analysing the way in which conversations are structured (Levinson, 1983). Discourse analysis uses the general methods of linguistics. It aims to discover the basic units of discourse and the rules that relate them. The most extreme version of this is the attempt to find a grammar for conversation in the same way as there are sentence and story grammars. Labov and Fanshel (1977), one of the most famous examples of the analysis of discourse, looked at the structure of psychotherapy episodes. Utterances are segmented into units such as speech, and conversational sequences are regulated by a set of sequencing rules that operate over these units. *Conversation analysis* is much more empirical, aiming to uncover general properties of the organisation of conversation without applying rules. Conversation analysis was pioneered by ethnomethodologists, who examine social behaviour in its natural setting. The data consist of tape-recordings and more latterly videos of transcripts of naturally occurring conversations.

Conversation is characterised by *turn-taking*: Speaker A says something, speaker B has a turn, and so on. A turn varies in length, and might contain more than one idea. Other speakers might speak during a turn in the form of back-channel communication, making sounds ("hmm hmm"), words ("yep"), or gestures (e.g. nodding) to show that the listener is still listening, is understanding, agrees, or whatever (Duncan & Niederehe, 1974). Turn structure is made explicit by the example of *adjacency pairs* (such as question–answer pairs, or greeting–greeting pairs, or offer–acceptance pairs). Of course the exact nature of the turns and their length depends upon the social settings: seminars are different from spontaneous drunken conversation. Nevertheless speakers manage to control conversations remarkably accurately. Less than 5% of conversation consists of the overlap of two speakers speaking at once, and the average gap between turns is on average just a few tenths of a second (Ervin-Tripp, 1979). Hence speakers must use quite a sophisticated mechanism for ensuring that turn-taking proceeds smoothly. Sacks, Schegloff and Jefferson (1974) proposed a local management system to do this. The minimal *turn-constructional unit* from which a turn is constructed is determined by syntactic and semantic structure, and by the intonational contour of the utterance (over which the speaker has a great deal of control). A speaker is initially assigned just one of these minimal units, and then a *transition relevance place* where a change of speaker might arise occurs. Sacks et al. discuss a number of rules that govern whether or not speakers actually do change at this. Gaze is important: we tend to look at our listeners when we are coming to the end of a turn, and hand gestures might be used to indicate the speaker wishes to continue. As important as visual cues might be, they cannot be the whole story, as we have no difficulty in ensuring smooth turn transitions in telephone conversations. Filled pauses indicate a wish to continue speaking. Speakers might deliberately invite a change of speakers by asking a question; otherwise a complex sequence of social rules comes into play. The advantage of the system discussed by Sacks et al. is that it can predict other characteristics of conversation such as when overlap (such as competing starts of turns, or where transitional relevance places have been misidentified) or gaps do occur.

This section has only been able to provide a flavour of the contents and methods of this area of research.

CONCLUDING SUMMARY

There are many similarities between understanding written text and spoken conversation. In each case the comprehender has to build a representation of what is being communicated. There are two viewpoints on how detailed this representation is. According to the constructionist viewpoint, we construct a detailed model of the discourse, using many elaborative inferences. According to the minimalist viewpoint, we make only those inferences we need to maintain the coherence of the representation. Bridging and anaphoric references are made automatically, whereas most elaborative references are made only later when necessary if recalling the text. Recently there has been a swing towards the minimalist position. Because of this, memory tasks are limited as a measure of on-line comprehension. We looked at a number of specific strategies that comprehenders use to resolve anaphoric ambiguity.

We read for the gist, and very quickly forget details of surface form. Inferences are integrated into our model as we go along, and we are very soon also unable to distinguish our inferences from what we originally heard.

Models of text processing must be able to explain how we represent knowledge, which material we remember, when and how we draw inferences, how anaphoric continuity is maintained, and when some material is foregrounded. Propositional networks and schema models can only do the first of these. Story grammars suffer from the problem that stories do not have the clearly delineated categories and terminal categories of sentences. The mental models approach is perhaps too constructionist, and it is not clear how mental models are actually represented. Kintsch's propositional network plus schema model is the currently the best worked out, but it is too early to say that it is the correct approach. Models in this area tend to be relatively under-specified and there is insufficient discriminating data. So far, connectionism has not made much of an impact in this area. At present it has focused on automatic, low-level processes, but it is likely that it will be important in the future.

There are additional problems that both speaker and listener face in conversation to ensure that the conversation proceeds smoothly. A number of turn-taking mechanisms are used to control this. On the whole, conversation is a co-operative enterprise. We have also briefly looked at pragmatics. Language is used to achieve a goal, and the goal might not be the literal meaning of what is said: language can have indirect as well as direct meanings. Each statement we make can be viewed as a type of speech act which has a particular goal. It is the comprehender's task to infer the intended meaning from the interaction of context, literal meaning, and assumptions about the structure of conversations (the co-operative principle). Much work remains to be done on the computations that underlie these inferences.

FURTHER READING

Spiro (1980) discusses text processing as a constructive process. For a short review of text comprehension, see Colley (1987). Fletcher (1994) reviews the literature on text memory. For a review of the role of inference in reading, see McKoon and Ratcliff (1992), Singer (1994), and van den Broek (1994). A good review of research on anaphors is given by Garnham (1985, 1987b), Garrod and Sanford (1994), and Sanford and Garrod (1994). For other experiments on the role of the discourse model in resolving anaphor, see Malt (1985). Stevenson (1993) reviews an excellent overview of mental representation with some emphasis on narrative and discourse processing. Models of text processing are reviewed by Kintsch (1994). Another early influential propositional network model was that of Norman and Rumelhart (1975). Brewer (1987) compares the mental model and schema approaches to memory. Additional empirical support of Kintsch's construction–integration model is provided in experiments described by Kintsch, Welsch, Schmalhofer, and Zimny (1990), and Perrig and Kintsch (1985). See Alba and Hasher (1983) for a detailed critical discussion of these schema formation. An overview of conversations and discourse is given by Ervin-Tripp (1993). For a detailed review of non-verbal behaviour and the structure of conversations, see Beattie (1983). Levinson (1983) is a good general text on all aspects of pragmatics. Gibbs (1974) reviews how we use language figuratively. Coulthard (1977) is a text specifically devoted to the analysis of discourse and conversation; see Coulthard (1992, 1994) for up-to-date reviews of discourse analysis. Sperber and Wilson (1987) is a summary of their book on relevance, with a peer commentary. Finally, Clark (1994) reviews the representation of discourse from the angle of production rather than comprehension.

CHAPTER EIGHT

Speech production and aphasia

INTRODUCTION

So far we have been concerned with the input processes of language. In this chapter we will examine the output of language, and in particular how we produce speech. We will follow the pattern of earlier chapters in first examining the data from normal subjects, and constructing a provisional model of speech production. We can then see whether and how data from brain-damaged patients can be integrated into this model.

The processes of speech production fall into three broad areas (Levelt, 1989). At the highest level are the processes of *conceptualisation* that concern the intentions of what to say and that determine the concepts that are to be expressed. These are sometimes also called *message-level* processes. The processes of *formulation* involve translating this conceptual representation into a linguistic form. Finally, the processes of *articulation* involve detailed phonetic and articulatory planning.

We will focus on the formulation process. It is clear that there are two major components to this: we have to select the individual words that we want to say, and we have to put them together to form a sentence. There has been rather more research on the details of lexical retrieval in production than on syntactic planning. Indeed, there has been considerably less research on speech production than on language comprehension and (single) visual word recognition in general. This is clear from the amount of space devoted to these topics in this book: five chapters on input, and only one on output. Clearly we do not spend disproportionately more time listening or reading than speaking, so why the imbalance? One obvious reason is that the investigation of production is much harder than the investigation of comprehension, primarily because it is difficult to control the input in experiments on production. In the case of experiments on word recognition, it is relatively easy to control the frequency, imageability, and visual appearance (or any aspect that is considered important) of the materials, but our thoughts are much harder to get under experimental control in this way than words. Similarly, as we saw in Chapter 5, it might not always be necessary to construct a syntactic representation of a sentence in order to derive its meaning. Yet when we speak, we clearly must produce a syntactic plan for what we say. Given this, it is perhaps surprising that more attention has not been paid to syntactic encoding in production, but the difficulties of controlling the input are substantial. One consequence of this imbalance between comprehension and production is that experiments have so far played a smaller role in production than in comprehension, although this imbalance is starting to change.

What other types of evidence then have been used to study production? First, there is the analysis of historical changes in vocabulary and pronunciation (Comrie, 1980). Second, there is the study of what to say and how to say it—the analysis of conversation and ethnomethodology (see Beattie, 1983, and the previous chapter). For example, Schenkein (1980) shows how speech may be repeated later in the conversation. Computer simulations and connectionist modelling are, as in other areas of psycholinguistics, becoming increasingly influential (although see Steedman & Johnson-Laird, 1980, for a discussion of non-connectionist simulations of deciding what to say, with particular emphasis on how we generate speech acts). Much has been learnt by the analysis of the distribution of hesitations or pauses in speech. Until now, however, by far the most influential data have been spontaneously occurring speech errors, or slips of the tongue.

HESITATION ANALYSIS

Hesitation analysis is concerned with the distribution of pauses and other dysfluencies in speech. We should distinguish between unfilled and filled pauses: an unfilled pause is simply a moment of silence, whereas a filled hesitation can be a filled pause (where a gap in the flow of words is filled with a sound such as "uh" or "um"), a repetition, a false start, or a parenthetical remark (such as "well" or "I mean"). Naturally unfilled pauses are easier to detect mechanically by the equipment used to measure pause duration, so analysis has focused upon them. It has been argued that pauses represent two types of difficulty, one in what might be called *microplanning* (due to retrieving particularly difficult words), and a second in *macroplanning* (due to planning the syntax and content of a sentence). The theoretical emphasis in the past has been that pausing predominately reflects semantic planning.

Pausing before individual words

Goldman-Eisler (1958, 1968) looked at the distribution of unfilled pauses (defined as longer than 250 milliseconds in the early work, and longer than 200 milliseconds in the later work) across time, using a device nicknamed the "pauseometer". Obviously there are gaps between speakers' "turns" in conversation, known as *switching pauses*, but there are many pauses within a single conversational turn by a particular speaker, approximately every five to eight words.

Goldman-Eisler (1958, 1968) showed that pauses are more likely to occur and to be of longer duration before words that are less *predictable* in the context of the preceding speech. *Predictability* reflects a number of notions, including word frequency and familiarity, and the preceding semantic and syntactic context. Pauses before less predictable words are hypothesised to reflect microplanning, and to correspond to a transient difficulty in lexical access. We know the meaning of the word we want to say but we cannot immediately retrieve its sound. Of course, not all hesitations precede less predictable words, and not all less predictable words are preceded by pauses. Furthermore, sections of repeated speech behave differently from pauses, tending to follow unpredictable words rather than preceding them, as though they are used to check that the speaker has selected the correct word (see Tannenbaum, Williams, & Hillier, 1965).

Beattie and Butterworth (1979) attempted to disentangle the effects of word frequency from contextual probability. They showed that the relationship between pausing and predictability did not appear to be attributable simply to word frequency, and concluded that the main component of predictability that determined hesitations was difficulty in semantic planning. Their study, however, did not rule out possible contributions from syntactic difficulty (Petrie, 1987). Furthermore, people often use appropriate hand gestures during these hesitations (Butterworth & Beattie, 1978). Suppose you are trying to retrieve the word "telephone", but are having difficulty; you pause just before you say it, and in that pause make a gesture appropriate to a telephone (such as making a dialling motion with your hand). This suggests that you know the meaning of what you want to say—that is, that the difficulty lies elsewhere other than in semantic planning. Indeed, as we shall see, this gesture evidence is entirely consistent with a two-stage model of lexical access in production: we first formulate a semantic specification, and phonological retrieval follows this. On this account the pause reflects a successful first stage, but a delay in the second stage, that of retrieving the particular phonological form of the word. This account ties in with the evidence from tip-of-the-tongue states below, which can be seen as an extreme version of microplanning pauses.

   The "tip-of-the-tongue state".   The tip-of-the-tongue (TOT) state is a more pronounced, yet nevertheless essentially transient, lexical access difficulty. It is the extreme form of a pause, but one where the word does not successfully come out at all. You are almost certainly familiar with this phenomenon: you know what the word is, yet you are unable to get the sounds out. TOTs are accompanied by strong "feelings of knowing" what the word is. They appear to be universal; they have even been observed in children as young as two (Elbers, 1985).
   Brown and McNeill (1966) were the first to examine the TOT state experimentally. They induced TOTs in subjects by reading them definitions of low frequency words, such as (1).

1.   "a navigational instrument used in measuring angular distances, especially the altitude of the sun, moon, and stars at sea"

Example (1) defines the word *sextant*. Brown and McNeill found that a proportion of the subjects will be placed in a TOT state by this task. Furthermore, they found that lexical retrieval is not an all-or-none affair: partial information can be retrieved, such as the number of syllables, the initial letter or sound, and the stress pattern; furthermore, subjects output near phonological neighbours like "secant", "sextet", and "sexton". We can think of TOTs as rather extreme versions of the pauses which occur before low predictability words. The TOT state shows us that we can be aware of the meaning of a word without being aware of its component sounds; and furthermore, that phonological representations are not unitary entities.
   Recently two theories of the origins of TOTs have emerged. These are called the *partial activation* and *blocking* or interference hypotheses. The partial activation hypothesis was first proposed by Brown (1970). The target items are inaccessible because they are only weakly represented in the system. Burke, MacKay, Worthley, and Wade (1991) provided evidence in favour of this model from both an experimental and a diary study in a group of young and old subjects. They argue that the

retrieval deficit involves weak links between the semantic and phonological systems. A broadly similar approach by Harley and MacAndrew (1992) localised the deficit within a two-stage model of lexical access, between the abstract lexical units and phonological forms (see below). At first sight Kohn et al. (1987) provided evidence contrary to the partial activation hypothesis in the form of a free association task. They showed that the partial information provided by subjects does not in time narrow or converge upon the target. However, A.S. Brown (1991) pointed out that subjects need not output the information in the order in which it comes to mind. Furthermore, in a noisy system there is no reason why each attempt at retrieval should give the same incorrect answer.

The blocking hypothesis, first mooted by Woodworth (1938), states that the target item is actively suppressed by a stronger competitor. This idea was tested by Jones and Langford (1987), who used a variant of the Brown and McNeill task known as *phonological blocking*. They presented a phonological neighbour of the target word and showed that this increases the chance of a TOT state occurring, while presenting a semantic neighbour does not. They interpreted this as showing that TOTs primarily arise as a result of competition. Jones (1989) further showed that the blocker or interloper is only effective if it is presented at the time of retrieval rather than just before. However, methodological problems with these experiments have recently been discussed by Perfect and Hanley (1992) and Meyer and Bock (1992). Exactly the same results are found with these materials when the blockers are not presented, suggesting that the original results were an artefact of the materials.

So far the TOT data best support the partial activation hypothesis, although the question is far from settled. They also suggest that the levels of semantic and phonological processing in lexical retrieval are distinct.

Pauses and sentence planning

Goldman-Eisler (1958, 1968) argued that in these pauses we plan the content of what we are about to say. She found that the difficulty of the speaking task also affected the pause rate, with more difficult tasks (for example, a task involving interpretation rather than simple description) leading to more pauses.

There has been some debate as to what constitutes an appropriate planning unit in spontaneous speech. Maclay and Osgood (1959) argued that the planning units must be larger than a single word because false starts involve corrections of the grammatical words associated with the unintended content-bearing words. Boomer (1965) argued that an appropriate unit of analysis corresponds to a *phonemic clause* which essentially has only one major stressed element within it, and which corresponds to a clause of the surface structure. He argued that the clause is planned in the hesitation at the start of the clause. Ford and Holmes (1978) used dual-task performance to monitor cognitive load during speech production. They argued that planning does not span sentences, and that planning a clause occurs primarily towards the end of the previous clause. They also concluded that the appropriate planning unit is the deep structure clause rather than the surface structure clause. However, this finding is controversial, as Holmes (1984; see also 1988) used a story continuation task to conclude that speakers plan in sentence clauses and may plan more than one sentence at a time. Clearly these results are highly task-sensitive. Levelt (1989) in a careful and detailed review of the literature concluded that the primary planning unit of speech is what are called *phonological phrases*. These are more or less the stretches of speech up to and including the lexical heads of each phrase (see Chapter 5).

What exactly is planned in the pauses? In particular, is the planning syntactic or semantic, or both? Goldman-Eisler (1968) claimed that pause time was not affected by the syntactic complexity of the utterances being produced, and concluded that planning is primarily semantic rather than syntactic. This conclusion is now considered controversial (see Petrie, 1987): one problem is that of what measure should be taken of syntactic complexity. At this stage it would be premature to rule out the possibility that macroplanning pauses represent planning both the semantic and syntactic content of a clause.

Henderson, Goldman-Eisler, and Skarbek (1966) proposed there were cognitive cycles in the planning of speech. In particular, phases of highly hesitant speech alternate with phases of more fluent speech; the hesitant phases also contain more filled pauses, and more false starts than the fluent phases. It is thought that most of the planning takes part in the hesitant phase, and in the fluent phase we merely say what we have just planned in the preceding hesitant phase (see Fig. 8.1). Butterworth (1975, 1980) argued that a cycle corresponds to an *idea*. He asked independent judges to divide other speakers' descriptions of their routes home into semantic units and compared these with hesitation cycles. An idea lasts for several clauses. One problem with this work is the way in which the units were identified by inspection of plots of unfilled pauses against articulation time. Jaffe, Breskin, and Gerstman (1972) showed that apparently cyclic patterns could be generated completely randomly. However, other phenomena (such as filled hesitations) also cluster within the planning phase of a cognitive cycle. For example, speakers tend to gaze less at their listeners during the planning phase, maintaining more eye contact during the execution

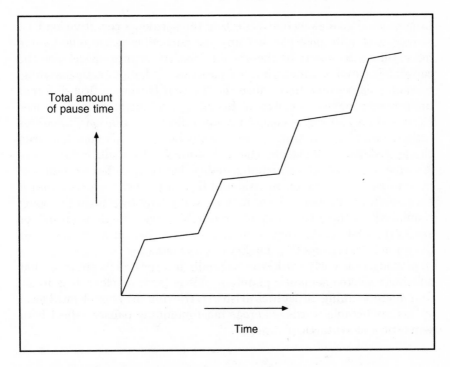

FIG. 8.1. Planning and execution phases: cognitive cycles in speech production.

phase (Beattie, 1980; Kendon, 1967). The use of gestures also differs (Beattie, 1983): speakers tend to use more *batonic gestures* (gestures used only for emphasis) in the hesitant phases, and more *iconic gestures* (gestures which in some way resemble the associated object) in the fluent phase (particularly before less predictable words). The observation that several features cluster together in hesitant phases suggests that these cycles are after all psychologically real.

Evaluation of research upon pauses

There are a number of problems with aspects of pause analysis. The first problem is that pauses might have more than one function. It is possible that speakers deliberately (though perhaps usually unconsciously) put pauses into their speech to make the listener's job easier, perhaps aiding them to segment speech, or to give them time to parse the speech. Lounsbury (1954) distinguished between *hesitation pauses*, which reflect planning by the speaker, and *juncture pauses*, which are put in by the speaker to mark major syntactic boundaries, perhaps for the convenience of the listener. Good and Butterworth (1980) provided experimental evidence that hesitations might be used to achieve some interactional goal as well as reflecting the speaker's cognitive load. Of course, it is quite possible that any one particular pause might serve more than one function: the speaker inserts it into speech for the convenience of the listener, but then also uses it for syntactic planning. Second, it is possible that pauses of different lengths reflect different underlying behaviours. Goldman-Eisler argued that *micropauses* (those shorter than 250 milliseconds) merely reflect articulation difficulties rather than planning time; more recently however this view has been challenged (see for example, Hieke, Kowal, & O'Connell, 1983). There is some measure of interchangeability between different types of hesitations: for example, Beattie and Bradbury (1979) showed that if speakers were dissuaded from making many lengthy pauses (by being "punished" by the appearance of a red light every time they paused for longer than 600 milliseconds), their pause rate indeed went down, but the number of repeats they made went up instead.

Although the early work was originally interpreted as showing that pausing reflected semantic planning, this is far from clear. It is likely that microplanning difficulties arise in retrieving the phonological form of less predictable words, whereas macroplanning pauses reflect both semantic and syntactic planning.

SPEECH ERRORS

Until fairly recently models of speech production rested primarily upon spontaneously occurring speech errors. Casual examination of our speech will reveal (in the unlikely event that you are unaware of this already) that it is far from perfect, but rife with errors. Analysis of these errors is one of the oldest research topics in psycholinguistics. Speech errors are frequently commented upon in everyday life. The case of the Reverend Dr. Spooner is quite commonly known; indeed, he gave his name to a particular type of error involving the exchange of initial consonants between words, the *spoonerism*. Some of Reverend Spooner's alleged spoonerisms are show in examples (2) to (4). (See Potter, 1980, for a discussion of whether Reverend Spooner's errors were in fact so frequent as to suggest an underlying pathology).

2.   Utterance: You have hissed all my mystery lectures.
     Target: ... missed all my history lectures.
3.   Utterance: In fact, you have tasted the whole worm.
     Target: ... wasted the whole term.
4.   Utterance: The Lord is a shoving leopard to his flock.
     Target: ... a loving shepherd.

Most people have also heard of the Freudian slip. In part of a general treatise on action slips or errors of action called *parapraxes*, Freud (1901/1975) noted the occurrence of slips of the tongue, and proposed that they revealed our repressed thoughts. In one example he gives, a professor said in a lecture, "In the case of female genitals, in spite of many *Versuchungen* (temptations)—I beg your pardon, *Versuche* (experiments) ..." Not all Freudian slips need arise from a repressed sexual thought. In another example he gives, the President of the Lower House of the Austrian Parliament opened a meeting with "Gentlemen, I take notice that a full quorum of members is present and herewith declare the sitting *closed!*" instead of open. Freud interpreted this as revealing the President's true thoughts that he secretly wished a potentially trouble-some meeting closed. However, Freud was not the first to study speech errors; a few years before, Meringer and Meyer (1895) provided what is now considered to be a more traditional analysis. Ellis (1980) re-analysed Freud's collection of corpus of speech errors in terms of the more process-oriented modern account of speech production outlined below.

The methodology behind speech error analysis is a simple one, but rather different from others described in this book. The most common method is to collect a large corpus of errors by recording as many errors as possible. Usually the researcher will interrupt the speaker when he or she detects the error, and ask the speaker what was the intended target, why they thought the error was made, and so on. Although this method introduces the possibility of observer bias, this appears to be surprisingly weak, if present at all. A comparison of error corpora against a smaller sample taken from a rigorous transcription of a sample of tape-recorded conversation (Garnham, Shillcock, Brown, Mill, & Cutler, 1982) suggests that the types and proportion of errors are very similar. Furthermore, it is possible to induce slips of the tongue artificially by, for example, getting subjects to read words out at speed (Baars, Motley, & Mackay, 1975). The findings from such studies corroborate the naturalistic data.

There are many different types of speech error. We can categorise them by considering the *linguistic units* involved in the error (for example, at the phonological feature, phoneme, syllable, morpheme, word, phrase, or sentence levels) and the error mechanism involved (such as the blend, substitution, addition, or deletion of units). Fromkin (1971/1973) argues that the existence of errors involving a particular unit shows these units are psychologically real. Table 8.1 gives some examples of speech errors from my own corpus which should make this clear. In any error there was the target that the speaker had in mind, and the erroneous utterance as actually produced; the erroneous part of the utterance is in italics.

TABLE 8.1
Examples of speech errors classified by speech unit and error mechanism

Type	Utterance	Target
Feature perseveration	Turn the kno*p*	knob
Phoneme anticipation	The *m*irst of May	first
Phoneme perseveration	God rest *re* merry gentlemen	ye
Phoneme exchange	Do you *r*eel *f*eally bad?	feel really bad
Affix deletion	The chimney cat*ch* fire	catches fire
Phoneme deletion	Back*g*ound lighting	background
Word blend	The *chung* of today	children + young
Word exchange	Guess whose *mind* came to *name*?	whose name came to mind
Morpheme exchange	I *random*ed some *samp*ly	I sampled some randomly
Word substitution	Get me a *fork*	spoon
Phrase blend	Miss you *a very much*	very much + a great deal

Let us now analyse a speech error in more detail to see what can be learnt from them. Consider the famous example of (5) from Fromkin (1971/1973).

5.   a weekend for maniacs—a *maniac* for *weekends*

The first thing to notice is that the sentence stress was left unchanged in this error, suggesting that stress is generated independently of the particular words involved. Even more strikingly, the plural morpheme "-s" was left at the end of the second word where it was originally intended to be in the first place: it did not move with "maniac". We say it was *stranded*. Furthermore, this plural morpheme was sounded as /z/ not as /s/. That is, the plural ending sounds consistent with the word that actually came before it, not with the word that was originally intended to come before it. (Plural endings are themselves voiced "/z/" if the final consonant of the word to which it is attached is voiced, as in "weekend", but are unvoiced "/s/" if the final consonant is unvoiced, as in "maniac".) This is an example of *accommodation* to the phonological environment.

Such examples tell us a great deal about speech production. Garrett's model, described below, is based upon a detailed analysis of such examples. However, Levelt et al. (1991a) argued that too much emphasis has been placed on errors, and that error analysis needs to be supported by experimental data. If these two approaches give conflicting results, the error data should take lower priority as they are only telling us about aberrant processing. There are three points that can be made in response to this. First, a complete model should be able to account for both experimental and speech error data. Second, the lines of evidence converge rather than giving conflicting results (Harley, 1993a). Third, it is possible to simulate spontaneously occurring speech errors experimentally, and these experimental simulations lead to the same conclusion as the natural errors. Baars, Motley, and MacKay (1975) required subjects to read rapidly pairs of words such as "darn bore" and "dart board". If subjects have to read these pairs from right to left, they make many spoonerisms. Furthermore, they are more likely to produce "barn door" (two real words) than they are the corresponding "bart doard"—an instance of the bias towards lexical outcomes also displayed in the naturalistic data.

Speech errors inform both our models of lexical retrieval in production and syntactic planning.

LEXICALISATION

Lexicalisation is the process in speech production whereby we turn the thoughts underlying words into sounds: we translate a semantic representation (the meaning) of a content word into its phonological representation of form (its sound). There are three main questions that must be considered. First, how many steps or stages are involved? Second, are these stages independent, or do they interact with one another? Third, what is the time course of the processes involved?

Fay and Cutler (1977) observed that there were two distinct types of whole word substitution speech error: semantic substitutions (such as examples 6 and 7), and phonological substitutions (such as examples 8 and 9). Phonological word substitutions are sometimes called *form-based* errors or *malapropisms*. (The word "malapropism" originally came from a character called Mrs. Malaprop in Sheridan's play *The Rivals*, who was always using words incorrectly, such as saying "reprehend" for "apprehend" and "epitaphs" for "epithets". Note that while Mrs. Malaprop produced these substitutions out of ignorance, the term is used slightly confusingly in psycholinguistics to refer to errors where the speaker knows perfectly well what the target should be.)

6.   fingers → *toes*
7.   husband → *wife*
8.   equivalent → *equivocal*
9.   historical → *hysterical*

Fay and Cutler argued that the occurrence of two types of word substitution suggests that the processes of word production and comprehension use the same lexicon, but in opposite directions. Items in the lexicon are arranged in phonological sequence to aid recognition, so that words that sound similar are close together. The lexicon is accessed in production by traversing a semantic network or decision tree. Hence the model can be said to be a search-based, single-level account of lexicalisation (see Fig. 8.2). Semantic errors occur when traversing the decision tree, and phonological errors occur when the final phonological form is selected. As we shall see in the next chapter, the argument that there is a single lexicon for comprehension and production is very controversial. If this is not the case, then some other

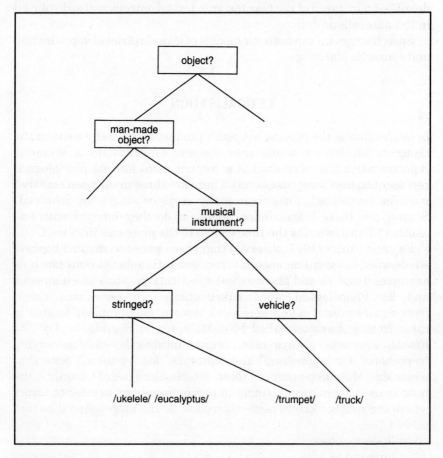

FIG. 8.2. Example a search-based single-level single lexicon model of lexicalisation, based on Fay and Cutler (1977).

mechanism will be necessary to account for the existence of malapropisms. A variant of this model was proposed by Butterworth (1982, 1989), who formulated it in terms of a two-stage process. In Butterworth's model an entry in a semantic lexicon is first selected, which gives a pointer to an entry in a separate phonological lexicon.

Interaction in lexicalisation. One problem with these models is that they predict that semantic and phonological processes should be independent in lexicalisation. That is, we should find semantic word substitutions and phonological substitutions, but no more *mixed substitutions* (the term was coined by Shallice & McGill, 1978). These are errors where the intrusion is both semantically and phonologically related to the target (e.g. examples 10 and 11). Obviously we need a formal definition of phonological similarity; here both the target and intrusion start with the same consonant, and contain the same number of syllables.

10.   comma → *colon*
11.   calendar → *catalogue*

Dell and Reich (1981) and Harley (1984) showed that far more mixed errors are found than chance would predict. Martin, Weisberg, and Saffran (1989) provided experimental evidence on the controlled elicitation of naming errors that also supports interaction. At the very least then the basic model must be modified, and this can be done in two ways. Butterworth (1982) proposed that a filter or editor checks the output to see that it is plausible; it is less likely to detect an error if the word output sounds like the target should have been, or is related in meaning. Such a mechanism, while it might be related to comprehension processes, is not parsimonious (see Stemberger, 1983). The alternative and currently preferred explanation is to permit interaction between semantic and phonological processes.

How many stages are there in lexicalisation?
Lexicalisation takes place in either one or two stages. According to the one-stage hypothesis, we go directly from the semantic level of processing to the phonological level of processing. According to the two-stage hypothesis, we go from the semantic level to an intermediate level where individual words (or *lexical units*) are represented in some abstract form; only then do we retrieve the phonological form of the words. The stage of specifying in a pre-phonological, abstract way the word that we are just about to say is called *lemma* selection; the second stage of specifying the actual concrete phonological form of the word is called *lexeme* or phonological form selection. It is likely that word

frequency effects in production are associated with the phonological forms rather than the lemmas (Jescheniak & Levelt, 1994). Kempen and Huijbers (1983) first proposed the hypothesis and terminology, on the basis of experiments of subjects describing simple visual scenes.

There is much evidence to favour the two-stage hypothesis. First, the different types of word substitution are readily explained, with semantic errors arising in lemma selection, and phonological errors in lexeme selection. The tip-of-the-tongue state is readily explained as success of the first stage of lexicalisation but failure of the second. We have already mentioned that work on hesitations and gestures during microplanning can be adduced as further evidence. Studies of picture naming by Levelt and his colleagues (Levelt et al., 1991; Schreifers, Meyer, & Levelt, 1990; see below for detailed discussion) provide experimental support, and the existence of different types of naming disorder or *anomia* in aphasic speakers, discussed in further detail later, provides neuropsychological corroboration. Further evidence comes from Wheeldon and Monsell's (1992) investigation of repetition priming in lexicalisation. Like repetition priming in visual word recognition, this effect is very long-lasting, spanning over a hundred intervening naming trials. They showed that naming a picture is facilitated by recently having produced the name by giving a definition or reading aloud. Prior production of a homophone (e.g. "weight" for "wait") is not an effective prime, so the source of the facilitation cannot be phonologically mediated. Instead, it must be semantic. Further evidence from Monsell, Matthews, and Miller (1992) looked at this effect in Welsh-English bilinguals. There was facilitation within a language, but not across (as long as the phonological forms of the words differed). Taken together the experiments show that both the meaning and phonological forms have to be activated for repetition priming in production to occur. In particular, they argue that repetition priming occurs as a result of the strengthening of the connections between the lemmas and phonological forms. These experiments also suggest that because repetition priming is so long-lasting it is related to frequency.

The motivation for a two-stage model has been most clearly explicated in reviews by Butterworth (1989) and Levelt (1992).

The time course of lexicalisation

Given that lexicalisation takes place in two stages, how do the two stages relate to one another? Are they independent, or do they interact? That is, does the second stage, phonological specification, only begin when the first stage, lemma retrieval, is complete, or does it begin while the first stage is still going on? If the latter is the case, then phonological processes should have some influence upon the abstract lemma selection:

that is, semantic and phonological processes should appear to overlap. The speech error evidence of mixed whole word substitutions is evidence for overlap or interaction between the two stages. To make this distinction concrete, suppose that you want to say the word "sheep". According to the two-stage hypothesis, you formulate the semantic representation underlying sheep, and use this to activate a number of competing abstract lexical items. Obviously in the first instance these will all be semantic relatives (like "sheep", "goat", "cow", etc.). The independence issue is this: before you start choosing the phonological form of the target word, how many of these competing units are left? According to the independence (modular) theory, only one: the target; according to the interactive theory, any number of them might be. Hence according to the interactive theory, when you intend to say "sheep", you might also be thinking of the phonological form /goʊt/, and this will in turn have an effect on the selection of "sheep". Another way of putting this is that according to the discrete models, the semantic-lexical and lexical-phonological stages cannot overlap, but according to the interactive model, they can. The issues involved are exactly those discussed in word recognition.

Levelt et al. (1991a) performed an elegant experiment to test between these two hypotheses. They looked for what is called a *mediated priming effect*: when you say "sheep", it primes or facilitates the recognition of the word "goat" (which obviously is a *semantic* relative of "sheep"); but does "goat" then go on to facilitate in turn one of its *phonological* neighbours, such as "goal"? They argue that the interactive model suggests that this mediated priming effect should occur, while the independence model states that it should not. The subjects' task was this: subjects were shown simple pictures of objects (such as a sheep) and had to name these objects as quickly as possible. This takes most people 500 to 800 milliseconds to do. In that time, subjects were given a word in an acoustic form through headphones (hearing "goal"); the subjects had to press a button as soon as they recognised this second word. That is, it was an acoustic lexical decision task. Levelt et al. found that there was no mediated priming for "goal": "sheep" speeded up subsequent processing of "goat", but not of "goal". Hence they argued no interaction occurred. Furthermore, in a separate experiment they showed that "sheep" only facilitates a semantic neighbour (e.g. "goat") early on in the naming task, while late on it only facilitates a phonological neighbour (e.g. "sheet").

Hence they concluded that in picture naming and lexicalisation, there is an early stage when semantic candidates are active (this is the lemma stage), and a late stage when phonological stages are active (the lexeme stage). Furthermore, these two stages are temporally discrete and do not overlap or interact.

However, a subsequent reply by Dell and O'Seaghdha (1991) questioned the original logic of the way Levelt et al. formulated the underlying hypotheses. They showed with simulations that a model that incorporated *local interaction* (between adjacent stages) could appear to be *globally modular*. This is because in these types of model, different types of information need not spread very far. In a similar way, Harley (1993a) showed that a model based upon interactive activation could indeed produce exactly this time course while permitting interaction between levels. Although there is still considerable debate (see Levelt et al., 1991b), the interactive model of lexicalisation is that which is currently most in favour.

The interactive activation model of lexicalisation

There is an emerging consensus among speech production theorists that lexicalisation can be described by spreading activation in a model similar to the interactive activation model of context effects in letter identification proposed by McClelland and Rumelhart (1981). Different versions of the same basic model have been described by Dell (1986), Dell and O'Seaghdha (1991), Harley (1993a), and Stemberger (1985). For example, in Harley's model lexicalisation proceeds in two stages. The meaning of a word is represented as a set of semantic features (see discussion of the Hinton and Shallice, 1991, and Plaut and Shallice, 1993a, model of deep dyslexia in Chapter 3, and the discussion of semantic representation in Chapter 6). These feed into a level of representation where abstract lexical representations equivalent to the lemmas are stored, and these in turn activate the phonological representations equivalent to lexemes. The basic architecture of the model is shown in Fig. 8.3; the rules that govern the behaviour of the network are similar to those in the McClelland and Rumelhart model described in Chapter 3. As we have just noted, computer simulations based on this model can also explain the picture naming data of Levelt et al. (1991a).

At this point it becomes difficult to distinguish empirically between the interactive and discrete models. One possible weakness of the interactive models is that they have many free parameters, and hence could potentially explain any pattern of results.

SYNTACTIC PLANNING

In a series of papers based primarily upon speech error analysis, Garrett (1975, 1976, 1980a, 1980b, 1982, 1988, 1992) has argued that speech production occurs via a series of levels of processing. This model is similar in nature to Fromkin's (1971/1973, 1993) *utterance generator*

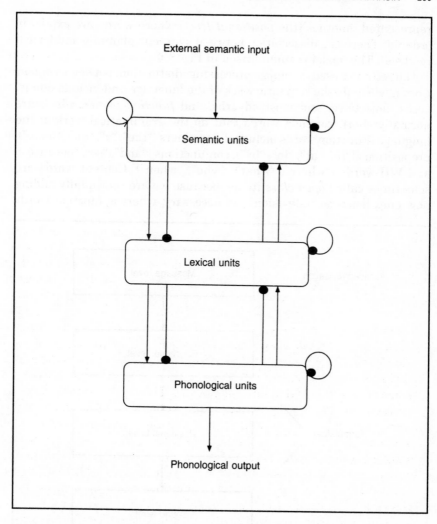

FIG. 8.3. Architecture of the interactive activation model of lexicalisation. (Based on Harley and MacAndrew, in press.) As in Fig. 3.4, arrows show excitatory connections, dots inhibitory connections. The semantic within-level connections are more complex, with partial connectivity, as indicated by the shaded dot.

model. Processing occurs serially, in that at any one stage of processing only one thing is happening; of course more than one thing is happening at different levels, because obviously even as we speak we might be planning what we are going to say next. However, these levels of processing do not *interact* with one another—that is, they are independent. The model distinguishes two major stages of syntactic planning, one (the *functional level*) where word order is not yet explicitly represented, another (the *positional level*) where words are explicitly ordered. There is a dissociation between syntactic planning and lexical retrieval. The model is summarised in Fig. 8.4.

Garrett proposed a major processing distinction between *content words*, which do the semantic work of the language and include nouns, verbs, adjectives, and most adverbs, and *function words*, which are normally short, common words that do the grammatical work of the language. Function words include determiners ("the", "a", "an", "some"), prepositions ("to", "at", "in", "by"), conjunctions ("and", "so", "because"), and WH-words ("where", "what", "who", "when"). Content words are sometimes called *open-class* items, because we are continually adding new ones (such as "television") as necessary, whereas function words

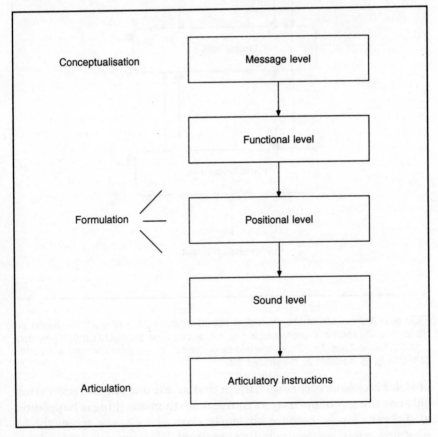

FIG. 8.4. Garrett's model of speech production, showing how the stages correspond to the processes of conceptualisation, formulation, and articulation. (Based on Garrett, 1975, 1976.)

comprise a relatively small, fixed-size set (approximately 360), and hence are sometimes called *closed-class* items. Further evidence that content and function words are processed differently—that is, that they come from distinct computational vocabularies—is that content words are sensitive to frequency in a lexical decision task, but function words are not, except in patients with Broca's aphasia (Bradley, Garrett, & Zurif, 1980). The exact interpretation of these results, however, has proved very controversial (see, for example, Gordon & Caramazza, 1982; Swinney, Zurif, & Cutler, 1980).

Evidence for Garrett's model of speech production

First, in morpheme exchanges such as (5), it is clear that the root or stem morpheme ("maniac") has been accessed independently of its plural affix—in this case the plural ending "-s". (In English affixes are either *prefixes*, which come before a word, or *suffixes*, which come after, and are always *bound morphemes*, in that they cannot occur without a stem; morphemes which can be found as words by themselves are called *free morphemes*. Bound morphemes can be either derivational or inflectional—see Chapter 1.) Because the bound morpheme has been left in its original place while the free morpheme has moved, we call this type of exchange morpheme *stranding*. In general, content words behave independently of and differently from the *grammatical elements*, which include inflectional bound morphemes and function words. This suggests that they are involved in different processing stages.

Second, as we also observed in (5), the plural suffix was produced correctly for the sentence as it was actually uttered, not as it was planned. This accommodation to the phonological environment suggests that the phonological specification of grammatical elements occurs rather late in speech production, certainly after the phonological forms of content words have been retrieved. This dissociation between specifying the sounds of content words and grammatical elements is of fundamental importance in the theory of speech production, and is one that will recur in our discussions of its pathology. Furthermore, in word exchange errors, the sentence stress is left unchanged, suggesting that this is specified independently of the content words.

These observations lead us to a general statement of Garrett's model. It is as though we specify a syntactic plan or frame for a sentence that consists of a series of slots into which content words are inserted. Word exchanges occur when content words are put into the wrong slot. Grammatical elements are part of the syntactic frame but their detailed phonological forms must be specified late.

An example of how a sentence is generated is shown in Table 8.2. We start with an intention to say a particular message; here, for example,

TABLE 8.2
An example of how we produce an utterance, based on Garrett's (1975, 1976)
model of speech production (for clarity, phonetic symbols are not used)

(A) Message level—intention to convey particular meaning activates appropriate propositions

(B) SUBJECT = "mother concept", VERB = "wipe concept", OBJECT = "plate concept"
TIME = past
NUMBER OF OBJECTS = MANY

(C) (DETERMINER) N_1 V [+PAST] (DETERMINER) N_2 [+PLURAL]

(D) /mother//wipe/ /plate/

(E) (DETERMINER) /mother/ /wipe/+[PAST] (DETERMINER) /plate/ + [PLURAL]

(F) /the/ /mother/ /wiped/ /the/ /plates/

(G) Low level phonological processing and articulation

about someone doing the washing up. This happens at the message level (A). There has been surprisingly little research on the message level; often it is just shown as a cartoon-like "thoughts" bubble. We choose what we are going to say and the general way in which we are going to say it, but it is very difficult to carry out research on it. It must surely be that the start of the production process must have a great deal in common with the end point of the comprehension process: perhaps, to borrow the terminology of the Kintsch model described in the previous chapter, "intention to convey message" schemata activate a number of propositions in our propositional network. The task of speech production is then to produce these parallel ideas one at a time: that is, they must be *linearised*. We go on to an abstract semantic specification with *functional* relationships specified (the functional level, B). Word exchanges occur at this stage, and as their absolute positions have not yet been specified, but their thematic roles have, they are constrained by syntactic category but not by the distance between the exchanging words. Next we generate an abstract syntactic frame for the planned sentence (C). The phonological representations of content words are then accessed from the lexicon using the semantic representation (D). These are then inserted into the syntactic planning frame where final positions are specified (the positional level, E). The function words and other grammatical elements are then phonologically specified to give the sound level representation (F). Sound exchanges occur at this stage and, as their absolute position is now specified, are constrained by distance. Other tidying up might then occur, as this is translated into a series of phonological features which then drive the articulatory apparatus (G).

It is a central hypothesis of this model that when parts of a sentence interact to produce a speech error, they must be elements of the same processing vocabulary. That is, certain types of error are never found, and things only exchange if they are involved in the same processing level. Garrett observed that content words almost always only exchange with other content words, and that function words exchange with other function words. This is an extraordinarily robust finding: in my corpus of several thousand speech errors, there is not a single instance of a content word exchanging with a function word. This then is further evidence that the two types of item are from computationally distinct vocabularies that are processed at different levels.

There are also very different constraints on word and sound exchange errors. Sounds only exchange across small distances, whereas words can exchange across phrases; words which exchange tend to come from the same syntactic class, whereas this is not a consideration in sound errors, which swap on words regardless of their syntactic class. In summary word exchange errors involve content words and are constrained by syntactic factors; sound errors are constrained by distance.

Evaluation of Garrett's model

The model is attractive and accounts for a great deal of the speech error evidence, but there are a number of problems which suggest that some aspects need to be changed. First, it is not at all clear that speech production is a serial process. There is clearly some evidence for at least local parallel processing in that we find word blend errors, which must be explained by two (or more) words being simultaneously retrieved from the lexicon (e.g. 12). More problematically, we find blends of phrases and sentences (e.g. 13). Furthermore, the locus of these blends is determined phonologically (Butterworth, 1982), so that the two phrases crossover where they sound most alike. This suggests that two alternative messages are processed in parallel from the message to the phonological levels. Furthermore, the message level can intrude into the utterance and lower levels of processing. These are called *non-plan-internal* errors (e.g. 14). These errors are *phonologically facilitated* in that the target and intrusion sound more alike than would be expected by chance alone (Harley, 1984)—just as with word substitution errors. Consider the following example (15) of a type of error known as environmental contamination (see also Harley 1990a), because the source of the intrusion is an object or name in the outside environment:

12. Utterance: It's difficult to *valify*. (Targets: validate + verify)

13.   Target 1: I'm making some tea.
       Target 2: I'm putting the kettle on.
       Utterance: *I'm making the kettle on.*
14.   Target: I've read all my library books.
       Utterance: I've *eaten* all my library books.
       Context: The speaker reported that he was hungry and was thinking of getting something to eat.
15.   Target: Get out of the car.
       Utterance: Get out of the *clark*.
       Context: The speaker was looking at a shop-front in the background that had the name "Clark's" printed upon it. The speaker reported that he was not aware of this at the time of speaking.

In example (15) from Harley (1984), the intruding item ("Clark's") is phonologically related to the target. We find that such a phonological relationship between the target and intrusions occurs more often than one would expect on a chance basis. Yet many of these cognitive intrusions clearly have a high-level or message level source. Hence speech production can involve parallel processing, with high-level processes constrained by low-level processes such as phonological similarity.

The constraint that processes are independent must also be weakened. We saw in our discussion of lexicalisation that mixed errors (e.g. 10 and 11) are more common than the independence hypothesis predicts. In general, all types of word substitution error display phonological facilitation. These data then are evidence for an interaction of semantic and phonological factors in lexicalisation. Furthermore, there is a word superiority or lexical bias effect in word blends and sound errors (Dell & Reich, 1981). From the examples in Table 8.1, consider the example of the spoonerism "feel really bad" being produced as "*reel feally bad*". The first element of the outcome, "reel", happens itself to be a word. Of course we would expect sound errors to form words sometimes by chance, but Dell and Reich showed that words are formed by such processes more often than is expected by chance. This then is evidence of an interaction between lexical and phonological processes. Priming effects found in the experiments by Bock (1982, 1987; see below) further suggest that levels of processing interact in syntactic planning. These findings all suggest that the levels of processing cannot be independent of one another but must interact.

A final problem about which little can be done, is that the distinction between content and function words is confounded with frequency (Stemberger, 1985), in that function words include some of the most common words of the language (for example, "the", "a"). Processing differences may reflect this rather than their being processed by different systems. However, the observation that bound morphemes behave like function words supports Garrett's hypothesis, as does neuropsychological data discussed below.

Interactive models of lexicalisation.   What modifications can be made to the Garrett model? The simplest approach is to permit interaction between levels. We discussed the interactive model of lexicalisation above. This mechanism underlies lexical insertion for content words, and feedback between the phonological and lemma levels explains the tendency to mixed substitution errors and phonological facilitation. This feedback also explains the lexical bias in sound errors; if phonemes exchange such that the exchange results in a word, these outcomes will receive supporting activation from the lexical level. Perhaps the most complete model of planning and phonological encoding in speech production is that of Dell (1986). Dell's model views spreading activation as a fundamental process, and makes extensive use of Garrett's concept of slots in a planning frame. Frames exist for words to form syntactic plans, morpheme roles to form complex words, and phoneme insertion to form words. Slots are always filled by the item from the appropriate category with the highest activation level. It must be said, however, that our understanding of syntactic encoding in production lags some considerable way behind our understanding of lexicalisation.

Processes of syntactic planning in production
Garrett's model tells us a great deal about the relative stages of syntactic planning, but says little about the syntactic processes themselves. These have been examined in an elegant series of experiments by Bock and her colleagues. First, word order in speech is determined by a number of factors which interact (Bock, 1982). For example, animate nouns tend to be the subjects of transitive sentences (McDonald, Bock, & Kelly, 1993), and conceptually more accessible items tend to be placed early in sentences (Bock & Warren, 1985; Bock, 1987; Kelly, Bock, & Keil, 1986). Generally, ease of lexical access affects syntactic planning. In summary, these experiments show that the grammatical role assignment component of syntactic planning is controlled by semantic-conceptual factors rather than by lexeme-related properties of words such as word lengths. Second, speakers construct sentences so as to as to provide "given" before "new" information (Bock & Irwin, 1980).

The task facing researchers in this area now is to examine the detailed mechanisms of syntactic planning. For example, how do we cope with dependencies between words, such as obtaining number agreement between subjects and verbs? For instance, we must ensure that we say "she does" and "they do". These processes have been investigated by Bock and Miller (1991), Bock and Cutting (1992), and Bock and Eberhard (1993), using a sentence-completion task designed to elicit agreement errors.

THE COGNITIVE NEUROPSYCHOLOGY OF SPEECH PRODUCTION: APHASIA

Aphasia is an impairment to speech production as a consequence of brain damage. Strictly the term means "without speech production", while dysphasia refers to an impairment of language abilities, but we will use it in its more inclusive and traditional sense. A major distinction has been made between *Broca's* and *Wernicke's aphasia*. These terms refer to what were once considered to be syndromes, or symptoms that cluster together, resulting from damage to different parts of the left hemisphere (with Broca's area towards the front, in the frontal lobe, and Wernicke's area towards the rear, in the posterior temporal lobe). Although recent debate has tended towards the conclusion that these labels are not particularly meaningful for psycholinguists, we shall use these terms as they provide convenient labels. They are also still meaningful for clinicians and neurologists, and they are still acceptable terms in those literatures. In summary, the early categorisation related more to the links between the characteristics of the impaired speech and anatomical regions of the brain, while currently the emphasis is upon developing more functional descriptions relating to psycholinguistic models of the impairments. This move is of course one aspect of the general development of cognitive neuropsychology. Another distinction often seen is between patients who are very *fluent* in their speech, and those who speech is *non-fluent*. Our aim here is to relate the individual symptoms of each complex to our model of speech production.

Broca's type aphasia
Broca's aphasia is characterised by slow, laborious, hesitant speech, with little intonation (called *dysprosody*) and with obvious articulation difficulties (called *speech apraxia*). There is also an obvious impairment of word order. At the most general level, Broca's type patients have a difficulty with sequencing units of the language. An example of Broca's aphasia is given in (16)—the dots indicate long pauses.

16. Ah ... Monday ... ah Dad and Paul ... and Dad ... hospital. Two ...
ah ... doctors ... and ah ... thirty minutes ... and yes ... ah ... hospital.
And er Wednesday ... nine o'clock. And er Thursday, ten o'clock...
doctors. Two doctors ... and ah ... teeth. (From Goodglass, 1976,
p. 278.)

Although many Broca's patients suffer from apraxia, not all obviously
have a syntactic disorder. However, we will focus on the syntactic
disorder as this is more revealing of the processes involved in speech
production. In traditional neuropsychology terms, such patients suffer
from what has been labelled *agrammatism*. Agrammatism actually has
two components. First, there is a *sentence construction deficit*, such that
patients have an impaired ability to output correctly ordered words: the
words do not form sentences, but look as though they are being output
one at a time. Second, some parts of speech are better preserved than
others: there is a *selective impairment of grammatical elements*, such
that content words are best preserved, and function words and word
endings (bound inflectional morphemes) are least well preserved.
Whether or not these two components are dissociable is an important
question.

The comprehension abilities of agrammatic aphasics.   It was once
believed that the comprehension abilities of agrammatic aphasics were
normal, but the data actually show a subtle impairment. Saffran,
Schwartz, and Marin (1980) reported that agrammatics'
sentence-picture matching abilities were impaired, and Caramazza and
Zurif (1976; see also Caramazza & Berndt, 1978) similarly found
impaired comprehension when semantic cues are eliminated. These
patients are particularly bad at reversible passives (e.g. "The dog was
chased by the cat" compared with "The flowers were watered by the
girl"—see Chapter 5). Linebarger, Schwartz, and Saffran (1983) found
that the ability to make *grammaticality judgements* was impaired in
these patients. This task requires patients to decide whether a
particular string of words is a grammatical sentence. In summary, this
suggests that the ability of agrammatics to parse sentences is impaired,
but this impairment is masked most of the time by their ability to make
use of semantic cues in comprehension. Grodzinsky (1989) proposed that
the comprehension of agrammatics is impaired because they do not have
the terminal nodes in their parse trees (see Chapter 5) that correspond
to closed-class words.

Recent research on the comprehension impairment in agrammatism
has centred on the issue of whether there is a disruption of the automatic
access of semantic and syntactic information from the lexicon (Friederici

& Kilborn, 1989; Haarmann & Kolk, 1991; Martin, Wetzel, Blossom-Stach, & Feher, 1989; Milberg, Blumstein, & Dworetzky, 1987; but see Tyler, Ostrin, Cooke, & Moss, 1995).

The psychological reality of agrammatism. There has been considerable debate as to whether terms such as Broca's aphasia and agrammatism have any place in modern neuropsychology. The debate centres on whether agrammatism is a coherent deficit: do agrammatics possess symptoms that consistently cluster together, and hence, is there a single underlying deficit that can account for them? If it is a meaningful syndrome, we should find that the sentence construction deficit, grammatical element loss, and a syntactic comprehension deficit should always co-occur. Recent studies find dissociations between these impairments by using single case studies (see, for example, Miceli, Mazzucci, Menn, & Goodglass, 1983; Saffran et al., 1980). This has methodological implications, for if there is no such syndrome as agrammatism, it is meaningless to perform group experiments upon what is in fact a functionally disparate group of patients. Instead, one should perform single case studies. This position has been advocated by Caramazza and his colleagues (see, for example, Badecker & Caramazza, 1985). In reply Caplan (1986) has argued that at the very least agrammatism is a convenient label. Although there might be sub-types, there is still a meaningful underlying deficit. This issue sparked considerable debate, both upon the status of agrammatism (see for example, Badecker & Caramazza, 1986, for a reply to Caplan) and upon the methodology of single case studies (see Bates, McDonald, MacWhinney, & Applebaum, 1991; Caramazza, 1991; McCloskey & Caramazza, 1988).

Explanations of agrammatism. An early explanation of agrammatism took the patients' articulation difficulties as central, and proposed that patients merely drop function words in an attempt to conserve resources. But agrammatism is much more than a loss of grammatical morphemes: there is also a sentence construction and syntactic comprehension deficit. Older theories attempt to find a single underlying cause for the three components. For example, Kean (1977) proposed a single *phonological deficit hypothesis*, later revised by Lapointe (1983), based on the assignment of stress to a syntactic frame. Kean argued that agrammatics omit items that are not what are called *phonological words*. Phonological words are items that can receive stress; in English these are items other than function words and inflections. Hence phonological words are just what are preserved in agrammatism. This hypothesis sparked considerable debate (see Caplan, 1992; Grodzinsky, 1984, 1990; Kolk, 1978). The central problem is that although it explains grammatical element loss, it does not account so well for the other components of the disorder.

Stemberger (1984) compared agrammatic errors with normal speech errors. He proposed that in agrammatics there is an increase in random noise and an increase in the threshold which it is necessary to exceed for access to occur. In these conditions substitutions and omissions, particularly of low frequency items, occur. He argued that agrammatism is a differential exacerbation of problems found in normal speech; this idea, that aphasic behaviour is just an extreme version of normal speech errors, is one frequently mentioned. Harley (1990b) made a similar proposal for the origin of *paragrammatisms*. These are errors involving misconstructed grammatical frames, and can be explained in terms of excessive substitutions. Again, however, these approaches do not explain all the characteristics of agrammatism. Although uninflected words are more common than inflected forms, the high frequency function words are more likely to be lost than content words, which are of lower frequency, on average. Stemberger argued that the syntactic structures involving function words are less frequent than structures which do not.

Perhaps the most plausible approach taken so far has been that of Schwartz (1987) to relate agrammatism to Garrett's model. Consider what would happen in this model if there was a problem translating from the functional level to the positional level. No sentence frame would be constructed, and no grammatical elements would be retrieved. This is what is observed. This does not provide an account of the comprehension deficit, but if this is a dissociable process then this would result from damage to other systems. The dissociation between the sentence construction deficit and grammatical element loss suggests that different processes must be responsible in Garrett's model for constructing the sentence frame and retrieving grammatical elements. Although the details remain to be worked out, this line of thought both supports and extends Garrett's model, and shows how neuropsychological impairments can be related to a model of normal processing.

Finally, a completely different approach is emerging that examines the possibility that agrammatism results from an impairment of working memory (Kolk & van Grunsven, 1985). Miyake, Carpenter, and Just (1994) simulated agrammatism in normal speakers by reducing their working memory capacity. This is an interesting idea, but it is too early to evaluate it in any detail (but see Caplan & Waters, in press).

Wernicke's type aphasia

Damage to Wernicke's area, which is the left temporal-parietal cortex, results in the production of fluent but often meaningless speech. As far as one can tell, speech forms well-formed sentences, with copious grammatical elements and with normal prosody. Comprehension is noticeably poor, and there are obvious major content word-finding difficulties. Zurif, Caramazza, Myerson, and Galvin (1974) found that patients were unable to pick the two most similar words from triads as "shark, mother, husband". Hence at first sight this appears to be the mirror image of Broca's-type aphasia. Just as we would expect from Garrett's model, there is a double dissociation between syntactic planning and grammatical element retrieval on the one hand (impaired in Broca's type but intact in Wernicke's type) and content word retrieval on the other (impaired in Wernicke's type but intact in Broca's type). This double dissociation supports the main principles of the model.

Jargon aphasia.   Jargon aphasia is an extreme type of fluent aphasia. Syntax is primarily intact but there are gross word-finding difficulties marked by content word substitutions or *paraphasias*. These include unrelated verbal paraphasias (e.g. 17); semantic paraphasias (18); and phonemic paraphasias (19). Of particular interest are *neologisms*, which are made up words not in a dictionary including distortions of real words (20) and abstruse paraphasias with no discernible relatives (21). As an example consider this description (22) of connected speech. This is a description by patient CB (from Buckingham, 1981, p.54) of the famous Boston "cookie theft" picture, which depicts a mother washing plates while the sink overfills.

17.   queen → *dog*
18.   queen → *king*
19.   queen → *keen*
20.   queen → *queet*
21.   queen → *robbli*
22.   "You mean like this boy? I mean [noy], and this, uh, [neoy]. This is a [kaynit], [kahken]. I don't say it, I'm not getting anything from it. I'm getting, I'm [dime] from it, but I'm getting from it. These were [eksprehsez], [ahgrashenz] and with the type of [mahkanic] is standing like this . . . and then the . . I don't know what she [goin] other than . . ."

Butterworth (1985) noted in his review that jargon aphasia changes with recovery, over time. A typical progression is: undifferentiated strings of phonemes; to neologistic speech; to word paraphasias and then perhaps circumlocutory phrases.

Butterworth (1979) examined hesitations before neologisms in the speech of patient KC, and found that they resemble those made by normal speakers before less predictable words. KC was more likely to hesitate before a neologism than a real word. The presence of pauses before neologisms at all argues against any account of neologisms relying upon disinhibition—that the lexical retrieval system is over-active. Butterworth instead argued that such errors arise when the patient is unable to activate any phonological form, and instead uses a *random phoneme generation device* to produce a pseudoword. Butterworth, Swallow, and Grimston (1981) examined the gestures in the pauses preceding the neologisms. They found that KC's use of gestures was the same as that of normal speakers, and they therefore concluded that the semantic system was intact in this patient. Butterworth (1985) argues that the first stage of lexical access (what we have called lemma retrieval) functions correctly, but the retrieval of the phonological forms fails. He also suggests that aphasic errors are accentuated normal slips of the tongue, and points to a large number of instances of word blend errors in KC's speech, combined with or perhaps caused by a failure in the mechanisms that normally check speech output. Ellis, Miller, and Sin (1983) found that the main determinant of probability of successful retrieval in jargon is word frequency. We would expect to have particular difficulty in retrieving low frequency items.

Another account of the origin of neologisms and jargon aphasia in terms of the traditional Garrett model of speech production is provided by Buckingham (1986). In particular, Buckingham posits disruption of the functioning of the device known as a *scan-copier* that is responsible for outputting the phonemes of a word into the syntactic frame in the correct order (Shattuck-Hufnagel, 1979). Buckingham (1981) pointed out that neologisms may actually have many different sources, but also invokes the notion of a random syllable generator.

Neologisms display appropriate syntactic accommodation, and their affixes appear correct for their syntactic environment (Butterworth, 1985). This is further support for the Garrett model, as content words are retrieved independently from their syntactic frames and inflections, and jargon is a disorder of lexical retrieval. All *Wernicke's-type* deficits can be seen as problems with the semantic-phonological access system. It is as yet unclear whether there are two sub-types, one involving a semantic impairment and one involving only a problem in the retrieval of phonological forms, although given the two stage model this would be expected.

Anomia

Anomia is an impairment of naming objects and pictures of objects, and can be found in isolation, or accompanying other disorders such as Wernicke's-type or mild Broca's aphasia. The two-stage model of lexicalisation suggests that there are two things that could go wrong in naming: we can have difficulty in retrieving the lemma from the semantic specification, or we could have difficulty in retrieving the phonological form given the lemma. As expected, we observe two types of anomia.

Anomia arising at the semantic level. Anomia at the semantic level is marked by an inability to use the semantic representation to select the correct lemma. Howard and Orchard-Lisle (1984) described a patient JCU, who had a general semantic disorder. Her naming of all types of object was substantially impaired, and she made many semantic errors. Her naming performance could be improved if she was given a phonological cue to the target such as its initial phoneme. However, these phonological cues could lead her astray; if she was given a cue to a close semantic relative of the target she would produce that. For example, the cue "l" would lead her to say "lion" in response to a picture of a tiger. Howard and Orchard-Lisle concluded that her processes of object recognition were normal. JCU scored highly on the *pyramids and palm trees* test. In this task the subject has to match a picture of an object to an associate. In the eponymous trial, the subject must match a picture of a pyramid to a picture of a palm tree rather than to one of a deciduous tree. This suggests that both object recognition processes and the underlying conceptual representation were intact. Howard and Orchard-Lisle concluded that JCU suffered from a semantic impairment such that there was interference between close semantic relatives. She was led to the approximate semantic domain such that the target word was distinguishable from semantically unrelated words, but the semantic representation was too impoverished to enable her to home in any more precisely.

The most striking evidence for involvement of the semantic level in naming disorders is when patients can name members of one semantic category (such as inanimate objects) better than another (such as animate objects). We discussed these category-specific semantic disorders in detail in Chapter 6.

Anomia without semantic impairment. Kay and Ellis (1987) described the case of EST. This patient knew the precise meaning of words, was good at all semantic tasks, but was very poor at retrieving any phonological information about the target. For example, he performed normally on the pyramids and palm trees test, and often offered detailed semantic information about the word he could not retrieve. He was not prone to interference from close semantic distracters. He was much better at retrieving high frequency words than low frequency. EST's problems appear to arise at the phonological level rather than at the semantic level.

Implications of semantic and phonological anomia. The two types of anomia support the idea that lexicalisation occurs in two stages. Semantic anomia can be explained as difficulty in retrieving the lemma, whereas non-semantic impairment can be explained as difficulty in retrieving the phonological representation after the lemma has been successfully accessed.

Connectionist modelling of aphasia

Aphasic speech has as yet not unleashed the same flurry of activity as there has been on dyslexic reading disorders. What research there has been has concentrated upon lexical retrieval problems, and, because the dominant models in this area are based upon spreading activation, modelling of speech production has worked within the interactive activation framework rather than the back-propagation framework. We will look at two connectionist models of lexicalisation in aphasia.

Martin and Saffran (1992) reported the case of patient NC, a young man who suffered a left hemisphere aneurysm that resulted in a pathological short short-term memory span and a disorder known as *deep dysphasia*. This is an aphasic analogue of deep dyslexia; it is a relatively rare disorder marked by an inability to repeat nonwords and the production of semantic errors in word repetition (see Howard & Franklin, 1988). Martin, Saffran, Dell, and Schwartz (1994) relate the lexicalisation component of Dell's (1986) model to NC's speech. They argue that the repetition errors arise because of a pathological increase in the rate at which the activation of units decays. Formal paraphasias arise because when the lexical unit corresponding to the target is activated, activation spreads to the appropriate phonological units. Feedback connections from the phonological to the lexical level ensure that lexical units corresponding to words that are phonologically similar to the target word become activated. Martin and Saffran argued that if the activation of lexical units decays pathologically quickly, then when this feedback occurs, the target lexical unit will be no more highly activated than other phonologically related lexical units that have been activated by phonological-lexical feedback. Repetition errors are accounted for by a similar mechanism. It is difficult to sustain the activation of the target lexical unit given rapid decay, particularly when it is hindered in other ways (such as when the target is low frequency, or supported by impoverished semantic representations).

Harley and MacAndrew (1992) lesioned a model of normal lexicalisation with the aim of producing some of the characteristics of aphasic paraphasias. They tested four hypotheses by lesioning our model. First, as we have seen, Martin and Saffran (1992) proposed that a pathological increase in the rate of decay leads to increased paraphasias and neologisms. In particular, they looked at lexical rather than global decay. Second, Harley (1990b) argued that the loss of within-level inhibitory connections would result in a pattern of impairments such that if lexical units were involved, neologisms and paraphasias would result, whereas if such connections between syntactic units were lost, paragrammatisms (Butterworth & Howard, 1987) would result. Third, Stemberger (1985) argued that normal speech errors result from noise in an interactive activation network. They tested the possibility that excessive random noise in a connectionist system could result in aphasic errors. Finally, Miller and Ellis (1987; see also Ellis, 1985) argued that neologisms result from the weakening of the connections between the semantic and lexical units. Harley and MacAndrew concluded that the final hypothesis would most likely result in more errors. Weakening the value of the parameter that governs the rate of spread of activation from semantic to lexical units often results in target and competing lexical items having high similar activation levels. It is at present unclear whether the predictions this model makes are correct (Nickels, 1995; Harley, 1995).

Evaluation of the contribution of aphasia research to models of normal processing

Taken together, the two main types of disorder support dissociations between the production of syntax and the retrieval of lexical forms, between the generation of syntax and the access of grammatical morphemes, and the retrieval of the phonology of content words. Garrett argued that content and function words are from different computational vocabularies, and this finding is confirmed. Schwartz (1987) interpreted agrammatism and jargon aphasia within the framework of Garrett's model. At present, this approach identifies the broad modules found in production rather than detailed mechanisms involved. It is not yet known whether it is consistent or inconsistent with the interactive models.

We have concentrated upon two major categories of aphasia because of what they tell us about normal speech production. There are however other types. In *global aphasia*, spontaneous speech, naming, and repetition are all severely affected. Speech abilities are not limited to the left hemisphere: disorders of language can arise from damage to the right hemisphere, even in right-handed people; this is called *crossed aphasia*. In *conduction aphasia* repetition is relatively impaired, although there is also some difficulty in naming and some comprehension impairment. *Transcortical aphasics* can repeat words relatively well. There are two types of transcortical aphasia depending on the precise lesion site: in *transcortical sensory aphasia* comprehension is impaired, output is fluent and may even include jargon, but repetition is relatively good; and in *transcortical motor aphasia* comprehension and repetition are very good, but there is very little spontaneous speech output. In principle, it should in the future be possible to relate each of these disorders to a more detailed model of normal production. Martin and Saffran (1990) have made a start in this direction, examining in detail the repetition abilities of patient ST, a transcortical sensory aphasic.

CONCLUDING SUMMARY

Speech production has been studied less than speech recognition because the variables involved are harder to control. Until recently most data have come from the study of hesitations and speech errors. Hesitations reflect, in part, planning by the speaker, although they may also serve social and segmentation functions. We can distinguish pauses attributable to microplanning, which probably represents transient difficulty in retrieving the phonological forms of less predictable words, from those attributable to macroplanning, which represents both semantic and syntactic planning, although there is some controversy as to whether syntactic planning is involved. The tip-of-tongue state can be seen as an extreme case of difficulty in microplanning.

Lexicalisation is the process of retrieving the phonological form of a word given its semantic specification. It is probably a two stage process, mediated by abstract lexical forms called lemmas. There has been considerable debate as to whether these two stages are independent or interact. Speech error data suggest they overlap, while picture-naming data suggest they are independent. Connectionist modelling suggests that both types of data can be explained by the interactive account.

The most influential model of global planning in speech production is that of Garrett. This models holds different types of processing to be independent. Processing occurs in stages, with a distinction between the functional and positional syntactic planning levels. The model is motivated primarily by speech error data which shows that different constraints operate on word exchange than on sound exchange errors, and that there is a fundamental distinction between content words and grammatical elements. The model is challenged by error data that prompt a more parallel, interactive explanation. Nevertheless, Garrett's model provides a generally accurate framework for how we produce speech.

The distinction between syntactic planning and semantic-phonological retrieval is also supported by the presence of double dissociations in the data. Disorders of syntactic planning are manifest in Broca's type patients, while disorders of content word selections are apparent in Wernicke's type patients. Agrammatism has three dissociable components: a sentence construction deficit, grammatical element loss, and impaired syntactic comprehension. These deficits relate to producing or comprehending the positional level in Garrett's model. Paraphasias and neologisms in fluent aphasia result from failures in content word retrieval: incorrect words or constructed strings of sounds are inserted into an otherwise intact planning frame. The status of these patterns of impairments as syndromes is highly controversial. There are two types of anomia, reflecting difficulties in accessing the lemma and phonological form levels in the two-stage lexicalisation model. Connectionist modelling of aphasia is still in its infancy.

FURTHER READING

For more on hesitations and pauses, see Beattie (1983) for a sympathetic review, Petrie (1987) for a critical review. A.S. Brown (1991) gives a general review of work on the tip-of-the tongue state. There is some debate as to whether speech and non-verbal gestures arise from a shared processing stage; for details of this debate see Butterworth and Hadar (1989), Feyereisen (1987), and McNeill (1985, 1987, 1989).

Brief overviews of the whole area are provided by Fromkin (1993) and Bock and Levelt (1994). A good review of the experimental literature is Levelt (1989). Levelt also discusses what might happen at the message level; Dennett (1991) also speculates about how the conceptualiser might work. Levelt further provides a detailed review of the low-level phonetic and articulatory processes in speech production. He discusses the size of the possible planning units in great detail. Bock (1989) and Bock and Loebell (1990) explore some properties of the syntactic frame.

For an overview of modern approaches to the neuropsychology of language, see Zurif and Swinney (1994). For further information on the neuropsychology of language, see Kolb and Whishaw (1990). For more on what cognitive neuropsychology tells us about normal speech production, see Caplan (1992), Ellis and Young (1988), and Schwartz (1987). For a review of the properties of agrammatism and its history, see Howard (1985). Neologisms are discussed in further detail by Buckingham (1986), Butterworth (1985), and Christman and Buckingham (1989). The methodological issues involved in cognitive neuropsychology have spawned a large literature of its own. Indeed, a special issue of the journal *Cognitive Neuropsychology* (1988, volume 5, issue 5) is completely devoted to this topic. For a more detailed discussion, see also Shallice (1988). The nature of agrammatism has always been central in this debate. See Harley (1993b) for a more detailed review of connectionist modelling of aphasia.

We noted in Chapter 1 that sign language is a full-blown language. As we might expect from this, after brain damage it breaks down in interesting ways. Ellis and Young (1988, Chapter 9) review the literature on the neuropsychology of sign languages and gestures.

In addition to speech production, there has of course been some research on writing, although less than on speaking. For a good overview, see Eysenck and Keane (1995) and Ellis (1993). The latter also a section on disorders of writing, the *dysgraphias*.

CHAPTER NINE

The structure of the language system

INTRODUCTION

In this chapter we will draw together many of the issues from previous ones. The architecture of a building indicates what it looks like, how its parts are arranged, its style, and how to get from one room to another. What is the architecture of the language system? How are its modules arranged, and how do they interact with one another? How many lexicons are there? How do we deal with ambiguity? How does context affect the operation of the sentence parsing mechanism? How does semantics interact with syntactic processing? What happens to the syntactic representation after parsing? This chapter discusses many issues that are at the cutting edge of psycholinguistics, and in some places there are more questions than answers.

Caplan (1992) describes the main characteristics of the language-processing system, based on Fodor's (1983) account of the modularity of mind. There are four main points. First, the language system is not a unitary structure, but is divided into a number of modules. We can say further that our initial assumption is that each module takes only one particular representation as input and delivers only one type of output. For example, the syntactic processor takes a word level representation and does not accept input directly from the acoustic level. In terms of Fodor (1983), such modules are said to be informationally encapsulated. We would have to revise this assumption if we find evidence for interaction or leakage between modules. That is, modularity is the simplest arrangement that is the default arrangement unless we find evidence to the contrary. Second, language processes are mandatory—they are activated obligatorily. We cannot help but read a word and access its meaning, even when it is to our advantage not to do so (as in the Stroop task). Third, language processes are generally operating unconsciously. Indeed, the detailed lower level processes are not open to conscious introspection. The second and third points are characteristic of automatic processing (Posner & Snyder, 1975; Shiffrin & Schneider, 1977). Finally, Caplan observes that most processing takes place very quickly and with great accuracy.

We can summarise this analysis as follows. First, what are the modules of the language processing system? Secondly, are they discrete or do they interact? In general, each of the previous chapters corresponds to a psycholinguistic module or set of modules. As we have seen, the issue of the extent to which they interact is very controversial.

THE STRUCTURE OF THE LANGUAGE SYSTEM

What modules of the language system can we identify? Clearly there is a semantic-conceptual system responsible for organising and accessing our world knowledge and for interacting with the perceptual system. We discussed the way in which word meanings might be represented in Chapter 6. At present, the most likely explanation is that they are decomposed into semantic features or micro-features, some of which might be fairly abstract. Features might be interconnected in a network, and at present we think that category membership is referenced by comparison with a prototype. It is present unclear whether there is an amodal unitary semantic store or whether initial contact with the conceptual system is made through modality-specific stores. The meanings of words can be connected together to form a propositional network which is operated on by schemata (particularly in comprehension—see Chapter 7) and the intention system (particularly in production—see Chapter 8).

When we see, hear, or produce a sentence, we have to recognise or produce the words (see Chapters 2, 3, 4, and 8) and decode or encode the syntax of the sentence (see Chapter 5). Little is known at present about the relationship between the syntactic encoder and decoder. Frazier (1990) subdivided the sentence-processing system into four modules. Two are *structural*: one computes constituent structure using pure syntactic information, another computes how the elements of these constituents should be bound together at the syntactic level (filler-gap dependencies). The third deals with assigning words to thematic roles (see Chapter 7), and the fourth computes referential relations. The last two do not look as though they could be informationally encapsulated, as world knowledge must surely be important here. But do they direct syntactic modules to do particular analyses (strong interaction), or maybe they just reject implausible analyses and get them to run again, as suggested by Fodor (1990)? We shall return to this issue in our discussion of syntactic ambiguity later in this chapter.

More is known about the modules of the word recognition and production systems. Each of these necessitates accessing the lexicon, and it is to the structure of the lexical system which we will now turn.

The lexicon

We have seen that there is some debate as to whether all semantic information is represented in a unitary store, or whether at least some information is represented in modality-specific stores. What about our mental dictionary, the lexicon? When we recognise a word, do we make contact with the same lexicon regardless of whether we are listening to speech or reading written language, or are there two *modality-specific* lexicons which we access appropriately? And is the lexicon that we end up at in word recognition the same as we start off from in production, or is there one lexicon for recognition and one for production?

It is apparent therefore that a number of alternatives are possible. The most parsimonious arrangement is that there is only one lexicon, used for the four tasks of reading, listening, writing and speaking. Then it is possible that there are four lexicons, one each for the tasks of writing, reading, speaking, and listening. Then there are two plausible intermediate positions where there are two lexicons. The first two-lexicon arrangement is separate lexicons for written (visual) language and spoken (verbal) language (each covering input and output tasks), the second is separate lexicons for input and output (each covering written and spoken language). That is, is the lexicon unitary, or is it *fractionated*?

Visual and verbal codes.   The first issue is whether the system we use to name words is distinct from other recognition systems. This can be examined most simply in the context of naming pictures of objects, the picture-naming task. To what extent can printed words prime and be primed by other types of material such as pictures? Pictures prime semantically related words in a lexical decision task (Carr, McCauley, Sperber, & Parmalee, 1982; McCauley, Parmalee, Sperber, and Carr (1980); Sperber, McCauley, Ragain, & Weil, 1979; Vanderwart, 1984) However, the magnitude of the between-modality priming effect (related pictures priming words and related words priming pictures) is substantially less than the size of the within-modality priming effect (pictures priming pictures, or words priming words). These findings suggest that the picture-naming and word recognition systems are distinct, although this is controversial (Glaser, 1992). These findings are sensitive to the particulars of the tasks used. Morton (1985) discussed differences in the details of experimental procedures that might account for different findings. For example, in experiments such as Durso and Johnson (1979) the pictures were presented very clearly; while in Warren and Morton (1982) they were presented tachistoscopically. Tachistoscopic recognition is analogous to stimulus degradation and produces a processing bottleneck not present in other experiments.

In Chapter 3 we saw that Winnick and Daniel (1970) showed that tachistoscopic recognition of a printed word was facilitated by the prior reading aloud of that word, while naming a picture or producing a word in response to a definition produced no subsequent facilitation of tachistoscopic recognition of those words. In response Morton divided the word recognition system into different sets of logogens for different modalities (e.g. input and output). Morton (1979b) revised the logogen model so that instead of one logogen for each word, there were two, modality-specific ones. Hence only visual inputs can facilitate subsequent visual identification of words, and auditorily presented primes cannot facilitate visually presented targets in tachistoscopic recognition.

Input and output: Word recognition and lexicalisation.   We saw in Chapter 8 that Fay and Cutler (1977) interpreted phonological word substitution speech errors (malapropisms) as evidence that the same lexicon was accessed in two different directions for speech production and comprehension. Monsell (1987) pointed out that this metaphor treats the lexicon as a spatial array with access as a process of aiming at a particular spot. In fact most of the data argue against a single lexicon used for both recognition and production. As we saw, malapropisms can be explained without recourse to a common lexicon in an interactive two-stage model of lexicalisation.

Indeed, Shallice, McLeod, and Lewis (1985) showed that having to monitor a list of auditorily presented words for a target created little interference on reading words aloud. Furthermore, listening to a word does not activate the same areas of the brain that are activated by reading a word aloud and word repetition, as shown by PET (positron emission topography) brain imaging (Petersen, Fox, Posner, Mintun, & Raichle, 1989). These pieces of evidence suggest that the speech input and output pathways are different.

Monsell (1987) discussed in detail the evidence that the same set of lexical units is not used in both production and perception: there is no evidence of interference between generating and identifying words, and different amounts of facilitation are found across different priming tasks in repetition priming experiments. However, he also argued that the input and output phonological pathways cannot be completely separate, because we find sub-lexical influences of speech production on speech perception. For example, Gordon and Meyer (1984) found that preparing to speak influences speech perception, so there must be some sharing of common mechanisms. Monsell tentatively argued that the interconnection between the speech production and recognition systems happens at a sub-lexical level such as the phonological buffer used in memory span tasks. (Baddeley, Lewis, & Vallar, 1984). The issue is far from being finally resolved, but two linked buffers, one for input and one for output, appear necessary.

Hence the conclusion is that there are different logogen systems for language production and recognition, with some overlap of sub-lexical mechanisms. A number of matters remain to be resolved. First, Dell (1988) suggested that the feedback connections in his interactive model of lexicalisation may be necessary for word recognition (see also Levelt et al., 1991b). This means in effect that interactions in speech production arise through leakage along the comprehension route. As we have just seen, evidence favours the view that the production and comprehension lexicons are distinct. Therefore where does the leakage occur? In general, we have seen that current evidence favours the view that both spoken and visual word recognition are autonomous (Chapters 2 and 3) yet lexicalisation appears to be interactive. It seems odd that one language system (production) is interactive while its mirror image (recognition) is autonomous, so why has this asymmetry arisen?

We have also seen that lexicalisation is a two-stage process, with an intermediate stage of abstract lemmas. To what do lemmas correspond in word recognition? As lemmas are abstract, the obvious correspondence is with visual and verbal input logogens. That is, lemmas are what are stored in the speech output lexicon.

In summary, experimental data from normal subjects suggests that spoken and visual word recognition make use of different mechanisms. There are distinct input and output lexicons, sharing a sub-lexical mechanism. We might also point out that there must be a direct connection from an early, pre-lexical auditory representation to a post-lexical phonological representation, as we have no difficulty in efficiently shadowing nonsense speech. This might involve the same sub-lexical phonological buffer. A number of issues about production and its relationship to comprehension remain unresolved, particularly concerning the differing amounts of interaction apparently found in each task.

Neuropsychological evidence.   There is a wealth of dissociations found between reading, writing, and visual and spoken word recognition. These are reflected in Ellis and Young's (1988) model (see Fig. 9.1), based mainly on neuropsychological data.

This model in their view represents the simplest possible structure of the lexical processing systems given neuropsychological constraints. They aimed to keep the number of boxes and connections to the minimum, and each route is supported by dissociation data. (We do not

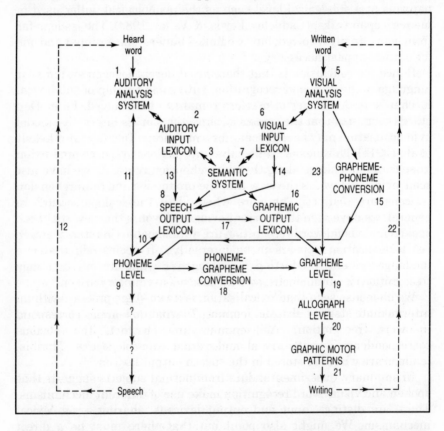

FIG. 9.1. Ellis and Young's (1988) model of the architecture of language processing. (Reprinted from Ellis, A.W., & Young, A W., 1988, *Human cognitive neuropsychology*, p.222. Hove: Lawrence Erlbaum Associates Ltd. Reprinted by permission.) Numbers refer to routes for which there is evidence from neuropsychological dissociation (see Ellis & Young for details).

have space to review these data in detail here, but see Ellis & Young, 1988, for details.) For example, some patients show *pure word deafness*, which as we saw in Chapter 2, means that they can speak, read, and write quite normally, but cannot understand speech. These patients however cannot repeat speech back; the existence of a separate speech input lexicon would only be supported by patients like this, but who also demonstrated intact repetition. That is, we need patients with word meaning deafness. As we saw, such case histories are rare, but have been reported by Bramwell (1897/1984) and Kohn and Friedman (1986). Anomics have difficulty in retrieving the name for objects, yet have perfect comprehension for those words. Beauvois and Dérouesné (1981) report a patient showing impaired spelling and intact lexical reading. It should be pointed out however that there is a scarcity of very clear-cut patients. Patients with anomia without dyslexia, for example, are rare. The neuropsychological data are not completely consistent, either; Behrmann and Bub (1992) argue on the basis of their patient MP that a single lexicon is involved in reading and writing.

Allport and Funnell (1981) also argued that we cannot have a separate amodal lexicon mediating between systems. They reviewed evidence from word-meaning deafness, phonological dyslexia, and deep dyslexia. They describe a number of patients that argue for a dissociation of cognitive and lexical functions. The semantic paraphasias of deep dyslexics rule out both any model where translation to a phonological code is a necessary condition to be able to access a cognitive code (as these patients understand the words without being able to do this), and they also rule out bi-directional connections between phonological, orthographic, and cognitive codes linked to a modality-independent lexicon (as is found in Forster's model). They point out that patients with word-meaning deafness are impaired in the comprehension of spoken words. Bramwell's patient could not comprehend spoken words, but could still write even irregular words to dictation. This is incompatible with any master file mediating lexical stores, and with obligatory phonological mediation of orthographic-to-cognitive codes.

There is an additional problem, which is one of distinguishing between problems of access versus problems of storage. We first met this problem in our discussion of semantic memory (see Chapter 6). Allport and Funnell (1981) argued that there is no evidence for independent lexicons in language production and comprehension. The evidence that motivated Morton to fractionate the logogen system is not necessarily an argument for distinct *lexicons*, only for distinct *access pathways* to logogens. They argue on the grounds of parsimony for the simpler model. Given that there must be distinct phonological and orthographic lexicons, they just have distinct input–output pathways. However, why should this argument not apply to all aspects of lexical access? Why should we not propose one lexicon with four different access mechanisms. This scheme is related to Monsell's (1987) procedural view of the lexicon. In this, the lexicon is a type of production system, with "demons" transcoding from one particular input domain to another output domain (including conceptual). On this account, Bramwell's patient lost the input-phonological to conceptual-functional pathway, while the input-phonological to output-orthographic pathway was preserved.

Evaluation of the structure of the lexicon.   It can be seen that the structure of the lexicon is a complex issue. The neuropsychological data strongly suggest that there are four different lexicons, one each for speaking, writing, and spoken and visual word recognition. Experimental data from normal subjects, while rather confusing, does not greatly contradict this conclusion.

An additional problem is that of distinguishing different *lexicons* from different access *mechanisms*. Suppose we have one lexicon, but four different methods of gaining access to it. In this case what is lost in the neuropsychological dissociations are not the lexical stores, but the access routes. The priming data from normal subjects can also be explained in this way if the access routes contribute in some way to the priming found. The possibility of different stores versus access mechanisms is a complex one, and the distinction is hard to test experimentally. At present this issue remains unresolved.

A final point on lexical organisation is that it is not too important whether words are represented in the lexicon in a local or distributed representation. In a distributed representation, words correspond to patterns of activations over units rather than to individual units (see the discussion of the Seidenberg & McClelland, 1989, model in Chapter 4). Hence the visual input lexicon corresponds to the hidden units in their model. In practice it is very difficult, perhaps impossible, to distinguish these possibilities. And given that individual words clearly do not correspond to individual neurons, they must be distributed to some extent.

Differences between visual and spoken word recognition and comprehension

There are clearly differences in processing the visual and auditory modalities. The immediate pre-lexical access code is unlikely to be the same; even if there is phonological recoding, it is unlikely to be obligatory in languages with deep orthography where there are many irregular words, such as English. The temporal demands of spoken and visual word recognition are very different. As previously noted, in normal circumstances we have access to a visual stimulus for much longer than an acoustic stimulus. Speech recognition is temporally constrained much more than visual word recognition. We have just seen that at the very least there are quite distinct pathways to word recognition, and probably distinct lexicons for visual and spoken word recognition.

It is even possible that fundamental variables have different effects in the two modalities. It is harder to find frequency effects in spoken language recognition than in visual word recognition (Bradley & Forster, 1987). In the cohort model frequency only affects the initial identification of a word, and identification of the spoken word is completed before the word's offset; hence any late decision task is likely to fail to detect it. Frequency effects are stronger for monosyllabic than polysyllabic words. Nevertheless, in normal circumstances the two systems develop closely in tandem. Apart from the youngest children, there is a very high correlation between auditory and visual comprehension skills (Palmer, MacLeod, Hunt, & Davidson, 1985).

Differences between the modalities may extend beyond word recognition. Kennedy, Murray, Jennings, and Reid (1989) argued that parsing is very different in the two modalities. In written language we have the opportunity to go back and re-analyse, but spoken language is gone very quickly, and we only have access to it via an input buffer.

Are lexical derivations fully listed?

How are morphologically complex words stored in the lexicon? Is there a full listing of all derivations of a word, so that are entries for "kiss", "kissed", "kisses" and "kissing"? We can call this the *full-listing hypothesis*. Or do we just list the stem ("kiss-"), and produce or decode the inflected items by applying a rule (add "-ed" to form past tense)? In this case, as English contains a large number of irregular derivations (e.g. "ran", "ate", "mice", "sheep"), we would have to list the exceptions separately. We can call this the *stem only plus rule and list of exceptions hypothesis* (Smith & Sterling, 1982; Taft, 1981). There is an intermediate position. It seems very uneconomical to list all inflections given that so many of them can be derived by a very simple rule, so the most commonly held version of the full-listing hypothesis states that only frequent and common words have a separate listing (Monsell, 1985; Sandra, 1990).

There are a number of experiments on the recognition of complex words. According to the stem only hypothesis, to recognise a morphologically complex word we must first strip off its affix, a process known as *affix stripping*. In a lexical decision task, words that look like they have a prefix (e.g. "interest", "result") but which in fact do not do so take longer to recognise than control words (Taft, 1981). It is as though subjects are trying to strip these words of their affixes but are then unable to find a match in the lexicon and have to reanalyse. Taft (1984) showed that subjects have difficulties with words such as "fined" that have a morphological structure different from that suggested by their homophones (here "find"). The subjects' task was to judge whether a visually presented word was a homophone. As subjects found this difficult to do, Taft argued that inflected words are represented in the lexicon as stem plus affix. However, it does not always necessarily take longer to recognise a word without a suffix than one with (Manelis & Tharp, 1977), although even then in some tasks they do.

Speech errors cast some light on the production side of this. We find errors where a dissociation occurs between the stems of lexical items and their affixes (the morpheme stranding errors discussed in Chapter 8). Affixes are also sometimes added incorrectly, anticipated, or deleted. Indeed, Garrett's speech production model rests upon a dissociation between content words and grammatical elements which are accessed at different times. (There is a contrary view: similar errors are also found involving other word final fragments. One needs to show that the fate of inflections is particularly different, and Butterworth, 1983, argued that it is not.) Finally, the neuropsychological evidence from affix loss in Broca's type disorders and affix addition to neologisms in jargon aphasia (Chapter 8) also suggests that affixes are added to stems.

In summary, the data support the stem-only model whereby morphologically complex words are decomposed into their stems by affix stripping, but morphologically complex high-frequency words may have their own lexical listing. Compound words whose meanings are not transparent from their components (e.g. "buttercup") will also be stored separately (Sandra, 1990).

INTERACTION BETWEEN SYSTEMS

We have just identified the main modules of the language system. To what extent do these modules operate independently of each other, and to what extent do they interact? This distinction between autonomy and interaction has been a recurring theme in previous chapters. We shall now look at what we can learn about it from studying how we cope with ambiguity in language.

Ambiguity arises in a number of ways. There are ambiguities associated with the segmentation of speech. Consider the spoken phrases "grey tape" with "great ape", and "ice cream" with "I scream":

in normal speech they sound the same. Some words have more than one meaning, and some sentences have more than one acceptable parse. Sentences are often temporarily ambiguous. How do we resolve the ambiguity? That is, how do we choose the appropriate meaning or *reading*? What role does context play in disambiguation, and at what stage is it used? We shall concentrate on lexical and syntactic ambiguity.

Lexical ambiguity

Ambiguity to do with words is called lexical ambiguity. Some words, called *homophones*, sound the same so that they are ambiguous when we hear them but not when we see them written down. Some examples of homophones are "knight" and "night", and "weight" and "wait". Some words called *homographs* are ambiguous when written down, and some of these may be disambiguated when pronounced (such as "lead"—as in "dog lead" and "lead" the metal).

Of most interest are *polysemous* words, which have multiple meanings. There are many examples of these in English, such as "bank", "straw", and "letter". Consider sentences (1) to (4). Some words are also syntactically ambiguous—"bank" can operate as a verb as well as a noun as in (5) or (6).

1. The fisherman put his catch on the bank.
2. The businessman put his money in the bank.
3. I got the mail and opened the letter.
4. The monk writing the manuscript to look a long time to form each letter.
5. I wouldn't bank on it if I were you.
6. The plane is going to bank suddenly to one side.

Most of the time we are probably not even aware of the ambiguity. Clearly we have somehow used the context of the sentence to disambiguate—that is, to select the appropriate sense. How do we do this? At what stage does context operate?

Models of lexical ambiguity.   There are three main models of resolving lexical ambiguity. When we come across an ambiguous word, do we go straight to the appropriate meaning, or do we access all of the senses and then choose between them? The three models differ in the position they take on this.

We can call the first model *context-guided single reading* lexical access (Glucksberg, Kreuz, & Rho, 1986; Schvaneveldt, Meyer, & Becker, 1976; Simpson, 1981). According to this model, the context restricts the access process so that only the relevant meaning is ever accessed. Traditionally this model has been out of favour because it is hard to see how the context can do this. This is less problematical with connectionist models, which are very good at satisfying multiple constraints. It is likely that connectionist models will be influential in the future in this area.

The second model is called *ordered access* (Hogaboam & Perfetti, 1975). All the meanings are accessed in order of their individual *meaning frequencies*, and then checked serially against the context to see if they are appropriate. For example, these days the financial sense of "bank" is used far more often in everyday speech than the riverside sense. In this case the financial sense has the higher meaning frequency. Perhaps it makes sense to check this against the context first, see if it is consistent, and only if it is not access the next sense?

The third model is called *multiple access* (Onifer & Swinney, 1981; Swinney, 1979). According to this model, when an ambiguous word is encountered, all meanings are activated, and the appropriate one is chosen when the context permits. There is a variant of this, hypothesising that if the ambiguity has not been resolved by the end of the clause, a meaning is selected whether or not there has been sufficient disambiguating context (Bever, Garrett, & Hurtig, 1973; Garrett, 1970; Lackner & Garrett, 1972). We can call this *variant multiple access but resolved at the end of clause*.

Broadly, we can characterise the context-sensitive selective access models as in the tradition of interactive models, with the multiple access models in the tradition of autonomy models.

Early evidence for multiple access. A number of experiments appear to show that we access routinely all the meanings of ambiguous words. They are based on the premise that if an ambiguous word is harder to process according to some measure than a control unambiguous word, even in a strongly biasing context, then this means that at some level the language-processing system has detected the ambiguity. For example, MacKay (1966) used a sentence completion task whereby subjects have to complete an initial sentence fragment (7 or 8) with an appropriate ending.

7. After taking the right turn at the intersection, I ...
8. After taking the left turn at the intersection, I ...

Subjects take longer to complete (7) rather than (8) because of the ambiguity of the word "right". This finding suggests that both senses are being considered, and the delay arises because the subject is making a choice. In a variant of this experiment, Bever et al. (1973) found that this effect is much stronger if the completion point is in the same clause as the ambiguous word (e.g. after "at the" rather than "I" ...).

In these sentences the ambiguity is unresolved by the context—both senses of "right" are appropriate here. Do we find that ambiguous words are more difficult even when the context biases us to one interpretation? Consider sentences (9) and (10). Here the context of "farmer" is strongly biasing towards the farmyard sense of "straw" rather than the sense of short drinking utensil. Foss (1970) used a technique called *phoneme monitoring* to show that ambiguous words take longer to process even when they are strongly biased by context. In this task the subject has to monitor spoken speech for a particular sound or phoneme, and press a button when they have detected it. In these sentences the target is /b/. Subjects are slower to detect the /b/ in (9) than in (10), ostensibly because they are slowed down by disambiguating the preceding word.

9.   The farmer put his straw *b*eside the machine.
10. The farmer put his hay *b*eside the machine.

The phoneme monitoring task however is sensitive to other linguistic variables, such as the length of the preceding word. Short words leave us little time to process them, whereas long words are often identified and processed before their end (see Chapter 2); it is as though processing of short words has to continue into the next. This processing carry-over delays identification of the phoneme for which subjects are monitoring. Mehler, Segui, and Carey (1978) showed that this effect disappears if the ambiguous words are properly controlled for length. It so happens that in English ambiguous words tend to be shorter than non-ambiguous words.

In the dichotic listening task different messages are presented to each ear. Subjects are told to attend to one ear and ignore the other. In experiments by Lackner and Garrett (1972) and MacKay (1973) the attended message was (11), and the unattended message either (12) or (13).

11. The spy *put out* the torch as a signal to attack.
12. The spy *extinguished* the torch in the window.
13. The spy *displayed* the torch in the window.

Afterwards subjects were asked to paraphrase the attended message. Their interpretation was affected by the unattended message which disambiguated the ambiguous phrase "put out".

Early evidence for selective access.   The experiments discussed so far suggest that all meanings of an ambiguous word are accessed in parallel. Other evidence contradicts this conclusion. Hogaboam and

Perfetti (1975) showed that the time taken to access meaning depends on frequency of use. They used an *ambiguity detection* task, which simply measures the time subjects take to detect the ambiguity. People are slow to detect ambiguity when the word occurs in its most frequent sense (14 rather than 15). This is because in (14) subjects access the common reading of "pen" automatically, integrate it with the context, and afterwards have to reanalyse to detect the ambiguity. In (15) subjects try the common sense, fail to integrate it with the context, and then access the second sense. Hence in this case the ambiguity is detected in routine processing. Holmes (1979) replicated this experiment in a comprehension task, controlling for the relative frequencies of each meaning using synonyms.

14.   The accountant filled his pen with ink.
15.   The farmer put the sheep in the pen.

Schvaneveldt et al. (1976) employed a successive lexical decision task. In this subjects see individual words presented in a stream, and they have to make lexical decisions to each word. In this case subjects become far less aware of relationships between successive words. The lexical decision time to triads of words such as (16–18) is the main experimental concern.

16.   save   bank   money
17.   river   bank   money
18.   day   bank   money

The fastest reaction time to "money" was in (16) where the appropriate meaning of "bank" had been primed by the first word ("save"). Reaction time was intermediate in control condition (18), but slowest in (17) where the incorrect sense had been primed. If all senses of "bank" had been automatically accessed when it was first encountered, then "money" should have been primed by "bank" whatever the first word. This result therefore supports selective access.

Swinney's (1979) experiment.   So far the evidence appears to be contradictory: there is some evidence in support of multiple access, and some in support of selective access. The results we find are very task-dependent, and these tasks are either *off-line* in the sense that they reflect processing times well after the ambiguity has been processed (such as ambiguity detection, dichotic listening, and sentence completion) or are tasks such as phoneme monitoring, which are pretty much on-line but are very sensitive to other variables. We need a task which tells us what is happening immediately we come across an ambiguous word. Such an experiment is reported by Swinney (1979), who used a cross-modal priming technique in which subjects have to respond to a visual lexical decision task while listening to correlated auditory material.

19.   Rumour had it that, for years, the government building had been plagued with problems. The man was not surprised when he found several (spiders, roaches, and other) bugs$_1$ in the corner$_2$ of his room.

In (19) the ambiguous word is "bugs". The phrase "spiders, roaches, and other" is a disambiguating context which strongly biases subjects towards the "insect" sense of "bugs" rather than the "electronic" sense; half the subjects saw this strongly disambiguating phrase. There was a visually presented lexical decision task either immediately after (point 1) or slightly later (point 2). The target in the lexical decision was either "ant" (associated with the biased sense), "spy" (associated with the irrelevant sense), or "sew" (a neutral control). Swinney found facilitation at point 1 for all the meanings of "bugs", including the irrelevant meaning, but found facilitation only for the relevant meaning at point 2. This suggests that when we first come across an ambiguous word, we automatically access all its meanings. However, we use context to make a very fast decision between the alternatives leaving only the consistent sense active.

Subsequent experiments have replicated and extended this result. Onifer and Swinney (1981) replicated the main finding using the same type of technique but where there was an asymmetry in the frequency of the senses of the ambiguous word, so that one meaning is much more frequent than the other. Tanenhaus, Leiman, and Seidenberg (1979) replicated using a naming task rather than lexical decision, and found that context-independent meaning faded after 200 milliseconds. Seidenberg, Tanenhaus, Leiman, and Bienkowski (1982) showed that when an ambiguous word such as "rose" is encountered, both senses (as in "flower" and "stood up") are activated, regardless of the semantic and syntactic contexts. That is, even the syntactically inappropriate sense of an ambiguous word becomes activated for a short while—that is, for a few hundred milliseconds, without reaching conscious awareness.

Recent work on lexical ambiguity.   In summary, the data so far suggest that when we hear or see an ambiguous word, we unconsciously access all the meanings immediately but use the context to reject very quickly all inappropriate senses. This process takes approximately 200 milliseconds. Less frequent meanings take longer to access because more evidence is needed to cross their threshold for being considered appropriate to the context. This suggests that the processes of lexical access are autonomous, or informationally encapsulated, in that all senses of the ambiguous word are output, but then semantic information is utilised very quickly to select the appropriate sense. This in turn suggests that the construction of the semantic representation of the sentence is happening more or less on a word-by-word basis, and there is some indication (from the result of Seidenberg et al., 1982) that it may even influence the construction of the syntactic representation. The precise timing of access depends on relative frequencies of meanings. For strongly biased words, the dominant word may be accessed first. When a related word is nearby, which can disambiguate through intra-lexical spreading activation, we find automatic access of the relevant meaning (Seidenberg et al., 1982). Hence the resolution of ambiguous words is unaffected by contextual effects except through lexical processing.

This view has recently been challenged in three ways. First, Glucksberg et al. (1986) consider possible artefacts (such as *backwards priming*; see Chapter 3) in the Swinney experiment. In the cross-modal design the subject hears the ambiguous word and then sees the visual target. However, the visual target may be available while the ambiguous prime is still being processed. Hence the visual target might be priming the supposed prime backwards in time, itself acting as a biasing context. Hence the apparent multiple access might be an artefact of the procedure, as all meanings will be activated, not necessarily by the biasing prior sentence context, but by the context provided by the target word. Glucksberg et al. eliminated this possible source of context by using nonwords as the visual targets. Nonwords cannot serve as biasing contexts even through backwards priming. But they can be forward primed by context, as context can make nonwords seem more word-like and therefore harder to reject (e.g. "abble" seems more word-like after "oranges, pears, and other fruit"). Hence it is still possible to measure lexical decision times for the nonwords. Otherwise this experiment replicated Onifer and Swinney (1981), using the same materials, who found non-context independent access, so there can be no lexical priming. Glucksberg et al. found using this procedure that context can constrain initial meaning activation, limiting lexical access to a single context-dependent sense. But even so the targets were still presented at the prime offsets, which might be relatively late: that is, all meanings might be activated but all but one rejected very quickly—such as before the end of the word. This result has recently been questioned by Burgess, Tanenhaus, and Seidenberg (1989), who argued that the interference effects obtained by Glucksberg et al. are post-lexical (see Chapter 3), and therefore that sentence context does not constrain the access of the relevant meaning.

Second, Tabossi (1988a,b) used cross-modal priming to show that sentential context which specifically constrains a property of the prime word did lead to selective facilitation. She argued for a modified version of context-dependency: not all aspects of semantic-pragmatic context can constrain search through the possible meanings, but only semantic features constraining specific semantic properties. For example, the context in (20) constrains closely the "sour" property of "lemon". Lemon primes "sour", the target presented visually for lexical decision immediately after the prime lemon. Hence the notion of context has been decomposed, with not all aspects of the context able to facilitate.

20.   The little boy shuddered eating a slice of lemon.

Moss and Marslen-Wilson (1993) pointed out however that the acoustic offset of the prime word may be too late to measure an effect, given that initial lexical access occurs very early, before words are completed. Moss and Marslen-Wilson also explored the way in which different prime-target relationships are influenced by different types of context. In addition they measured early, before prime offset. Normatively semantically associated targets were primed independent of context, while access to semantic property targets was affected by the semantic context. Semantic properties were not automatically accessed whenever heard, but can be modulated by prior context, even at the earliest probe position. Hence this finding again indicates that neither exhaustive or selective access models may be quite right, in that what we find depends upon the detailed relationship between the context and the meanings of the word.

Third, extensive use has been made recently of studying eye movements, which are thought to reflect on-line processing. Studies making use of this technique (e.g. Duffy, Morris, & Rayner, 1988; Rayner & Frazier, 1989) have shown that the time subjects take gazing at ambiguous words depends on the location of the disambiguating context (in particular, whether it is before or after the ambiguous word), and whether the alternative meanings of the ambiguous word are relatively equal or highly discrepant in frequency. Simpson (1994) described these two types of ambiguous words as *balanced* and *unbalanced* respectively. When the disambiguating context comes before the ambiguity, if the dominant meaning is relevant then there is no difference between balanced and unbalanced ambiguous words, but if the less frequent meaning is appropriate we find that unbalanced words have longer gaze durations than balanced ones. If the disambiguating context comes after the ambiguity, we find that subjects spend longer looking at balanced ambiguous words than unbalanced, which take the same time as control words. This suggests that if there is no disambiguating context at the time we come across the ambiguous word, the dominant meaning of unbalanced words is retrieved immediately; for balanced words, however, where both meanings are equally likely, there is an increase in processing load. When the context comes before, the dominant sense is accessed automatically, and having to access the less frequent meaning makes processing more difficult. In effect, context that biases towards the less frequent sense turns unbalanced words into the more difficult balanced ones.

Evaluation of work on lexical ambiguity. We can distinguish two basic approaches to how we eventually select the appropriate sense of ambiguous words. On the autonomous view, we automatically access all the multiple senses of a word, and use the context to select the appropriate reading. We can further distinguish two versions of this autonomy position. According to the strong autonomy thesis, we only make a choice at the end of a major syntactic unit, such as a clause. Semantic processing can only begin when the parser has completed its initial analysis, or analyses if the lexical ambiguity also leads to syntactic ambiguity (see next section). According to the weak autonomy thesis, semantic information can access the appropriate sense of the word very quickly (as long as no syntactic ambiguity is also involved). On the interactive view, the context enables selective access of the appropriate sense of the ambiguous word. So far the data just favour the weak autonomy position, but the experiments used in this area are very sensitive to properties of the target and context length. Whether or not and when we get context-sensitive priming in these cross-modal experiments depends on the details of the semantic relationship between the target and prime. Early experiments using off-line tasks found contradictory results for both multiple and context-specific selective access. Later experiments using more sophisticated cross-modal priming indicated multiple access with rapid resolution. More recent experiments still have questioned this, suggesting that associative relationships may be able to access the appropriate meaning automatically and selectively, and that processing difficulty depends upon the relative frequencies of the alternative senses of the ambiguous word, and the relative position of the disambiguating context. Hence the way in which lexical ambiguity is dealt with is an interaction between the characteristics of the ambiguous word and the type of disambiguating context.

A number of questions remain: in particular, how does context exert its influence in selecting the right meaning? How does *semantic integration* occur? It is possible that connectionist models will be relevant here in the near future. MacDonald, Pearlmutter, and Seidenberg (1994) begin to address this issue, and also address the relationship between lexical and syntactic ambiguity.

Syntactic ambiguity and garden path sentences

The issue of syntactic ambiguity is again most relevant to the issue of whether or not parsing is autonomous or interactive. According to the autonomy thesis, we can only start semantic work after we have completely parsed a major syntactic unit. That is, we must wait until the end of a clause before semantic processing can start. According to the interactionist thesis, the construction of a semantic representation and its utilisation can begin right away, so that semantic information can guide parsing. So does semantic information constrain how parsing of ambiguous phrases takes place (the interactive view), or choosing between parsed alternatives, or forcing the syntactic module to reparse or *backtrack* (the autonomous view)?

There are different types of ambiguity involving more than one word. The simplest are perhaps the bracketing or scope ambiguities of example (21), which could be interpreted either in the sense of (22) or (23).

21.   old men and women leave first
22.   ([old men] and women)
23.   (old [men and women])

More complex are structural ambiguities associated with parsing. We have already discussed syntactic preferences in parsing ambiguous structures such as in sentence (24) in Chapter 5. Now consider example (25):

24.   Boris said that Vlad finished it yesterday.
25.   I saw the Pennines flying to Glasgow.

Many of us would not initially recognise a sentence such as (25) as ambiguous. On consideration, this might be because one of its two meanings is so semantically anomalous (the interpretation that I looked up and saw a mountain range in the sky flying to a city) that it does not appear to be even considered. This is the central issue in coping with ambiguity. To what extent does semantic information interact with syntactic processing?

We must distinguish between standing (or permanent) ambiguity, when you get to the end of the sentence and it is still not disambiguated, and local ambiguity, where material is temporarily or locally ambiguous, but is disambiguated by subsequent material. Many sentences are temporarily ambiguous; indeed, any sentence starting "the" is, as either an adjective or noun can follow. It is only in the more extreme cases that we become aware of this, and these are called garden path sentences.

Consider an early experiment on temporary structural ambiguity by Tyler and Marslen-Wilson (1977). They used a *sentence continuation* task in which subjects hear one of two versions of the beginning of a sentence (26) and (27) over headphones. They are then given either the word "is" or "are" visually, and have to continue the sentence in an appropriate way. They are faster at producing an appropriate continuation in an appropriate context than without one. This suggests that there is interaction in language processing: the message level influences the processing of working out the syntactic structure. However, a non-interactive explanation has been proposed by Forster (1979). He argued that all interpretations of a sentence are generated, and the ambiguity is resolved later. That is, the context does not affect the low-level processes.

26.   If you walk too near the runway, landing planes …
27.   If you've been trained as a pilot, landing planes …

Hence when processing ambiguous sentences, similar questions apply as with processing ambiguous words. Do we process all the alternatives in parallel until definitive information exists that enables us to make a positive conclusion, or do we choose the best bet on the basis of current information? A parallel multiple-path parser uses all possible interpretations of an ambiguous constituent to construct multiple interpretations in parallel. A single path parser makes a choice on the basis of the syntactic best bet, perhaps in an interactive parser making use of other sources of information.

In practice the autonomy view has become identified with the position that we initially construct the most plausible parse tree on syntactic grounds alone, and reparse if this later turns out to be unacceptable. The interactive view has become the view that parsing is guided by semantic considerations, and that the garden path phenomenon is a semantic and not syntactic effect. We shall review the evidence for these positions.

Garden path sentences.   The ambiguity in (24) and (25) above is permanent in the sense that it is still unresolved by the end of the sentence. Syntactic ambiguity may be also be transient, in the sense that later material disambiguates. The most researched examples of transient syntactic ambiguity are *garden path sentences*—so called because the early part of a sentence biases you strongly to one interpretation that subsequently turns out to be wrong. The existence of garden path sentences is at first sight some evidence for a single path parser.

28.   The horse raced past the barn fell.
29.   The log floated past the bridge sank.
30.   The ship sailed round the Cape sank.
31.   The old man the boats.

Consider (28) from Bever (1970). The verb "raced" is ambiguous in that it could be a main verb (the most frequent sense) or a past participle. If we hear this sentence, up to the final, unexpected word "fell" this sentence could be interpreted in the normal straightforward way. When we come across the last word we realise we have been led up the garden path because our original analysis is wrong, and apparently have to go back and re-analyse (to arrive at the interpretation of "The horse that was raced past the barn was the one that fell"—some people take some time to work out what the correct interpretation is). That is, we try to parse as simple noun followed by a prepositional phrase. In fact, it contains a *reduced relative* clause (a relative clause that is "reduced" because it lacks the *relative pronoun* "which" or "that"). Two main questions arise here: do we access all interpretations and choose between them? Or does semantics influence our choice as we parse? The simplest theory is that when we begin parsing we select the one interpretation, and only come up with an alternative when it does not work. The second issue is if we really do backtrack, is this really because of syntactic factors, or is it semantic factors that have led us up the garden path?

In Chapter 5 we distinguished between first pass and second pass parsing. We need to consider further whether the first stage constructs only one initial phrase structure—the *serial model*—or whether it constructs all possible interpretations of an ambiguous string in parallel—the *parallel model* (Mitchell, 1994). The phenomenon of garden path sentences clearly supports the serial model. According to the autonomy or garden path theory, the first pass is automatic and affected only by syntactic factors such as minimal attachment and late closure (Frazier & Rayner, 1982; Rayner & Frazier, 1987). The first pass is carried out by a purely structure-driven *syntactic processor*. If the results of the first pass turn out to be incompatible with further syntactic, pragmatic, or semantic and thematic information generated by an independent *thematic processor*, then a second pass is necessary to revise the parse tree. This is called a *structure-driven* model of parsing. On the interactive position (e.g. Altmann & Steedman, 1988), non-syntactic context can affect the first pass. Altmann and Steedman (1988) proposed an incremental parser that understands sentences on a word-by-word basis, or incrementally. At each word alternative syntactic interpretations are generated in parallel, and then discriminated against using context. They call this "weak" interaction, as opposed to strong interaction, where context actually guides the parsing process so that only one alternative is generated. On this view, as semantic factors guide parsing, it must be semantic considerations which in this case must lead us up the garden path. This type of approach is called the *discourse-driven* model of parsing.

Evidence for autonomy. Frazier and Rayner (1982) argued that the parser tries to attach each new word to the clause currently being constructed—a principle known as *late closure* (see Chapter 5). Hence (32) is unambiguous and does not cause the parser any problem, but (33) is troublesome for this reason and leads to a garden path. They found reading time longer for (33) than (32), and in (33) the first fixation in the disambiguating region was longer.

32. Since Jay always jogs a mile and a half this seems a short distance to him.
33. Since Jay always jogs a mile and a half seems a very short distance to him.
34. The defendant examined by the lawyer turned out to be unreliable.
35. The evidence examined by the lawyer turned out to be unreliable.

Ferreira and Clifton (1986) also argued that semantic factors do not affect reading time and therefore argued that the syntactic processor is autonomous. The noun-verb-noun strategy (the canonical order strategy of Chapter 5) takes the word "examined" to be the main verb, and "examined" requires an agent. "The defendant" in (34) is animate and can fulfil this role so this structure is ambiguous; in (35) "the evidence" is inanimate and cannot. However, the semantic inconsistency of sentences such as (35) does not prevent garden pathing of (34). They argue that semantics does not prevent or cause garden pathing, but can speed recovery from it. The ambiguity is very short in duration, and is resolved by the following word, "by" (see Clifton & Ferreira, 1989; Taylor & Taylor, 1990).

Evidence for interaction. On the interactive account then we would expect semantic factors to affect whether or not we get garden pathed. What is the evidence that this is the case? One frequently used technique is that of making speeded *grammaticality judgements*. In this task subjects see a string of words, and have to decide as quickly as possible whether the string is grammatical or not. Subjects on the whole are more likely to misidentify garden path sentences as non-grammatical in this task than non-garden path sentences. Crain and Steedman (1985) used this technique to show that an appropriate semantic context can eliminate syntactic garden paths. Sentence (36) was incorrectly judged ungrammatical far more often than the structurally identical but semantically more plausible sentence (37).

36. The teachers taught by the Berlitz method passed the test.
37. The children taught by the Berlitz method passed the test.

They argued that there is no such thing as a truly neutral semantic context: even when it is absent from the sentence, subjects bring prior knowledge and expectations to the experiment. Crain and Steedman argued that parsing is not autonomous, and that all syntactic parsing preferences can be explained semantically. At first, all syntactic alternatives are considered in parallel, and semantic considerations then rapidly select among them. Semantic difficulty is based upon the amount of information that has to be assumed: the more assumptions that have to be made, the harder the sentence is to process. Hence sentences such as (38) are difficult compared with (39) because, as in (39), the existence of only one horse is assumed. This assumption is incompatible with the actual semantic representation needed to understand (38)—that there are a number of horses but it was the one that was raced past the barn which was the one which fell. That is, if a unique referent can be found for a definite noun phrase then the following phrase (called the *postnominal*) will initially be interpreted as modifying that noun phrase. This is called the *referential hypothesis*.

38. The horse raced past the barn fell.
39. The horse raced past the barn quickly.

Milne (1982) also argued that it is semantic factors rather than syntactic that lead to garden paths. Consider the three sentences (40–42). The first two are potential garden path sentences, but only the first causes difficulty, because only this sentence sets up semantic expectancies.

40.   The granite rocks during the earthquake.
41.   The granite rocks were by the seashore.
42.   The table rocks during the earthquake.

Holmes et al. (1987) used a *self-paced reading* task to argue that readers are not always led up the garden path as often as has been claimed. In self-paced reading subjects press a button to obtain each new word of the sentence. They found that reading time for an ambiguous phrase did not decrease even if it was preceded by a phrase that should have disambiguated it. Therefore they concluded that garden path effects are not due to being led up the garden path in the sense of having chosen an incorrect parse and having to backtrack, but rather that such sentences are syntactically more complex and need more processing time. More specifically, they argued that Frazier and Rayner's (1982) results that were originally attributed to minimal attachment were not in fact due to garden path effects, but to the extra complexity involved in coping with two sets of clausal relations (as in "Vlad knew the schedule" and "the schedule was wrong") rather than one (43 versus 44). (The minimal attachment strategy is that comprehenders syntactically structure as each word is encountered; at points of potential ambiguity they select the simplest structure, which is that which requires the fewest syntactic nodes to be postulated; see Chapter 5 and Fig. 5.4).

43.   Vlad knew the schedule (by heart).
44.   Vlad knew the schedule (was wrong).

Hence (44) should be harder to process than (43). Now consider (45).

45.   Vlad knew that the schedule was wrong.

Here the addition of the word "that"—an *overt complementiser*—should disambiguate the ambiguity present in "Vlad knew" between the potential alternative structures of (43) and (44). As (45) should then have been disambiguated, the reading time for the final phrase "was wrong" in (45) should be shorter than for the same phrase in (44), where it is that phrase that resolves the ambiguity. Holmes et al. (1987) found no difference, and argued that support for minimal attachment had been weakened. They argued that such sentences with clausal complements are always inherently difficult.

In reply, Rayner and Frazier (1987) replicated their experiment with eye movement measurements rather than subject-paced reading times. They found a different pattern of results. This points to another difficulty, that different techniques give different results. In particular, self-paced reading might measure late processes that are not picked up in eye movement measurements. They also noted that some materials were odd. To take an extreme example, consider (46) where a tensed complement is used without an overt complementiser. They concluded that minimal attachment is indeed reflected in first pass reading times.

46.   The vampire observed the behaviour of the bats was abnormal.

Altmann, Garnham, and Dennis (1992) used eye movement measurements to investigate how context affects garden pathing. It is argued that eye movements get at the first pass of parsing. Consider sentence (47).

47.   The fireman told the man that he had risked his life for to install a smoke detector.

Autonomy theory predicts that (47) should always lead to a garden path. We always start to parse "the man" as a simple noun phrase because this has a simpler structure than the alternative (which turns out to be the correct analysis), as the head of a complex noun phrase. The referential hypothesis of the incremental interactive theory of Crain and Steedman (1985) and Altmann and Steedman (1988; see also Steedman & Altmann, 1989) states that the resolution of ambiguities in context depends upon whether a unique referent can be found. The context can bias the parser towards or away from garden pathing. The null context induces a garden path. Previous context however such as preceding this ambiguous relative structure with a relative supporting referential context (such as by providing more than one possible referent for "the man"—for example, "A fireman braved a dangerous fire in a hotel. He rescued one of the guests at great danger to himself. A crowd of men gathered around him.") will bias the parser towards a relative clause interpretation and prevent garden pathing. Eye movement measurements verified this prediction. Measurements of difficulty associated with garden pathing could be attributable to longer average reading times per character in the ambiguity region, and an increased probability of regressive eye movements. Altmann et al. in particular distinguished between first pass reading times that are followed by a leftwards regression, and those followed by a rightwards movement to of the region of interest. They showed that it is important to separate these two components, and showed that reading times defined by regressive (leftwards) movement is a better measure. When syntactic information leads to ambiguity and a garden path is possible then the parser proceeds to construct a syntactic representation on the basis of the best semantic bet.

Finally, it is unclear whether the supposedly purely syntactic principles of minimal attachment and late closure might not be better explained by semantic biases. Taraban and McClelland (1988) compared self-paced reading times for sentences such as (48) and (49).

48.   The thieves stole all the paintings in the museum while the guard slept.
49.   The thieves stole all the paintings in the night while the guard slept.

Sentence (49) is a minimal attachment structure but (48) is not. Taraban and McClelland found that (48) is read faster than (49), because, they argue, all the words up to "museum" and "night" bias subjects towards the non-minimal interpretation. They concluded that violations of the purely syntactic process of the attachment of words to the developing structural representation do not slow down reading, but violations of the semantic process of assigning words to thematic roles does.

Lexical guidance in parsing.   Recent work suggests that parsing can be guided by lexical information, and that the verb plays a particularly important role (Clifton et al., 1984; Ford et al., 1982; Holmes, 1987; Mitchell, 1987; Mitchell & Holmes, 1985). As we have seen (Chapters 2, 3, and 4), a great deal of information is retrieved in lexical access. Does parsing make use of information other than part-of-speech (that is, whether a word is noun, verb, adjective, and so forth)? In particular, does it use detailed syntactic information available about verbs, such as whether they take a direct object, and the types of complement structures they can take? And exactly when does lexical guidance have its effect?

The issue here is whether detailed lexical information influences the first stage of parsing (constructing the preliminary phrase structure) or the second (the evaluation or monitor stage), or both. This is a controversial topic and there is a wealth of evidence to support both the early and late-only positions. Models which make use of verb information at an early stage consider each of the alternative sentence frames. According to Ford et al. (1982), the lexical information retrieved for each verb tells the initial parser what kinds of structure are associated with it, and the strength or likelihood of each alternative. If later information contradicts that initial structure, then we are garden pathed. Hence lexical guidance plays an important role in leading us up the garden path, and helping us to avoid it. Holmes (1987) also argued that detailed lexical information about verbs does direct the initial parsing strategies. If this is the case, parsing preferences can be explained by lexical guidance; and thematic information can be used to eliminate the garden path effect in these reduced relative sentences. Similar conclusions have been reached by Boland, Tanenhaus, and Garnsey (1990); Holmes, Stowe, and Cupples (1989); Tanenhaus, Carlson, and Trueswell (1989); and Trueswell, Tanenhaus, and Kello (1993).

On the other hand, in garden path models lexical information does not have an early influence, and only one structure is constructed initially, on the basis of pure syntactic information. In support of this, Mitchell (1987), on the basis of data from a self-paced reading task, concluded that the initial stage only makes use of part-of-speech information, and that detailed information from the verb only affects the second, evaluative, stage of processing. Consider sentences (50) and (51). In (50), according to garden path theory, the parser prefers to assign the phrase "the doctor" as direct object of "visited" (to comply with late closure, keeping the first phrase open for as long as possible). As expected subjects were garden pathed by (50). However, in (51) lexical guidance should tell the parser that "sneezed" cannot take a direct object. Nevertheless, subjects are still led up the garden path with (51); hence the initial parse must be ignoring verb control information.

50.   After the child had visited the doctor prescribed a course of injections.
51.   After the child had sneezed the doctor prescribed a course of injections.

If this is the case the initial parse is both very short-sighted and autonomous. Similarly, Ferreira and Henderson (1990) reported data from eye movements and word-by-word self-paced reading of ambiguous sentences. They also argued that these data suggest that verb information does not affect the initial parse, although it might guide the second stage of re-analysis. Frazier (1989) similarly argued that detailed lexical information has no effect upon the first stage of parsing. Further evidence about the complex way in which lexical guidance can affect parsing comes from detailed analyses of reaction times and speed-error trade-offs throughout the time course of parsing (McElree, 1993).

In summary, as the conflicting data have yet to be entirely resolved, it is at present unclear whether the first stage of parsing is autonomous and unable to use lexical guidance.

Evaluation of work on garden path sentences.   There is a great deal of work on transient syntactic ambiguity and a great deal of it seems to lead to contradictory conclusions. At present, on balance the evidence just favours an autonomous or modular system whereby syntactic processes occur independently of semantic and contextual processes. Having said that it is difficult to explain away all the findings that suggest that contextual information can influence the on-line construction of a syntactic representation. In this case we are led up the garden path not by syntactic factors, but our semantic expectations. The data can perhaps be reconciled in the two-stage or two-pass parsing model. In the first stage, a preliminary phrase structure is created on the basis of purely syntactic information, perhaps limited to knowledge only of the part-of-speech of words, guided by principles such as late closure and minimal attachment. The second parsing stage, where the structures are evaluated for consistency and plausibility, has access to many more types of information, including lexical guidance. Garden paths arise when the structure created by the first stage turns out to be invalid and the structure has to be recomputed. However, this is still a very active research area. Papers have recently been published which argue for the autonomous, structure-driven parsing model (Mitchell, Corley, & Garnham, 1992; Mitchell & Corley, 1994), whereas other recent papers argue for the interactive, discourse-driven model (Altmann, Garnham, & Henstra, 1994). Clearly we are some way from a consensus.

Many people might think that garden path sentences are rather odd: often there would be pauses in normal speech and commas in written language, which, although strictly optional, are usually there and prevent the ambiguity in the first place. For example, Rayner and Frazier (1987) intentionally omitted punctuation in order to mislead the subjects' parsers. Deletion of the *complementiser* "that" can also produce misleading results (Trueswell et al., 1993). In such cases it is possible that these sentences are not telling us as much about normal parsing as we think. There is evidence that punctuation such as commas can influence the course of on-line parsing (Mitchell & Holmes, 1985).

Ambiguous filler-gap dependencies.   A final sort of temporary structural ambiguity concerns filler-gap dependencies. Sometimes the object of a sentence is moved elsewhere in the sentence, leaving a gap (sometimes called *trace*). There is no gap in (52), but in (53) "sharpen" is a transitive verb, and the object "sword" has been moved from it leaving a gap (indicated by __).

52.   Which sword is sharpest?
53.   Which sword did Vlad sharpen __ yesterday?

There are two syntactic strategies for filling a gap (J.D. Fodor, 1978). The first is to postulate a gap after any verb that can be used transitively and is not followed immediately by a noun phrase. If this fails, the second strategy comes into play only when necessary—such as if you reach the end of the sentence and there is still no obvious filler. Sentence (54) is ambiguous between interpretations (55) and (56).

54. Vlad, I like to tell jokes.
55. Vlad, I like $_{[t]}$ to tell jokes.
56. Vlad, I like to tell $_{[t]}$ jokes.
57. This is the girl the teacher wanted $_{[t_1]}$ to talk to $_{[t_2]}$.
58. This is the girl the teacher wanted $_{[t_1]}$ to talk.

Frazier et al. (1983) noted that sentences of the form of (57) are understood 100 milliseconds faster (as measured by reading times) than those of the form of (58). When the parser detects a gap, it fills it with the a filler, the most recent potential dislocated constituent. This leads to the correct outcome in (57): here the constituent "the teacher" goes into the gap t_1, leaving "the girl" to go into t_2. In (58) however it is "the girl" that should go into the gap t_1, and not the most recent constituent. This delays processing, leading to the slower reading times.

CONCLUDING SUMMARY

There is not a single language system, but a number of corrected modules. Do they interact or are they autonomous? This central issue has dominated research in syntax and word recognition and production. There is probably not a unitary lexicon in which an amodal representation is stored for each of the four language tasks reading, writing, speaking, and listening, but one lexicon for each task. Much of the evidence comes from neuropsychological dissociations. The issue is complicated by the problem of distinguishing between four different stores, and four different access routes to one store.

There are many cases where there is more than one interpretation for a string of phonemes, word, phrase, or sentence: that is, there is a great deal of ambiguity in language. Our problem in lexical ambiguity is in selecting the appropriate sense of a word for the given context. We have seen that the main issue is whether disambiguation occurs through multiple access, when we access automatically all the senses of a word and then use the context to select the appropriate one, or selective access, where we access either the appropriate meaning straightaway, or try the different senses of the word against the context in the order of their frequency of occurrence. More recent studies show that the detailed pattern of results depends upon the relative frequencies of the alternative senses of the word, and the precise relationship between the context and the ambiguous word. At present we consider that the way in which lexical ambiguity is dealt with is an interaction between the precise characteristics of the ambiguous word and the type of disambiguating context.

Structural ambiguity arises when a sentence has more than one syntactic analysis. This often happens transiently at least. The extreme case of transient syntactical ambiguity is the garden path sentence, where we have the sense of having selected an incorrect structural analysis. A similar issue applies here as with lexical ambiguity: do we parse all alternative structural analyses in parallel, and make a choice using disambiguating information when it is available, or do we do parse in the most likely way and then backtrack if it turns out to be incorrect? Both of these are versions of an autonomous model of parsing as only syntactic information is used to guide parsing. Current evidence from studies of garden pathing supports the serial model, in that we appear to construct only one initial syntactic structure. Furthermore, do we use semantic information to guide the parsing process so that we construct only the semantically most plausible semantic interpretation? Can thematic information about verbs prevent garden pathing and direct the first stage of parsing? This is the interactive position. It is hard to draw any definite conclusion, but so far evidence just favours the autonomous view. We should note that there is no such thing as a truly neutral context: even if it is not supplied by the sentence, subjects bring their own knowledge and expectations to the experimental task.

Finally we should return to the related issue raised in Chapters 2 and 3 on whether or not high-level context can affect lower level processing such as word recognition. Both spoken and visual word recognition appear to be largely autonomous up to the stage of lexical access. In summary we have distinguished the main modules of the language processing system, and we can say that: word recognition is autonomous, lexicalisation is interactive, syntactic production is interactive, parsing is autonomous. Why some of these modules should appear to be autonomous while others are interactive is rather unsatisfactory, and is at present a mystery.

It is possible that the study of the development of language might inform our understanding of the mature process. We will look at these developmental issues in Chapters 10 and 11.

FURTHER READING

For a full review of picture naming, see Glaser (1992) and Morton (1985). Allport and Funnell (1981) review many of the issues concerning lexical fractionation; they argue for the reparability of cognitive and lexical codes. Monsell (1987) is a comprehensive review of the literature on the fractionation of the lexicon. Ellis and Young (1988, Chapter 8) provide a detailed discussion of the neuropsychological evidence for their proposed architecture of the language system. Bradley and Forster (1987) review the differences between spoken and visual word recognition.

Simpson (1984) reviews the early work on lexical ambiguity, and Simpson (1994) reviews the later work. Mitchell (1994) reviews syntactic ambiguity. Johnson-Laird (1983) discusses different types of parsing system with special reference to garden path sentences.

Many references in Chapter 5 on parsing are also relevant to the topic of syntactic ambiguity. Altmann (1989a) is an edited collection of excellent if technical papers that provide an overview of more contemporary approaches on syntactic ambiguity. Altmann (1988) reviews models of syntactic ambiguity, and Norris (1987) reviews the work on interaction and garden path sentences; see also Clifton, Speer, and Abney (1991) for a review of work on syntactic ambiguity.

CHAPTER TEN

Language, thought, and the precursors of language

INTRODUCTION

This chapter examines the relationship between language and other cognitive and biological processes. We will begin by examining the requirements for language acquisition: what biological, social, and cognitive precursors are necessary for a child to acquire language normally? Do adults have to talk to children in a special way for them to learn language? What affects the rate of linguistic development? What are the consequences of different types of impairment or deprivation upon language? Does the form of our language influence or determine the way in which we think, or is the form of our language dependent upon more general cognitive factors?

Philosophy has produced two very different views on how we obtain knowledge. The *rationalists* (such as Plato and Descartes) maintained that certain fundamental ideas are innate—that is, they are present from birth. The *empiricists* (such as Locke and Hume) rejected this doctrine of innate ideas, maintaining that all knowledge is derived from experience. Among the most influential work of the empiricists was that of Locke (1690/1975). Locke argued that all knowledge held by the rationalists to be innate could be acquired through experience. According to him, the mind at birth is a *tabula rasa*—a "blank sheet of paper" upon which sensations write and determine future behaviour. The rationalist–empiricist controversy is alive today. Chomsky's work in general and his views on language acquisition are very much in the rationalist camp, and it is easy to see strong empiricist threads in Piaget. (Piaget argued that cognitive structures are not innate.) Although we must be wary of simplifying the debate by trying to label contrasting views as rationalist or empiricist, the questions of which processes are innate, and which processes must be in place for language to develop, are of fundamental importance.

Many animals are clearly able to solve some problems without language, and we saw in Chapter 1 that the extent to which language tuition in apes improves performance on other cognitive tasks is questionable. This suggests that language is not essential for problem solving and thought. Although this may seem obvious, it has not always been considered so. Among the early approaches to examining the relationship between language and thought, the behaviourists thought that thought was speech. Young children speak their thoughts aloud; this becomes internalised so that covert speech is thought. Thought is nothing more than small motor movements. Watson (1913) said "thought processes are really motor habits in the larynx." Jacobsen (1932) found some evidence for this because thinking often is accompanied by covert speech. Jacobsen detected electrical activity in the throat muscles when subjects were asked to think. But is thought possible without these small motor movements? Smith, Brown, Thomas, and Goodman (1947) used curare to paralyse temporarily all the voluntary muscles of a volunteer (Smith, who clearly deserved to be first author on this one). Despite being unable to make any motor movement of the speech apparatus, he later reported that he had been able to think and solve problems. Hence there is more to thought than moving the vocal apparatus. Moreover, although animals can solve some problems without language, perhaps this is an important limitation. Does language further set us apart from animals because it enables new and more advanced forms of thought?

We can list the logically possible alternatives; each of them has been championed at some time or other. First, cognitive development determines language development. This is the viewpoint adopted by Piaget and his followers. Second, language and cognition are independent faculties (Chomsky's position). Third, language and cognition originate independently but become inter-dependent; the relationship is complex (Vygotsky's position). Finally, the idea that language determines cognition is known as the Sapir-Whorf hypothesis.

THE BIOLOGICAL BASIS OF LANGUAGE DEVELOPMENT

What are the biological precursors of language? That is, how is language development related to the development of brain functions? How do biological processes interact with social factors? In Chapter 2 we saw how the abilities of infants to perceive speech are very advanced. This is strong evidence that these abilities at least are innate.

An important concern is the development of lateralisation of function. The two hemispheres of the brain are in part specialised for different tasks: broadly, the left hemisphere is particularly concerned with analytic, time-based processing, while the right hemisphere is particularly concerned with holistic, spatially-based processing. An important consequence of this is that for the great majority (96%) of right handers language functions are predominately localised in the left hemisphere. (According to Rasmussen & Milner, 1977, even 70% of left handers are left-hemisphere dominant.) We can distinguish initially between two models of how this lateralisation occurs. The *invariance hypothesis* states that the left hemisphere is specialised for language at birth and it is only if it is damaged over a wide area, involving both anterior and posterior brain locations, that the right hemisphere can take over language functions (Rasmussen & Milner, 1975). Language has a special affinity for the left hemisphere owing to special innate anatomical organisation and will not abandon it unless an entire centre is destroyed, and even then one might only find a partial shift in function. The *maturation hypothesis* states that the two hemispheres are similar at birth with respect to language but the left hemisphere matures to become specialised for language functions. *Maturation* means that the neural hardware is not fully developed by birth but instead develops at least in part afterwards. The best known version of the maturation hypothesis is Lenneberg's (1967) *critical period hypothesis*.

The critical period hypothesis

The critical period hypothesis has two components. First, certain biological events can only happen in this early period. Second, certain linguistic events must happen to the child during this period for development to proceed normally. It is argued that language is acquired most efficiently during the critical period.

The idea of a critical period for development is not unique to humans. Many songbirds such as the chaffinch are born with the rudiments of a song, but must be exposed to the male song of their species between the ages of ten and fifteen days in order to acquire it normally. Furthermore, birds display hemispheric specialisation in that only one hemisphere controls the song (see Demers, 1988, for more detail) Evidence for a critical period for human linguistic development comes from a number of sources.

Evidence from aphasia. Lenneberg's main source of evidence came from an examination of the development of lateralisation. He argued that at birth, the left and right hemispheres of the brain are equipotential in that, in principle, either could take over any role. Lateralisation occurs as a result of maturation, developing rapidly through years two to five, then slowing down and is complete in puberty. (Others such as Krashen, 1973, place the end of the critical period rather earlier, around the age of five, but this does not change the essence of the proposal.) Lenneberg argued that the brain possesses a degree of flexibility early on, in that, if necessary, functions can develop in alternative locations in the brain.

The primary motivation for this comes from differences in recovery after brain damage at different ages. As we have seen, in adults primary language functions are localised in the left hemisphere, and damage to this consequently leads to significant language impairment. Young children, however, can apparently recover completely from brain damage, with the younger the child, the better being the chances of a complete recovery. Indeed, the entire function of the left hemisphere can be taken over by the right if the child is young enough. There are a number of cases of complete *hemidecortication* where an entire hemisphere is removed as a drastic treatment of exceptionally severe epilepsy. Such an operation upon an adult would almost totally destroy all speech abilities. If performed upon children who are young enough—that is, during their critical periods—they seem able to recover almost completely. Furthermore, it is possible that *crossed aphasia*, where right hemisphere lesions lead to a language deficit, might be more common in children. (This however is heavily disputed; for contrary evidence and discussion see Woods & Teuber, 1973). All this suggests that the brain is not lateralised at birth but that this emerges gradually throughout childhood. At birth, the two hemispheres have the same potential—hence the name *equipotentiality*—but their functions become more rigid as a consequence of maturation. This period of maturation is the critical period.

The picture is probably not this simple. First, there are problems with the research on hemidecorticates. Dennis and Whitaker (1976, 1977) agreed with the general picture that left hemidecortication in young children results in no *severe* aphasia, but found that left hemi-decorticates subsequently have particular difficulties in understanding complex syntax relative to right hemidecorticates. It is thought that the right hemisphere cannot completely accommodate to taking over all language functions. Bishop (1983) presents methodological criticisms of this work: the number of subjects is very small; it is necessary to match for IQ; and when one does so there is a large overlap with normal performance. It is not clear that non-decorticates of the same age would have performed any better.

Furthermore, there are clear signs that some lateralisaton is present at a very early age. Entus (1977) looked at three week old infants using a sucking dishabituation paradigm. Exploring the cognitive and perceptual abilities of infants this young is obviously difficult and complex methodologies are necessary. In this task, the experimenter monitors changes in the infant's sucking rate as stimuli are presented (they are trained to suck rapidly to ensure the stimulus is continued): stimuli that are perceived to be different by the child produce a change in the sucking rate. She found a more marked change in the sucking rate when speech stimuli were presented to the right ear (and therefore a left hemisphere advantage), and an advantage for non-speech stimuli when presented to the left ear (indicating a right hemisphere advantage). Molfese (1977) used evoked potentials (a measure of the brain's electrical activity) and found hemispheric differences to speech and non-speech in infants as young as one week. A summary of the criticisms can be found in Bishop (1993), but this work suggests that the left hemisphere is specialised for language at least to some degree from birth.

Second language and the critical period.   The critical period hypothesis is traditionally used to explain why second language acquisition is so difficult for older children and adults, while younger children apparently have less difficulty. Johnson and Newport (1989) refine the formulation of the critical period hypothesis to clarify the way in which it accounts for second language acquisition. They distinguished two further hypotheses, both of which assume that humans have a superior capacity for learning language early in life. The *exercise hypothesis* further maintains that unless this capacity is exercised early, it is lost. The *maturational state hypothesis* on the other hand states that this capacity disappears or declines as maturation progresses regardless of other factors. Both hypotheses predict that children will be better than adults in acquiring the first language; only the maturational hypothesis predicts that children will be superior at second language learning. Indeed, it is possible under the exercise hypothesis that, all other things being equal, adults might be better than children because of their better learning skills. Research has addressed the issue of whether there is an age-related block on second language learning.

Contrary to popular opinion, Snow (1983) concluded that in fact adults were no worse than young children at learning a second language, and indeed might even be better. We often think children are better at learning the first and second languages, but they spend much more time being exposed to and learning language than adults, which makes a fair comparison very difficult. Snow and Hoefnagel-Hohle (1978) compared English children and adults in the first year of living in Holland learning Dutch. The young children (3–4 years old) scored lowest of all. Experimental and anecdotal evidence suggests that adults learning a language have a persistent foreign accent, and phonological development might be the one area for which there is a critical period.

On the other hand, Johnson and Newport (1989) found some evidence for a critical period for second language acquisition. They looked at native Korean and Chinese immigrants to the USA aged between 3 and 39 years, and found a large advantage for earlier over later arriving immigrants in making judgements about whether a sentence was grammatically correct or not, with a linear relationship up to puberty.

Adults seem to have an initial advantage in learning a second language, but the eventual attainment level of children appears to be better (see Krashen, Long, & Scarcella, 1982, for a review). Newport and Johnson conclude that their data best support the maturational state hypothesis. That is, our capacity for acquiring language declines regardless of whether or not we receive appropriate input during the critical period. However, rather than finding an all-or-none critical period, Newport and Johnson found evidence of a gradual, linear decline through it. The evidence for a critical period of some aspects of syntactic development and even more strongly, phonological development (Flege & Hillenbrand, 1984), seems particularly strong. Second language acquisition is not a perfect test of the hypothesis, however, because the speakers have usually acquired at least some of a first language. What happens if we cannot acquire a first language during the critical period?

Linguistic deprivation during the critical period. It is a corollary of the critical period hypothesis that unless children receive linguistic input during the critical period they will not acquire language normally. The strongest version of the hypothesis is of course that without input during this period children cannot acquire language at all. Supporting evidence comes from reports of wild or *feral children* who have been abandoned at birth and deprived of language in childhood. One type, *wolf children*, receive their name from when children are reputedly brought up by wolves as wolf cubs (such as Romulus and Remus). This is a particular example of cross-fostering by another animal species. Another type, *attic children*, get their name from lengthy confinement in places such as attics. James IV of Scotland was reputedly one of the first to perform such an experiment (around the year 1500), abandoning two children in the wild. Later he found that they spoke "very good Hebrew". In better documented cases, not surprisingly, the feral children have no language at all when found, but more importantly for our purposes appear to find language difficult to acquire despite intensive training. One of the most famous of these cases was the "Wild Boy of Aveyron", a child found in isolated woods in the south of France in 1800. Despite attempts by an educationalist named Dr. Itard to socialise the boy, given the name Victor, and to teach him language, he never learnt more than two words. (This story was subsequently turned into a film by François Truffault, *L'enfant sauvage*.) More recent reports of feral children involving apparent cross-fostering include the wolf children of India (Singh & Zingg, 1942) and the monkey boy of Burundi (Lane & Pillard, 1978). These cases describe events that happened some time ago and what actually happened is now usually unclear. Furthermore, we do not know why these children were abandoned in the first place: it is certainly conceivable that they were retarded before abandonment, and therefore might have been language-impaired anyway.

It is less easy to apply this argument to the unfortunate child known as "Genie" (Curtiss, 1977). Genie was a child who was apparently normal at birth, but suffered severe linguistic deprivation. From the age of 20 months until she was taken into protective custody by the Los Angeles police at the age of 13 years 9 months, she had been isolated in a small room, most of the time strapped into a potty chair. Her father was extraordinarily intolerant of noise, so there was virtually no speech in the house—not even overheard from a radio or television. Genie was punished if she made any sounds. The only contact she had with other people was a few minutes each day when her mother fed her baby food, and occasionally when her father and older brother barked at her like dogs. This represents extreme social, physical, nutritional, and linguistic deprivation. Not surprisingly, Genie's linguistic abilities were virtually non-existent. What is of particular interest to us is whether she managed to learn language subsequently, as at the age of nearly 14 the critical period is hypothesised to be finished or almost finished. With training, Genie learned some language skills. However, her syntactic development always remained retarded relative to her vocabulary. She uses few question words, far fewer grammatical words, tends to form negatives only by adding negatives to the start of sentences. She failed to acquire the use of inflectional morphology, the passive transformation, and the use of auxiliary verbs. Furthermore, unlike most right-handed children, she showed a left ear, right hemisphere advantage for speech sounds. There could be a number of reasons for this, including left hemisphere degeneration, the inhibition of the left hemisphere by the right, or the left hemisphere now performing some other function. Unfortunately tests for dyspraxia were not administered. Also, because of financial and legal difficulties, the research did not continue for as long as might have been hoped, and hence many questions are still unanswered. (Genie is now in an adult foster home.) In summary, Genie shows that it is possible to learn some language outside the critical period, but also that syntax appears to have some privileged role. The amount of language that can be learnt after the critical period certainly seems very limited.

Of course, given that Genie was subjected to extreme types of deprivation other than linguistic (such as malnutrition and social deprivation), these cannot be ruled out as having an explanatory role in her later linguistic difficulties. Furthermore, there has been no agreement over whether Genie was retarded before her period of confinement. Indeed, her father locked her away precisely because he considered her to be severely retarded, in the belief that he was protecting her.

On the other hand, there is some clear evidence that children can completely recover from early linguistic deprivation as long as they are "rescued" early enough. Mason (1942) describes the case of Isabelle, a child who was kept in seclusion with her deaf-mute mother until the age of six and a half. After this, she passed through the normal phases of language development at a greatly accelerated rate, and after 18 months was highly linguistically competent.

Hearing children of hearing-impaired parents. In principle, the hearing children of deaf parents should provide a cleaner test, although of course the extent of linguistic deprivation is never as extreme. Sachs, Bard, and Johnson (1981) reported the case of "Jim", a hearing child of deaf parents whose only exposure to spoken language until he entered nursery at the age of three was the television. His intonation was abnormally flat, his articulation poor, and his grammar very idiosyncratic. For example, Jim produced utterances such as "House. Two house. Not one house. That two house." This example shows that Jim acquired the concept of plurality but not that it is usually marked by an "-s" inflection, although normally this is one of the earliest grammatical morphemes a child learns. Utterances such as "Going house a fire truck" suggest that Jim constructed his own syntactic rules based upon stating a phrase followed by specifying the topic of that phrase—the opposite of the usual word order in English. Although this is an incorrect rule, it does emphasise the drive to create syntactic rules (see below on the language bioprogramme hypothesis). Jim's case suggests that exposure to language alone is not sufficient: it must be in an appropriate interactional context.

Evaluation of the critical period hypothesis.   We can reject a strong version of the critical period hypothesis on two grounds. Children can acquire some language outside it, and lateralisation does not occur wholly within it. In particular, some lateralisation is present from birth or before. Nevertheless, it is possible to defend a weakened version of it. A critical period appears to be involved in early phonological development and the development of syntax. This tie-up between the development of syntax and its biological precursors is interesting, because it can be connected with Chomsky's claim that language is innate and species-specific. According to this view, an innate language acquisition device is a necessary precursor of language development. All in all, most of the data appear to support the invariance hypothesis rather better than the maturation hypothesis.

There is evidence that the critical period does not apply only to spoken language. Newport (1990) found evidence of a critical period for the congenitally deaf learning American Sign Language, particularly concerning the use of morphologically inflected signs. Once again, there was a continuous linear decline rather than a sudden drop-off at puberty. Of course adults can learn sign language, but it is argued they learn it less efficiently.

Finally, there is some debate as to why there is a critical period for language. Bever (1981) argued that it is a normal property of growth, arising from a loss of plasticity as cells and processes become more specialised and more independent. On the other hand, Hurford (1991) argued that the critical period arises as a result of evolutionary processes. This argument is made convincing by the support of computer simulations of the evolution of language in a population.

THE DRIVING FORCE OF LANGUAGE ACQUISITION

What makes language acquisition happen? We have seen that there are some biological precursors to language, but assuming these are intact, what then transforms a non-speaking, non-comprehending infant into a linguistically competent individual? The lines between the empiricist camp of the behaviourists, who argued that language was entirely learnt, and the rationalist camp of those such as Chomsky, who argue that there must be an important innate language-specific component, are very clear. In between there is a position such as Piaget's, where general cognitive principles can arise from innate dispositions, but the development of these general cognitive principles is then sufficient to account for language acquisition.

Learning theory

To what extent can language acquisition be explained by learning alone via conditioning and reinforcement? The classic statement of the position was Skinner's (1957) book *Verbal behavior*. Skinner argued that language was acquired by the same mechanisms of conditioning and reinforcement that were thought at the time to govern all other aspects of animal and human behaviour (see also Chapter 1). There is however clear evidence against this position.

First, adults (generally) correct only the truth and meaning of children's utterances, not the syntax (Brown & Hanlon, 1970; see example 1). Indeed, attempts by adults to correct incorrect syntax and phonology usually make no difference. Examples (2) and (3) are from de Villiers and de Villiers (1979). At the age of eighteen months their son Nicholas went from correctly producing the word turtle to pronouncing it "kurka", in spite of all attempts at correction, and clearly being able to produce the constituent sounds. In the second example the mother does not correct a blatant grammatical solecism because the meaning is apparent and correct.

1. Child: Doggie (pointing at a horse).
    Adult: No, that's a horsie (stressed).

2. Adult: Say "Tur"
    Child: Tur
    Adult: Say "Tle"
    Child: Tle
    Adult: Say "Turtle"
    Child: Kurka

3. Child: Mama isn't boy, he a girl.
    Adult: That's right.

4. Child: My teacher holded the rabbits and we patted them.
    Adult: Did you say teacher held the baby rabbits?
    Child: Yes.
    Adult: What did you say she did?
    Child: She holded the baby rabbits and we patted them.
    Adult: Did you say she held them tightly?
    Child: No, she holded them loosely.

Parents rarely correct grammar and if they try to do so the corrections have little effect (see example 4, from Bellugi, 1970). Parents may provide some *noisy feedback* in that certain discourse patterns vary in frequency depending on the grammaticality of the child's utterances (see Bohannon, MacWhinney, & Snow, 1990; Bohannon & Stanowicz, 1988; Demetras, Post, & Snow, 1986; Hirsh-Pasek, Treiman, & Schneiderman, 1984; Moerk, 1991; Morgan & Travis, 1989). For example, the parent is more likely to repeat the child's utterance if it is grammatical. However, this type of feedback seems far too weak to have any effect on the course of acquisition (Marcus, 1993). As we shall see, the debate about whether or not children receive *negative evidence*—that is, information about which strings of words are not grammatical—is important, because without negative feedback children would have to rely on internal mechanisms (such as innate principles) to help them learn the grammar.

The second piece of evidence against a conditioning theory of language learning is that some words (such as "no!") are clearly understood before they are ever produced. Third, the pattern of acquisition of irregular past verb tenses and irregular plural nouns is curious and not as would be expected by learning theory. Some examples of irregular forms are "gived" for "gave", and "mouses" for "mice". The sequence observed is correct, incorrect, then correct. It can be explained if a general rule has been learned but applied incorrectly (e.g. "form past tenses by adding '-ed'"; "form plurals by adding '-s'"). This is an example of what is called U-shaped development: performance starts off at a good level, but then becomes worse, before improving again. U-shaped development is indicative of a developing system that has to learn both rules and exceptions to those rules. Fourth, as we saw in Chapter 4, there are arguments based upon the structure of language. Fifth, babbling is not random, and imitation is not important: hearing babies of deaf parents babble normally. In general, language acquisition appears very rule-based.

Is language input degenerate? The role of child-directed speech

Chomsky showed that children cannot learn language by conditioning. Instead, they acquire a set of rules or grammar. But neither, he argued (Chomsky, 1965), could they learn this by environmental exposure alone, because the speech they hear is a *degenerate input*. (This is sometimes also known as the *poverty of the stimulus* argument.) By this he meant that the speech children hear is far from ideal for learning a language. On the one hand, it is full of slips of the tongue, false starts, and hesitations; words and sounds run into one another. They hear defective sentences without these being labelled as defective. On the other, there does not seem to be enough information in the language which children hear for them to be able to learn the grammar. That is, they are not normally exposed to examples of grammatical constructions that would enable them to deduce the grammar. All in all, Chomsky considered it to be impossible that a child could deduce the structure of the grammar solely on the basis of such an input. Instead, the design of the grammar must be innate.

At least the first part of this claim is now controversial because of research on the special way in which adults (particularly mothers) talk to children (Snow, 1972, 1994). This special way of talking to children is called *motherese*, or *child-directed speech*, or CDS, and is commonly known as *baby talk*. Adults talk in a simplified way to children, taking care to make their speech easily recognisable. The topics of sentences are to do with the "here and now"; they are phonologically simplified (baby words such as "moomoo" and "geegee"); there are more pauses, utterances are shorter, the speech is slower, and it is clearly segmented. There is more repetition and redundancy. There are fewer word endings than in normal speech, sentences are shorter, and prosody is exaggerated. Messer (1980) showed that there is a great deal of repetition in the speech of mothers to their children, and they focus upon shared activities. Language teachers are more likely to use basic level nouns (Hall, 1994). Speech is specifically directed towards the child and marked by a high pitch (Garnica, 1977). Furthermore, these differences are more marked the younger the child; hence adults reliably speak in a higher pitch to two year olds than to five year olds. The most important words in sentences received special emphasis. In fact the term "motherese" is something of a misnomer. Although mothers use it more, fathers use it too (Hladik & Edwards, 1984), and even children use it when speaking to younger children (Shatz & Gelman, 1973).

What determines the level of simplification used in motherese? Cross (1977) proposed the linguistic feedback hypothesis, which states that mothers in some way tailor the amount of simplification they provide depending on how much the child appears to need. Snow (1977) pointed out that mothers produce motherese before infants are old enough to produce any feedback on the level of simplification. She proposed a *conversational hypothesis* in that what was important were the mothers' expectations of what the child needed to know and could understand. More recently, Cross, Johnson-Morris, and Nienhuys (1980) provided evidence from a study of motherese to hearing-impaired children suggesting that a number of factors might be operating, and that elements of both the feedback and conversational hypotheses are operating. The form of motherese also interacts in a complex way with the social setting: maternal speech contains more nouns during toy play, but more verbs during non-toy play (Goldfield, 1993).

Child-directed speech gradually fades away as the child gets older. It is sensitive to the child's comprehension level rather than their production level (Clarke-Stewart, Vanderstoep, & Killian, 1979). Hence speech intended for children seems to be specially marked in order to make it stand out from background noise, and is simplified so that the task of discovering the referents of words and understanding the syntactic structure is easier than it would otherwise be. In this respect Chomsky's claim about children only being exposed to a degraded input does not hold up to scrutiny.

However, there is some controversy about the difference motherese actually makes to development. Do children require a syntactically and phonologically simplified input in order to be able to acquire language? The evidence suggests not, although the data are not entirely consistent. First, although its use is widespread, it is not, however, universal across all cultures (Heath, 1983; Pye, 1986). Furthermore, there is great variation in the styles of social interaction and the form of motherese across different cultures (Lieven, 1994). Data from a longitudinal study by Ellis and Wells (1980) suggests that the rate of linguistic development is not simply correlated with the complexity of the children's input. What seems to be important is not merely the *form* of what is said to the children, but, perhaps not surprisingly, the *content*. In particular the children who learn fastest are those who receive most encouragement and acknowledgement of their utterances. Questioning and directing children's attention to the environment were also good facilitators, and particularly features of the environment that were salient to the child (such as repeated household activities). Cross (1978) demonstrated the value of extended replies by adults, those replies which amplify the comments of the children. The children who showed the most rapid linguistic development were those whose mothers both asked their children more questions and who gave more extensive replies to their children's questions (Howe, 1980). Finally, it is possible that motherese has an effect on linguistic development at a very early stage, at just over one year (Hampson & Nelson, 1993). Even though motherese might not be *necessary* for language development, it might nevertheless facilitate it (see Pine, 1994, for a recent review).

If the form of motherese appears to make little difference to linguistic development, what is its purpose? One possibility is that it serves some other function, such as creating and maintaining a bond between the adult and child. Harris and Coltheart (1986) proposed that the syntactic simplification is a side-effect of the simplification of the context and restricted content. Needless to say, both of these factors might be operative. If motherese does not however help linguistic development, what about Chomsky's original argument that language acquisition is very difficult given such an impoverished input? How do children nevertheless acquire it so successfully? Chomsky argued that they do so because they come ready equipped for the task.

What might be innate in language? The language acquisition device

Chomsky (1965, 1968, 1986) argued that language acquisition must be guided by innate constraints. We saw in Chapter 5 that Chomsky argued that language is a special faculty not dependent on other cognitive or perceptual processes. It is acquired, he argued, at a time when the child is incapable of complex intellectual achievements, and therefore could not be dependent upon intelligence, cognition, or experience. Because the language they hear is degenerate, children cannot acquire a grammar by exposure to language alone. Help is provided by the innate structure called the *language acquisition device* (LAD). In Chomsky's later work the LAD is replaced by the idea of *universal grammar*. This is a theory of the primitives and rules of inferences that would enable the child to learn any natural grammar. Hence it is the principles and parameters that constrain language acquisition.

Obviously languages vary, superficially greatly, and children are faced with the task of learning the particular details of their language. For Chomsky (1981) this is the process of *parameter setting*. A parameter is a universal aspect of a language that can take on one of a small number of positions. The parameters are set through the child's exposure to a particular language. Another way of looking at it is that the LAD does not prescribe details of particular languages but rather sets boundaries of what acquired languages can look like; languages are not free to vary in every possible way, but are restricted. For example, no language yet discovered forms questions by inverting the order of words in the declarative form of the sentence. The LAD can be thought of as a set of switches that constrain the possible shape of the grammars the child can acquire; exposure to a particular language sets these switches to a particular position. These constraints must be general enough to apply across all languages; that is, as innate constraints clearly cannot be language-specific. Instead, there must be aspects of language that are *universal*. Chomsky argues that there are enormous deep similarities between languages, and the differences are actually quite superficial. As Pinker (1994) says, a visiting Martian would conclude that apart from different vocabularies, humans surely speak the same language.

Linguistic universals. Linguistic universals are features of language that can be found in most languages. (According to Chomsky they are truly universal in the sense that these features can be defined independently of any language, and when they do occur in particular languages they can be identified by their characteristics within the general theory.) Chomsky distinguished between substantive and formal universals. Substantive universals concern the categories of syntax, semantics and phonology that are common to all languages. The presence of the noun and verb categories is an example of a substantive universal. The distinction is so fundamental that it can arise in the absence of linguistic input: "David", a deaf child with virtually no exposure to language, used one type of gesture corresponding to nouns, and another type for verbs (Goldin-Meadow, Butcher, Mylander, & Dodge, 1994). A formal universal concerns the general form of syntactic rules. These are universal constraints on the form of syntactic rules. One of the goals of universal grammar is to specify these universals.

An interesting example of a linguistic universal is word order. Greenberg (1963) examined word order and morphology in 30 very different languages and found 45 universals. For example, he examined the primary order of subject, object, and verb (English is a SVO language: its dominant order is subject–verb–object). He noted that we do not find all possible combinations; in particular, there seems to be an aversion to placing the object first. The proportions found are shown in Table 10.1.

There are three possible reasons why universals exist. First, they might be part of the innate component of the grammar. Second, they might be part of an innate component of cognition, which then leads to their incorporation in all languages. Third, they might be such strong features of the environment that they are imposed on each of us from birth, and this is reflected in their presence in all languages. In practice it might be very difficult to distinguish between these alternatives. Take

TABLE 10.1
Different word orders found as percentages of languages (based on Greenberg, 1963)

subject	object	verb	44%
subject	verb	object	35%
verb	subject	object	19%
verb	object	subject	2%
object	verb	subject	0%
object	subject	verb	0%

as an example the presence of categories of nouns and verbs in all languages. This reflects the distinction between objects and actions. Is such a distinction innate? Or is this such an overwhelming property of the environment that it does not need to be. Furthermore, even though universals might now have become fossilised as an innate component of our grammar, this might be because they started off as important environmental features. These difficult psychological, evolutionary, linguistic, and philosophical problems might never be solved.

Pidgins and creoles.   Further evidence that there is a strong biological drive to learn syntax comes from the study of pidgin and creole languages. Pidgins are simplified languages that were developed for use in communication between speakers of different languages that were forced into prolonged contact (such as by slavery) in places such as the Caribbean and Hawaii. A creole is a pidgin language which has become the native tongue of the children of the pidgin speakers. Whereas pidgins are highly simplified syntactically, creole languages are complete, syntactically rich sentences that appear to be the spontaneous *creation* of the first generation of children born into mixed linguistic communities (see Bickerton, 1981, 1984; the latter includes a peer commentary). Creoles are not restricted to spoken language: hearing-impaired children develop a creole sign language if exposed to a signing pidgin (Pinker, 1994). It is as though there is a biological drive to develop syntax, even when it is not present in the adult form of communication. Bickerton calls this the *language bioprogramme hypothesis*: children have an innate drive to create a grammar that will make a language even in the absence of proper environmental input.

Genetic linguistics.   Further evidence that aspects of language are innate comes from studies of *genetic linguistics*. This is a relatively new subject, and concerns specific language disabilities for which there appears to be a genetic basis. For example, *specific language impairment* or SLI runs in families (Gopnik, 1990a,b; Gopnik & Crago, 1991; Leonard, 1989; see Gopnik, 1992, for a review). One British family, known as the K's, display SLI, and a study of the heritability of the disorder suggests a single dominant gene is involved. People with SLI have a near normal IQ on tests of non-verbal performance. However, their speech is slow and effortful, replete with grammatical errors, particularly involving pronouns and inflections.

Formal approaches to language learning.   How do children learn the rules of grammar? Most accounts stress the importance of *induction* in learning rules: induction is the process of forming a rule by generalising from specific instances. One aspect of the poverty of the stimulus argument is that children come to learn rules that could not be learnt from the input (Lightfoot, 1982). Hence children are exposed to sentences like (5) and (6). Sentence (7) however is ungrammatical. Children are not exposed to it and then told it is ungrammatical, yet they still come to know this. Lightfoot argued that as they can acquire rules that are not derivable from the input, they must have additional help. This additional help must be innate.

5.   Whom did the vampire meet in the castle?
6.   Whom did you believe that the vampire met in the castle?
7.   * Whom did you see the vampire that met in the castle?

Gold (1967) showed that the mechanism of induction is not in itself sufficiently powerful to enable a language to be learned (this is known as *Gold's theorem*). If language learners are presented only with positive data, they can only learn regular or type 3 languages (those that can be generated by a finite state automaton; see Chapter 5). As we have seen, human language is substantially more powerful than a type 3 grammar. In other words, human language cannot be acquired by induction only from positive exemplars of sentences of the language. That is, they need *negative evidence*. Furthermore, the extent to which children use negative data is, as we have seen above, also questionable. Hence induction cannot be the only mechanism of language acquisition. This finding was seized upon by those arguing the importance of innate constraints as further evidence that they are necessary. The area of research that tries to reconcile these apparently incompatible claims, and which generally examines the processes of how language learning might occur, is known as *learnability theory* or *formal learning theory*.

Pinker (1984) attempted to bring together learnability theory and the developmental evidence. He placed a number of constraints upon acquisition. First, the acquisition mechanisms must begin with no specific knowledge of the child's native language—that is, the particular language to be learned. Each intermediate rule system is the result of the interaction of specified acquisition mechanisms with the preceding rule system on the basis of the input received in the interim. Pinker stressed the continuity between the grammar of the child and the adult grammar. He argues that the target adult grammar to which the developmental process strives is best served by *lexical functional grammar* (see Chapter 5). Pinker argued that the child is innately equipped with a large number of the components of the grammar. For example, he argued that the categories "noun" and "verb" are innate, as is a predisposition to induce phrase structure rules. Even though they are supplied with these categories, they still have to assign words to them. As we shall see in the next chapter, this is not a trivial problem. Pinker argued that the *linking rule* that links a syntactic category such as "verb" on to a thematic role such as "agent" must be innate.

More general innate accounts. Other researchers agree that the child must come to language learning with innate help, but this assistance need not be as language-specific as a LAD. Slobin (1970, 1973, 1985) has argued that children are not born with structural constraints such as particular categories, but a system of processing strategies that guide their inductions. Slobin stressed the role of general cognitive development, and examined a great deal of cross-cultural evidence. Slobin (1973) proposed a number of processing strategies that could account for this acquisition process (see Table 10.2). Slobin emphasised that syntactic constructions are of independent semantic significance to the child, and this is an additional constraint upon acquisition. For Slobin, certain cognitive functions are privileged; for example, the child tried to map speech first onto objects and events.

In a similar vein, Taylor and Taylor (1990) listed a number of factors that characterise language acquisition (Table 10.3). These principles apply to learning other skills as well. Of course, other factors (albeit biological, cognitive, or social) may in turn underlie these principles.

Bootstrapping. In some ways the first steps in language acquisition are the hardest. Once a few words, rules, and principles have been acquired, these can serve as the basis of learning more complex information. This process of using some simple information to acquire more complex is known as *bootstrapping* (after the idea of trying to lift yourself up by your bootstraps).

TABLE 10.2
Some general principles of acquisition (based on Slobin, 1973)

1. Pay attention to the ends of words.
2. The phonological form of words can be systematically modified.
3. Pay attention to the order of morphemes and words.
4. Avoid interruption or rearrangement of units.
5. Underlying semantic relations should be clearly marked.
6. Avoid exceptions.
7. The use of grammatical markers should make semantic sense.

TABLE 10.3
Pragmatic factors affecting acquisition
(based on Taylor & Taylor, 1990)

Simple and short before complex and long

Gross before subtle distinctions

Perceptually salient (in terms of size, colour etc.) first

Personal before non-personal

Here and now before those displaced in time and space

Concrete before abstract

Frequent and familiar before less frequent and unfamiliar

Regular before irregular forms (though interacts with frequency)

Items in isolation before capturing relationships

Whole first, then analysed into parts, then mature whole

At the centre of this problem is the question of how children begin to work out the meaning of what they hear before they acquire the rules of the grammar? Macnamara (1972) proposed that in the first stage, the child focuses upon individual content words. In this way a small lexicon is acquired. Information pertaining to word order is ignored at this stage. The child can combine the meanings of the individual words with the context to determine the speaker's intended meaning. For example, a child who sees Mummy drop a ball, knows the meaning of the words "Mummy", "drop", and "ball", and who hears the sentence "Mummy dropped the ball" can work out the intended meaning of that utterance. In doing so, the child can also take the first steps towards mapping words onto roles in sentences. One of the earliest observations is that the default sentence order (in English at least, as we have seen) is subject (or agent), action, and object (or person or thing acted upon). The nature of motherese (in referring to the here and now and using syntactically simplified constructions) facilitates this process.

Pinker (1984, 1989) used a version of Macnamara's (1972) idea that meaning is used to work out syntax, known as the *semantic bootstrapping hypothesis* (see below). He argued that the child first learns the meaning of some content words, and uses these to construct semantic representations of some simple input sentences. With the surface structure of a sentence and knowledge about its meaning the child is in a position to make an inference about its underlying structure. Hence having innate power is an advantage. The problem is that it might be too powerful. After all, the processes of language acquisition are slow and full of errors. There is a fine balance between a developmental system that is innately constrained as Pinker proposes, and yet unconstrained enough to give rise to all these false starts. Pinker also therefore attempts to show that developmental phenomena cannot be accounted for by simpler mechanisms. This is a difficult area, and doubtless a great deal of work remains to be done.

Problems with innate accounts.   Although innate accounts have the advantage of providing a simple explanation for many otherwise mysterious phenomena, they have a number of disadvantages. First, the predictions they make are not always borne out by the data. Bowerman (1990) showed that the verbs which Pinker's semantic bootstrapping account predicts should be easiest for children to map onto thematic roles are often actually those which they find more difficult. Braine (1988a,b), in detailed reviews of Pinker's theory, questions the need for semantic bootstrapping, and examines the evidence against the existence of very early phrase structure rules. Braine concludes that *semantic assimilation* theory (Schlesinger, 1988) gives a better account of early syntactic development because it does not need to postulate the existence of innate structures. According to this account, early semantic categories develop into early syntactic categories without any abrupt transition. At any early age children use an "agent–action" sentence schema. This can be used to analyse new NP-VP sequences even if this is not strictly an appropriate analysis. The important point is that it is possible to give an account of early syntactic development without having to assume that syntactic categories are innate (see also Chapter 11).

Finally, many people consider there is something unsatisfactory about innate principles. This is because it is easy to fall back on a nativist explanation if it is not easy to see a non-nativist alternative. This is not always a fair criticism, but it is important to be explicit about which principles are innate and how they operate. The best way of countering those researchers who see this as a negative approach would be to show where the principles come from and how they work: for example, by showing which genes control language development and how. As Braine (1992) asked, exactly how do we get from genes laid down at conception to syntactic categories two and a half years later? We are a long way away from being to able to answer this question (but see Pinker, 1994, for some suggestions about this). Finally, nativist accounts tend not to to give enough emphasis to the importance of the social precursors of language. It is possible that social factors can do a great deal of the work for which innate principles have been proposed. (See below for further details of this approach, and the next chapter for details of how social mechanisms might obviate the need for particular principles).

THE COGNITION HYPOTHESIS:
COGNITIVE PRECURSORS TO LANGUAGE

According to Piaget, development takes place in a sequence of well-defined stages. In order to reach a certain stage of development, the child must have gone through all the preceding stages. Piaget identified four principal stages of cognitive development. At birth the child has only innate reflexes, and in the first stage, which Piaget called the *sensori-motor period*, behaviour is organised around its sensory or motor effects. This stage lasts through infancy until the child is about two years old. A primary development in this period is the attainment of the concept of *object permanence*—that is, realising that objects have continual existence and do not disappear as soon as they go out of view. Indeed, Piaget divided the sensori-motor period up into six sub-stages depending upon the progress made towards object permanence. Next comes the *pre-operational stage*, which lasts until the age of about six. This stage is characterised by *egocentric* thought. The most specific way of looking at this is that these children are unable to adopt alternative viewpoints to their own; a more general way is that they are unable to change their point of view. The *concrete operational* stage lasts until the age of about 12. The child is able to adopt alternative viewpoints. This is best illustrated with the classic *conservation task*. In this task water is poured from a short wide glass to a tall thin glass, and the child is asked if the amounts of water are the same. A pre-operational child will reply the tall glass has more water in; a concrete operational child will correctly say they both contain the same amount. In the *formal operations* stage the adolescent is not limited to concrete thinking, being able to reason abstractly and logically. The main mechanisms of cognitive development are assimilation and accommodation. Assimilation is the way in which information is abstracted from the world to fit existing cognitive structures; accommodation is the way in which cognitive structures are adjusted in order to accommodate otherwise incompatible information.

According to Piaget, language is a social and cognitive process like any other and therefore clearly has cognitive prerequisites; it is dependent on other cognitive and perceptual processes and clearly follows cognitive stages of development. Piaget (1967) argued that "the structures that characterise thought have their roots in action and in sensori-motor structures that are far deeper than thought." Adult speech is socialised and has communicative intent, whereas early language is *egocentric*. Piaget (1923/1955) went on to distinguish three different types of early egocentric speech: repetition or *echolalia* (where children simply repeat their or others' utterances); *monologues* (when children talk to themselves, apparently just speaking their thoughts out loud); and group or *collective monologues* (where two or more children appear to be taking appropriate turns in a conversation but actually just produce monologues). For Piaget, cognitive and social egocentrism are related.

The cognition hypothesis states that language needs certain cognitive precursors in order to develop (e.g. Sinclair-de-Zwart, 1973). For example, the child has to attain the stage of object permanence in order to be able to acquire concepts of objects and names (nouns). This explains why there is an explosion in vocabulary size around 18 months. But Corrigan (1978) showed that there was no correlation between the development of object permanence and linguistic development once age was partialled out. We can also observe comprehension of names up to 6 months earlier. An important, though at first small, class of early words are relational words (e.g. "no", "up", "more", "gone"). The first relational words depend on object permanence, and are linked to its emergence (McCune-Nicolich, 1981). Words that relate to changes in the state of objects still present in the visual field (e.g. "up", "move") emerge before those (e.g. "all gone") that relate to absent objects (Tomasello & Farrar, 1984, 1986).

The language development of deaf and blind children
The linguistic development of deaf children is disadvantaged, but their cognitive development is relatively spared. The cognitive development of blind children is obviously greatly impaired, but their linguistic development is relatively spared. This should provide a good test of the mutual influences of linguistic and cognitive development.

Hearing-impaired children. It is obvious that the development of spoken language is impaired in deaf or hearing-impaired children. There is some evidence (e.g. Mohay, 1982) that deaf children spontaneously start using and combining increasingly complex gestures in the absence of sign language. This at least shows that there is a strong need for humans to attempt to communicate in some way. However, given adequate tuition, the time course of the acquisition of sign language runs remarkably in parallel. Meier (1991) argued that deaf children using sign language pass the same linguistic "milestones" at about the same ages as do hearing children (and perhaps some milestones actually before hearing children).

Results on the cognitive consequences of deafness have proved rather mixed. In an early experiment, Conrad and Rush (1965) found differences in coding in memory tasks between hearing and deaf children. This is not surprising given the involvement of acoustic or phonological processing in short-term or working memory (see Baddeley, 1990, for a summary). If rigorous enough controls are used, it can be demonstrated that these indeed reflect *differences* in the memory systems rather than inferiority of the hearing-impaired systems (Conrad, 1979). Furth (1966, 1971) found that compared with hearing children, performance on Piagetian tasks was relatively normal. A review of results on tasks such as conservation gave a range of results, from no impairment to one to two years; the evidence was mixed. Furth (1973) showed that deaf adolescents had more difficulty with symbolic logic than hearing children. Furth interpreted these data as evidence for the Piagetian hypothesis that language is not necessary for normal cognitive development. Any differences between deaf and hearing children arise, he argued, out of the lack of experiences and training of the deaf children.

However, most deaf children learn some kind of sign language at a very early age, so this conclusion is premature. Indeed, Best (1973) found that the more exposure to sign language deaf children had, the better their performance upon the Piagetian tasks. Clearly there are differences in cognitive development between hearing-impaired and non-hearing-impaired children, but it is not obviously the case that one group is superior to the other.

Visually-impaired children.   The cognitive development of blind or visually-impaired children is retarded. The smaller range of experiences available to the child, the relative lack of mobility, the decreased opportunity for social contact, and the decreased control of the child's own body and environment, all take their toll on cognitive development (Lowenfeld, 1948). The development of the concept of object permanence is primarily dependent upon the senses of hearing and touch, and this leads to delay in the attainment of the concept, and necessarily a very different type of concept.

Some (but not all) blind children take longer to say their first words (Lewis, 1987). This result is controversial: Bigelow (1987) found that the first 50 words were acquired between the mean ages of 1;4 (shorthand for "one year four months") and 1;9, compared with the 1;3 to 1;8 found in sighted children by Nelson (1973). The earliest words appear to be similar to those of normal children, although there appears to be a general reduction in the use of object names (Bigelow, 1987). Not surprisingly, unlike in the case of sighted children, names do not refer to objects salient in the visual world, but instead to objects salient in the auditory and tactile domains (e.g. the names of musical instruments;

"dirt"; "powder"). Instead, blind children use more action words than sighted children. The earliest words also appear to be used rather differently. They appear to be used to comment on the child's own actions, in play, or in imitation rather than for communication or referring to objects or events. Indeed, Dunlea (1984) argued that as blind children were not using words beyond the context in which they were first learnt, the use of words as symbols was at least delayed. Vocabulary acquisition is generally slower. Syntactic development is marked by the use of far more repeated phrases than is normally found. Direct repetition is also more common. This use of repeated phrases carries over into later development. There is difficulty with pronouns—in particular "you" is often used for "I". The understanding of some particular words is bound to be different: Landau and Gleitman (1985) describe the case of a three year old child who, when asked to look up, reached her arms over her head. The other curious finding is that function words are much less common early on (Bigelow, 1987). Furthermore, blind children do not ask questions of the type "what's that?" "what?" or use modifiers, which account for the earliest function words of sighted children. This might also reflect the fact that their parents adapt their own language to the needs of the children, providing more spontaneous labelling.

Hence the linguistic development of blind children is very different from that of sighted children. The differences however seem to be the obvious ones that one would expect given the nature of their disability. We cannot conclude immediately that there is a more general impairment to syntactic development that results from a mediating stage of impaired cognitive processing.

Even if there were, the picture would be complicated by the observation that any linguistic deficit may not necessarily arise solely as a consequence of differences in cognitive development. For example, the development of mutual gaze and the social precursors of language will necessarily be different; and sighted parents of blind children still tend to talk about objects that are visually prominent.

Evaluation of evidence from deaf and blind children. It is difficult to draw any conclusion from a comparison of deaf and blind children. The cognitive development of deaf children generally proceeds better than it should if language were primary, and the linguistic development of blind children generally proceeds better than it should if cognition were primary. Deaf children learn sign language, and blind children acquire excellent coping strategies. Indeed, we can go further and argue that the linguistic development of deaf children and the cognitive development of blind children both proceed better than we might expect.

Language development in children with learning difficulties

Another clear test of the cognition hypothesis should be an examination of the linguistic abilities of children with learning difficulties. Surely if cognitive development drives linguistic development, then slow cognitive development should be reflected in slow linguistic development? On the whole, there is a gross correlation between intelligence and language development. Speech is often delayed and deficient (e.g. Johnson & Ramsted, 1983). On the other hand, Yamada (1990) described the case of "Laura". Laura's linguistic competence far outstrips her other cognitive abilities. Yamada argued that Laura displayed severe and widespread impairments in all cognitive domains (her IQ was estimated at 41), yet appeared unimpaired at complex syntactic and morphological constructions. Furthermore, factors that cause problems in cognitive tasks do not do so in linguistic tasks; hence while non-linguistic tasks involving hierarchical reasoning are very difficult for Laura, her ability to use grammatical hierarchies is intact. Although her short-term memory is very short she can still produce complex syntactic constructions. Yamada concluded that cognitive and linguistic processes are distinct, and that as normal language can develop when there is severe general cognitive impairment, cognitive precursors are not essential for linguistic development. The situation is not completely straightforward, however, as not all Laura's linguistic abilities were spared. Along similar lines, Bellugi, Bihrle, Jernigan, Trauner, and Doherty (1991) describe Williams syndrome. This rare genetic disorder leads to physical abnormalities (affected children are sometimes called "elfin-faced" or "pixie people") and a very low IQ, typically around 50, yet the speech of such people is very fluent and grammatically correct. Indeed, they are particularly fond of unusual words.

Cases such as Laura's and children with Williams syndrome are clearly difficult for any position that either argues for interaction between cognitive and linguistic development or for the primacy of cognitive factors. Indeed, given our description of specific language impairment above, the evidence favours a double dissociation between language skills and general cognitive abilities.

Evaluation of the cognition hypothesis

There is no clear evidence for a strong version of the cognition hypothesis. Children acquire some language abilities before they obtain object permanence, and there is little supporting evidence from an examination of the mentally handicapped or a comparison of deaf and blind children. Indeed, Bruner (1964) argued that aspects of cognitive performance are facilitated by language. The possibility that linguistic training would improve performance of the conservation task was tested by Sinclair-de-Zwart (1969), and found only to have an indirect effect. Linguistic training does not affect basic cognitive processes but helps in description and in focusing upon the relevant aspects of the task.

Cognitive processes clearly continue to develop beyond infancy. For example, working memory capacity increases through childhood from about 2 at age 2–3, to the adult span of 7 plus or minus 2 in late childhood, and there might also be changes in the structure of memory (McShane, 1991). For example, the amount young children rehearse is less. This should have obvious consequences for linguistic processes such as parsing, particularly that of complex structures which need to be stored. There has been some debate on the role working memory subsequently plays in language. It has been argued that patients with severely limited working memory spans show no impairments to their parsing and comprehension abilities, although this is controversial (see Howard & Butterworth, 1989; Vallar & Baddeley, 1987, 1989). The precise effect of memory development on complex parsing abilities throughout childhood largely remains to be explored.

There is currently little active research on the Piagetian approach to language. The emphasis has instead shifted to the communicative precursors of language and the social-interactionist account.

SOCIAL PRECURSORS TO LANGUAGE

We noted above that it is difficult to disentangle the specific effects of linguistic deprivation in feral children from other factors such as malnutrition, and perhaps more obviously relevant, social deprivation. Cases such as that of Jim point to the importance of exposure to language in a socially meaningful situation. It is clearly not enough to be exposed to language; something more is necessary. We have already seen in our discussion of child-directed speech that adults tend to talk to children about objects that are in sight and about events that have just happened: the "here and now". The usefulness of this is obvious (for example, in associating names with objects), and it is clear that learning language just by watching television is going to be very limited in this respect. To be effective early language learning must take place in a social setting. (Obviously this and talking about the "here and now" usually go closely together.)

Social interactionists stress the development of language through interaction with other people (Bruner, 1983; Durkin, 1987; Farrar, 1990; Gleason, Hay & Crain, 1989). According to social interactionists, there is little evidence for a biologically determined critical period apart from perhaps for the acquisition of accent. Hence although biological and cognitive processes may be necessary for language development, they are not sufficient. Language development must occur in the context of meaningful social interaction. To emphasise this, Bruner (1983) contrasted the idea of a LAD with that of a LASS (*language acquisition socialisation system*).

Bruner (1975) has stressed the importance of the social setting in acquiring language. In many respects his views are similar to those of Piaget, but he places more emphasis upon social development. Bruner stressed the importance of the social setting of the mother–child dyad in helping the child to work out the meaning of utterances to which they are exposed. Although child-directed speech is an important mechanism, the social dyad achieves much more than a particular way of talking. For example, the important distinction between agents and objects is first made clear in turn-taking (and games based on turn-taking) with the mother. Mutual gaze may be important in discovering the referents of words. Bruner suggested that some of these social skills, or the way in which they are used in learning language, may be innate. Establishing joint attention is another important social device.

Notwithstanding innate principles and learning mechanisms, children learn at least some aspects of language in social settings using skills that are to some extent under social control. Feedback from adults about their communicative efficiency plays a vital role in development. For example, as we shall see in Chapter 11, the social-communicative setting can play a vital role in acquiring word meanings by restricting the domain of discourse (Tomasello, 1992). Along the same lines, it may also facilitate the task of learning the grammar of the language. We saw above that there has been a great deal of debate about the role of negative evidence in language acquisition, and that its limitations have been used to justify the existence of innate principles. It is possible that the necessity of innate principles might be reduced if negative evidence is taken into account acting in combination with the social setting (Sokolov & Snow, 1994). The development of communicative competence is an essential prerequisite of language acquisition.

Turn-taking in early conversation.   There is more to learning to use language than just learning the meanings of words and a grammar. As we have seen in Chapter 6, conversations have a structure. Clearly we do not always talk all at once; we appear to take turns in conversations. Furthermore, at the very least children have to learn to listen and to pay some attention when they are spoken to. How does this ability to interact in conversational settings develop? There is some evidence that it develops at a very early age. Schaeffer (1975) proposed that the origins of turn-taking lie in feeding. In feeding sucking occurs in bursts interspersed with pauses which appear to act as a signal to mothers to play with the baby, to cuddle it, or to talk to it. He also noted that mothers and babies rarely vocalise simultaneously. Snow (1977) observed that mothers respond to their babies' vocalisations as if their yawns and burps were utterances. Hence the precursors of conversation are present at an early age and might emerge from other activities. The gaze of mother and child also seem to be correlated; in particular, the mother quickly turns her gaze to whatever the baby is looking at. Hence again co-operation emerges at an early age. Although in these cases it is the mother who is apparently sensitive to the pauses of the child, there is further evidence that babies of just a few weeks of age are differentially sensitive to features of their environment. Trevarthen (1975) found that babies visually track and try to grab inanimate objects, but make other responses to people such as waving and what he called *pre-speech*—small movements of the mouth, rather like a precursor of talking. The exact role of this pre-speech is unclear, but certainly by the end of the first six months the precursors of social and conversational skills are apparent, and infants have developed the ability to elicit communicative responses.

Evaluation of social interactionist accounts.   Few would argue with the central theme of the social-interactionist approach: to be effective, language acquisition must take place in a meaningful social setting. But can this approach in itself account for all features of language acquisition? All the evidence which has been used to support the nativist position can be used to weaken the social-interactionist account. One particular disadvantage of this approach is that until recently, such accounts were often vague about the details of how social interactions influence development. Social interactions are mediated by cognitive processes, and the key to a sophisticated theory lies in explicating this relationship.

LANGUAGE AND THOUGHT: THE PRIMACY OF LANGUAGE?

We have considered the Chomskyan position that language and cognition are independent faculties, and the Piagetian position that cognitive development drives language development. In this section we will look at two approaches which stress the influence of language in cognition.

Interdependence of language and thought: Vygotsky

Vygotsky (1934/1962) argued for a complex relationship between language and thought, based upon his observations of inner speech, egocentric speech, and child monologues. He proposed that speech and thought have different ontogenetic roots (that is, different origins within an individual). In particular, early on speech has a pre-intellectual stage, whereas thought is non-verbal. In this stage words are not symbols for the objects they denote, but are actual properties of the objects. So up to some point in development, about age two, they are independent; however, they become connected. Then language and thought become interdependent, giving *verbal thought*: thought becomes verbal, and speech becomes rational. Children's monologues become internalised to become *inner speech*. Unlike Piaget, Vygotsky then considered that subsequent cognitive development was determined in part by language.

Vygotsky contrasted his theory with that of Piaget's, using experiments that manipulated the strength of social constraints. Piaget argued that egocentric speech arises because of insufficient socialisation, and withers away as the child learns to communicate by taking into account the point of view of the listener. For Vygotsky the reverse is the case. Egocentric speech serves the function of self-guidance that eventually becomes internalised as inner speech, and is only vocalised because the child has not yet learnt how to internalise it. The boundaries between child and listener are confused, so that self-guiding speech can only be produced in a social context. He found that egocentric speech (as measured by what he called the *coefficient of egocentricity*) decreased when the child's feeling of being understood lessened (such as when the listener was at another table). This is the reverse he claimed of what Piaget would predict. However, these experiments are difficult to evaluate because Vygotsky omitted many procedural details and measurements that are necessary for a full evaluation. It is surprising that they have not been repeated under more stringent conditions. Until then, and until this type of theory is more fully specified, it is difficult to evaluate the significance of Vygotsky's ideas.

The Sapir-Whorf hypothesis

The central idea of the Sapir-Whorf hypothesis is that the form of our language determines the structure of our thought processes: it affects the way we remember things and the way in which we perceive the world. It was originally proposed by a linguist, Edward Sapir, and a fire insurance engineer and amateur linguist, Benjamin Lee Whorf (see Whorf, 1956a,b). Although Whorf is most closely associated with anthropological evidence based on the study of American Indian languages, the idea came to him from his work in fire insurance. He noted that accidents sometimes happened because, he thought, people were misled by words—as in the case of a worker who threw a cigarette end into an "empty" drum of petrol. Far from being empty, the drum was full of petrol vapour, with explosive results.

The Sapir-Whorf hypothesis really comprises two distinct central ideas that are often confounded. First, *linguistic relativism* is the idea that different languages map onto the world in different ways. Second, *linguistic determinism* holds that the form and characteristics of our language determine the way in which we think, remember, perceive. Taken together, they form the Sapir-Whorf hypothesis.

Miller and McNeill (1969) distinguished between three versions of the Sapir-Whorf hypothesis. In the strong version, language determines thought. In a weaker version, language affects only perception. In the weakest version, language differences affect processing on certain tasks where linguistic encoding is important. It is the weakest version that has proved easiest to test.

Anthropological evidence.   The first line of evidence is anthropological, and concerns the intertranslatability of languages. Whorf analysed native American Indian languages such as Hopi, Nootka, Apache, and Aztec. He argued that each language imposes its own "world view" on its speakers. For example, he concluded that as Hopi contains no words or grammatical constructions that refer to time, Hopi speakers must have a different conception of time from us. Whorf's data is now considered highly unreliable (Malotki, 1983). Furthermore, translation can be very idiosyncratic. Take as an example Whorf's (1940/1956b) analysis of "clear dripping spring" in (8).

8.   "We might isolate something in nature by saying 'It is a dripping spring'. Apache erects the statement on a verb *ga*: 'be white (including clear, uncoloured, and so on)'. With a prefix *no*—the meaning of downward motion enters: 'whiteness moves downward'. Then *to*, meaning both 'water' and 'spring', is prefixed. The result corresponds to our 'dripping spring', but synthetically it is 'as water, or springs, whiteness moves downward'. How utterly unlike our way of thinking!" (Whorf, 1940/1956b, p.241.)

Whorf's translation is very idiosyncratic, and it is far from clear from it that speakers of Apache actually dissect the world in different ways (Clark & Clark, 1977; Pinker, 1994). For example, both languages have separate elements for "clear", "spring", and "moving downwards". Why should the expression not have been translated "It is a clear dripping spring"? The appeal of such translations is further diminished when it is realised that Whorf based his claim not on interviews with Apache speakers, but on an analysis of their recorded grammar. Lenneberg and Roberts (1956) pointed out the circularity in the reasoning that because languages differ, thought patterns differ because of the differences in the languages. An independent measure of thought patterns is necessary before a causal conclusion can be drawn.

Vocabulary differentiation has been used to support the Whorfian hypothesis. Because some cultures have single words available for concepts that others may take many to describe, it is argued that those cultures view the world differently. For example, Boas (1911) reported that Eskimo has four different words for snow; there are thirteen Philippine words for rice. An amusing debunking of some of these claims can be found in Pullum (1989). Whorf (1940/1956b) inflated the number to seven, and drew a comparison with English, which has only one word for snow regardless of whether it is falling, on the ground, slushy, and so on. The number of types of snow the Eskimo were supposed to have then varied with subsequent indirect reporting, apparently reaching its maximum in an editorial in the New York Times on February 9, 1984, with "one hundred", to "two hundred" in a Cleveland television weather forecast. In fact, Eskimo only has two words or roots for types of snow: "qanik", for "snow in the air" or "snowflake"; and "aput", for "snow on the ground". This story reiterates the importance of always checking sources. Note also that we do actually have several words for different types of snow, including slush, sleet, and blizzard.

In any case, such data are unlikely to have any perceptual effect. We can learn new words for snow: people learning to ski readily do so, and this does not apparently change the way in which they perceive the world, even though it might change the way in which we respond to it. For example, you might choose not to go skiing on certain types of snow. Vocabulary differences reflect experience and expertise.

Grammatical differences between languages.   Carroll and Casagrande (1958) examined the cognitive consequences of grammatical differences in the English and Navaho languages. The form of the class of verbs concerning handling used in Navaho depends upon the shape and rigidity of the object being handled. Endings for the verb corresponding to "carry", for example, vary depending upon whether a rope or a stick is being carried. Carroll and Casagrande therefore argued that speakers of Navaho should pay more attention to the properties of objects that determine the endings than do English speakers, and in particular they should group instances of objects according to their form. As all the children were bilingual, the comparison was made between more Navaho-dominant and more English-dominant Navaho children. The more Navaho-dominant children did indeed group objects more by form rather than colour compared to the English-dominant group. However, a control group of non-Native American English speaking children grouped even more according to form, behaving like the Navaho children were predicted to behave! It is therefore not clear what conclusions can be drawn from this study.

A second example is that Chinese does not have a subjunctive mood that enables English speakers to encode easily *counter-factuals* such as "If I had gone to the library, I would have met Dirk". Bloom (1981, 1984) argued that Chinese speakers find it harder to reason counter-factually. They are more easily overloaded on processing loads such as memory than languages which support these forms. Au (1983, 1984) countered that the sentences used by Bloom were not good idiomatic Chinese. Liu (1985) also argued that it is possible to argue counter-factually in Chinese. The form taken to do so might be longer than the English subjunctive construction, which might account for any differences that do arise.

Indirect effects of language on cognition.   There is more evidence that language can have an indirect effect on cognition, particularly on tasks where linguistic encoding is important. Carmichael, Hogan and Walter (1932) looked at the effects of learning a verbal label on subjects' memory for nonsense pictures (see Fig. 10.1). They found that the recall of the pictures was affected by the label which the subjects had associated with the pictures. Santa and Ranken (1972) showed that arbitrary verbal labels aided the recall of nonsense shapes.

Duncker (1945) explored the phenomenon known as *functional fixedness* using the "box and candle" problem, where subjects have to construct a device using commonplace materials so that a candle can burn down to its bottom while attached to the wall. The easiest solution is to use the box containing the materials as a support; subjects however take a long time to think of this, because they fixate on the box's function as container. Glucksberg and Weisberg (1966) showed that the labelling of objects can strengthen or weaken the functional fixedness effect depending on the appropriateness of the label.

Hence work on memory and problem solving supports the weakest version of the Whorfian hypothesis. Language can facilitate or hinder performance on some cognitive tasks, particularly those where linguistic encoding is routinely important.

Colour coding and memory for colour.   The most fruitful way of investigating the strong version of the Sapir-Whorf hypothesis has proved to be analysis of the way in which we name and remember

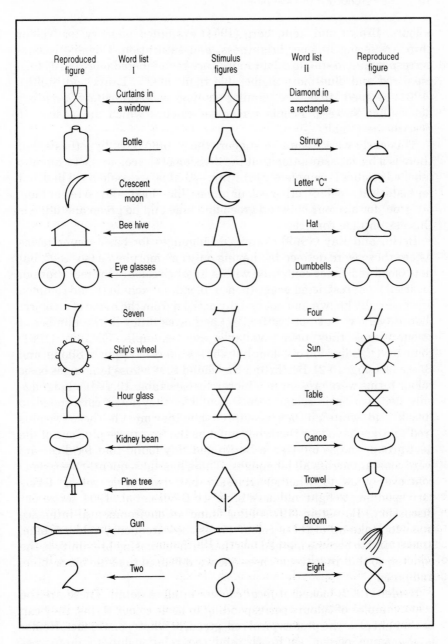

FIG. 10.1. Example stimuli and responses showing the effect of verbal labels. (Reprinted from Carmichael, L., Hogan, H.P., & Walter, A.A., 1932. An experimental study of the effect of language on the reproduction of visually presented forms. *Journal of Experimental Psychology*, 15, 73–86, p.80.)

colours. Brown and Lenneberg (1954) examined memory for "colour chips" differing in hue, brightness, and saturation. Codable colours corresponding to simple colour names are remembered more easily (e.g. ideal red and blue more memorable than "bled"). Lantz and Stefflre (1964) argued that the similar notion *communication accuracy* determines success. People remember colours which are easiest to describe best of all.

This early work seems to support the Sapir-Whorf hypothesis, but there is a basic assumption that the division of the colour spectrum into labelled colours is completely arbitrary—that is, we could have had, but for historical accident, other colour names, like "bled" and no red or blue, or "grue" for a colour between green and blue and no green and blue. Is this assumption correct?

Berlin and Kay (1969) examined languages for basic colour terms where these were defined by: having only one morpheme (so "red", but not "blood red"); not contained within another colour (so "red", but not "scarlet"); not restricted usage (hence "blond" is excluded); and common and generally known and not usually derived from the name of an object (hence "yellow" but not "saffron"). Languages differ in the number of colour terms they have available. For example, Gleason (1961) compared the division of colour hues by speakers of English, Shona, and Bassa (see Fig. 10.2). Berlin and Kay found that across languages basic colour terms were present in a hierarchy (see Table 10.4). If a language only has two basic colour terms available, they must correspond to "black" and "white"; if they have three then they must be these two plus "red"; if they have four then they must be the first three plus one of the next group, and so on. Hence Berlin and Kay found that focal colours were constant across all languages. (There has subsequently been some controversy as to whether Russian has two basic colour terms corresponding to light and dark blue; see Davies et al., 1991, for recent discussion.) Bornstein (1973) later found an environmental influence upon the take-up of these colour terms. Low-frequency colours (blue, green) tend to become merged together with increasing proximity to the equator, so that in extreme cases one word is used to name black, blue, and green.

Heider (1972) looked at *focal colours* in more detail. These are the best examples of colours corresponding to basic colour terms: they can be thought of as the prototypical red, green, or whatever. (In fact, Heider is the same person as Rosch, and the relationship to prototypes discussed in Chapter 6 is apparent.) The Dani of New Guinea have just two colour terms, "mili" (black) and "mola" (white). She taught the Dani made-up names for other colours. They learned names more easily for other focal colours than for non-focal colours They could remember focal

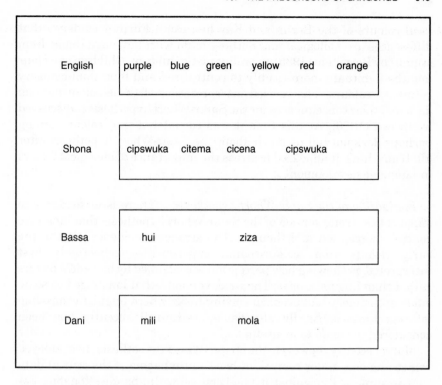

FIG. 10.2. Use of colour terms in English, Shona, Bassa, and Dani. (Based on Glucksberg, 1988, p.228, and Gleason, 1961, p.4.)

colours more easily than non-focal, even those for which they did not have a name. Children also prefer focal colours. In a similar way, English speakers attend to differences between light and dark blue in exactly the same way as Russian speakers, even though the latter have names for these regions (Laws, Davies, & Andrews, 1995).

In conclusion it seems that the division of the colour spectrum is not arbitrary, but is based on the physiology of the colour vision system. The six most sensitive points of the visual system correspond to the first six

TABLE 10.4
A hierarchy of colour names (based on Berlin & Kay, 1969)

BLACK	WHITE		
RED			
YELLOW	GREEN	BLUE	
BROWN			
PURPLE	PINK	ORANGE	GREY

focal colours of the Berlin and Kay hierarchy. Further evidence that differences are biological and nothing to do with language comes from studies by Bornstein (1985) on prelinguistic children. Children aged four months habituate more readily to central red and blue than category boundary colours. The revised interpretation of these colour-naming data and their consequences for the Sapir-Whorf hypothesis is discussed by Brown (1976). At this time it was considered that colour naming perhaps does not tell us much about the Sapir-Whorf hypothesis after all. If anything, it appeared to stress the importance of biological factors in language development.

Evaluation of the Sapir-Whorf hypothesis.   There is no evidence to support the strong version of the Sapir-Whorf hypothesis that language controls perception and thought. The strongest evidence, that of the early results from colour-coding experiments, is actually best interpreted as showing how perception is controlled by biological factors rather than linguistic ones. The weak version—that language has some effect on memory and problem solving tasks where linguistic encoding is important—is hardly surprising, and until recently has been considered to vague to be useful.

More recently however the Sapir-Whorf hypothesis has enjoyed something of a minor revival, at least in that some of the critical data that is supposedly against it has been shown to be questionable. For example, details of 19 out of the 20 languages originally detailed in the Berlin and Kay (1969) were in fact bilingual speakers living in San Francisco, and the use of colour categories by bilingual speakers differs systematically from that of monolingual speakers. In particular, the colour categorisation of bilinguals comes to resemble that of monolingual speakers of their second language, whatever their first. This in itself would give rise to an artefactual universality in colour categorisation. There are also methodological problems with the expanded set of 98 languages studied later by Berlin and Kay (Cromer, 1991; Hickerson, 1971). The criteria Berlin and Kay (1969) used for naming basic colour terms are suspect (Michaels, 1977). In any case, the criteria seem to have been inconsistently applied, and it is possible that the basic colour terms of many languages were omitted (Hickerson, 1971).

Furthermore, there were problems with the materials used in the original studies by Heider. The focal colours are perceptually more discriminable than the non-focal colours in the specific Berlin and Kay array used in that they were perceptually more distant from their neighbours. When the materials are corrected for this artefact, Lucy and Shweder (1979) found that focal colours were not remembered any better than non-focal colours. On the other hand, a measure of communication accuracy did predict memory performance. This finding suggests that having a convenient colour label can indeed assist colour memory. Kay and Kempton (1984) showed that although English speakers display categorical perception of colours that lay on either side of a colour name boundary, such as blue and green, speakers of the Mexican Indian language Tarahumara, who do not have names for blue and green, do not. Hence having an available name can at least accentuate the difference between two categories.

Finally, Hunt and Agnoli (1991) have argued that the weak version of the hypothesis is not after all too vague to be useful. The most plausible version of the Whorfian hypothesis states that if a thought expressible in one language cannot be expressed so easily in another, then that difference will have consequences in the ease with which cognitive processes can be carried out and acquired. At the very least, having one word for a concept rather than having to use a whole sentence reduces memory load. They give some specific examples of how differences between languages might lead to slight differences in cognitive style. For example, the structure of number names in Chinese is different from that in English. In Chinese there are only 14 basic number terms (0–10, 100, 1000, and 10,000). English has the additional terms for those in the teens. Hence an English-speaking child has to learn a special word for 11, "eleven", while the Chinese child only has to produce "ten and one". English-speaking children have difficulty in learning to count in the teen range while Chinese-speaking children do not (see Hunt & Agnoli, 1991).

We have seen in this book a number of cases where different languages exemplify different properties that are bound to have cognitive consequences. For example, the absence of irregular words in shallow orthographies such as Serbo-Croat and Italian must surely be reflected in differences between their reading systems and those of speakers of languages such as English. Furthermore, as we saw in our discussion of dyslexia in Japanese, differences between languages can lead to differences in the effects of brain damage. In summary, although there is little evidence that language controls perception and thought, a weaker version of the hypothesis is still justifiable and useful.

Language use and social processes

Does the way in which we use language affect the way society treats groups of people, or in which groups of people function in society? These hypotheses take as their starting point some version of the Sapir-Whorf hypothesis.

The sociologist Bernstein (1961) attempted to explain the perceived relative educational disadvantage of working compared with middle class children by saying that working class children learn an *impoverished language*. He called the language used by middle class children an *elaborated code*, and that used by working class children a *restricted code*. It is not clear however what causal role this plays. Of course marked dialect differences between teachers and pupils who come from different social classes may cause communication problems, but is far from obvious that the working class dialect is impoverished compared to the middle class dialect: it is just different. Dialects and "class languages" and their political consequences are widely held to be of considerable importance, as evinced by, for example, the discussion by Stalin (1954/1972).

Another example of the social importance of the relationship between language and thought is in the effect of language upon disadvantaged sections of society. Some of the strongest arguments for non-sexist language have been proposed by Spender (1980). It is argued, for example, that using the word "man" to refer to all humanity has the association that males are more important than females; or using a word like "chairman" (rather than a more gender-neutral term such as "chair" or "chairperson") encourages the view that the normal expectation is that the chair will be a man. Such a theory is obviously dependent upon some form of the Sapir-Whorf hypothesis being tenable. There has been surprisingly little empirical work in this area.

CONCLUDING SUMMARY

Attempts to find a simple relationship between language and thought have proved difficult. We can dismiss any simple relationship between the two; any relationship is likely to be complex. Support can be found for aspects of each of the four possible relationships between language and thought: that language has a large innate component and develops independently of other faculties (the viewpoint associated with Chomsky and Pinker); that aspects of cognitive development facilitate some aspects of linguistic development (the cognition hypothesis); that language and thought have separate roots but become interdependent later in childhood (Vygotsky's position); and that differences in language affect performance on memory and on some cognitive tasks (the weak version of the Sapir-Whorf hypothesis). The strong versions of these hypotheses have probably all got to be rejected. For example, there is no clear correlation between the stages of cognitive and linguistic development. Children do not have to attain object permanence before they can start naming objects. There is no evidence that language affects perception.

It is important to note that these particular findings that support the weak version of these hypotheses are not contradictory. Consider this scenario. Grammar, particularly syntax, has an innate component that predisposes the child to acquire a particular type of grammar. At birth, the brain shows some signs of lateralisation for speech and non-speech processing, and this proceeds throughout childhood. The language acquisition device must be activated by exposure to language; if this does not happen early enough then normal syntax cannot be acquired. Parents and others facilitate language acquisition by making speech to young children and its referents very clear. As language develops, the relationship between linguistic and cognitive processes becomes more closely entwined. Egocentric speech becomes internalised to form the inner speech that we believe guides much of our thought. Differences between languages can have some effect upon the cognitive styles of the members of those communities. Language can also affect performance on tasks such as problem solving and memory where linguistic encoding is important. It is a simplification to pick out biological, cognitive, and social factors in isolation and say that this is the driving force of language acquisition. Instead, language acquisition occurs because of a complex interaction between these processes.

FURTHER READING

Gleason and Ratner (1993) give an overview of language development covering many of the topics in this and the next chapter. See Cottingham (1984) for a discussion of rationalism and empiricism. A general overview of cognitive development is provided by Flavell, Miller, and Miller (1993) and by McShane (1991). Piattelli-Palmarini (1980) edited a collection of papers that arose from the famous debate between Chomsky and Piaget on the relationship between language and thought, and the contributions of nativism versus experience, at the Royaumont Abbey near Paris in 1975. Piattelli-Palmarini (1994) summarised and updated this debate. Lewis (1987) discusses general issues concerning the effects of different types of disability upon linguistic and cognitive development. For more on language acquisition in the blind, see the collection of papers in Mills (1983). Kyle and Woll (1985) is a textbook on sign language and the consequences of its use upon cognitive development. Cromer's (1991) book provides a good critical overview of this area, and indeed of many of the topics in this chapter. Gallaway and Richards (1994) is a collection of papers covering recent research on child-directed speech and the role of the environment; the final chapter by Richards and Gallaway (1994) provides an overview.

An excellent source of readings on the critical period and how language develops in exceptional circumstances is Bishop and Mogford (1993). For a more detailed review of the critical period and second language hypothesis see McLaughlin (1984). A popular account of Genie and other attic children plus an outline of their importance is given by Ryman (1993). Description of the neurology of hemispheric specialisation can be found in Kolb and Whishaw (1990). Other cases of linguistic deprivation are discussed by Skuse (1993). Cases of hearing children of deaf parents and their implications are reviewed by Schiff-Myers (1993). See Harris (1982) for a full review of cognitive prerequisites to language. Social precursors of language are discussed in more detail in Harris and Coltheart (1986). Details of innate mechanisms and learnability theory are discussed by McShane (1991). A convincing defence of the position that language has an important innate component is presented by Pinker (1994); see also Pinker (1989) for more on formal approaches to language acquisition; see also Elman (1993). For more on language acquisition as parameter setting, see Stevenson (1988). For more on the early language of blind children, see Dunlea (1989), and for more on language in deaf, blind, and handicapped children, Cromer (1991). For the effects of linguistic training on cognitive performance, see Dale (1976). This book also discusses the Sapir-Whorf hypothesis in detail.

See Glucksberg (1988) for an overview of the relationship between language and thought. Fodor (1972) and Newman and Holzman (1993) review the work of Vygotsky and its impact. For a detailed review of the Sapir-Whorf hypothesis in general and the experiments on colour coding in particular, see Lucy (1992). Clark and Clark (1977) provide an extensive review of the relationship between language and thought, with particular emphasis on developmental issues.

CHAPTER ELEVEN

Language development

INTRODUCTION

In this chapter we will look at how language develops from infancy to adolescence. There is a clear progression in the course of language development, but whether or not discontinuous stages are involved is contentious. From about the age of 6 months, infants start babbling. It has been argued that around this time they start noticing that particular strings of sounds co-occur with particular situations (Jusczyk, 1982, MacKain, 1982): for example, whenever the sounds "mummy" are made, mother is there. Children start producing their first words around the age of 10 or 11 months. The single words are sometimes thought of as forming single word utterances. Around the age of 18 months, as we have seen in the previous chapter, there is a rapid explosion in vocabulary size, and around this time two-word speech emerges. The vocabulary explosion and onset of two-word speech is strongly correlated (Bates, Bretherton, & Snyder, 1988; Nelson, 1973). Before children produce utterances that are grammatically correct by adult standards, they produce *telegraphic speech* which contains a number of words but with some grammatical elements absent (Brown & Bellugi, 1964). As grammatical elements appear, they do so in a relatively fixed order for a particular language. The two-word stage is followed at the age of approximately 2 years 6 months by increasingly complex sentences.

In practice, it is quite difficult to carry out controlled experiments on large numbers of young children. Nevertheless, there are some *cross-sectional* studies which look at the performance of a group of children at a particular age, perhaps compared with a group of children at a different age. One problem with the cross-sectional methodology is that there is enormous linguistic variation between children of the same age. Not only are some children linguistically more advanced, there are also differences in linguistic style between children. Because of this, observational and diary studies have also been important methodologies. Longitudinal studies of individual children, often the experimenters' own, have been particularly influential. Because of this, most of the literature concerns a surprisingly small number of children, and one possible consequence of this is that variation between individuals in development has been underestimated.

In this chapter we will concentrate on the development of children's productions, divided into the main topics of phonological, semantic, and syntactic development, because these are the topics upon which most research has been carried out. It should be remembered however that the development of production and comprehension are intimately related. We have discussed the development of reading skills in Chapter 4.

PHONOLOGICAL DEVELOPMENT

Infants appear to be sensitive to speech sounds from a very early age. We looked at the perceptual abilities of infants in some detail in Chapter 2. It is clear that young children are particularly sensitive to speech sounds. For example, Eimas, Siqueland, Jusczyk, and Vigorito (1971) showed that infants as young as one month old could distinguish between two syllables that differed in only one distinctive phonological feature (e.g. voicing in /pa/ versus /ba/). They did this using a sucking dishabituation technique (see Chapter 2). Eimas et al. played the different sounds and found they could elicit changes in the sucking rate. Furthermore they found that perception was categorical, as the infants were only sensitive to changes in voice onset time that straddled the adult boundaries: that is, the categories used by the babies were the same as those used by adults.

How does the production of early sounds develop?

Babbling

From about the age of 6 months to 10 months, before infants start speaking, they make speech-like sounds known as *babbling*. Babbling is clearly more language-like than other early vocalisations such as crying and cooing, and consists of strings of vowels and consonants combined into sometimes lengthy series of syllables, usually with a great deal of repetition, such as "bababa gugugu", sometimes with an apparent intonation contour. There are two types of babbling (Oller, 1980): *reduplicated babble* is characterised by repetition of consonant-vowel syllables, often producing the same pair for a long time (e.g. "babababab"); *non-reduplicated* or variegated babble is characterised by strings of non-repeated syllables (e.g. "bamido"). Babbling lasts for 6 to 9 months, fading out as the child produces the first words. It appears to be universal: deaf infants also babble (Sykes, 1940), although it is now known that they produce slightly different babbling patterns, suggesting that speech perception plays some role (Oller, Eilers, Bull, & Carney, 1985). Across many countries, the 12 most frequent consonants constitute 95% of babbled consonants (Locke, 1983), although babbling patterns differ slightly across languages, again suggesting that speech perception determines some aspects of babbling (de Boysson-Bardies, Sagart, & Durand, 1984; de Boysson-Bardies, Halle, Sagart, & Durand, 1989).

What is the relationship between babbling and later speech? The *continuity hypothesis* (Mowrer, 1960) states that babbling is a direct precursor of language. In babbling, it was argued, the child produces all of the sounds that are to be found in all of the world's languages. This is then gradually narrowed down, by reinforcement by parents and others, and lack of exposure to sounds within a particular language, to the set of sounds in the relevant language. The extreme version of this is of course the behaviourist account of language development discussed in the previous chapter: words are acquired by the processes of reinforcement and shaping of random babbling sounds. At first sight there is some evidence for this. Initially babbling is universal, and as we saw above it does become modified by exposure to the language to which the child is exposed. There are a number of problems with the continuity hypothesis. Many sounds, such as consonant clusters, are not produced at all in babbling. Also parents are not selective about reinforcement in babbling; they reinforce all vocalisations indiscriminately.

The *discontinuity hypothesis* states that babbling bears no simple relationship to later development. Jakobson (1968) postulated two stages in the development of sounds. In the first stage children babble, producing a wide range of sounds that do not emerge in any particular order and that are not obviously related to later development. The second stage is marked by the sudden disappearance of many sounds that were previously in their repertoires (e.g. /l/ and /r/). Some sounds are dropped temporarily, re-emerging perhaps many months later, whereas some are dropped altogether. Jakobson argued that it is only in this second stage that children are learning the phonological contrasts appropriate to their particular language, and these contrasts are acquired in an invariant order. Although Jakobson observed that there was a silent period between babbling and early speech, in fact there is probably some overlap (Menyuk, Menn, & Silber, 1986). Indeed, there seem to be some phonological sequences that are repeated that are neither clearly babbling nor words. These can be thought of as *protowords*. Early words might be embedded in variegated babble. There are preferences for certain phonetic sequences that are found later in early speech (Oller, Wieman, Doyle, & Ross, 1976). This points to some continuity between babbling and early speech.

There is thus no clear evidence for either the continuity or the discontinuity hypothesis. What then is the function of babbling? Clark and Clark (1977) proposed that there is an indirect relationship between babbling and speech, in that babbling provides practice at gaining control over the articulatory tract.

Later phonological development

Early speech uses a much restricted set of sounds compared with those found in the babbling of just a few months before, including some sounds that were only rarely or not all produced then. It is clearly not the case that young children do this to focus upon phonological distinctions one by one until they are acquired, because words will often be changed after they have been mastered. Instead children appear to be *hypothesis testing*, with each new hypothesis necessitating change in the pronunciation of words already mastered, either directly as a consequence of trying out a new rule, or indirectly as a result of a shift of attention. Jakobson (1968) proposed that the way in which children master the contrasts between sounds is related to the sound structure of languages. He argued that children learn the contrasts in an order that is universal across languages. Furthermore, the order of acquisition of the contrasts is predictable from a comparison of the languages of the world: the phonological contrasts that are most widespread are acquired first, whereas those that are to be found in only a few languages are acquired last. One weakness of this approach is that because the theory emphasises the acquisition of contrasts, other features of phonological development are missed or cannot be explained (see Kiparsky & Menn, 1977). In addition, there are often clear exceptions to any systematic simplification of a child's phonological structure. Children can often produce a word containing a particular phonological string when all other similar words are simplified or omitted.

Simplification of output. It is well-known that young children simplify the words they produce. According to Jakobson (1968), at least one reason why this happens is because the child has not yet learnt the appropriate phonological contrasts. For example, a child produces "fish" as "fis" because he or she has not yet mastered the distinction between palatal and alveolar fricatives (see Chapter 2). Jakobson further argued that the order in which these contrasts are learnt reflects their frequency in the child's language, so that rarely used sounds will be acquired relatively late. We have just seen that this cannot be the complete story, because there are too many exceptions, and that the children are at least aware of the contrasts even if they cannot always apply them. A second reason that has been proposed is that children are using phonological rules to change the perceived forms into ones that they can produce (Menn, 1980; Smith, 1973). One problem with this is that children sometimes alternate between different forms of simplification. A third possibility is that simplifications are a by-product of the development of the speech production system (Gerken, 1994). This hypothesis makes use of the development of statistical regularities in connectionist models, but it is too early to evaluate this third explanation for why children simplify their output.

Smith (1973) described four ways in which children simplify the words they produce, with a general tendency towards producing shorter strings. They often omit the final consonant, they reduce consonant clusters, they omit unstressed syllables, and they repeat syllables. Younger children often substitute easier sounds (such as those in the babbling repertoire) for more difficult sounds (those not to be found in the babbling repertoire). This effect is found across all languages. Nevertheless, the children can still correctly perceive the sounds they cannot yet produce (Smith, 1973).

SINGLE WORD UTTERANCES

Words are produced from the age of about one. New words are added slowly in the first year, so that by the age of 18–24 months the child has a vocabulary of about 50 words. At this stage the vocabulary explosion mentioned in the previous chapter occurs. We have also seen that comprehension precedes production. Nelson (1973) examined the first 10 words produced by children and found that important person names, animals, food, and toys were the categories most commonly referred to. However, children differ greatly in their earliest words. Indeed, she was able to divide the children into two groups: *expressive* children emphasise people and feelings, and *referential* children emphasise objects. The different types of first words used by young children have later consequences. The referential group acquired vocabulary more quickly, whereas the expressive group made faster syntactic development.

Greenfield and Smith (1976) found that early words may refer to many different roles, not just objects, and further proposed that the first utterances may always name roles. For example, the early word "mama" might be used to refer to particular actions carried out by the mother. Generally, the earliest words can be characterised as referring to either things that move (such as people, animals, vehicles) and to things that can be moved (such as food, clothes, toys). Moving things tend to be named before movable things. Places and the instruments of actions are very rarely named.

There is some debate as to whether the earliest referential words may differ in their use and representation from later ones (McShane, 1991). In particular, the child's earliest use of reference appears to be qualitatively different from later. The youngest children name objects spontaneously or give names of objects in response to questions quite rarely, in marked contrast to their behaviour at the end of the second year. The vocabulary explosion does appear to be linked with the ability to name objects, as the bulk of the explosion is marked at first by a large number of new object names.

SEMANTIC DEVELOPMENT

It would be surprising if children got the meanings of words right every time. Consider the size of the task. A mother says to a child sitting in a pram: "Isn't the moon pretty?". How of all the things in the environment does the child pick out the referent for "moon"? It is not immediately obvious that the referent is both an object and an object in the visual field. Even when the child has picked out the appropriate referent, substantial problems remain. It has to learn that "moon" refers to the object, not some property such as "being silver coloured" or "round". What are the properties of the visual object that are important? The child has to learn that the word "moon" refers to the same thing, even when its shape changes (from crescent to full moon). The task then of associating names with objects and actions is an enormous one. Errors are therefore only to be expected. Sentences (1) and (2) are examples of errors in acquiring meaning from Clark and Clark (1977):

1. Mother pointed out and named a dog "bow-wow".
    Child later applies "bow-wow" to dogs, but also to cats, cows, and horses.

2. Mother says sternly to child: "Young man, you did that on purpose."
    When asked later what "on purpose" means, child says: "It means
    you're looking at me."

What are the features that determine the child's first guess at the
meaning of words? How do the first guesses become corrected so that
they converge upon the way adults use words?

Clark and Clark (1977) argued that, in the very earliest stages of
development, the child must start with two assumptions about the
purpose of language: language is for communication, and language
makes sense in context. From then on they can form hypotheses about
what the words mean, and develop strategies for using and refining
those meanings.

Semantic and conceptual development

Children's semantic development is dependent upon their conceptual
development. They can only map meanings into the concepts they have
available at that time. In this respect, linguistic development must
follow cognitive development. Of course, not all concepts may be marked
by linguistic distinctions. There must surely be some innate processes,
if only to categorise, so the child is born with the ability to form concepts.
Quinn and Eimas (1986) suggest that categorisation is part of the innate
architecture of cognition.

The first words emerge out of shared reference (see the previous
chapter on the social precursors of language). However, there are
well-known philosophical objections to a simple look and name, or
ostensive model of learning the first words (Quine, 1960). Ostensive
means pointing—this conveys the idea of acquiring simple words by a
parent pointing at a dog and saying "dog", and the child attaching the
name to the object. The problem is simply that the child does not know
which attribute of input is being labelled: for all the child knows, it could
be that the word "dog" is supposed to pick out just the dog's feet, or the
whole category of animals, or its brown colour, or the barking sound it
makes, or its smell, or the way it is moving, and so on. One thing that
makes the task slightly easier is that we have seen on our discussion of
motherese in the previous chapter that adults stress the most important
words, and children selectively attend to the stressed parts of the speech
they hear (Gleitman & Wanner, 1982). Nevertheless, the problem is
obvious and enormous.

There are three ways round this problem. The first is that there is an
innate basis to the hypotheses they make (Fodor, 1981). We have evolved
such that we are more likely to attach the word "dog" to the object "dog",
rather than to its colour, or some even more abstruse concept such as

"the hairy thing I see on Mondays". The second is that the child uses some means other than ostensive definition to map words onto concepts (McShane, 1991). As yet no plausible such mechanism has been proposed that could wholly achieve this, although as we shall see, it is possible that the role of social factors has been greatly underestimated. The third is that the cognitive system is *constrained* in its interpretations, and makes use of a number of *lexical principles* to help to establish the referent of a new word (Golinkoff, Hirsh-Pasek, Bailey, & Wenger, 1992; Golinkoff, Mervis, & Hirsh-Pasek, 1994). Hence the cognitive system may be constrained so that it tends to treat ostensive definitions as labels for whole objects; Markman (1990) called this the *whole object assumption*. There is some evidence that adults are sensitive to this constraint: Ninio (1980) found that when talking to children adults almost wholly use ostensive definition to refer to whole objects rather than parts or attributes. When adults deviate from this, they try to make it clear—for example, by mentioning the name of the whole object as well. Of course, not all early words name objects, so additional constraints would be necessary. Another might be a *mutual exclusivity assumption*, whereby each object can only have one label (Markman & Wachtel, 1988). Soja, Carey, and Spelke (1991; but see Landau, Jones, & Smith, 1992; Soja, Carey & Spelke, 1992) argue that the sorts of inferences children make vary according to the type of object being referred to. For example, if the speaker is talking about a solid object, the child assumes the word refers to the whole object, but if the speaker is talking about a non-solid substance, then the child infers that the word refers to parts or properties of the substance. Finally, as children acquire words, new strategies become available. For example, they may be biased to assign words to objects for which they do not already have names (the *novel name-nameless category* or N3C principle; Mervis & Bertrand, 1994). Later on, when the child's vocabulary is larger and their linguistic abilities more sophisticated, explicit definition becomes possible. Hence superordinate and subordinate terms can be explicitly defined by constructions such as "Tables, chairs, and sofas are all types of furniture." This is another example of bootstrapping in action.

We noted in the previous chapter the importance of the social setting upon language development. Early words may be constrained so that they are only used in particular discourse settings (Levy & Nelson, 1994; see also Nelson, Hampson, & Shaw, 1993). It now seems likely however that the social setting also plays an important role in learning word meaning. Recent work has emphasised the role of the social setting in learning new words as a supplement or alternative to innate or cognitive constraints. Tomasello (1992) argued that social and pragmatic factors could have an important influence on language development. Our initial problem is that the simple ostensive or "look and name" model of semantic development does not explain why children associate words with particular aspects of the environment. We have examined a number of possible innate and cognitive constraints that might account for this. The problem would be greatly simplified if the adult and child establish through any other available communicative means that the discourse is focusing upon a particular dimension. For example, if it has been established that the domain of discourse is "colour", then the word "pink" will be used to name not the pig, but its colour. Adults and children *interact* in determining the focus of early conversation. The importance of pragmatic and communicative factors is shown in a study by Tomasello and Kruger (1992), who surprisingly showed that young children are better at learning new verbs when adults are talking about actions that have yet to happen than when they are used ostensively to refer to actions that are ongoing. This must be because the impending action contains a great deal of pragmatic information which the infant can use, perhaps in combinations with past associations. Tomasello and Barton (1994) elaborate on how social-pragmatic cues help children to learn new words. In summary, the social setting can serve the same role as innate principles in enabling the child to determine the reference without knowing the language. Joint attention with adults, or *inter-subjectivity*, is an essential component of learning a language.

A number of other points can be made. Children appear to vary in the importance they assign to different concepts, and this leads to individual differences and preferences for learning words. The first use of "dog" varies from four-legged mammal shaped objects, to all furry objects (including inanimate objects such as coats and hats), to all moving objects (Clark & Clark, 1977). In each case the same basic principle is operating: a child forms a hypothesis about what a word refers to and tries it out. The hypotheses however differs from child to child.

Brown (1958) was among the earliest to suggest that children infer that the denotation of words corresponds to what was later known as the basic level (see Chapter 6; see also Hall, 1993, Hall & Waxman, 1993). Rosch et al. (1976) found that the bulk of early words were indeed basic level terms. Superordinate concepts seem particularly difficult to acquire (Markman, 1989). Only later, after the constraint biasing children to basic level terms weakens, do taxonomic hierarchies begin to develop. Later on particular cues become important. Mass nouns in particular seem to aid children in learning hierarchical taxonomies (Markman, 1985, 1989), flagging superordinate category names. As such, they are syntactically restricted, which is apparent when we try to substitute one for another. Hence although we can say "this is a table", "this is a furniture" is incorrect; similarly "this is a ring" but not "this is a jewellery"; and a final example, "this is a pound" but not "this is a money". Of course, not all superordinate terms are mass nouns and restricted in this way, but this does appear to be an important cue.

Finally, there are syntactic cues to word meaning. Brown (1958) first proposed that children may use part-of-speech as a cue to meaning. For example, 17-month-olds are capable of attending to the difference between noun phrase syntax as in "This is Sib" and count noun syntax as in "This is a sib". This is obviously a useful cue for determining whether the word refers to an object or is a proper name. The general capacity to use syntax to infer meaning is an example of bootstrapping, more specifically syntactic bootstrapping (Gleitman, 1990).

Evaluation of research on semantic development. Approaches that make use of constraints on how children relate words to the world are not without their problems. First, we are still faced with the problem of where these constraints themselves come from. Are they innate, and part of the language acquisition device? Second, they are actually more biases than constraints, as children sometimes go against them (Nelson, 1988, 1990; but see also Behrend, 1990; Kuczaj, 1990). Furthermore, very early words (those used before the vocabulary explosion) often violate the constraints (Barrett, 1986). For example, Bloom (1973) noted that a young child uses "car" to refer to cars, but only when watched from a certain location. The constraints only appear to come into operation around 18 months, which is difficult to explain if they are indeed a component of the language acquisition device. (It is of course possible that the attainment of the concept of object permanence interacts with this.) Third, whereas it is relatively easy to think of constraints that apply to concrete objects and substances, it is less easy to do so for abstract objects and actions. The alternative viewpoint, primarily espoused by Nelson (1988, 1990), is that there are no constraints on early lexical development, and that children are not continually forming and testing hypotheses, but that instead language development is better seen as a process of social convergence between adult and child, emphasising communicability. We have seen that the role of social and pragmatic constraints in early acquisition might have been greatly underestimated.

Errors in early meaning
One useful way of finding out about the features of the environment that are important for learning meaning, and the way it then develops, is by looking more closely at these mistakes children make. Early meanings may overlap with adult meanings in four ways: the early meaning might

be exactly the same as the adult meaning; it might overlap but go beyond it; it might be too restricted; or there might be no overlap at all. Words that have no overlap with adult usage get abandoned very quickly: Bloom (1973) observed that in the earliest stages of talking inappropriate names are used for objects and actions, but these are then dropped very quickly. Although as we saw in the previous chapter, conditioning and reinforcement cannot be the main driving forces of language acquisition, this is not to say that they play no role. Words which have no overlap in meaning with the adult usage are likely to provide no reinforcement in communication. Most research has concentrated upon the use of words that go beyond the adult usage.

Over-extensions and under-extensions.   E. Clark (1973) was one of the first to look at *over-extensions* (sometimes called *over-generalisations*) in detail. Over-extensions are common in early language and appear to be found across all languages. Table 11.1 gives some examples of early over-extensions. They are very common in development. Rescorla (1980) found that one third of the first 75 words were over-extended, including early high-frequency words. The examples in Table 11.1 make clear that over-extensions are often based upon perceptual attributes of the object. Shape in particular is an important characteristic, but the examples also show that over-extensions are possible on the basis of the properties of movement, size, texture, and sound of the object referred to. Perceptual attributes however are not the only basis of over-generalisation. Nelson (1974) proposed that functional attributes are more important than perceptual

TABLE 11.1
Examples of over-extensions (from Clark & Clark, 1977)

Referent	Domain of application
Moon	Cakes, round marks on window, round postcards, letter "O"
Ball	Apples, grapes, eggs, anything round
Bars of cot	Toy abacus, toast rack with parallel bars, picture of columned building
Stick	Cane, umbrella, ruler, all stick-like objects
Horse	Cow, calf, pig, all four-legged animals
Toy goat on wheels	Anything that moves
Fly	Specks of dirt, dust, all small insects, toes
Scissors	All metal objects
Sound of train	Steaming coffee pot, anything that made a noise

ones. However, Bowerman (1978) and E. Clark (1973) both found that appearance usually takes precedence over function. That is, children over-extend based upon a perceptual characteristic such as shape even when the object in the domain of application clearly have different functions, and the child may be aware of that.

McShane and Dockrell (1983) pointed out that many reports of over-extensions failed to distinguish persistent from occasional errors. They argued that occasional errors tell us little about the child's semantic representation, perhaps arising only from filling a transient difficulty in accessing the proper word with the most available one. Such transient over-generalisations are more akin to adult word substitution speech errors (see Chapter 8), and as such would tell us little about normal semantic development. Hence it is important to show that words involved in real over-extensions are permanently over-extended, and also that the same words are over-extended in comprehension. If a word is over-extended because the representation of its meaning is incomplete, the pattern of comprehension of that word by the child should also reflect this.

To this end, Thomson and Chapman (1977) showed that young children also over-extended the meanings of words in comprehension as well as production. They found that many words that were over-extended in production by a group of 21- to 27-month-old children were over-extended. However, not all words over-extended in production were over-extended in comprehension. Most children chose the appropriate adult referent for about half the words they over-extended in comprehension. Clark and Clark (1977) hypothesised that these data suggest that over-extensions develop in two stages. In the earliest stage, the child focuses upon an attribute, usually perceptual, and then uses the new word to refer to that attribute. However, with more exposure they realise that the word has a more specific meaning, but they do not know the other words that would enable them to be more precise. In this later stage then they use the over-extended word rather as shorthand for "like it". Hence the child might know that there is more to being a ball than being round, yet when confronted with an object like the moon, not having the word "moon" call it "ball" meaning "the-thing-with-the-same-shape-as-a-ball".

There is some controversy surrounding these findings. Fremgen and Fay (1980) argued that the results of Thomson and Chapman (1977) were an experimental artefact in that the children were repeatedly tested on the same words and this might have led to the children changing their response either out of boredom or to please the experimenter. When Fremgen and Fay tested children only once on each word, they failed to find comprehension overextensions in words over-extended in production. The situation is complex, however, as Chapman and Thomson (1980) showed that in their original sample there was no evidence of an increase in the number of over-extensions across trials, which would have been expected if Fremgen and Fay's hypothesis was correct. Behrind (1988) also found over-extensions in comprehension in children as young as 13 months.

Children understand the words they cannot produce; hence the general argument is that over-extensions are performance errors. An alternative viewpoint was proposed by Mervis and Canada (1983), who argued that at least some comprehension errors are competence errors. That is, the basic-level categories of children and adults are different: the category structures of children are different.

The related concept of *under-extensions* is that of when words are used more specifically than their meaning—such as using the word "round" to refer only to balls. The number of under-extensions might be dramatically under-recorded, because usually the construction will appear to be true. For example, if a child points at the moon and says "round", this utterance is clearly correct, even if the child thinks that this is the name of the moon.

Theoretical accounts of over- and under-extensions. Three types of theory have been proposed to account for these data. They correspond to approaches to adult lexical semantics. They are the semantic feature hypothesis, the functional core hypothesis, and the prototype hypothesis. They all share the framework that over-generalisations can be thought of as occurring because of a lexical representation that is incomplete with that of the adult, whereas under-extensions occur because the developing representation is more specific than that of the adult.

The *semantic feature hypothesis* (E. Clark, 1973) is based upon a decompositional theory of lexical semantics. As we have seen in Chapter 6, this approach states that the meaning of a word can be specified in terms of a set of semantic features. Over- and under-extensions occur as a result of a mismatch between the features of the word as used by the child compared with the complete adult representation. The child samples from the features, primarily on perceptual grounds. Over-extensions occur when the set of features is incomplete; under-extensions occur when additional spurious features are developed (such as the meaning of "round" including something like [+ silvery white and in the sky]). Semantic development consists primarily of acquiring new features and reducing the mismatch by restructuring the lexical representations until the features used by the adult and child converge. The features are acquired in an order from most to least general.

At first sight this theory looks very plausible. However, problems with this approach are discussed by Atkinson (1982) and Barrett (1978). Any theory of lexical development based upon a semantic feature theory of meaning will inherit the same problems as the original theory. As we have seen in Chapter 6, there are serious problems with the semantic feature theory. In particular, we must be able to point to plausible, simple features in all domains, and this is not always easy, even for the kind of concrete objects and actions that young children talk about. Atkinson (1982) in particular pointed to the central problem that the features proposed to account for the data are ad hoc. Also, on the one hand the developmental theory cannot easily be related to any plausible general semantic theory; and neither on the other hand can it be related to an independent theory of perceptual development.

Nelson (1974, 1979) attempted to relate over-extensions to other data, particularly the nature of the earliest words. The *functional core hypothesis* is an attempt to link and explain these data. Generalisation is not restricted to perceptual similarity; functional features are also stressed. In many other respects this is similar to the featural account.

The *prototype hypothesis* (Bowerman, 1978) states that lexical development consists of acquiring a prototype that corresponds to the adult version. Although Atkinson (1982) argued that the main drawback of this approach is the theoretically under-specified notion of a prototype, we have seen that this is now emerging as the most promising account of semantic representation. Therefore any account of over-extensions that attempts to relate them to this theory must be taken very seriously. There is also a substantial body of evidence in its favour. For example, Richards (1979) pointed out that children learn basic level terms first. Over-extensions may probably be explained better in terms of concept development and basic category use. Kay and Anglin (1982) found prototypicality effects in over- and under-extensions. The more prototypical of a category was the referent, the more likely it is that the conceptual prototype name would be extended to include the referent. Words are less likely to be extended for more peripheral category members. This suggests that the concepts are not fully developed but clustered around just a few prototypical exemplars.

In summary, the strengths and weaknesses of these developmental theories are the same as those of the corresponding adult theories. Therefore it is not surprising that a theory that relates over-extensions to the developing semantic prototypes is currently the most promising.

New approaches to semantic development. How then do prototypes develop? Barrett (1978) argued that the key features in learning the meaning of a word are those that maximally contrast it from related words. For example, the denotation of "dog" is learnt by learning the contrast between dogs and similar animals (such as cats) rather than simply learning the prototypical features of dogs. In the revised version of this model (Barrett, 1982), although contrasts are still important, they are not what are acquired first. Instead words are initially mapped onto prototypical representations; the most salient prototypical features are used to group the word with words sharing similar features, and contrastive features are then used to distinguish between semantically similar words.

This *contrastive hypothesis* has become particularly influential over the last few years. (See Clark, 1987, for a recent exposition.) However, there are some problems that remain to be solved. When new words are acquired, because features are contrasted with existing features, the meaning should not overlap with that of existing words: it should find a gap, as it were. Gathercole (1987) however has pointed out that this is not always the case. If anything, contrast appears to be used later rather than earlier as an organising principle of semantic development. Neither is it likely to be the only principle driving semantic development. There comes a point when it is no longer useful for semantic development to make a contrast (for example, between black cats and white cats), and the contrastive hypothesis says nothing about this.

Evaluation of work on early semantic development
It is unlikely that only one principle is operating in semantic development. On the one hand, children have to learn appropriate contrasts between words and objects, but they must not learn inappropriate or too many contrasts. The idea of the developing prototype is currently the most useful account of semantic development and errors in development, but a great deal of work remains to be done. As this is just the sort of domain where the learning of regularities and the relationship between many complex inputs and outputs is important, we might expect connectionism to make a useful contribution here. However as yet there has been no research on this topic. One obvious problem is that it is most unclear how to model the input to semantic development. How should the salient perceptual and functional attributes of objects and actions be encoded? Finally, we should not underestimate the importance of the social setting of language development.

The later development of meaning
Children stop over-extending at around the age of 2½ years. At this point they start asking questions such as "What's the name of that?", and vocabulary develops quickly from then on. From this point, a good

guide to the order of acquisition of words is the semantic complexity of the semantic domain under consideration. Words with simpler semantic representations are acquired first. For example, the order of acquisition of dimensional terms used to describe size matches their relative semantic complexity, and are acquired in the sequence in (3).

3. big – small
    tall – short, long – short
    high – low
    thick – thin
    wide – narrow, deep – shallow

"Big" and "small" are the most general of these terms, and these are acquired first. "Wide" and "narrow" are the most specific terms, and are also used to refer to the secondary dimension of size, and hence these are late-acquired. The other terms are intermediate in complexity and are acquired in between; it is also possible to account for the order of their acquisition in terms of their semantic complexity (Bierwisch, 1970; Clark & Clark, 1977; Wales & Campbell, 1970).

Does comprehension always precede production?

Comprehension usually precedes production. Quite often contextual cues are strong enough for the child to get the gist of an utterance without perhaps being able to understand the details. In such cases there is no question of the child being able to produce language immediately after being first exposed to a particular word or structure. Furthermore, as we have seen, even when a child starts producing a word or structure, it might not be produced in the same way as an adult would use it (e.g. over-extensions). There is more to development than a simple lag, however. The order of comprehension and production is not always preserved: words that are comprehended first are not always produced first (Clark & Hecht, 1983). Early comprehension and production vocabularies may differ quite markedly (Benedict, 1979). There are even cases of words being produced before there is any comprehension for their meaning (Leonard, Newhoff, & Fey, 1980).

The development of negatives.   However, studies of different types of negatives confirm that children are generally aware of semantic distinctions and the different senses of different constructions before they are able to produce them all. Bloom (1970) noted that children at the two-word stage used the word "no" in three different senses. These senses later became differentiated in the same developmental sequence, and became marked by their own constructions. First, the negative as rejection became marked by the use of "don't". Non-existence then became marked by replacing constructions such as "no lights" with "no more lights". Finally denial becomes marked by the use of the word "not". McShane (1980) confirmed this pattern, adding two additional senses of "no": to comment on a failed action, and also as a contradiction in conversation.

EARLY SYNTACTIC DEVELOPMENT

In the previous chapter we looked at what motivates the child to learn grammar. In this section we will describe how syntax develops. As we have seen a stage of single word speech (sometimes called *holophrastic speech*) precedes a stage of two-word utterances. Following this, early speech is *telegraphic*, in that grammatical morphemes may be omitted (a phenomenon reminiscent of agrammatism). We can broadly distinguish between *continuous theories*, whereby children are thought to have knowledge of grammatical categories from the very earliest stages (e.g. Bloom, 1994; Brown & Bellugi, 1964; Menyuk, 1969; Pinker, 1984), and *discontinuous theories*, whereby early multi-word utterances are not governed by adult-like rules (Bowerman, 1973; Braine, 1963; Maratsos, 1983). For the continuous theories, the child's task is to attach particular words to innate grammatical categories, and hence bootstrap their way into grammar (Bloom, 1994; Pinker, 1984). Superimposed on this is the extent to which the theory emphasises the semantic richness of the early utterances. For all approaches an important question is how do children discover the syntactic categories to which words belong?

Two-word grammars
Soon after the vocabulary explosion, the first two word utterances appear. There is a gradation between one word and two word utterances in the form of two single words juxtaposed (Bloom, 1973). Children remain in the two-word phase for some time.

Early research focused upon uncovering the grammar that underlies early language. It was hoped that detailed longitudinal studies of a few children would reveal the way in which adult grammar was acquired. Early multi-word speech is commonly said to be *telegraphic* in that it consists primarily of content words, with many of the function words absent (Brown & Fraser, 1963; Brown & Bellugi, 1964). It would be a mistake to characterise telegraphic speech as consisting only of content words, as can be seen from the following discussion of pivot grammar. Braine (1963) studied three children from when they started to form two-word utterances (at about the age of 20 months). He identified a small number of what he called *pivot words*. These were words which were used frequently and always occurred in the same fixed position in every sentence. Pivot words were not used alone and not found in conjunction with other pivot words. Most pivot words (called P_1 words) were to be found in the initial position, although a smaller group (the P_2 words) were to be found in the second position. There was a larger group of what Braine called *open words* which were used less frequently and which varied in the position in which they were used, but were usually placed second. This idea that sentences are formed from a small number of pivot words is called *pivot grammar*. Hence most two-word sentences were of the form (P_1 + open) words (e.g. "pretty boat", "pretty fan", "other milk", "other bread") with a smaller number of (open + P_2) forms (e.g. "push it"). Some (open + open) constructions (e.g. "milk cup"), and some utterances consisting only of open words, are also to be found.

Brown (1973) took a similar longitudinal approach with three children named "Adam", "Eve", and "Sarah". Samples of their speech were recorded over a period of years from when they started to speak until the production of complex multi-word utterances. Brown observed that the children appeared to be using different rules to adults, but rules nevertheless. This idea that children learn rules but apply them inappropriately is an important concept. They produced utterances such as "more nut", "a hands", and "two sock". Brown proposed a grammar similar to pivot grammar, whereby noun phrases were to be rewritten according to the rule NP→ (modifier + noun). The category of "modifier" did not correspond to any single adult syntactic category, containing articles, numbers, and some (demonstrative) adjectives and (possessive) nouns. As the children grew older, however, these distinctions emerged, and the grammar became more complex.

Problems with the early grammar approaches.   Bowerman   (1973) pointed to a number of problems in these early studies. She reviewed language development across a number of cultures, particularly English and Finnish. She concluded that the rules of pivot grammar were far from universal. Indeed, they did not fully capture the speech of American children. She confirmed that young children use a small number of words in relatively fixed positions, but not the other properties ascribed to pivot words. On closer analysis she found that the open class was not undifferentiated, using instead a number of classes. Harris and Coltheart (1986) pointed out that the children in the Bowerman study might have been linguistically more advanced, with the obvious consequence of the likelihood of increased syntactic differentiation.

Bloom (1970) pointed out that in emphasising the syntactic structure of these simple utterances, these early grammatical approaches failed to capture their semantic richness. The movement towards placing more emphasis on the context and content of children's utterances, rather than just upon their form, became known as *rich interpretation*. Hence it became apparent that two-word utterances with the same form could be used in different ways. In one famous example Bloom noted that the utterance "mommy sock" by a child called Kathryn was used on one occasion to refer to the mother's sock, and on another to refer to the action of the child having her sock put on by the mother. Bloom argued that it was essential to observe the detailed context of each utterance.

The rich interpretation methodology has its own problems. In particular, the observation of an appropriate context and the attribution of the intended meaning of a child's utterance to a particular utterance in that context is a subjective judgement by the observer. It is difficult to be certain, for example, that the child really did have two different meanings in mind for the "mommy sock" utterance above.

In summary, it is difficult to uncover a simple grammar for early development that is based on syntactic factors alone. An additional problem is that the order of words in early utterances is not always consistent.

Semantic approaches to early syntactic development

The apparent failure of pure syntactic approaches to early development, and the emerging emphasis on the semantic richness of early utterances, led to an emphasis upon semantic accounts of early grammars, often in terms aligned to Fillmore's (1968) notion of case grammar (see Chapters 5 and 7). Examples of grammars based on this include Schlesinger (1971), and Slobin (1970). Aspects of Brown's (1973) grammar were also derived from this: for instance, he observed that 75% of two-word utterances could be described in terms of only 11 semantic relations (see Table 11.2 for examples).

Evaluation of semantic approaches.   There is some appeal to this approach in the way in which it de-emphasises syntax and innate structures, and emphasises mechanisms such as bootstrapping, but it has its problems. First, as with case grammar, there is a lack of agreement upon the necessary semantic categories. Second, it is unclear whether children are conceptually able to make these distinctions. Third, this approach does not give any account of the other 25% of Brown's observed utterances. Fourth, the order of acquisition and the emergence of rules differs across children. Finally, Braine (1976) argued

TABLE 11.2
Eleven important early semantic relations and examples
(from Brown, 1973)

Attributive	"big house"
Agent – Action	"Daddy hit"
Action – Object	"hit ball"
Agent – Object	"Daddy ball"
Nominative	"that ball"
Demonstrative	"there ball"
Recurrence	"more ball"
Non-existence	"all-gone ball"
Possessive	"Daddy chair"
Entity + Locative	"book table"
Action + Locative	"go store"

that this approach was too general: the evidence is best described by children learning rules about specific words rather than general semantic categories. For example, when children learn the word "more", is this a case of learning that word "more" specifically combines with entities, or is it more generally the case that they understand that it represents the idea of "recurrence plus entities"? If the latter is the case then when children learn the word "more" they should be able to use other available recurrence terms (e.g. "another") freely in similar ways; however, they do not. Hence the child appears to be learning specific instances rather than just semantic categories. Braine gives the example of a child who learnt to use "other" mostly only with nouns denoting food and clothing. Braine concluded that children use a combination of general and specific rules.

The formation of syntactic categories

As we saw in Chapter 5, one of the most basic requirements of parsing and understanding language is that words are identified as belonging to major syntactic categories such as nouns, verbs, and adjectives. How do children learn these categories and which words belong to them? One view is that the primary basis is innate (Pinker, 1984). In some ways this is rather a negative hypothesis; it is difficult to prove, and a major piece of supporting evidence is the negative finding of being unable to account for the emergence of these categories in any other way.

On the *constructivist-semantic* or *meaning-first* view, grammatical classes are first constructed on a semantic basis (e.g. Gleitman, 1981, Macnamara, 1982). A gross distinction is that nouns correspond to objects, adjectives to attributes, and verbs to actions. But the true picture is much more complex than this. So one of the major failings of a semantic approach to early grammar is that semantics alone cannot provide a direct basis for syntax. It is possible, however, that early semantic categories could underlie syntactic categories (McShane, 1991). For example, as we have just noted many early-acquired nouns denote objects. But this is obviously not true of many nouns (e.g. "sleep", "truth", "time", "love", "happiness") used to refer to salient abstract concepts. It has nevertheless been proposed that the category of "noun" emerges based upon a semantic category of objecthood (Gentner, 1982; Slobin, 1981). Bates and MacWhinney (1982) proposed that abstract nouns later become assimilated to the category because the words behave in the same way as do the more prototypical nouns; for example, they occupy the same sorts of positions in sentences.

Verbs are more difficult to account for in this way. Although a prototypical verb might be an action, a large number of important early verbs do not refer to actions (e.g. "love", "think", "want", "need", "see"). Many early verbs refer to states. However, many adjectives describe states (e.g. "hungry", "nice"). Hence if the early syntactic prototype for verbs is based upon the semantic notions of actions and states, one might occasionally expect errors where adjectives get used as verbs (e.g. "I hungries"). However such constructional errors are never found (McShane, 1991). Therefore it seems unlikely that children are inducing the early verb prototype from a pure semantic notion. Instead, Maratsos (1982) proposed that early syntactic categories are formed on the basis of shared grammatical properties. For example, in English nouns can occupy first positions in declarative sentences. Once one category has been formed bootstrapping facilitates the acquisition of subsequent ones: adjectives come before and modify or specify nouns, verbs come between nouns, and so on. Maratsos also proposed that the types of modifications that words can undergo are pointers to syntactic categories. For example, if a word can be modified by adding "-ed" and "-ing" to the end, then it must be a verb. But inflectional systems are complex and contain many irregularities.

Although it would be premature to reject the notion that syntactic categories develop as prototypes based on semantic information, another view is now emerging (Bloom, 1994; Levy & Schlesinger, 1988). More recent work emphasises how children can acquire syntactic categories from a very early age with very little or no semantic information. This approach exemplifies how children might view language as a rule-governed "puzzle" which has to be solved. Children as young as two easily acquire gender inflections in languages such as Hebrew, even though these syntactic constructions have very little semantic basis and contribute little to the meaning of the message (Levy, 1983, 1988). Gender may play an important role in marking word boundaries, and may be particularly prominent to children if they are viewing language as a "puzzle". Children acquiring Hebrew attend to syntactic regularities before they attend to semantic regularities (Levy, 1988). Syntactic cues are far more effective than semantic cues for acquiring the distinction between count nouns (which can represent objects, such as "broomstick") and mass nouns (which represent substances or classes of things, such as "water" or "furniture"). It is possible to say "a broomstick", but not "a water"; similarly we can say "much water" but not "much broomstick". We can pluralise count nouns ("broomsticks" is acceptable) but not mass nouns ("waters" is not acceptable). Children seem to acquire the distinction not by noting that count and mass nouns can correspond to objects versus substances, but by making use of these syntactic cues (Gathercole, 1985, Gordon, 1985). Children do not miscategorise nouns whose semantic properties are inappropriate, but instead make use of the syntactic information.

This new approach to acquiring syntactic categories claims that children perform a *distributional analysis* on the input data (Gathercole, 1985; Levy & Schlesinger, 1988; Valian, 1986). This means that children essentially search for syntactic regularities without semantic (or innate) information. The very latest work uses connectionist modelling of distributional analysis to show how categories can be acquired on a statistical basis alone (Elman, 1990; Finch & Chater, 1992). This approach shows how syntactic categories can be acquired without explicit knowledge of syntactic rules or semantic information. Instead, all that is necessary is statistical information about how words tend to cluster together. This approach also answers the criticism that a distributional analysis of syntactic categories is beyond children's computational abilities (Pinker, 1984).

Once a few words have been identified as belonging to particular categories, further development is more straightforward. The semantic bootstrapping hypothesis proposes that children make use of mapping between cognition and grammar such as "all names of objects are count nouns" (Pinker, 1984). In this way semantic information is used to determine syntactic categories. The opposing view is that of syntactic bootstrapping (Gleitman, 1990), whereby syntactic information is used to acquire the meaning of some words. The intermediate position is that children use non-syntactic constraints to apply the meanings of a small number of words, and then use semantic bootstrapping, or knowledge of syntax, to determine their grammatical categories. Once a few categories have been acquired in this way, and greater syntactic competence has been achieved, the process is easier. It may then be the case that later on syntactic information might be used to derive semantic information about more abstract words.

Evaluation of work on learning syntactic categories.   In summary, the relationship between the development of syntax and the development of semantics is likely to be a complex one. Early work stressed the importance of semantic information in the acquisition of syntactic categories, but more recent work has shown how these categories can be acquired with little or no semantic information. Children probably learn syntactic categories through a distributional analysis of the language. It is unlikely that we need to postulate innate principles. Connectionist modelling may be very useful in this domain.

Later syntactic development

Brown (1973) suggested that the mean length of utterance (MLU) is a useful way of charting the progress of syntactic development. This is the mean length of an utterance measured in morphemes averaged over many words. Brown divided early development into five stages based upon MLU. Naturally MLU increases as the child gets older; we find an even better correlation with age if single word utterances are omitted from the analysis (Klee & Fitzgerald, 1985). This approach is rather descriptive and there is not much relationship with age from age five on. Nevertheless, it is a convenient and much used measure.

The rule-based nature of linguistic development is clear from the work of Berko (1958). She argued that if children used rules their use should be apparent even with words they had not used before. They should be able to use appropriate word endings even for imaginary words. Berko used nonsense words to name pictures of strange animals and people doing odd actions. For example, she would point to a drawing and say: "This is a wug. This is another one. Now there are two __." The children would fill in the gap with the appropriate plural ending "wugs". In fact, they could use rules to generate possessives ("the bik's hat"), past tenses ("he ricked yesterday"), and number agreement in verbs ("he ricks every day").

The development of order of acquisition of grammatical morphemes is relatively constant across children (James & Khan, 1982). The earliest acquired is the present progressive (e.g. "kissing"), followed by spatial prepositions, plurals, possessive, articles, and the past tense in different forms.

Verb inflections: Acquiring the past tense.   The development of the past tense has come under particular scrutiny. Brown (1973) observed that the youngest children use verbs in uninflected forms. Brown argued what has since been observed by others (and see earlier on comprehension preceding production): that children seem to be aware of the meaning of the different syntactic roles before they could use the inflections. That is, the youngest children use the simplest form to convey all of the syntactic roles (see earlier on rich interpretation). Very quickly however they learn to use the appropriate inflections: past tenses to convey the sense of time (usually marked by adding "-ed"), the use of the "-ing" ending, number modification, and modification by combination with auxiliaries. Although regular verbs can be modified by applying a simple rule (e.g. form the past tense by adding "-ed"), a large number of verbs are irregular.

In the previous chapter we mentioned the time course of development of irregular verbs and nouns, and used this as evidence for the claim that linguistic development is primarily rule-based. We noted that this is an apparent example of U-shaped development: behaviour changes from good performance (here on the past tenses of irregular verbs), to poor performance, before improving again. We observed that in the poor performance phase, children make a large number of over-regularisation errors (e.g. Brown, 1973; Cazden, 1968; Kuczaj, 1977). The traditional view has been that this shows that children learn explicit rules by induction. One problem with this account is that it presupposes that children have the verb category over which to induce in the first place (McShane, 1991). Also regular and irregular forms coexist (Kuczaj, 1977). The proportion of over-regularisations never rose above 46% in 14 children studied by Kuczaj (1977), suggesting that a very general, powerful rule is not induced. Hence McShane concluded that over-regularisations arise as the by-product of the verb-category formation process.

Recent connectionist modelling of this area has generated substantial controversy. Rumelhart and McClelland (1986) simulated the acquisition of the past tense using back-propagation. The input consisted of the root form of the verb, and the output the inflected form. Words were represented as phonemes in the form of Wickelphones (see Chapter 4). The important point here was the training schedule. This was designed to mimic the type of exposure that children have. At first the model was trained on 10 of the highest frequency words, 8 of which happened to be irregular. After 10 training cycles 410 medium-frequency verbs were introduced for another 190 learning trials. Finally 86 low-frequency verbs were introduced. The model behaved as do children: initially it produced the correct output, but then began to over-regularise. Rumelhart and McClelland pointed out that the model behaved in a rule-like way, without explicitly learning or having been taught a rule. Instead, the behaviour emerged as a consequence of the statistical properties of the input. If true, this might be an important general point about language acquisition.

What are the problems with this account? First, the way in which the medium-frequency, largely regular verbs are all introduced in one block on trial 11 is quite unlike what happens to children, where exposure is cumulative and gradual (McShane, 1991). The most substantial criticisms of this work were made by Pinker and Prince (1988; see also Lachter & Bever, 1988). Pinker and Prince argued that Rumelhart and McClelland represented properties local to verbs that are general properties of the language. In particular, irregular verbs are not really totally irregular. It is possible to predict which verbs are likely to be irregular, and the way in which that irregularity will be made manifest. This is because irregular verbs still obey the general phonological constraints of the language. Hence it is possible that irregular forms are derived by general phonological rules. Pinker and Prince also point out that there is no explicit representation for a word in Rumelhart and McClelland's (1986) model. Instead, it is represented as a distributed pattern of activation (see Chapter 3). Pinker and Prince argue that words as explicit units play a vital role in the acquisition process. Finally, Pinker and Prince argued that the simulation's U-shaped development resulted directly from its training schedule. The drop in performance of the model occurred when the number of regular verbs in the training vocabulary was suddenly increased. There is no such discontinuity in the language to which young children are exposed.

Further work, such as that of Plunkett and Marchman (1991, 1993) has addressed some of these problems. They argued that connectionist networks can model the acquisition of verb morphology, but many more factors have to be taken into account. In particular, they proposed that the training set must more realistically reflect what happens with children. Rather than present all the verbs to be learned in one go, or with a sudden discontinuity as in the original Rumelhart and McClelland model, they gradually increased the number of verbs the system must learn, to simulate the gradual increase in children's vocabulary size. They concluded that U-shaped learning can be displayed by a network even when there are no discontinuities in the training. MacWhinney and Leinbach (1991) reached similar conclusions.

One outcome of the modelling work by Rumelhart and McClelland has been to focus attention on the details of how children acquire a skill such as forming the past tense (e.g. Marchman & Bates, 1994; Marcus et al., 1992). As a side effect of this work, we now know much more than we did before.

Cross-linguistic differences.   Languages differ in their syntactic complexity. For example, English is relatively constrained in its use of word order, whereas other languages (such as Russian) are more highly inflected and have freer word order. Not surprisingly, these differences lead to differences in the detail of language acquisition.

What is perhaps surprising is the amount of uniformity in language acquisition across languages. For example, stage 1 speech (covering the period with the first multi-word utterances, up to MLU of 2.0) seems largely uniform across the world (Dale, 1976; Slobin, 1970). There are some differences: young Finnish children do not produce yes/no questions (Bowerman, 1973). This is because Finnish cannot form questions by rising intonation, and relies on an interrogative inflection. Differences emerge in later development. Plural marking is an extremely complex process in Arabic, but relatively simple in English. Hence plural marking is acquired early in English-speaking children, but is not entirely mastered until the teenage years for Arabic-speaking children (see McCarthy & Prince, 1990; Prasada & Pinker, 1993). In complex inflectional languages such as Russian, development generally progresses from the most concrete (e.g. plurals) first to the most abstract later (e.g. gender usually has no systematic semantic basis; see Slobin, 1966b; but see also the work on Hebrew by Levy, 1988, discussed earlier).

The development of syntactic comprehension.   As children grow older it is easier to carry out experiments, and as their communicative competence increases emphasis shifts onto the development of their comprehension strategies. The basic preference of older children is to form sentences with the canonical order of noun-verb-noun corresponding to subject-action-object. However young children are more difficult to carry out suitable experiments upon, and present a more confused picture. They tend to respond yes to every question, to see the self as agent, to treat whatever is nearest to their pushing hand as the agent, and to make animate nouns agents (Bridges, 1980). Not only does this show that experiments are difficult to perform, but also that early comprehension uses a lot of pragmatic strategies. These may vary from child to child.

It is possible to trace the development of the ability to comprehend syntactic constructions such as asking questions and the use of the passive. We have touched upon some of the relevant points in the development of the passive in our discussion of adult syntax. The sorts of difficulties children have with the passive form are exactly those we might expect on that basis. The youngest children have difficulties with passives because, in terms of Bever's (1970) description of surface structure parsing strategies, they are inappropriately applying the standard canonical order strategy and hence erroneously map actor into object and vice versa. Older children (around 3 years old) start to map the roles of passives as adults do, but they make mistakes depending upon the semantic context of the utterance. This is exactly as we would expect on the basis of the Slobin (1966a) experiment on reversible and irreversible passives: children have particular difficulty with reversible passives; that is, when there are no straightforward semantic cues available to assist them. Harris (1978) showed that animacy is an important cue in the development of passives. Animate things tend to get placed earlier in the sentence: hence, in a picture description task, when the object being acted upon was animate (such as a boy being run over by a car), a passive construction tended to be used to put the animate object first ("the boy was run over by the car"). Animacy is obviously an important factor in reversible versus irreversible constructions. The type of verb also matters: young children find passives with action verbs easier than stative verbs such as "remember" (Sudhalter & Braine, 1985).

BILINGUALISM AND SECOND LANGUAGE LEARNING

There is not space here to cover the topics of bilingualism and second language acquisition in detail, but it is important to address briefly the main issues. We have already seen in the previous chapter (Chapter 10) that the idea of a critical period for language development is controversial. The commonly held assumption that it is more difficult for older children and adults to learn another language, given the same amount of exposure in the same way, is not necessarily correct. Important questions still remain: How does second language acquisition differ from first? How do children and adults store the two sets of words in their lexicons? How do the children manage to keep the languages apart? How do they learn to recognise that two distinct languages are involved?

Bilingualism
If a speaker is fluent in two languages, then they are said to be *bilingual*. The commonly held image of a bilingual person is one brought up in such cultures where they are exposed to two languages from birth. It is not necessary for them to be equally fluent, but at least they should be very competent in the second language. (Of course, more rarely some people

are trilingual—or above, multilingual—that is, fluent in three or more languages.) There are some parts of the world where this is quite common (to mention just a few examples: North Wales and Welsh-English; Canada and French-English; and many ethnic minorities within a culture). Weinreich (1953) proposed that there were three types of bilingualism depending on the way in which the two languages are learned. The ideal representation is called *compound bilingualism*. Here the labels in the two different languages are jointly connected to a common concept. This totally integrated arrangement could only arise when equal prominence was given to each language in childhood. In *co-ordinate bilingualism* there are parallel sets of word–concept pairs, and the second language is connected to a new conceptual structure, even though this overlaps with the first. This situation arises when the learning situation for the second language is less ideal. The case where the second language develops so that it is entirely parasitic on the first language is known as *subordinate bilingualism*. The co-ordinate and subordinate types of bilingualism arise when one language is learned before another. However, it is not at all easy to distinguish between these categories in practice, and it is not clear that order of acquisition is quite so fundamental as Weinreich originally considered (Bialystok & Hakuta, 1994). The modern emphasis is on examining the structure of the bilingual lexicon (or lexicons).

Early work reported diary studies such as that of Leopold (1939–1949). Leopold was a German linguist, whose daughter Hildegard had an American mother and lived from an early age in the USA. German was used in the home at first, but this soon gave way to English, the environment language. This shows that the child can quickly (within 6 months) forget the old language and pick up a new one if they move to another country. Initially the two languages are undifferentiated, mixed up, but differentiation emerges (Vihman, 1985). We observe *language mixing* where words combine, such as an English suffix added to a German root, or where English words put into a French syntactic structure, or answering questions in one language with answers in another (Redlinger & Park, 1980; Swain & Wesche, 1975). *Code switching* (sometimes called language switching) is the name of the tendency of bilinguals when speaking to other bilinguals to switch from one language to another, often to more appropriate words or phrases. This processes is highly variable between individuals, and there is no obvious processing cost attached (see Nishimura, 1986).

How many lexicons are there in a bilingual speaker? Is there a separate store for each language, or just one common store? The evidence is complex, but suggests that a mixture of common and separate stores is used in individuals (Taylor & Taylor, 1990). For example, concrete words, cognates (words in different languages that have the same root and meaning and which look similar), and culturally similar words act as though they are stored in common; abstract and other words act as though they are in separate stores. The amount of repetition priming is much greater and longer-lasting within than between languages (Kirsner, Smith, Lockhart, King, & Jain, 1984). In separate store models, the two languages connected via an underlying amodal conceptual system that is hypothesised to be the same interface as that which interfaces between language and pictures (Potter, So, von Eckardt, & Feldman, 1984; see also Schwanenflugel & Rey, 1986). Steering between these two extremes, Grosjean and Soares (1986) argued that the language system is flexible in a bilingual speaker and that its behaviour depends upon the circumstances. In unilingual mode, when the input and output are limited to only one of the available languages, and perhaps when the other speakers involved are unilingual in that language, interaction between the language systems is kept to a minimum; the bilingual tries to switch off the second language. In the bilingual mode, both language systems are active and interact. How speakers have strategic control over their language systems is a topic that largely remains to be explored.

Finally, it appears that bilingual children suffer no obvious disadvantages from learning two languages simultaneously (Snow, 1993). There might be some initial delay in learning vocabulary items in one language, but this delay is soon made up, and of course the total, bilingual vocabulary of the children is much greater. Indeed, bilingual children show an advantage in acquiring and using metalinguistic skills (such as knowing that a word is an arbitrary name for something) over monolingual children (Hakuta & Diaz, 1985).

Second language acquisition

If a child or adult has already become competent at a language and then attempts to learn another, we speak of second language acquisition. A number of methods have been used to teach a second language. The traditional method is based on translation from one to another, with lectures in grammar in the primary language. *Direct* methods (such as the Berlitz method) on the other hand carry out all teaching in the second language (L2), with emphasis on conversational skills. The *audiolingual* method emphasises speaking and listening before reading and writing. The *immersion* method teaches a group of learners exclusively through the medium of the foreign language. Perhaps the most natural method of learning a new language is *submersion*, where the learner is surrounded exclusively by speakers of L2, usually in the foreign country.

Krashen (1982) proposed five important hypotheses concerning language acquisition which together form the *monitor model* of second language learning. Central to his approach is a distinction between *language learning* (which is what traditional methods emphasise) and *language acquisition* (which is more akin to what children do naturally). Learning emphasises explicit knowledge of grammatical rules, whereas acquisition emphasises their unconscious use. Although learning has its role, to be more successful second language acquisition should place more emphasis on acquisition. The first of the five hypotheses is the *acquisition and learning distinction hypothesis*. Children acquire their first language largely unconsciously and automatically. Earlier views that stressed the importance of the critical period maintained that adults could only learn a second language. Krashen argued that adults can indeed acquire the second language, at least in part. (This claim is supported by observing that hearing-impaired adults can learn sign language.) The second hypothesis is the *natural order in acquisition hypothesis*. The order of acquisition of syntactic rules, and the types of errors of generalisation made, are the same in both languages.

The third and fourth hypotheses are central to Krashen's whole approach. The third is the *monitor hypothesis*. It states that the acquisition processes create sentences in the second language, but learning enables the development of a monitoring process to check and edit this output, but only if there is sufficient time in the interaction. (Hence it is difficult to employ the monitor in spontaneous conversation.) The monitor uses knowledge of the rules rather than the rules themselves. (This is reminiscent of Chomsky's competence–performance distinction). The fourth is the *comprehensible input hypothesis*. In order to move from one stage to the next, given the natural order hypothesis, the acquirer must understand the meaning and the form input from the next highest stage. This hypothesis stresses the role of comprehension. There are two sub-hypotheses. First, production does not need to be taught: it emerges itself in time, given understanding. Second, the input at the next highest level need not contain only information from that level. Finally, the fifth is the *active filter hypothesis*. Attitude and emotional factors are very important in second language acquisition and account for a lot of the apparent difference in the facility in which adults and children can learn a second language.

Krashen's approach provides a useful framework, and being one of the earliest models has proved one of the most influential. However, to date there has been surprisingly little experimental evidence to support all the assumptions, and many of his claims are now considered questionable (see McLaughlin, 1987).

Making second language acquisition easier. Second language is often characterised by a phase or phases of *silent periods* when few productions are offered despite obvious development of comprehension. Classroom teaching methods that force students to speak in these silent periods might be doing more harm than good. Newmark (1966) argued that this has the effect of forcing the speaker back onto the rules of the first language. Hence silent periods should be respected.

Krashen's idea central idea is to make second language acquisition more like first by providing *comprehensible input*. The immersion method, involving complete exposure to L2, exemplifies these ideas. Whole schools in Montreal, Canada contain English-speaking children who are taught in French in all subjects from first year (Bruck, Lambert, & Tucker, 1976). Immersion seems to have no deleterious effects, and is if anything beneficial beyond bilingualism (e.g. mathematics). The French acquired is very good but not perfect: there is a slight accent, and syntactic errors are sometimes made (see Chapter 10 on the critical period).

Sharpe (1992) identified what he called the "four Cs" of successful modern language teaching. These are *communication* (the main purpose of learning a language is aural communication, and successful teaching emphasises this); *culture* (which means learning about the culture of the speakers of the language and de-emphasising direct translation); *context* (which is similar to providing comprehensible input); and giving the learners *confidence*. These points may seem obvious, but they are often neglected in traditional, grammar-based methods of teaching foreign languages.

Finally, some particular methods of learning second languages are of course better than others. Ellis and Beaton (1993) reviewed what facilitates learning foreign language vocabulary. They concluded that simple rote repetition is best for learning to produce the new words, but that using keywords is best for comprehension. Naturally learners want to be able to do both, so a combination of techniques is the optimum strategy.

CONCLUDING SUMMARY

Language acquisition can be seen both as a process of hypothesis testing and learning statistical regularities. We have examined semantic, syntactic, and phonological development. In each case learning appears to be constrained, but there is considerable disagreement upon how these constraints should be specified. Related to this issue is that of the extent to which language acquisition depends upon innate language-specific principles. For example, it is not clear whether the way in which young children relate words to features of the world is constrained by specific innate limitations on the types of hypotheses which can be generated, or on more general principles such as "attach words to whole objects in the first instance", or some combination of these. Certainly, children seem to make use of constraints in attaching words to objects and events, even if the origin of these constraints is debatable. Examination of the "errors" children make in using their first words, particularly over-extensions, has been fruitful. It seems likely that these are best accounted for in terms of the developing prototype underlying word meaning with some principle of contrast. It is important to remember the role of social and pragmatic factors in development and how joint attention can help establish the referents of new words.

We have also traced the time course of language acquisition. After babbling, development progresses through a one-word stage, a two-word utterance stage, to sentences of increasing length and grammatical complexity. Early speech is telegraphic in that grammatical elements are often omitted. When these emerge, they do so gradually in an order that is largely constant within in a language. We have looked at attempts to derive early grammars based on both purely syntactic and also on semantic considerations. The relationship between the development of syntax and semantics is likely to be complex, but it seems that the ability of young children to learn syntactic categories by a distributional analysis has been previously underestimated.

Among the features of later syntactic development, the development of the morphology of the past tense of verbs has come in for particular scrutiny. Connectionist modelling has been particularly influential but controversial in this area.

We have also looked briefly at bilingualism at second language acquisition. Contrary to popular belief, it is not necessarily harder to learn a second language. Normally the conditions are such that it is much more difficult learning the second language than the first. Unlike infants, adults and older children do not usually have prolonged exposure to the new language without having to respond until they are ready, and the learning situation is much more stressful. Traditional learning methods do not stress the role of comprehensible input. Methods which do this such as the immersion method are much more successful. There are a number of ways in which second language acquisition in adults could be facilitated.

FURTHER READING

Naturally this chapter can only provide a sketch of language development and an indication of the main issues. There are many texts that describe language development in far more detail than can be attempted in a single chapter. Some recent examples include Owens (1988) for an introductory approach, and Fletcher and Garman (1986) for a more advanced set of readings. Fletcher and MacWhinney (1995) is a set of advanced surveys of the complete area of child language analogous to that of Gernsbacher (1994) on general psycholinguistics. Bloom (1994) reviewed current controversial issues in the area. Atkinson (1982) provides a theoretical analysis of a number of aspects of acquisition, particularly on semantic development. A comprehensive and up-to-date collection of review readings in the major areas of language acquisition is provided by L. Bloom (1993). A survey of cognitive and linguistic development, with emphasis on how these processes arise from infancy, is provided by the book by P. Bloom (1993). Gerken (1994) reviews phonological development. Markman (1989) covers the development of categorisation and word meaning in depth. Merriman (1986) provides a critical review of theories of early semantic development. Clark (1993) describes her most recent work on lexical development. See Dale (1976) and Slobin (1982) for more on cross-linguistic comparisons of language development.

Similarly there are many reference works on bilingualism and second language acquisition. See Snow (1993) for an introductory one chapter overview. Recent examples of more detailed reviews include Kilborn (1994) and Klein (1986). Books covering the area in greater depth include Bialystok and Hakuta (1994), Harris (1992), Romaine (1995), Schreuder and Weltens (1993), and Schwanenflugel (1991).

See also the further reading at the end of the previous chapter.

CHAPTER TWELVE

New directions

INTRODUCTION

This chapter is rather different from the others in that it is not organised around any one component of the language system or its acquisition. In this chapter, I will try to summarise the present status of the psychology of language, and indicate where it is likely to go in the future. We will look again at the themes raised in the first chapter.

By now I hope that you have been convinced that psycholinguists have made great progress in understanding the processes involved in human language. In this book we have traced language processes from the lower levels to the higher. We started with the lowest level, speech and visual word recognition, and worked through parsing to the higher cognitive levels of comprehension. We looked at processes which involve the extraction and representation of meaning and intention. We then examined speech production, which involves the flow of information in the reverse order: from meaning to sound. Each of the early chapters more or less corresponds to a putative psycholinguistic processing module. Although usefully pedagogically, this description bears little resemblance to the history of psycholinguistics. This has been, unsurprisingly, much more haphazard. If we place the real birth of modern psycholinguistics sometime around Chomsky's (1957) review of Skinner's *Verbal behavior*, its infancy would correspond to the period in the early and mid-1960s attempting to relate language processing to transformational grammar. Since then, it has achieved independence and flourished on all fronts. Furthermore, I hope that I have convinced you that the cognitive approach to psycholinguistics has taught us a very great deal indeed. Nevertheless, it is doubtful whether we would say that psycholinguistics has passed adolescence. Many questions remain, and indeed, in some respects, the more we learn the more questions are raised.

Let us now return to the main themes which were outlined in Chapter 1. Then we will look at some possible developments in the near future of psycholinguistics.

THEMES: A REPRISE

Five main themes were raised in the introduction. These were an emphasis on uncovering the actual processes involved, the relationship of apparently different language processes to one another, the issue of modularity, the sensitivity of our results to the particular experimental techniques employed, and the application of the findings of psycholinguistics to real world problems.

First, as we have seen, modern psycholinguistics is founded upon data. Careful experiments have clearly told us a great deal about the processes involved in language. However, as in all science, there are two main ways of doing things. We can call these the *bottom-up* and the *top-down* approaches to science. In the bottom-up mode, psycholinguists are driven by experimental results. Perhaps there is a novel finding, or a prediction from a theory that does not come out as predicted. A model is then constructed to account for these findings. Alternatively, a theory might be bolstered by having its predictions verified. Either way, experimental results drive theoretical advances. (This approach includes data from single case studies, as well as naturalistic data such as speech errors and hesitation analysis.) A top-down approach does not necessarily worry too much about the data in the first instance, but instead tries to develop a theoretical framework which can then be used to make sense of the data. Predictions are then derived from formalisations of these frameworks and then tested. We might compare these approaches with experimental and theoretical physics. In the past examples of top-down approaches have included linguistics and symbolic AI. Currently the most influential top-down approach is connectionism. Of course these modes of thought are not exclusive.

Second, we have tried where possible to relate language processes to each other. This was emphasised particularly in Chapter 9. However, a great deal remains to be done on this.

Third, a recurring theme of this book has been the distinction between modular and interactive models. In modular models, the boxes of the diagrams used to represent the structure of language systems carry out their computations independently of the others, and other boxes only get access to the final output. Put rather crudely, interactive models allow boxes to fiddle around with the contents of other boxes while they are still processing, or are allowed to start processing on the basis of early or preliminary outputs rather than having to wait for the final thing. This issue has recurred through every chapter on adult psycholinguistics: spoken and visual word recognition, parsing, lexicalisation, and syntactic planning in speech production. The picture is not yet totally clear, but whereas in the not-too-distant past interactive models were in favour, the trend is definitely now to recognising that a great deal of language processing is modular. We also noted in the introduction that researchers become perhaps unduly emotive about this topic. The alternative approach is to dispense with broad, general considerations, and focus upon the details of what happens. For example, Altmann (1989b) suggested that rather than focusing upon broad issues such as interaction and autonomy in parsing, it is preferable to concentrate on what information is used and when.

Fourth, we have seen that our results are on occasion very sensitive to the particular techniques we employ. This means that in addition to having a theory about the principal object of study, we need to have a theory about the tools themselves. Perhaps this is most clearly exemplified by the debate about lexical decision and naming and whether they measure the same stages of lexical access.

Finally, psycholinguistics should address many practical issues. We can discern five key applications. First, we now know a great deal about reading, and this can be applied to improving methods of teaching reading (Chapters 3 and 4). Second, these techniques should also be of use in helping children with language disabilities; for example, the study of developmental dyslexia has aroused much interest (Chapters 4 and 10). Third, psycholinguistics helps us to improve the way in which the acquisition of foreign languages can be improved in children and adults (Chapters 10 and 11). Fourth, we have greatly increased our understanding of how language can be disrupted by brain damage (Chapters 2, 4, 6, and 8). This has had consequences for the treatment and rehabilitation of brain-damaged patients (e.g. see Howard & Hatfield, 1987). Fifth, there are obvious advantages if we could develop computers that can understand and produce language. This is a complex task, but an examination of how humans perform these tasks has been revealing. Generally, computers are better at lower level tasks such as word recognition. Higher level, integrative processes involve a great deal of context (Chapters 6 and 7), and this has proved a major stumbling block for work in the area.

In addition to these five themes, we noted in Chapter 1 that modern psycholinguistics is eclectic. In particular, we have made use of data from cognitive neuropsychology and techniques of connectionist modelling. Both have greatly enhanced our understanding of normal processing, and both are likely to remain influential for some time to come.

Cognitive neuropsychology

We have seen that the study of impairments to the language system has cast light on virtually every aspect of psycholinguistics. For example, it is has provided a major motivation for the dual-route model of reading (Chapter 4); it has enhanced our understanding of the development of reading and spelling (Chapter 4); it has provided interesting if complex data that any theory of semantics must explain (Chapter 6); it has bolstered the two-stage model of lexicalisation (Chapter 8); and it has been revealing about the nature of syntactic planning and parsing (Chapter 8).

It is sometimes thought that cognitive neuropsychology has been more influential in Britain than elsewhere (particularly the United States). For example, group studies are still frequently reported overseas, but they have almost completely been replaced by single case studies in British studies. Even if this geographical localisation is the case, it does not undermine its true value. There are also many notable exceptions, such as the pioneering work of Caramazza and colleagues on the methodology of cognitive neuropsychology (see Chapter 8). Finally, there are signs that this approach is becoming widespread elsewhere (see, for example, the work discussed in Chapter 8 of Martin & Saffran, 1992; Martin et al., 1994; and Saffran et al., 1980).

Connectionism

Connectionism has revolutionised psycholinguistics over approximately the last ten years. What are its virtues that have made it so attractive? First, as we have seen, unlike traditional AI, it has neural plausibility. It is based on a metaphor of the brain, in that processing takes place in lots of simple, massively interconnected neuron-like units. It is important not to get too carried away with this metaphor, but at least we have the feeling that we are starting off with the right sort of models. Second, just like traditional AI, connectionism has the virtue that modelling forces us to be totally explicit about our theories. This has had two major consequences. First, recall that many psycholinguistic models are specified as *box and arrow* diagrams (see for examples Figs. 3.3 and

9.1). This approach is sometimes called, rather derogatorily, *boxology*. It is certainly not unique to psycholinguistics, and such an approach is not as bad as is sometimes hinted. It at least gives rise to an understanding of the architecture of the language system—what the "boxes" of the language system are, and how they are related to others. However, connectionism has meant that we have had to focus on the processes that take place inside the boxes of our models. In some cases (such as the acquisition of past tense), this has led to a detailed re-examination of the evidence. Second, connectionism has forced us to consider in detail the representations used by the language system. This has lead to a healthy debate, even if the first representations used by connectionist modellers turn out later not to be the correct ones. (For example, see Chapter 11 and the debate on using Wickelfeatures as a representation of phonology in the input to the system that learns the past tenses of verbs.) Third, the emphasis on learning in many connectionist models focuses on the developmental aspect that is hopefully leading to an integration of adult and developmental psycholinguistics.

Connectionist neuropsychology. Very recently, one big growth area has been the intersection of connectionism and cognitive neuropsychology in the use of connectionist modelling to simulate neuropsychological disorders. This approach has been called *connectionist neuropsychology.* Models are developed of the intact process, and then the effects of "lesioning" parts of the network are systematically explored. We have seen examples in surface and deep dyslexia (Chapter 4), category-specific disorders (Chapter 6), and aphasia (Chapter 8). The assumptions of connectionist neuropsychology are discussed by Harley (1993b) and Plaut and Shallice (1993a).

SOME GROWTH AREAS

Having looked at where psycholinguistics has come from, where is it going next? There is no particular reason to expect a revolution in the way we examine or understand language. To some extent, the next ten years are likely to see progress in solving the same sorts of problems using the same sorts of techniques. (Hopefully, of course, our models should be more sophisticated, and our experimental techniques more refined.) However, the focus of interest does change: for example, there is not the same interest in evaluating theories of transformational grammar now as there was in the sixties. So here are some possible growth areas in psycholinguistics in the near future. The list is rather arbitrary and perhaps personal, and some of these points have been covered in greater detail in earlier chapters. Nevertheless, this selection gives some flavour of global trends in the subject. Generally, the trend is towards more inclusive models covering more complex phenomena. For example, now our processing of morphologically simple words is relatively well understood, interest is growing in words are morphologically more complex (e.g. Marslen-Wilson et al., 1994; Taft, 1985, 1987).

Language and the brain

There has not been much emphasis on the localisation of language functions in the brain so far in this book. However, new techniques of brain imaging are gradually becoming more accurate and more accessible. A number of techniques for examining the brain's activity have been around for some time. These include EEG (electro-encephalograms) and ERP (event-related potentials), both of which measure the electrical activity of the brain by electrodes on the scalp. However, CAT (computerised axial tomography), MRI ([nuclear] magnetic resonance imaging), and PET (positron emission topography) scans provide more accessible data in the form of easily understandable "pictures of the living brain". These techniques are still prohibitively expensive for most of us, and their temporal and spatial resolution are currently relatively poor. However, this situation is likely to improve.

When this happens, these techniques could potentially tell us a number of things. In particular, they might tell us a great deal about the time course of processes, and when different sources of information are made use of. As such, they might be particularly revealing about issues concerning modularity. Suppose in a brain scan taken during the lexicalisation of a single word we detect both semantic and phonological areas active simultaneously. (This assumes that the system is physically modular to this extent, which seems the case, given the data from aphasia.) This might be evidence for interaction. In effect, we could plot the graphs for the time course of processing directly. The problem in interpretation is that it is hard to be sure exactly what is causing any activity.

This problem means that, for the moment at least, the utility of brain imaging is likely to be restricted to the processing of single items. Suppose we see during sentence processing that the parsing and semantic areas are active at the same time. This could be a result of interaction, or could reflect the parsing of one part of the sentence and the semantic integration of earlier material. It might even reflect the subject parsing a sentence and thinking dimly about what's for tea that night. It might be possible to tease them apart but we will need clever experiments to do this.

Some recent examples of work in monitoring brain activity include evidence from ERP about what happens in the sentence-verification task (Kounios & Holcomb, 1992). They also show that concrete and abstract words are processed differently, supporting dual-code theory (Kounios & Holcomb, 1994), and word frequency and sentence context interact (van Petten & Kutas, 1990). Posner and Carr (1992) review recent work on what such techniques tell us about the anatomical constraints on word recognition. We saw in Chapter 9 that listening to a word does not activate the same areas of the brain which are activated by reading a word aloud and word repetition, as shown by PET brain imaging (Petersen et al., 1989), suggesting that the speech input and output pathways are different. We can also use ERPs to examine the time course of activation when we process ambiguous words (van Petten & Kutas, 1987), hence contributing to our understanding of lexical ambiguity. ERPs can also be used to monitor the flurry of activity that occurs when we detect a trace during parsing (Garnsey et al., 1989; Kluender & Kutas, 1993; see Chapter 5).

One particularly useful observation is that a negative evoked potential found 400 milliseconds after the event (and hence called the N400) is sensitive to semantic processing (Kounios & Holcomb, 1992; Kutas & Hillyard, 1980) and indicative of violations of semantic expectancy (Nigram, Hoffman, & Simons, 1992). This can be used to map out time course of syntactic and semantic processing, and has been used to argue that syntactic processing is autonomous (Neville, Nicol, Barss, Forster, & Garrett, 1991). The use of brain imaging in neuropsychology is obvious, as it enables researchers to identify the lesion site without an autopsy. The outputs of brain scans are being increasingly presented in the case study literature.

In summary, data from brain activity is interesting but very complex and difficult to interpret. At present, the techniques have relatively poor spatial and temporal accuracy. The use of such techniques is also likely to be limited by the extent to which representations are distributed. They will not be able to locate individual words as these will be distributed with others over the same neural substrate.

Connectionism

So far connectionism has focused mainly on low-level processes, such as recognising individual words. It is likely that modellers will turn their attention to processes higher in the chain, such as parsing and syntax (some preliminary work includes Chalmers, 1990; Elman, 1991; McClelland, St. John, & Taraban, 1989; Waltz & Pollack, 1985). As this happens, it is possible that connectionist principles will have to be modified somewhat to take account of the complexities and interactions involved. One possible way in which this might happen is the widespread adoption of what are called hybrid models. These combine connectionist and symbolic modelling techniques (e.g. Hendler, 1989). Finally, there remain many developmental issues to which connectionism, with its emphasis on learning, seems ideally suited.

Cognitive neuropsychology

We have just seen that cognitive neuropsychology is becoming more fashionable in the United States. It is likely that this trend will continue. At present, progress depends upon finding theoretically interesting case studies, and this of course is a matter of time, luck, and hard searching. Time is likely to throw up some interesting phenomena and dissociations. We have also seen that connectionist neuropsychology is a burgeoning area, and this is likely to continue. We still await comprehensive connectionist accounts of many important phenomena such as phonological dyslexia and agrammatism. Another possible development is that of detailed modelling of individual single case studies.

Developmental

We can expect the more widespread use of developmental data to help resolve adult questions. For example, the study of how children learn and represent word meanings might be revealing about adult semantic representation. Altmann (in press) relates parsing mechanisms that cope with ambiguity to an attentional mechanism rooted in early language acquisition. There is also much more scope for connectionist modelling in this area.

Integrative models

Eventually, a full understanding of psycholinguistics would entail an understanding of the nature of all the components of the language processor, and how they are related to each other. We saw in Chapter 9 (Fig. 9.1) how a start has been made on the word recognition system by Ellis and Young (1988), based primarily on neuropsychological data. Indeed, it might turn out that cognitive neuropsychology will have a particularly important role to play in this enterprise. In particular, the relationship between language processes and short-term memory is important. The extent to which short-term memory plays a role in processes as diverse as speech perception, word repetition, parsing, comprehension, and learning to speak and read has already excited much research in both impaired and unimpaired speakers (see

Gathercole & Baddeley, 1990; Howard & Butterworth, 1989; Martin & Breedin, 1992; Martin & Saffran, 1990; Vallar & Baddeley, 1987, 1989; Waters, Caplan, & Hildebrandt, 1991).

The semantic-conceptual interface. One important goal of any integrative theory is to specify how the language system interfaces with other cognitive systems. That is, what is the final output of comprehension and the initial input to production? It is likely these are going to be the same. In Chapter 6 we saw how currently the most likely proposal about the form of the output is a propositional representation associated with the activation of goal and other schemata (see the description of Kintsch's model in that chapter). In Chapter 8, we saw that the conceptualiser that creates the input to the production system has been much neglected. In Chapter 9, we saw that the work of people like Jackendoff (1983) has begun to put restrictions on the interface between the semantic and cognitive systems. Clearly much remains to be done in this important area, and we can only hope that over the next few years some progress is made.

Cross-linguistic comparisons
This book has largely been about experiments on speakers of the English language. This bias does not just reflect my bias, because most of the work carried out has been on English. There is an assumption here about cross-linguistic constancy: that many of the processes involved in language are universal. That is, it is a testable assumption that the architecture of the language system is constant across all speakers, whatever language they speak, but the representations and detailed processes involved may vary. That is, we all share the same hard-wired modules, but they vary slightly in what they do.

Chomsky's ideas have been very influential in this respect. You will remember that according to this position language is an innate faculty specified by the language acquisition device (LAD). All languages, because they are governed by the form of the LAD, are similar at some deep level. Variation between languages boils down to differences in vocabulary, and the parameters set by the exposure to a particular language. For example, we saw in Chapter 5 that languages differ in whether they are "head first" or "head last". In Chapter 2 we saw that the pre-lexical code varies between languages. English uses a stress-based representation, whereas French uses a syllable-based representation. Nevertheless, in both cases there is a pre-lexical representation which is used to access the lexical code, and this is constrained by the properties of the speech recognition module, which probably does not enable the use of top-down information. Similarly,

Perfetti and Zhang (1995) examine Chinese character identification. The Chinese writing system is entirely logographic, yet phonological information is activated during identification. Perfetti and Zhang argue that there is a universal principle of phonological encoding in reading. In summary, although spoken and written languages differ with obvious consequences for the superficial form of the language processes, at a fundamental level the language processor has a universal architecture. Cross-linguistic comparisons help us to constrain the nature of this architecture.

Languages differ at all levels, as will be apparent from this book, including the phonemes used by different languages, the phonological strings which different languages find acceptable (their *phonotactic constraints*), vocabulary, the regularity of grapheme-phoneme correspondences, the extent of word gender and inflections, and in the syntactic rules employed. What are the consequences of these differences? Much research remains to be done on this.

There are many areas where it is useful to compare languages. First, the observation that there are similar constraints on syntactic rules has been used to motivate the concept of universal grammar (Chapter 5). We also saw in Chapter 5 that examining a single language (English) might have given us a distorted view of the parsing process. Second, similarities and differences in languages have consequences for language development (Chapters 10 and 11). For example, we saw that cross-linguistic analysis of the development of gender argues against a semantic basis for the development of syntactic categories. Third, what can analysis of different languages which map orthography onto phonology in different ways tell us about reading (Chapter 4)? And do different languages break down in different ways after brain damage? Cross-linguistic approaches to aphasia have recently been reviewed by Bates and Wulfeck (1989), and Bates, Wulfeck, and MacWhinney (1991).

CONCLUDING SUMMARY

The eventual goal of psycholinguistics is a detailed and unified theory of language and how it relates to other cognitive processes. The more we know, in some ways the harder psycholinguistics gets to do. Cutler (1981) observed that the list of variables which had to be controlled in psycholinguistics experiments was large and growing, and there were many that were rarely considered. Here is Cutler's list for experiments on single words: syntactic class, ambiguity, surface and deep frequency, length, association, age of acquisition, autobiographical associations, categorisability, concreteness, digram frequency, imagery, goodness, letter frequency, number of meanings, orthographic regularity, meaningfulness, emotionality, recognition threshold, position of recognition point, and morphology. Since then we have discovered that not only the neighbours of words are important, but that their properties are also. And this is before we have begun to consider constraints on processing units larger than a word. Cutler asked: Will we be able to run any psycholinguistic experiments at all in 1990? The answer is clearly "yes", but it is getting more difficult, and we have to make a number of carefully justified assumptions.

There remains a great deal to do in psycholinguistics. If this book has inspired any reader to investigate further and even actually contribute to the subject, it has served its purpose.

FURTHER READING

My description of the bottom-up and top-down modes of doing psycholinguistics is of course a big simplification. Most people have heard about the importance of falsification in science; for a review of the philosophy of science, see Chalmers (1982). Many of the more speculative ideas are to be found in books written for a general audience. These include Dennett (1991) on the conceptualiser and the evolution of language, and Pinker (1994) on the evolution and genetic basis of language. Kutas and van Petten (1994) review research on event-related potentials relevant to psycholinguistics.

Appendix:
Connectionism

INTRODUCTION

This appendix provides a more formal and detailed treatment of connectionism than it has been possible to provide in the main text. It can be skipped, but will hopefully be comprehensible to anyone with a knowledge of basic algebra. If you find the mathematics daunting, it is worth persevering, as it is impossible to obtain a true understanding of connectionism without it. For more detailed and comprehensive coverage, see the further reading.

Connectionism has become the preferred term to describe a class of models that all have in common the principle that processing occurs through the action of many simple, inter-connected units; *parallel distributed processing* (PDP) and *neural networks* are other commonly used terms that are almost synonymous. In all connectionist models there are two very important concepts. The first is that there are these many processing units connected together. The second is that energy or activation spreads around the network. Activation spreads around the network modified by the strengths of the connections between units. Units have activation levels which are modified by the amount of activation they receive from other units.

There are many types of connectionist model. One useful distinction is between models that do not learn and models that do. For our purposes the most important examples of the models that do not learn are those based upon interactive activation and competition, and of models that do, those trained using back-propagation. It is useful to distinguish between the *architecture* of a network, which describes the layout of the network—how many units there are and how they are connected to each other, the *algorithm* that determines how activation spreads around the network, and the *learning rule*, if appropriate, that specifies how the network learns.

We will look at two approaches which have been the most influential in psycholinguistics. Other important learning algorithms which have been used include Hebbian learning and the Boltzmann machine (Hinton & Sejnowski, 1986); see the further reading for details of these.

INTERACTIVE ACTIVATION MODELS

McClelland and Rumelhart (1981) and Rumelhart and McClelland (1982) presented a model called *interactive activation* with competition (IAC). It is one of the earliest connectionist models, and its original purpose was to account for word context effects on letter identification. The TRACE model of spoken word recognition (McClelland & Elman, 1986) is very similar, but differs in that the architecture has no inhibitory connections between levels.

The model consists of many simple processing units arranged in three levels. There is an input level of visual feature units, a level where units correspond to individual letters, and an output level where each unit corresponds to a word. Each unit is connected to each unit in the level immediately before and after it. Each of these connections is either excitatory (that is positive, or *facilitatory*) or *inhibitory* (negative). Excitatory connections make the units at the end more active, whereas inhibitory connections make them less active. Furthermore, each unit is connected to each other unit within the same level by an inhibitory connection. See Fig. 3.4 for a graphical representation of this architecture.

When a unit becomes activated, it sends off energy, or *activation*, simultaneously along the connections to all the other units to which it is connected. If it is connected by a facilitatory connection, it will increase the activation of the unit at the other end of the connection, whereas if it is connected by an inhibitory connection, it will decrease the activation at the other end. Hence if the unit corresponding to the letter "T" in the initial letter position becomes activated, it will increase the activation level of the word units corresponding to "TAKE" and "TASK", but decrease the activation level of "CAKE". Because units are connected to all other units at the same level by inhibitory connections, as soon as a unit becomes activated, it starts inhibiting all the other units at that level. Various equations summarised below determine the way in which activation flows between units, is summed by units, and is used to change the activation level of each unit at each time step. As we saw in Chapter 3, over time, the pattern of activation settles down or *relaxes* into a stable configuration so that only one word remains active.

Basic equations of the interactive activation model

As we have seen, in this model activation spreads to neighbouring units via connections. Connections have numbers or *weights* which determine how much activation spreads along that connection, and hence how quickly activation builds up at the unit at the end of the connection. Hence the total activation, called net_i, arriving at each unit i from j connections is shown in equation (1). Put in words, this means it is the sum (Σ) of the products of the output activation (a_j) of all the units that input to it and the weights on the connection between the input and receiving unit (w_{ji}).

$$net_i = \sum_j a_j . w_{ji} \tag{1}$$

An example should makes this clear. Figure A.1 shows part of a very simple network. There are four input units to one destination unit. The total amount of activation arriving at the destination unit will be the sum of all the products of the outputs of the units that input to it with the appropriate weights on the connections: that is, $((1 \times +0.2) + (0 \times -0.5) + (1 \times +0.7) + (1 \times -0.1)) = +0.8$. This is in general how all units in all connectionist networks become activated. The idea is that this is a simplified model of a neuron. Neurons become excited or inhibited by all the other neurons which make contact with them.

Finally, further equations are needed to determine what happens to a unit in each processing cycle after it receives an input. In the IAC model, each unit changes its activation level depending on how much or how little input it receives, and whether that input is overall positive (excitatory) or negative (inhibitory). In each cycle the change in activation of a unit i, Δa_i, is given by equations (2) and (3).

$$\Delta a_i = (max - a_i)net_i - decay(a_i - rest) \qquad \text{if } net_i > 0 \tag{2}$$

$$\Delta a_i = (a_i - min)net_i - decay(a_i - rest) \qquad \text{otherwise} \tag{3}$$

where *rest* is the unit's resting level of activation, *decay* a parameter that makes the unit tend to decay back to its resting level in the absence of new input, *min* the unit's minimum permitted level of activation, and *max* the unit's maximum permitted level of activation.

Processing takes place in cycles, which represent the passage of time. At the end of each cycle the activation levels of all the units in the

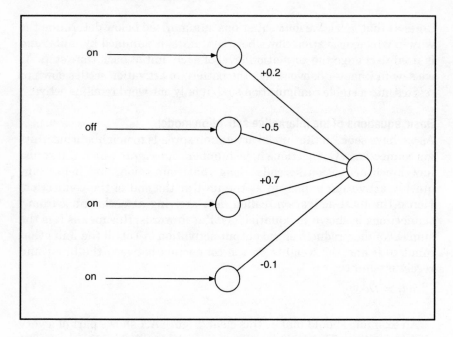

FIG. A.1. A simplified connectionist unit or "neuron". This takes converts multiple inputs (derived from the weighted output of other units) and converts them to a single output.

network are updated. In the next cycle the process is repeated using the new activation levels.

BACK-PROPAGATION

The simplest type of network architecture that can be trained by back-propagation has three layers or levels. Again, each typically contains many simple units. These are called the input, hidden, and output levels (see Fig. 4.3 for an example). As in the IAC model, each of the units in these layers has an activation level, and each unit is connected to all the units in the next level by a weighted connection, which can be either excitatory or inhibitory. These networks *learn* to associate an input pattern with an output pattern using a learning rule called back-propagation.

The connections in the network all start off with random weights. Suppose we want to associate the input pattern of graphemes D O G with the output pattern of sounds or phonemes /d/ /ɒ/ /g/—that is, we want the model to learn how to pronounce the printed word "DOG". One pattern of activation over the input units corresponds to "DOG". In the

Figure for simplicity I have made the representation a local one—that is, one unit corresponds to "D", one to "O", one to "G", and so on. In more realistic models these patterns are usually *distributed* so that "DOG" is represented by a pattern of activation over the input units with no one single unit corresponding to any one single letter. Hence "DOG" might be represented by input unit 1 on, input unit 2 off, input unit 3 on, and so on. These units then pass activation on to the hidden units according to the values of the connections between the input and hidden units. Activation is then summed by each unit in the hidden layer in just the same way it is in the interactive activation model discussed above. In models which learn using back-propagation the output of a unit is a complex function of its input: there must be a non-linear relationship between the two, given by a special type of function called the *logistic function*. The output O_u of a unit is related to its input by equation (4),

$$O_u = \frac{1}{(1 + e^{-netinput_u})} \tag{4}$$

where e is the exponential constant, with a value of approximately 2.71828.

Each unit has an individual threshold or *bias*. (This is usually implemented by attaching an additional unit, the bias unit, which is always on, to each principle unit. The value of the weights between the bias and other units can be learned like any other weights.)

Activation is then passed on from the hidden to the output units, and so eventually the output units end up with an activation value. But as we started off with totally random values, they are very unlikely to be the correct ones. We wanted as the target output the most activated output units to correspond to the phonemes /d/ /ɒ/ /g/, but the actual output is going to be totally random, maybe something close to /k/ /i/ /j/. What the learning rule does then is to modify the connections in the network so that the output will be a bit less like what it actually produced, and a bit more like what it should be. It does this in a way which is very like what happens in calculating the mean squared error in an analysis of variance. The difference between the actual and target outputs is computed, and the values of all the weights from the hidden to the output units are adjusted slightly to try to make this difference smaller. This process is then *back-propagated* to change the weights on the connections between the input and the hidden units. The whole process can then be repeated for a different input–output (e.g. grapheme–phoneme) pair.

The back-propagation learning rule is based on the *generalised delta rule*. The rule for changing the weights following the presentation of a particular pattern p is given by (5), where j and i index adjacent upper and lower layers in the network, t_{pj} is the jth component of the desired target pattern, o_{pj} the corresponding jth component of the actual output pattern p, and i_{pi} is the ith component of the input pattern.

$$\Delta_p w_{ij} = (t_{pj} - o_{pj}) \cdot i_{pi} \tag{5}$$

The error for the output units is given by Equation (6), and that for the hidden units by (7), where l and m are connecting layers. The weight change is given by (8).

$$\delta_{pj} = (t_{pj} - o_{pj}) \cdot o_{pj} \cdot (I - o_{pj}) \tag{6}$$

$$\delta_{pl} = {}^{m}o_{pl} \cdot (1 - o_{pl}) \cdot \Sigma \, \delta_{pm} \cdot w_{lm} \tag{7}$$

$$\Delta w_{ij(n+1)} = \eta \cdot (\delta_{pj} \cdot o_{pi}) + \alpha \cdot \Delta w_{ij(n)} \tag{8}$$

There are two new constants in (8): η is the learning rate, which determines how quickly the network learns, and α is the momentum term, which stops the network changing too much and hence overshooting on any learning cycle. Needless to say, this training process cannot be completed in a single step. It has to be repeated many times, but gradually the values of actual and desired outputs converge. Naturally you have to be cautious about the composition of the training set of materials. For example, if you are interested in word frequency, you have to encode it in the training in some way, perhaps by presenting more input–output pairings of frequent words more often. Interestingly, if you then present the network with an item that it has not seen before, it can manage it quite well. That is, although the network has not been taught any explicit rules of pronunciation, it behaves as though it has learned them, and can *generalise* appropriately.

You should bear in mind that this description is something of a simplification. Why you need hidden units in such a model, what happens if you do not, and how you select how many units to have are interesting issues in themselves.

FURTHER READING

Bechtel and Abrahamsen (1991) and Quinlan (1991) are both excellent textbooks on connectionism. The two volume set Parallel Distributed Processing (Rumelhart, McClelland, & the PDP research group, 1986; McClelland, Rumelhart, & the PDP research group, 1986) are classics. Caudill and Butler (1992), McClelland and Rumelhart (1988), and Orchard and Phillips (1991) all provide exercises and programs on a floppy disk.

References

Aitchison, J. (1994). *Words in the mind: An introduction to the mental lexicon* (2nd ed.). Oxford: Blackwell.

Alba, J.W., & Hasher, L. (1983). Is memory schematic? *Psychological Bulletin, 93,* 203–231.

Allport, D.A. (1977). On knowing the meaning of words we are unable to report: The effects of visual masking. In S. Dornic (Ed.), *Attention and performance VI* (pp. 505–534). Hillsdale, NJ: Lawrence Erlbaum Associates Inc.

Allport, D.A., & Funnell, E. (1981). Components of the mental lexicon. *Philosophical Transactions of the Royal Society of London, Series B, 295,* 397–410.

Altmann, G.T.M. (1988). Ambiguity, parsing strategies, and computational models. *Language and Cognitive Processes, 3,* 73–97.

Altmann, G.T.M. (Ed.). (1989a). *Parsing and interpretation.* Hove, UK: Lawrence Erlbaum Associates Ltd.

Altmann, G.T.M. (1989b). Parsing and interpretation: An introduction. *Language and Cognitive Processes, 4,* 1–19.

Altmann, G.T.M. (Ed.). (1990). *Cognitive models of speech processing.* Cambridge, MA: MIT Press.

Altmann, G.T.M. (in press). Accounting for parsing principles: From parsing preferences to language acquisition. In T. Inui & J.L. McClelland (Eds.), *Attention and performance XVI.* Cambridge, MA: MIT Press.

Altmann, G.T.M., Garnham, A., & Dennis, Y. (1992). Avoiding the garden path: Eye movements in context. *Journal of Memory and Language, 31,* 685–712.

Altmann, G.T.M., Garnham, A., & Henstra, J. (1994). Effects of syntax in human sentence parsing: Evidence against a structure-based proposal mechanism. *Journal of Experimental Psychology: Learning, Memory, and Cognition, 20,* 209–216.

Altmann, G.T.M., & Shillcock, R.C. (Eds.). (1993). *Cognitive models of speech processing.* Hove, UK: Lawrence Erlbaum Associates Ltd.

Altmann, G.T.M., & Steedman, M.J. (1988). Interaction with context during human sentence processing. *Cognition, 30,* 191–238.

Anderson, J.R. (1976). *Language, memory, and thought.* Hillsdale, NJ: Lawrence Erlbaum Associates Inc.

Anderson, J.R. (1983). *The architecture of cognition.* Cambridge, MA: Harvard University Press.

Anderson, J.R. (1985). *Cognitive psychology and its implications* (2nd ed.). New York: W.H. Freeman.

Anderson, J.R., & Bower, G.H. (1973). *Human associative memory.* Washington: Winston and Sons.

Anderson, R.C., & Pichert, J.W. (1978). Recall of previously unrecallable information following a shift in perspective. *Journal of Verbal Learning and Verbal Behavior, 12,* 1–12.

Andrews, S. (1989). Frequency and neighborhood effects on lexical access: Activation or search. *Journal of Experimental Psychology: Learning, Memory and Cognition, 15,* 802–814.

Antos, S.J. (1979). Processing facilitation in a lexical decision task. *Journal of Experimental Psychology: Human Perception and Performance, 5,* 527–545.

Armstrong, S., Gleitman, L.R., & Gleitman, H. (1983). What some concepts might not be. *Cognition, 13,* 263–274.

Atkinson, M. (1982). *Explanations in the study of child language development.* Cambridge: Cambridge University Press.

Au, T.K. (1983). Chinese and English counterfactuals: The Sapir-Whorf hypothesis revisited. *Cognition, 15,* 155–187.

Au, T.K. (1984). Counterfactuals: In reply to Alfred Bloom. *Cognition, 17,* 289–302.

Austin, J.L. (1976). *How to do things with words* (2nd ed.). Oxford: Oxford University Press. (First edition published 1962.)

Baars, B.J., Motley, M.T., & MacKay, D.G. (1975). Output editing for lexical status from artificially elicited slips of the tongue. *Journal of Verbal Learning and Verbal Behavior, 14,* 382–291.

Bach, E., Brown, C., & Marslen-Wilson, W.D. (1986). Crossed and nested dependencies in German and Dutch: A psycholinguistic study. *Language and Cognitive Processes, 1,* 249–262.

Backman, J.E. (1983). Psycholinguistic skills and reading acquisition: A look at early readers. *Reading Research Quarterly, 18,* 466–479.

Baddeley, A.D. (1990). *Human memory: Theory and practice.* Hove, UK: Lawrence Erlbaum Associates Ltd.

Baddeley, A.D., Ellis, N.C., Miles, T.R., & Lewis, V.J. (1982). Developmental and acquired dyslexia: A comparison. *Cognition, 11,* 185–199.

Baddeley, A.D., Lewis, V.J., & Vallar, G. (1984). Exploring the articulatory loop. *Quarterly Journal of Experimental Psychology, 36A,* 233–252.

Badecker, W., & Caramazza, A. (1985). On considerations of method and theory governing the use of clinical categories in neurolinguistics and cognitive neuropsychology: The case against agrammatism. *Cognition, 20,* 97–125.

Badecker, W., & Caramazza, A. (1986). A final brief in the case against agrammatism: The role of theory in the selection of data. *Cognition, 24,* 277–282.

Baillet, S.D., & Keenan, J.M. (1986). The role of encoding and retrieval processes in the recall of text. *Discourse Processes, 9*, 247–268.

Balota, D.A. (1994). Visual word recognition: The journey from features to meaning. In M.A. Gernsbacher (Ed.), *Handbook of psycholinguistics* (pp. 303–358). San Diego: Academic Press.

Balota, D.A., & Chumbley, J.I. (1984). Are lexical decisions a good measure of lexical access? The role of word frequency in the neglected decision stage. *Journal of Experimental Psychology: Human Perception and Performance, 10*, 340–357.

Balota, D.A., & Chumbley, J.I. (1985). The locus of word-frequency effects in the pronunciation task: Lexical access and/or production? *Journal of Memory and Language, 24*, 89–106.

Balota, D.A., & Chumbley, J.I. (1990). Where are the effects of frequency on visual word recognition tasks? Right where we said they were! Comment on Monsell, Doyle, and Haggard (1989). *Journal of Experimental Psychology: General, 119*, 231–237.

Balota, D.A., & Lorch, R.F. (1986). Depth of automatic spreading activation: Mediated priming effects in pronunciation but not in lexical decision. *Journal of Experimental Psychology: Human Perception and Performance, 10*, 340–357.

Banks, W.P., & Flora, J. (1977). Semantic and perceptual processing in symbolic comparison. *Journal of Experimental Psychology: Human Perception and Performance, 3*, 278–290.

Baron, J., & Strawson, C. (1976). Use of orthographic and word-specific knowledge in reading words aloud. *Journal of Experimental Psychology: Human Perception and Performance, 2*, 386–393.

Barrett, M.D. (1978). Lexical development and overextension in child language. *Journal of Child Language, 5*, 205–219.

Barrett, M.D. (1982). Distinguishing between prototypes: The early acquisition of the meaning of object names. In S.A. Kuczaj (Ed.), *Language development: Vol. 1: Syntax and semantics* (pp. 313–334). New York: Springer-Verlag.

Barrett, M.D. (1986). Early semantic representations and early word-usage. In S.A. Kuczaj & M.D. Barrett (Eds.), *The development of word meaning: Progress in cognitive development research* (pp. 39–67). New York: Springer-Verlag.

Barron, R.W. (1981). Reading skills and reading strategies. In C.A. Perfetti & A.M. Lesgold (Eds.), *Interactive processes in reading* (pp. 299–328). Hillsdale, NJ: Lawrence Erlbaum Associates Inc.

Barron, R.W. (1986). Word recognition in early reading: A review of the direct and indirect access hypothesis. *Cognition, 24*, 93–119.

Barron, R.W., & Baron, J. (1977). How children get meaning from printed words. *Child Development, 48*, 587–594.

Barry, C., & Richardson, J.T.E. (1988). Accounts of oral reading in deep dyslexia. In H.A. Whitaker (Ed.), *Phonological processes and brain mechanisms* (pp. 118–171). New York: Springer-Verlag.

Barsalou, L.W. (1985). Ideals, central tendency, and frequency of instantiation as determinants of graded structure in categories. *Journal of Experimental Psychology: Learning, Memory, and Cognition, 11*, 629–654.

Bartlett, F.C. (1932). *Remembering: A study in experimental and social psychology*. Cambridge: Cambridge University Press.

Bates, E., Bretherton, I., & Snyder, L. (1988). *From first words to grammar: Individual differences and dissociable mechanisms.* Cambridge: Cambridge University Press.

Bates, E., & MacWhinney, B. (1982). Functionalist approaches to grammar. In E. Wanner & L.R. Gleitman (Eds.), *Language acquisition: The state of the art* (pp. 173–218). Cambridge: Cambridge University Press.

Bates, E., Masling, M., & Kintsch, W. (1978). Recognition memory for aspects of dialog. *Journal of Experimental Psychology: Human Learning and Memory, 4,* 187–197.

Bates, E., McDonald, J., MacWhinney, B., & Applebaum, M. (1991). A maximum likelihood procedure for the analysis of group and individual data in aphasia research. *Brain and Language, 40,* 231–265.

Bates, E., & Wulfeck, B. (1989). Comparative aphasiology: A cross-linguistic approach to language breakdown. *Aphasiology, 3,* 111–142.

Bates, E., Wulfeck, B., & MacWhinney, B. (1991). Cross-linguistic research in aphasia: An overview. *Brain and Language, 41,* 123–148.

Battig, W.F., & Montague, W.E. (1969). Category norms for verbal items in 56 categories: A replication and extension of the Connecticut category norms. *Journal of Experimental Psychology Monograph, 80,* 1–46.

Beattie, G.W. (1980). The role of language production processes in the organisation of behaviour in face-to-face interaction. In B. Butterworth (Ed.), *Language production: Vol. 1: Speech and talk* (pp. 69–107). London: Academic Press.

Beattie, G.W. (1983). *Talk: An analysis of speech and non-verbal behaviour in conversation.* Milton Keynes: Open University Press.

Beattie, G.W., & Bradbury, R.J. (1979). An experimental investigation of the modifiability of the temporal structure of spontaneous speech. *Journal of Psycholinguistic Research, 8,* 225–247.

Beattie, G.W., & Butterworth, B. (1979). Contextual probability and word frequency as determinants of pauses and errors in spontaneous speech. *Language and Speech, 22,* 201–211.

Beauvois, M.-F. (1982). Optic aphasia: A process of interaction between vision and language. *Philosophical Transactions of the Royal Society of London Series B, 298,* 35–47.

Beauvois, M.-F., & Derouesné, J. (1979). Phonological alexia: Three dissociations. *Journal of Neurology, Neurosurgery and Psychiatry, 42,* 1115–1124.

Beauvois, M.-F., & Derouesné, J. (1981). Lexical or orthographic agraphia. *Brain, 104,* 21–49.

Bechtel, W., & Abrahamsen, A. (1991). *Connectionism and the mind.* Oxford: Blackwell.

Becker, C.A. (1976). Allocation of attention during visual word recognition. *Journal of Experimental Psychology: Human Perception and Performance, 2,* 556–566.

Becker, C.A. (1980). Semantic context effects in visual word recognition: An analysis of semantic strategies. *Memory and Cognition, 8,* 439–512.

Becker, C.A., & Killion, T.H. (1977). Interaction of visual and cognitive effects in word recognition. *Journal of Experimental Psychology: Human Perception and Performance, 3,* 389–407.

Behrend, D.A. (1988). Overextensions in early language comprehension: Evidence from a signal detection approach. *Journal of Child Language, 15,* 63–75.

Behrend, D.A. (1990). Constraints and development: A reply to Nelson (1988). *Cognitive Development, 5*, 313–330.

Behrmann, M., & Bub, D. (1992). Surface dyslexia and dysgraphia: Dual routes, single lexicon. *Cognitive Neuropsychology, 9*, 209–251.

Bellugi, U. (1970). Learning the language. *Psychology Today, 4*, 32–35.

Bellugi, U., Bihrle, A., Jernigan, T., Trauner, D., & Doherty, S. (1991). Neuropsychological, neurological, and neuroanatomical profile of Williams syndrome. *American Journal of Medical Genetics Supplement, 6*, 115–125.

Benedict, H. (1979). Early lexical development: Comprehension and production. *Journal of Child Language, 6*, 183–200.

Berko, J. (1958). The child's learning of English morphology. *Word, 14*, 150–177.

Berlin, B., & Kay, P. (1969). *Basic color terms: Their universality and evolution.* Berkeley and Los Angeles: University of California Press.

Berndt, R.S., & Mitchum, C.C. (1990). Auditory and lexical information sources in immediate recall: Evidence from a patient with a deficit to the phonological short-term store. In G. Vallar & T. Shallice (Eds.), *Neuropsychological implications of short-term memory* (pp. 115–144). Cambridge: Cambridge University Press.

Bernstein, B. (1961). Social structure, language, and learning. *Educational Research, 3*, 163–176.

Berwick, R.C., & Weinberg, A.S. (1983a). The role of grammars in models of language use. *Cognition, 13*, 1–61.

Berwick, R.C., & Weinberg, A.S. (1983b). Reply to Garnham. *Cognition, 15*, 271–276.

Besner, D., & Swan, M. (1982). Models of lexical access in visual word recognition. *Quarterly Journal of Experimental Psychology, 34A*, 313–325.

Besner, D., Twilley, L., McCann, R.S., & Seergobin, K. (1990). On the connection between connectionism and data: Are a few words necessary? *Psychological Review, 97*, 432–446.

Best, B.J. (1973). *Classificatory development in deaf children: Research on language and cognitive development.* Occasional Paper No. 15, Research, Development and Demonstration Center in Education of Handicapped Children, University of Minnesota.

Bever, T.G. (1970). The cognitive basis for linguistic structures. In J.R. Hayes (Ed.), *Cognition and the development of language* (pp. 279–362). New York: Wiley.

Bever, T.G. (1981). Normal acquisition processes explain the critical period for language learning. In K.C. Diller (Ed.), *Individual differences and universals in language aptitude* (pp. 176–198). Rowley, MA: Newbury House.

Bever, T.G., Garrett, M.F., & Hurtig, R. (1973). The interaction of perceptual processes and ambiguous sentences. *Memory and Cognition, 1*, 277–286.

Bever, T.G., & McElree, B. (1988). Empty categories access their antecedents during comprehension. *Linguistic Inquiry, 19*, 35–45.

Bialystok, E., & Hakuta, K. (1994). *In other words: The science and psychology of second-language acquisition.* New York: Basic Books.

Bickerton, D. (1981). *Roots of language.* Ann Arbor, MI: Karoma.

Bickerton, D. (1984). The language bioprogram hypothesis. *Behavioral and Brain Sciences, 7*, 173–221.

Bickerton, D. (1986). More than nature needs? A reply to Premack. *Cognition, 23*, 73–79.

Bierwisch, M. (1970). Semantics. In J. Lyons (Ed.), *New horizons in linguistics* (Vol. 1, pp. 166–185). Harmondsworth, Middlesex: Penguin.

Bigelow, A. (1987). Early words of blind children. *Journal of Child Language, 14*, 47–56.

Bishop, D. (1983). Linguistic impairment after left hemidecortication for infantile hemiplegia? A reappraisal. *Quarterly Journal of Experimental Psychology, 35A*, 199–207.

Bishop, D. (1993). Language development after focal brain damage. In D. Bishop & K. Mogford (Eds.), *Language development in exceptional circumstances*. Hove, UK: Lawrence Erlbaum Associates Ltd.

Bishop, D., & Mogford, K. (Eds.). (1993). *Language development in exceptional circumstances*. Hove, UK: Lawrence Erlbaum Associates Ltd.

Black, J.B., & Wilensky, R. (1979). An evaluation of story grammars. *Cognitive Science, 3*, 213–229.

Bloom, A.H. (1981). *The linguistic shaping of thought: A study in the impact of thinking in China and the West*. Hillsdale, NJ: Lawrence Erlbaum Associates, Inc.

Bloom, A.H. (1984). Caution—the words you use may affect what you say: A response to Au. *Cognition, 17*, 275–287.

Bloom, L. (1970). *Language development: Form and function in emerging grammars*. Cambridge, MA: MIT Press.

Bloom, L. (1973). *One word at a time: The use of single word utterances before syntax*. The Hague: Mouton.

Bloom, L. (1993a). *The transition from infancy to language: Acquiring the power of expression*. Cambridge: Cambridge University Press.

Bloom, P. (Ed.) (1993b). *Language acquisition: Core readings*. New York: Harvester Wheatsheaf.

Bloom, P. (1994). Recent controversies in the study of language acquisition. In M.A. Gernsbacher (Ed.), *Handbook of psycholinguistics* (pp. 741–780). San Diego: Academic Press.

Blumstein, S.E., Cooper, W.E., Zurif, E.B., & Caramazza, A. (1977). The perception and production of voice-onset time in aphasia. *Neuropsychologia, 15*, 19–30.

Blumstein, S.E., & Stevens, K.N. (1979). Acoustic invariance in speech production: Evidence from measurements of the spectral characteristics of stop consonants. *Journal of the Acoustical Society of America, 66*, 1001–1017.

Boas, F. (1911). Introduction to The Handbook of North American Indians (Vol. 1). *Bureau of American Ethology Bulletin, 40* (Part 1).

Bock, J.K. (1982). Toward a cognitive psychology of syntax: Information processing contributions to sentence formulation. *Psychological Review, 89*, 1–47.

Bock, J.K. (1987). An effect of accessibility of word forms on sentence structure. *Journal of Memory and Language, 26*, 119–137.

Bock, J.K. (1989). Closed-class immanence in sentence production. *Cognition, 31*, 163–186.

Bock, J.K., & Cutting, J.C. (1992). Regulating mental energy: Performance units in language production. *Journal of Memory and Language, 31*, 99–127.

Bock, J.K., & Eberhard, K. M. (1993). Meaning, sound and syntax in English number agreement. *Language and Cognitive Processes, 8*, 57–99.

Bock, J.K., & Irwin, D.E. (1980). Syntactic effects of information availability in sentence production. *Journal of Verbal Learning and Verbal Behavior, 19*, 467–484.

Bock, J.K., & Levelt, W.J.M. (1994). Language production: Grammatical encoding. In M.A. Gernsbacher (Ed.), *Handbook of psycholinguistics* (pp. 945–984). San Diego: Academic Press.

Bock, J.K., & Loebell, H. (1990). Framing sentences. *Cognition, 35*, 1–39.

Bock, J.K., & Miller, C.A. (1991). Broken agreement. *Cognition, 23*, 45–93.

Bock, J.K., & Warren, R.K. (1985). Conceptual accessibility and syntactic structure in sentence formulation. *Cognition, 21*, 47–67.

Boden, M.A. (1977). *Artificial intelligence and natural man*. Brighton: Harvester.

Bohannnon, J.N., MacWhinney, B., & Snow, C.E. (1990). No negative evidence revisited: Beyond learnability or who has to prove what to whom. *Developmental Psychology, 26*, 221–226.

Bohannon, J.N., & Stanowicz, L. (1988). The issue of negative evidence: Adult responses to children's language errors. *Developmental Psychology, 24*, 684–689.

Boland, J.E., Tanenhaus, M.K., & Garnsey, S.M. (1990). Evidence for the immediate use of verb control information in sentence processing. *Journal of Memory and Language, 29*, 413–432.

Bolinger, D.L. (1965). The atomization of meaning. *Language, 41*, 555–573.

Boomer, D.S. (1965). Hesitations and grammatical encoding. *Language and Speech, 8*, 148–158.

Bornstein, M.H. (1973). Qualities of colour vision in infancy. *Journal of Experimental Child Psychology, 19*, 401–419.

Bornstein, S. (1985). On the development of colour naming in young children: Data and theory. *Brain and Language, 26*, 72–93.

Borsley, R.D. (1991). *Syntactic theory: A unified approach*. London: Edward Arnold.

Bower, G.H., Black, J.B., & Turner, T.J. (1979). Scripts in memory for text. *Cognitive Psychology, 11*, 177–220.

Bowerman, M. (1973). *Learning to talk: A cross linguistic study of early syntactic development, with special reference to Finnish*. Cambridge: Cambridge University Press.

Bowerman, M. (1978). The acquisition of word meanings: An investigation into some current conflicts. In N. Waterson & C.E. Snow (Eds.), *The development of communication* (pp. 263–287). Chichester: Wiley.

Bowerman, M. (1990). Mapping thematic roles onto syntactic functions: Are children helped by innate linking rules? *Linguistics, 28*, 1253–1289.

Bowles, N.L., & Poon, L.W. (1985). Effects of priming in word retrieval. *Journal of Experimental Psychology: Learning, Memory, and Cognition, 11*, 272–283.

Bradley, D.C., & Forster, K.I. (1987). A reader's view of listening. *Cognition, 25*, 103–134.

Bradley, D.C., Garrett, M.F., & Zurif, E.B. (1980). Syntactic deficits in Broca's aphasia. In D. Caplan (Ed.), *Biological studies of mental processes* (pp. 269–286). Cambridge, MA: MIT Press.

Bradley, L., & Bryant, P. (1978). Difficulties in auditory organization as a possible cause of reading backwardness. *Nature, 271*, 746–747.

Bradley, L., & Bryant, P. (1983). Categorizing sounds and learning to read—A causal connection. *Nature, 301*, 419–421.

Braine, M.D.S. (1963). The ontogeny of English phrase structure: The first phase. *Language, 39*, 1–13.

Braine, M.D.S. (1976). Children's first word combinations. *Monographs of the Society for Research in Child Development, 41* (Serial No. 164).

Braine, M.D.S. (1988a). Review of Language learnability and language development by S. Pinker. *Journal of Child Language, 15,* 189–219.

Braine, M.D.S. (1988b). Modeling the acquisition of linguistic structure. In Y. Levy, I.M. Schlesinger, & M.D.S. Braine (Eds.), *Categories and processes in language acquisition* (pp. 217–259). Hillsdale, NJ: Lawrence Erlbaum Associates Inc.

Braine, M.D.S. (1992). What sort of innate structure is needed to "bootstrap" into syntax? *Cognition, 45,* 77–100.

Bramwell, B. (1897). Illustrative cases of aphasia. *Lancet, 1,* 1256–1259. Reprinted in *Cognitive Neuropsychology, (1984) 1,* 249–258.

Bransford, J.D., Barclay, J.R., & Franks, J.J. (1972). Sentence memory: A constructive versus interpretive approach. *Cognitive Psychology, 3,* 193–209.

Bransford, J.D., & Johnson, M.K. (1973). Consideration of some problems of comprehension. In W.G. Chase (Ed.), *Visual information processing* (pp. 383–438). New York: Academic Press.

Bresnan, J. (1978). A realistic transformational grammar. In M. Halle, J. Bresnan, & G.A. Miller (Eds.), *Linguistic theory and psychological reality* (pp. 1–59). Cambridge, MA: MIT Press.

Brewer, W.F. (1987). Schemas versus mental models in human memory. In P. Morris (Ed.), *Modelling cognition* (pp. 187–197). Chichester: J. Wiley & Sons.

Bridges, A. (1980). SVO comprehension strategies reconsidered: The evidence of individual patterns of response. *Journal of Child Language, 7,* 89–104.

Britton, B.K., Muth, K.D., & Glynn, S.M. (1986). Effects of text organization on memory: Test of a cognitive effect hypothesis with limited exposure time. *Discourse Processes, 9,* 475–487.

Bronowski, J., & Bellugi, U. (1970). Language, name, and concept. *Science, 168,* 669–673.

Brown, A.S. (1991). A review of the tip-of-the-tongue experience. *Psychological Bulletin, 109,* 204–223.

Brown, G.D.A. (1987). Resolving inconsistency: A computational model of word naming. *Journal of Memory and Language, 26,* 1–23.

Brown, G.D.A., & Ellis, N.C. (1994). Issues in spelling research: An overview. In G.D.A. Brown & N.C. Ellis (Eds.), *Handbook of spelling: Theory, process and intervention* (pp. 3–25). London: John Wiley & Sons.

Brown, G.D.A., & Watson, F.L. (1987). First in, first out: Word learning age and spoken word frequency as predictors of word familiarity and word naming latency. *Memory and Cognition, 15,* 208–216.

Brown, G.D.A., & Watson, F.L. (1994). Spelling-to-sound effects in single-word reading. *British Journal of Psychology, 85,* 181–202.

Brown, P. (1991). DEREK: The direct encoding routine for evolving knowledge. In D. Besner & G.W. Humphreys (Ed.), *Basic processes in reading: Visual word recognition* (pp. 104–147). Hillsdale, NJ: Lawrence Erlbaum Associates Inc.

Brown, R. (1957). Linguistic determinism and the part of speech. *Journal of Abnormal and Social Psychology, 55,* 1–5.

Brown, R. (1958). *Words and things.* New York: Free Press.

Brown, R. (1970). Psychology and reading: Commentary on chapters 5 to 10. In H. Levin & J.P. Williams (Eds.), *Basic studies on reading* (pp. 164–187). New York: Basic Books.

Brown, R. (1973). *A first language: The early stages*. London: George Allen and Unwin.

Brown, R. (1976). In memorial tribute to Eric Lenneberg. *Cognition, 4,* 125–154.

Brown, R., & Bellugi, U. (1964). Three processes in the acquisition of syntax. *Harvard Educational Review, 34,* 133–151.

Brown, R., & Fraser, C. (1963). The acquisition of syntax. In C. Cofer & B. Musgrave (Eds.), *Verbal behavior and learning: Problems and processes* (pp. 158–209). New York: McGraw-Hill.

Brown, R., & Hanlon, C. (1970). Derivational complexity and order of acquisition in child speech. In J.R. Hayes (Ed.), *Cognition and the development of language* (pp. 11–53). New York: John Wiley & Sons.

Brown, R., & Lenneberg, E.H. (1954). A study in language and cognition. *Journal of Abnormal and Social Psychology, 49,* 454–462.

Brown, R., & McNeill, D. (1966). The "tip of the tongue" phenomenon. *Journal of Verbal Learning and Verbal Behavior, 5,* 325–337.

Bruce, D.J. (1958). The effects of listeners' anticipations in the intelligibility of heard speech. *Language and Speech, 1,* 79–97.

Bruck, M., Lambert, W.E., & Tucker, G.R. (1976). Cognitive and attitudinal consequences of bilingual schooling: The St. Lambert project through grade six. *International Journal of Psycholinguistics, 6,* 13–33.

Bruner, J.S. (1964). The course of cognitive growth. *American Psychologist, 19,* 1–15.

Bruner, J.S. (1975). From communication to language—a psychological perspective. *Cognition, 3,* 255–287.

Bruner, J.S. (1983). *Child's talk: Learning to use language*. New York: Norton.

Bryant, P., & Bradley, L. (1983). Psychological strategies and the development of reading and writing. In M. Martlew (Ed.), *The psychology of written language: Developmental and educational perspectives* (pp. 163–178). Chichester: John Wiley & Sons Ltd.

Bryant, P., & Impey, L. (1986). The similarity between normal readers and developmental and acquired dyslexics. *Cognition, 24,* 121–137.

Bub, D., Black, S., Hampson, E., & Kertesz, A. (1988). Semantic encoding of pictures and words: Some neuropsychological observations. *Cognitive Neuropsychology, 5,* 27–66.

Bub, D., Cancelliere, A., & Kertesz, A. (1985). Whole-word and analytic translation of spelling to sound in a non-semantic reader. In K.E. Patterson, J.C. Marshall, & M. Coltheart (Eds.), *Surface dyslexia: Neuropsychological and cognitive studies of phonological reading* (pp. 15–34). Hove, UK: Lawrence Erlbaum Associates Ltd.

Buckingham, H.W. (1981). Where do neologisms come from? In J.W. Brown (Ed.), *Jargonaphasia* (pp. 39–62). New York: Academic Press.

Buckingham, H.W. (1986). The scan-copier mechanism and the positional level of language production: Evidence from phonemic paraphasia. *Cognitive Science, 10,* 195–217.

Burgess, C., Tanenhaus, M.K., & Seidenberg, M.S. (1989). Context and lexical access: Implications of nonword interference for lexical ambiguity resolution. *Journal of Experimental Psychology: Learning, Memory, and Cognition, 15,* 620–632.

Burke, D., MacKay, D.G., Worthley, J.S., & Wade, E. (1991). On the tip of the tongue: What causes word finding failures in young and older adults? *Journal of Memory and Language, 30,* 237–246.

Butterworth, B. (1975). Hesitation and semantic planning in speech. *Journal of Psycholinguistic Research, 4*, 75–87.

Butterworth, B. (1979). Hesitation and the production of neologisms in jargon aphasia. *Brain and Language, 8*, 133–161.

Butterworth, B. (1980). Evidence from pauses in speech. In B. Butterworth (Ed.), *Language production: Vol. 1: Speech and talk* (pp. 155–176). London: Academic Press.

Butterworth, B. (1982). Speech errors: Old data in search of new theories. In A. Cutler (Ed.), *Slips of the tongue and language production* (pp. 73–108). Amsterdam: Mouton.

Butterworth, B. (1983). Lexical representation. In B. Butterworth (Ed.), *Language production: Vol. 2: Development, writing, and other language processes* (pp. 257–294). London: Academic Press.

Butterworth, B. (1985). Jargon aphasia: Processes and strategies. In S. Newman & R. Epstein (Eds.), *Current perspectives in dysphasia* (pp. 61–96). Edinburgh: Churchill Livingstone.

Butterworth, B. (1989). Lexical access in speech production. In W. Marslen-Wilson (Ed.), *Lexical representation and process* (pp. 108–135). Cambridge, MA: MIT Press.

Butterworth, B., & Beattie, G.W. (1978). Gesture and silence as indicators of planning in speech. In R.N. Campbell & P.T. Smith (Eds.), *Recent advances in the psychology of language: Vol. 4: Formal and experimental approaches* (pp. 347–360). London: Plenum.

Butterworth, B., Campbell, R., & Howard, D. (1986). The uses of short-term memory: A case study. *Quarterly Journal of Experimental Psychology, 38A*, 705–737.

Butterworth, B., & Hadar, U. (1989). Gesture, speech, and computational stages: A reply to McNeill. *Psychological Review, 96*, 168–174.

Butterworth, B., & Howard, D. (1987). Paragrammatisms. *Cognition, 26*, 1–37.

Butterworth, B., Swallow, J., & Grimston, M. (1981). Gestures and lexical processes in jargonaphasia. In J. Brown (Ed.), *Jargonaphasia* (pp. 113–124). New York: Academic Press.

Butterworth, B., & Wengang, Y. (1991). The universality of two routines for reading: Evidence from Chinese dyslexia. *Proceedings of the Royal Society of London Series B, 245*, 91–95.

Campbell, R., & Butterworth, B. (1985). Phonological dyslexia and dysgraphia: A developmental case with associated deficits of phonemic processing and awareness. *Quarterly Journal of Experimental Psychology, 37A*, 435–475

Caplan, D. (1972). Clause boundaries and recognition latencies. *Perception and Psychophysics, 12*, 73–76.

Caplan, D. (1986). In defense of agrammatism. *Cognition, 24*, 263–276.

Caplan, D. (1992). *Language: Structure, processing, and disorders.* Cambridge, MA: MIT Press.

Caplan, D., & Waters, G.S. (in press). Aphasic disorders of syntactic comprehension and working memory capacity. *Cognitive Neuropsychology.*

Caramazza, A. (1986). On drawing inferences about the structure of normal cognitive systems from the analysis of patterns of impaired performance. *Brain and Cognition, 5*, 41–66.

Caramazza, A. (1991). Data, statistics, and theory: A comment on Bates, McDonald, MacWhinney, and Applebaum's "A maximum likelihood procedure for the analysis of group and individual data in aphasia research." *Brain and Language, 41*, 43–51.

Caramazza, A., & Berndt, R.S. (1978). Semantic and syntactic processes in aphasia: A review of the literature. *Psychological Bulletin, 85*, 898–918.

Caramazza, A., & Zurif, E.B. (1976). Dissociation of algorithmic and heuristic processes in language comprehension: Evidence from aphasia. *Brain and Language, 3*, 572–582.

Carmichael, L., Hogan, H.P., & Walter, A.A. (1932). An experimental study of the effect of language on the reproduction of visually presented forms. *Journal of Experimental Psychology, 15*, 73–86.

Carpenter, P.A., & Just, M.A. (1977). Reading comprehension as eyes see it. In M.A. Just & P.A. Carpenter (Eds.), *Cognitive processes in comprehension* (pp. 109–140). Hillsdale, NJ: Lawrence Erlbaum Associates Inc.

Carr, T.H., McCauley, C., Sperber, R.D., & Parmalee, C.M. (1982). Words, pictures and priming: On semantic activation, conscious identification and the automaticity of information processing. *Journal of Experimental Psychology: Human Perception and Performance, 8*, 757–777.

Carr, T.H., & Pollatsek, A. (1985). *Recognizing printed words: A look at current models. Reading research: Advances in theory and practice* (Vol. 5, pp. 1–82). New York: Academic Press.

Carroll, J.B., & Casagrande, J.B. (1958). The function of language classifications in behavior. In E.E. Maccoby, T.M. Newcomb, & E.L. Hartley (Eds.), *Readings in social psychology* (3rd ed., pp. 18–31). New York: Holt, Rinehart & Winston.

Carston, R. (1987). Review of Gavagai! or the future history of the animal language controversy, by David Premack. *Mind and Language, 2*, 332–349.

Castles, A., & Coltheart, M. (1993). Varieties of developmental dyslexia. *Cognition, 47*, 149–180.

Caudhill, M., & Butler, C. (1992). *Understanding neural networks: Computer explorations* (Vols. 1 & 2). Cambridge, MA: MIT Press.

Cazden, C.B. (1968). The acquisition of noun and verb inflections. *Child Development, 39*, 433–448.

Chalmers, A.F. (1982). *What is this thing called science?* (2nd ed.). Milton Keynes: Open University Press.

Chalmers, D.J. (1990). Syntactic transformations on distributed representations. *Connection Science, 2*, 53–62.

Chambers Twentieth Century Dictionary. (1977). Edinburgh: W & R Chambers.

Chang, T.M. (1986). Semantic memory: Facts and models. *Psychological Bulletin, 99*, 199–220.

Chapman, R.S., & Thomson, J. (1980). What is the source of overextension errors in comprehension testing of two-year-olds? A reply to Fremgen and Fay. *Journal of Child Language, 7*, 575–578.

Chertkow, H., & Bub, D. (1990). Semantic memory loss in Alzheimer-type dementia. In M. Schwartz (Ed.), *Modular deficits in Alzheimer-type dementia* (pp. 207–244). Cambridge, MA: MIT Press.

Chertkow, H., Bub, D., & Seidenberg, M.S. (1989). Priming and semantic memory in Alzheimer's disease. *Brain and Language, 36*, 420–446.

Chomsky, N. (1957). *Syntactic structures*. The Hague: Mouton.

Chomsky, N. (1959). Review of "Verbal behavior" by B. F. Skinner. *Language*, *35*, 26–58.

Chomsky, N. (1965). *Aspects of the theory of syntax*. Cambridge, MA: MIT Press.

Chomsky, N. (1968). *Language and mind*. New York: Harcourt Brace.

Chomsky, N. (1981). *Lectures on government and binding*. Dordrecht: Foris.

Chomsky, N. (1986). *Knowledge of language*. New York: Praeger Special studies.

Chomsky, N. (1988). *Language and problems of knowledge: The Managua lectures*. Cambridge, MA: MIT Press.

Chomsky, N. (1991). Linguistics and cognitive science: Problems and mysteries. In A. Kasher (Ed.), *The Chomskyan turn* (pp. 26–53). Oxford: Blackwell.

Christman, S.S., & Buckingham, H.W. (1989). Jargonaphasia. In C. Code (Ed.), *The characteristics of aphasia* (pp. 111–130). Hove, UK: Lawrence Erlbaum Associates Ltd.

Chumbley, J.I., & Balota, D.A. (1984). A word's meaning affects the decision in lexical decision. *Memory and Cognition*, *12*, 590–606.

Cirilo, R.K., & Foss, D.J. (1980). Text structure and reading time for sentences. *Journal of Verbal Learning and Verbal Behavior*, *19*, 96–109.

Clark, E.V. (1973). What's in a word? On the child's acquisition of semantics in his first language. In T.E. Moore (Ed.), *Cognitive development and the acquisition of language* (pp. 65–110). New York: Academic Press.

Clark, E.V. (1987). The principle of contrast: A constraint on language acquisition. In B. MacWhinney (Ed.), *Mechanisms of language acquisition*. Hillsdale, NJ: Lawrence Erlbaum Associates Inc.

Clark, E.V. (1993). *The lexicon in acquisition*. Cambridge: Cambridge University Press.

Clark, E.V., & Hecht, B.F. (1983). Comprehension and production. *Annual Review of Psychology*, *34*, 325–247.

Clark, H.H. (1973). The language-as-fixed effect fallacy: A critique of language statistics in psychological research. *Journal of Verbal Learning and Verbal Behavior*, *12*, 335–359.

Clark, H.H. (1977a). Bridging. In P.N. Johnson-Laird & P.C. Wason (Ed.), *Thinking: Readings in cognitive science* (pp. 411–420). Cambridge, UK: Cambridge University Press.

Clark, H.H. (1977b). Inferences in comprehension. In D. LaBerge & S.J. Samuels (Eds.), *Basic processes in reading: Perception and comprehension* (pp. 243–263). Hillsdale, NJ: Lawrence Erlbaum Associates Inc.

Clark, H.H. (1994). Discourse in production. In M.A. Gernsbacher (Ed.), *Handbook of psycholinguistics* (pp. 985–1022). San Diego : Academic Press.

Clark, H.H., & Clark, E.V. (1977). *Psychology and language: An introduction to psycholinguistics*. New York: Harcourt Brace Jovanovich.

Clark, H.H., & Haviland, S.E. (1977). Comprehension and the given-new contract. In R.O. Freedle (Ed.), *Discourse production and comprehension* (pp. 1–40). Norwood, NJ: Ablex.

Clark, H.H., & Wilkes-Gibbs, D. (1986). Referring as a collaborative process. *Cognition*, *22*, 1–39.

Clarke, R., & Morton, J. (1983). Cross modality facilitation in tachistoscopic word recognition. *Quarterly Journal of Experimental Psychology*, *35A*, 79–96.

Clarke-Stewart, K., Vanderstoep, L., & Killian, G. (1979). Analysis and replication of mother-child relations at 2 years of age. *Child Development, 50*, 777–793.

Clifton, C., & Ferreira, F. (1987). Discourse structure and anaphora: Some experimental results. In M. Coltheart (Ed.), *Attention and Performance XII: The psychology of reading* (pp. 635–654). Hove, UK: Lawrence Erlbaum Associates Ltd.

Clifton, C., & Ferreira, F. (1989). Ambiguity in context. *Language and Cognitive Processes, 4*, 77–103.

Clifton, C., Frazier, L., & Connine, C. (1984). Lexical and syntactic expectations in sentence comprehension. *Journal of Verbal Learning and Verbal Behavior, 23*, 696–708.

Clifton, C., Speer, S., & Abney, S.P. (1991). Parsing arguments: Phrase structure and argument structure as determinants of initial parsing decisions. *Journal of Memory and Language, 30*, 251–271.

Cohen, G. (1983). *The psychology of cognition* (2nd ed.). London: Academic Press.

Colby, K.M. (1975). *Artificial paranoia.* New York: Pergamon Press.

Cole, R.A. (1973). Listening for mispronunciations: A measure of what we hear during speech. *Perception and Psychophysics, 13*, 153–156.

Cole, R.A., & Jakimik, J. (1980). A model of speech perception. In R.A. Cole (Ed.), *Perception and production of fluent speech* (pp. 133–163). Hillsdale, NJ: Lawrence Erlbaum Associates Inc.

Coleman, L., & Kay, P. (1981). Prototype semantics. *Language, 57*, 26–44.

Colley, A.M. (1987). Text comprehension. In J.R. Beech & A.M. Colley (Eds.), *Cognitive approaches to reading* (pp. 113–138). Chichester: John Wiley & Sons.

Collins, A.M., & Loftus, E.F. (1975). A spreading-activation theory of semantic processing. *Psychological Review, 82*, 407–428.

Collins, A.M., & Quillian, M.R. (1969). Retrieval time from semantic memory. *Journal of Verbal Learning and Verbal Behavior, 8*, 240–247.

Coltheart, M. (1980). Deep dyslexia: A right hemisphere hypothesis. In M. Coltheart, K.E. Patterson, & J.C. Marshall (Eds.), *Deep dyslexia* (pp. 326–380). (2nd ed. 1987). London: Routledge & Kegan Paul.

Coltheart, M. (Ed.) (1987a). *Attention and performance XII: The psychology of reading.* Hove, UK: Lawrence Erlbaum Associates Ltd.

Coltheart, M. (1987b). Varieties of developmental dyslexia: A comment on Bryant and Impey. *Cognition, 27*, 97–101.

Coltheart, M., Besner, D., Jonasson, J.T., & Davelaar, E. (1979). Phonological encoding in the lexical decision task. *Quarterly Journal of Experimental Psychology, 31*, 489–507.

Coltheart, M., Curtis, B., Atkins, P., & Haller, M. (1993). Models of reading aloud: Dual-route and parallel-distributed-processing approaches. *Psychological Review, 100*, 589–608.

Coltheart, M., Davelaar, E., Jonasson, J.T., & Besner, D. (1977). Access to the internal lexicon. In S. Dornic (Ed.), *Attention and performance VI* (pp. 535–555). London: Academic Press.

Coltheart, M., Masterson, J., Byng, S., Prior, M., & Riddoch, M.J. (1983). Surface dyslexia. *Quarterly Journal of Experimental Psychology, 35*, 469–495.

Coltheart, M., Patterson, K.E., & Marshall, J.C. (Eds.) (1987). *Deep dyslexia* (2nd ed.). London: Routledge & Kegan Paul. (1st ed., 1980.)

Coltheart, M., & Rastle, K. (1994). Serial processing in reading aloud: Evidence for dual-route models of reading. *Journal of Experimental Psychology: Human Perception and Performance, 20*, 1197–1211.

Coltheart, V., & Leahy, J. (1992). Children's and adults' reading of nonwords: Effects of regularity and consistency. *Journal of Experimental Psychology: Learning, Memory, and Cognition, 18*, 718–729.

Comrie, B. (1980). Diachronic arguments for the psychological reality of abstract phonology: A critical review. In B. Butterworth (Ed.), *Language production: Vol. 1: Speech and talk* (pp. 271–296). London: Academic Press.

Connine, C.M. (1990). Effects of sentence context and lexical knowledge in speech processing. In G.T.M. Altmann (Ed.), *Cognitive models of speech processing* (pp. 281–294). Cambridge, MA: MIT Press.

Connine, C.M., & Clifton, C. (1987). Interactive use of lexical information in speech perception. *Journal of Experimental Psychology: Human Perception and Performance, 13*, 291–319.

Conrad, C. (1972). Cognitive economy in semantic memory. *Journal of Experimental Psychology, 92*, 149–154.

Conrad, R. (1979). *The deaf school child: Language and cognitive function.* London: Harper Row.

Conrad, R., & Rush, M.L. (1965). On the nature of short-term memory encoding by the deaf. *Journal of Speech and Hearing Disorders, 30*, 336–343.

Corballis, M.C. (1992). On the evolution of language and generativity. *Cognition, 44*, 197–226.

Corbett, A.T., & Chang, F. (1983). Pronoun disambiguation: Accessing potential antecedents. *Memory and Cognition, 11*, 383–394.

Corbett, A.T., & Dosher, B.A. (1978). Instrument inferences in sentence encoding. *Journal of Verbal Learning and Verbal Behavior, 17*, 479–492.

Corrigan, R. (1978). Language development as related to stage 6 object permanence development. *Journal of Child Language, 5*, 173–189.

Coslett, H.B. (1991). Read but not write "idea": Evidence for a third reading mechanism. *Brain and Language, 40*, 425–443.

Cottingham, J. (1984). *Rationalism.* London: Paladin.

Coulthard, M. (1977). *An introduction to discourse analysis.* London: Longman.

Coulthard, M. (Ed.) (1992). *Advances in spoken discourse analysis.* London: Routledge.

Coulthard, M. (Ed.) (1994). *Advances in written text analysis.* London: Routledge.

Crain, S., & Steedman, M.J. (1985). On not being led up the garden path: The use of context by the psychological parser. In D. Dowty, L. Karttunen, & A. Zwicky (Eds.), *Natural language parsing* (pp. 320–358). Cambridge: Cambridge University Press.

Cromer, R.F. (1991). *Language and thought in normal and handicapped children.* Oxford: Blackwell.

Cross, T.G. (1977). Mothers' speech adjustments: The contribution of selected child listener variables. In C.E. Snow & C.A. Ferguson (Eds.), *Talking to children: Language input and acquisition* (pp. 151–188). Cambridge: Cambridge University Press.

Cross, T.G. (1978). Mother's speech and its association with rate of linguistic development in young children. In N. Waterson & C.E. Snow (Eds.), *The development of communication* (pp. 199–216). Chichester: Wiley.

Cross, T.G., Johnson-Morris, J.E., & Nienhuys, T.G. (1980). Linguistic feedback and maternal speech: Comparisons of mothers addressing hearing and hearing-impaired children. *First Language, 1*, 163–189.

Cuetos, F., & Mitchell, D.C. (1988). Cross-linguistic differences in parsing: Restrictions on the use of the late closure strategy in Spanish. *Cognition, 30*, 73–105.

Curtiss, S. (1977). *Genie: A psycholinguistic study of a modern-day "wild child"*. London: Academic Press.

Cutler, A. (1981). Making up materials is a confounded nuisance, or: Will we be able to run any psycholinguistic experiments at all in 1990? *Cognition, 10*, 65–70.

Cutler, A., & Butterfield, S. (1992). Rhythmic cues to speech segmentation: Evidence from juncture misperception. *Journal of Memory and Language, 31*, 218–236.

Cutler, A., Mehler, J., Norris, D., & Segui., J. (1986). The syllable's differing role in the segmentation of French and English. *Journal of Memory and Language, 25*, 385–400.

Cutler, A., Mehler, J., Norris, D., & Segui., J. (1992). The monolingual nature of speech segmentation by bilinguals. *Cognitive Psychology, 24*, 381–410.

Cutler, A., & Norris, D. (1988). The role of strong syllables in segmentation for lexical access. *Journal of Experimental Psychology: Human Perception and Performance, 14*, 113–121.

Dagenbach, D., Carr, T.H., & Wilhelmsen, A. (1989). Task-induced strategies and near-threshold priming: Conscious influences on unconscious perception. *Journal of Memory and Language, 28*, 412–443.

Dale, P.S. (1976). *Language development: Structure and function* (2nd ed.). New York: Holt, Rinehart & Winston.

D'Andrade, R.G., & Wish, M. (1985). Speech act theory in quantitative research on interpersonal behavior. *Discourse Processes, 8*, 229–259.

Daneman, M., & Carpenter, P.A. (1980). Individual differences in working memory and reading. *Journal of Verbal Learning and Verbal Behavior, 19*, 450–466.

Davidoff, J., & de Bleser, R. (1993). Optic aphasia: A review of past studies and reappraisal. *Aphasiology, 7*, 135–154.

Davies, I., Corbett, G., Laws, G., McGurk, H., Moss, A., & Smith, M.W. (1991). Linguistic basicness and colour information processing. *International Journal of Psychology, 26*, 311–327.

de Boysson-Bardies, B., Halle, P., Sagart, L., & Durand, C. (1989). A cross-linguistic investigation of vowel formants in babbling. *Journal of Child Language, 16*, 1–17.

de Boysson-Bardies, B., Sagart, L., & Durand, C. (1984). Discernible differences in the babbling of infants according to target language. *Journal of Child Language, 11*, 1–15.

DeCasper, A.J., & Fifer, W.P. (1980). Of human bonding: Newborns prefer their mothers' voices. *Science, 208*, 1174–1176.

de Groot, A.M.B. (1984). Primed lexical decision: Combined effects of the proportion of related prime-target pairs and the stimulus onset asynchrony of prime and target. *Quarterly Journal of Experimental Psychology, 36A*, 253–280.

Dell, G.S. (1986). A spreading-activation theory of retrieval in sentence production. *Psychological Review, 93*, 283–321.

Dell, G.S. (1988). The retrieval of phonological forms in production: Tests of predictions from a connectionist model. *Journal of Memory and Language, 27*, 124–142.

Dell, G.S., & O'Seaghdha, P.G. (1991). Mediated and convergent lexical priming in language production: A comment on Levelt et al. (1991). *Psychological Review, 98*, 604–614.

Dell, G.S., & Reich, P.A. (1981). Stages in sentence production: An analysis of speech error data. *Journal of Verbal Learning and Verbal Behavior, 20*, 611–629.

Demers, R.A. (1988). Linguistics and animal communication. In F.J. Newmeyer (Ed.), *Linguistics: The Cambridge Survey: Vol. 3: Language: Psychological and biological aspects* (pp. 314–335). Cambridge: Cambridge University Press.

Demetras, M.J., Post, K.N., & Snow, C.E. (1986). Feedback to first language learners: The role of repetitions and clarification questions. *Journal of Child Language, 13*, 275–292.

Den Heyer, K. (1985). On the nature of the proportion effect in semantic priming. *Acta Psychologica, 60*, 25–38.

Den Heyer, K., Briand, K., & Dannenbring, G.L. (1983). Strategic factors in a lexical decision task: Evidence for automatic and attention driven processes. *Memory and Cognition, 10*, 358–370.

Dennett, D.C. (1991). *Consciousness explained*. London: Penguin.

Dennis, M., & Whitaker, H.A. (1976). Language acquisition following hemidecortication: Linguistic superiority of the left over the right hemisphere. *Brain and Language, 3*, 404–433.

Dennis, M., & Whitaker, H.A. (1977). Hemispheric equipotentiality and language acquisition. In S.J. Segalowitz & F.A. Gruber (Eds.), *Language development and neurological theory* (pp. 93–106). New York: Academic Press.

de Renzi, E., & Lucchelli, F. (1994). Are semantic systems separately represented in the brain? The case of living category impairment. *Cortex, 30*, 3–25.

Deutsch, J.A. (1960). *The structural basis of behavior*. Chicago: University of Chicago Press.

de Villiers, P.A., & de Villiers, J.G. (1979). *Early language*. London: Fontana/Open Books.

Dooling, D.J., & Lachman, R. (1971). Effects of comprehension on retention of prose. *Journal of Experimental Psychology, 88*, 216–222.

Doyle, J.R., & Leach, C. (1988). Word superiority in signal detection: Barely a glimpse, yet reading nonetheless. *Cognitive Psychology, 20*, 283–318.

Duffy, S.A., Morris, R.K., & Rayner, K. (1988). Lexical ambiguity and fixation times in reading. *Journal of Memory and Language, 27*, 429–446.

Duncan, S.E., & Niederehe, G. (1974). On signaling that it's your turn to speak. *Journal of Experimental Social Psychology, 10*, 234–247.

Duncker, K. (1945). On problem-solving. *Psychological Monographs, 58*, (5, Whole No. 270).

Dunlea, A. (1984). The relation between concept formation and semantic roles: Some evidence from the blind. In L. Feagans, C. Garvery, & R.M. Golinkoff (Eds.), *The origins and growth of communication* (pp. 224–243). Norwood, NJ: Ablex.

Dunlea, A. (1989). *Vision and the emergence of meaning: Blind and sighted children's early language*. Cambridge: Cambridge University Press.

Durkin, K. (1987). Minds and language: Social cognition, social interaction and the acquisition of language. *Mind and Language, 2*, 105–140.

Durso, F.T., & Johnson, M.K. (1979). Facilitation in naming and categorizing repeated pictures and words. *Journal of Experimental Psychology: Human Learning and Memory, 5*, 449–459.

Ehrlich, S.F., & Rayner, K. (1981). Contextual effects on word perception and eye movements during reading. *Journal of Verbal Learning and Verbal Learning Behavior, 20*, 641–655.

Eimas, P.D., Miller, J.L., & Jusczyk, P.W. (1987). On infant speech perception and the acquisition of language. In S. Harnad (Ed.), *Categorical perception* (pp. 161–195). New York: Cambridge University Press.

Eimas, P.D., Siqueland, E.R., Jusczyk, P.W., & Vigorito, J. (1971). Speech perception in infants. *Science, 171*, 303–306.

Elbers, L. (1985). A tip-of-the-tongue experience at age two? *Journal of Child Language, 12*, 353–365.

Ellis, A.W. (1980). On the Freudian theory of speech errors. In V.A. Fromkin (Ed.), *Errors in linguistic performance* (pp. 123–132). New York: Academic Press.

Ellis, A.W. (1985). The production of spoken words: A cognitive neuro-psychological perspective. In A.W. Ellis (Ed.), *Progress in the psychology of language* (Vol. 2, pp. 107–145). Hove, UK: Lawrence Erlbaum Associates Ltd.

Ellis, A.W. (1993). *Reading, writing and dyslexia: A cognitive analysis* (2nd ed.). Hove, UK: Lawrence Erlbaum Associates Ltd.

Ellis, A.W., & Marshall, J.C. (1978). Semantic errors or statistical flukes: A note on Allport's "On knowing the meaning of words we are unable to report". *Quarterly Journal of Experimental Psychology, 30*, 569–575.

Ellis, A.W., Miller, D., & Sin, G. (1983). Wernicke's aphasia and normal language processing: A case study in cognitive neuropsychology. *Cognition, 15*, 111–144.

Ellis, A.W., & Young, A.W. (1988). *Human cognitive neuropsychology*. Hove, UK: Lawrence Erlbaum Associates Ltd.

Ellis, N.C., & Beaton, A. (1993). Factors affecting the learning of foreign language vocabulary: Imagery keyword mediators and phonological short-term memory. *Quarterly Journal of Experimental Psychology, 46A*, 533–558.

Ellis, R., & Wells, G. (1980). Enabling factors in adult-child discourse. *First Language, 1*, 46–62.

Elman, J.L. (1990). Finding structure in time. *Cognitive Science, 14*, 179–211.

Elman, J.L. (1991). Distributed representations, simple recurrent networks, and grammatical structure. *Machine Learning, 7*, 195–225.

Elman, J.L. (1993). Learning and development in neural networks: The importance of starting small. *Cognition, 48*, 71–99.

Elman, J.L., & McClelland, J.L. (1988). Cognitive penetration of the mechanisms of perception: Compensation for coarticulation of lexically restored phonemes. *Journal of Memory and Language, 27*, 143–165.

Entus, A.K. (1977). Hemispheric asymmetry in processing of dichotically presented speech sounds. In S.J. Segalowitz & F.A. Gruber (Eds.), *Language development and neurological theory* (pp. 63–73). New York: Academic Press.

Eriksen, C.W., Pollack, M.D., & Montague, W.E. (1970). Implicit speech: Mechanisms in perceptual encoding? *Journal of Experimental Psychology, 84*, 502–507.

Ervin-Tripp, S. (1979). Children's verbal turn-taking. In E. Ochs & B.B. Schieffelin (Eds.), *Developmental pragmatics* (pp. 391–414). New York: Academic Press.

Ervin-Tripp, S. (1993). Conversational discourse. In J. Berko Gleason & N.B. Ratner (Eds.), *Psycholinguistics* (pp. 238–271). Fort Worth: Holt, Rhinehart & Winston.

Eysenck, M.W., & Keane, M.T. (1995). *Cognitive psychology: A student's handbook* (3rd ed.). Hove, UK: Lawrence Erlbaum Associates Ltd.

Fabb, N. (1994). *Sentence structure.* London: Routledge & Kegan Paul.

Faglioni, P., & Botti, C. (1993). How to differentiate retrieval from storage deficit: A stochastic approach to semantic memory modeling. *Cortex, 29,* 501–518.

Farah, M.J., & Commentators. (1994). Neuropsychological inference with an interactive brain: A critique of the "locality" assumption. *Behavioral and Brain Sciences, 17,* 43–104.

Farah, M.J., Hammond, K.M., Mehta, Z., & Ratcliff, G. (1989). Category-specificity and modality-specificity in semantic memory. *Neuropsychologia, 27,* 193–200.

Farah, M.J., & McClelland, J.L. (1991). A computational model of semantic memory impairment: Modality-specificity and emergent category-specificity. *Journal of Experimental Psychology: General, 120,* 339–357.

Farrar, M.J. (1990). Discourse and the acquisition of grammatical morphemes. *Journal of Child Language, 17,* 607–624.

Fay, D., & Cutler, A. (1977). Malapropisms and the structure of the mental lexicon. *Linguistic Inquiry, 8,* 505–520.

Feitelson, D., Tehori, B.Z., & Levinberg-Green, D. (1982). How effective is early instruction in reading? Experimental evidence. *Merrill-Palmer Quarterly, 28,* 458–494.

Fera, P., & Besner, D. (1992). The process of lexical decision: More words about a parallel distributed processing model. *Journal of Experimental Psychology: Learning, Memory, and Cognition, 18,* 749–764.

Ferreira, F., & Clifton, C. (1986). The independence of syntactic processing. *Journal of Memory and Language, 25,* 348–368.

Ferreira, F., & Henderson, J.M. (1990). Use of verb information in syntactic parsing: Evidence from eye movements and word-by-word self-paced reading. *Journal of Experimental Psychology: Learning, Memory, and Cognition, 16,* 555–568.

Feyereisen, P. (1983). Gestures and speech, interactions and separations: A reply to McNeill. *Psychological Review, 94,* 493–498.

Fillmore, C.J. (1968). The case for case. In E. Bach & R.T. Harms (Eds.), *Universals of linguistic theory* (pp. 1–90). New York: Holt, Rhinehart & Winston.

Finch, S., & Chater, N. (1992). Bootstrapping syntactic categories. *Proceedings of the 14th Annual Conference of the Cognitive Science Society* (pp. 820–825). Hillsdale, NJ: Lawrence Erlbaum Associates Ltd.

Fischler, I. (1977). Semantic facilitation without association in a lexical decision task. *Memory and Cognition, 5,* 335–339.

Fischler, I., & Bloom, P.A. (1979). Automatic and attentional processes in the effects of sentence contexts on word recognition. *Journal of Verbal Learning and Verbal Behavior, 18,* 1–20.

Flavell, J.H., Miller, P.H., & Miller, S. (1993). *Cognitive development* (3rd ed.). Englewood Cliffs, NJ: Prentice-Hall.

Flege, J.E., & Hillenbrand, J. (1984). Limits on phonetic accuracy in foreign language speech production. *Journal of the Acoustical Society of America, 76,* 708–721.

Fletcher, C.R. (1986). Strategies for the allocation of short-term memory during comprehension. *Journal of Memory and Language, 25,* 43–58.

Fletcher, C.R. (1994). Levels of representation in memory for discourse. In M.A. Gernsbacher (Ed.), *Handbook of psycholinguistics* (pp. 589–608). San Diego: Academic Press.

Fletcher, P., & Garman, M. (1986). *Language acquisition* (2nd ed.). Cambridge: Cambridge University Press.

Fletcher, P., & MacWhinney, B. (Eds.). (1995). *Handbook of child language.* Oxford: Blackwell.

Flores d'Arcais, G.B., Saito, H., & Kawakami, M. (1995). Phonological and semantic activation in reading Kanji characters. *Journal of Experimental Psychology: Learning, Memory, and Cognition, 21,* 34–42.

Fodor, J.A. (1972). Some reflections on L.S. Vygotsky's thought and language. *Cognition, 1,* 83–95.

Fodor, J.A. (1975). *The language of thought.* Hassocks, Sussex: Harvester Press.

Fodor, J.A. (1978). Tom Swift and his procedural grandmother. *Cognition, 6,* 229–247.

Fodor, J.A. (1979). In reply to Philip Johnson-Laird. *Cognition, 7,* 93–95.

Fodor, J.A. (1981). The present status of the innateness controversy. In J.A. Fodor, *Representations* (pp. 257–316). Brighton: Harvester Press.

Fodor, J.A. (1983). *The modularity of mind.* Cambridge, MA: MIT Press.

Fodor, J.A. (1985). Précis and multiple book review of the Modularity of mind. *Behavioral and Brain Sciences, 8,* 1–42.

Fodor, J.A., & Bever, T.G. (1965). The psychological reality of linguistic segments. *Journal of Verbal Learning and Verbal Behavior, 4,* 414–420.

Fodor, J.A., Bever, T.G., & Garrett, M.F. (1974). *The psychology of language.* New York: McGraw-Hill.

Fodor, J.A., & Garrett, M.F. (1967). Some syntactic determinants of sentential complexity. *Perception and Psychophysics, 2,* 289–296.

Fodor, J.A., Garrett, M.F., Walker, E.C.T., & Parkes, C.H. (1980). Against definitions. *Cognition, 8,* 263–367.

Fodor, J.D. (1978). Parsing strategies and constraints on transformations. *Linguistic Inquiry, 9,* 427–473.

Fodor, J.D. (1990). Thematic roles and modularity: Comments on the chapters by Frazier and Tanenhaus et al. In G.T.M. Altmann (Ed.), *Cognitive models of speech processing* (pp. 434–456). Cambridge, MA: MIT Press.

Fodor, J.D., Fodor, J.A., & Garrett, M.F. (1975). The psychological unreality of semantic representations. *Linguistic Inquiry, 6,* 515–531.

Fodor, J.D., & Frazier, L. (1980). Is the human sentence parsing mechanism an ATN? *Cognition, 8,* 418–459.

Ford, M., Bresnan, J., & Kaplan, R.M. (1982). A competence-based theory of syntactic closure. In J. Bresnan (Ed.), *The mental representation of grammatical relations* (pp. 727–796). Cambridge, MA: MIT Press.

Ford, M., & Holmes, V.M. (1978). Planning units and syntax in sentence production. *Cognition, 6,* 35–53.

Forster, K.I. (1976). Accessing the mental lexicon. In R.J. Wales & E.C.T. Walker (Eds.), *New approaches to language mechanisms* (pp. 257–287). Amsterdam: North Holland.

Forster, K.I. (1979). Levels of processing and the structure of the language processor. In W.E. Cooper & E.C.T. Walker (Eds.), *Sentence processing: Psycholinguistic studies presented to Merrill Garrett* (pp. 27–85). Hillsdale, NJ: Lawrence Erlbaum Associates Inc.

Forster, K.I. (1981a). Frequency blocking and lexical access: One mental lexicon or two? *Journal of Verbal Learning and Verbal Behavior, 20,* 190–203.

Forster, K.I. (1981b). Priming and effects of sentence and lexical contexts on naming time: Evidence of autonomous lexical processing. *Quarterly Journal of Experimental Psychology, 33A,* 465–495.

Forster, K.I. (1989). Basic issues in lexical processing. In W.D. Marslen-Wilson (Ed.), *Lexical representation and process* (pp. 75–107). Cambridge, MA: MIT Press.

Forster, K.I. (1994). Computational modeling and elementary process analysis in visual word recognition. *Journal of Experimental Psychology: Human Perception and Performance, 20,* 1292–1310.

Forster, K.I., & Chambers, S.M. (1973). Lexical access and naming time. *Journal of Verbal Learning and Verbal Behavior, 12,* 627–635.

Forster, K.I., & Davis, C. (1984). Repetition priming and frequency attenuation in lexical access. *Journal of Experimental Psychology: Learning, Memory, and Cognition, 10,* 680–698.

Foss, D.J. (1970). Some effects of ambiguity upon sentence comprehension. *Journal of Verbal Learning and Verbal Behavior, 9,* 699–706.

Foss, D.J. (1982). A discourse on semantic priming. *Cognitive Psychology, 14,* 590–607.

Foss, D.J., & Blank, M.A. (1980). Identifying the speech codes. *Cognitive Psychology, 12,* 1–31.

Foss, D.J., & Gernsbacher, M.A. (1983). Cracking the dual code: Toward a unitary model of phoneme identification. *Journal of Verbal Learning and Verbal Behavior, 22,* 609–632.

Foss, D.J., & Swinney, D.A. (1973). On the psychological reality of the phoneme: Perception, identification, and consciousness. *Journal of Verbal Learning and Verbal Behavior, 12,* 246–257.

Fouts, R.S., Fouts, D.H., & van Cantford, T.E. (1989). The infant Loulis learns signs from cross-fostered chimpanzees. In R.A. Gardner, B.T. Gardner, & T.E. van Cantford (Eds.), *Teaching sign language to chimpanzees* (pp. 280–292). Albany, NY: Suny Press.

Fouts, R.S., Shapiro, G., & O'Neil, C. (1978). Studies of linguistic behaviour in apes and children. In P. Siple (Ed.), *Understanding language through sign language research* (pp. 163–185). London: Academic Press.

Fouts, R.S., Hirsch, A.D., & Fouts, D.H. (1982). Cultural transmission of a human language in a chimpanzee mother–infant relationship. In H.E. Fitzgerald, J.A. Mullins, & P. Cage (Eds.), *Child nurturance* (Vol. 3, pp. 159–193). New York: Plenum Press.

Francis, W.N., & Kuçera, H. (1982). *Frequency analysis of English usage.* Boston: Houghton Mifflin.

Franklin, S., Howard, D., & Patterson, K.E. (1994). Abstract word deafness. *Cognitive Neuropsychology, 11,* 1–34.

Frauenfelder, U.H., & Peeters, G. (1990). Lexical segmentation and TRACE: An exercise in simulation. In G.T.M. Altmann (Ed.), *Cognitive models of speech processing* (pp. 50–86). Cambridge, MA: MIT Press.

Frauenfelder, U.H., & Tyler, L.K. (1987). The process of spoken word recognition: An introduction. *Cognition, 25*, 1–20.

Frazier, L. (1987a). Sentence processing: A tutorial review. In M. Coltheart (Ed.), *Attention and performance, XII: The psychology of reading* (pp. 559–586). Hove, UK: Lawrence Erlbaum Associates Ltd.

Frazier, L. (1987b). Syntactic processing: Evidence from Dutch. *Natural Language and Linguistic Theory, 5*, 519–560.

Frazier, L. (1989). Against lexical generation of syntax. In W.D. Marslen-Wilson (Ed.), *Lexical representation and process* (pp. 505–528). Cambridge, MA: MIT Press.

Frazier, L. (1990). Exploring the architecture of the language processing system. In G.T.M. Altmann (Ed.), *Cognitive models of speech processing* (pp. 409–433). Cambridge, MA: MIT Press.

Frazier, L., & Clifton, C. (1989). Successive cyclicity in the grammar and parser. *Language and Cognitive Processes, 4*, 93–126.

Frazier, L., Clifton, C., & Randall, J. (1983). Filling gaps: Decision principles and structure in sentence comprehension. *Cognition, 13*, 187–222.

Frazier, L., Flores d'Arcais, G.B., & Coolen, R. (1993). Processing discontinuous words: On the interface between lexical and syntactic processing. *Cognition, 47*, 219–249.

Frazier, L., & Fodor, J.D. (1978). The sausage machine: A new two-stage parsing model. *Cognition, 6*, 291–325.

Frazier, L., & Rayner, K. (1982). Making and correcting errors during sentence comprehension: Eye movements in the analysis of structurally ambiguous sentences. *Cognitive Psychology, 14*, 178–210.

Frederiksen, J.R., & Kroll, J.F. (1976). Spelling and sound: Approaches to the internal lexicon. *Journal of Experimental Psychology: Human Perception and Performance, 2*, 361–379.

Frege, G. (1892). Über Sinn und Bedeutung. *Zeitschrifte für Philosophie und Philosophische Kritik, 100*, 25–50. Translated in P.T. Geach & M. Black (Eds.), Philosophical writings of Gottlob Frege (1952). Oxford: Blackwell.

Fremgen, A., & Fay, D. (1980). Overextensions in production and comprehension: A methodological clarification. *Journal of Child Language, 7*, 205–211.

Freud, S. (1975). *The psychopathology of everyday life.* (Trans. A. Tyson.) Harmondsworth: Penguin. (Originally published 1901.)

Friederici, A., & Kilborn, K. (1989). Temporal constraints on language processing: Syntactic priming in Broca's aphasia. *Journal of Cognitive Neuroscience, 1*, 262–272.

Frith, U. (1985). Beneath the surface of developmental dyslexia. In K.E. Patterson, J.C. Marshall, & M. Coltheart (Eds.), *Surface dyslexia* (pp.301–330). Hove, UK: Lawrence Erlbaum Associates Ltd.

Fromkin, V.A. (1971/1973). The non-anomalous nature of anomalous utterances. *Language, 51*, 696–719. Reprinted in V.A. Fromkin (Ed.) (1973), *Speech errors as linguistic evidence* (pp. 215–242). The Hague: Mouton.

Fromkin, V.A. (1993). Speech production. In J. Berko Gleason & N.B. Ratner (Eds.), *Psycholinguistics* (pp. 272–301). Fort Worth: Holt, Rhinehart & Winston.

Fromkin, V.A., & Rodman, R. (1978). *An introduction to language* (2nd ed.). New York: Holt, Rhinehart & Winston.

Funnell, E. (1983). Phonological processes in reading: New evidence from acquired dyslexia. *British Journal of Psychology, 74*, 159–180.

Funnell, E., & Sheridan, J. (1992). Categories of knowledge? Unfamiliar aspects of living and non-living things. *Cognitive Neuropsychology, 9*, 135–153.

Furth, H. (1966). *Thinking without language*. London: MacMillan.

Furth, H. (1971). Linguistic deficiency and thinking: Research with deaf subjects 1964–69. *Psychological Bulletin, 75*, 58–72.

Furth, H. (1973). *Deafness and learning: A psychosocial approach*. Belmont, CA: Wadsworth.

Gallaway, C., & Richards, B.J. (Eds.) (1994). *Input and interaction in language acquisition*. Cambridge: Cambridge University Press.

Ganong, W.F. (1980). Phonetic categorization in auditory word perception. *Journal of Experimental Psychology: Human Perception and Performance, 6*, 110–125.

Gardner, R.A., & Gardner, B.T. (1969). Teaching sign language to a chimpanzee. *Science, 165*, 664–672.

Gardner, R.A., & Gardner, B.T. (1975). Evidence for sentence constituents in the early utterances of child chimpanzee. *Journal of Experimental Psychology: General, 104*, 244–267.

Gardner, R.A., van Cantfort, T.E., & Gardner, B.T. (1992). Categorical replies to categorical questions by cross-fostered chimpanzees. *American Journal of Psychology, 105*, 27–57.

Garnham, A. (1983a). Why psycholinguists don't care about DTC: A reply to Berwick and Weinberg. *Cognition, 15*, 263–270.

Garnham, A. (1983b). What's wrong with story grammars. *Cognition, 15*, 145–154.

Garnham, A. (1985). *Psycholinguistics: Central topics*. London: Methuen.

Garnham, A. (1987a). *Mental models as representation of discourse and text*. Chichester: Horwood.

Garnham, A. (1987b). Understanding anaphora. In A.W. Ellis (Ed.), *Progress in the psychology of language* (Vol. 3, pp. 253–300). Hove, UK: Lawrence Erlbaum Associates Ltd.

Garnham, A., & Oakhill, J. (1992). Discourse processing and text representation from a "mental models" perspective. *Language and Cognitive Processes, 7*, 193–204.

Garnham, A., Oakhill, J., & Cruttenden, H. (1992). The role of implicit causality and gender cue in the interpretation of pronouns. *Language and Cognitive Processes, 7*, 231–255.

Garnham, A., Oakhill, J., Ehrlich, M.-F., & Carreiras, M. (1995). Representations and processes in the interpretation of pronouns: New evidence from Spanish and French. *Journal of Memory and Language, 34*, 41–62.

Garnham, A., Oakhill, J., & Johnson-Laird, P.N. (1982). Referential continuity and the coherence of discourse. *Cognition, 11*, 29–46.

Garnham, A., Shillcock, R.C., Brown, G.D.A., Mill, A.I.D., & Cutler, A. (1982). Slips of the tongue in the London-Lund corpus of spontaneous conversation. In A. Cutler (Ed.), *Slips of the tongue and language production* (pp. 251–263). Amsterdam: Mouton.

Garnica, O. (1977). Some prosodic and paralinguistic features of speech to young children. In Snow, C.E., & Ferguson, C.A. (Eds.), *Talking to children: Language input and acquisition* (pp. 63–88). Cambridge: Cambridge University Press.

Garnsey, S.M., Tanenhaus, M.K., & Chapman, R.M. (1989). Evoked potentials and the study of sentence comprehension. *Journal of Psycholinguistic Research, 18*, 51–60.

Garrett, M.F. (1970). Does ambiguity complicate the perception of sentences? In G.B. Flores d'Arcais & W.J.M. Levelt (Eds.), *Advances in psycholinguistics* (pp. 48–60). Amsterdam: North Holland.

Garrett, M.F. (1975). The analysis of sentence production. In G. Bower (Ed.), *The psychology of learning and motivation* (Vol. 9, pp. 133–177). New York: Academic Press.

Garrett, M.F. (1976). Syntactic processes in sentence production. In R.J. Wales & E.C.T. Walker (Eds.), *New approaches to language mechanisms* (pp. 231–255). Amsterdam: North Holland.

Garrett, M.F. (1980a). Levels of processing in sentence production. In B. Butterworth (Ed.), *Language production: Vol. 1: Speech and talk* (pp. 177–220). London: Academic Press.

Garrett, M.F. (1980b). The limits of accommodation. In V. Fromkin (Ed.), *Errors in linguistic performance: Slips of the tongue, ear, pen, and hand* (pp. 263–271). New York: Academic Press.

Garrett, M.F. (1982). Production of speech: Observations from normal and pathological language use. In A.W. Ellis (Ed.), *Normality and pathology in cognitive functions* (pp. 19–76). London: Academic Press.

Garrett, M.F. (1988). Processes in language production. In F.J. Newmeyer (Ed.), *Linguistics: The Cambridge Survey: Vol. 3: Language: Psychological and biological aspects* (pp. 69–96). Cambridge: Cambridge University Press.

Garrett, M.F. (1992). *Disorders of lexical selection*. Cognition, 42, 143–180.

Garrett, M.F., Bever, T.G., & Fodor, J.A. (1966). The active use of grammar in speech perception. *Perception and Psychophysics, 1*, 30–32.

Garrod, S.C., & Sanford, A.J. (1977). Interpreting anaphoric relations: The integration of semantic information while reading. *Journal of Verbal Learning and Verbal Behavior, 16*, 77–90.

Garrod, S.C., & Sanford, A.J. (1994). Resolving sentences in a discourse context: how discourse representation affects language understanding. In M.A. Gernsbacher (Ed.), *Handbook of psycholinguistics* (pp. 675–698). San Diego: Academic Press.

Gathercole, S.E., & Baddeley, A.D. (1990). Phonological memory deficits in language disordered children: Is there a causal connection? *Journal of Memory and Language, 29*, 336–360.

Gathercole, V.C. (1985). "He has too much hard questions": The acquisition of the linguistic mass–count distinction in much and many. *Journal of Child Language, 12*, 395–415.

Gathercole, V.C. (1987). The contrastive hypothesis for the acquisition of word meaning: A reconsideration of the theory. *Journal of Child Language, 14*, 493–531.

Gazdar, G., Klein, E., Pullum G.K., & Sag, I.A. (1985). *Generalized phrase structure grammar*. Oxford: Blackwell.

Gentner, D. (1981). Verb structures in memory for sentences: Evidence for componential representation. *Cognitive Psychology, 13*, 56–83.

Gentner, D. (1982). Why nouns are learned before verbs: Linguistic relativity vs. natural partitioning. In S.A. Kuczaj (Ed.), *Language development: Vol. 2: Language, thought, and culture* (pp. 301–334). Hillsdale, NJ: Lawrence Erlbaum Associates Inc.

Gergely, G., & Bever, T.G. (1986). Related intuitions and the mental representation of causative verbs in adults and children. *Cognition, 23,* 211–277.

Gerken, L (1994). Child phonology: Past research, present questions, future direction. In M.A. Gernsbacher (Ed.), *Handbook of psycholinguistics* (pp. 781–820). San Diego: Academic Press.

Gernsbacher, M.A. (1984). Resolving 20 years of inconsistent interactions between lexical familiarity and orthography, concreteness, and polysemy. *Journal of Experimental Psychology: General, 113,* 256–281.

Gernsbacher, M.A. (1994). (Ed.) *Handbook of psycholinguistics.* San Diego: Academic Press.

Gernsbacher, M.A., & Hargreaves, D.J. (1988). Accessing sentence participants: The advantage of first mention. *Journal of Memory and Language, 27,* 699–717.

Gernsbacher, M.A., Hargreaves, D.J., & Beeman, M. (1989). Building and accessing clausal representations: The advantage of first mention versus the advantage of clause recency. *Journal of Memory and Language, 28,* 735–755.

Gerrig, R. (1986). Processes and products of lexical access. *Language and Cognitive Processes, 1,* 187–196.

Gibbs, R.W. Jnr. (1986). What makes some indirect speech acts conventional? *Journal of Memory and Language, 25,* 181–196.

Gibbs, R.W. Jnr. (1994). Figurative thought and figurative language. In M.A. Gernsbacher (Ed.), *Handbook of psycholinguistics* (pp. 411–446). San Diego: Academic Press.

Gilhooly, K.J. (1984). Word age-of-acquisition and residence time in lexical memory as factors in word naming. *Current Psychological Research, 3,* 24–31.

Glanzer, M., & Ehrenreich, S.L. (1979). Structure and search of the internal lexicon. *Journal of Verbal Learning and Verbal Behavior, 18,* 381–398.

Glaser, W.R. (1992). Picture naming. *Cognition, 42,* 61–105.

Gleason, H.A. (1961). *An introduction to descriptive linguistics.* New York: Holt, Rinehart & Winston.

Gleason, J.B., Hay, D., & Crain, L. (1989). The social and affective determinants of language development. In M. Rice & R. Schiefelbusch (Eds.), *The teachability of language* (pp. 171–186). Baltimore: Paul Brookes.

Gleason, J.B., & Ratner, N.B. (1993). Language development in children. In J.B. Gleason & N.B. Ratner (Eds.), *Psycholinguistics* (pp. 301–350). Fort Worth: Harcourt Brace Jovanovich.

Gleitman, L.R. (1981). Maturational determinants of language growth. *Cognition, 10,* 105–113.

Gleitman, L.R. (1990). The structural sources of word meaning. *Language Acquisition, 1,* 3–55.

Gleitman, L.R., & Wanner, E. (1982). Language acquisition: The state of the state of the art. In E. Wanner & L.R. Gleitman (Eds.), *Language acquisition: The state of the art* (pp. 3–48). Cambridge: Cambridge University Press.

Glucksberg, S. (1988). Language and thought. In R.J. Sternberg & E.E. Smith (Eds.), *The psychology of human thought* (pp. 214–241). Cambridge: Cambridge University Press.

Glucksberg, S., Kreuz, R.J., & Rho, S.H. (1986). Context can constrain lexical access: Implications for models of language comprehension. *Journal of Experimental Psychology: Learning, Memory and Cognition, 12,* 323–335.

Glucksberg, S., & Weisberg, R.W. (1966). Verbal behavior and problem solving: Some effects of labelling in a functional fixedness problem. *Journal of Experimental Psychology, 71*, 659–664.

Glushko, R.J. (1979). The organization and activation of orthographic knowledge in reading aloud. *Journal of Experimental Psychology: Human Perception and Performance, 5*, 674–691.

Gold, E.M. (1967). Language identification in the limit. *Information and Control, 16*, 447–474.

Goldfield, B.A. (1993). Noun bias in maternal speech to one-year-olds. *Journal of Child Language, 20*, 85–99.

Goldiamond, I., & Hawkins, W.F. (1958). Vexierversuch: The logarithmic relationship between word-frequency and recognition obtained in the absence of stimulus words. *Journal of Experimental Psychology, 56*, 457–463.

Goldin-Meadow, S., Butcher, C., Mylander, C., & Dodge, M. (1994). Nouns and verbs in a self-styled gesture system: What's in a name? *Cognitive Psychology, 27*, 259–319.

Goldinger, S.D., Luce, P.A., & Pisoni, D.B. (1989). Priming lexical neighbours of spoken words: Effects of competition and inhibition. *Journal of Memory and Language, 28*, 501–518.

Goldman-Eisler, F. (1958). Speech production and the predictability of words in context. *Quarterly Journal of Experimental Psychology, 10*, 96–106.

Goldman-Eisler, F. (1968). *Psycholinguistics: Experiments in spontaneous speech*. London: Academic Press.

Golinkoff, R.M., Hirsh-Pasek, K., Bailey, L.M., & Wenger, N.R. (1992). Young children and adults use lexical principles to learn new nouns. *Developmental Psychology, 28*, 99–108.

Golinkoff, R.M., Mervis, C.B., & Hirsh-Pasek, K. (1994). Early object labels: The case for lexical principles. *Journal of Child Language, 21*, 125–155.

Good, D.A., & Butterworth, B. (1980). Hesitancy as a conversational resource: Some methodological implications. In H.W. Dechert & M. Raupach (Eds.), *Temporal variables in speech* (pp. 145–152). The Hague: Mouton.

Goodglass, H. (1976). Agrammatism. In H. Whitaker and H.A. Whitaker (Eds.), *Studies in neurolinguistics* (Vol. 1, pp. 237–260). New York: Academic Press.

Gopnik, M. (1990a). Dysphasia in an extended family. *Nature, 344*, 715.

Gopnik, M. (1990b). Feature blindness: A case study. *Language Acquisition, 1*, 139–164.

Gopnik, M. (1992). A model module? *Cognitive Neuropsychology, 9*, 253–258.

Gopnik, M., & Crago, M.B. (1991). Familial aggregation of a developmental language disorder. *Cognition, 29*, 1–50.

Gordon, B., & Caramazza, A. (1982). Lexical decision for open- and closed-class words: Failure to replicate differential frequency sensitivity. *Brain and Language, 15*, 143–160.

Gordon, P. (1985). Evaluating the semantic categories hypothesis: The case of the count/mass distinction. *Cognition, 20*, 209–242.

Gordon, P. & Meyer, D.E. (1984). Perceptual-motor processing of phonetic features. *Journal of Experimental Psychology: Human Perception and Performance, 10*, 153–178.

Goswami, U. (1988). Orthographic analogies and reading development. *Quarterly Journal of Experimental Psychology, 40A*, 239–268.

Goswami, U. (1993). Towards an interactive analogy model of reading development: Decoding vowel graphemes in beginning reading. *Journal of Experimental Child Psychology, 56*, 443–475.

Goswami, U., & Bryant, P. (1990). *Phonological skills and learning to read.* Hove, UK: Lawrence Erlbaum Associates Ltd.

Gough, P.B. (1972). One second of reading. In J.F. Kavanaugh & I.G. Mattingly (Eds.), *Language by ear and by eye* (pp. 331–358). Cambridge, MA: MIT Press.

Graesser, A.C., Singer, M., & Trabasso, T. (1994). Constructing inferences during narrative text comprehension. *Psychological Review, 101*, 371–395.

Grainger, J. (1990). Word frequency and neighborhood frequency effects in lexical decision and naming. *Journal of Memory and Language, 29*, 228–244.

Grainger, J., O'Regan, K., Jacobs, A.M., & Segui, J. (1989). On the role of competing word units in visual word recognition: The neighbourhood frequency effect. *Perception and Psychophysics, 45*, 189–195.

Greenberg, J.H. (1963). Some universals of grammar with particular reference to the order of meaningful elements. In J.H. Greenberg (Ed.), *Universals of language* (pp. 58–90). Cambridge, MA: MIT Press.

Greene, J. (1972). *Psycholinguistics.* Harmondsworth: Penguin.

Greenfield, P.M., & Smith, J.H. (1976). *The structure of communication in early language development.* New York: Academic Press.

Grice, H.P. (1975). Logic and conversation. In P. Cole & J. Morgan (Eds.), *Syntax and semantics: Vol. 3: Speech acts* (pp. 41–58). New York: Academic Press.

Grober, E.H., Beardsley, W., & Caramazza, A. (1978). Parallel function in pronoun assignment. *Cognition, 6*, 117–133.

Grodzinsky, Y. (1984). The syntactic characterization of agrammatism. *Cognition, 16*, 88–120.

Grodzinsky, Y. (1989). Agrammatic comprehension of relative clauses. *Brain and Language, 37*, 480–499.

Grodzinsky, Y. (1990). *Theoretical perspectives on language deficits.* Cambridge, MA: MIT Press.

Grosjean, F. (1980). Spoken word recognition processes and the gating paradigm. *Perception and Psychophysics, 28*, 267–283.

Grosjean, F., & Gee, J.P. (1987). Prosodic structure and spoken word recognition. *Cognition, 25*, 135–155.

Grosjean, F., & Soares, C. (1986). Processing mixed language: Some preliminary findings. In J. Vaid (Ed.), *Linguistics processing in bilinguals: Psycholinguistic and neuropsychological perspectives* (pp. 145–179). Hillsdale, NJ: Lawrence Erlbaum Associates Inc.

Haarmann, H., & Kolk, H.H.J. (1991). Syntactic priming in Broca's aphasics: Evidence for slow activation. *Aphasiology, 5*, 247–263.

Haberlandt, K. (1994). Methods in reading research. In M.A. Gernsbacher (Ed.), *Handbook of psycholinguistic research* (pp. 1–32). San Diego: Academic Press.

Hakuta, K., & Diaz, R. (1985). The relationship between degree of bilingualism and cognitive ability: A critical discussion and some new longitudinal data. In K.E. Nelson (Ed.), *Children's language* (Vol. 5, pp. 319–344). Hillsdale, NJ: Lawrence Erlbaum Associates Inc.

Hall, D.G. (1993). Basic-level individuals. *Cognition, 48*, 199–221.

Hall, D.G. (1994). How mothers teach basic-level and situation-restricted count nouns. *Journal of Child Language, 21*, 391–414.

Hall, D.G., & Waxman, S.R. (1993). Assumptions about word meaning: Individuation and basic-level kinds. *Child Development, 64*, 1550–1570.

Halle, M., & Stevens, K.N. (1962). Speech recognition: A model and a program for research. *IRE Transactions of the Professional Group on Information Theory, 8*, 155–159.

Hampson, J., & Nelson, K. (1993). The relation of maternal language to variation in rate and style of language acquisition. *Journal of Child Language, 20*, 313–342.

Hampton, J.A. (1979). Polymorphous concepts in semantic memory. *Journal of Verbal Learning and Verbal Behavior, 18*, 441–461.

Hampton, J.A. (1981). An investigation of the nature of abstract concepts. *Memory and Cognition, 9*, 149–156.

Hankamer, J., & Sag, I.A. (1976). Deep and surface anaphora. *Linguistic Inquiry, 7*, 391–428.

Harley, T.A. (1984). A critique of top-down independent levels models of speech production: Evidence from non-plan-internal speech production. *Cognitive Science, 8*, 191–219.

Harley, T.A. (1990a). Environmental contamination of normal speech. *Applied Psycholinguistics, 11*, 45–72.

Harley, T.A. (1990b). Paragrammatisms: Syntactic disturbance or failure of control? *Cognition, 34*, 85–91.

Harley, T.A. (1993a). Phonological activation of semantic competitors during lexical access in speech production. *Language and Cognitive Processes, 8*, 291–309.

Harley, T.A. (1993b). Connectionist approaches to language disorders. *Aphasiology, 7*, 221–249.

Harley, T.A. (1995). Connectionist models of anomia: A reply to Nickels. *Language and Cognitive Processes, 10*, 47–58.

Harley, T.A., & MacAndrew, S.B.G. (1992). Modelling paraphasias in normal and aphasic speech. *Proceedings of the 14th Annual Conference of the Cognitive Science Society* (pp. 378–383). Hillsdale, NJ: Lawrence Erlbaum Associates Inc.

Harley, T.A., & MacAndrew, S.B.G. (in press). Interactive models of lexicalisation: Some constraints from speech error, picture naming, and neuropsychological data. In J. Levy, D. Bairaktaris, J. Bullinaria, & D. Cairns (Eds.), *Connectionist models of memory and language*. London: UCL Press.

Harris., M. (1978). Noun animacy and the passive voice: A developmental approach. *Quarterly Journal of Experimental Psychology, 30*, 495–504.

Harris, M., & Coltheart, M. (1986). *Language processing in children and adults*. London: Routledge & Kegan Paul.

Harris, P.L. (1982). Cognitive prerequisites to language? *British Journal of Psychology, 73*, 187–195.

Harris, R.J. (1977). Comprehension of pragmatic implications in advertising. *Journal of Applied Psychology, 63*, 603–608.

Harris, R.J. (1978). The effect of jury size and judge's instructions on memory for pragmatic implications from courtroom testimony. *Bulletin of the Psychonomic Society, 11*, 129–132.

Harris, R.J. (Ed.) (1992). *Cognitive processing in bilinguals*. Amsterdam: North Holland.

Harris, Z.S. (1951). *Methods in structural linguistics*. Chicago: University of Chicago Press.

Hart, J., Berndt, R.S., & Caramazza, A. (1985). Category-specific naming deficit following cerebral infarction. *Nature, 316,* 439–440.

Haviland, S.E., & Clark, H.H. (1974). What's new? Acquiring new information as a process of comprehension. *Journal of Verbal Learning and Verbal Behavior, 13,* 515–521.

Hayes, C. (1951). *The ape in our house.* New York: Harper.

Hayes, K.J., & Nissen, C.H. (1971). Higher mental functions of a home-raised chimpanzee. In A.M. Schrier & F. Stollnitz (Eds.), *Behaviour of nonhuman primates* (Vol. 4, pp. 60–115). New York: Academic Press.

Heath, S.B. (1983). *Ways with words.* Cambridge: Cambridge University Press.

Heider, E.R. (1972). Universals in colour naming and memory. *Journal of Experimental Psychology, 93,* 10–20.

Henderson, A., Goldman-Eisler, F., & Skarbek, A. (1966). Sequential temporal patterns in speech. *Language and Speech, 8,* 236–242.

Henderson, L. (1982). *Orthography and word recognition in reading.* London: Academic Press.

Henderson, L. (1987). Word recognition: A tutorial review. In M. Coltheart (Ed.), *Attention and performance XII: The psychology of reading* (pp. 171–200). Hove, UK: Lawrence Erlbaum Associates Ltd.

Hendler, J.A. (1989). Marker-passing over microfeatures: Towards a hybrid symbolic/connectionist model. *Cognitive Science, 13,* 79–106.

Hendrix, G.G. (1979). Encoding knowledge in partitioned networks. In N.V. Findler (Ed.), *Associative networks: Representation and use of knowledge by computers* (pp. 51–92). New York: Academic Press.

Herman, L.M., Richards, D.G., & Wolz, J.P. (1984). Comprehension of sentences by bottlenosed dolphins. *Cognition, 16,* 129–219.

Herrnstein, R., Loveland, D., & Cable, C. (1977). Natural concepts in pigeons. *Journal of Experimental Psychology: Animal learning and memory, 2,* 285–302.

Hickerson, N.P. (1971). Review of "Basic Color Terms". *International Journal of American Linguistics, 37,* 257–270.

Hieke, A.E., Kowal, S.H., & O'Connell, D.C. (1983). The trouble with "articulatory" pauses. *Language and Speech, 26,* 203–214.

Hinton, G.E. (1992). How neural networks learn from experience. *Scientific American, 267,* (3, September), 105–109.

Hinton, G.E., Plaut, D.C., & Shallice, T. (1993). Simulating brain damage. *Scientific American, 269,* (4, October), 58–65.

Hinton, G.E., & Sejnowski, T.J. (1986). Learning and relearning in Boltzmann machines. In D.E. Rumelhart, J.L. McClelland, & the PDP Research Group. (1986). *Parallel distributed processing: Explorations in the microstructure of cognition* (Vol. 1: Foundations, pp. 282–317). Cambridge, MA: MIT Press.

Hinton, G.E, & Shallice, T. (1991). Lesioning an attractor network: Investigations of acquired dyslexia. *Psychological Review, 98,* 74–95.

Hintzman, D.L. (1986). "Schemata abstraction" in a multiple-trace memory model. *Psychological Review, 93,* 411–428.

Hirsh-Pasek, K., Kemler-Nelson, D.G., Jusczyk, P.W., Cassidy, K. W., Druss, B., & Kennedy, L. (1987). Clauses are perceptual units for young infants. *Cognition, 26,* 269–286.

Hirsh-Pasek, K., Reeves, L.M., & Golinkoff, R.M. (1993). Words and meaning: From primitives to complex organisation. In J. Berko Gleason & N.B. Ratner (Eds.), *Psycholinguistics* (pp. 134–199). Fort Worth: Harcourt Brace.

Hirsh-Pasek, K., Treiman, R., & Schneiderman, M. (1984). Brown and Hanlon revisited: Mothers' sensitivity to ungrammatical forms. *Journal of Child Language, 11*, 81–88.

Hladik, E.G., & Edwards, H.T. (1984). A comparative analysis of mother-father speech in the naturalistic home environment. *Journal of Psycholinguistic Research, 13*, 321–332.

Hockett, C.F. (1960). The origin of speech. Scientific American, 203, 89–96.

Hodgson, J.M. (1991). Informational constraints on pre-lexical priming. *Language and Cognitive Processes, 6*, 169–205.

Hoffman, J.E., & MacMillan, F.W. (1985). Is semantic priming automatic? In M.I. Posner & O.S. Marin (Eds.), *Attention and performance X1* (pp. 585–599). Hillsdale, NJ: Lawrence Erlbaum Associates Inc.

Hogaboam, T.W., & Perfetti, C.A. (1975). Lexical ambiguity and sentence comprehension: The common sense effect. *Journal of Verbal Learning and Verbal Behavior, 14*, 265–275.

Holender, D. (1986). Semantic activation without conscious identification in dichotic listening, parafoveal vision, and visual masking: A survey and appraisal. *The Behavioral and Brain Sciences, 9*, 1–23.

Hollan, J.D. (1975). Features and semantic memory: Set-theoretic or network model? *Psychological Review, 82*, 154–155.

Holmes, V.M. (1979). Accessing ambiguous words during sentence comprehension. *Quarterly Journal of Experimental Psychology, 31*, 569–589.

Holmes, V.M. (1984). Sentence planning in a story continuation task. *Language and Speech, 27*, 115–134.

Holmes, V.M. (1987). Syntactic parsing: In search of the garden path. In M. Coltheart (Ed.), *Attention and performance, XII: The psychology of reading* (pp. 587–599). Hove, UK: Lawrence Erlbaum Associates Ltd.

Holmes, V.M. (1988). Hesitations and sentence planning. *Language and Cognitive Processes, 3*, 323–361.

Holmes, V.M., Kennedy, A., & Murray, W.S. (1987). Syntactic structure and the garden path. *Quarterly Journal of Experimental Psychology, 39A*, 277–293.

Holmes, V.M., & O'Reagan, J.K. (1981). Eye fixation patterns during the reading of relative clause sentences. *Journal of Verbal Learning and Verbal Behavior, 20*, 417–430.

Holmes, V.M., Stowe, L., & Cupples, L. (1989). Lexical expectations in parsing complement-verb sentences. *Journal of Memory and Language, 28*, 668–689.

Holyoak, K.J., & Glass, A.L. (1975). The role of contradictions and counter-examples in the rejection of false sentences. *Journal of Verbal Learning and Verbal Behavior, 14*, 215–239.

Howard, D. (1985). Agrammatism. In S. Newman & R. Epstein (Eds.), *Current perspectives in dysphasia* (pp. 1–31). Edinburgh: Churchill Livingstone.

Howard, D., & Butterworth, B. (1989). Short-term memory and sentence comprehension: A reply to Vallar and Baddeley, 1987. *Cognitive Neuropsychology, 6*, 455–463.

Howard, D., & Franklin, S. (1988). *Missing the meaning?* Cambridge, MA: MIT Press.

Howard, D., & Hatfield, F.M. (1987). *Aphasia therapy: Historical and contemporary issues.* Hove, UK: Lawrence Erlbaum Associates Ltd.

Howard, D., & Orchard-Lisle, V. (1984). On the origin of semantic errors in naming: Evidence from the case of a global aphasic. *Cognitive Neuropsychology, 1*, 163–190.

Howe, C. (1980). Language learning from mothers' replies. *First Language, 1*, 83–97.

Howes, D.H., & Solomon, R.L. (1951). Visual duration threshold as a function of word probability. *Journal of Experimental Psychology, 41*, 401–410.

Huddleston, R. (1984). *Introduction to the grammar of English*. Cambridge: Cambridge University Press.

Humphreys, G.W. (1985). *Attention, automaticity, and autonomy in visual word processing*. Reading research: Advances in theory and practice (Vol. 5, pp. 253–310). New York: Academic Press.

Humphreys, G.W., & Bruce, V. (1989). *Visual cognition*. Hove, UK: Lawrence Erlbaum Associates Ltd.

Humphreys, G.W., & Evett, L.J. (1985). Are there independent lexical and non-lexical routes in word processing? An evaluation of the dual-route theory of reading. *Behavioral and Brain Sciences, 8*, 689–740.

Hunt, E., & Agnoli, F. (1991). The Whorfian hypothesis: A cognitive psychology perspective. *Psychological Review, 99*, 377–389.

Hurford, J.R. (1991). The evolution of the critical period for language acquisition. *Cognition, 40*, 159–201.

Jackendoff, R. (1977). X̄ Syntax: *A study of phrase structure*. Cambridge, MA: MIT Press.

Jackendoff, R. (1983). *Semantics and cognition*. Cambridge, MA: MIT Press.

Jacobs, A.M., & Grainger, J. (1994). Models of visual word recognition— Sampling the state of the art. *Journal of Experimental Psychology: Human Perception and Performance, 20*, 1311–1334.

Jacobsen, E. (1932). The electrophysiology of mental activities. *American Journal of Psychology, 44*, 677–694.

Jaffe, J., Breskin, S., & Gerstman, L.J. (1972). Random generation of apparent speech rhythms. *Language and Speech, 15*, 68–71,

Jakobson, R. (1968). *Child language, aphasia and phonological universals*. The Hague: Mouton.

James, S.L., & Khan, L.M.L. (1982). Grammatical morpheme acquisition: An approximately invariant order? *Journal of Psycholinguistic Research, 11*, 381–388.

Jared, D., McRae, K., & Seidenberg, M.S. (1990). The basis of consistency effects in word naming. *Journal of Memory and Language, 29*, 687–715.

Jared, D., & Seidenberg, M.S. (1991). Does word identification proceed from spelling to sound to meaning? *Journal of Experimental Psychology: General, 120*, 358–394.

Jarvella, R.J. (1971). Syntactic processing of connected speech. *Journal of Verbal Learning and Verbal Behavior, 10*, 409–416.

Jaynes, J. (1977). *The origin of consciousness in the breakdown of the bicameral mind*. Boston: Houghton Mifflin.

Jescheniak, J.D., & Levelt, W.J.M. (1994). Word frequency effects in speech production: Retrieval of syntactic information and of phonological form. *Journal of Experimental Psychology: Learning, Memory, and Cognition, 20*, 824–843.

Job, R., Miozzo, M., & Sartori, G. (1993). On the existence of category-specific impairments. A reply to Parkin and Stewart. *Quarterly Journal of Experimental Psychology, 46A*, 511–516.

Johnson, J.R., & Ramsted, V. (1983). Cognitive development in preadolescent language impaired children. *British Journal of Disorders of Communication, 18*, 49–55.

Johnson, J.S., & Newport, E.L. (1989). Critical period effects in second language learning: The influence of maturational state on the acquisition of English as a second language. *Cognitive Psychology, 21*, 60–99.

Johnson, R.E. (1970). Recall of prose as a function of the structural importance of the linguistic units. *Journal of Verbal Learning and Verbal Behavior, 9*, 12–90.

Johnson-Laird, P.N. (1975). Meaning and the mental lexicon. In A. Kennedy & A. Wilkes (Eds.), *Studies in long-term memory* (pp. 123–142). London: John Wiley.

Johnson-Laird, P.N. (1983). *Mental models.* Cambridge: Cambridge University Press.

Johnson-Laird, P.N. (1978). What's wrong with Grandma's guide to procedural semantics: A reply to Jerry Fodor. *Cognition, 6*, 249–261.

Johnson-Laird, P.N., Herrman, D.J., & Chaffin, R. (1984). Only connections: A critique of semantic networks. *Psychological Bulletin, 96*, 292–315.

Johnston, R.S. (1983). *Developmental deep dyslexia.* Cortex, 19, 133–139.

Jolicoeur, P., Gluck, M.A., & Kosslyn, S.M. (1984). Pictures and names: Making the connection. *Cognitive Psychology, 16*, 243–275.

Jones, G.V. (1985). Deep dyslexia, imageability, and ease of predication. *Brain and Language, 24*, 1–19.

Jones, G.V. (1989). Back to Woodworth: Role of interlopers in the tip-of-the-tongue phenomenon. *Memory and Cognition, 17*, 69–76.

Jones, G.V., & Langford, S. (1987). Phonological blocking in the tip of the tongue state. *Cognition, 26*, 115–122.

Jones, G.V., & Martin, M. (1985). Deep dyslexia and the right-hemisphere hypothesis for semantic paralexia: A reply to Marshall and Patterson. *Neuropsychologia, 23*, 685–688.

Jorm, A.F. (1979). The cognitive and neurological basis of developmental dyslexia: A theoretical framework and review. *Cognition, 7*, 19–32.

Jusczyk, P.W. (1982). Auditory versus phonetic coding of speech signals during infancy. In J. Mehler, E.C.T. Walker, & M. Garrett (Eds.), *Perspectives on mental representation* (pp. 361–387). Hillsdale, NJ: Lawrence Erlbaum Associates Inc.

Just, M.A., & Carpenter, P.A. (1980). A theory of reading: From eye fixations to comprehension. *Psychological Review, 87*, 329–354.

Kail, R., & Nippold, M.A. (1984). Unconstrained retrieval from semantic memory. *Child Development, 55*, 944–951.

Kaplan, R.M. (1972). Augmented transition networks as psychological models of sentence comprehension. *Artificial Intelligence, 3*, 77–100.

Kaplan, R.M., & Bresnan, J. (1982). Lexical-functional grammar: A formal system for grammatical representation. In J. Bresnan (Ed.), *The mental representation of grammatical relations* (pp. 173–281). Cambridge, MA: MIT Press.

Katz, J.J. (1977). The real status of semantic representations. *Linguistic Inquiry, 8*, 559–584.

Katz, J.J., & Fodor, J.A. (1963). The structure of a semantic theory. *Language, 39*, 170–210.

Katz, N., Baker, E., & Macnamara, J. (1974). What's in a name? A study of how children learn common and proper names. *Child Development, 45,* 469–473.

Kay, D.A., & Anglin, J.M. (1982). Overextension and underextension in the child's expressive and receptive speech. *Journal of Child Language, 9,* 83–98.

Kay, J. (1985). Mechanisms of oral reading: A critical appraisal of cognitive models. In A.W. Ellis (Ed.), *Progress in the psychology of language* (Vol. 2, pp. 73–105). Hove, UK: Lawrence Erlbaum Associates Ltd.

Kay, J., & Bishop, D. (1987). Anatomical differences between nose, palm, foot. Or, the body in question: Further dissection of the processes of sub-lexical spelling-sound translation. In M. Coltheart (Ed.), *Attention and performance XII: The psychology of reading* (pp. 449–469). Hove, UK: Lawrence Erlbaum Associates Ltd.

Kay, J., & Ellis, A.W. (1987). A cognitive neuropsychological case study of anomia: Implications for psychological models of word retrieval. *Brain, 110,* 613–629.

Kay, J., & Marcel, A.J. (1981). One process, not two in reading aloud: Lexical analogies do the work of nonlexical rules. *Quarterly Journal of Experimental Psychology, 33A,* 397–414.

Kay, P., & Kempton, W. (1984). What is the Sapir-Whorf hypothesis? *American Anthropologist, 86,* 65–79.

Kean, M-L. (1977). The linguistic interpretation of aphasic syndromes: Agrammatism in Broca's aphasia, an example. *Cognition, 5,* 9–46.

Keenan, J.M., MacWhinney, B., & Mayhew, D. (1977). Pragmatics in memory: A study of natural conversation. *Journal of Verbal Learning and Verbal Behavior, 16,* 549–560.

Kellogg, W.N., & Kellogg, L.A. (1933). *The ape and the child.* New York: McGraw-Hill.

Kelly, M.H., Bock, J.K., & Keil, F.C. (1986). Prototypicality in a linguistic context: Effects on sentence structure. *Journal of Memory and Language, 25,* 59–74.

Kempen, G., & Huijbers, P. (1983). The lexicalization process in sentence production and naming: Indirect election of words. *Cognition, 14,* 185–209.

Kendon, A. (1967). Some functions of gaze direction in social interaction. *Acta Psychologica, 26,* 22–63.

Kennedy, A., Murray, W.S., Jennings, F., & Reid, C. (1989). Parsing complements: Comments on the generality of the principle of minimal attachment. *Language and Cognitive Processes, 4,* 51–76.

Keysar, B. (1989). On the functional equivalence of literal and metaphorical interpretations of discourse. *Journal of Memory and Language, 28,* 375–385.

Kiger, J.I., & Glass, A.L. (1983). The facilitation of lexical decisions by a prime occurring after the target. *Memory and Cognition, 11,* 356–365.

Kilborn, K. (1994). Learning language late: Second language acquisition in adults. In M.A. Gernsbacher (Ed.), *Handbook of psycholinguistics* (pp. 917–944). San Diego: Academic Press.

Kimball, J. (1973). Seven principles of surface structure parsing in natural language. *Cognition, 2,* 15–47.

Kintsch, W. (1974). *The representation of meaning in memory.* Hillsdale, NJ: Lawrence Erlbaum Associates Inc.

Kintsch, W. (1979). On modelling comprehension. *Educational Psychologist, 14,* 3–14.

Kintsch, W. (1988). The use of knowledge in discourse processing: A construction-integration model. *Psychological Review, 95*, 163–182.

Kintsch, W. (1994). The psychology of discourse processing. In M.A. Gernsbacher (Ed.), *Handbook of psycholinguistics* (pp. 721–740). San Diego: Academic Press.

Kintsch, W., & Keenan, J.M. (1973). Reading rate and retention as a function of the number of propositions in the base structure of sentences. *Cognitive Psychology, 5*, 257–274.

Kintsch, W., & van Dijk, T.A. (1978). Toward a model of text comprehension and production. *Psychological Review, 85*, 363–394.

Kintsch, W., & Vipond, D. (1979). Reading comprehension and readability in educational practice and psychological theory. In L.G. Nilsson (Ed.), *Perspectives in memory research* (pp. 329–366). Hillsdale, NJ: Lawrence Erlbaum Associates Inc.

Kintsch, W., Welsch, D., Schmalhofer, F., & Zimny, S. (1990). Sentence memory: A theoretical analysis. *Journal of Memory and Language, 29*, 133–159.

Kiparsky, P., & Menn, L. (1977). On the acquisition of phonology. In J. Macnamara (Ed.), *Language learning and thought* (pp. 47–78). New York: Academic Press.

Kirsner, K., Smith, M., Lockhart, R.S., King, M.L., & Jain, M. (1984). The bilingual lexicon: Language-specific units in an integrated network. *Journal of Verbal Learning and Verbal Behavior, 23*, 519–539.

Klapp, S.T. (1974). Syllable-dependent pronunciation latencies in number naming, a replication. *Journal of Experimental Psychology, 102*, 1138–1140.

Klapp, S.T., Anderson, W.G., & Berrian, R. (1973). Implicit speech in reading considered. *Journal of Experimental Psychology, 100*, 368–374.

Klatt, D.H. (1979). Speech perception: A model of acoustic–phonetic analysis and lexical access. *Journal of Phonetics, 7*, 279–312.

Klatt, D.H. (1980). Speech perception: A model of acoustic-phonetic analysis and lexical access. In R.A. Cole (Ed.), *Perception and production of fluent speech* (pp. 243–288). Hillsdale, NJ: Lawrence Erlbaum Associates Inc.

Klatt, D.H. (1989). Review of selected models of speech perception. In W. Marslen-Wilson (Ed.), *Lexical representation and process* (pp. 169–226). Cambridge, MA: MIT Press.

Klee, T., & Fitzgerald, M.D. (1985). The relation between grammatical development and mean length of utterance in morphemes. *Journal of Child Language, 12*, 251–269.

Klein, W. (1986). *Second language acquisition.* Cambridge: Cambridge University Press.

Klima, E.S., & Bellugi, U. (1979). *The signs of language.* Cambridge, MA: Harvard University Press.

Kluender, K.R. (1994). Speech perception as a tractable problem in cognitive science. In M.A. Gernsbacher (Ed.), *Handbook of psycholinguistics* (pp. 173–218). San Diego: Academic Press.

Kluender, R., & Kutas, M. (1993). Bridging the gap: Evidence from ERPs on the processing of unbounded dependencies. *Journal of Cognitive Neuroscience, 5*, 196–214.

Kohn, S.E., & Friedman, R.B. (1986). Word-meaning deafness: A phonological-semantic dissociation. *Cognitive Neuropsychology, 3*, 291–308.

Kohn, S.E., Wingfield, A., Menn, L., Goodglass, H., Gleason, J.B., & Hyde, M. (1987). Lexical retrieval: The tip-of-the-tongue phenomenon. *Applied Psycholinguistics, 8*, 245–266.

Kolb, B., & Whishaw, I.Q. (1990). *Fundamentals of human neuropsychology* (3rd ed.). New York: WH Freeman and Co.

Kolk, H.H.J. (1978). The linguistic interpretation of Broca's aphasia: A reply to M-L. Kean. *Cognition, 6*, 353–361.

Kolk, H.H.J., & van Grunsven, M. (1985). Agrammatism as a variable phenomenon. *Cognitive Neuropsychology, 2*, 347–384.

Komatsu, L.K. (1992). Recent views of conceptual structure. *Psychological Bulletin, 112*, 500–526.

Koriat, A. (1981). Semantic facilitation in lexical decision as a function of prime-target association. *Memory and Cognition, 9*, 587–598.

Kornai, A., & Pullum, G.K. (1990). The X-bar theory of phrase structure. *Language, 66*, 24–50.

Kounios, J., & Holcomb, P.J. (1992). Structure and process in semantic memory: Evidence from event-related brain potentials and reaction times. *Journal of Experimental Psychology: General, 121*, 459–479.

Kounios, J., & Holcomb, P.J. (1994). Concreteness effects in semantic processing: ERP evidence supporting dual-coding theory. *Journal of Experimental Psychology: Learning, Memory, and Cognition, 20*, 804–823.

Krashen, S.D. (1973). Lateralization, language learning and the critical period: Some new evidence. Language Learning, 23, 63–74.

Krashen, S.D. (1982). *Principles and practices in second language acquisition.* Oxford: Pergamon.

Krashen, S.D., Long, M., & Scarcella, R. (1982). Age, rate, and eventual attainment in second language acquisition. In S.D. Krashen, R. Scarcella, & M. Long (Eds.), *Child-adult differences in second language acquisition* (pp. 161–172). Rowley, MA: Newbury House.

Kremin, H. (1985). Routes and strategies in surface dyslexia and dysgraphia. In K.E. Patterson, J.C. Marshall, & M. Coltheart (Eds.), *Surface dyslexia: Neuropsychological and cognitive studies of phonological reading* (pp. 105–137). Hove, UK: Lawrence Erlbaum Associates Ltd.

Kuçera, H., & Francis, W.N. (1967). *Computational analysis of present-day American English.* Providence, RI: Brown University Press.

Kuczaj, S.A. (1977). The acquisition of regular and irregular past tense forms. *Journal of Verbal Learning and Verbal Behavior, 16*, 589–600.

Kuczaj, S.A. (1990). Constraining constraint theories. *Cognitive Development, 5*, 341–344.

Kuhl, P.K. (1981). Discrimination of speech by non-human animals: Basic auditory sensitivities conducive to the perception of speech-sound categories. *Journal of the Acoustical Society of America, 70*, 340–349.

Kutas, M., & Hillyard, S.A. (1980). Reading senseless sentences: Brain potentials reflect semantic incongruity. *Science, 207*, 203–205.

Kutas, M., & van Petten, C. (1994). Psycholinguistics electrified: Event-related brain potential investigations. In M.A. Gernsbacher (Ed.), *Handbook of psycholinguistics* (pp. 83–143). San Diego: Academic Press.

Kyle, J.G., & Woll, B. (1985). *Sign language: The study of deaf people and their language.* Cambridge: Cambridge University Press.

Labov, W. (1973). The boundaries of words and their meanings. In C-J. Bailey & R.W. Shuy (Eds.), *New ways of analyzing variations in English* (pp. 340–373). Washington, DC: Georgetown University Press.

Labov, W., & Fanshel, D. (1977). *Therapeutic discourse: Psychotherapy as conversation*. New York: Academic Press.

Lachter, J., & Bever, T.G. (1988). The relation between linguistic structure and associative theories of language learning: A constructuve critique of some connectionist learning models. *Cognition, 28*, 195–247.

Lackner, J.R., & Garrett, M.F. (1972). Resolving ambiguity: Effects of biasing context in the unattended ear. *Cognition, 1*, 359–372.

Lakatos, I. (1970). Falsification and the methodology of scientific research programmes. In I. Lakatos & A. Musgrave (Eds.), *Criticism and the growth of knowledge* (pp. 91–196). Cambridge: Cambridge University Press.

Lakoff, G. (1987). *Women, fire, and dangerous things*. Chicago: University of Chicago Press.

Landau, B., & Gleitman, L.R. (1985). *Language and experience: Evidence from the blind child*. Cambridge, MA: Harvard University Press.

Landau, B., Jones, S., & Smith, L. (1992). Perception, ontology, and naming in young children: Commentary on Soja, Carey, and Spelke. *Cognition, 43*, 85–91.

Landauer, T.K., & Freedman, J.L. (1968). Information retrieval from long-term memory: Category size and recognition time. *Journal of Verbal Learning and Verbal Behavior, 7*, 291–295.

Lane, H., & Pillard, R. (1978). *The wild boy of Burundi*. New York: Random House.

Langacker, R. (1987). *Foundations of cognitive grammar*. Stanford: Stanford University Press.

Lantz, D., & Stefflre, V. (1964). Language and cognition revisited. *Journal of Abnormal Psychology, 69*, 472–481.

Lapointe, S. (1983). Some issues in the linguistic description of agrammatism. *Cognition, 14*, 1–39.

Laws, G., Davies, I., & Andrews, C. (1995). Linguistic structure and non-linguistic cognition: English and Russian blues compared. *Language and Cognitive Processes, 10*, 59–94.

Laxon, V., Masterson, J., & Coltheart, V. (1991). Some bodies are easier to read: The effect of consistency and regularity on children's reading. *Quarterly Journal of Experimental Psychology, 43A*, 793–824.

Laxon, V., Masterson, J., Pool, M., & Keating, C. (1992). Nonword naming: Further exploration of the pseudohomophone effect in terms of orthographic neighborhood size, graphemic changes, spelling-sound consistency, and reader accuracy. *Journal of Experimental Psychology: Learning, Memory, and Cognition, 18*, 730–748.

Lenneberg, E.H. (1962). Understanding language without ability to speak: A case report. *Journal of Abnormal and Social Psychology, 65*, 419–425.

Lenneberg, E.H. (1967). *The biological foundations of language*. New York: Wiley.

Lenneberg, E.H., & Roberts, J.M. (1956). *The language of experience*. Memoir 13, Indiana University Publications in Anthropology and Linguistics.

Leonard, L.B. (1989). Language learnability and specific language impairment in children. *Applied Psycholinguistics, 10*, 179–202.

Leonard, L.B., Newhoff, M., & Fey, M.E. (1980). Some instances of word usage without comprehension. *Journal of Child Language, 7*, 186–196.

Leopold, W.F. (1939–1949). *Speech development of a bilingual child: A linguist's record* (5 vols.). Evanston, IL: Northwestern University Press.

Levelt, W.J.M. (1989). *Speaking: From intention to articulation.* Cambridge, MA: MIT Press.

Levelt, W.J.M. (1992). Accessing words in speech production: Stages, processes and representations. *Cognition, 42,* 1–22.

Levelt, W.J.M., Schriefers, H., Vorberg, D., Meyer, A.S., Pechmann, T., & Havinga, J. (1991a). The time course of lexical access in speech production: A study of picture naming. *Psychological Review, 98,* 122–142.

Levelt, W.J.M., Schriefers, H., Vorberg, D., Meyer, A.S., Pechmann, T., & Havinga, J. (1991b). Normal and deviant lexical processing: Reply to Dell and O'Seaghdha (1991). *Psychological Review, 98,* 615–618.

Levinson, S. (1983). *Pragmatics.* Cambridge: Cambridge University Press.

Levy, E., & Nelson, K. (1994). Words in discourse: A dialectical approach to the acquisition of meaning and use. *Journal of Child Language, 21,* 367–389.

Levy, Y. (1983). It's frogs all the way down. *Cognition, 15,* 75–93.

Levy, Y. (1988). The nature of early language: Evidence from the development of Hebrew morphology. In Y. Levy, I.M. Schlesinger, & M.D.S. Braine (Eds.), *Categories and processes in language acquisition* (pp. 73–98). Hillsdale, NJ: Lawrence Erlbaum Associates Inc.

Levy, Y., & Schlesinger, I.M. (1988). The child's early categories: Approaches to language acquisition theory. In Y. Levy, I.M. Schlesinger, & M.D.S. Braine (Eds.), *Categories and processes in language acquisition* (pp. 261–276). Hillsdale, NJ: Lawrence Erlbaum Associates Inc.

Lewis, V. (1987). *Development and handicap.* Oxford: Blackwell.

Liberman, A.M., Cooper, F.S., Shankweiler, D.P., & Studdert-Kennedy, M. (1967). Perception of the speech code. *Psychological Review, 74,* 431–461.

Liberman, A.M., Harris, K.S., Hoffman, H.S., & Griffith, B.C. (1957). The discrimination of speech sounds within and across phoneme boundaries. *Journal of Experimental Psychology, 53,* 358–368.

Liberman, A.M., & Mattingly, I.G. (1985). The motor theory of speech perception revised. *Cognition, 21,* 1–36.

Liberman, I.Y., Shankweiler, D.P., Fischer, F.W., & Carter, B. (1974). Explicit syllable and phoneme segmentation in the young child. *Journal of Experimental Child Psychology, 18,* 201–212.

Lieven, E.V.M. (1994). Crosslinguistic and crosscultural aspects of language addressed to children. In C. Gallaway & B.J. Richards (Eds.), *Input and interaction in language acquisition* (pp. 56–73). Cambridge: Cambridge University Press.

Lightfoot, D. (1982). *The language lottery: Toward a biology of grammars.* Cambridge, MA: MIT Press.

Lindsay, P.H., & Norman, D.A. (1977). *Human information processing* (2nd ed.). New York: Academic Press.

Linebarger, M.C., Schwartz, M.F., & Saffran, E.M. (1983). Sensitivity to grammatical structure in so-called agrammatic aphasics. *Cognition, 13,* 361–392.

Liu, L.G. (1985). Reasoning counter-factually in Chinese: Are there any obstacles? *Cognition, 21,* 239–270.

Lively, S.E., Pisoni, D.B., & Goldinger, S.D. (1994). Spoken word recognition: Research and theory. In M.A. Gernsbacher (Ed.), *Handbook of psycholinguistics* (pp. 265–302). San Diego: Academic Press.

Locke, J. (1690). *Essay concerning human understanding*. (Ed. P.M. Nidditch, 1975.) Oxford: Clarendon.

Locke, J.L. (1983). *Phonological acquisition and change*. New York: Academic Press.

Loftus, E.F. (1973). Category, dominance, instance dominance, and categorization time. *Journal of Experimental Psychology, 97*, 70–74.

Loftus, E.F. (1975). Leading questions and the eyewitness report. *Cognitive Psychology, 7*, 560–572.

Loftus, E.F. (1979). *Eyewitness testimony*. Cambridge, MA: Harvard University Press.

Lorch, R.F., Balota, D.A., & Stamm, E.G. (1986). Locus of inhibition effects in the priming of lexical decisions: Pre- or post-lexical access. *Memory and Cognition, 9*, 587–598.

Lounsbury, F.G. (1954). Transitional probability, linguistic structure and systems of habit-family hierarchies. In C.E. Osgood & T.A. Sebeok (Eds.), *Psycholinguistics: A survey of theory and research problems* (pp. 93–101). Bloomington: Indiana University Press. (Reprinted 1965.)

Lowenfeld, B. (1948). Effects of blindness on the cognitive functions of children. *Nervous Child, 7*, 45–54.

Luce, P.A., Pisoni, D.B., & Goldinger, S.D. (1990). Similarity neighbourhoods of spoken words. In G.T.M. Altmann (Ed.), *Cognitive models of speech processing* (pp. 122–147). Cambridge, MA: MIT Press.

Luce, R.D. (1993). *Sound and hearing: A conceptual introduction*. Hillsdale, NJ: Lawrence Erlbaum Associates Inc.

Lucy, J.A. (1992). *Language diversity and thought*. Cambridge: Cambridge University Press.

Lucy, J.A., & Shweder, R.A. (1979). Whorf and his critics: Linguistic and non-linguistic influences on colour memory. *American Anthropologist, 81*, 581–615.

Lupker, S.J. (1984). Semantic priming without association: A second look. *Journal of Verbal Learning and Verbal Behavior, 23*, 709–733.

Lyons, J. (1977a). *Chomsky* (2nd ed.). London: Fontana. (First edition 1970.)

Lyons, J. (1977b). *Semantics* (Vol. 1). Cambridge: Cambridge University Press.

Lyons, J. (1977c). *Semantics* (Vol. 2). Cambridge: Cambridge University Press.

MacDonald, M.C. (1989). Priming effects from gaps to antecedents. *Language and Cognitive Processes, 4*, 35–56.

MacDonald, M.C., Just, M.A., & Carpenter, P.A. (1992). Working memory constraints on the processing of syntactic ambiguity. *Cognitive Psychology, 24*, 56–98.

MacDonald, M.C., Pearlmutter, N. J., & Seidenberg, M.S. (1994). The lexical nature of syntactic ambiguity resolution. *Psychological Review, 101*, 676–703.

MacKain, C. (1982). Assessing the role of experience in infant speech discrimination. *Journal of Child Language, 9*, 323–350.

MacKay, D.G. (1966). To end ambiguous sentences. *Perception and Psychophysics, 1*, 426–436.

MacKay, D.G. (1973). Aspects of the theory of comprehension, memory and attention. *Quarterly Journal of Experimental Psychology, 25*, 22–40.

Maclay, H., & Osgood, C.E. (1959). Hesitation phenomena in spontaneous English speech. *Word, 15*, 19–44.

Macnamara, J. (1972). Cognitive basis of language learning in infants. *Psychological Review, 79*, 1–13.

Macnamara, J. (1982). *Names for things: A study of human learning.* Cambridge, MA: MIT Press.

MacWhinney, B., & Leinbach, J. (1991). Implementations are not conceptualizations: Revising the verb learning model. *Cognition, 40,* 121–157.

MacWhinney, B., & Pleh, C. (1988). The processing of restrictive relative clauses in Hungarian. *Cognition, 29,* 95–141.

Malotki, E. (1983). *Hopi time: A linguistic analysis of temporal concepts in the Hopi language.* Berlin: Mouton.

Malt, B.C. (1985). The role of discourse structure in understanding anaphora. *Journal of Memory and Language,* 24, 271–289.

Mandler, J.M. (1978). A code in the node: The cue of a story schema in retrieval. *Discourse Processes, 1,* 14–35.

Mandler, J.M., & Johnson, N.S. (1977). Remembrance of things parsed: Story structure and recall. *Cognitive Psychology, 9,* 111–191.

Mandler, J.M., & Johnson, N.S. (1980). On throwing out the baby with the bathwater: A reply to Black and Wilensky's evaluation of story grammars. *Cognitive Science, 4,* 305–312.

Manelis, L., & Tharp, D.A. (1977). The processing of affixed words. *Memory and Cognition, 5,* 690–695.

Maratsos, M.P. (1982). The child's construction of grammatical categories. In E. Wanner & L.R. Gleitman (Eds.), *Language acquisition: The state of the art* (pp. 240–266). Cambridge: Cambridge University Press.

Maratsos, M.P. (1983). Some current issues in the study of the acquisition of grammar. In J.H. Flavell, & E.M. Markman (Eds.), *Handbook of child psychology: Vol. 3: Cognitive development* (pp. 707–786). (P.H. Mussen, Series Editor). New York: Wiley.

Marcel, A.J. (1980). Surface dyslexia and beginning reading: A revised hypothesis of the pronunciation of print and its impairments. In M. Coltheart, K.E. Patterson, & J.C. Marshall (Eds.), *Deep dyslexia* (pp. 227–258). (2nd ed. 1987). London: Routledge and Kegan Paul.

Marcel, A.J. (1983a). Conscious and unconscious perception: Experiments on visual making and word recognition. *Cognitive Psychology, 15,* 197–237.

Marcel, A.J. (1983b). Conscious and unconscious perception: An approach to the relations between phenomenal experience and perceptual processes. *Cognitive Psychology, 15,* 238–300.

Marchman, V., & Bates, E. (1994). Continuity in lexical and morphological development: A test of the critical mass hypothesis. *Journal of Child Language, 21,* 339–366.

Marcus, G.F. (1993). Negative evidence in language acquisition. *Cognition, 46,* 53–85.

Marcus, G.F., Ullman, M., Pinker, S., Hollander, M., Rosen, T.J., & Xu, F. (1992). Overregularization in language acquisition. *Monographs of the Society for Research in Child Development, 57,* serial no. 228.

Marcus, M.P. (1980). *A theory of syntactic recognition for natural language.* Cambridge, MA: MIT Press.

Markman, E.M. (1985). Why superordinate category terms can be mass nouns. *Cognition, 19,* 311–353.

Markman, E.M. (1989). *Categorization and naming in children.* Cambridge, MA: MIT Press.

Markman, E.M. (1990). Constraints children place on word meanings. *Cognitive Science, 14,* 57–77.

Markman, E.M., & Wachtel, G.F. (1988). Children's use of mutual exclusivity to constrain the meaning of words. *Cognitive Psychology, 20*, 121–157.

Marr, D. (1982). *Vision: A computational investigation in to the human representation and processing of visual information.* San Francisco: WH Freeman.

Marsh, G., Desberg, P., & Cooper, J. (1977). Developmental changes in strategies of reading. *Journal of Reading Behaviour, 9*, 391–394.

Marsh, G., Friedman, M.P., Welch, V., & Desberg, P. (1981). A cognitive-developmental theory of reading acquisition. In T.G. Waller & G.E. Mackinnon (Eds.), *Reading research: Advances in theory and practice* (Vol. 3, pp. 199–221). New York: Academic Press.

Marshall, J.C. (1970). The biology of communication in man and animals. In J. Lyons (Ed.), *New horizons in linguistics* (Vol. 1, pp. 229–242). Harmondsworth: Penguin.

Marshall, J.C., & Newcombe, F. (1966). Syntactic and semantic errors in paralexia. *Neuropsychologia, 4*, 169–176.

Marshall, J.C., & Newcombe, F. (1973). Patterns of paralexia: A psycholinguistic approach. *Journal of Psycholinguistic Research, 2*, 175–199.

Marshall, J.C., & Newcombe, F. (1980). The conceptual status of deep dyslexia: An historical perspective. In M. Coltheart, K.E. Patterson, & J.C. Marshall (Eds.), *Deep dyslexia* (pp. 1–21). (2nd ed. 1987). London: Routledge & Kegan Paul.

Marshall, J.C., & Patterson, K.E. (1985). Left is still left for semantic paralexias: A reply to Jones and Martin. *Neuropsychologia, 23*, 689–690.

Marslen-Wilson, W.D. (1973). Linguistic structure and speech shadowing at very short latencies. *Nature, 244*, 522–523.

Marslen-Wilson, W.D. (1975). Sentence perception as an interactive parallel process. *Science, 189*, 226–228.

Marslen-Wilson, W.D. (1976). Linguistic descriptions and psychological assumptions in the study of sentence perception. In R.J. Wales & E.C.T. Walker (Eds.), *New approaches to language mechanisms* (pp. 203–230). Amsterdam: North Holland.

Marslen-Wilson, W.D. (1984). Spoken word recognition: A tutorial review. In H. Bouma & D.G. Bouwhis (Eds.), *Attention and performance X: Control of language processes* (pp. 125–150). Hove, UK: Lawrence Erlbaum Associates Ltd.

Marslen-Wilson, W.D. (1987). Functional parallelism in spoken word recognition. *Cognition, 25*, 71–102.

Marslen-Wilson, W.D. (1989). (Ed.) *Lexical representation and process.* Cambridge, MA: MIT Press.

Marslen-Wilson, W.D. (1990). Activation, competition, and frequency in lexical access. In G.T.M. Altmann (Ed.), *Cognitive models of speech processing* (pp. 148–172). Cambridge, MA: MIT Press.

Marslen-Wilson, W.D., & Tyler, L.K. (1980). The temporal structure of spoken language understanding. *Cognition, 8*, 1–71.

Marslen-Wilson, W.D., Tyler, L.K., Waksler, R., & Older, L. (1994). Morphology and meaning in the English mental lexicon. *Psychological Review, 101*, 3–33.

Marslen-Wilson, W.D., & Warren, P. (1994). Levels of perceptual representation and process in lexical access: Words, phonemes, and features. *Psychological Review, 101*, 653–675.

Marslen-Wilson, W.D., & Welsh, A. (1978). Processing interactions and lexical access during word recognition in continuous speech. *Cognitive Psychology, 10*, 29–63.

Martin, N., & Saffran, E.M. (1990). Repetition and verbal STM in transcortical sensory aphasia: A case study. *Brain and Language, 39*, 254–288.

Martin, N., & Saffran, E.M. (1992). A computational account of deep dysphasia: Evidence from a single case study. *Brain and Language, 43*, 240–274.

Martin, N., Saffran, E.M., Dell, G.S., & Schwartz, M.F. (1994). Origins of paraphasias in deep dysphasia: Testing the consequences of a decay impairment to an interactive spreading activation model of lexical retrieval. *Brain and Language, 47*, 609–660.

Martin, N., Weisberg, R.W., & Saffran, E.M. (1989). Variables influencing the occurrence of naming errors: Implications for models of lexical retrieval. *Journal of Memory and Language, 28*, 462–485.

Martin, R.C. (1982). The pseudohomophone effect: The role of visual similarity in non-word decisions. *Quarterly Journal of Experimental Psychology, 34A*, 395–410.

Martin, R.C., & Breedin, S.D. (1992). Dissociations between speech perception and phonological short-term memory deficits. *Cognitive Neuropsychology, 9*, 509–534.

Martin, R.C., Wetzel, W.F., Blossom-Stach, C., & Feher, E. (1989). Syntactic loss versus processing deficit: An assessment of two theories of agrammatism and syntactic comprehension deficits. *Cognition, 32*, 157–191.

Mason, M.K. (1942). Learning to speak after six and one half years silence. *Journal of Speech and Hearing Disorders, 7*, 295–304.

Massaro, D.W. (1988). Some criticisms of connectionist models of human performance. *Journal of Memory and Language, 27*, 213–234.

Massaro, D.W. (1989). Testing between the TRACE model and the fuzzy logical model of speech perception. *Cognitive Psychology, 21*, 398–421.

Massaro, D.W. (1994). Psychological aspects of speech perception: Implications for research and theory. In M.A. Gernsbacher (Ed.), *Handbook of psycholinguistics* (pp. 219–264). San Diego: Academic Press.

Massaro, D.W., & Cohen, M.M. (1991). Integration versus interactive activation: The joint influence of stimulus and context in perception. *Cognitive Psychology, 23*, 558–614.

Massaro, D.W., & Cohen, M.M. (1994). Visual, orthographic, phonological, and lexical influences in reading. *Journal of Experimental Psychology: Human Perception and Performance, 20*, 1107–1128.

Masson, M.E.J. (1995). A distributed memory model of semantic priming. *Journal of Experimental Psychology: Learning, Memory, and Cognition, 21*, 3–23.

Masterson, J., Coltheart, M., & Meara, P. (1985). Surface dyslexia in a language without irregularly spelled words. In K.E. Patterson, J.C. Marshall, & M. Coltheart (Eds.), Surface dyslexia: *Neuropsychological and cognitive studies of phonological reading* (pp. 215–223). Hove, UK: Lawrence Erlbaum Associates Ltd.

Mauner, G., Tanenhaus, M.K., & Carlson, G.N. (1995). A note on parallelism effects in processing deep and surface Verb-phrase anaphora. *Language and Cognitive Processes, 10*, 1–12.

Mazuka, R. (1991). Processing of empty categories in Japanese. *Journal of Psycholinguistic Research, 20*, 215–232.

McCann, R.S., & Besner, D. (1987). Reading pseudohomophones: Implications for models of pronunciation assembly and the locus of word frequency effects in naming. *Journal of Experimental Psychology: Human Perception and Performance, 13*, 14–24.

McCarthy, J.J., & Prince, A. (1990). Foot and word in prosodic morphology: The Arabic broken plural. *Natural Language and Linguistic Theory, 8*, 209–283.

McCauley, C., Parmalee, C.M., Sperber, R.D., & Carr, T.H. (1980). Early extraction of meaning from pictures and its relation to conscious identification. *Journal of Experimental Psychology: Human Perception and Performance, 6*, 265–276.

McClelland, J.L. (1979). On the time relations of mental processes: An examination of systems of processes in cascade. *Psychological Review, 86*, 287–330.

McClelland, J.L. (1987). The case for interactions in language processing. In M. Coltheart (Ed.), *Attention and performance XII: The psychology of reading* (pp. 3–36). Hove, UK: Lawrence Erlbaum Associates Ltd.

McClelland, J.L. (1991). Stochastic interactive processes and the effect of context on perception. *Cognitive Psychology, 23*, 1–44.

McClelland, J.L. & Elman, J.L. (1986). The TRACE model of speech perception. *Cognitive Psychology, 18*, 1–86.

McClelland, J.L., & Rumelhart, D.E. (1981). An interactive activation model of context effects in letter perception: Part 1. An account of the basic findings. *Psychological Review, 88*, 375–407.

McClelland, J.L., & Rumelhart, D.E. (1988). *Explorations in parallel distributed processing*. Cambridge, MA: MIT Press.

McClelland, J.L., Rumelhart, D.E., & the PDP Research Group. (1986). *Parallel distributed processing: Vol. 2: Psychological and biological models*. Cambridge, MA: MIT Press.

McClelland, J.L., St. John, M., & Taraban, R. (1989). Sentence comprehension: A parallel distributed processing approach. *Language and Cognitive Processes, 4*, 287–335.

McCloskey, M. (1980). The stimulus familiarity problem in semantic memory research. *Journal of Verbal Learning and Verbal Behavior, 19*, 485–504.

McCloskey, M., & Caramazza, A. (1988). Theory and methodology in cognitive neuropsychology: A response to our critics. *Cognitive Neuropsychology, 5*, 583–623.

McCloskey, M., & Glucksberg, S. (1978). Natural categories: Well-defined or fuzzy sets? *Memory and Cognition, 6*, 462–472.

McCune-Nicolich, L. (1981). The cognitive bases of relational words in the single word period. *Journal of Child Language, 8*, 15–34.

McDonald, J.L., Bock, J.K., & Kelly, M.H. (1993). Word order and world order: Semantic, phonological, and metrical determinants of serial position. *Cognitive Psychology, 25*, 188–230.

McElree, B. (1993). The locus of lexical preference effects in sentence comprehension: A time-course analysis. *Journal of Memory and Language, 32*, 536–571.

McKoon, G., & Ratcliff, R. (1986). Inferences about predictable events. *Journal of Experimental Psychology: Learning, Memory, and Cognition, 15*, 326–338.

McKoon, G., & Ratcliff, R. (1989). Semantic associations and elaborative inference. *Journal of Experimental Psychology: Learning, Memory, and Cognition, 12*, 82–91.

McKoon, G., & Ratcliff, R. (1992). Inference during reading. *Psychological Review, 99*, 440–466.

McKoon, G., Ratcliff, R., & Seifert, C.M. (1989). Making the connection: Generalized knowledge structures in story understanding. *Journal of Memory and Language, 28*, 711–734.

McLaughlin, B. (1984). *Second language acquisition in childhood* (2nd ed.). Hillsdale, NJ: Lawrence Erlbaum Associates Inc.

McLaughlin, B. (1987). *Theories of second-language learning*. London: Arnold.

McNamara, T.P. (1992). Theories of priming: I. Associative distance and lag. *Journal of Experimental Psychology: Learning, Memory, and Cognition, 18*, 1173–1190.

McNamara, T.P. (1994). Theories of priming: II. Types of prime. *Journal of Experimental Psychology: Learning, Memory, and Cognition, 20*, 507–520.

McNeill, D. (1985). So you think gestures are nonverbal? *Psychological Review, 92*, 350–371.

McNeill, D. (1987). So you think gestures are nonverbal! Reply to Feyereisen. *Psychological Review, 94*, 499–504.

McNeill, D. (1989). A straight path—to where? Reply to Butterworth and Hadar. *Psychological Review, 96*, 175–179.

McShane, J. (1980). *Learning to talk*. Cambridge: Cambridge University Press.

McShane, J. (1991). *Cognitive Development*. Oxford: Blackwell.

McShane, J., & Dockrell, J. (1983). Lexical and grammatical development. In B. Butterworth (Ed.), *Speech production: Vol. 2: Development, writing, and other language processes* (pp. 51–99). London: Academic Press.

Medin, D.L. (1989). Concepts and conceptual structure. *American Psychologist, 44*, 1469–1481.

Mehler, J. (1963). Some effects of grammatical transformations on the recall of English sentences. *Journal of Verbal Learning and Verbal Behavior, 2*, 346–351.

Mehler, J. (1981). The role of syllables in speech processing: Infant and adult data. *Philosophical Transactions of the Royal Society of London, Series B, 295*, 333–352.

Mehler, J., Dommergues, J., Frauenfelder, U.H., & Segui, J. (1981). The syllable's role in speech segmentation. *Journal of Verbal Learning and Verbal Behavior, 20*, 298–305.

Mehler, J., Jusczyk, P.W., Lambertz, G., Halstead, N., Bertoncini, J., & Amiel-Tison, C. (1988). A precursor of language acquisition in young infants. *Cognition, 29*, 143–178.

Mehler, J., Segui, J., & Carey, P.W. (1978). Tails of words: Monitoring ambiguity. *Journal of Verbal Learning and Verbal Behavior, 17*, 29–35.

Meier, R. P. (1991). Language acquisition by deaf children. *American Scientist, 79* (January-February), 60–70.

Menn, L. (1980). Phonological theory and child phonology. In G.H. Yeni-Komshian, J.F. Kavanagh, & C.A. Ferguson (Eds.), *Child phonology* (Vol. 1, pp. 23–41). New York: Academic Press.

Menyuk, P. (1969). *Sentences children use*. Cambridge, MA: MIT Press.

Menyuk, P., Menn, L., & Silber, R. (1986). Early strategies for the perception and production of words and sounds. In P. Fletcher & M. Garman (Eds.), *Language acquisition* (2nd ed., pp. 198–222). Cambridge: Cambridge University Press.

Meringer, R., & Mayer, K. (1895). *Versprechen und Verlesen: Eine Pyschologisch-Linguistische Studie*. Stuttgart: Gössen.

Merriman, W.E. (1986). How children learn the reference of concrete nouns: A critique of the current hypotheses. In S.A. Kuczaj & M.D. Barrett (Eds.), *The development of word meaning: Progress in cognitive development research* (pp. 1–38). New York: Springer-Verlag.

Mervis, C.B., & Bertrand, J. (1994). Young children and adults use lexical principles to learn new nouns. *Child Development, 65*, 1646–1662.

Mervis, C.B., & Canada, K. (1983). On the existence of competence errors in early comprehension: A reply to Fremgen & Fay and Chapman & Thomson. *Journal of Child Language, 10*, 431–440.

Mervis, C.B., Catlin, J., & Rosch, E. (1975). Relationships among goodness-of-example, category norms, and word frequency. *Bulletin of the Psychonomic Society, 7*, 283–284.

Messer, D. (1980). The episodic structure of maternal speech to young children. *Journal of Child Language, 7*, 29–40.

Meyer, A.S., & Bock, K. (1992). The tip-of-the-tongue phenomenon: Blocking or partial activation? *Memory and Cognition, 20*, 715–726.

Meyer, D.E., & Schvaneveldt, R.W. (1971). Facilitation in recognizing pairs of words: Evidence of a dependence between retrieval operations. *Journal of Experimental Psychology, 90*, 227–235.

Meyer, D.E., Schvaneveldt, R.W., & Ruddy, M.G. (1974). Loci of contextual effects on visual word recognition. In P.M.A. Rabbitt & S. Dornic (Eds.), *Attention and performance V* (pp. 98–118). New York: Academic Press.

Miceli, G., Mazzucci, A., Menn, L., & Goodglass, H. (1983). Contrasting cases of Italian agrammatic aphasia without comprehension disorder. *Brain and Language, 19*, 65–97.

Michaels, D. (1977). Linguistic relativity and color terminology. *Language and Speech, 20*, 333–343.

Milberg, W., Blumstein, S.E., & Dworetzky, B. (1987). Processing of lexical ambiguities in aphasia. *Brain and Language, 31*, 138–150.

Miller, D., & Ellis, A.W. (1987). Speech and writing errors in "neologistic jargonaphasia": A lexical activation hypothesis. In M. Coltheart, G. Sartori, & R. Job (Eds.), *The cognitive neuropsychology of language* (pp. 235–271). Hove, UK: Lawrence Erlbaum Associates Ltd.

Miller, G.A., Heise, G.A., & Lichten, W. (1951). The intelligibility of speech as a function of the text of the test materials. *Journal of Experimental Psychology, 41*, 329–355.

Miller, G.A., & Johnson-Laird, P.N. (1976). *Language and perception*. Cambridge: Cambridge University Press.

Miller, G.A., & McKean, K.E. (1964). A chronometric study of some relations between sentences. *Quarterly Journal of Experimental Psychology, 16*, 297–308.

Miller, G.A., & McNeill, D. (1969). Psycholinguistics. In G. Lindzey & E. Aronson (Eds.), *The handbook of social psychology* (Vol. 3, pp. 666–794). Reading, MA: Addison-Wesley.

Miller, J.L. (1981). Effects of speaking rate on segmental distinctions. In P.D. Eimas & J.L. Miller (Eds.), *Perspectives on the study of speech* (pp. 39–74). Hillsdale, NJ: Lawrence Erlbaum Associates Inc.

Miller, J.L., & Jusczyk, P.W. (1989). Seeking the neurobiological bases of speech perception. *Cognition, 33*, 111–137.

Mills, A.E. (Ed.) (1983). *Language acquisition in the blind child: Normal and deficient*. London: Croom Helm.

Milne, R.W. (1982). Predicting garden path sentences. *Cognitive Science, 6*, 349–373.

Milsark, G. (1983). On length and structure in sentence parsing. *Cognition, 13*, 129–134.

Minsky, M. (1975). A framework for representing knowledge. In P.H. Winston (Ed.), *The psychology of computer vision* (pp. 211–277). New York: McGraw-Hill.

Mitchell, D.C. (1987). Lexical guidance in human parsing: Locus and processing characteristics. In M. Coltheart (Ed.), *Attention and performance, XII: The psychology of reading* (pp. 601–618). Hove, UK: Lawrence Erlbaum Associates Ltd.

Mitchell, D.C. (1987). Reading and syntactic analysis. In J.R. Beech & A.M. Colley (Eds.), *Cognitive approaches to reading* (pp. 87–112). Chichester: John Wiley & Sons Ltd.

Mitchell, D.C. (1994). Sentence parsing. In M.A. Gernsbacher (Ed.), *Handbook of psycholinguistic research* (pp. 375–410). San Diego: Academic Press.

Mitchell, D.C., & Corley, M.M.B. (1994). Immediate biases in parsing: Discourse effects or experimental artifacts? *Journal of Experimental Psychology: Learning, Memory, and Cognition, 20*, 217–222.

Mitchell, D.C., Corley, M.M.B., & Garnham, A. (1992). Effects of context in human sentence parsing: Evidence against a discourse-based proposal mechanism. *Journal of Experimental Psychology: Learning, Memory, and Cognition, 18*, 69–88.

Mitchell, D.C., & Holmes, V.M. (1985). The role of specific information about the verb in parsing sentences with local structural ambiguity. *Journal of Memory and Language, 24*, 542–559.

Miyake, A., Carpenter, P.A., & Just, M.A. (1994). A capacity approach to syntactic comprehension disorders: Making normal adults perform like aphasic patients. *Cognitive Neuropsychology, 11*, 671–717.

Moerk, E. (1991). Positive evidence for negative evidence. *First Language, 11*, 219–251.

Mohay, H. (1982). A preliminary description of the communication systems evolved by two deaf children in the absence of a sign language model. *Sign Language Studies, 34*, 73–90.

Molfese, D.L. (1977). Infant cerebral asymmetry. In S.J. Segalowitz & F.A. Gruber (Eds.), *Language development and neurological theory* (pp. 21–35). New York: Academic Press.

Monsell, S. (1985). Repetition and the lexicon. In A.W. Ellis (Ed.), *Progress in psychology of language* (Vol. 2, pp. 147–195). Hove, UK: Lawrence Erlbaum Associates Ltd.

Monsell, S. (1987). On the relation between lexical input and output pathways for speech. In A. Allport, D. Mackay, W. Prinz, & E. Sheerer (Eds.), *Language perception and production: Shared mechanisms in listening, speaking, reading, and writing* (pp. 273–311). London: Academic Press.

Monsell, S. (1991). The nature and locus of word frequency effects in reading. In D. Besner & G.W. Humphreys (Ed.), *Basic processes in reading: Visual word recognition* (pp. 148–197). Hillsdale, NJ: Lawrence Erlbaum Associates Inc.

Monsell, S., Doyle, M.C., & Haggard, P.N. (1989). Effects of frequency on visual word recognition tasks: Where are they? *Journal of Experimental Psychology: General, 118*, 43–71.

Monsell, S., Matthews, G.H., & Miller, D.C. (1992). Repetition of lexicalization across languages: A further test of the locus of priming. *Quarterly Journal of Experimental Psychology,, 44A*, 763–783.

Montague, R. (1974). *Formal philosophy: Selected papers of Richard Montauge* (Ed. R. H. Thomason). London: Yale University Press.

Morais, J., Bertelson, P., Cary, L., & Alegria, J. (1986). Literacy training and speech segmentation. *Cognition, 24*, 45–64.

Morais, J., & Kolinsky, R. (1994). Perception and awareness in phonological processing: The case of the phoneme. *Cognition, 50*, 287–297.

Morgan, J.L., & Travis, L. L. (1989). Limits on negative information in language input. *Journal of Child Language, 16*, 531–552.

Morrison, C.M., Ellis, A.W., & Quinlan, P.T. (1992). Age of acquisition, not word frequency, affects object naming, not object recognition. *Memory and Cognition, 20*, 705–714.

Morrow, D.G., Bower, G.H., & Greenspan, S.L. (1989). Updating situation models during narrative comprehension. *Journal of Memory and Language, 28*, 292–312.

Morton, J. (1969). Interaction of information in word recognition. *Psychological Review, 76*, 165–178.

Morton, J. (1970). A functional model for human memory. In D.A. Norman (Ed.), *Models of human memory* (pp. 203–260). New York: Academic Press.

Morton, J. (1979a). Word recognition. In J. Morton & J.C. Marshall (Eds.), *Psycholinguistics series. Vol. 2: Structures and processes* (pp. 107–156). London: Paul Elek.

Morton, J. (1979b). Facilitation in word recognition: Experiments causing change in the logogen model. In P.A. Kolers, M.E. Wrolstad, & M. Bouma (Eds.), *Processing of visible language* (pp. 259–268). New York: Plenum.

Morton, J. (1984). Brain-based and non-brain-based models of language. In D. Caplan, A.R. Lecours, & A. Smith (Eds.), *Biological perspectives in language* (pp. 40–64). Cambridge, MA: MIT Press.

Morton, J. (1985). Naming. In S. Newman & R. Epstein (Eds.), *Current perspectives in dysphasia* (pp. 217–230). Edinburgh: Churchill Livingstone.

Morton, J., & Long, J. (1976). Effect of word transition probability on phoneme identification. *Journal of Verbal Learning and Verbal Behavior, 15*, 43–51.

Morton, J., & Patterson, K.E. (1980). A new attempt at an interpretation, or, an attempt at a new interpretation. In M. Coltheart, K.E. Patterson, & J.C. Marshall (Eds.), *Deep dyslexia* (pp. 91–118). (2nd ed. 1987). London: Routledge and Kegan Paul.

Moss, H.E., & Marslen-Wilson, W.D. (1993). Access to word meanings during spoken language comprehension: Effects of sentential semantic context. *Journal of Experimental Psychology: Learning, Memory, and Cognition, 19*, 1254–1276.

Mowrer, O.H. (1960). *Learning theory and symbolic processes*. New York: John Wiley and Sons.

Murphy, G.L. (1985). Processes of understanding anaphora. *Journal of Memory and Language, 24*, 290–303.

Murphy, G.L., & Medin, D.L. (1985). The role of theories in conceptual coherence. *Psychological Review, 92*, 289–316.

Nebes, R.D. (1989). Semantic memory in Alzheimer's disease. *Psychological Bulletin, 106,* 377–394.

Neely, J.H. (1977). Semantic priming and retrieval from lexical memory: Roles of inhibitionless spreading activation and limited capacity attention. *Journal of Experimental Psychology: General, 106,* 226–254.

Neely, J.H. (1991). Semantic priming effects in visual word recognition: A selective review of current findings and theories. In D. Besner & G.W. Humphreys (Ed.), *Basic processes in reading: Visual word recognition* (pp. 264–336). Hillsdale, NJ: Lawrence Erlbaum Associates Inc.

Neely, J.H., Keefe, D.E., & Ross, K. (1989). Semantic priming in the lexical decision task: Roles of prospective prime-generated expectancies and retrospective relation-checking. *Journal of Experimental Psychology: Learning, Memory, and Cognition, 15,* 1003–1019.

Neisser, U. (1981). John Dean's memory: A case study. *Cognition, 9,* 1–22.

Nelson, K. (1973). Structure and strategy in learning to talk. *Monographs of the Society for Research in Child Development, 38* (serial no. 149).

Nelson, K. (1974). Concept, word, and sentence: Inter-relations in acquisition and development. *Psychological Review, 81,* 267–285.

Nelson, K. (1979). Features, contrasts and the FCH: Some comments on Barrett's lexical development hypothesis. *Journal of Child Language, 6,* 139–146.

Nelson, K. (1987). What's in a name? Reply to Seidenberg and Petitto. *Journal of Experimental Psychology: General, 116,* 293–296.

Nelson, K. (1988). Constraints on word meaning? *Cognitive Development, 3,* 221–246.

Nelson, K. (1990). Comment on Behrend's "Constraints and development". *Cognitive Development, 5,* 331–339.

Nelson, K., Hampson, J., & Shaw, L.K. (1993). Nouns in early lexicons: Evidence, explanations and implications. *Journal of Child Language, 20,* 61–84.

Neville, H., Nicol, J.L., Barss, A., Forster, K.I., & Garrett, M.F. (1991). Syntactically based sentence processing classes: Evidence from event-related brain potentials. *Journal of Cognitive Neuroscience, 3,* 151–165.

Newman, F., & Holzman, L. (Eds.) (1993). *Lev Vygotsky: Revolutionary scientist.* London: Routledge.

Newmark, L. (1966). How not to interfere with language learning. *International Journal of American Linguistics, 32,* 77–83.

Newport, E.L. (1990). Maturational constraints on language learning. *Cognitive Science, 14,* 11–28.

Nickels, L. (1995). Getting it right? Using aphasic naming errors to evaluate theoretical models of spoken word production. *Language and Cognitive Processes, 10,* 13–45.

Nigram, A., Hoffman, J.E., & Simons, R.F. (1992). N400 to semantically anomalous pictures and words. *Journal of Cognitive Neuroscience, 4,* 15–22.

Ninio, A. (1980). Ostensive definition in vocabulary teaching. *Journal of Child Language, 7,* 565–573.

Nishimura, M. (1986). Intrasentential code-switching: The case of language assignment. In J. Vaid (Ed.), *Language processing in bilinguals* (pp. 123–143). Hillsdale, NJ: Lawrence Erlbaum Associates Inc.

Norman, D.A., & Rumelhart, D.E. (1975). Memory and knowledge. In D.A. Norman, D.E. Rumelhart, and the LNR Research Group (Eds.), *Explorations in cognition* (pp. 3–32). San Francisco: Freeman.

Norris, D. (1984). The effects of frequency, repetition, and stimulus quality in visual word recognition. *Quarterly Journal of Experimental Psychology, 36A*, 507–518.

Norris, D. (1986). Word recognition: Context effects without priming. *Cognition, 22*, 93–136.

Norris, D. (1987). Syntax, semantics, and garden paths. In A.W. Ellis (Ed.), *Progress in the psychology of language* (Vol. 3, pp. 233–252). Hove, UK: Lawrence Erlbaum Associates Ltd.

Norris, D. (1990). A dynamic-net model of human speech recognition. In G.T.M. Altmann (Ed.), *Cognitive models of speech processing* (pp. 87–104). Cambridge, MA: MIT Press.

Norris, D. (1994). A quantitative multiple-levels model of reading aloud. *Journal of Experimental Psychology: Human Perception and Performance, 20*, 1212–1232.

Norris, D., & Brown, G.D.A. (1985). Race models and analogy theories: A dead heat? Reply to Seidenberg. *Cognition, 20*, 155–168.

Nosofsky, R.M. (1991). Tests of an exemplar model for relating perceptual classification and recognition memory. *Journal of Experimental Psychology: Human Perception and Performance, 17*, 3–27.

Oakhill, J. (1994). Individual differences in children's text comprehension. In M.A. Gernsbacher (Ed.), *Handbook of psycholinguistics* (pp. 821–848). San Diego: Academic Press.

Obusek, C.J., & Warren, R.M. (1973). Relation of the verbal transformation and the phonemic restoration effects. *Cognitive Psychology, 5*, 97–107.

Oller, D.K. (1980). The emergence of sounds of speech in infancy. In G.H. Yeni-Komshian, J.F. Kavanagh, & C.A. Ferguson (Eds.), *Child phonology* (Vol. 1, pp. 93–112). New York: Academic Press.

Oller, D. K., Eilers, R.E., Bull, D.H., & Carney, A. E. (1985). Prespeech vocalizations of a deaf infant: A comparison with normal metaphonological processes. *Journal of Speech and Hearing Research, 28*, 47–63.

Oller, D. K., Wieman, L.A., Doyle, W.J., & Ross, C. (1976). Infant babbling and speech. *Journal of Child Language, 3*, 1–11.

Olson, R.K. (1994). Language deficits in "specific" reading ability. In M.A. Gernsbacher (Ed.), *Handbook of psycholinguistics* (pp. 895–916). San Diego: Academic Press.

Onifer, W., & Swinney, D.A. (1981). Accessing lexical ambiguities during sentence comprehension: Effects of frequency of meaning and contextual bias. *Memory and Cognition, 9*, 225–236.

Orchard G.A., & Philips, W. A. (1991). *Neural computation: A beginner's guide*. Hove, UK: Lawrence Erlbaum Associates Ltd.

Osgood, C.E., & Sebeok, T.A. (Eds.) (1954). *Psycholinguistics: A survey of theory and research problems* (pp. 93–101). Bloomington: Indiana University Press. (Reprinted 1965.)

O'Sullivan, C., & Yeager, C.P. (1989). Communicative context and linguistic competence: The effects of social setting on a chimpanzee's conversational skills. In R.A. Gardner, & T.E. van Cantford (Eds.), *Teaching sign language to chimpanzees* (pp. 269–279). Albany, NY: Suny Press.

Owens, R.E. Jr. (1988). *Language development: An introduction* (2nd ed.). Columbus: Merril.

Paap, K.R., Newsome, S., McDonald, J.E., & Schvaneveldt, R.W. (1982). An activation-verification model for letter and word recognition: The word superiority effect. *Psychological Review, 89*, 573–594.

Pachella, R.G. (1974). The interpretation of reaction time in information processing research. In B.H. Kantowitz (Ed.), *Human information processing: Tutorials in performance and cognition* (pp. 41–82). Hillsdale, NJ: Lawrence Erlbaum Associates Inc.

Paget, R. (1930). *Human speech*. New York: Harcourt Brace.

Paivio, A. (1971). *Imagery and verbal processes*. London: Holt, Rhinehart and Winston.

Paivio, A., Yuille, J.C., & Madigan, S. (1968). Concreteness, imagery, and meaningfulness values of 925 nouns. *Journal of Experimental Psychology Monographs, 76*.

Palmer, J., MacLeod, C.M., Hunt, E., & Davidson, J.E. (1985). Information processing correlates of reading. *Journal of Verbal Learning and Verbal Behavior, 24*, 59–88.

Parkin, A.J. (1982). Phonological recoding in lexical decision: Effects of spelling-to-sound regularity depend on how regularity is defined. *Memory and Cognition, 10*, 43–53.

Parkin, A.J., & Stewart, F. (1993). Category-specific impairments? No. A critique of Sartori et al. *Quarterly Journal of Experimental Psychology, 46A*, 505–509.

Patterson, F. (1981). *The education of Koko*. New York: Holt, Rhinehart & Winston.

Patterson, K.E. (1980). Derivational errors. In M. Coltheart, K.E. Patterson, & J.C. Marshall (Eds.), *Deep dyslexia* (pp. 286–306). (2nd ed. 1987). London: Routledge and Kegan Paul.

Patterson, K.E., & Besner, D. (1984). Is the right hemisphere literate? *Cognitive Neuropsychology, 3*, 341–367.

Patterson, K.E., & Coltheart, V. (1987). Phonological processes in reading: A tutorial review. In M. Coltheart (Ed.), *Attention and performance XII: The psychology of reading* (pp. 421–447). Hove, UK: Lawrence Erlbaum Associates Ltd.

Patterson, K.E., Marshall, J.C., & Coltheart, M. (1985). Surface dyslexia in various orthographies: Introduction. In K.E. Patterson, J.C. Marshall, & M. Coltheart (Eds.), (1985). *Surface dyslexia: Neuropsychological and cognitive studies of phonological reading* (pp. 209–214). Hove, UK: Lawrence Erlbaum Associates Ltd.

Patterson, K.E., Marshall, J.C., & Coltheart, M. (Eds.) (1985). *Surface dyslexia: Neuropsychological and cognitive studies of phonological reading*. Hove, UK: Lawrence Erlbaum Associates Ltd.

Patterson, K.E., & Morton, J. (1985). From orthography to phonology: An attempt at an old interpretation. In K.E. Patterson, J.C. Marshall, & M. Coltheart (Eds.), *Surface dyslexia: Neuropsychological and cognitive studies of phonological reading* (pp. 335–359). Hove, UK: Lawrence Erlbaum Associates Ltd.

Patterson, K.E., Seidenberg, M.S., & McClelland, J.L. (1989). Connections and disconnections: Acquired dyslexia in a computational model of reading processes. In R.G.M. Morris (Ed.), *Parallel distributed processing: Implications for psychology and neurobiology* (pp. 131–181). Oxford: Clarendon Press.

Patterson, K.E., Vargha-Khadem, F., & Polkey, C.E. (1989). Reading with one hemisphere. *Brain, 112*, 39–63.

Pavlov, I.P. (1927/1960). *Lectures on conditioned reflexes*. (Trans. G.V. Anrep). New York: Dover.

Pearce, J.M. (1987). *An introduction to animal cognition*. Hove, UK: Lawrence Erlbaum Associates Ltd.

Perfect, T.J., & Hanley, J.R. (1992). The tip-of-the-tongue phenomenon: Do experimenter-presented interlopers have any effect? *Cognition, 45*, 55–75.

Perfetti, C.A. (1994). Psycholinguistics and reading ability. In M.A. Gernsbacher (Ed.), *Handbook of psycholinguistics* (pp. 849–886). San Diego: Academic Press.

Perfetti, C.A., & Zhang, S. (1995). Very early phonological activation in Chinese reading. *Journal of Experimental Psychology: Learning, Memory and Cognition, 21*, 24–33.

Perrig, W., & Kintsch, W. (1985). Propositional and situational representations of text. *Journal of Memory and Language, 24*, 503–518.

Peters, P.S., & Ritchie, R.W. (1973). Context-sensitive immediate constituent analysis: Context-free language revisited. *Mathematical Systems Theory, 6*, 324–333.

Petersen, S.E., Fox, P.T., Posner, M.I., Mintun, M.E., & Raichle, J. (1989). Positron emission tomographic studies of the processing of single words. *Journal of Cognitive Neuroscience, 1*, 153–170.

Petrie, H. (1987). The psycholinguistics of speaking. In J. Lyons, R. Coates, M. Deuchar, & G. Gazdar (Eds.), *New horizons in linguistics* (Vol. 2, pp. 336–366). Harmondsworth: Penguin.

Piaget, J. (1923). *The language and thought of the child*. (Trans. M. Gabain, 1955). Cleveland: Meridian.

Piaget, J. (1967). *Six psychological studies*. New York: Vintage Books.

Piattelli-Palmarini, M. (Ed.) (1980). *Language and learning: the debate between Jean Piaget and Noam Chomsky*. London: Routledge & Kegan Paul.

Piattelli-Palmarini, M. (1989). Evolution, selection, and cognition: From "learning" to parameter setting in biology and the study of language. *Cognition, 31*, 1–44.

Piattelli-Palmarini, M. (1994). Ever since language and learning: Afterthoughts on the Piaget-Chomsky debate. *Cognition, 50*, 315–346.

Pine, J.M. (1994). The language of primary caregivers. In C. Gallaway & B.J. Richards (Eds.), *Input and interaction in language acquisition* (pp. 15–37). Cambridge: Cambridge University Press.

Pinker, S. (1984). *Language learnability and language development*. Cambridge, MA: MIT Press.

Pinker, S. (1989). *Learnability and cognition*. Cambridge, MA: MIT Press.

Pinker, S. (1994). *The language instinct*. Harmondsworth: Allen Lane.

Pinker, S., & Bloom, P. (1990). Natural language and natural selection. *Behavioral and Brain Sciences, 13*, 707–784.

Pinker, S., & Prince, A. (1988). On language and connectionism: Analysis of a parallel distributed processing model of language acquisition. *Cognition, 28*, 59–108.

Pisoni, D.B., & Luce, P.A. (1987). Acoustic-phonetic representations in word recognition. *Cognition, 25*, 21–52.

Pisoni, D.B., & Tash, J. (1974). Reaction times to comparisons within and across phonetic categories. *Perception and Psychophysics, 15*, 285–290.

Plaut, D.C., & McClelland, J.L. (1993). Generalizing with componential attractors: Word and nonword reading in an attractor network. In W. Kintsch (Ed.), *Proceedings of the Fifteenth Annual Conference of the Cognitive Science Society* (pp. 824–829). Hillsdale, NJ: Lawrence Erlbaum Associates Inc.

Plaut, D.C., & Shallice, T. (1993a). Deep dyslexia: A case study of connectionist neuropsychology. *Cognitive Neuropsychology, 10*, 377–500.

Plaut, D.C., and Shallice, T. (1993b). Perseverative and semantic influences on visual object naming errors in optic aphasia: A connectionist account. *Journal of Cognitive Neuroscience, 5*, 89–117.

Plunkett, K., & Marchman, V. (1991). U-shaped learning and frequency effects in a multi-layered perceptron: Implications for child language acquisition. *Cognition, 38*, 1–60.

Plunkett, K., & Marchman, V. (1993). From rote learning to system building: Acquiring verb morphology in children and connectionist nets. *Cognition, 48*, 21–69.

Pollatsek, A., Bolozky, S., Well, A.D., & Rayner, K. (1981). Asymmetries in the perceptual span for Israeli readers. *Brain and Language, 14*, 174–180.

Posner, M.I., & Carr, T.H. (1992). Lexical access and the brain: Anatomical constraints on cognitive models of word recognition. *American Journal of Psychology, 105*, 1–26.

Posner, M.I., & Keele, S.W. (1968). On the genesis of abstract ideas. *Journal of Experimental Psychology, 77*, 353–363.

Posner, M.I., & Snyder, C.R.R. (1975). Facilitation and inhibition in the processing of signals. In P.M.A. Rabbitt & S. Dornic (Eds.), *Attention and Performance V* (pp. 669–682). New York: Academic Press.

Postal, P. (1964). *Constituent Structure: A study of contemporary models of syntactic description*. Bloomington, IN: Research Center for the Language Sciences.

Postman, L., & Keppel, G. (1970). *Norms of word associations*. New York: Academic Press.

Potter, J.M. (1980). What was the matter with Dr. Spooner? In V.A. Fromkin (Ed.), *Errors in linguistic performance* (pp. 13–34). New York: Academic Press.

Potter, M.C., So, K.F., Von Eckardt, B., & Feldman, L.B. (1984). Lexical and conceptual representation in beginning and proficient bilinguals. *Journal of Verbal Learning and Verbal Behavior, 23*, 23–38.

Potts, G.R., Keenan, J.M., & Golding, J.M. (1988). Assessing the occurrence of elaborative inferences: Lexical decision versus naming. *Journal of Memory and Language, 27*, 399–415.

Prasada, S., & Pinker, S. (1993). Generalisation of regular and irregular morphological patterns. *Language and Cognitive Processes, 8*, 1–56.

Premack, D. (1971). Language in chimpanzee? *Science, 172*, 808–822.

Premack, D. (1976a). *Intelligence in ape and man*. Hillsdale, NJ: Lawrence Erlbaum Associates Inc.

Premack, D. (1976b). Language and intelligence in ape and man. *American Scientist, 64*, 674–683.

Premack, D. (1985). "Gavagai!" or the future history of the animal language controversy. *Cognition, 19*, 207–296.

Premack, D. (1986a). *Gavagai! or the future history of the animal language controversy*. Cambridge, MA: MIT Press.

Premack, D. (1986b). Pangloss to Cyrano de Bergerac: "nonsense, it's perfect!" A reply to Bickerton. *Cognition, 23*, 81–88.

Premack, D. (1990). Words: What are they, and do animals have them? *Cognition, 37*, 197–212.

Premack, D., & Woodruff, G. (1978). Does the chimpanzee have a theory of mind? *Behavioral and Brain Sciences, 1*, 515–526.

Pring, L. (1981). Phonological codes and functional spelling units: Reality and implications. *Perception and Psychophysics, 30,* 573–578.

Pullum, G.K. (1989). The great Eskimo vocabulary hoax. *Natural Language and Linguistic Theory, 7,* 275–281.

Pye, C. (1986). Quiché Mayan speech to children. *Journal of Child Language, 13,* 85–100.

Quine, W.V.O. (1960). *Word and object.* Cambridge, MA: MIT Press.

Quinlan, P.T. (1991). *Connectionism and psychology.* New York: Harvester Wheatsheaf.

Quinn, P.C., & Eimas, P.D. (1986). On categorization in early infancy. *Merrill-Palmer Quarterly, 32,* 331–363.

Rack, J.P., Snowling, M.J., & Olson, R.K. (1992). The nonword reading deficit in developmental dyslexia: A review. *Reading Research Quarterly, 27,* 29–43.

Radford, A. (1981). *Transformational syntax: A student's guide to Chomsky's extended standard theory.* Cambridge: Cambridge University Press (1981).

Rasmussen, T., & Milner, B. (1975). Clinical and surgical studies of the cerebral speech areas in man. In K.J. Zulch, O. Creutzfeldt, & G.C. Galbraith (Eds.), *Cerebral localization* (pp. 238–257). New York: Springer-Verlag.

Rasmussen, T., & Milner, B. (1977). The role of early left brain injury in determining lateralization of cerebral speech functions. *Annals of the New York Academy of Sciences, 299,* 355–369.

Rayner, K., & Frazier, L. (1987). Parsing temporarily ambiguous complements. *Quarterly Journal of Experiment Psychology, 39A,* 657–673.

Rayner, K., & Frazier, L. (1989). Selection mechanisms in reading lexically ambiguous words. *Journal of Experimental Psychology: Learning, Memory, and Cognition, 15,* 779–790.

Rayner, K., & Pollatsek, A. (1989). *The psychology of reading.* Englewood Cliffs, NJ: Prentice-Hall.

Rayner, K., Well, A.D., & Pollatsek, A. (1980). Asymmetry of the effective visual field in reading. *Perception and Psychophysics, 27,* 537–544.

Read, C., Zhang, Y., Nie, H., & Ding, B. (1986). The ability to manipulate speech sounds depends on knowing alphabetic writing. *Cognition, 24,* 31–44.

Reber, A.S., & Anderson, J.R. (1970). The perception of clicks in linguistic and nonlinguistic messages. *Perception and Psychophysics, 8,* 81–89.

Redlinger, W., & Park, T.Z. (1980). Language mixing in young bilinguals. *Journal of Child Language, 7,* 337–352.

Reicher, G.M. (1969). Perceptual recognition as a function of meaningfulness of stimulus materials. *Journal of Experimental Psychology, 81,* 274–280.

Remez, R.E. (1994). A guide to research on the perception of speech. In M.A. Gernsbacher (Ed.), *Handbook of psycholinguistics* (pp. 145–172). San Diego: Academic Press.

Rescorla, L. (1980). Overextension in early language development. *Journal of Child Language, 7,* 321–335.

Richards, B.J., & Gallaway, C. (1994). Conclusions and directions. In C. Gallaway & B.J. Richards (Eds.), *Input and interaction in language acquisition* (pp. 253–269). Cambridge: Cambridge University Press.

Richards, M.M. (1979). Sorting out what's in a word from what's not: Evaluating Clark's semantic features acquisition theory. *Journal of Experimental Child Psychology, 27,* 1–47.

Riddoch, M.J., & Humphreys, G.W. (1987). Visual object processing in optic aphasia: A case of semantic access agnosia. *Cognitive Neuropsychology, 4,* 131–185.

Riddoch, M.J., Humphreys, G.W., Coltheart, M., & Funnell, E. (1988). Semantic systems or system? Neuropsychological evidence re-examined. *Cognitive Neuropsychology, 5*, 3–25.

Rips, L.J., Shoben, E.J., & Smith, E.E. (1973). Semantic distance and the verification of semantic relations. *Journal of Verbal Learning and Verbal Behavior, 12*, 1–20.

Rips, L.J., Smith, E.E., & Shoben, E.J. (1975). Set-theoretic and network models reconsidered: A comment on Hollan's "Features and semantic memory". *Psychological Review, 82*, 156–157.

Romaine, S. (1995). *Bilingualism* (2nd ed.). Oxford: Blackwell.

Rosch, E. (1973). Natural categories. *Cognitive Psychology, 4*, 328–350.

Rosch, E. (1978). Principles of categorization. In E. Rosch & B. Lloyd (Eds.), *Cognition and categorization* (pp. 27–48). Hillsdale, NJ: Lawrence Erlbaum Associates Inc.

Rosch, E., & Mervis, C.B. (1975). Family resemblances: Studies in the internal structure of categories. *Cognitive Psychology, 7*, 573–605.

Rosch, E., Mervis, C.B., Gray, W., Johnson, D., & Boyes-Braem, P. (1976). Basic objects in natural categories. *Cognitive Psychology, 8*, 382–439.

Ross, B.H., & Bower, G.H. (1981). Comparisons of models of associative recall. *Memory and Cognition, 9*, 1–16.

Rosson, M.B. (1983). From SOFA to LOUCH: Lexical contributions to pseudoword pronunciation. *Memory and Cognition, 11*, 152–160.

Rubenstein, H., Lewis, S.S., & Rubenstein, M.A. (1971). Evidence for phonemic recoding in visual word recognition. *Journal of Verbal Learning and Verbal Behavior, 10*, 645–658.

Rubin, D.C. (1980). 51 properties of 125 words: A unit analysis of verbal behavior. *Journal of Verbal Learning and Verbal Behavior, 19*, 736–755.

Rumelhart, D.E. (1975). Notes on a schema for stories. In D.G. Bobrow and A.M. Collins (Eds.), *Representation and understanding: Studies in Cognitive Science* (pp. 211–236). New York: Academic Press.

Rumelhart, D.E. (1977). Understanding and summarizing brief stories. In D. LaBerge & S.J. Samuels (Eds.), *Basic processes in reading: Perception and comprehension* (pp. 265–303). Hillsdale, NJ: Lawrence Erlbaum Associates Inc.

Rumelhart, D.E. (1980). On evaluating story grammars. *Cognitive Science, 4*, 313–316.

Rumelhart, D.E., & McClelland, J.L. (1982). An interactive activation model of context effects in letter perception: Part 2. The contextual enhancement effect and some tests and extensions of the model. *Psychological Review, 89*, 60–94.

Rumelhart, D.E., & McClelland, J.L. (1986). On learning the past tense of English verbs. In D.E. Rumelhart & J.L. McClelland & the PDP Research Group, *Parallel distributed processing: Vol. 2. Psychological and biological models* (pp. 216–271). Cambridge, MA: MIT Press.

Rumelhart, D.E., McClelland, J.L., & the PDP Research Group. (1986). *Parallel distributed processing: Vol. 2: Foundations*. Cambridge, MA: MIT Press.

Ryman, R. (1993). *Genie*. London: Joseph.

Sachs, J.S. (1967). Recognition memory for syntactic and semantic aspects of connected discourse. *Perception and Psychophysics, 2*, 437–442.

Sachs, J., Bard, B., & Johnson, M.L. (1981). Language with restricted input: case studies of two hearing children of deaf parents. *Applied Psycholinguistics, 2*, 33–54.

Sacks, H., Schegloff, E.A., & Jefferson, G. (1974). A simplest systematics for the organization of turn-taking in conversation. *Language, 50*, 696–735.

Saffran, E.M., Bogyo, L.C., Schwartz, M.F., & Marin, O.S.M. (1980). Does deep dyslexia reflect right hemisphere reading? In M. Coltheart, K.E. Patterson, & J.C. Marshall (Eds.), *Deep dyslexia* (pp. 381–406). (2nd ed., 1987). London: Routledge and Kegan Paul.

Saffran, E.M., Marin, O.S.M., & Yeni-Komshian, G.H. (1976). An analysis of speech perception in word deafness. *Brain and Language, 3*, 209–228.

Saffran, E.M., Schwartz, M.F., & Marin, O.S.M. (1980). Evidence from aphasia: Isolating the components of a production model. In B. Butterworth (Ed.), *Language production: Vol. 1: Speech and talk* (pp. 221–241). London: Academic Press.

Sag, I.A., & Hankamer, J. (1984). Toward a theory of anaphoric processing. *Linguistics and Philosophy, 7*, 325–345.

Samuel, A.G. (1981). Phonemic restoration: Insights from a new methodology. *Journal of Experimental Psychology: General, 110*, 474–494.

Samuel, A.G. (1987). The effect of lexical uniqueness on phonemic restoration. *Journal of Memory and Language, 26*, 36–56.

Samuel, A.G. (1990). Using perceptual-restoration effects to explore the architecture of perception. In G.T.M. Altmann (Ed.), *Cognitive models of speech processing* (pp. 295–314). Cambridge, MA: MIT Press.

Sandra, D. (1990). On the representation and processing of compound words: Automatic access to constituent morphemes does not occur. *Quarterly Journal of Experimental Psychology, 42A*, 529–567.

Sanford, A.J., & Garrod, S.C. (1981). *Understanding written language*. Chichester: John Wiley.

Sanford, A.J. & Garrod, S.C. (1994). Selective processing in text understanding. In M.A. Gernsbacher (Ed.), *Handbook of psycholinguistics* (pp. 699–720). San Diego: Academic Press.

Santa, J.L., & Ranken, H.B. (1972). Effects of verbal coding on recognition memory. *Journal of Experimental Psychology, 93*, 268–278.

Sartori, G., & Job, R. (1988). The oyster with four legs: A neuropsychological study on the interaction of visual and semantic information. *Cognitive Neuropsychology, 5,* 105–132.

Sartori, G., Miozzo, M., & Job, R. (1993). Category-specific impairments? Yes. *Quarterly Journal of Experimental Psychology, 46A*, 489–504.

Sasanuma, S. (1980). Acquired dyslexia in Japanese: Clinical features and underlying mechanisms. In M. Coltheart, K.E. Patterson, & J.C. Marshall (Eds.), *Deep dyslexia* (pp. 48–90). (2nd ed., 1987). London: Routledge & Kegan Paul.

Savage, G.R., Bradley, D.C., & Forster, K.I. (1990). Word frequency and the pronunciation task: The contribution of articulatory fluency. *Language and Cognitive Processes, 5*, 203–236.

Savage-Rumbaugh, E.S. (1987). Communication, symbolic communication, and language: A reply to Seidenberg and Petitto. *Journal of Experimental Psychology: General, 116*, 288–292.

Savage-Rumbaugh, E.S., & Lewin, R. (1994). *Kanzi: The ape at the brink of the human mind*. London: Doubleday.

Savage-Rumbaugh, E.S., McDonald, K., Sevcik, R.A., Hopkins, W.D., & Rupert, E. (1986). Spontaneous symbol acquisition and communicative use by pygmy chimpanzees (Pan paniscus). *Journal of Experimental Psychology: General, 115*, 211–235.

Savage-Rumbaugh, E.S., Rumbaugh, D.M., & Boysen, S. (1978). Linguistically mediated tool use and exchange by chimpanzees. *Behavioral and Brain Sciences, 1*, 539–554.

Savin, H.B., & Bever, T.G. (1970). The nonperceptual reality of the phoneme. *Journal of Verbal Learning and Verbal Behavior, 9*, 295–302.

Savin, H.B., & Perchonock, E. (1965). Grammatical structure and the immediate recall of English sentences. *Journal of Verbal Learning and Verbal Behavior, 4*, 348–353.

Schaeffer, B., & Wallace, R. (1969). Semantic similarity and the comprehension of word meanings. *Journal of Experimental Psychology, 82*, 343–346.

Schaeffer, B., & Wallace, R. (1970). The comparison of word meanings. *Journal of Experimental Psychology, 86*, 144–152.

Schaeffer, H.R. (1975). Social development in infancy. In R. Lewin (Ed.), *Child alive* (pp. 32–39). London: Temple Smith.

Schank, R.C. (1972). Conceptual dependency: A theory of natural language understanding. *Cognitive Psychology, 3*, 552–631.

Schank, R.C. (1975). *Conceptual information processing*. Amsterdam: North Holland.

Schank, R.C. (1982). *Dynamic memory*. Cambridge: Cambridge University Press.

Schank, R.C., & Abelson, R. (1977). *Scripts, plans, goals and understanding*. Hillsdale, NJ: Lawrence Erlbaum Associates Inc.

Schenkein, J. (1980). A taxonomy for repeating action sequences in natural conversation. In B. Butterworth (Ed.), *Language production: Vol. 1: Speech and talk* (pp. 21–48). London: Academic Press.

Schiff-Myers, N. (1993). Hearing children of deaf parents. In D. Bishop & K. Mogford (Eds.), *Language development in exceptional circumstances*. Hove, UK: Lawrence Erlbaum Associates Ltd.

Schlesinger, I.M. (1971). Production of utterances and language acquisition. In D.I. Slobin (Ed.), *The ontogenesis of grammar* (pp. 63–102). New York: Academic Press.

Schlesinger, I.M. (1988). The origin of relational categories. In Y. Levy, I.M. Schlesinger, & M.D.S. Braine (Eds.), *Categories and processes in language acquisition* (pp. 121–178). Hillsdale, NJ: Lawrence Erlbaum Associates Inc.

Schneider, W., & Shiffrin, R.M. (1977). Controlled and automatic human information processing: I. Detection, search and attention. *Psychological Review, 84*, 1–66.

Schober, M.F., & Clark, H.H. (1989). Understanding by addressees and overhearers. *Cognitive Psychology, 21*, 211–232.

Schreuder, R., & Weltens, B. (Eds.) (1993). *The bilingual lexicon*. Amsterdam: Benjamins.

Schriefers, H., Meyer, A.S., & Levelt, W.J.M. (1990). Exploring the time course of lexical access in language production: Picture–word interference studies. *Journal of Memory and Language, 29*, 86–102.

Schuberth, R.E., & Eimas, P.D. (1977). Effects of context n the classification of words and non-words. *Journal of Experimental Psychology: Human Perception and Performance, 3*, 27–36.

Schvaneveldt, R.W., Meyer, D.E., & Becker, C.A. (1976). Lexical ambiguity, semantic context, and visual word recognition. *Journal of Experimental Psychology: Human Perception and Performance, 2*, 243–256.

Schwanenflugel, P.J. (Ed.) (1991). *The psychology of word meanings.* Hillsdale, NJ: Lawrence Erlbaum Associates Inc.

Schwanenflugel, P.J., & Rey, M. (1986). Interlingual semantic facilitation: Evidence for a common representational system in the bilingual lexicon. *Journal of Memory and Language, 25*, 605–618.

Schwartz, M.F. (1987). Patterns of speech production deficit within and across aphasia syndromes: Application of a psycholinguistic model. In M. Coltheart, G. Sartori, & R. Job (Eds.), *The cognitive neuropsychology of language* (pp. 163–199). Hove, UK: Lawrence Erlbaum Associates Ltd.

Schwartz, M.F., Marin, O.S.M., & Saffran, E.M. (1979). Dissociations of language function in dementia: A case study. *Brain and Language, 7*, 277–306.

Schwartz, M.F., Saffran, E.M., & Marin, O.S.M. (1980). Fractionating the reading process in dementia: Evidence for word-specific print-to-sound associations. In M. Coltheart, K.E. Patterson, & J.C. Marshall (Eds.), *Deep dyslexia* (pp. 259–269). London: Routledge & Kegan Paul.

Searle, J.R. (1969). *Speech acts.* Cambridge: Cambridge University Press.

Searle, J.R. (1975). Indirect speech acts. In P. Cole & J.L. Morgan (Eds.), *Syntax and semantics: Vol. 3: Speech acts* (pp. 59–82). New York: Academic Press.

Searle, J.R. (1979). Metaphor. In A. Ortony (Ed.), *Metaphor and thought* (pp. 92–123). Cambridge: Cambridge University Press.

Seidenberg, M.S. (1988). Cognitive neuropsychology and language: The state of the art. *Cognitive Neuropsychology, 5*, 403–426.

Seidenberg, M.S., & McClelland, J.L. (1989). A distributed developmental model of word recognition. *Psychological Review, 96*, 523–568.

Seidenberg, M.S., & McClelland, J.L. (1990). More words but still no lexicon. Reply to Besner et al. (1990). *Psychological Review, 97*, 447–452.

Seidenberg, M.S., & Petitto, L.A. (1979). Signing behavior in apes: A critical review. *Cognition, 7*, 177–215.

Seidenberg, M.S., & Petitto, L.A. (1987). Communication, symbolic communication, and language: Comment on Savage-Rumbaugh, Macdonald, Sevcik, Hopkis, and Rubert (1986). *Journal of Experimental Psychology: General, 116*, 279–287.

Seidenberg, M.S., Plaut, D.C., Petersen, A.S., McClelland, J.L., & McRae, K. (1994). Nonword pronunciation and models of word recognition. *Journal of Experimental Psychology: Human Perception and Performance, 20*, 1177–1196.

Seidenberg, M.S., Tanenhaus, M.K., Leiman, J.M., & Bienkowski, M. (1982). Automatic access of the meanings of ambiguous words in context: Some limitations of knowledge-based processing. *Cognitive Psychology, 14*, 489–537.

Seidenberg, M.S., Waters, G.S., Barnes, M.A., & Tanenhaus, M.K. (1984). When does irregular spelling or pronunciation influence word recognition? *Journal of Verbal Learning and Verbal Behavior, 23*, 383–404.

Seidenberg, M.S., Waters, G.S., Sanders, M., & Langer, P. (1984). Pre- and post-lexical loci of contextual effects on word recognition. *Memory and Cognition, 12*, 315–328.

Seifert, C.M., McKoon, G., Abelson, R.P., & Ratcliff, R. (1986). Memory connections between thematically similar episodes. *Journal of Experimental Psychology: Learning, Memory, and Cognition, 12*, 220–231.

Seifert, C.M., Robertson, S.P., & Black, J.B. (1985). Types of inference generated during reading. *Journal of Memory and Language, 24*, 405–422.

Seymour, P.H.K. (1987). Individual cognitive analysis of competent and impaired reading. *British Journal of Psychology, 78*, 483–506.

Seymour, P.H.K. (1990). Developmental dyslexia. In M.W. Eysenck (Ed.), *Cognitive psychology: An international review* (pp. 135–196). Chichester: John Wiley.

Shallice, T. (1988). *From neuropsychology to mental structure*. Cambridge: Cambridge University Press.

Shallice, T., & McCarthy, R. (1985). Phonological reading: From patterns of impairment to possible procedure. In K.E. Patterson, J.C. Marshall, & M. Coltheart (Eds.), *Surface dyslexia: Neuropsychological and cognitive studies of phonological reading* (pp. 361–397). Hove, UK: Lawrence Erlbaum Associates Ltd.

Shallice, T., & McGill, J. (1978). The origins of mixed errors. In J. Requin (Ed.), *Attention and performance VII* (pp. 193–208). Hillsdale, NJ: Lawrence Erlbaum Associates Inc.

Shallice, T., McLeod, P., & Lewis, K. (1985). Isolating cognitive modules with the dual task paradigm: Are speech perception and production separate processes? *Quarterly Journal of Experimental Psychology, 37A*, 507–532.

Shallice, T., & Warrington, E.K. (1975). Word recognition in a phonemic dyslexic patient. *Quarterly Journal of Experimental Psychology, 27*, 187–199.

Shallice, T., & Warrington, E.K. (1980). Single and multiple component central deep dyslexic syndromes. In M. Coltheart, K.E. Patterson, & J.C. Marshall (Eds.), *Deep dyslexia* (pp. 199–145). (2nd ed., 1987). London: Routledge & Kegan Paul.

Shallice, T., Warrington, E.K., & McCarthy, R. (1983). Reading without semantics. *Quarterly Journal of Experimental Psychology, 35A*, 111–138.

Shannon, C.E., & Weaver, W. (1949). *The mathematical theory of communication*. Urbana, IL: University of Illinois Press.

Sharpe, K. (1992). Communication, culture, context, confidence: The four Cs of primary modern language teaching. *Language Learning Journal, 6*, 13–14.

Shattuck-Hufnagel, S. (1979). Speech errors as evidence for a serial ordering mechanism in speech production. In W.E. Cooper & E.C.T. Walker (Eds.), *Sentence processing: Psycholinguistic studies presented to Merrill Garrett* (pp. 295–342). Hillsdale, NJ: Lawrence Erlbaum Associates Inc.

Shatz, M., & Gelman, R. (1973). The development of common skills: Modifications in the speech of young children as a function of the listener. *Monograph of the Society for Research in Child Development, 152*.

Shelton, J.R., & Martin, R.C. (1992). How semantic is automatic semantic priming? *Journal of Experimental Psychology: Learning, Memory, and Cognition, 18*, 1191–1209.

Shiffrin, R.M., & Schneider, W. (1977). Controlled and automatic human information processing: II. Perceptual learning, automatic attending, and a general theory. *Psychological Review, 84*, 127–190.

Simpson, G.B. (1981). Meaning dominance and semantic context in the processing of lexical ambiguity. *Journal of Verbal Learning and Verbal Behavior, 20*, 120–136.

Simpson, G.B. (1984). Lexical ambiguity and its role in models of word recognition. *Psychological Bulletin, 96*, 316–340.

Simpson, G.B. (1994). Context and the processing of ambiguous words. In M.A. Gernsbacher (Ed.), *Handbook of psycholinguistic research* (pp. 359–374). San Diego: Academic Press.

Sinclair-de-Zwart, H. (1969). Developmental psycholinguistics. In D. Elkind & J.H. Flavell (Eds.), *Studies in cognitive development* (pp. 315–366). Oxford: Oxford University Press.

Sinclair-de-Zwart, H. (1973). Language acquisition and cognitive development. In T.E. Moore (Ed.), *Cognitive development and the acquisition of language* (pp. 9–26). New York: Academic Press.

Singer, M. (1994). Discourse inference processes. In M.A. Gernsbacher (Ed.), *Handbook of psycholinguistics* (pp. 479–516). San Diego: Academic Press.

Singer, M., & Ferreira, F. (1983). Inferring consequences in story comprehension. *Journal of Verbal Learning and Verbal Behavior, 22*, 437–448.

Singh, J.A.L., & Zingg, R.M. (1942). *Wolf children and feral man.* Hamden, CT: Shoe String Press. (Reprinted 1966, New York: Harper & Row.)

Skinner, B.F. (1957). *Verbal behavior.* New York: Appleton-Century-Crofts.

Skuse, D.H, (1993). Extreme deprivation in early childhood. In D. Bishop, D., & K. Mogford, K. (Eds.), *Language development in exceptional circumstances* (pp. 29–46). Hove, UK: Lawrence Erlbaum Associates Ltd.

Slobin, D.I. (1966a). Grammatical transformations and sentence comprehension in childhood and adulthood. *Journal of Verbal Learning and Verbal Behavior, 5*, 219–227.

Slobin, D.I. (1966b). The acquisition of Russian as a native language. In F. Smith & G.A. Miller (Eds.), *The genesis of a language: A psycholinguistic approach* (pp. 129–248). Cambridge, MA: MIT Press.

Slobin, D.I. (1970). Universals of grammatical development in children. In G. Flores d'Arcais & W.J.M. Levelt (Eds.), *Advances in psycholinguistics* (pp. 174–186) Amsterdam: North Holland.

Slobin, D.I. (1973). Cognitive prerequisites for the development of grammar. In C.A. Ferguson & D.I. Slobin (Eds.), *Studies of child language development* (pp. 175–208). New York: Holt, Rhinehart & Winston.

Slobin, D.I. (1981). The origins of grammatical encoding of events. In W. Deutsch (Ed.), *The child's construction of language* (pp. 185–199). London: Academic Press.

Slobin, D.I. (1982). Universal and particular in the acquisition of language. In E. Wanner & L.R. Gleitman (Eds.), *Language acquisition: The state of the art* (pp. 128–170). Cambridge: Cambridge University Press.

Slobin, D.I. (1985). Crosslinguistic evidence for the language-making capacity. In D.I. Slobin (Ed.), *The crosslinguistic study of language acquisitions: Vol. 2: Theoretical issues* (pp. 1157–1249). Hillsdale, NJ: Lawrence Erlbaum Associates Inc.

Smith, E.E., & Medin, D.L. (1981). *Categories and concepts.* Harvard: Harvard University Press.

Smith, E.E., Shoben, E.J., & Rips, L.J. (1974). Structure and process in semantic memory: A featural model for semantic decisions. *Psychological Review, 81*, 214–241.

Smith, N.V. (1973). *The acquisition of phonology: A case study.* Cambridge: Cambridge University Press.

Smith, P.T., & Sterling, C.M. (1982). Factors affecting the perceived morphophonemic structure of written words. *Journal of Verbal Learning and Verbal Behavior, 21,* 704–721.

Smith, S.M., Brown, H.O., Thomas, J.E.P., & Goodman, L.S. (1947). The lack of cerebral effects of d-tubocurarine. *Anesthesiology, 8,* 1–14.

Snodgrass, J.G. (1984). Concepts and their surface representation. *Journal of Verbal Learning and Verbal Behavior, 23,*3–22.

Snodgrass, J.G., & Vanderwart, M. (1980). A standardised set of 260 pictures: Norms for name agreement, image agreement, familiarity, and visual complexity. *Journal of Experimental Psychology: Human Learning and Memory, 6,* 174–215.

Snow, C.E. (1983). Age differences in second language acquisition: Research findings and folk psychology. In K. Bailey, M. Long, & S. Peck (Eds.), *Second language acquisition studies* (pp. 141–150). Rowley, MA: Newbury House.

Snow, C.E. (1972). Mothers' speech to children learning language. *Child Development, 43,* 549–565.

Snow, C.E. (1977). The development of conversation between mothers and babies. *Journal of Child Language, 4,* 1–22.

Snow, C.E. (1993). Bilingualism and second language acquisition. In J.B. Gleason & N.B. Ratner (Eds.), *Psycholinguistics* (pp. 391–416). Fort Worth: Harcourt Brace Jovanovich.

Snow, C.E. (1994). Beginning from baby talk: Twenty years of research on input and interaction. In C. Gallaway & B.J. Richards (Eds.), *Input and interaction in language acquisition* (pp. 3–12). Cambridge: Cambridge University Press.

Snow, C.E., & Hoefnagel-Hohle, M. (1978). The critical period for language acquisition: Evidence from second language learning. *Child Development, 49,* 1114–1128.

Snowling, M.J. (1983). The comparison of acquired and developmental disorders of reading. *Cognition, 14,* 105–118.

Snowling, M.J. (1987). *Dyslexia: A cognitive developmental perspective.* Oxford: Blackwell.

Soja, N.N., Carey, S., & Spelke, E.S. (1991). Ontological categories guide young children's inductions of word meaning: Object terms and substance terms. *Cognition, 38,* 179–211.

Soja, N.N., Carey, S., & Spelke, E.S. (1992). Perception, ontology, and word meaning. *Cognition, 45,* 101–107.

Sokolov, J.L., & Snow, C.E. (1994). The changing role of negative evidence in theories of language development. In C. Gallaway & B.J. Richards (Eds.), *Input and interaction in language acquisition* (pp. 38–55). Cambridge: Cambridge University Press.

Spender, D. (1980). *Man made language.* London: Routledge & Kegan Paul.

Sperber, D., & Wilson, D. (1986). *Relevance: Communication and cognition.* Oxford: Blackwell.

Sperber, D., & Wilson, D. (1987). Précis of Relevance: Communication and cognition. *Behavioral and Brain Sciences, 10,* 697–754.

Sperber, R.D., McCauley, C., Ragain, R.D., & Weil, C.M. (1979). Semantic priming effects on picture and word processing. *Memory and Cognition, 7,* 339–345.

Spiro, R.J. (1980). Constructive processes in prose comprehension and recall. In R.J. Spiro, B.C. Bruce, & W.F. Brewer (Eds.), *Theoretical issues in reading comprehension* (pp. 245–278). Hillsdale, NJ: Lawrence Erlbaum Associates Inc.

Stabler, E.P.Jr. (1983). How are grammars represented? *Behavioral and Brain Sciences, 6*, 391–421.

Stalin, J.V. (1954). *Marxism and problems of linguistics*. (Trans. unknown, 1972.) Peking: Foreign Language Press.

Stanners, R.F., Jastrzembski, J.E., & Westwood, A. (1975). Frequency and visual quality in a word-nonword classification task. *Journal of Verbal Learning and Verbal Behavior, 14*, 259–264

Stanovich, K.E., & Bauer, D.W. (1978). Experiments on the spelling-to-sound regularity effect in word recognition. *Memory and Cognition, 6*, 410–415.

Stanovich, K.E., Cunningham, A.E., & Cramer, B. (1984). Assessing phonological awareness in kindergarten children: Issues of task comparability. *Journal of Experimental Child Psychology, 38*, 175–190.

Stanovich, K.E., & West, R.F. (1979). Mechanisms of sentence context effects in reading: Automatic activation and conscious attention. *Memory and Cognition, 6*, 115–123.

Stanovich, K.E., & West, R.F. (1981). The effect of sentence context on ongoing word recognition: Tests of a two-process theory. *Journal of Experimental Psychology: Human Perception and Performance, 7*, 658–672.

Steedman, M.J., & Altmann, G.T.M. (1989). Ambiguity in context: A reply. *Language and Cognitive Processes, 4*, 105–122.

Steedman, M.J., & Johnson-Laird, P.N. (1980). The production of sentences, utterances, and speech acts: Have computers anything to say? In B. Butterworth (Ed.), *Language production: Vol. 1: Speech and talk* (pp. 111–142). London: Academic Press.

Stemberger, J.P. (1983). Distant context effects in language production: A reply to Motley et al. *Journal of Psycholinguistic Research, 12*, 555–560.

Stemberger, J.P. (1984). Structural errors in normal and agrammatic speech. *Cognitive Neuropsychology, 1*, 281–313.

Stemberger, J.P. (1985). An interactive activation model of language production. In A.W. Ellis (Ed.), *Progress in the psychology of language* (Vol. 1, pp. 143–186). Hove, UK: Lawrence Erlbaum Associates Ltd.

Stevens, K.N. (1960). Toward a model for speech recognition. *Journal of the Acoustical Society of America, 32*, 47–55.

Stevenson, R. (1988). *Models of language development*. Milton Keynes: Open University Press.

Stevenson, R. (1993). *Language, thought, and representation*. Chichester: John Wiley & Sons.

Stewart, F., Parkin, A.J., & Hunkin, N.M. (1992). Naming impairments following recovery from herpes simplex encephalitis: Category-specific? *Quarterly Journal of Experimental Psychology, 44A*, 261–284.

Stillings, N.A., Feinstein, M.H., Garfield, J.L., Rissland, E.L., Rosenbaum, D.A., Weisler, S.E., & Baker-Ward, L. (1987). *Cognitive Science: An introduction*. Cambridge, MA: MIT Press.

Sudhalter, V., & Braine, M.D.S. (1985). How does comprehension of passives develop? *Journal of Child Language, 12*, 455–470.

Sulin, R.A., & Dooling, D.J. (1974). Intrusion of a thematic idea in retention of prose. *Journal of Experimental Psychology, 103*, 255–262.

Swain, M., & Wesche, M. (1975). Linguistic interaction: Case study of a bilingual child. *Language Sciences, 17*, 17–22.

Swinney, D.A. (1979). Lexical access during sentence comprehension: (Re)consideration of context effects. *Journal of Verbal Learning and Verbal Behavior, 18*, 545–569.

Swinney, D.A., Zurif, E.B., & Cutler, A. (1980). Effects of sentential stress and word class upon comprehension in Broca's aphasics. *Brain and Language, 10*, 132–144.

Sykes, J.L. (1940). A study of the spontaneous vocalizations of young deaf children. *Psychological Monograph, 52*, 104–123.

Tabossi, P. (1988a). Accessing lexical ambiguity in different types of sentential context. *Journal of Memory and Language, 27*, 324–340.

Tabossi, P. (1988b). Effects of context on the immediate interpretation of unambiguous words. *Journal of Experimental Psychology: Learning, Memory, and Cognition, 14*, 153–162.

Taft, M. (1981). Prefix stripping revisited. *Journal of Verbal Learning and Verbal Behavior, 20*, 289–297.

Taft, M. (1982). An alternative to grapheme-phoneme conversion rules? *Memory and Cognition, 10*, 465–474.

Taft, M. (1984). Evidence for abstract lexical representation of word structure. *Memory and Cognition, 12*, 264–269.

Taft, M. (1985). The decoding of words in lexical access: A review of the morphographic approach. In D. Besner, T.G. Waller, & G.E. MacKinnon (Eds.), *Reading research: Advances in theory and practice* (Vol. 5, pp. 83–123). Orlando, FL: Academic Press.

Taft, M. (1987). Morphographic processing: The BOSS re-emerges. In M. Coltheart (Ed.), *Attention and Performance XII: The psychology of reading* (pp. 265–279). Hove, UK: Lawrence Erlbaum Associates Ltd.

Tanaka, J.W., & Taylor, M. (1991). Object categories and expertise: Is the basic level in the eye of the beholder? *Cognitive Psychology, 23*, 457–482.

Tanenhaus, M.K., & Carlson, G.N. (1989). Lexical structure and language comprehension. In W.D. Marslen-Wilson (Ed.), *Lexical representation and process* (pp. 529–561). Cambridge, MA: MIT Press.

Tanenhaus, M.K., & Carlson, G.N. (1990). Comprehension of deep and surface verbphrase anaphors. *Language and Cognitive Processes, 5*, 257–280.

Tanenhaus, M.K., Carlson, G.N., & Trueswell, J.C. (1989). The role of thematic structure in interpretation and parsing. *Language and Cognitive Processes, 4*, 211–234.

Tanenhaus, M.K., Leiman, J.M., & Seidenberg, M.S. (1979). Evidence for multiple stages in the processing of ambiguous words in syntactic contexts. *Journal of Verbal Learning and Verbal Behavior, 18*, 427–440.

Tanenhaus, M.K., & Lucas, M. (1987). Context effects in lexical processing. *Cognition, 25*, 213–234.

Tannenbaum, P.H., Williams, F., & Hillier, C.S. (1965). Word predictability in the environments of hesitations. *Journal of Verbal Learning and Verbal Behavior, 4*, 134–140.

Taraban, R., & McClelland, J.L. (1988). Constituent attachment and thematic role assignment in sentence processing: Influences of content-based expectations. *Journal of Memory and Language, 27*, 597–632.

Taylor, I., & Taylor, M.M. (1990). *Psycholinguistics: Learning and using language*. Englewood Cliffs, NJ: Prentice Hall International.

Temple, C.M. (1987). The nature of normality, the deviance of dyslexia and the recognition of rhyme: A reply to Bryant and Impey (1986). *Cognition, 27,* 103–108.

Temple, C.M., & Marshall, J. (1983). A case study of developmental phonological dyslexia. *British Journal of Psychology, 74,* 517–533.

Terrace, H.S., Petitto, L.A., Sanders, R.J., & Bever, T.G. (1979). Can an ape create a sentence? *Science, 206,* 891–902.

Thompson, C.R., & Church, R.M. (1980). An explanation of the language of a chimpanzee. *Science, 208,* 313–314.

Thomson, J., & Chapman, R.S. (1977). Who is "Daddy" revisited: The status of two-year-olds' overextended words in use and comprehension. *Journal of Child Language, 4,* 359–375.

Thorndyke, P.W. (1977). Cognitive structures in comprehension and memory of narrative discourse. *Cognitive Psychology, 9,* 77–110.

Thorndyke, P.W., & Hayes-Roth, B. (1979). The use of schemata in the acquisition and transfer of knowledge. *Cognitive Psychology, 11,* 82–106.

Tomasello, M. (1992). The social bases of language acquisition. *Social Development, 1,* 67–87.

Tomasello, M., & Barton, M. (1994). Learning words in nonostensive contexts. *Developmental Psychology, 30,* 639–650.

Tomasello, M., & Farrar, M.J. (1984). Cognitive bases of lexical development: Object permanence and relational words. *Journal of Child Language, 11,* 477–493.

Tomasello, M., & Farrar, M.J. (1986). Object permanence and relational words: A lexical training study. *Journal of Child Language, 13,* 495–505.

Tomasello, M., & Kruger, A. (1992). Joint attention on actions: Acquiring verbs in ostensive and non-ostensive contexts. *Journal of Child Language, 19,* 311–333.

Trevarthen, C. (1975). Early attempts at speech. In R. Lewin (Ed.), *Child alive* (pp. 62–80). London: Temple Smith.

Trueswell, J.C., Tanenhaus, M.K., & Kello, C. (1993). Verb-specific constraints in sentence processing: Separating effects of lexical preference from garden paths. *Journal of Experimental Psychology: Learning, Memory, and Cognition, 19,* 528–553.

Tulving, E. (1972). Episodic and semantic memory. In E. Tulving & W. Donaldson (Eds.), *Organization of memory* (pp. 381–403). New York: Academic Press.

Turvey, M.T. (1973). On peripheral and central processes in vision. *Psychological Review, 80,* 1–52.

Tweedy, J.R., Lapinski, R.H., & Schvaneveldt, R.W. (1977). Semantic-context effects on word recognition: Influence of varying the proportion of items presented in an appropriate context. *Memory and Cognition, 5,* 84–89.

Tyler, L.K. (1990). The relationship between sentential context and sensory input: Comments on Connine's and Samuel's chapters. In G.T.M. Altmann (Ed.), *Cognitive models of speech processing* (pp. 315–323). Cambridge, MA: MIT Press.

Tyler, L.K., & Marslen-Wilson, W.D. (1977). The on-line effects of semantic context on syntactic processing. *Journal of Verbal Learning and Verbal Behavior, 16,* 683–692.

Tyler, L.K., Ostrin, R.K., Cooke, M., & Moss, H.E. (1995). Automatic access of lexical information in Broca's aphasics: Against the automaticity hypothesis. *Brain and Language, 48,* 131–162.

Tyler, L.K. & Wessels, J. (1983). Quantifying contextual contributions to word-recognition processes. *Perception and Psychophysics, 34,* 409–420.

Valian, V. (1986). Syntactic categories in the speech of young children. *Developmental Psychology, 22,* 562–579.

Vallar, G., & Baddeley, A.D. (1987). Phonological short-term store and sentence processing. *Cognitive Neuropsychology, 4,* 417–438.

Vallar, G., & Baddeley, A.D. (1989). Developmental disorders of verbal short-term memory and their relation to sentence comprehension: A reply to Howard and Butterworth. *Cognitive Neuropsychology, 6,* 465–473.

van den Broek, P. (1994). Comprehension and memory of narrative texts: Inference and coherence. In M.A. Gernsbacher (Ed.), *Handbook of psycholinguistics* (pp. 539–588). San Diego: Academic Press.

van Orden, G.C. (1987). A rows is a rose: Spelling, sound and reading. *Memory and Cognition, 15,* 181–198.

van Orden, G.C., & Goldinger, S.D. (1994). Interdependence of form and function in cognitive systems explains perception of printed words. *Journal of Experimental Psychology: Human Perception and Performance, 20,* 1269–1291.

van Orden, G.C., Johnston, J.C., & Hale, B.L. (1988). Word identification in reading proceeds from spelling to sound to meaning. *Journal of Experimental Psychology: Learning, Memory, and Cognition, 14,* 371–386.

van Orden, G.C., Pennington, B.F., & Stone, G.O. (1990). Word identification in reading and the promise of subsymbolic psycholinguistics. *Psychological Review, 97,* 488–522.

van Petten, C., & Kutas, M. (1987). Ambiguous words in context: An event-related potential analysis of the time course of meaning activation. *Journal of Memory and Language, 26,* 188–208.

van Petten, C., & Kutas, M. (1990). Interactions between sentence context and word frequency in event-related potentials. *Memory and Cognition, 18,* 380–393.

Vanderwart, M. (1984). Priming by pictures in lexical decision. *Journal of Verbal Learning and Verbal Behavior, 23,* 67–83.

Varney, N.L. (1984). Phonemic imperception in aphasia. *Brain and Language, 21,* 85–94.

Venezky, R.L. (1970). *The structure of English orthography.* The Hague: Mouton.

Vihman, M.M. (1985). Language differentiation by the bilingual infant. *Journal of Child Language, 12,* 297–324.

Vipond, D. (1980). Micro- and macroprocesses in text comprehension. *Journal of Verbal Learning and Verbal Behavior, 19,* 276–296.

von Frisch, K. (1950). *Bees, their vision, chemical senses, and language.* Ithaca, NY: Cornell University Press.

von Frisch, K. (1974). Decoding the language of bees. *Science, 185,* 663–668.

Vygotsky, L. (1934). *Thought and language.* (Trans. E. Hanfman & G. Vakar, 1962) Cambridge, MA: MIT Press.

Wales, R.J., & Campbell, R. (1970). On the development of comparison and the comparison of development. In G.B. Flores d'Arcais & W.J.M. Levelt (Ed.), *Advances in psycholinguistics* (pp. 373–396). Amsterdam: North Holland.

Walker, C.H., & Yekovich, F.R. (1987). Activation and use of script-based antecedents in anaphoric reference. *Journal of Memory and Language, 26,* 673–691.

Walker, S. (1987). Review of Gavagai! or the future history of the animal language controversy, by David Premack. *Mind and Language, 2*, 326–332.

Wall, R. (1972). *Introduction to mathematical linguistics.* Englewood Cliffs, NJ: Prentice-Hall.

Waltz, D.L., & Pollack, J.B. (1985). Massively parallel parsing: A strongly interactive model of natural language interpretation. *Cognitive Science, 9*, 51–74.

Wanner, E. (1980). The ATN and the sausage machine: Which one is baloney? *Cognition, 8*, 209–225.

Wanner, E., & Maratsos, M.P. (1978). An ATN approach to comprehension. In M. Halle, J.W. Bresnan, & G.A. Miller (Eds.), *Linguistic theory and psychological reality* (pp. 119–161). Cambridge, MA: MIT Press.

Warren, C., & Morton, J. (1982). The effects of priming on picture recognition. *British Journal of Psychology, 73*, 117–129.

Warren, R.M. (1970). Perceptual restoration of missing speech sounds. *Science, 167*, 392–393.

Warren, R.M., & Warren, R.P. (1970). Auditory illusions and confusions. *Scientific American, 223*, 30–36.

Warrington, E.K. (1975). The selective impairment of semantic memory. *Quarterly Journal of Experimental Psychology, 27*, 635–657.

Warrington, E.K. (1981). Concrete word dyslexia. *British Journal of Psychology, 72*, 175–196.

Warrington, E.K., & McCarthy, R. (1983). Category specific access dysphasia. *Brain, 106*, 859–878.

Warrington, E.K., & McCarthy, R. (1987). Categories of knowledge: Further fractionation and an attempted integration. *Brain, 110*, 1273–1296.

Warrington, E.K., & Shallice, T. (1979). Semantic access dyslexia. *Brain, 102*, 43–63.

Warrington, E.K., & Shallice, T. (1984). Category-specific semantic impairments. *Brain, 107*, 829–854.

Wason, P.C. (1965). The contexts of plausible denial. *Journal of Verbal Learning and Verbal Behavior, 4*, 7–11.

Waters, G.S., Caplan, D., & Hildebrandt, N. (1991). On the structure of verbal short-term memory and its functional role in sentence comprehension: Evidence from neuropsychology. *Cognitive Neuropsychology, 8*, 81–126.

Watson, J.B. (1913). Psychology as the behaviorist views it. *Psychological Review, 20*, 158–177.

Weinreich, U. (1953). *Languages in contact.* The Hague: Mouton.

Weizenbaum, J. (1966). ELIZA - A computer program for the study of natural language communication between man and machine. *Communications of the Association for Computing Machinery, 9*, 36–45.

Werker, J.F., & Tees, R.C. (1984). Cross-language speech development: Evidence for perceptual reorganization during the first year of life. *Infant Behavior and Development, 7*, 49–63.

West, R.F., & Stanovich, K.E. (1978). Automatic contextual facilitation in readers of three ages. *Child Development, 49*, 727–727.

West, R.F., & Stanovich, K.E. (1982). Source of inhibition in experiments on the effect of sentence context on word recognition. *Journal of Experimental Psychology: Learning, Memory, and Cognition, 8*, 385–399.

West, R.F., & Stanovich, K.E. (1986). Robust effects of syntactic structure on visual word processing. *Memory and Cognition, 14*, 104–112.

Whaley, C.P. (1978). Word-nonword classification time. *Journal of Verbal Learning and Verbal Behavior, 17*, 143–154.

Wheeldon, L.R., & Monsell, S. (1992). The locus of repetition priming of spoken word production. *Quarterly Journal of Experimental Psychology, 44A*, 723–761.

Wheeler, D. (1970). Processes in word recognition. *Cognitive Psychology, 1*, 59–85.

Whittlesea, B.W.A. (1987). Preservation of specific experiences in the representation of general knowledge. *Journal of Experimental Psychology: Learning, Memory, and Cognition, 13*, 3–17.

Whorf, B.L. (1956a). *Language, thought, and reality: Selected writings of Benjamin Lee Whorf*. New York: Wiley.

Whorf, B.L. (1956b). Science and linguistics. In J.B. Carroll (Ed.), *Language, thought and reality: Selected writings of Benjamin Lee Whorf* (pp. 207–219). (Originally published 1940.) Cambridge, MA: MIT Press.

Wickelgren, W.A. (1969). Context-sensitive coding, associative memory, and serial order in (speech) behavior. *Psychological Review, 76*, 1–15.

Wilding, J. (1990). Developmental dyslexics do not fit in boxes: Evidence from the case studies. *European Journal of Cognitive Psychology, 2*, 97–131.

Wilensky, R. (1983). Story grammars versus story points. *Behavioral and Brain Sciences, 6*, 579–623.

Wilkins, A.J. (1971). Conjoint frequency, category size, and categorization time. *Journal of Verbal Learning and Verbal Behavior, 10*, 382–385.

Wilks, Y. (1976). Parsing English II. In E. Charniak & Y. Wilks (Eds.), *Computational semantics* (pp. 155–184). Amsterdam: North-Holland.

Williams, P.C., & Parkin, A.J. (1980). On knowing the meaning of words we are unable to report—Confirmation of a guessing explanation *Quarterly journal of Experimental Psychology, 32*, 101–107.

Wingfield, A., & Klein, J.F. (1971). Syntactic structure and acoustic pattern in speech perception. Perception and *Psychophysics, 9*, 23–25.

Winnick, W.A., & Daniel, S.A. (1970). Two kinds of response priming in tachistoscopic recognition. *Journal of Experimental Psychology, 84*, 74–81.

Winograd, T.A. (1972). *Understanding natural language*. New York: Academic Press.

Winston, P.H. (1984). *Artificial Intelligence*. Reading, MA: Addison-Wesley.

Wittgenstein, L. (1953). *Philosophical Investigations*. (Trans. G.E.M. Ancombe.) Oxford: Blackwell.

Woodruff, G., & Premack, D. (1981). Primitive mathematical concepts in the chimpanzee: proportionality and numerosity. *Nature, 293*, 568–570.

Woods, B.T., & Teuber, H.-L. (1973). Early onset of complementary specialization of cerebral hemispheres in man. *Transactions of the American Neurological Association, 98*, 113–117.

Woods, W.A. (1970). Transition network grammars for natural language analysis. *Communications of the Association for Computing Machinery, 13*, 591–606.

Woods, W.A. (1975). What's in a link? Foundations for semantic networks. In D.G. Bobrow & A.M. Collins (Ed.), *Representation and understanding: Studies in cognitive science* (pp. 35–82). New York: Academic Press.

Woodworth, R.S. (1938). *Experimental psychology*. New York: Holt.

Yamada, J.E. (1990). *Laura: A case for the modularity of language*. Cambridge, MA: MIT Press.

Yekovich, F.R., & Thorndyke, P.W. (1981). An evaluation of alternative models of narrative schema. *Journal of Verbal Learning and Verbal Behavior, 20,* 454–469.

Yule, G. (1985). *The study of language.* Cambridge: Cambridge University Press.

Zaidel, E., & Peters, A.M. (1981). Phonological encoding and ideographic reading by the disconnected right hemisphere. *Brain and Language, 14,* 205–234.

Zurif, E.B., Caramazza, A., Myerson, P., & Galvin, J. (1974). Semantic feature representations for normal and aphasic language. *Brain and Language, 1,* 167–187.

Zurif, E.B., & Swinney, D.A. (1994). The neuropsychology of language. In M.A. Gernsbacher (Ed.), *Handbook of psycholinguistics* (pp. 1055–1074). San Diego: Academic Press.

Zwitserlood, P. (1989). The locus of the effects of sentential-semantic context in spoken-word processing, *Cognition, 32,* 25–64.

Author index

Subject index